Getting Into the
ACT

Official Guide to the ACT Assessment

Second Edition

Written and endorsed by ACT

Information for Life's Transitions

A Harvest Book

Harcourt Brace & Company, Publishers
San Diego New York London

ACT endorses the *Code of Fair Testing Practices in Education,* a statement of guidelines for those who develop, administer, and use educational tests and data. The *Code* sets forth criteria for fairness in four areas: developing and selecting appropriate tests, interpreting test scores, striving for fairness, and informing test takers. ACT is committed to ensuring that each of its testing programs upholds the *Code*'s standards for appropriate test development practice and use.

A copy of the full *Code* may be obtained free of charge from ACT Publications, P.O. Box 168, Iowa City, Iowa 52243-0168, 319-337-1429.

Inquiries concerning this publication should be mailed to:
    ACT Publications
    P.O. Box 168
    Iowa City, Iowa 52243-0168

Printed in the United State of America

Library of Congress Catalog Card Number: 97-073482

ISBN 0-15-600535-2

Second edition

N M L K J I H G F

Contents

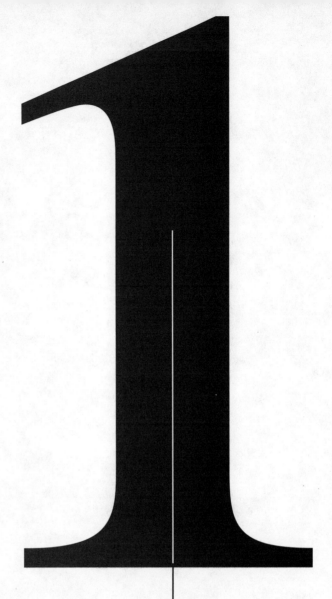

Part 1: Overview

1

Getting Started

The purpose of this book is to supplement the booklet *Preparing for the ACT Assessment* by providing information about the ACT test to as many students as possible. You'll learn about many topics, including the following:

■ the content of the exam
■ the procedures you'll follow when you're actually taking the exam
■ the types of questions you can expect to find on the exam
■ suggestions on how you might approach the questions
■ general test-taking strategies

You'll also find actual ACT tests you can use for practice and detailed explanatory answers to help with your review.

This book is intended to help you **know what to expect** when you take the ACT test so you can relax and concentrate on doing your best. The more you know about what to expect on **any** test you take, the more likely it is that your performance on that test will accurately reflect your overall preparation and achievement in the areas it measures. Knowing what to expect can help reduce any nervousness you may feel as you approach the test. Not only will this information make you more comfortable, it can also help keep your performance on the test from being unfairly hampered by outside factors, like worrying about what's going to happen next.

Knowing what to expect on a test can reduce your nervousness.

About This Book

The ACT Assessment measures your understanding of what you've been taught in courses that you are expected to have completed by the time you enter college. Just as it has taken you years to learn all this material, it will take some time to review the material for the ACT test. You can't expect to thoroughly review the material for this test in a night or two. However, any review should be helpful to you, even if it just makes you more comfortable when you actually sit down to take the ACT test.

This book is divided into three main parts:

Part 1: **Overview.** This includes the purpose of the ACT test, how to register for it, what to expect at the test center, and general test-taking strategies. This part is identified by a black bar on the edge of the right-hand pages.

Part 2: **The Tests.** This part takes you step-by-step through each of the four individual tests of the ACT Assessment (English, Mathematics, Reading, and Science Reasoning) and provides illustrative and sample items. This part is identified by a gray bar on the edge of the right-hand pages.

Part 3: **Practice Tests and Scoring.** Two complete ACT tests with answer explanations are included, as well as instructions on how to score your tests and interpret your test scores. This part is identified by the absence of shaded bars on the pages.

Each of these three parts serves a different purpose. Part 1 gives a general overview of the ACT test, including basic information about getting ready for the test. Part 2 gives specific information about the four individual tests: English, Mathematics, Reading, and Science Reasoning. The content covered in each of these four individual tests is reviewed, and specific test-taking strategies for each section are discussed. Part 3 lets you practice taking the ACT test and gives you help on items you missed as well as ideas about what you may need to study more.

Working Through This Book

Some suggestions for using this book to prepare for the ACT test, based on questions that students often ask, are given below.

How do I use this book?

Each of the three parts of this book is intended to give you information about different aspects of the ACT test. The first part answers general questions about the ACT test and test taking. The second part takes you through a thorough review of each of the four individual tests of the ACT Assessment (English, Mathematics, Reading, and Science Reasoning) and provides illustrative and sample items from previous ACT tests. The third part allows you to practice taking the exam with real ACT tests.

Should I work through this entire book?

There are many reasons to purchase and use a test preparation book. Perhaps you have taken the ACT test before and want to improve your score. Perhaps you want to practice taking the ACT test under conditions similar to the actual testing conditions. You may want to brush up on some specific mathematics concepts to bring up your Mathematics Test scores. Maybe you would feel most comfortable if you could do a thorough review of all of the content covered by the ACT test. Each of these very different reasons requires a different strategy for using this book. Once you decide on **your** reasons for using this book, you can then map out a study plan that is best suited to your needs. The answers to the following questions will help guide you in this effort.

What does the test measure?

There are two sections that can help answer this question. The first part of Chapter 2, "About the ACT Test," gives you an overview of what the test measures in general, and the first part of **each section** of Chapter 4 gives you a more in-depth view of each of the four individual tests that make up the ACT Assessment (English, Mathematics, Reading, and Science Reasoning).

What do I need to know about taking standardized tests like the ACT test?

Chapter 2 tells you all you need to know about the test before you walk into the test center. Chapter 3 gives you some general hints about taking standardized tests. Each of the four sections of Chapter 4 begins with a general overview of an individual test of the ACT Assessment and gives hints throughout to help you work successfully through that individual test. Finally, in Chapter 5 you can become familiar with the ACT test by taking it under actual testing conditions.

How do I register for the ACT test?

"Registering for the ACT Test" in Chapter 2 deals specifically with registering for the ACT test.

What should I expect on the day of the test?

The section in Chapter 2 called "At the Test Center" should answer your questions about the test center. Taking the practice tests in Chapter 5 under conditions similar to those of the actual test (for example, eliminating distractions, timing yourself, using an answer sheet) will also help you learn what to expect.

I've already taken the ACT test. How can I improve my ACT test scores?

If you want to improve your score on a particular area of the ACT test, you can review that section and try the associated practice items in Chapter 4. You can also take the ACT practice tests in Chapter 5. The best way to improve your ACT scores in any specific test area (English, Mathematics, Reading, or Science Reasoning) is to review the content that makes up that individual test. For example, if you find that your English Test scores are lower than you would like them to be, try going to your English teacher and asking for help. You can show your teacher the practice tests on which you have done poorly and ask for extra help in those areas.

I have trouble in English. How can I do my best on the English Test of the ACT Assessment?

You can review the English section of Chapter 4, work through the sample questions, and then take the practice ACT tests in Chapter 5. Asking your English teacher for help is another good strategy.

I have trouble in mathematics. How can I do my best on the Mathematics Test of the ACT Assessment?

You can review the Mathematics section of Chapter 4, work through the sample questions, and then take the practice ACT tests in Chapter 5. Asking your math teacher for help is another good strategy.

I have trouble in reading. How can I do my best on the Reading Test of the ACT Assessment?

You can review the Reading section of Chapter 4, work through the sample questions, and then take the practice ACT tests in Chapter 5. Asking your English teacher for help is another good strategy.

I have trouble in science. How can I do my best on the Science Reasoning Test of the ACT Assessment?

You can review the Science Reasoning section of Chapter 4, work through the sample questions, and then take the practice ACT tests in Chapter 5. Asking your science teacher for help is another good strategy.

All I care about is practice, practice, practice. How can this book help me?

Take the two practice ACT tests in Chapter 5. For more sample items, see Chapter 4. There is also another sample ACT test in *Preparing for the ACT Assessment*, a free booklet you can get from your counselor or at the address printed on the front cover of this book.

What do my ACT test scores mean? How are they calculated?

Chapter 6 describes how your scores are calculated and what they mean.

*I feel overwhelmed. How can I get an answer to **all** these questions?*

If you're unsure where to begin, there's no better place than the beginning. Work your way through the entire book, one step at a time.

I don't have enough time to prepare as thoroughly as I'd like. What should I do?

You could take one of the practice tests to see where you most need to focus your efforts. If any of your individual test scores are much lower than you'd expect, focus your efforts on those areas first. Then, as time permits, study other areas that you feel need work.

Before You Begin

As you use this book to help you prepare for the ACT test, remember that everyone learns and studies differently. Some people study best when they are by themselves. Others need to work with fellow students to do their best. Still others function best in a structured class with a teacher leading them through their studies. You should use whatever method works best for you. Keep in mind, however, that when you actually take the ACT Assessment, it will be just you and the test.

We recommend that you break your study time into one-hour segments (except when you're taking the timed practice tests, of course). If you want to study for more than one hour in a day, that's fine—just make sure you take a break each half hour, even if it's only to stretch and give your mind a chance to absorb what you've learned.

2

The ACT Assessment: Inside and Out

About the ACT Test

The ACT test is an examination designed to measure academic achievement in four major curriculum areas: English, mathematics, reading, and natural sciences. Materials covered on the four tests that make up the ACT Assessment correspond very closely to topics covered in typical high school classes. Each of the four individual tests—English, Mathematics, Reading, and Science Reasoning—is described in detail in Chapter 4 of this book.

The ACT test isn't an IQ test—it doesn't measure your basic intelligence. It's an **achievement** test that's been carefully designed—using surveys of classroom teachers, reviews of curriculum guides for schools all over the country, and advice from curriculum specialists and college faculty—to be one of several effective tools for evaluating your readiness for college work.

The four individual tests that make up the ACT Assessment consist of questions that measure your skills and knowledge. You're **not** required to memorize facts or vocabulary to do well on the ACT test. Of course, all the terms, formulas, and other facts you've learned over the years will be useful to you when you take the ACT test, but last-minute cramming—for instance, memorizing 5,000 vocabulary words or the entire periodic table of chemical elements or the significance of a long list of dates like April 10, 1849, and May 22, 1931*—while no doubt an exciting way to spend a Saturday night, won't directly improve your performance on the ACT test.

What you **can** do to improve your performance—on the ACT test or any exam—is to find out ahead of time what you'll be expected to know or do and to think about how you can use your unique abilities to your best advantage.

First sale of canned rattlesnake meat, 1931.

*Walter Hunt created and patented the safety pin on April 10, 1849.

The first sale of canned rattlesnake meat was by Floridian Products Corporation on May 22, 1931.

Registering for the ACT Test

Selecting a test date

One of the first decisions you'll need to make is **when** to take the ACT test. There are several factors to consider:

- When is the ACT test being offered near your home?
- When does each college or scholarship agency you're interested in need to have your ACT test scores?
- Where do you stand in your high school coursework?
- Are you planning to take the ACT test more than once?

Let's take a look at each of these considerations in turn.

The ACT test is offered nationally several times a year, between September and June. However, it's not offered at every test center on each test date. If you need to take the ACT test on a day other than Saturday because of religious reasons, you'll want to be especially attentive in selecting a test date because the non-Saturday dates are less frequent and are held at fewer test centers.

One of the first things you should find out, then, is where and when the ACT test is being offered in your area. Your high school guidance counselor should be able to give you that information. It's also printed in the booklet *Registering for the ACT Assessment*, which is available free from your school counselor. (See the inside front cover of this book for information on requesting a copy if it's not available from your high school.) Select a test date and location that is convenient for you. Often, your own or a neighboring school will serve as a test center.

One important decision you need to make is whether you should take the ACT test during your junior or your senior year in high school. A number of factors will affect this decision. First, you should find out when colleges you're interested in need to have your test scores. Is there a special program or scholarship for which you want to apply? If so, is there a deadline by which you need to have test scores submitted to the college or agency? It normally takes about four weeks after your test date for your scores to be reported (if there are any problems matching your answer sheet to your registration, it can take up to seven weeks), so be sure to allow enough time. You may not be certain yet which school or program you'll decide on. That's okay. Just be sure you're doing everything, including taking the ACT test, early enough to keep all your options open.

Another consideration in deciding when to take the ACT test is where you stand in your high school coursework. If you're in a college-prep program and taking a lot of courses in English, mathematics, and science in your sophomore and junior years, it may be wise for you to take the ACT test in your junior year, while those subjects are still fresh in your memory. If, on the other hand, you're studying material covered on the ACT test during your senior year, it's reasonable to assume that your performance on the ACT test might be better then.

Perhaps you'll decide to take the ACT test more than once, in hopes of improving your score. In that case, it's probably better to take the exam in your junior year to allow time for a second try.

There are several advantages to taking the ACT test in your junior year:

- You probably will have completed much of the coursework corresponding to the material covered on the ACT test.
- You'll have your ACT test scores and other information in time to help make decisions about your final year of high school coursework. (For example, you may decide to take additional classes in an area in which your test score was lower than you want it to be.)
- Colleges will know of your interest and have your scores in time to contact you during the summer before your senior year, when many of them like to send information about such things as admissions, advanced placement, and special programs to prospective students.
- You'll have your ACT test scores and information from colleges in time to make decisions about visiting campuses or contacting schools.
- You'll have the opportunity to take the ACT test again if you feel your scores don't accurately reflect your achievement.

Colleges will have your scores in time to Contact you during the summer before your senior year.

Test information release

On certain test dates, you may request (for an additional fee) a copy of the test questions used to determine your score, a copy of your answers, a list of the correct answers, and a copy of the table used to convert raw scores (the number of questions you answered correctly on each individual test) to reported scores (the scores that appear on your score report). The service isn't offered for all test dates, so if you're interested in receiving this information, you'll need to check the dates in *Registering for the ACT Assessment* to be sure you're choosing a test date on which the service is available.

Registering

You can usually get an ACT test registration packet from your high school counselor. If no registration packets are available, you or your counselor can write or call ACT for them. The address and phone number appear inside the front cover of this book.

The ACT test registration packet includes a copy of the booklet *Registering for the ACT Assessment.* The booklet describes the steps you need to take to register for the ACT test and lists the deadlines.

Beginning in the fall of 1997, you can register in new ways rather than by completing a registration folder. For example, you can register on the World Wide Web (http://www.act.org) or through ACT's College Connector, if that software is available at your high school. Or, if you are in high school and have taken the ACT Assessment on a national test date within the last two years, your record should be available for **re**registration by phone. There is an additional fee for using the telephone service. Complete instructions, fees, and phone numbers are listed in the registration booklet. If you register on the Web, through College Connector, or reregister by phone, you must pay using MasterCard or VISA.

No matter which method you choose to register, ACT will send you an admission ticket to confirm your registration and to give you specific information about where and when to report to take the test. Read your admission ticket carefully as soon as it arrives to make sure all the information is correct, including the names of the colleges to which you want your scores sent. If you need to make corrections before the test date, follow the instructions on the back of the admission ticket.

You are guaranteed a seat and test booklet at a test center only if you register by the deadline for a test date. If you miss the late registration deadline but have a pressing need to test on the next test date, you can try to test as a "standby" examinee. Testing as a standby is more costly, and you are **not** guaranteed a seat or test booklet. If you decide to take your chance as a standby, be sure to follow the instructions for standby testing in the registration booklet exactly. You must bring a completed registration folder and fee payment with you to the test center, along with acceptable identification. Standby examinees will be admitted only after all registered students have been seated.

Registering under special circumstances

See the registration booklet for instructions for special registration—for example, if your religious beliefs prevent you from taking the exam on Saturday and there are no non-Saturday test centers in your area or if you have a diagnosed disability and require testing accommodations.

If you have a diagnosed disability and documentation of extended time accommodations in school, you *may* be eligible to test on selected national test dates with extended time. Details about the procedures for applying to test with extended time and the amount of time provided are in the registration booklet. To test with extended time, you **must** register by the deadline for the desired test date so your documentation may be reviewed and arrangements made. (Extended time is **not** available for standby examinees.)

At the Test Center

Arriving at the test center

You'll be asked to report to the test center by 8:00 a.m on your test date. The doors will be closed after that, and no one arriving late will be admitted. Under no circumstances will you be admitted after the first timed test has begun, so **be sure** to arrive on time.

You may need to walk a few blocks to get to the test center, or you may need to drive several hours, perhaps to an unfamiliar city. Whatever your situation, be certain to allow plenty of time. If the test is being administered in a place that's new to you, you might consider finding the location the night before the test or even a few days in advance.

Test centers vary considerably. You may be taking the ACT test in your own high school, at a local community college, or in a large building on a nearby university campus. Your surroundings may be quite familiar, or they may be uncomfortably new. If they're new, allow yourself a few extra minutes to get used to the place. Then try to forget about your surroundings so that you can concentrate on the test.

It's probably best to bring with you **only** the things you'll need that morning, since other materials will just be in your way. Be sure to bring:

■ several sharpened **pencils with erasers,**
■ your **admission ticket,**
■ **acceptable identification** (see the registration booklet for details), and
■ an **acceptable calculator** if you wish to use one on the Mathematics Test (acceptable calculators are described in the registration booklet and in the free booklet *Preparing for the ACT Assessment*).

If you need **glasses or contacts** for reading, bring them too, of course.

Because you will probably want to pace yourself, bring a **watch.** Although the test supervisor will announce when there are 5 minutes remaining on each individual test, not all testing rooms have wall clocks.

Bring with you only the things you'll need that morning.

What to wear? Try making this decision ahead of time so you'll have one less thing to think about on the morning of the test. Keep in mind that the building used for administering the ACT test is often one not normally used on a Saturday. As a result, you may find that the heat or air conditioning has been turned off. It's a good idea to dress in layers so that you can adjust to the temperature you find in your testing room.

Remember, too, that you're going to be sitting in the same place for more than three hours. Wearing something you're especially comfortable in may make you better able to relax and concentrate on the test. For many people, what they're wearing can make a difference in how they feel about themselves. Picking something you like and feel good wearing may give you a little extra boost of confidence.

It's a good idea to dress in layers so you can adjust to the temperature you find in your room.

What to expect at the test center

The way **check-in procedures** are handled at a particular test center depends on such things as how many students are taking the ACT test at that center. You may find that all students are met at a central location and directed from there to different classrooms. You may find signs posted, telling you that everyone whose last name falls between certain letters should report directly to a particular room. However this part of the check-in is handled at your center, you can anticipate that certain things will be done, including verification of your identity.

You will be asked for your admission ticket and acceptable identification. To be admitted to take the ACT test, you **must** present acceptable identification or be personally recognized by one of the test center personnel. Examples of acceptable identification include current identification issued by your school, employer, or city/state/federal government on which both your name and current photograph appear; a recognizable *individual* photograph of you in a school yearbook or other publication, printed within the last year and with your first and last name in the caption; or a school letter of identification, which must include your name and full physical description and be on school letterhead signed in ink by you in the presence of a school official (not a relative) and signed in ink by that official. Complete explanations of acceptable forms of identification and examples of unacceptable forms of identification appear in the registration booklet. **Be sure** that you have one of the acceptable forms of identification before you go to the test center. Otherwise, you will not be allowed to test.

In the room you'll be directed to a seat by a room supervisor or proctor (a member of the testing staff). If you are left-handed, let the room supervisor know so that an appropriate desk or table can be made available to you. If there is any problem with your desk, let the room supervisor know.

You'll be asked to put away **everything** except your identification, admission ticket, and pencils. You'll be allowed to have your calculator on your desk only during the Mathematics Test. Nothing else will be allowed in the testing room: no dictionaries, no books or other reading materials, no scratch paper or notes, no highlighting pens, no radios or earphones, no pagers or cellular phones, no food or drink—nothing except your pencils, identification, and admission ticket. If your watch has an alarm, you'll be asked to turn the alarm off so it won't disturb others.

Eating, drinking, and the use of tobacco are not allowed in the testing room, but you can have a snack before the test or during the break, as long as you eat it outside the testing room.

Even though every room is different, you should expect an environment that is quiet, well lighted, and reasonably comfortable. If you have problems with the testing environment, let your room supervisor know immediately.

While you're waiting for the test to begin, you may find yourself getting anxious or jittery. That's perfectly normal. Most of us get nervous in new situations. People handle this nervousness in different ways.

Some people find it helpful to practice **mental and physical relaxation techniques.** If this appeals to you, try alternately flexing and relaxing your muscles, beginning at your toes and moving up through your shoulders, neck, and arms. Meanwhile, imagine yourself in a quiet, peaceful place: at the beach, in the mountains, or just in your favorite lounge chair. Breathe deeply and smoothly.

Relax... imagine yourself in a quiet, peaceful place...

Other people like to **control that nervous energy** and turn it to their advantage. For them, concentrating on the task at hand and shutting everything else out of their minds is the most helpful strategy. If this is your style, you may even want to close your eyes and imagine yourself already working on the exam, thinking about how it will feel to move confidently and smoothly through the tests.

If you have the chance, try out the two approaches on some classroom tests and see which one works better for you. The important thing is to keep the ACT test in perspective. Try not to let it become "larger than life." Remember, it's just one part of a long academic career.

Instructions will be read for each of the four ACT tests, but it's helpful to know them in advance. You'll find the test directions in the sample tests in this book.

Be sure to ask about any aspect of the test-taking procedure that is not perfectly clear to you. After all, how can you expect to do your best if you're worrying about a procedural detail? Testing staff will be available throughout the exam. In fact, they'll be moving quietly around the room while you're working. If you have a question about the administration of the test (not about any of the test questions), raise your hand and quietly ask for information.

During the exam, **you may find yourself getting tired.** If so, check your posture to make sure you're sitting up straight. It's difficult to get enough air in your lungs when you're slouching. You'll stay more alert and confident if you have a steady supply of fresh oxygen going to your brain.

You might want to practice those relaxation techniques again, too, because tension contributes to fatigue. During the short breaks between the individual tests, you might find it helpful to stretch your neck and shoulder muscles, rotate your shoulders, stretch back in your chair, and take some long, deep breaths.

You can expect a slightly longer break (approximately 10 minutes) at the end of the second test. During this break, it's a good idea to stand up, walk around a little, stretch, and relax. You may wish to get a drink, go to the rest room, have a snack, or chat with friends. It's important to keep in mind, though, that you still have work requiring concentration ahead of you. It's also important to return to the room quickly. Your room supervisor will start the third section of the test promptly, and you'll need to be back at your desk and ready to go on time.

If you become ill during the test, you certainly may turn in your test materials and leave if you need to. Let your room supervisor know that you are ill and whether you wish to have your answer sheet scored. One caution: once you've decided to leave the test center, you won't be allowed to return and continue—so **be sure** that leaving is what you want to do. You might try simply closing your eyes or putting your head on the desk for a minute first; then if you feel better, you'll be able to continue.

Summary

This chapter should help you to understand how to get ready to take the ACT test. Knowing the basics of how to register for the ACT test should get you through that process pretty smoothly. By now, you should have a fair idea of what to expect at the test center and know where to find more information: in the ACT test registration booklet (*Registering for the ACT Assessment*) and in *Preparing for the ACT Assessment*. Now that you know the basic information, you should be ready to move on to the ACT test itself.

3
General Test-Taking Strategies

The first thing you should realize is that you've been preparing for the ACT test for **years.** The best possible preparation for a college admission test is active, thoughtful high school coursework. If you've been taking challenging courses, paying attention in class, doing your homework, and thinking about the assignments, you've already done most of the preparation you need to take the ACT test.

Another important part of the preparation that you've already completed is your previous test-taking experience. Just think about all the quizzes, tests, and exams you've taken in ten or more years of school. Think about all the tests you've taken outside of school, too: swimming tests, driving tests, qualifying tests for team sports, and quizzes in popular magazines (for example, "What Kind of Friend Are You?"). Tests of all kinds have become a major part of our lives. They help us make informed decisions, give us one way to compare ourselves with others and to measure our own progress, show us how various products stack up against each other, and help assure us that people performing important roles in our lives are qualified to do so.

An important thing to remember is that **none** of these tests alone makes you qualified to do something; it's the work you do and the skills you learn **before** you take a test that make you qualified. Just taking the driving test, for instance, didn't make you a qualified driver. It was all the parallel parking you did, your knowledge of standard road signs, the skills you developed in your driver's education class, all the things you observed in years of watching other people drive, and your desire to become a licensed driver that gave you the skills you needed. These are the things that made you a qualified driver, one who could pass that test.

Getting Ready

It might be helpful to compare taking the ACT test (or any other important exam) to playing an important match in tennis, or performing in a music concert, or facing another team in debate, or acting in a play. The best way to get ready for a game or performance is to prepare actively: practice the skills required, learn strategies to enable you to demonstrate your strengths, exercise your mind and body, and learn how to deal with the stress of the moment in order to turn it to your advantage.

To get ready for an important test, you need to prepare in much the same way. You need to exercise your mind (for example, through discussion, reading, problem solving), take care of your body (it's difficult for your mind to function well when your body is hungry or tired), and develop strategies (for example, find out in advance as much as you can about the test so you'll know what to expect).

It's a good idea to think about how you'll use what you know in order to do your best on the ACT test. What kind of approach and preparation for this exam will allow you to best demonstrate the abilities and skills you've developed over the years? How can you make sure that you'll do your best?

The suggestions in this chapter are designed to help you build on the preparation that you have already completed. They're taken from advice gathered over years—from education specialists, from testing specialists, and from people who, like you, have taken lots of tests. Read the advice, try it out, and see how it fits with what you already know about the way you take tests. Realize that **you can choose how you will take the ACT test.** Then make intelligent choices about what will work for you.

Mental Preparation

As we've said before, the best mental preparation for the ACT test is solid schoolwork. However, there are some things you can do to prepare for the test and to boost your confidence as well. The following tips will help make you feel calm and mentally confident so that you'll do your very best on the ACT test.

Get organized

If you know that you are going to be taking the ACT test, you should begin preparing well in advance. Don't leave preparation to the last minute. As the test date moves closer, organize a plan to help you do your best on the exam. Getting organized involves everything from assembling the materials you need to take the test (see your registration packet for details) to practicing specific test-taking strategies that will help you do your best. This chapter outlines many different aspects of successful test preparation.

Keep the test in perspective

Remembering that the ACT test is only a small part of the long process of your education and training will help you keep it in perspective. So will remembering that the ACT test and tests like it are designed to provide **you** with information. When you have completed the ACT test, you will receive valuable information that you can use to help make decisions about your future educational plans.

Another way to keep the ACT test in perspective is to remind yourself that it's you taking the test, not the test taking you. **Put yourself in charge** as you go into the test. That's the best way to ensure that you do as well on the test as you can.

Strategies

Learn as much as you can about the ACT test

Before you take the ACT test, the first thing you should do is find out as much about the exam as you can. This advice may seem obvious, but it's surprising how many people just walk into the test and take their chances. Surprises may be fine for a birthday party, but they can be very upsetting when they turn up on tests. The more you know about the ACT test in advance, the more confident you can feel.

Where can you find information about the ACT test? You may find that one good place to look for information is right in your school. Talk to other students who have taken the test and ask them for their impressions. Talk to **several** students so you're not swayed by only one person's experience. Talk to your **teachers and school counselors,** too. Very often they can give you excellent advice based not only on their knowledge of the test but also on what they know about your abilities. Another potential source of information is your public or school library. You can also ask your school counselor for a copy of *Preparing for the ACT Assessment*, a free booklet published by ACT.

Familiarize yourself with the content of the four individual ACT tests (English, Mathematics, Reading, and Science Reasoning) included on the ACT test. Review the information about the four individual ACT tests provided in this book. Note which content areas make up a large proportion of the four individual tests and which do not. The specific topics included in each content area are examples of possible topics; they do not include all of the possibilities. Know what to expect on the test day. Familiarize yourself with the information in this book, your registration packet, and the free booklet *Preparing for the ACT Assessment*.

Once you know **what** to expect, you can concentrate on **how** to do the work. For instance, once you know that the ACT Mathematics Test covers trigonometry skills, you can focus your attention on the properties of triangles, if you need review in that area.

Maybe this seems obvious to you, but focusing attention on the task at hand is often harder than it sounds. Don't let preparing for the ACT test seem like an overwhelming job. Cutting that large task into smaller pieces will make preparing much more manageable. Training yourself to concentrate your mental energies on small, manageable jobs instead of letting yourself be distracted by all sorts of other interesting things will have long-term benefits, including making it easier for you to prepare mentally for the ACT test or any test.

Refresh your knowledge and skills in the content areas

Once you have a good idea of the content of the four individual ACT tests, review those content areas you have studied but do not have fresh in your mind. You also may want to spend time refreshing your knowledge in the content areas that make up large portions of the individual tests.

Identify the content areas you have not studied

If you find that the four individual ACT tests contain many unfamiliar content areas, consider taking courses to help you gain knowledge in those areas before you take the ACT test. Because the ACT test measures knowledge acquired over a period of time, it is unlikely that a "cram" course covering material that is unfamiliar to you will help you improve your scores. Longer, full-term courses in the subject matter will be most helpful to you because they aim to improve your knowledge in a subject area.

Plan your study time

When an exam like the ACT test is far in the future, it's pretty easy to put off preparing for it. Something else always seems to come up: going on a date, seeing a movie, watching your favorite television show, even cleaning your room may seem more interesting than studying for a test that's still in the hazy future. Somehow the days disappear, though, and you find yourself frantically cramming the night before the test, overwhelmed by just how much material you have to cover.

If this sounds familiar, try setting up a reasonable schedule for studying for the ACT test. **Set aside small amounts of time** for studying over an extended period—days, weeks, or even months—so you won't have so much to do at the end that you feel swamped. Sometimes it's too easy to scrap the whole plan once there's a small change in it, so **make your schedule flexible** enough to allow for a surprise homework assignment or some unexpected fun. And find a way to **reward yourself** as you get the work done, even if it's just a checklist you can mark to show your progress.

In setting up a schedule to prepare for the ACT test, refer to the suggestions in Chapter 1 for some ideas. Figure out how you can best use the materials in this book, estimate the time you want and need to spend, and plan a schedule that will allow you to complete the materials at least several days before your scheduled exam date. If something interferes with your plan, don't discard your schedule, just make it a more manageable one. You can benefit from **any** plan, even if it's scaled down from your original one.

An important part of mental preparation is learning to appreciate and use your particular abilities. It is important to know your abilities and to make your study decisions based on what **you** need to do.

Develop a positive mental attitude

In addition to learning the material you'll be tested on and reviewing it to make sure it's fresh in your mind, it's important to go into the ACT test with a good mental attitude, confident that you can do your best. While confidence obviously isn't enough by itself to ensure good performance on a test, a real lack of confidence can hurt your performance. Be confident in your ability to do well on the ACT test. **You can do well!** You just need to be prepared to work hard.

Some small changes can make a surprising difference. For example, how you imagine yourself taking the exam may affect how well you actually do. Negative thoughts have a way of turning into negative actions. So **practice positive thinking:** imagine yourself meeting the challenge of the exam with ease, successfully. The day of the test, tell yourself you intend to do your best, and act as if you mean it. You probably won't get a perfect score, but that's not the point. You want to be sure you do as well as you can against the most important

Develop a positive mental attitude.

measure: your own capabilities. The real satisfaction doesn't lie in meeting somebody else's expectations for you, but in knowing that you've met your own expectations—that you've done your personal best.

Physical Preparation

You may wonder why physical preparation is important for an exam such as the ACT test. After all, taking an exam isn't exactly like playing a game of soccer. So why should you prepare yourself physically?

Think of the body as the mind's support system. Being sure that your body is at peak performance the morning you take the ACT test will help your mind work at its peak too.

Exercise

This is not the time to neglect your usual exercise. Be sure you get plenty of physical activity in the days before the exam. Hiking, running, walking, biking, swimming, basketball, soccer—all the aerobic exercises you regularly enjoy will improve your body's performance.

Diet

Diet is also important. You've probably heard the standard advice: "Be sure to **eat a good breakfast** before you take the test." That sounds like sensible advice, but what exactly is a "good breakfast"? Different people have different opinions.

On test day you should probably select the healthiest breakfast **you** are accustomed to. If you routinely eat a very light breakfast, choose your **best** light breakfast—don't switch to something entirely new. If you usually have a bowl of cereal and juice, for example, you probably shouldn't have a huge stack of pancakes the morning of the ACT test. On the other hand, if you're accustomed to a substantial breakfast, it would be a mistake to skip breakfast altogether or to eat significantly less than you're used to. A sugary breakfast will probably work against you. While it may give you an initial charge of energy to start the morning, that energy will most likely burn off before you're halfway through.

When planning what to eat the morning of the test, you may want to consider that while eating and drinking are not allowed in the testing room, you can have a snack before the test or during the break. (You can expect a ten-minute break at the end of the second test.)

Somebody may suggest to you that you'll do better on the test if you "take something." This simply isn't true. The effect on your body of taking drugs not prescribed for you by a medical doctor is negative. Period.

What exactly is a "good breakfast"?

Rest

Get plenty of sleep the night before the test so you will be in good physical condition for taking it. How much sleep is "plenty"? Again, keep in mind **your** typical schedule. If you routinely go to bed at 11:00 p.m., this is probably not the time to stay up until 2:30 a.m. On the other hand, going to bed at 8:00 p.m. may also be a mistake. If you suddenly go to bed much earlier than your body is used to, you may find yourself tossing and turning for hours, and you'll be more tired than you would have been if you'd watched television or read or shot baskets during that time.

Advice you hear about physical preparation for tests often focuses on just the day before a test. You'll find, however, that the amount of sleep and exercise you get—not just the day before the test, but for days and even weeks before—will make a difference in how you feel and how you are able to perform on the test. Similarly, it's not just what you eat for breakfast the morning of test day, but what you've eaten for several days before that gives you the power you need to perform well.

Going to bed much earlier than your body is used to may be a mistake.

Test-Taking Strategies

As with most skills, test-taking skill varies from person to person. In this chapter we've listed a few basic test-taking strategies that apply to nearly every test you take, as well as to the ACT test. You've probably used most of these strategies before. Recognizing that you know how to use them—and that they are valuable—should help you approach the ACT test with confidence.

Take a practice test

The best way to anticipate what it will be like to take the ACT test is to take a sample version of it. You'll find a practice ACT test in the free booklet *Preparing for the ACT Assessment*. You'll also find two complete ACT tests in this book. (See Chapter 5 for the tests and Chapter 6 for suggestions on how to score them.) You may want to practice some of the strategies outlined in this chapter when you take the practice tests.

Learn to pace yourself

The ACT test, like many tests, **must** be completed within a specific and limited amount of time. Working quickly and efficiently is one of the skills necessary for conveying how much you've learned on the topic being tested.

Pacing yourself on a multiple-choice test can be quite simple. As an example, for the Mathematics Test, which consists of 60 multiple-choice questions, one possibility is to simply divide the amount of time available for the test by the number of questions you'll have to answer. One problem with this, on some tests, is that you may come up with a length of time that doesn't mean much. Do you have any clear idea of how long 80 seconds is, for example? Another problem may be that the amount of time sounds so short it's scary, and you can talk yourself into feeling panicky.

Another option is to divide the total number of questions into smaller groups and figure out how much time you have for each group. If you prefer this approach, try to keep the math simple. For example, if you have a total of 30 questions to answer in one hour, think of it as either two groups of 15 questions at 30 minutes for each group, or three groups of 10 questions at 20 minutes for each group. Then check your watch to see how closely you're keeping to that schedule as you're taking practice ACT tests. If after 10 questions you've used only 18 minutes, you'll know that you're doing well. On the other hand, if those first 10 questions have taken 23 minutes, you'll probably want to pick up the pace if you can. You will probably also want to set aside several minutes at the end of each individual test for a quick review of your work.

On the English, Reading, and Science Reasoning Tests, you may want to pace yourself by figuring out a certain amount of time to spend reading each passage and then determining how much time you have left to spend on the associated questions. For example, if you have four passages to cover in 40 minutes, you would allow yourself roughly 10 minutes for each passage and the related questions. If you spend 5 minutes reading a passage, then you would know that you have roughly 5 minutes to spend on the questions associated with the passage. Chapter 4 contains more detailed ideas about how to pace yourself on each of the four ACT tests.

You won't want to drift off into fascinating speculation about how many isopods — whatever they are — you can fit on a petri dish.

No matter how you choose to pace yourself while taking the ACT test, don't let your concern about time get in the way of your work. Don't try to push yourself to work so fast that you begin to feel out of control or to make careless errors. After all, answering 60 questions so quickly that, through carelessness, you miss 20 doesn't give you a better score than answering 50 more slowly and missing only 10.

The ACT test has been designed so that most people taking it are able to finish each individual test. Many people have time to go back and check their work on each test too. So, while you won't want to lose time by daydreaming or drifting off into fascinating speculation prompted by one of the test questions ("Say, how many isopods can you fit on a petri dish, anyway?"), you shouldn't worry unnecessarily about time either. Use all of the time available so you can do your very best on the test.

We've included the time available for each individual test of the ACT Assessment in the information in Chapter 4. Use the practice tests in this book to check your own working pace and see if you, like most people, will have time to finish each ACT test and go back and check your work. Perhaps working through the practice tests will let you know at what pace you need to work in order to finish within the available time. If so, you'll want to keep that in mind when you take the actual test.

If you wish to keep track of your pace while taking the ACT test, bring a watch. Not all testing centers have wall clocks. The test supervisor will announce when there are 5 minutes left on each test.

Know the directions and understand the answer sheet

It's easy to ignore directions, no matter what we're doing. Have you ever seen anyone read **all** the directions for installing a new appliance, or putting a child's toy together, or changing the time on a digital watch? Many of us are more likely to just forge ahead—do whatever we're doing the way we think it ought to be done, regardless of what a manufacturer had in mind.

Putting the instructions aside and "winging it" is probably all right at home (sometimes the entertainment value may even be worth the frustration), but you're not working under a time deadline at home. If something goes wrong or doesn't make sense, you can always undo what you've done and start over. With an exam such as the ACT test, you need to get it right the first time.

On the day that you take the ACT test, the directions for each test will be read to you. However, it is helpful to know them in advance—it will save you time and worry. For example, the English, Reading, and Science Reasoning Tests of the ACT Assessment ask for the "best" answer, while the Mathematics Test asks for the "correct" answer. This simple difference in the instructions signals an important distinction you need to keep in mind as you're working through those tests. Because only one answer is "correct" in the Mathematics Test, you'll want to be sure your understanding of the question and your calculations are precise—so that your answer matches one, and only one, of the possible answers. In the other areas, more than one of the possible answers may arguably be "correct," and you'll need to be careful to select the "best" answer among those potentially "correct" ones. You'll find the directions for each test in the practice ACT tests in this book.

Before you take the ACT test, become familiar with the answer sheet as well. Knowing in advance how to use the answer sheet will save you time and worry when you take the actual test and also help you to take it.

Strategies

Read carefully and thoroughly

Just as it's important to read and understand the **directions** for a test, it's also important to read and understand each **question** on the test. As you've probably discovered somewhere along the line, you can miss even the simplest test question by reading carelessly and overlooking an important word or detail. Some questions on the ACT test, for instance, require more than one step, and the answer to each preliminary step may be included as an answer choice. If you read these questions too quickly, you can easily make the mistake of choosing a plausible answer that relates to a preliminary step but is the incorrect answer to the question.

Take the time to read each question carefully and thoroughly before deciding on your answer. Make sure you understand **exactly** what the question asks and what you are to do to answer it. You may want to underline or circle key words in the test booklet. Reread the item if you are confused.

Watch the question's wording. Look for words such as *not* or *least*, especially when they are not clearly set off through the use of underlining, capital letters, or bold type. Don't make careless errors because you only skimmed the question or the options. Pay close attention to qualifying words such as *all, most, some, none—always, usually, seldom, sometimes, never—best, worst—highest, lowest—smaller, larger*. (There are many other qualifying words; these are only a few examples of related groups.) When you find a qualifier in one of the responses to a question, a good way to determine whether or not the response is the best answer is to substitute related qualifiers and see which makes the best statement. For example, if a response says "Tests are always difficult," you might test the truth of the word *always* by substituting *sometimes* and the other words related to *always*. If any of the words other than the one in the answer makes the best statement, then the response is not the best answer.

Pay close attention to modifying or limiting phrases in the statement. For instance, a question in the Reading Test might have the following as a possible answer: "Lewis and Clark, the great British explorers, began their historic trip to the West Coast by traveling up the Mississippi." The answer is incorrect because Lewis and Clark were not British, but were U.S. citizens. (You would not be expected to know from memory that Lewis and Clark were U.S. citizens; that information would be included in the passage.)

Read all the answer choices before selecting one. Questions on the ACT test often include answer choices that seem plausible but that aren't quite correct. Even though the first answer choice may appeal to you, the correct or best answer may be farther down the list.

Decide on strategies for answering easier and harder questions

Many people work quickly through an entire individual test (English, Mathematics, Reading, or Science Reasoning) answering only those questions they're pretty sure about the first time and skipping the others. Then they go back and work more slowly through the questions they found difficult at first. There are several advantages to this approach:

■ You have the satisfaction of moving along quickly, accomplishing a lot in a short period of time.

■ When you return to a tough question, you may have remembered something important in the meantime. (It's like putting part of your brain "on special assignment" while you go on to the rest of the test.)

■ You can be sure you'll get to **all** the questions you can answer easily before you run out of time.

The biggest possible disadvantage to this approach is that, if you're marking your answer sheet at the same time that you're answering the questions, you have to be **very careful** about where you're marking your answers on your answer sheet. If you skip a question in your test booklet, be sure to skip the question on your answer sheet too. You'll probably want to put a check or a star by each of these questions in your test booklet—**not on your answer sheet**—so that you can find them easily later on, when you're ready to return to them. (Remember: unless you're instructed otherwise, **you can write in the ACT test booklet** as much as you like.)

Decide on a strategy for marking your answer sheet

Many people find that writing their answers in the test booklet as they work through the questions on an individual test and saving 5 minutes at the end of each individual test in order to fill in their answer sheet helps them avoid making errors in marking their answer sheets. You may want to try this strategy to see if it works for you.

Decide on a strategy for guessing

Should you guess or not? On some standardized tests, you're penalized for each incorrect answer. On the ACT test, however, your raw score is based on the number of questions you get right—there's no deduction for wrong answers.

Because **you're not penalized for guessing on the ACT test,** it's to your advantage to answer each question. Here's a good way to proceed:

1) When you come to a question that stumps you, see if you can eliminate at least a couple of the choices.
2) If you still aren't sure about the answer, take your best guess.

If you can rule out one or two of the possible answers, the odds are better that you'll select the right response. You don't need a perfect reason to eliminate one answer and choose another. Sometimes an intelligent guess is based on a hunch—on something you may know but don't have time to consciously recognize in a timed-test situation.

Maybe you've heard some advice about how to answer questions when you don't know the correct answer, such as "When in doubt, choose C," or "When in doubt, select the longest (or shortest) alternative," or "If NONE OF THE ABOVE (or a similar response) is among the answer choices, select it." While these bits of advice may hold true now and then, you should know that the questions on the ACT test have been carefully written to make these strategies ineffective. The best advice is to rule out any of the possible answers you can on the basis of your knowledge and then, if necessary, make your best guess.

Decide on a strategy for changing your mind

You think that you might have marked the wrong answer choice on a certain question. Do you go with your original answer or change it to the new answer? People may tell you to always go with your first response. And surely everyone has had the experience of agonizing over a response, trying to decide whether to change it, then doing so only to find out later that the first answer was the right one.

However, some research by education and testing specialists suggests that you **should** change your answer when you change your mind. If you're like the people tested in that research, your second answer is more likely to be the correct one.

So, how can you decide what you should do? Unfortunately, there's no easy advice that will suit every test taker and every situation. What you should do depends upon **you** and your test-taking methods. Before you change an answer, think about how you approached the question in the first place. Give some weight to the reasons why you now believe another answer is better. Don't mechanically follow an arbitrary rule just because it works for somebody else. Know yourself; then trust yourself to make intelligent, informed decisions.

Plan to check your work

When you get to the end of one of the four individual ACT tests, you may feel you've done quite enough. After all, you've just spent from 30 to 60 minutes hassling with questions that didn't seem to want to be answered. You're tired, and you just want to use that extra 5 minutes for a nap. Maybe you look around the room and see other people who have closed both their test booklets and their eyes.

Hard as it may be, try to keep your energy going until time is called so you can go back through that test and check your answers. (Remember: you're allowed to work on only one test at a time.) You also may want to set aside a few minutes to mark your answer sheet for that test all at once after you've checked your answers.

Here are some suggestions for checking your answers:

■ Be sure you've marked all your answers in the proper places on the answer sheet.

■ Be certain you've answered **all** the questions on your answer sheet, even the ones you weren't sure about. (Of course, you must be very careful to stop marking ovals when time is called.)

■ When you reach the end of the Mathematics Test, check your calculations. You may check your calculations using the math booklet as scratch paper or using a calculator. (Calculators are now allowed for use **only** on the Mathematics Test; see your registration booklet for details.)

■ Check your answer sheet for stray pencil marks that may be misread by the scoring machine.

■ Be sure you've marked only one answer on your answer sheet for each question.

■ If there are too many questions for you to check all of your answers, be sure to check those that you feel most uncertain about first, then any others that you have time for.

Have a panic strategy

When you're under pressure during a test, an unexpected question or something small like breaking a pencil can be very upsetting. For many students, the natural tendency at such times is to panic. Panic detracts from test performance by causing students to become confused and discouraged and to have trouble recalling information that they know.

It's a good idea to have a strategy ready for dealing with panic that might arise while you take the ACT test. One good panic strategy is to give yourself a brief "time out." To do this, take slow, deep breaths and let yourself relax. Put the test temporarily out of mind. Close your eyes if you want. Visualize yourself confidently resuming work on the test, turning in a completed test paper, and leaving the room with a feeling of having done your best work. Allow 20 to 30 seconds for your time out. That's probably all you'll need to get your panic under control and start back to work on the test.

Summary

All the strategies outlined in this chapter are merely suggestions intended to give you ideas about good preparation habits and strategies for getting through the ACT test in the best, most efficient manner possible. Some of the strategies will work for you, others won't. Feel free to pick and choose from among all the strategies in this chapter, and the more specific strategies in Chapter 4, so that you have a test-taking plan that works best for **you.**

Strategies

Part 2: The Tests

4

Test Format and Content

The ACT test is made up of four individual tests, each of which is designed to measure academic achievement in a major area of high school study: English, mathematics, reading, and natural sciences. This chapter contains four sections; each describes one of the four tests in detail, gives examples of the kinds of questions you're likely to find on that test, and offers some suggestions for approaching those questions and that test as a whole.

The example questions in each section of this chapter are taken from actual ACT tests, but the way they're presented and discussed varies somewhat in each section.

The questions you'll find discussed in the English and Reading sections are taken from sample passages and questions that immediately follow the discussions. The English example questions that are discussed are taken from a complete English Test. The Reading examples are taken from six sample passages and accompanying questions. (So, while there are 60 example Reading questions in this chapter, there are only 40 Reading questions in an actual test.) Not all of the sample questions with each of the passages in the English and Reading sections are used as examples in the discussions; therefore, keys are provided at the end of each of these sections for you to check your answers. If you want to use the English and Reading sample passages and questions for practice, you may want to do that before reading the discussions of the tests. Or you may prefer to read the discussions first, and then to work through the sample passages and questions with the benefit of the information you've just read.

Each example question in the Mathematics section of this chapter is followed immediately by a discussion of the question. In the Science Reasoning section you'll find four sample passages, each accompanied by five questions and each followed by a discussion of those five example questions. Keys are provided at the end of each of these sections for you to check your answers.

However you approach this chapter, before you begin you may find it helpful to take a look at the following charts to give yourself an idea of the makeup of the ACT Assessment as a whole and of its individual tests.

ACT Assessment English Test 75 items, 45 minutes		
Content/Skills	**Proportion of Test**	**Number of Items**
Usage/Mechanics	**.53**	**40**
Punctuation	.13	10
Basic Grammar and Usage	.16	12
Sentence Structure	.24	18
Rhetorical Skills	**.47**	**35**
Strategy	.16	12
Organization	.15	11
Style	.16	12
Total	**1.00**	**75**
Scores reported: Usage/Mechanics (40 items) Rhetorical Skills (35 items) Total test score (75 items)		

ACT Assessment Mathematics Test 60 items, 60 minutes		
Content Area	**Proportion of Test**	**Number of Items**
Pre-Algebra	.23	14
Elementary Algebra	.17	10
Intermediate Algebra	.15	9
Coordinate Geometry	.15	9
Plane Geometry	.23	14
Trigonometry	.07	4
Total	**1.00**	**60**
Scores reported: Pre-Algebra/Elementary Algebra (24 items) Intermediate Algebra/Coordinate Geometry (18 items) Plane Geometry/Trigonometry (18 items) Total test score (60 items)		

ACT Assessment Reading Test		
40 items, 35 minutes		
Reading Content	**Proportion of Test**	**Number of Items**
Prose Fiction	.25	10
Humanities	.25	10
Social Studies	.25	10
Natural Sciences	.25	10
Total	**1.00**	**40**

Scores reported: Arts/Literature (Prose Fiction, Humanities: 20 items)
Social Studies/Sciences (Social Studies, Natural Sciences: 20 items)
Total test score (40 items)

ACT Assessment Science Reasoning Test			
40 items, 35 minutes			
Content Area*	**Format**	**Proportion of Test**	**Number of Items**
Biology	Data Representation	.38	15
Earth/Space Sciences	Research Summaries	.45	18
Chemistry Physics	Conflicting Viewpoints	.17	7
Total		**1.00**	**40**

Scores reported: Total test score (40 items)

*Note: Content areas are distributed over the different formats.

ACT Assessment English Test

On the ACT English Test, you have 45 minutes to read five passages, or essays, and answer 75 multiple-choice questions about them—an average of 15 questions per passage. The passages on the English Test cover a variety of subjects; the example passages that follow this discussion range from a personal essay about using a fanny pack to a historical essay about the beginnings of radio broadcasting.

Content of the ACT English Test

The ACT English Test is designed to measure your ability to accomplish the wide variety of decisions involved in revising and editing a given piece of writing. An important part of revision and editing decisions is a good understanding of the conventions of standard written English. You may not always use "standard written English" in casual writing (for instance, when you're writing to a friend) or in conversation. In casual writing or conversation, we often use slang expressions that have special meanings with friends our own age or in our part of the country. Because slang can become outdated (Does anybody say "groovy" anymore?) and regional terms might not be familiar to students everywhere (Do you and your friends say "soda," or "soft drink," or "pop"?), this test emphasizes the standard written English that is taught in schools around the country.

Questions on the English Test fall into two categories:

■ **Usage/Mechanics** (punctuation, grammar and usage, sentence structure)
■ **Rhetorical Skills** (writing strategy, organization, style)

You'll receive a score for all 75 questions, and two subscores—one based on 40 Usage/Mechanics questions and the other based on 35 Rhetorical Skills questions.

You will **not** be tested on spelling or on how well you can recall specific rules of grammar. Grammar and usage are tested only within the context of the essay, not by questions like "Must an appositive always be set off by commas?" Likewise, you won't be tested directly on your vocabulary, although the better your vocabulary is, the better equipped you'll be to answer questions that involve choosing the most appropriate word.

Like the other tests in the ACT Assessment, the English Test doesn't require you to memorize what you read. The questions and essays are side-by-side for easy reference. This is **not** a memorization test.

The questions discussed below are taken from the example passages and questions that follow on pages 68–79. If you prefer, you can work through the example passages and questions before you read the rest of this discussion. On the other hand, if you wish to better understand the English Test, you may want to first read the discussion, then work through the example passages and questions.

Types of Questions on the ACT English Test

Usage/Mechanics questions always refer to an underlined portion of the essay. You must decide on the best choice of words and punctuation for that underlined portion. Usually, your options include NO CHANGE, which means that the essay is best as it's written. Sometimes you'll also have the option of completely removing the underlined portion. For example, question 55 (from the passage and questions on pages 74–76) offers you the option of removing the phrase "it's control for" from the sentence.

Years later, the Radio Law of 1927 was
$\overline{54}$
enacted. It authorized it's control for licensing
$\overline{55}$
and of policing the broadcasters.

55. A. NO CHANGE
   B. controlling
   C. the control of
   D. OMIT the underlined portion.

In this example, the best answer is not to omit the underlined portion but to replace it with **C.**

Rhetorical Skills questions may refer to an underlined portion, or they may ask about a section of the essay or an aspect of the essay as a whole. For example, in the following question (from the passage and questions on pages 70–72), you're given a sentence to be added to the passage and the purpose of that sentence, and then you're asked to decide the most logical and appropriate place in the essay to add that sentence for that purpose.

---

30. The writer intends to add the following sentence to the essay in order to provide a comparison that would help underline the challenges that Bessie Coleman faced:

> Her dream of becoming the world's first black woman pilot seemed as remote in Chicago as it had been in Oklahoma.

In order to accomplish this purpose, it would be most logical and appropriate to place this sentence after the:

F. first sentence in Paragraph 2.
G. first sentence in Paragraph 3.
H. last sentence in Paragraph 3.
J. first sentence in Paragraph 5.

In this example, the best answer is **G,** because the first sentence in Paragraph 3 describes Coleman's inability to find flying lessons in Chicago.

Let's take a look now at some of the kinds of questions you're likely to find on the ACT English Test in each of the two categories. If you want to know what an individual question looks like in the context of the passage it appears in, turn to the pages indicated. You can also use those passages and questions for practice, either before or after reading this discussion.

Usage/Mechanics

Usage/Mechanics questions focus on the conventions of punctuation, grammar and usage, and sentence structure and formation.

Punctuation questions involve identifying and correcting the following misplaced, missing, or unnecessary punctuation marks:

- commas
- apostrophes
- colons and semicolons
- parentheses and dashes ( ) –
- periods, question marks, and exclamation points

These questions address not only the "rules" of punctuation but also the use of punctuation to express ideas clearly. For example, you should be prepared to show how punctuation can be used to indicate possession or to set off a parenthetical element.

Usage/Mechanics
- *using phrases in sentences*
- *punctuation ~ • misplased • missing or • unnecssesary.*
- *how punctuation used*

In many punctuation questions, the words in every choice will be identical but the commas or other punctuation will vary. It's important to read the choices carefully in order to notice the presence or absence of commas, semicolons, colons, periods, and other punctuation. The following example of a punctuation question comes from the passage and questions on pages 68–70.

It was sleek,

eye-catching, and best of all; appeared to be
2

actually functional.

2. F. NO CHANGE
   G. eye-catching, and, best, of all
   H. eye-catching and best of all,
   J. eye-catching, and, best of all,

It may help you to read through this sentence without paying attention to the punctuation so you can identify the grammatical construction of it. There is a series of adjectives: "sleek, eye-catching, and . . . appeared to be actually functional." There is also a short parenthetical phrase (a kind of aside), "best of all," between the next-to-last and last item in the series. So, you have two punctuation matters to consider in this question. What punctuation should you use to deal with the items in a series and the parenthetical phrase?

Items in a series are usually separated by commas. (It might be good to keep in mind that when the next-to-last and last items are separated by a conjunction like *and,* a comma after the next-to-last item is often considered optional.) Parenthetical phrases are usually set off from the rest of the sentence with commas, dashes, or parentheses. None of the options for question 2 propose dashes or parentheses. It is possible to use no punctuation at all for a very short parenthetical phrase that fits easily into the flow of the sentence. The phrase "best of all" occurs in the middle of a punctuated series, so it would be more helpful to the reader if it were set off using punctuation. **J** is the only option for placing a comma before and after "best of all," and it also proposes a comma after the next-to-last item in the series.

You might have decided that this was the best way to punctuate the sentence before even looking at the four options given, then matched **J** with your own choice and put that down as your answer. A way to double-check your answer if you are in doubt is to consider other possible solutions to a punctuation problem and then to make sure none of the answer choices match those other possible solutions.

Grammar and usage questions involve choosing the best word or words in a sentence based on considerations of the conventions of grammar and usage. Some examples of poor and better phrases are given below.

- Grammatical agreement

  Subject and verb

  "The owner of the bicycles *are* going to sell them"

  should be:

  "The owner of the bicycles *is* going to sell them."

  Pronoun and antecedent

  "Susan and Mary left *her* briefcases in the office"

  should be:

  "Susan and Mary left *their* briefcases in the office."

  Adjectives and adverbs with corresponding nouns and verbs

  "Danielle spread frosting *liberal* on the cat"

  should be:

  "Danielle spread frosting *liberally* on the cat."

- Verb forms

  "Fritz had just *began* to toast Lydia's marshmallows when the rabbits stampeded"

  should be:

  "Fritz had just *begun* to toast Lydia's marshmallows when the rabbits stampeded."

- Pronoun forms and cases

  "Seymour and Svetlana annoyed *there* parents all the time"

  should be:

  "Seymour and Svetlana annoyed *their* parents all the time."

  "After the incident with the peanut butter, the zebra and *me* were never invited back"

  should be:

  "After the incident with the peanut butter, the zebra and *I* were never invited back."

- Comparative and superlative modifiers

"My goldfish is *more smarter* than your brother"

should be:

"My goldfish is *smarter* than your brother."

"Your brother, however, has the *cuter* aardvark that I've ever seen"

should be:

"Your brother, however, has the *cutest* aardvark that I've ever seen."

My goldfish is smarter than your brother.

- Idioms

"An idiom is an established phrase that follows no particular grammatical rule yet can be looked *down* in the dictionary"

should be:

"An idiom is an established phrase that follows no particular grammatical rule yet can be looked *up* in the dictionary."

Questions dealing with pronouns sometimes have to do with using the proper form and case of the pronoun. Often, however, they address a pronoun's agreement with its antecedent or referent. In such cases, it's important to consider the entire sentence, and sometimes the preceding sentence, in order to make sure you know what the antecedent is. Consider the following question (from the passage and questions on pages 72–74).

When Hank Aaron

stretched out a sinewy arm to pull one down,
<u></u>
　　　37

striding up to a rack of ash-hewn bats, he became a
<u></u>
　　　37

modern-day knight selecting <u>their</u> lance.
　　　　　　　　　　　　　38

38. **F.** NO CHANGE
　　G. there
　　H. his
　　J. one's

Here, the possessive pronoun in question refers back to "a modern-day knight." In an indirect way, it also refers back to Hank Aaron, since he is the person being described as a modern-day knight. The third-person plural pronoun *their* (**F**) does not agree in number with the antecedent, "a modern-day knight." Option **G,** *there,* is a word that functions as an adverb, noun, or pronoun; it is often confused with the possessive pronoun *their.* Because *there* cannot be used to refer to a person, it is incorrect. **J** does show singular possession through the use of the apostrophe plus *s,* but the indefinite pronoun *one* is used to refer to a person who is not specifically named. The context of this sentence calls for the specificity offered by the personal pronoun *his* (**H**).

Sentence structure questions involve the effective formation of sentences, including dealing with relationships between and among clauses, placement of modifiers, and shifts in construction. Below are some examples:

- Subordinate or dependent clauses

    "These hamsters are excellent pets *because providing* hours of cheap entertainment."

    This sentence could be rewritten as:

    "These hamsters are excellent pets *providing* hours of cheap entertainment."

    It could also be revised as:

    "These hamsters are excellent pets *because they provide* hours of cheap entertainment."

- Run-on sentences

    "We discovered that the entire family had been devoured by *anteaters it* was horrible."

    This sentence should actually be two:

    "We discovered that the entire family had been devoured by *anteaters. It* was horrible."

- Comma splices

    "The anteaters had terrible *manners, they* just ate and ran."

    This sentence could be rewritten as:

    "The anteaters had terrible *manners. They* just ate and ran."

    It could also be rewritten as:

    "The anteaters had terrible *manners; they* just ate and ran."

Anteater belatedly displaying good manners.

■ Sentence fragments

"*When he* found scorpions in his socks."

This needs a subject to let us know who "he" is and what he did:

"*Julio didn't lose his temper when he* found scorpions in his socks."

■ Misplaced modifiers

"*Snarling and snapping, Juanita attempted to control her pet turtle.*"

Unless Juanita was doing the snarling and snapping, the sentence should be rewritten:

"Snarling and snapping, *the pet turtle resisted Juanita's attempt to control it.*"

It could also be rewritten this way:

"Juanita attempted to control her pet turtle, *which snarled and snapped.*"

■ Shifts in construction

"We sat down to the table to eat, but before we began, John *says* grace."

This should be rewritten as:

"We sat down to the table to eat, but before we began, John *said* grace."

"Hamsters should work at the most efficient pace that *one* can."

This should be rewritten as:

"Hamsters should work at the most efficient pace that *they* can."

Many questions about sentence structure and formation will ask you about how clauses and phrases are linked. This means that you may have to consider punctuation or the lack of punctuation, which can create problems like comma splices, run-on sentences, or sentence fragments. You also may have to consider various words that can be used to link clauses and phrases: conjunctions like *and, but, because,* and *when,* and pronouns like *who, whose, which,* and *that.* The following question (from the example passage and questions on pages 72–74) is a good example of a sentence structure question.

Babe Ruth, Ted Williams, Joe DiMaggio,

Roberto Clemente—names like these will echo through

<u>time that are</u> trumpet calls to storied battles fought
₃₅

and won in ages past.

35. A. NO CHANGE
    B. time like
    C. time in which
    D. time, which is like

What would be the best way to link the phrase "trumpet calls to storied battles fought and won in ages past" to the independent clause "names like these will echo through time"? You might be able to readily come up with an answer to this question that matches one of the answer choices given. Another approach would be to look at each answer choice and test it out.

Option **A** proposes using the pronoun *that* to link the phrase and the clause. Let's see if the clause makes sense if we substitute the preceding noun, which would be the most logical antecedent, for the pronoun: "time are trumpet calls to storied battles fought and won in ages past." That just doesn't sound right to the ear. Let's do the same with the pronoun *which* in **C:** "in time trumpet calls to storied battles fought and won in ages past." This clause should sound like a sentence, but it sounds like a sentence fragment. Let's try **D:** "time is like trumpet calls to storied battles fought and won in ages past." This sounds like a sentence, but it's a sentence that doesn't make much sense.

Option **B** proposes a different approach to linking this phrase to the main clause: using the preposition *like* (meaning "in the manner of, similar to"). In this approach the phrase becomes a prepositional phrase describing *echo,* the verb of the main clause. The prepositional phrase helps to describe how these names will echo: "like trumpet calls to storied battles fought and won in ages past." That works from the standpoint of both sentence structure and logic. (You may have been told by teachers to avoid using *like* in writing, but it does have a place in good writing.)

Rhetorical Skills

Rhetorical Skills questions focus on writing strategy, organization, and style.

Writing strategy questions focus on the choices made and strategies used by a writer in the act of composing or revising an essay. These questions may ask you to make decisions concerning the appropriateness of a sentence or essay in relation to a particular audience or purpose; the effect of adding, revising, or deleting supporting material; or the effective choice of an opening, transitional, or closing sentence.

The following question (from the example passage and questions on pages 77–79) is a fairly typical example of the kinds of writing decisions that strategy questions ask you to make:

[2]

Some are very serious; running is a
<u>65</u>
discipline for them. 66 They run hard and gracefully, easily passing the rest of us. Their clothing looks comfortable and functional. I see them doing stretching exercises to warm up and cooling-down exercises after they run.

[3]

67 They wear expensive, fashionable outfits, perfectly fit and sleek, always new-looking. Neither these runners nor their <u>clothes,</u> ever look
<u>68</u>
sweaty or messy. One young man ran for two hours, and his sweatband was dry, his hair in place, and his shoes unscuffed. Such runners don't so much exercise as perform.

67. The writer wishes to begin Paragraph 3 with a sentence that strengthens the focus of the paragraph, while providing a transition from Paragraph 2. Which of the following would be the best choice?

A. Some runners run for health reasons.
B. Some runners run to be admired.
C. Runners come in a wide range of ages.
D. Some people like money and the things money can buy.

It's important to read the question very carefully. Notice that the answer should fulfill two purposes: it should provide an opening sentence for Paragraph 3 that will help focus the paragraph and that will also provide a transition from the preceding paragraph. In a writing strategy question such as this, it is very likely that there will be no usage or mechanics problems in the sentences offered as options. The best answer will be the most effective and appropriate one in terms of the purpose stated in the question.

Probably the best way to approach this question is to read through the rest of Paragraph 3 in order to get a good understanding of its content. You may be able to rule out some of the choices simply on this basis. For example, **A** and **C,** which mention running for health reasons and the age range of runners, respectively, have very little in common with the rest of the paragraph. **D** offers some possibilities, especially in terms of the sentence that would immediately follow it in the paragraph. But the sentence in **D** doesn't specifically refer to runners; it just says that "people like money and the things money can buy." The first two paragraphs of the essay indicate that the writer is focusing specifically on the different types of runners that he or she has encountered while running.

Option **B** works best here. It adds a new piece of information—"some runners run to be admired"—but it's a statement that ties together the various descriptions in the paragraph. The fact that some runners wear expensive and fashionable outfits and always look neat and well groomed could be chalked up to those runners' vanity. This sentence also offers a nice parallel to and comparison with the opening sentence of the preceding paragraph: "Some [runners] are very serious; running is a discipline for them."

Organization questions deal with issues of order, coherence, and unity in an essay. For example, you may be asked about the organization of ideas (the most logical order for sentences within a paragraph or paragraphs within an essay) or the relevance of particular statements in the context of the essay.

The following question (from the example passage and questions on pages 72–74) is a good example of the kind of question you'll find about the organization of an essay:

And when glints of the afternoon sun shone off Mickey Mantle's colossal bat, there will have to be seen
—————
39
for one brief, stirring moment the glimmer of the jewels in King Arthur's own mighty sword, Excalibur.

So there he stood, that learned professor of
——
40
mine, lecturing about the ideas, that have engaged
—————
41
people's minds for centuries.

40. F. NO CHANGE
G. (Begin new paragraph) To summarize,
H. (Do NOT begin new paragraph) So
J. (Do NOT begin new paragraph) Yet

This is another case where two different issues must be considered in order to come up with the best answer. The two issues, however, are not entirely unrelated: you need to decide whether there should be a paragraph break at this point and what word or phrase would provide the most logical transition to this sentence from what precedes it. For both of these issues, it's important to understand not only what is stated in this sentence but also what is stated in the sentences surrounding it.

The essay is primarily a writer's reminiscence of a philosophy professor who loved baseball and the Boston Red Sox so much that he accomplished the remarkable feat of teaching a philosophy class while listening to the World Series. The second paragraph of the essay, however, consists of a digression on the mythical qualities of baseball. A paragraph break at the underlined portion for question 40 seems the most logical thing to do, because this sentence returns the reader to the description of "that learned professor of mine." Thus, you can safely rule out **H** and **J,** which call for no paragraph break at this point.

Options **F** and **G** both offer an acceptable decision concerning the paragraph break, but they propose different ways of introducing the sentence. **G** proposes using the phrase "to summarize," but it's hard to understand the logic of that. What is the sentence summarizing? It's certainly not summarizing the previous paragraph. **F** proposes the word *so,* which the writer uses to help the essay get back on its main track. In effect, *so* says, "Because, in some general way, of all that I have said in the preceding paragraph about the mythical quality of baseball, there he stood, that learned professor of mine, lecturing. . . ."

We might agree that the writer of this essay could have come up with a better way to introduce this sentence, but the key point here is that **F** is an acceptable answer, and it's the best answer among the four choices given. It's good for you to remember that the answer you first think up might not always be among the answer choices. There is often more than one way to solve a writing problem, so you have to stay open to every acceptable possibility.

Style questions involve effective word choices in terms of writing style, tone, clarity, and economy. Sometimes a phrase or sentence that isn't technically ungrammatical is nevertheless confusing because it's poorly written. Sometimes there's a word or phrase that clashes with the tone of the essay. Good writing also involves eliminating ambiguous pronoun references, excessively wordy or redundant material, and vague or awkward expressions.

Like most writing strategy and organization questions, style questions require a general understanding of the essay as a whole. The following style question (from the example passage and questions on pages 77–79) focuses on the issues of economy and clarity in writing:

Although some look as
$\overline{70}$
though they were once athletes, most seem to be

grimly performing to their doctor's prescription.

70. F. NO CHANGE
    G. seem to be retired athletes, looking
    H. seemingly look to be
    J. look to be

As is often the case with this type of question, a good grasp of vocabulary in context will help you immensely. The word *look* or *looking* appears in each answer choice—what does it mean here? One of the most common definitions of *look* is "to see; to exercise the power of vision." There are a variety of possible definitions, but the one that best fits this context is "to seem; to have the appearance or likelihood of being." Once you've figured that out, **G** and **H** become clearly redundant and unnecessarily wordy. You might have already had a hunch along those lines.

Option **J**'s problem isn't wordiness or redundancy so much as it is awkwardness. The phrase "look to be" sounds acceptable enough (in fact, later in this sentence we find "seem to be performing"), but "look to be as though" just doesn't sound like something someone would say or write. As it's used in this construction, the phrase "to be" doesn't seem to add any meaning to the sentence. Option **F** is clearly a better choice, providing a more concise and fluent sentence.

The questions provided here are a small sample of the kinds of questions that might be on the test. The previous question, for example, is only one kind of style question; it doesn't cover all the territory of "style" that might be addressed on the test. The example passages and questions at the end of this section have all the examples referred to in this chapter as they would appear in a test. These example passages and questions and the practice tests in Chapter 5 will provide you with a thorough understanding of the ACT Assessment English Test.

Strategies for Taking the ACT English Test

Pace yourself

The ACT English Test contains 75 questions to be completed in 45 minutes, which works out to exactly 36 seconds per question. Spending 1 to 1½ minutes skimming through each passage leaves you about 30 seconds to respond to each question. If you are able to spend less time than that on each question, you can use the remaining time allowed for this test to review your work and to return to the questions that were most difficult for you. Another way to think of it is that you have 45 minutes to read and answer the questions for five passages, giving you a maximum of 9 minutes for each passage and its questions.

Be aware of the writing style used in the passages

The five passages cover a variety of topics and are written in a variety of styles. It's important that you take into account the writing style used in each passage as you respond to the questions.

Some of the passages will be anecdotes or narratives written from an informal, first-person point of view. Others will be more formal essays, scholarly or informative in nature, often written in the third person. Some questions will ask you to choose the best answer based not on its grammatical correctness but on its consistency with the style and tone of the passage as a whole. An expression that's too breezy for an essay on the life of President Herbert Hoover might be just right for a personal narrative about a writer's attempt at learning to skateboard.

Be sure to consider a question's context before you choose an answer

Some people find it helpful to skim a passage and its questions before trying to answer those questions. Particularly with questions involving writing strategy and organization, it can help to have some of the questions in mind before you begin carefully reading the passage. If there are questions about the order of sentences within a paragraph, or about the order of paragraphs within a passage, you may want to answer those questions first to make sure that the major elements of the passage are ordered logically. Understanding the order of the passage may make it easier for you to answer some of the other questions.

As you're answering each question, be sure to read at least a sentence or two **beyond** the sentence containing the portion being questioned. You may need to read even more than that to make sure you understand what the writer is trying to say.

Examine the underlined portions of the passage

Before responding to a question identified by an underlined portion, check for a stated question preceding the options. If there is one, it will provide you with some guidelines for deciding on the best choice. Whether there is a stated question or not, you should carefully examine what is underlined in the passage. Consider the features of writing that are included in the underlined portion. The options for each question will contain changes in one or more aspects of writing.

Note the differences in the options

Many of the questions that refer to underlined portions will involve more than one aspect of writing. Examine each option and note how it differs from the others. Consider **all** the features of writing that are included in each option. (Be careful not to select an answer that corrects one error but creates a different one.)

Determine the best answer

There are at least two approaches you can take to determine the best answer to a question about an underlined portion. One approach is to reread the sentence or sentences containing the underlined portion, substitute each of the possible options in turn, and determine the best choice. Another approach is to decide how the underlined portion might best be phrased in standard written English or in terms of the particular question posed, then to look for your phrasing among the options offered. If the underlined portion is correct as it is, select the "NO CHANGE" option.

If you can't decide which option is best, you may want to mark the question in your test booklet so you can return to it later. Remember: you're not penalized for guessing, so after you've eliminated as many options as you can, take your best guess.

Watch for questions about the entire passage or a section of the passage

Some questions ask about a section of the passage. They are identified by a question number in a box at the appropriate point in the passage, rather than by an underlined portion. Here's an example from the sample passage and questions on pages 68–70:

The fanny

pack <u>would then enable me</u> to achieve a previously
        9

unimagined level of personal fitness. 10

10. Suppose that the writer were to change the end of the preceding sentence from "a previously unimagined level of personal fitness" to read simply "better health." If made, this change would cause this sentence to be more:

   F. dramatic.
   G. unreasonable.
   H. fantastic.
   J. straightforward.

The best answer for this question is **J;** "better health" is a more straightforward phrase than "personal fitness."

Some other questions ask about an aspect of the passage as a whole. These are placed at the end of the passage, following boxed instructions like these:

Questions 59 and 60 ask about the preceding passage as a whole.

You may want to read any questions that ask about the passage as a whole first so you can keep them in mind while you're reading through the passage. For questions about a section of the passage or the passage as a whole, you must decide the best answer on the basis of the particular writing or revision problem presented in the question.

Reread the sentence, using your selected answer

Once you have selected the answer you feel is best, reread the corresponding sentence or sentences in the passage, substituting the answer you've selected for the underlined portion or for the boxed numeral. Sometimes an answer that sounds fine out of context doesn't "fit" within the sentence or passage. Be sure to keep in mind both the punctuation marks and words in each possible response; sometimes just the omission of a comma can make an important difference.

Avoid making new mistakes

Beware of correcting mistakes in the passage and, in your haste, picking a response that creates a new mistake. The following question (from the example passage and questions on pages 70–72) illustrates the possibility of doing that.

[1] While <u>they're, she had as</u> one of her

instructors Anthony Fokker, the famous aircraft

designer.

23. **A.** NO CHANGE
    B. they're
    C. there,
    D. there, she had as

Options **C** and **D** would both correct the problem that the contraction *they're* (they are) presents in the underlined portion. However, notice that **C** would introduce a new problem because it creates a sentence fragment. ("While there, one of her instructors, Anthony Fokker, the famous aircraft designer.") The best answer is **D.**

Be observant, especially in questions where the responses have similar wording. One comma or apostrophe can make all the difference, as the following question (from the example passage and questions on pages 68–70) illustrates:

The <u>packs zipper</u>

compartments could hold all manner of things: keys,

sweatbands, and candy bars.

6. **F.** NO CHANGE
    G. pack zippers's
    H. packs' zippered
    J. pack's zippered

It probably only took you a moment to reject **G,** "pack zippers's compartments," as not sounding much like standard written English. The phrases "zipper compartments" and "zippered compartments" both sound acceptable, but should the preceding word be *packs, pack's,* or *packs'*? You need to decide whether an apostrophe is needed at all and, if so, whether the noun taking the ownership should be singular or plural. (The best answer is **J.**)

Be aware of the connotations of words

Vocabulary isn't tested in an isolated way on the ACT English Test. Nevertheless, a good vocabulary and an awareness of not only the dictionary definitions of words but also the connotations (feelings and associations) suggested by those words will help you do well on the test.

The following question (from the passage and questions on pages 68–70) asks you to think about how certain words and their connotations can function in terms of the rest of the essay.

Granted, I found room for my house keys and wallet,

but every time I tried to stuff a large bag of chips

into one of the zippered compartments, <u>resulting</u>
                                          12

was a bag filled with millions of minuscule potato

chip fragments. ☐13

13. The way in which the words *millions* and *minuscule* function in the preceding sentence might best be described as being:
   A. exaggeration working on behalf of humor.
   B. understatement acting to restrict the essay's dramatic impact.
   C. accuracy intended to mask the writer's disgust with fanny packs.
   D. nonsense working to further the writer's strongly impassioned prose style.

The words *millions* and *minuscule* in an informative or scientific essay certainly might provide accuracy, as **C** suggests. One might also imagine a piece of writing where these words would be intentionally nonsensical, as **D** proposes. In this lighthearted personal essay on fanny packs, however, these words connote, or imply, an exaggeration (a writing technique also known as hyperbole). The writer doesn't mean literally "millions of minuscule potato chip fragments" here, but wants to overstate the magnitude of the error of trying to carry a bag of chips in a fanny pack, so the best answer is **A.**

In questions such as this one, you have to focus on what the words mean and what associations the words have for the typical reader.

Be careful with two-part questions

Some questions require extra thought because you have to decide not only which option is best but also which supporting reason for an option is most appropriate or convincing. The following question occurs at the end of the example passage on early radio broadcasting on pages 74–76. Each option begins with either a yes or no response, followed by a supporting reason for that response.

---

60. The writer has been asked to write an essay assessing the development of modern technologies after the First World War. Would this essay fulfill that assignment?

F. Yes; the writer focuses exclusively on the commercial possibilities of radio.

G. Yes; the writer focuses on the need for federal regulation in the world of broadcasting.

H. No; the writer focuses on the commercial possibilities of radio, just one technology.

J. No; the writer focuses on the contrast between early radio and radio broadcasting of today.

Once you decide whether the essay would or would not fulfill the assignment described in the question, you need to decide which reason or explanation provides the most appropriate support for the answer and is most accurate in terms of the essay. Sometimes the supporting reason may not accurately reflect the essay (the explanation in **J,** for example). Sometimes the reason accurately reflects the essay but doesn't logically support the answer to the question. For example, it is true, as **F** states, that the writer of this essay focuses on the commercial possibilities of radio, but this reason does not support the answer that this essay assesses the development of modern technologies after the First World War. **H** is the best answer because the essay does not assess the development of new technologies after the First World War, but focuses on the commercial possibilities of radio, which is just one technology.

Watch for interdependent questions

Sometimes you'll find that the best way for you to answer questions about a passage is **not** necessarily in their numbered order. Occasionally, you'll find it easier to answer a question after you've answered the one that follows it. Or you might find two questions about different elements of the same sentence, in which case it may help you to consider them both together.

In general, you may find it helpful to look for questions about the best order for paragraphs within a passage and answer those questions first. Do the same for questions about sentence order within a paragraph and questions about where to add a sentence or sentences in a passage. Otherwise you risk missing relationships that are obvious only when the elements have been ordered or added properly.

In the following example (from the example passage and questions on pages 74–76), you can see that it would be difficult to answer question 59 without taking into consideration your answer to question 50. If you decide that the most logical sequence of sentences for Paragraph 2 is something other than what is presented in the passage, that decision would affect two of question 59's placement choices for the sentence to be added. Which are actually the first and last sentences of Paragraph 2? If you do decide to reorder the sentences of Paragraph 2, it might help you to pencil in the correct order of the sentences in your test booklet. Just cross out the sentence numbers in the brackets and write in the correct order. (The best answers to questions 50 and 59 are **F** and **B.**)

---

[2]

[1] Then a vice president of Westinghouse, looking for a way to make the transmission of radio signals more profitable, <u>decided</u> on a two-fold
48
strategy. [2] First, he would entice an audience with daily programming of great variety. [3] Second, he would sell this audience the radio receivers necessary to listen to this entertainment. [4] The <u>plan succeeded</u>
49
beyond anyone's expectations. 50

50. Which of the following sequences of sentences will make Paragraph 2 most logical?
   F. NO CHANGE
   G. 1, 4, 3, 2
   H. 2, 1, 3, 4
   J. 4, 1, 2, 3

59. The writer wishes to add the following sentence to the essay:

   Nowadays, no matter where you are, it's hard to be far from a radio.

   If added, this sentence would best support and most logically be placed:

   A. before the first sentence of Paragraph 2.
   B. after the last sentence of Paragraph 2.
   C. before the last sentence of Paragraph 3.
   D. after the last sentence of Paragraph 4.

In the next example (from the example passage and questions on pages 77–79), it may be helpful to consider questions 74 and 75 together, because they're contained in the same sentence. First answer the question that seems easier to you. Once you've solved that problem in the sentence, turn to the other question.

<u>Similarly, running</u> may itself be a boring
₇₄
sport, but the other runners, an interesting selection

of <u>humanity, can</u> make it fun.
₇₅

74. **F.** NO CHANGE
    G. However, running
    H. Running
    J. Furthermore, running

75. **A.** NO CHANGE
    B. humanity; can
    C. humanity. Can
    D. humanity can

Questions 74 and 75 deal with different kinds of writing problems. Question 74 is about choosing the most logical transitional word, and question 75 is about the appropriate use of punctuation. Yet, you may find that answering question 75, for example, makes question 74 seem less daunting. Try penciling in your answer choice to one question so that you can read more easily through the rest of the sentence while responding to the other question. (The best answers for questions 74 and 75 are **H** and **A,** respectively.)

Remember that this section is only an overview of the English Test. Directly or indirectly, a question may test you in more than one of the areas mentioned, so it's important not to become overly concerned with categorizing a question before you answer it. And, while awareness of the types of questions can help you be a more critical and strategic test taker, just remember: the **type** of question you're answering isn't important. The most important thing is to focus on what the question asks and do your best to pick out the best answer, given the rest of the essay.

SAMPLE PASSAGE I

Fanny Pack

Although the name—*fanny pack*—did not

appeal to <u>me as</u> the product itself did. It was sleek,
₁

<u>eye-catching, and best of all;</u> appeared to be
₂

actually functional. Pocketless shorts have always

posed a problem for those who jog or bike. No

doubt the fear of being caught <u>without so much as</u>
₃

a dollar bill or an identification card was the reason

<u>I'm keeping its</u> spot by the television set warm.
₄

    The fanny pack provided an easy solution

for the shortcomings of shorts without pockets,

<u>though</u> it would allow me to break free from the TV
₅

to explore the outdoor world. The <u>packs zipper</u>
₆

compartments could hold all manner of things: keys,

sweatbands, and candy bars. If too much exercise

left me thirsty, I could reach into the special pocket

for my wallet and buy something cold and refreshing.

No question about it—the fanny pack was the

total solution!

1. A. NO CHANGE
   B. myself, though
   C. me,
   D. me, like

2. F. NO CHANGE
   G. eye-catching, and, best, of all
   H. eye-catching and best of, all,
   J. eye-catching, and, best of all,

3. A. NO CHANGE
   B. for as little as
   C. like
   D. OMIT the underlined portion.

4. F. NO CHANGE
   G. it kept a
   H. I kept my
   J. it's kept the

5. A. NO CHANGE
   B. therefore,
   C. because
   D. and

6. F. NO CHANGE
   G. pack zippers's
   H. packs' zippered
   J. pack's zippered

Imagining that I myself might become as sleek and
7

dashing as the fanny pack. Who knows, I thought, with
8
a little ingenuity I might be able to pack enough into
the thing for some *really* long trips. The fanny
pack would then enable me to achieve a previously
9

unimagined level of personal fitness. [10]

What I hadn't counted on, however, was the
relations of its size for my necessities. When I
11
laid everything out on the kitchen table, I realized I
couldn't fit everything I needed into the pack.
Granted, I found room for my house keys and wallet,
but every time I tried to stuff a large bag of chips
into one of the zippered compartments, resulting
12
was a bag filled with millions of minuscule potato
chip fragments. [13]

7. **A.** NO CHANGE
   B. Imagination leading me to think
   C. I began to imagine
   D. I will have imagined

8. **F.** NO CHANGE
   G. Who could have known that, thinking that
   H. He knew that
   J. Not having had that thought, with

9. **A.** NO CHANGE
   B. had since enabled me
   C. enabling
   D. since enabling me

10. Suppose that the writer were to change the end of the
    preceding sentence from "a previously unimagined
    level of personal fitness" to read simply "better
    health." If made, this change would cause this sentence
    to be more:

    F. dramatic.
    G. unreasonable.
    H. fantastic.
    J. straightforward.

11. **A.** NO CHANGE
    B. relative size of
    C. relationship with
    D. relatively sizing as to

12. **F.** NO CHANGE
    G. as a result
    H. the result
    J. thus resulting

13. The way in which the words *millions* and *minuscule*
    function in the preceding sentence might best be
    described as being:

    A. exaggeration working on behalf of humor.
    B. understatement acting to restrict the essay's dra-
       matic impact.
    C. accuracy intended to mask the writer's disgust
       with fanny packs.
    D. nonsense working to further the writer's strongly
       impassioned prose style.

Because my dream of taking fitness to new
levels by racing around the countryside with my
faithful fanny pack died a sad death. I found
other uses for my investment, however. It turns out
to be the perfect place to store my remote control
and *TV Guide*.

14. F. NO CHANGE
    G. Whereas,
    H. Yet
    J. So,

15. A. NO CHANGE
    B. was dead
    C. expired as
    D. dying

SAMPLE PASSAGE II

Bessie Coleman: In Flight

[1]

After the final performance of one last
practice landing, the French instructor nodded to the
young African-American woman at the controls and
jumped down to the ground. Bessie Coleman was on
her own now. She lined up the nose of the open

cockpit biplane on the runway's center mark, she gave
the engine full throttle, and took off into history.

[2]

It was a long journey from the American
Southwest she'd been born in 1893, to these French skies.

The year in which she was born was about a century ago.
There hadn't been much of a future for her in Oklahoma

then. After both semesters of the two-semester year
at Langston Industrial College, Coleman headed for
Chicago to see what could be done to realize a dream.

16. F. NO CHANGE
    G. one finally ultimate
    H. one final
    J. one last final

17. A. NO CHANGE
    B. off
    C. along
    D. OMIT the underlined portion.

18. F. NO CHANGE
    G. mark,
    H. mark, Coleman
    J. mark that

19. A. NO CHANGE
    B. Southwest that she'd been
    C. Southwest, where she'd been
    D. Southwest, she was

20. F. NO CHANGE
    G. It is now just about a century since the year of her birth.
    H. Just about a century has passed since the year of her birth.
    J. OMIT the underlined portion.

21. A. NO CHANGE
    B. a year
    C. a year like two full semesters
    D. one year filled with two semesters

Ever since she saw her first airplane when she was a little girl, Coleman had known that someday, somehow, she would fly.

[3]

Try as she might, however, Coleman could not obtain flying lessons anywhere in the city. Then she sought aid from Robert S. Abbott of the *Chicago Weekly Defender*. The newspaperman got in touch with a flight school in France that was willing to teach this determined young woman to fly.

[4]

[1] While they're, she had as one of her instructors Anthony Fokker, the famous aircraft designer. [2] Bessie Coleman took a quick course in French, should she settle her affairs, and sailed for Europe. [3] Coping with a daily foreign language and flying in capricious, unstable machines held together with baling wire was daunting, but Coleman persevered. [26]

[5]

On June 15, 1921, Bessie Coleman, earned an international pilot's license, issued by the International Aeronautical Federation. Not only was she the first black woman to win her pilot's wings, she was the first American woman to hold this coveted license.

22.　F.　NO CHANGE
　　G.　Abbott:
　　H.　Abbott, whose
　　J.　Abbott;

23.　A.　NO CHANGE
　　B.　they're
　　C.　there,
　　D.　there, she had as

24.　F.　NO CHANGE
　　G.　as if to settle
　　H.　to settle
　　J.　settled

25.　A.　NO CHANGE
　　B.　(Place after *with*)
　　C.　(Place after *flying*)
　　D.　(Place after *in*)

26.　Which of the following sequences of sentences will make Paragraph 4 most logical?
　　F.　NO CHANGE
　　G.　1, 3, 2
　　H.　2, 1, 3
　　J.　3, 2, 1

27.　A.　NO CHANGE
　　B.　Coleman earned an international pilot's license
　　C.　Coleman, earned an international pilot's license
　　D.　Coleman earned an international pilot's license;

[6]

She was ready for a triumphant return to the

United States to barnstorm and lecture proof that if
                                           —————
                                            28

the will is strong enough for one's dream can be
         ————————————
                29

attained.

28. F. NO CHANGE
    G. lecture and proof
    H. lecture, proof
    J. lecture proof,

29. A. NO CHANGE
    B. stronger than
    C. strongly enough,
    D. strong enough,

Question 30 asks about the preceding passage as a whole.

---

30. The writer intends to add the following sentence to the essay in order to provide a comparison that would help underline the challenges that Bessie Coleman faced:

    Her dream of becoming the world's first black woman pilot seemed as remote in Chicago as it had been in Oklahoma.

    In order to accomplish this purpose, it would be most logical and appropriate to place this sentence after the:

    F. first sentence in Paragraph 2.
    G. first sentence in Paragraph 3.
    H. last sentence in Paragraph 3.
    J. first sentence in Paragraph 5.

SAMPLE PASSAGE III

Philosophy and Baseball

In the fall of 1967, the Boston Red Sox were

playing in the World Series. I was a freshman at a

university that was located in the Midwest at the
—————————————————————————————
                      31

time, enrolled in a philosophy course that met at two

in the afternoon. The course was taught by a native

Bostonian. He wanted to watch the games on television,

but he was too responsible to cancel class. So he

conducted classes, those October afternoons, while

actually listening to the games on a small transistor

radio propped up inside his lectern, the volume

turned down so that only he could hear.

31. A. NO CHANGE
    B. midwestern university then
    C. midwestern university
    D. university which was in the Midwest

32 Baseball is unique among

American sports by its ability to appeal to a
33

love resembling that of a child of fable and
34

legend. Babe Ruth, Ted Williams, Joe DiMaggio,

Roberto Clemente—names like these will echo through

time that are trumpet calls to storied battles fought
35

and won in ages past. 36 When Hank Aaron

stretched out a sinewy arm to pull one down,
37

striding up to a rack of ash-hewn bats, he became a
37

modern-day knight selecting their lance. And
38

when glints of the afternoon sun shone off Mickey

Mantle's colossal bat, there will have to be seen
39

for one brief, stirring moment the glimmer of the

jewels in King Arthur's own mighty sword, Excalibur.

32. Which of the following sentences, if inserted at this point, would provide the most effective transition to the second paragraph?
   F. Accounting for this kind of behavior is easy.
   G. Most of the students in the class were not fond of this instructor.
   H. Today, most World Series games are played in the evening.
   J. He did a remarkable job, considering how distracted he must have been.

33. A. NO CHANGE
   B. as
   C. in
   D. because

34. F. NO CHANGE
   G. love that seems to occur during childhood
   H. love like that of children
   J. childlike love

35. A. NO CHANGE
   B. time like
   C. time in which
   D. time, which is like

36. Which of the following sentences, if added at this point, would most effectively lead the reader from the generalization in the preceding sentence to the specific examples that follow?
   F. These heroes of baseball embodied the ancient legends, bringing them to life.
   G. Baseball, of course, is not the only sport that provides heroes.
   H. Those battles lasted for nine innings, unless a tie led to extra innings.
   J. The truly great thing about it is that these men are as human as you or I.

37. A. NO CHANGE
   B. strode up to a rack of ash-hewn bats, stretching out a sinewy arm to pull one down,
   C. strode up to a rack of ash-hewn bats to stretch out a sinewy arm, pulling one down,
   D. pulled one down, stretching out his sinewy arm as he strode up to a rack of ash-hewn bats,

38. F. NO CHANGE
   G. there
   H. his
   J. one's

39. A. NO CHANGE
   B. will
   C. can
   D. could

So there he stood, that learned professor of
40

mine, lecturing about the ideas, that have engaged
41

people's minds for centuries. Then he'd interrupt

himself to announce, with smiling eyes, that the Sox

had taken a two-to-nothing lead. Here was a

man who's mind was disciplined
42

inside his schoolbook to contemplate
43

the collected wisdom of the ages—and he

was behaving like a boy with a contraband

comic opened. On those warm October days, as

the afternoon sun dances and plays on the domes
44

and spires of the university, the philosophers

had to stand aside, for the professor's imagination
45

had transported him to the Boston of his youth.
45

40. F. NO CHANGE
    G. (Begin new paragraph) To summarize,
    H. (Do NOT begin new paragraph) So
    J. (Do NOT begin new paragraph) Yet

41. A. NO CHANGE
    B. ideas that
    C. ideas. That
    D. ideas, which

42. F. NO CHANGE
    G. man whose
    H. man, who's
    J. man that's

43. A. NO CHANGE
    B. (Place after *ages*)
    C. (Place after *boy*)
    D. (Place after *opened* and end sentence with a period)

44. F. NO CHANGE
    G. dances, playing
    H. danced and played
    J. dancing and playing

45. Which of the alternatives would conclude this sentence so that it supports the writer's principal reflections on the professor's behavior?
    A. NO CHANGE
    B. due to the fact that the professor was about to hand out a test.
    C. while the professor told the class about King Arthur and the Knights of the Round Table.
    D. as the professor recounted all the great baseball stars he'd seen play.

SAMPLE PASSAGE IV

Tuning In During the Twenties

[1]

Modern broadcasting began to develop after

the First World War. Before 1920, radio was simply

a useful way to send electrical signals ashore from a

ship at sea, or, from one "ham" operator to another.
46

46. F. NO CHANGE
    G. ship, at sea, or
    H. ship at sea or;
    J. ship at sea or

The new technology associated with movies and airplanes was already developing rapidly by the time soldiers started returning from European trenches in 1918. The vast potential of the airwaves, therefore, had scarcely been touched.

[2]

[1] Then a vice president of Westinghouse, looking for a way to make the transmission of radio signals more profitable, decided on a two-fold strategy. [2] First, he would entice an audience with daily programming of great variety. [3] Second, he would sell this audience the radio receivers necessary to listen to this entertainment. [4] The plan succeeded
49
beyond anyone's expectations. 50

[3]

The federal Radio Division in Washington, D.C., was created to license stations, because it had no
51
power to regulate them. Broadcasters multiplied wildly, some helping themselves to the more desirable frequencies, others increasing their transmission power at will. Chaos means things were out of control.
52

[4]

Yet even in the midst of such anarchy,

some commercial possibilities and organizations
53
saw clearly of a medium whose regulation seemed
53

47. A. NO CHANGE
B. however,
C. also,
D. in fact,

48. F. NO CHANGE
G. but had a decision
H. deciding
J. yet decided

49. A. NO CHANGE
B. successful planning was
C. success plan was
D. plans succeeding

50. Which of the following sequences of sentences will make Paragraph 2 most logical?
F. NO CHANGE
G. 1, 4, 3, 2
H. 2, 1, 3, 4
J. 4, 1, 2, 3

51. A. NO CHANGE
B. since
C. thus
D. but

52. Which of the alternatives provides the most logical and succinct conclusion for Paragraph 3?
F. NO CHANGE
G. Chaos reigned.
H. There were some problems.
J. The government was always in control.

53. A. NO CHANGE
B. some saw clearly the commercial possibilities and organizations
C. some organizations saw clearly the commercial possibilities
D. organizations saw clearly some possible commercials

whose
who's

imminent. In 1926, RCA paid the American

Telephone & Telegraph Company one million dollars

for station WEAF in New York City—and NBC was

born. Years later, the Radio Law of 1927 was
    54

enacted. It authorized it's control for licensing
                      55
and of policing the broadcasters.

[5]

The RCA executives who created the
                        56
powerful NBC network were right to see that

sizable profits would come from this new medium.

Even in 1930 for example an hour's advertising on
                    57
nationwide radio to forty-seven cities cost $10,180.

Advertising turned broadcasting into an industry,

and the untapped potential of the airwaves

began to be realized.
    58

54. F. NO CHANGE
    G. A year later,
    H. Factually,
    J. In conclusion,

55. A. NO CHANGE
    B. controlling
    C. the control of
    D. OMIT the underlined portion.

56. F. NO CHANGE
    G. which
    H. having
    J. as

57. A. NO CHANGE
    B. Even in 1930; for example
    C. Even, in 1930 for example,
    D. Even in 1930, for example,

58. F. NO CHANGE
    G. begins realizing it.
    H. began reality.
    J. began it's realizing.

Questions 59 and 60 ask about the preceding passage as a whole.

---

59. The writer wishes to add the following sentence to the essay:

    Nowadays, no matter where you are, it's hard to be far from a radio.

    If added, this sentence would best support and most logically be placed:

    A. before the first sentence of Paragraph 2.
    B. after the last sentence of Paragraph 2.
    C. before the last sentence of Paragraph 3.
    D. after the last sentence of Paragraph 4.

60. The writer has been asked to write an essay assessing the development of modern technologies after the First World War. Would this essay fulfill that assignment?

    F. Yes; the writer focuses exclusively on the commercial possibilities of radio.
    G. Yes; the writer focuses on the need for federal regulation in the world of broadcasting.
    H. No; the writer focuses on the commercial possibilities of radio, just one technology.
    J. No; the writer focuses on the contrast between early radio and radio broadcasting of today.

SAMPLE PASSAGE V

The Joy of Running

[1]

I keep in shape by running on an indoor track several times a week. There are many advantages to running as a sport, of which the top two advantages are: I never have to reserve a court or find teammates;

teammates are usual in many sports; I can run at

my convenience and I can set my own pace. Just

running is, however, rather boring, so I've made it interesting by watching the other runners. [64]

[2]

Some are very serious; running is a

discipline for them. [66] They run hard and gracefully, easily passing the rest of us. Their clothing looks comfortable and functional. I see them doing stretching exercises to warm up and cooling-down exercises after they run.

61. **A.** NO CHANGE
    B. sport, of which a few of the many advantages are:
    C. sport, which I will now list:
    D. sport:

62. **F.** NO CHANGE
    G. those who play tennis do have to worry about courts;
    H. although running is hard on one's feet;
    J. I need only shoes for equipment;

63. **A.** NO CHANGE
    B. convenience, and;
    C. convenience; and
    D. convenience and,

64. Which of the following sentences, if added here, would best introduce the variety of runners discussed in the rest of the essay?
    F. Runners as a group take their hobby very seriously.
    G. For fun, I've divided runners into groups, and I assign each runner I see to a group.
    H. Running is excellent exercise and many people really have fun doing it.
    J. Some people run by themselves and others like to run in marathons.

65. **A.** NO CHANGE
    B. serious, as to them
    C. serious; since
    D. serious and,

66. The writer wishes to add information here that will explain and further support the point made in the preceding sentence. Which of the following sentences will do that best?
    F. They like the discipline and are very serious about their running.
    G. They run with a single-minded intensity that is admirable but intimidating.
    H. When they run, they run with both discipline and great seriousness.
    J. Running is for them a very serious discipline and they are intensely devoted to it.

[3]

67 They wear expensive, fashionable

outfits, perfectly fit and sleek, always new-looking.

Neither these runners nor their clothes, ever look
                                        ———
                                         68
sweaty or messy. One young man ran for two hours,

and his sweatband was dry, his hair in place, and his

shoes unscuffed. Such runners don't so much exercise

as perform.

[4]

Then there are the middle-aged people, some

older and in worse shape than I. Many of them are

functionally dressed in old shorts and T-shirts. Like

me, they don't run very fast, and they would walk
                                    ——————
                                       69

a lap every now and then. Although some look as
                                         ————
                                          70
though they were once athletes, most seem to be

grimly performing to their doctor's prescription.

[5]

Some runners, of all ages, are there to lose

weight. 71 Others run for fun, like children at

play, and still others seem to see the track as a social

club, a place to meet friends.

67. The writer wishes to begin Paragraph 3 with a sentence that strengthens the focus of the paragraph, while providing a transition from Paragraph 2. Which of the following would be the best choice?
   A. Some runners run for health reasons.
   B. Some runners run to be admired.
   C. Runners come in a wide range of ages.
   D. Some people like money and the things money can buy.

68. F. NO CHANGE
    G. clothes do they
    H. clothes—
    J. clothes

69. A. NO CHANGE
    B. if they would
    C. they used to
    D. they

70. F. NO CHANGE
    G. seem to be retired athletes, looking
    H. seemingly look to be
    J. look to be

71. The writer wants to describe how the runners mentioned in the preceding sentence run. Which of the following sentences, if added here, will do that best?
    A. They labor determinedly.
    B. They know running helps you lose weight.
    C. Running is at least as good for weight loss as tennis or swimming.
    D. Losing weight is what it's all about for them.

[6]

My favorite social runners are a pair of young

women. Fashionably garbed and on the alert for
_____
72

young men. They listen to a Walkman radio, not

unusual among runners, but they have one

between them with two sets of earphones.

Blithely running along the earphone cord dangles
_____
73

between them.

[7]

Similarly, running may itself be a boring
_____
74

sport, but the other runners, an interesting selection

of humanity, can make it fun.
_____
75

72. F. NO CHANGE
G. women fashionably
H. women; fashionably
J. women, and fashionably

73. A. NO CHANGE
B. Dangling, they run blithely along, the earphone cord
C. Running blithely along, the earphone cord dangles
D. They run blithely along, the earphone cord dangling

74. F. NO CHANGE
G. However, running
H. Running
J. Furthermore, running

75. A. NO CHANGE
B. humanity; can
C. humanity. Can
D. humanity can

Answer Key for English Test Sample Items

1. C	26. H	51. D
2. J	27. B	52. G
3. A	28. H	53. C
4. H	29. D	54. G
5. D	30. G	55. C
6. J	31. C	56. F
7. C	32. F	57. D
8. F	33. C	58. F
9. A	34. J	59. B
10. J	35. B	60. H
11. B	36. F	61. D
12. H	37. B	62. J
13. A	38. H	63. C
14. J	39. D	64. G
15. A	40. F	65. A
16. H	41. B	66. G
17. A	42. G	67. B
18. G	43. D	68. J
19. C	44. H	69. D
20. J	45. A	70. F
21. B	46. J	71. A
22. F	47. B	72. G
23. D	48. F	73. D
24. J	49. A	74. H
25. C	50. F	75. A

ACT Assessment Mathematics Test

The ACT Mathematics Test asks you to answer 60 multiple-choice questions in 60 minutes. The questions are designed to measure your achievement of the mathematical knowledge, skills, and reasoning techniques that are taught in high school mathematics courses and needed for college mathematics courses; therefore, they cover a wide variety of concepts, techniques, and procedures. Naturally, some questions will require computation, but you are allowed to use a calculator on the Mathematics Test, whenever and wherever you choose. You'll need to understand basic mathematical terminology and to recall some basic mathematical principles and formulas. However, the questions on the test are designed to emphasize your ability to reason mathematically, not to test your computation ability or your ability to recall definitions, theorems, or formulas.

Content of the ACT Mathematics Test

As you saw in the chart on page 42, the questions on the ACT Mathematics Test are drawn from the following six categories:

- **Pre-Algebra**
- **Elementary Algebra**
- **Intermediate Algebra**
- **Coordinate Geometry**
- **Plane Geometry**
- **Trigonometry**

You will receive a score for all 60 questions, and three subscores: a Pre-Algebra/Elementary Algebra subscore based on 24 questions, an Intermediate Algebra/Coordinate Geometry subscore based on 18 questions, and a Plane Geometry/Trigonometry subscore based on 18 questions.

Pre-algebra questions involve solving problems using the mathematics that you probably learned before you took your first math course in high school—things like operations using whole numbers, fractions, decimals, and integers; numbers raised to positive integer powers and square roots of numbers; ratio, proportion, and percent; multiples and factors of integers; absolute value; ordering numbers from least to greatest or greatest to least; linear equations with one variable; simple probability and counting the number of ways something can happen; representation and interpretation of data in charts, tables, and graphs; and simple descriptive statistics like mean, median, and mode.

Elementary algebra questions test your ability to solve problems that involve topics like using variables to express functional relationships, substitution, operations on polynomials, factoring and solving simple quadratic equations (the kind that can be solved by factoring), linear inequalities with one variable, and properties of integer exponents and square roots.

Intermediate algebra questions ask you to apply your knowledge, skills, and reasoning ability to solve problems that involve more advanced topics of algebra like the quadratic formula, radical and rational expressions, inequalities and absolute value equations, sequences, systems of equations, quadratic inequalities, functions, matrices, roots of polynomials, and complex numbers.

Coordinate geometry questions deal with the real number line and the (x,y) coordinate plane. They cover number line graphs as well as graphs of points, lines, polynomials, and other curves in the (x,y) coordinate plane. They also cover relationships between equations and graphs, slope, parallel and perpendicular lines, distance, midpoints, and conics.

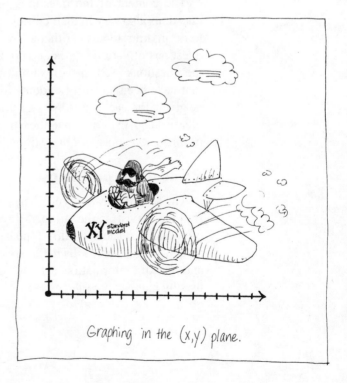

Graphing in the (x,y) plane.

Plane geometry questions test your grasp of topics that are usually part of high school geometry. Included are the properties and relations of plane figures (triangles, rectangles, parallelograms, trapezoids, and circles); angles, parallel lines, and perpendicular lines; translations, rotations, and reflections; proof techniques; simple three-dimensional geometry; and measurement concepts like perimeter, area, and volume.

Trigonometry questions cover the trigonometric ratios defined for right triangles; the values, properties, and graphs of the trigonometric functions; trigonometric identities; and trigonometric equations.

The right triangle family.

Types of Questions on the ACT Mathematics Test

The content of the questions on the ACT Mathematics Test varies; the questions also vary in their complexity and in the amount of thinking you have to do in order to answer them. The rest of this section gives you examples of questions of various types and complexities from all six content areas. All of the questions used in the examples are from actual ACT Mathematics Tests that have been taken by students from across the country. A solution strategy is given for each question. As you read and work through each example, please keep in mind that the strategy given is just one way to solve the problem. A variety of other strategies will also work for each question.

Basic math problems

The sort of question you're probably the most familiar with (and probably find the easiest) is the stripped-down, bare-bones, garden-variety, basic math problem. Problems of this type are simple and straightforward. They test readily identifiable skills in the six content areas, usually have very few words and no extra information, ask the very question you'd expect them to ask, and usually have a numeric answer.

Question 1 is a good example of a basic math problem from pre-algebra.

---

1. What is 4% of 1,100 ?

   A.   4
   B.   4.4
   C.   40
   D.   44
   E.   440

This problem has very few words, asks a direct question, and has a numeric answer. The solution is simple: convert 4% to a decimal and multiply by 1,100 to get $(0.04)(1,100) = 44$. You probably wouldn't need your calculator on this problem, but remember that you may use it if you wish.

Question 2 is a basic elementary algebra problem.

---

2. For all x, $(x + 4)(x - 5) = ?$

   F. $x^2 - 20$
   G. $x^2 - x - 20$
   H. $2x - 1$
   J. $2x^2 - 1$
   K. $2x^2 - x + 20$

You should know what to do to answer the question the instant you read the problem—use the distributive property (FOIL—Firsts, Outside, Inside, Lasts) and get $x(x - 5) + 4(x - 5) = x^2 - 5x + 4x + 4(-5) = x^2 - x - 20$. On this problem, you probably wouldn't use your calculator.

Question 3 is an example of a basic problem from intermediate algebra.

---

3. If $x + y = 1$, and $x - y = 1$, then $y = ?$

   A. -1

   B. 0

   C. $\frac{1}{2}$

   D. 1

   E. 2

This problem gives you a system of linear equations with unknowns x and y and asks for the value of y. You might be able to solve this problem intuitively—the only number that can be added to and subtracted from another number and give the same result for the problem ($x + y$ and $x - y$ both give 1) is 0, so y must be 0. Or, you could use algebra and reason that, because $x + y$ and $x - y$ both equal 1, they equal each other, and $x + y = x - y$ gives $2y = 0$, so $y = 0$. Although some calculators have graphing or matrix functions for solving problems of this type, using a calculator on this problem would probably take most students longer than solving it with one of the strategies given here.

Question 4 is an example of a basic problem in coordinate geometry.

---

4. What is the slope of the line containing the points
(–2,7) and (3,–3) ?

F. 4

G. $\frac{1}{4}$

H. 0

J. $-\frac{1}{2}$

K. –2

This problem has a few more words than some of the other examples of basic problems you've seen so far, but the most important word is "slope." Seeing that you are given two points, you would probably think of the formula that defines the slope of a line through two points:

$$\frac{y_1 - y_2}{x_1 - x_2}.$$

Applying the formula gives $\frac{7-(-3)}{-2-3}$, or –2.

There are also some basic plane geometry problems on the ACT Mathematics Test. Question 5 is a good example.

---

5. If the measure of an angle is $37\frac{1}{2}°$, what is the measure of its supplement, shown in the figure below?

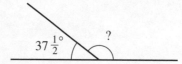

A. $52\frac{1}{2}°$

B. $62\frac{1}{2}°$

C. $127\frac{1}{2}°$

D. $142\frac{1}{2}°$

E. Cannot be determined from the given information

Like many geometry problems, this problem has a figure. The figure tells you what you are given (an angle of $37\frac{1}{2}°$) and what you're asked to find (its supplement, marked by "?"). There really isn't anything you need to mark on the figure, because all the important information is already there. If you know that the sum of the measure of an angle and the measure of its supplement equals $180°$, a simple subtraction gives the correct answer ($142\frac{1}{2}°$). If you are used to doing most computations on your calculator, you may want to use it on this problem for subtraction.

A word of caution is in order here. You probably noticed that "Cannot be determined from the given information" is one of the options for question 5. Statistics gathered over the years for the ACT Mathematics Test show that "Cannot be determined from the given information" is chosen by many students even when it is not the correct option. You should **not** think that whenever "Cannot be determined from the given information" is an option, it is automatically the correct answer. It isn't, as question 5 demonstrates. Later in this section, there's a question for which "Cannot be determined from the given information" **is** the correct answer. Be sure to work out each problem that has this answer choice and choose it only when you are convinced that it actually is the correct answer.

You'll find basic trigonometry problems, like question 6, on the ACT Mathematics Test.

---

6. What is the sine of ∠A in the triangle below?

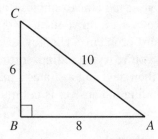

F. 0.30
G. 0.50
H. 0.60
J. 0.75
K. 0.80

This question asks you to find the sine of ∠A in the triangle that is shown in the figure. If you have studied trigonometry, you've seen questions like this before. The lengths of all three sides of the triangle are given on the figure, even though only two are actually needed for finding sin ∠A. The extra information is there not to confuse you, but rather to test your ability to sort out the information that you need from the information that you are given. Picking 6 (the length of the side opposite ∠A) and 10 (the length of the hypotenuse) and forming the ratio $\frac{6}{10}$ gives the correct answer, 0.60.

Basic math problems in settings

Basic math problems in settings are what people often call "word problems" or "story problems." They typically describe situations from everyday life where you need to apply mathematics in order to find the answer to a question. The major difference between this type of problem and the basic math problems that you've seen in the examples so far is that the problem isn't set up for you—you have to set it up yourself. Most people find this to be the most difficult part of word problems. The key steps are reading the problem carefully, deciding what you're trying to find, sorting out what you really need from what's given, and then devising a strategy for finding the answer. Once the problem is set up, finding the answer is not much different than solving a basic math problem.

You can find basic math problems in settings in all of the content areas. Question 7 is an example from pre-algebra.

---

7. What is the total cost of 2.5 pounds of bananas at $0.34 per pound and 2.5 pounds of tomatoes at $0.66 per pound?

   A. $1.00
   B. $2.40
   C. $2.50
   D. $3.50
   E. $5.00

Here, you're asked to find the total cost of some bananas and tomatoes. The important information is that the total cost includes 2.5 pounds of bananas at $0.34 per pound and 2.5 pounds of tomatoes at $0.66 per pound. A straightforward solution strategy would be to multiply to find the cost of the bananas and the cost of the tomatoes and then add to find the total cost. Now, the problem you're left with is very basic—calculating $2.5(0.34) + 2.5(0.66)$. Using your calculator might save time and avoid computation errors, but if you see that $2.5(0.34) + 2.5(0.66) = 2.5(0.34 + 0.66) = 2.5(1.00) = 2.50$, you might be able to do the computation more quickly in your head.

Basic elementary algebra problems can be in settings also. Question 8 is an example.

---

8. The relationship between temperature expressed in degrees Fahrenheit (F) and degrees Celsius (C) is given by the formula

$$F = \frac{9}{5}C + 32$$

If the temperature is 14 degrees Fahrenheit, what is it in degrees Celsius?

F. -10
G. -12
H. -14
J. -16
K. -18

In this problem, you're given a relationship (in the form of an equation) between temperatures expressed in degrees Fahrenheit (F) and degrees Celsius (C). You're also given a temperature of 14 degrees Fahrenheit and asked what the corresponding temperature would be in degrees Celsius. Your strategy would probably be to substitute 14 into the equation in place of the variable F. This leaves you with a basic algebra problem—solving the equation $14 = \frac{9}{5}C + 32$ for C. Before going on to the next problem, it would probably be a good idea to check your answer, which should be $C = -10$, by substituting -10 for C, multiplying by $\frac{9}{5}$ and adding 32 to see if the result is 14. Checking doesn't take long, and you might catch an error.

Question 9 is an example of an intermediate algebra problem in a setting.

---

9. Amy drove the 200 miles to New Orleans at an average speed 10 miles per hour faster than her usual average speed. If she completed the trip in 1 hour less than usual, what is her usual driving speed, in miles per hour?

- **A.** 20
- **B.** 30
- **C.** 40
- **D.** 50
- **E.** 60

After reading the problem, you know that it is about travel and that the basic formula "distance equals the rate multiplied by the time" ($D = rt$) or one of its variations ($r = \dfrac{D}{t}$ or $t = \dfrac{D}{r}$) will probably be useful. For travel problems, a table is often an efficient way to organize the information. Because the problem asks for Amy's usual speed (rate), it would probably be wise to let the variable r represent her usual speed. You might organize your table like this:

	Distance	Rate	Time
Usual trip	200	r	$\dfrac{200}{r}$
This trip	200	$r + 10$	$\dfrac{200}{r + 10}$

Then, because the time for this trip $\left(\dfrac{200}{r + 10}\right)$ is 1 hour less than the time for the usual trip $\left(\dfrac{200}{r}\right)$, solving $\dfrac{200}{r + 10} = \dfrac{200}{r} - 1$ will give the answer. Solving this equation is a matter of using routine algebra skills and procedures. The solution, $r = 40$, answers the question, "What is her usual driving speed?" A quick check that driving 200 miles at 40 miles per hour (mph) takes 5 hours and that driving 200 miles at 50 mph (which is 10 mph faster) takes 4 hours (which is 1 hour less) should convince you that your answer is correct.

Coordinate geometry problems can be in settings too. Question 10 is an example.

---

10. A map is laid out in the standard (x,y) coordinate plane. How long, in units, is an airplane's path on the map as the airplane flies along a straight line from City A located at $(20,14)$ to City B located at $(5,10)$?

   F. $\sqrt{1,201}$

   G. $\sqrt{241}$

   H. $\sqrt{209}$

   J. 7

   K. $\sqrt{19}$

In this problem, you're told that you will be working with the (x,y) coordinate plane and that you will need to find a distance. The distance formula should immediately come to mind. All you need is two points, and those are given. The problem now becomes a basic math problem—applying the distance formula:

$$\sqrt{(x_1 - x_2)^2 + (y_1 - y_2)^2} = \sqrt{(20 - 5)^2 + (14 - 10)^2} = \sqrt{241}.$$

Your calculator might be useful in finding $(20 - 5)^2 + (14 - 10)^2$, but you should not press the square root key because most of the answer choices are in radical form.

A geometry problem in a setting is illustrated by question 11.

---

11. A person 2 meters tall casts a shadow 3 meters long. At the same time, a telephone pole casts a shadow 12 meters long. How many meters tall is the pole?

   A. 4
   B. 6
   C. 8
   D. 11
   E. 18

Question 11 has no figure, which is sometimes the case with geometry problems. It might be wise to draw your own figure and label it with the appropriate numbers from the problem. "A person 2 meters tall casts a shadow 3 meters long" is a pretty good clue that you should draw a right triangle with the vertical leg labeled 2 and the horizontal leg labeled 3, and "a telephone pole casts a shadow 12 meters long" suggests that you should draw another right triangle with the horizontal leg labeled 12. Finding how many meters tall the pole is amounts to finding the length of the other leg of your second triangle, which you would label with a variable, say x. Your figure would be similar to this:

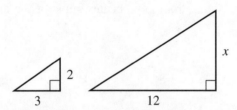

The triangles are similar (they're both right triangles and the angle that the sun's rays make with the ground is the same for both because the shadows were measured at the same time), so finding the height of the pole amounts to setting up and solving a proportion between corresponding sides of the triangles—a basic math problem. Your proportion might be $\frac{3}{12} = \frac{2}{x}$. Cross multiply to get $3(x) = 12(2)$, or $3x = 24$, and solve to get $x = 8$. Because the numbers are quite simple to work with, you probably wouldn't use your calculator on this problem.

Last (but not least), question 12 shows an example of a trigonometry problem in a setting.

---

12. The hiking path to the top of a mountain makes, at the steepest place, an angle of 20° with the horizontal, and it maintains this constant slope for 500 meters, as illustrated below. Which of the following is the closest approximation to the change in elevation, in meters, over this 500-meter section?

(Note: You may use the following values, which are correct to 2 decimal places:
cos 20° ≈ .94; sin 20° ≈ .34; tan 20° ≈ .36)

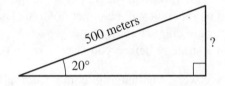

F.   20
G.   170
H.   180
J.   250
K.   470

This problem has a figure, and the figure is labeled with all the necessary information, including a question mark to tell you what you need to find. To set the problem up, you need to decide which of the trigonometric ratios involves the hypotenuse and the side opposite the given angle of a right triangle. Once you decide that the sine ratio is appropriate, the problem you have left to solve is a basic trigonometry problem: $\sin 20° = \frac{x}{500}$, or $500 \sin 20° = x$. Then, using the value for sin 20° given in the note, calculate $x = 500(.34) = 170$. You may want to use your calculator to avoid computation errors.

Very challenging problems

The ACT Mathematics Test emphasizes reasoning ability, so it naturally has problems that can be very challenging. Because these problems are designed to test your understanding of mathematical concepts and your ability to pull together what you have learned in your math classes, they will probably be unlike those you usually see. Some will be in settings, and some won't. Some will have figures, and some won't. Some will have extra information that you'll have to sort out, and some won't have enough information so the correct answer will be "Cannot be determined from the given information." Some will have numeric answers, some will have answers that are expressions or equations that you have to set up, and some will have answers that are statements for you to interpret and judge. On some questions your calculator will be helpful, and on others it will be better not to use it. All of the questions will share one important characteristic, however—they will challenge you to think hard and plan a strategy before you start to solve them.

Problems that are very challenging come from all six content areas. Question 13 is a very challenging pre-algebra problem.

---

13. If 537^{102} were calculated, it would have 279 digits. What would the digit farthest to the right be (the ones digit)?

   A. 1
   B. 3
   C. 4
   D. 7
   E. 9

You certainly wouldn't want to calculate 537^{102} by hand, and your calculator doesn't display enough digits for you to be able to read off the ones digit for this very large number, so you have to figure out another way to "see" the ones digit. A good place to start might be to look at the ones digit for powers of 7 because 7 is the ones digit of 537. Maybe there will be a pattern: $7^0 = \mathbf{1}$, $7^1 = \mathbf{7}$, $7^2 = 4\mathbf{9}$, $7^3 = 34\mathbf{3}$, $7^4 = 2,40\mathbf{1}$, $7^5 = 16,80\mathbf{7}$, $7^6 = 117,64\mathbf{9}$, $7^7 = 823,54\mathbf{3}$. It looks like the pattern of the ones digits is 1, 7, 9, 3, 1, 7, 9, 3, ⋯, with the sequence of these 4 digits repeating over and over. Now, if you can decide where in this pattern the ones digit of 537^{102} falls, you'll have the problem solved. You might organize a chart like this:

Ones digit	1	7	9	3
Powers of 7	0 4	1 5	2 6	3 7

The next row would read "8 9 10 11" to show that the ones digits of 7^8, 7^9, 7^{10}, and 7^{11}, respectively, are 1, 7, 9, and 3. You could continue the chart row after row until you got up to 102, but that would take a lot of time. Instead, think about where 102 would fall. It looks like the numbers in the first column are multiples of 4, so 100 would fall there because it is a multiple of 4. Then 101 would be in the second column, and 102 would fall in the third column. Therefore, the ones digit of 537^{102} is 9.

Question 14 is an elementary algebra problem designed to challenge your ability to think mathematically.

---

14. If $a < -1$, which of the following best describes a general relationship between a^3 and a^2 ?

F. $a^3 > a^2$

G. $a^3 < a^2$

H. $a^3 = a^2$

J. $a^3 = -a^2$

K. $a^3 = \dfrac{1}{a^2}$

Here you are told that $a < -1$ and then you are asked for the relationship between a^3 and a^2. By stopping to think for a moment before trying to manipulate the given inequality or experimenting with numbers plugged into the answer choices, you might realize that if $a < -1$, then a is a negative number, so its cube is a negative number. Squaring a negative number, however, gives a positive number. Every negative number is less than every positive number, so the correct relationship between a^3 and a^2 is $a^3 < a^2$. Of course, there are other ways to approach the problem.

For a very challenging intermediate algebra problem, look at question 15.

---

15. If $\left(\frac{4}{5}\right)^n = \sqrt{\left(\frac{5}{4}\right)^3}$, then $n = ?$

    A. $-\frac{3}{2}$

    B. -1

    C. $-\frac{2}{3}$

    D. $\frac{2}{3}$

    E. $\frac{3}{2}$

In this problem, you're asked to find the value of a variable, but the variable is in the exponent. After some thought you might decide to try to rewrite $\sqrt{\left(\frac{5}{4}\right)^3}$ so that it is $\frac{5}{4}$ raised to a power. You should remember that the square root is the same as the $\frac{1}{2}$ power, so, after using some properties of exponents, $\sqrt{\left(\frac{5}{4}\right)^3} = \left(\left(\frac{5}{4}\right)^3\right)^{\frac{1}{2}} = \left(\frac{5}{4}\right)^{\frac{3}{2}}$. Now at least the left side and the right side of the equation have the same form, but the bases of the two expressions aren't the same—they're reciprocals. In thinking about the connection between reciprocals and exponents, you might realize that taking the opposite of the exponent (that is, making it have the opposite sign) will "flip" the base, because $a^{-n} = \frac{1}{a^n}$. So now, with $\left(\frac{4}{5}\right)^n = \left(\frac{4}{5}\right)^{-\frac{3}{2}}$, $n = -\frac{3}{2}$.

There are also coordinate geometry problems that are very challenging. Question 16 is an example.

---

16. In the standard (x,y) plane, the triangle with vertices at $(0,0)$, $(0,k)$, and $(2,m)$, where m is constant, changes shape as k changes. What happens to the triangle's area, expressed in square coordinate units, as k increases starting from 2 ?

   F. The area increases as k increases.
   G. The area decreases as k increases.
   H. The area always equals 2.
   J. The area always equals m.
   K. The area always equals $2m$.

This problem might seem confusing at first, because there are two different variables and there is no figure to help you sort things out. You're told that m is a constant but that k changes. So, to help get you started, you could pick a value for m, say $m = 1$. Then, at least you can start sketching a figure. The point $(0,k)$ is on the y-axis and k increases starting with 2, so you could start by drawing a figure similar to this:

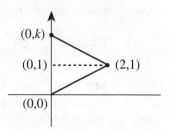

You can see the triangle that the problem mentions. If you think of the segment from $(0,0)$ to $(0,k)$ as the base and the segment from $(2,1)$ to $(0,1)$ as the height, you can see that as k increases, the base of the triangle gets longer but the height remains the same. From geometry, you know that the area of a triangle is given by $\frac{1}{2}$(base)(height). Therefore, the area will increase as the base gets longer, so, in other words, the area will increase as k increases. You should be able to reason that for any value of m, the result would have been the same, and you can feel confident that the correct answer is the first answer choice.

For a very challenging geometry problem, look at question 17.

---

17. In the figure below, $\overline{AB} \cong \overline{AC}$ and $\overline{BC}$ is 10 units long. What is the area, in square inches, of $\triangle ABC$?

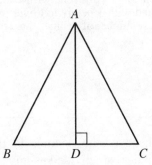

A. 12.5

B. 25

C. $25\sqrt{2}$

D. 50

E. Cannot be determined from the given information

This problem has a figure, but none of the information given is marked on the figure. It would probably be wise to mark the figure yourself to indicate which sides are congruent and which side is 10 units long. You need to find the area of $\triangle ABC$, and you know that the base $\overline{BC}$ is 10 units long. You need the measure of the height $\overline{AD}$ before you can apply the formula for the area of a triangle. You might ask yourself, "Is there any way to get the height?" If you were given the measure of one of the angles or the measure of one of the congruent sides, you might be able to find the height, but no other information is given. With a little more thought, you should realize that the height can be any positive number because there are infinitely many isosceles triangles with base 10 units long. You conclude that there is not enough information to allow you to solve this problem, and the correct answer choice is the last one: "Cannot be determined from the given information."

This is the example that was mentioned earlier where "Cannot be determined from the given information" is the correct answer. Remember not to jump to a hasty conclusion when "Cannot be determined from the given information" is an answer choice. Sometimes it is the right answer, but sometimes it isn't.

Problems that are very challenging can be in settings, too. Question 18 is an example from pre-algebra.

---

18. A bag of pennies could be divided among 6 children, or 7 children, or 8 children, with each getting the same number, and with 1 penny left over in each case. What is the smallest number of pennies that could be in the bag?

   F.   22
   G.   43
   H.   57
   J.   169
   K.   337

In this problem, whenever the pennies in the bag (which contains an unknown number of pennies) are divided evenly among 6 children, 7 children, or 8 children, there is always 1 penny left over. This means that if you take the extra penny out of the bag, then the number of pennies left in the bag will be divisible (with no remainder) by 6, 7, and 8. You should ask yourself, "What is the smallest number that is divisible by 6, 7, and 8?" In mathematical terminology, you're looking for the least common multiple of 6, 7, and 8. One way to find the least common multiple is to use the prime factorizations of the three numbers and to find the product of the highest power of each prime that occurs in one or more of the three numbers. This process will yield $2^3 \cdot 3 \cdot 7 = 168$ ($168 \div 6 = 28$, $168 \div 7 = 24$, and $168 \div 8 = 21$). But wait! You're not quite finished. Remember to add back in the penny that you took out of the bag originally to make the divisions come out even. Thus, your answer is 169.

Question 19 is an example of an elementary algebra word problem that is very challenging.

---

19. There are n students in a class. If, among those students, $p\%$ play at least 1 musical instrument, which of the following general expressions represents the number of students who play NO musical instrument?

A. np

B. $.01np$

C. $\dfrac{(100-p)n}{100}$

D. $\dfrac{(1-p)n}{.01}$

E. $100(1-p)n$

This is an example of a problem that has a mathematical expression as its answer. Finding an expression to answer a question usually makes you think more than finding a numerical answer because the variables require you to think abstractly. In this problem, you are told that out of a class of n students, $p\%$ play one or more musical instruments. Finding the percent of students who play no musical instruments is simple: $(100 - p)\%$. To find the number of students who play no musical instruments, you'd probably want to convert $(100 - p)\%$ to a decimal and multiply by n. If $100 - p$ were a number, you'd automatically move the decimal point two places to the left without thinking. But, since there's no decimal point to move in $100 - p$, you have to think about what you need to do to convert $(100 - p)\%$ to a decimal. Moving the decimal point two places to the left is the same as dividing by 100, so $(100 - p)\%$ as a decimal is $\dfrac{100 - p}{100}$, and the number of students who play no musical instruments is $\dfrac{(100 - p)n}{100}$.

Question 20 is an example of a coordinate geometry problem that has a setting and is very challenging.

---

20. Starting at her doorstep, Ramona walked down the sidewalk at 1.5 feet per second for 4 seconds. Then she stopped for 4 seconds, realizing that she had forgotten something. Next she returned to her doorstep along the same route at 1.5 feet per second. The graph of Ramona's distance (d) from her doorstep as a function of time (t) would most resemble which of the following?

F.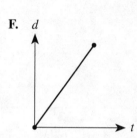

J.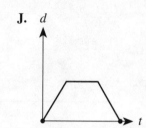

G.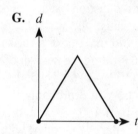

K.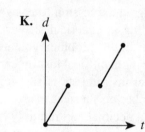

H.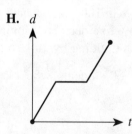

This problem is different from any of the problems you've seen so far because its answer is a graph. And, instead of giving you an equation and asking you to identify the equation's graph, this problem describes a situation and asks you to decide which graph represents the situation. You need to think about what the description of each of Ramona's activities says in terms of distance as a function of time and what each activity would translate into graphically. For example, at first Ramona walked at a constant rate down the sidewalk. Therefore, she moved farther away from her doorstep as time elapsed and her distance from her doorstep increased at a constant rate as time increased. So, the first part of the graph should be a line segment with a positive slope. Unfortunately, all five graphs start out this way, so none of the options can be eliminated at this point. The next thing Ramona did was stop for 4 seconds. If she stood still, her distance from her doorstep would not change even though time was still elapsing. This part of the graph should then reflect a constant value for d as time increases. It should be a horizontal line segment. This information allows you to eliminate options **F, G,** and **K,** because they do not have a horizontal segment. Ramona's next activity helps you decide between **H** and **J.** Ramona walked back home at the same rate along the same route as before. On her way back home, her distance from her doorstep decreased at a constant rate as elapsed time increased. This would be graphed as a line segment with a negative slope, and therefore **J** is the correct graph.

Another word problem that challenges you to think mathematically is question 21.

---

21. An object detected on radar is 5 miles to the east, 4 miles to the north, and 1 mile above the tracking station. Among the following, which is the closest approximation to the distance, in miles, that the object is from the tracking station?

  A. 6.5
  B. 7.2
  C. 8.3
  D. 9.0
  E. 10.0

This problem is about computing a distance, but it's a distance in three-dimensional space and there isn't a picture to help you. For this problem, it might be helpful for you to draw a sketch of the situation. Your sketch might be a "box" like this:

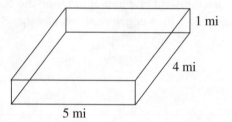

You need to find the length of the diagonal from the lower left corner of the front of the box to the top right corner of the back of the box. This is the hypotenuse of a right triangle ($\triangle OBR$ on the figure redrawn below with certain vertices marked) that has its right angle at B. One leg of this triangle has length 1, but the other leg is $\overline{BR}$, and you don't know the length of $\overline{BR}$.

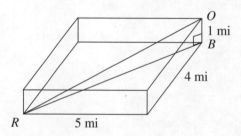

A closer look shows that $\overline{BR}$ is the hypotenuse of $\triangle RAB$ (shown on the figure below), which has its right angle at A and legs that measure 5 and 4.

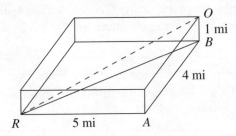

Using the Pythagorean theorem gives $BR = \sqrt{5^2 + 4^2} = \sqrt{41}$. Now you can use the Pythagorean theorem again to get $OR = \sqrt{\left(\sqrt{41}\right)^2 + 1^2} = \sqrt{42}$, which is about 6.5.

Grouped questions

Sometimes the Mathematics Test contains grouped questions, usually two or three questions per group, that all relate to the same information, which is often presented in a graph or chart. Questions 22–24 illustrate a group of questions that relate to the same information.

Use the following information to answer questions 22–24.

At both Quick Car Rental and Speedy Car Rental, the cost, in dollars, of renting a full-size car depends on a fixed daily rental fee and a fixed charge per mile that the car is driven. However, the daily rental fee and the charge per mile are not the same for the 2 companies. In the graph below, line Q represents the total cost for Quick Car Rental and line S represents the total cost for Speedy Car Rental.

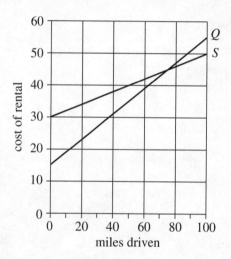

22. Robert plans to rent a full-size car for 1 day and drive only 50 miles. If his only consideration is to incur the least cost, which company should he choose?

F. Quick Car Rental, because the cost is $5.00 less.
G. Quick Car Rental, because the cost is $15.00 less.
H. Either company, because the costs are equal.
J. Speedy Car Rental, because the cost is $5.00 less.
K. Speedy Car Rental, because the cost is $15.00 less.

23. If you rent a full-size car from Quick Car Rental for 1 day, how much more would the total rental cost be if you drove the car 78 miles than if you drove it 77 miles?

   A. $0.10
   B. $0.15
   C. $0.20
   D. $0.40
   E. $0.55

24. What would be the total cost of renting a full-size car from Speedy Car Rental for 1 day and driving the car 150 miles?

   F. $ 60
   G. $ 75
   H. $ 85
   J. $ 90
   K. $120

Once you've looked at the information given for a group of questions, you can use the same sorts of strategies to answer the questions that you would use on any question on the ACT Mathematics Test. Question 22 requires you to read the graph and compare the costs of renting a car from the 2 companies, assuming that the car is going to be driven 50 miles. In the graph, the cost for Speedy Car Rental appears to be about $40, and the cost of Quick Car Rental appears to be about $35. These points are marked on the graph that is redrawn below.

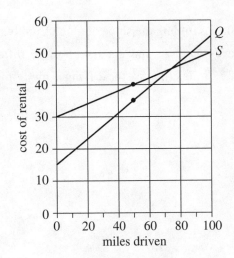

So Robert will incur the least cost if he rents from Quick Car Rental because that cost is $5 less.

Question 23 requires you to determine how much more Robert would pay if he rented a car from Quick Car Rental and drove 78 miles than if he drove 77 miles. Using mathematical concepts might be a better approach than trying to read the graph, because you might not be able to read the graph accurately enough. You know from coordinate geometry that, in the standard (x,y) coordinate plane, the slope of a line gives the rate of change in y per unit change in x, which is exactly what you want to find in this problem—how much the cost at Quick Car Rental changes when the car is driven 1 more mile. Two points that are easy to read accurately off the graph are $(0,15)$ and $(50,35)$, labeled on the redrawn graph below.

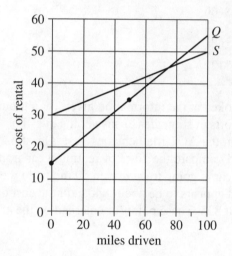

Using the formula for finding the slope of a line from two given points, you calculate the slope as $\frac{35-15}{50-0}$ and get 0.4. So, the difference for driving 78 miles instead of 77 miles (that is, for driving 1 more mile) is $0.40.

In question 24, you are asked for the cost of renting a car from Speedy Car Rental and driving it 150 miles. You can't simply read the cost off the graph, because 150 isn't on the graph. But you can find an equation of the line for Speedy Car Rental and then plug 150 into the equation. Recall that if you know two points (x_1, y_1) and (x_2, y_2) on a line, you can find an equation for the line using the two-point form for an equation of a line: $y - y_1 = \frac{y_2 - y_1}{x_2 - x_1}(x - x_1)$. Here, you can use two points that are easy to read off the graph, like $(0,30)$ and $(100,50)$, shown on the redrawn graph below, to get $y - 30 = \frac{50 - 30}{100 - 0}(x - 0)$ or $y = 0.20x + 30$. Then when $x = 150$, $y = 0.20(150) + 30 = 60$. So, $60 is the answer.

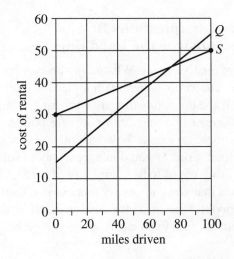

As you have seen in the sample questions in this section, the Mathematics Test includes all types of questions. Some will be easy for you, and some will be hard. They will all require you to demonstrate as much as possible about what you know and can do in mathematics.

Answer Key for Mathematics Test Sample Items

1. D	9. C	17. E
2. G	10. G	18. J
3. B	11. C	19. C
4. K	12. G	20. J
5. D	13. E	21. A
6. H	14. G	22. F
7. C	15. A	23. D
8. F	16. F	24. F

Strategies for Taking the ACT Mathematics Test

Pace yourself

There are 60 questions for you to answer in 60 minutes, which allows you an average of 1 minute per problem. Some problems will take you less than 1 minute, and some will take you more. Don't spend too much time on any one question. You should keep a close eye on your watch to make sure you work at a pace that will allow you to finish the test in the 60 minutes allotted. When determining your pace, be aware that the questions are arranged in order of difficulty: the question that ACT predicts will be the easiest for most students is first and the question predicted to be the hardest for most students is last.

Answer all the easy questions first, then go back to answer the hard ones

Easy and *hard* are relative terms. What might be easy for one student might be hard for another. You know which math topics are easy for you and which are hard. Answer all the questions that are easy for you and then go back to the hard ones. Remember that you don't get more points for answering hard questions. All questions, no matter how easy or hard, count equally toward your Mathematics total score. If you don't see a way to solve a problem, or if the method you're using seems to be taking a lot of time, skip the question and move on to questions that you can answer more easily. Don't forget, however, to mark in the test booklet (never on the answer sheet) all those questions that you skip so that you can find them easily when you go back to them later.

Answer all questions

Answer all questions even if you have no idea how to solve some of them. If you're stumped and have time, eliminate as many of the options as you can and then guess from among the ones that remain. If time is running out and you don't have time to eliminate any of the options, guess anyway. Even a wild guess has a 20% chance of being correct, but a blank has no chance of being correct. Remember, your score is based solely on the number of questions you answer correctly—there is no penalty for guessing and no penalty for wrong answers.

Read each problem carefully

Read carefully enough so you know what you're trying to find before you start looking for it, and so you know what you have to work with to help you find it. Remember that you don't necessarily have to use all the information you're given. Watch for cases where the information given is insufficient for solving the problem, but be fairly certain before you mark "Cannot be determined from the given information" that you haven't missed some information and that there isn't an alternate strategy that would enable you to solve the problem from the given information.

Look for information in the options

Sometimes looking at the options will provide valuable information about the form of the answer. For example, the options can tell you whether your answer should be left in radical form or converted to a decimal approximation, whether you should spend time reducing a probability to lowest terms, or whether your polynomial answer should be left in factored form or multiplied out. For some problems, you have to analyze the options as part of your solution strategy. For example, when a question asks "Which of the following statements is true?" and the statements are the five options, there is often no way to proceed except by examining each option in turn. Sometimes, using the options gives you an alternate way to solve a problem. For example, suppose you're trying to solve a quadratic equation and you can't get the quadratic expression to factor and can't remember the quadratic formula. You might be able to get the correct answer by substituting the options, in turn, into the equation until one works. This strategy should be used very sparingly, however, because it is usually more time-consuming than other strategies.

Use figures wisely and whenever you can

Whether the figure is given or you sketch your own, for visual learners there is truth in the old saying, "A picture is worth a thousand words." The marks you add to given figures (for example, dimensions that are given in the question but aren't on the figure or that you calculate in the process of solving the problem, marks to show congruences, auxiliary lines like perpendiculars and diagonals) and the figures you draw yourself often help you see the relationships more clearly.

Use your calculator wisely

A calculator will be helpful on the Mathematics Test only if you are very familiar with the one you bring to the test and you use it wisely during the test. Trying to use a calculator that you are not very familiar with or trying to use a calculator on every problem can have disastrous effects. Experimenting with the capabilities of a new calculator during the testing session or using a calculator in situations where a non-calculator approach would be better can cost you precious time. Bring the calculator that you are most familiar with— the one you use in your math classes or at home. Don't worry that other students have more sophisticated calculators than yours; the type of calculator that students use should not make a difference in their scores. Use your calculator wisely; remember that a non-calculator strategy is often better than a calculator strategy. And don't believe everything your calculator tells you. Make sure the numbers it gives you are reasonable and make sense.

Think!

Your head is by far a more powerful and efficient problem-solving tool than your pencil or your calculator. Think before you plunge in and begin working on a problem. Don't panic if you suddenly can't remember a formula or all of the steps of a procedure you've been taught. There might be another way to do the problem that will work just as well. For example, you don't have to write and solve an equation for every algebra word problem. You might be able to reason through such a problem and get the correct answer without an equation. Sometimes it's best to let your common sense about numbers take over.

Show your work

You have certainly heard this before—probably in every math class you've ever taken. Of course, you're not going to have time during the test to write down every step for every problem the way you might on a homework assignment, but writing down at least some of what you are thinking and doing as you solve a problem will be worth the time it takes. It may be important, as a way of record keeping, to write down numbers that you plug into your calculator, and the intermediate results it gives you, in the process of solving a problem. If you don't write anything down and your answer for a problem doesn't match any of the answer choices, your only alternative is to start over. But, if you have at least something written down, you may be able to go back over your work and find your mistake. Also, if you have time at the end of the test to go back and check your answers, having something written down will enable you to check over your work more quickly.

Check your answers

Before you leave a question, make sure your answer makes sense. Don't believe everything your calculator tells you; make sure that the answer your calculator displays makes sense to you and that your answer actually answers the question. For example, if a problem about oranges and apples asks for the number of apples, make sure your answer doesn't give the number of oranges, or if a problem asks for the altitude of a triangle, make sure your answer isn't the hypotenuse. Remember, if you have time left after answering all of the questions on the Mathematics Test, use it wisely and go back and check your work.

Triangle contemplating its altitude.

ACT Assessment Reading Test

The ACT Reading Test is designed to measure your skill in reading. The Reading Test asks you to answer 40 questions—10 questions about each of four passages—in 35 minutes. The passages in the Reading Test come from published materials such as books and magazines and are like those a first-year college student can expect to read.

Content of the ACT Reading Test

The ACT Reading Test contains one passage from each of the following four categories:

■ **Prose Fiction** (intact short stories or excerpts from short stories or novels)
■ **Humanities** (architecture, art, dance, ethics, film, language, literary criticism, music, philosophy, radio, television, theater)
■ **Social Studies** (anthropology, archaeology, business, economics, education, geography, history, political science, psychology, sociology)
■ **Natural Sciences** (anatomy, astronomy, biology, botany, chemistry, ecology, geology, medicine, meteorology, microbiology, natural history, physiology, physics, technology, zoology)

Your Reading Test score will tell you how you did on all 40 questions of the Reading Test. You'll also receive a Social Studies/Sciences subscore (based on how you do on the 20 questions in the social studies and natural sciences sections of the test), and an Arts/Literature subscore (based on how you do on the 20 questions in the humanities and prose fiction sections of the test).

You'll have 35 minutes to read the Reading Test's four passages and answer the 40 multiple-choice questions. This means you'll have about 8 to 9 minutes to read each passage and answer the questions that follow. That's not a lot of time, but it's more than you might think. Once you've read through this section, you'll have a better idea of what the Reading Test is all about and what you need to do in order to do your best on it.

The Reading Test evaluates your ability to understand the passages that appear in the test. It does not test your ability to remember relevant facts from outside the passage. You don't need to be knowledgeable about the subject area that a passage covers in order to do well on the questions, but you do need to read attentively and to think carefully about what you read. The passages may deal with subjects you're familiar with, or you may know almost nothing about the subjects of the passages. It doesn't matter, though: the passages contain all the information you need to answer the questions.

Types of Passages on the ACT Reading Test

Just as going to see the latest action movie is different from watching a wildlife special on public television, reading a novel or short story is a different experience from reading a scientific essay. As you read the different passages in the Reading Test, you may find it helpful to keep their essential differences in mind.

Prose Fiction

Prose fiction passages generally include a narration of events and revelation of character. Think about how you read fiction. What do you look for? Do you read fiction hoping to find facts, or to be entertained? Although we learn a great deal when we read fiction, most of us read for the story—to "find out what happens"—or because we're interested in the characters. The questions on prose fiction passages ask about the kinds of things you pay attention to when you read a short story or novel—plot, characters, and mood, among other things.

As you read a prose fiction passage, don't just note events. Try to be aware of the passage's mood or tone, the relationships of the characters, and the emotion implied by what the characters say as well as how they say it. A writer often uses dialogue not only to explain a situation to a reader, but also to reveal character. Refer to the sample passages on pages 132 and 134 for examples of the type of prose fiction passage you can expect on the ACT Reading Test.

Humanities

Humanities passages tend to describe or analyze ideas or works of art. Although some humanities passages taken from personal essays may seem a bit like prose fiction passages, there is one important difference: the personal essays are written as fact, and prose fiction is, well, fiction.

Humanities passages are typically informative pieces, although at times you'll be very aware of the writer's presence and point of view. Sometimes a question will ask you to project the writer's likely response to a hypothetical argument or situation, based on what the passage tells you about the writer's opinions and what the language implies.

These passages might have characters, but they're not characters like those in a short story. Rather, they're historical figures or prominent contemporary people—people who have actually lived. You won't be making the same kind of inferences about them as you might about fictional characters. In these passages, the kinds of relationships you'll be asked to infer or identify are those between events, ideas, people, trends, or modes of thought. Refer to the sample passage on page 142 for an example of the type of humanities passage you can expect on the ACT Reading Test.

Yes, I really lived...

Characters in humanities passages are people who have actually lived.

Social Studies

Social studies passages typically present information gathered by research (rather than through scientific experimentation). A social studies passage might be about Japanese history, or political action committees, or a psychological experiment. You'll find names, dates, and concepts in these passages, and you'll need to pay close attention to what name goes with what concept in a discussion of political systems and to keep track of who said what in a passage discussing different views of a constitutional amendment. Watch for cause-effect relationships, comparisons, and sequences of events. Pay careful attention to the specifics, especially the way in which they help you shape an idea of the passage's subject. Refer to the sample passage on page 136 for an example of the type of social studies passage you can expect on the ACT Reading Test.

Natural Sciences

This kind of passage usually presents a science topic and an explanation of the topic's significance. A natural sciences passage requires a different sort of analysis than a prose fiction passage does. For instance, in a natural sciences passage, the author is typically concerned with the relationships between natural phenomena, not the relationships between characters. As with social studies passages, you should pay special attention to cause-effect relationships, comparisons, and sequences of events. Keep track of any specific laws, rules, and theories that are mentioned, but don't try to memorize them.

Many of the Reading Test's nonfiction passages, especially natural sciences passages, will include some specialized or technical language. Don't let new words throw you. If knowing the meaning of a word is necessary to answer a question, the passage will provide clues to its meaning. Do your best to figure it out from the context, and then go on. Don't devote extra time to it unless it comes up later in one of the questions. Refer to the sample passages on pages 138 and 140 for examples of the type of natural sciences passage you can expect on the ACT Reading Test.

Types of Questions on the ACT Reading Test

On the Reading Test, all of the questions fall into one of two basic categories: referring and reasoning. **Referring** questions ask you to find or use information that is clearly stated in the passage. **Reasoning** questions ask you to do more: they ask you to take information that's either stated or implied in the passage and use it to answer more complex questions.

You shouldn't worry about these categories while you're taking the Reading Test. It's most important that you focus on the questions themselves and on what they ask you about a given passage. Because each passage is different, the kinds of questions you see will vary from passage to passage. Still, there are some general types of questions you're likely to encounter. Most questions will ask you to do one of the following:

■ identify important details
■ identify the main point of a paragraph or passage
■ make comparisons between characters or ideas
■ identify cause-effect relationships
■ make generalizations about events or characters
■ determine the meaning of unfamiliar words from the context of the passage
■ make reasonable inferences about events, ideas, or characters
■ identify an author's point of view

This list gives you an idea of what kinds of questions are asked most frequently on the Reading Test. Sometimes Reading Tests contain other types of questions, but don't worry. Just make sure you read each passage and its questions carefully. You'll find that the information you need to determine the best answer for a question is always available in the passage. Questions that illustrate each of the most common types of questions on the Reading Test follow.

Representative ACT Reading Test Questions

Details. Some test questions ask you to pick out significant details mentioned in a passage. A detail can be something as seemingly simple as a characteristic of a person, place, or thing, or a particular date, as with the question below from the passage and questions on pages 132–133.

---

1. In what year did Lewis Barber Fletcher's wife and friends first hear about his momentous train trip?

    A. 1891
    B. 1896
    C. 1941
    D. 1946

You'll need to read the passage carefully to get the correct answer here. If you simply read the passage's first sentence and assume that that date—the only one printed in the passage—is the answer, you'll get the question wrong. You need to read the next sentence, starting on line 4, to know that the answer is **C,** not **A.** This date is important to the passage: the fact that it took so long for his family to hear about the trip tells us a lot about Lewis Barber Fletcher.

Details questions in dense natural sciences passages can be more challenging. Look, for example, at this question (from the passage and questions on pages 140–141):

---

48. The author of the passage feels that the feature which contributes to the Great Horned Owl's somewhat human appearance is its:

    F. operculum.
    G. pre-aural flap.
    H. facial disks.
    J. asymmetrical ears.

You have to work through a lot of information in the first paragraph before you find the right answer to this question. If you read closely, you'll find that the information you need (in lines 18–21) indicates that the best answer is **H.**

Questions about details occasionally ask you to find the one detail that does **not** support a particular point or situation. You need to pay careful attention to these questions. When you answer them you need to remember that the usual form of the question is being reversed. Here's an example of this kind of "reverse" question (from the passage and questions on pages 140–141):

---

44. According to the passage, all of the following contribute to the owl's extraordinary sound scanning EXCEPT its:

    F. facial muscles.
    G. operculum.
    H. beak.
    J. feathers.

From the information in lines 15–35, you know that an owl's facial muscles and feathers, working together, are critical to its hearing. This means that neither **F** nor **J** is the best answer. (Remember: this question asks what does **not** contribute to the "owl's extraordinary sound scanning.") Lines 27–35 tell us of the importance of the operculum to the owl's hearing, which means **G** can't be the answer, either. There's no evidence anywhere that the owl's beak has anything to do with its exceptional hearing, so **H** is the correct answer to the question.

Main Idea. To answer this kind of question you need to be able to identify the focus of a passage or of a paragraph in a passage. You shouldn't count on finding this information summed up in the first paragraph of a passage or in the first sentence of a paragraph. You may have been advised to make the first sentence of each paragraph the "topic sentence" in your own writing, but not every writer does that. You'll need to figure out what the author's main point is in a paragraph or in an entire passage by reading the paragraph or passage carefully.

Main idea questions can be very straightforward. The following question, based on the passage about Beethoven on pages 142–143, is very direct:

---

51. The main idea of the passage is that:

A. the distinction between the Classical period of music and the Romantic period of music is artificial.

B. the music of the Classical period is far superior to the music of the Romantic period.

C. Beethoven was such a masterful musician that he virtually transformed the musical forms of his day.

D. Beethoven was a power-hungry individual who sublimated his music to his quest for political power.

If you read the passage carefully, you will know that the author thinks that Beethoven was a great and influential composer—the whole passage is about the importance of his music. Options **A** and **B**, which talk about the differences between music of the Classical period and the Romantic period, are pretty clearly not the main idea of this passage, but what about **D?** The fourth paragraph (lines 35–44) addresses Beethoven's personality and tells us that "Biographers have emphasized Beethoven the wretched man." This is interesting information to have, but it is a minor point if you look at what the passage as a whole says. Therefore, **C** is the correct answer.

Main idea questions often ask about individual paragraphs, but they do not always use the words "main idea." In the following, the paragraph in question has several pieces of information but nothing that you would be able to call a "main idea." Therefore, the "main idea" type of question is asked in a somewhat different way here. The following question is from the passage and questions on pages 138–139.

---

38. One of the main observations made in the next-to-last paragraph (lines 73–85) is that:

F. current law can be seen as encouraging truck drivers to drive at unsafe times.

G. truck drivers should work different hours every day.

H. truck drivers find it difficult to cover their required daily mileage.

J. the accidents truck drivers have occur when they've driven more than 14 hours.

The issue in this paragraph is not **H,** how many miles truck drivers cover, nor is it **J,** the number of accidents that truck drivers who work more than 14 hours a day have. One of the main observations made in this paragraph is that truck drivers might be better off working the same hours every day, which is the opposite of **G.** To answer this question correctly, you need to be able to see that **F** is simply paraphrasing information found in lines 77–78: "current law fosters the practice of driving at bad times."

Comparison. You're most likely to find comparison questions in passages that contain a lot of information, for instance social studies and natural sciences passages, which are more likely to contain data or points of view that can be compared to one another. This kind of test question can make you process a lot of information—you may be asked to weigh one concept against another and identify a significant difference between the two. But comparison questions aren't always overly complicated.

The question below (from the passage and questions on pages 140–141) is a good example of the kind of comparison question you might see in a natural sciences passage.

---

49. The author of the passage compares the ears of owls and humans, and states that one way in which an owl's ears are superior is that the owl:

 A. has a pre-aural flap, which triangulates.
 B. uses them for low-frequency hearing.
 C. can direct its operculum at the sound source.
 D. has a larger left ear than right ear.

This question refers to the passage's comparison of owl and human ears and asks you to remember what makes an owl's ear superior to a human ear. Lines 27–31 is where the author makes the comparison. He first explains a similarity between the ears (which tells you **A** can't be right), and then notes the thing that makes owl hearing superior: the owl's ability to direct its ear toward a sound source. To choose the correct answer, **C,** you have to remember that the pre-aural flap is called the operculum (lines 27–28).

Cause-effect. Cause-effect questions can be asked about prose fiction passages—sometimes one character's actions cause another character to react in a certain way. Cause-effect questions also arise in natural sciences passages where a process may be described sequentially. Sometimes the answer to a cause-effect question is stated in the passage; sometimes you must put together the information you've read and work out the answer on your own.

Here's an example of a very direct cause-effect question, from the example passage and questions on pages 136–137.

---

27. According to the account of tansu-making in the passage, improved wood-planing techniques resulted in:

   A. a need to change the types of wood used.
   B. the need to apply thicker wood finishes.
   C. the use of thinner wood.
   D. a renewed interest in black-and-gold lacquered finishes.

The answer to this question is clearly stated in lines 70–73, where the passage says that "Thick pieces of wood originally used became thinner around 1900, when improved wood planing techniques resulted in mass-produced tansu of diminished quality." The answer is **C**.

Below is an example of a more complicated cause-effect question, from the passage and questions on pages 140–141.

---

46. According to the passage, an owl that dives into a snowbank and emerges holding a mouse was able to capture its prey most probably because the:

   F. owl heard the mouse in the snowbank, figured out its location, and attacked.
   G. owl was actually able to see into the snowbank and spot the mouse.
   H. mouse made a noise in a tonal range identical to the owl's tonal range.
   J. owl read the mouse's pellets and realized exactly where it would be.

This question tests your ability to apply information from one part of the passage to another part; it also asks you to understand a particular cause-effect situation and make an inference based on what you know from the passage. The last sentence of the passage mentions owls plunging into snowdrifts and emerging holding mice in their talons, and the rest of the last paragraph suggests how an owl might do this. Specifically, the passage states that owls are especially sensitive to the high-frequency sounds that mice make, which helps to explain how an owl would be able to find and catch a mouse in a snowbank. So, **F** is the correct answer.

Generalization. This type of question usually asks you to take a lot of information, digest it, and then find a simple, or at least a shorter, way to answer the question being asked. A generalization question may involve interpreting words or behavior, or it may ask you to make some kind of general observation or draw a conclusion about an entire passage or the nature of an argument an author is making. Consider the following question (from the passage and questions on pages 134–135):

---

19. As he is depicted in the passage, the editor-in-chief is best described as a man who became:

- **A.** a good bit more cynical about astrological predictions.
- **B.** more cheerful as he looked toward the future.
- **C.** less easygoing than before but more professional overall.
- **D.** much easier to work with but overall less happy.

The answer to this question can be found by reading the passage's last paragraph, which describes how the editor-in-chief's behavior changed after he had a personal horoscope written for himself. Once you digest the last paragraph, it's easy to see that the editor-in-chief's behavior is not what is described in **A, B,** or **C,** and that **D** offers a generalization that works.

Vocabulary. Vocabulary questions test the meaning of words in context. This means that they ask you to figure out the meaning of a word, even if it's a word you don't know, from the sentence in which the word appears. (Sometimes you'll need to look at the sentences before or after the sentence in which the word appears, too.)

Look at the question below (from the passage and questions on pages 136–137) and see how it is worded. Most vocabulary questions will look like this.

---

25. As it is used in the passage, the word *patina* (line 58) most nearly means the:

  A. design carved in the wood of the chests.
  B. original finish applied to the chest.
  C. destruction of the wood by smoke and heat.
  D. surface appearance of the wood.

From the context, it is clear that *patina* has something to do with the tansu, which we know from the first paragraph were made of wood. The sentence in which *patina* is used says that "those [tansu] in original condition show a lovely natural patina" (lines 57–58). There is nothing in the passage that suggests that *patina* means a design carved in a tansu (**A**). The tansu referred to in this sentence—"large kitchen tansu" (line 55)—were "rarely finished" (lines 56–57), so **B** is not the best answer. A natural patina is described as occurring on tansu "in original condition" (line 57), which rules out **C**. Lines 58–59 tell us that a *patina* develops from exposure to smoke and heat, suggesting the best answer, **D**.

Sometimes the words tested have more than one meaning, and you'll have to read the passage closely to determine which meaning the question is asking for. The following question (from the passage and questions on pages 140–141) is an example of this kind of vocabulary item.

---

42. As it is used in line 62, the word *marked* most nearly means:

  F. noticeable.
  G. slight.
  H. scientific.
  J. written down.

Because one meaning of *marked* is "written down," it would be tempting to guess **J** as the answer for this question. However, *marked* is used differently in line 62 of the passage. For that context, **F** is the best answer. The other two options are not suggested by the context of *marked:* information in the paragraph suggests that the increase in nightly catch is more than just "slight," which rules out **G,** and the owl's increase is not "scientific" (**H**), although efforts to determine the size of an owl's catch might be.

Inferences. To infer something is to arrive at a conclusion by reasoning from the evidence that is available. By that definition, most referring questions ask you to make inferences. But here, "inferences" refers to a particular type of question. Inferences questions often begin with "It can reasonably be inferred from the passage," but will sometimes start with "The passage suggests" or "It is implied in the passage" or "It can reasonably be concluded from the passage." What all this means is that the answer to this kind of question won't be something stated directly in the passage. To choose the correct answer for this type of question, you're going to have to find the option that best paraphrases something that's been said in the passage.

Here's a good example of an inferences question (from the passage and questions on pages 134–135):

---

12. It can reasonably be inferred from the passage that the narrator worked very carefully on the editor-in-chief's horoscope because the narrator:

   F. wanted to earn his thousand crowns fair and square.
   G. hoped to affect the editor-in-chief's actions.
   H. had always wanted to do the editor-in-chief a favor.
   J. did not want the editor-in-chief to know he was a nuclear scientist.

To answer this question, you need to pay attention to various clues in the passage. For instance, in lines 75–76, the narrator says that a horoscope can "greatly influence, even dictate, the way people act." We can infer that the narrator didn't like the editor-in-chief, who had "ruined the lives" of many of the narrator's friends (line 64). The passage also tells us, in lines 73–75, that while writing the editor-in-chief's horoscope, the narrator consulted regularly with R., whose boss was the editor-in-chief. Finally, in the last paragraph, we learn that the horoscope does in fact change the editor-in-chief's behavior for the better. Putting all this information together makes it easy to find the right answer, **G.**

The following question (from the passage and questions on pages 140–141) is a good example of an inferences question that doesn't use the word *inferred* or *implied,* but asks you in a different way to infer something.

---

47. The passage suggests that one quite unusual feature of owl hearing is that the owl:

   A. enjoys the low-pitched sound of its own voice.
   B. can usually guess at a sound's point of origin.
   C. hears its own tonal range best.
   D. does not hear its own tonal range best.

The author doesn't give us the answer, **D,** directly. What he says, in lines 50–53, is that "owls hear higher-frequency sounds better than the lower-pitched sounds made by their own voices. Almost all other animals hear their own tonal range best." Given that information, it seems pretty reasonable to say that the fact that an owl doesn't hear its own tonal range best is something unusual about an owl's hearing.

Point of View. You will feel the presence of the author more strongly in some passages than others. In a straightforward social studies passage, where the author tries to be objective in reporting the results of a survey, it may not be easy to identify the author's feelings. In other passages, though, how the author feels is an important aspect of the passage. Consider the following question (from the passage and questions on pages 142–143):

---

53. The attitude of the author of the passage toward Beethoven is apparently one of:

   A. admiration.
   B. disdain.
   C. ambivalence.
   D. envy.

The correct answer for this question is **A:** throughout the passage, the author expresses admiration for Beethoven. This is made clear by the way the author refers to Beethoven's accomplishments—"titanic" (line 8), for example—and also by arguments that the author makes. For instance, in the fourth paragraph (lines 35–44), the author argues that Beethoven's faults do not directly detract from, or even affect, his worth as an artist.

Strategies for Taking the ACT Reading Test

Pace yourself

Before you read the first passage of the Reading Test, you may want to take a quick look through the entire Reading Test. If you choose to do this, flip through the pages and look at each of the passages and their questions. (Note that the passages begin on the pages to your left, and the questions follow.) You don't need to memorize anything—you can look at any of the Reading Test passages and questions during the time allotted for that test.

Some readers find that looking quickly at the questions first gives them a better idea of what to look for as they're reading the passage. If you're a slow reader, though, this may not be a good strategy. If you **do** decide to preview the questions, don't spend too much time on them—just scan for a few key words or ideas that you can watch for when you read the passage. To see what approach works best for you, you might want to try alternating between the two approaches—previewing the questions and not previewing the

questions—as you work through the practice tests in this book. Remember that when you take the ACT test for real, a clock will be ticking. Plan your approach for the Reading Test before you take the actual ACT test.

Because your time will be limited, it's probably not a good idea to try a strategy for the first time on the test.

Before you begin your careful reading of each passage, here are some things you'll want to remember:

Use the time allotted

You have 35 minutes to read four passages and answer 40 questions. You'll probably want to pace yourself so you don't spend too much time on any one passage or question. If you take 2 to 3 minutes to read each passage, then you'll have about 35 to 40 seconds to answer each question associated with the passage. Some of the questions will take less time, which will allow you more time for the more challenging ones.

Because time is limited, you should be very careful in deciding whether to skip more difficult questions. If you skip the difficult questions from the first passage until you work through the entire Reading Test, for example, you may find that you've forgotten so much of the first passage that you have to reread it before you can answer the question that puzzled you the first time through. It will probably work better for you to think of the test as four approximately 9-minute units and to try to complete all the questions for a passage within its allotted time.

Think of an overall strategy that works for you

Are you the kind of person who likes to get the big picture first, then carefully go over your work? Do you like to answer the questions you're sure of right away and then go back and puzzle out the tougher ones? Or are you something of a perfectionist? (Do you find it hard to concentrate on a question until you know you got the one before it right?) There isn't any right way or wrong way to approach the Reading Test—just make sure the way you choose is the way that works best for you.

Getting the "big picture."

Keep the passage as a whole in mind

Your initial look at the whole Reading Test should give you some ideas about how to approach each passage. Notice that there are short paragraphs with subject headings in front of each passage. These "advance organizers" tell you the subject matter of the passage, where the passage comes from, who wrote it, and sometimes a little information about the passage. Occasionally, an advance organizer will define a difficult word or concept for you. Reading the advance organizers carefully should help you be more organized as you approach each passage.

Always remember that the Reading Test asks you to refer and reason on the basis of the passage. You may know a lot about the subject of some of the passages you read, but try not to let what you already know influence the way you answer the questions. There's a reason why many questions begin with "According to the passage" or "It can be reasonably inferred from the passage." If you read and understand the passage well, the rest will take care of itself. During the Reading Test, you can refer back to the passages as often as you like.

Find a strategy for approaching each question

First, you should read the question carefully so you know what it asks. Look for the best answer: read and consider all the options, even though you may feel you have identified the best one. Keep asking yourself whether you can justify your choice as the best answer.

Some people find it useful to answer the easy questions first and skip the difficult ones (being careful, of course, to mark the answer sheet correctly and to mark in the test booklet the questions they skipped). Then they go back and consider the difficult questions. When you're working on a test question and are not certain about the answer, try to eliminate options you're sure are incorrect. If you can rule out a couple of options, you'll improve your chances of getting the question right. Keep referring back to the passage for information.

Reading Strategies summary

The sample passages and questions used as examples in this section can be found on the following pages. They come from ACT tests that thousands of students have already taken. Remember, the questions in this section do not represent every type of question you're likely to see, but they should give you a good overall idea of the kinds of questions you'll see when you take the ACT Reading Test. If you want a more complete picture of what the ACT Reading Test will look like, there are two complete Reading Tests included in the two practice ACT tests on pages 173 and 349 in Chapter 5. And remember that the best way to do well on the ACT Reading Test is to have a solid understanding of each passage—the best thing you can do is to read carefully.

Sample Passage I

PROSE FICTION: This passage is adapted from the short story "The Boy on the Train" by Arthur Robinson (©1988 by Arthur Robinson).

In 1891, at the age of five, Lewis Barber Fletcher traveled alone from Jacksonville, Florida, to the little town of Camden, thirty-one miles northwest of Utica, in upstate New York. Fifty years later, his wife, child-
5 ren, and friends heard about his trip for the first time when this item appeared on the editorial page of the *Utica Daily Press* under a standing head, "50 Years Ago Today in the Press": "Lewis B. Fletcher, 5, arrived in Utica yesterday on a New York Central train on his
10 way to join his mother in Camden. He was traveling alone from Jacksonville, Florida." A friend spotted the item and phoned Mrs. Fletcher, who called her husband at his office and read it to him. She had to read it twice before he got it straight; he was hard of hearing and
15 even with an amplifying device on his telephone often had trouble understanding, mostly because he became tense when he had to use it. When he understood what she had read him, he gave an embarrassed "Ha!" and said he had forgotten about the trip. There was no
20 further discussion—he disliked talking about personal matters at his office, possibly suspecting that all work stopped while the help listened for material for gossip. When he came home that evening, he had already read the item at work, clipped it, stuck it in his billfold, and
25 developed an attitude toward it—a sort of amused, self-conscious pride that seemed to say yes, he had traveled nearly fourteen hundred miles by himself when he was five, with two changes of train, one of them involving a ferry from Jersey City to Manhattan, and had managed
30 the whole thing, as he had everything else in his life, by strict application to business.

The item was a sort of one-day sensation. Two clippings were put away in a photograph album, and the subject was pretty much forgotten. Sarah, the youngest
35 child, occasionally resurrected it when the family was together at Christmas, or, in later years, during vaca-tions at the elder Fletchers' place outside Utica. In the evening, when their parents had gone to bed and the children stayed up talking, Sarah might say in a rever-
40 ential tone, "Can you imagine him traveling alone from Jacksonville to Camden when he was five?" The two others—Howard, the oldest, and Edward—would say they could imagine it, that it was the easiest thing in the world to imagine. The picture they'd then conjure up
45 was of a five-year-old old man with white hair, steel-rimmed bifocals, and a hearing aid that he kept turned off to save the flat, half-pint-shaped battery.

Edward did wonder that his father seemed to have forgotten about a trip that should have been a momen-
50 tous experience for a five-year-old. He decided that his father may have felt there was something shameful about it and the shame had caused him to repress the memory. The children were dimly aware that their paternal grandparents had separated in Jacksonville and
55 were later divorced, and that their grandmother had

brought up Lewis and Reginald in Camden, but they didn't know any details. What Edward learned later was that right after the separation their grandmother had returned to Camden with Reginald, leaving Lewis with
60 their grandfather. The grandfather, who wasn't much good, had apparently decided he didn't want Lewis and had put him on a train for the two-day trip to his mother's. It was not an amusing picture: a five-year-old had been left behind by his mother and then sent off
65 alone by his father—abandoned by one, rejected by the other. Edward would try to imagine him without white hair, hearing aid, or steel-rimmed bifocals, a small boy with brown hair and a grave face, being taken to the train by his father, so dumb with misery and fright that
70 he couldn't cry, knowing only that he was going some-where out there into unknown space.

Edward went over the trip from time to time, adding details, trying to get inside the boy to experi-ence his anxiety and despair and very likely his distrust
75 of people on the train, whose brief, unctuous kind-nesses betrayed their fear of ending up with him on their hands.

This was the image of his father that could move Edward, and it seemed to bear no relation to the
80 anxiety-ridden old man in his early forties who sat all evening with a *Saturday Evening Post* in his lap, his hands clasped over his stomach and his thumbs revolving first one way and then the other while he went over and over whatever was worrying him.

1. In what year did Lewis Barber Fletcher's wife and friends first hear about his momentous train trip?
   A. 1891
   B. 1896
   C. 1941
   D. 1946

2. Lewis Barber Fletcher's children, listed from oldest to youngest, are:
   F. Sarah, Howard, and Edward.
   G. Sarah, Edward, and Howard.
   H. Howard, Sarah, and Edward.
   J. Howard, Edward, and Sarah.

3. The person responsible for informing the Fletcher family about the trip Lewis Barber Fletcher had taken in 1891 was:

   A. an unnamed friend of the family.
   B. a client of Lewis Barber Fletcher.
   C. a friend's daughter by the name of Sarah.
   D. the narrator of this story.

4. According to the passage, Lewis Barber Fletcher was:

   F. abandoned by his mother and rejected by his father.
   G. abandoned by his grandfather and rejected by his mother.
   H. abandoned by his grandmother and rejected by his mother.
   J. rejected by his grandfather and his father.

5. It was Edward's father's habit, when nervous, to:

   A. turn off his hearing aid.
   B. be shamed by bad memories.
   C. look at newspaper clippings.
   D. twiddle his thumbs.

6. As it is used in lines 39–40, the word *reverential* most nearly means:

   F. very loud.
   G. inaudible.
   H. amused.
   J. awed.

7. One of the main points of the second paragraph (lines 32–47) is that:

   A. everyone found Lewis Barber Fletcher's trip very amusing and they mentioned it frequently.
   B. Howard and Edward found Lewis Barber Fletcher's trip to be fascinating and easy to reconstruct.
   C. the Fletcher children found it hard to imagine their father as a little child.
   D. Lewis Barber Fletcher looked exactly the same as an old man as he had as a child.

8. It is implied in the fourth paragraph (lines 72–77) that the people Lewis Barber Fletcher met on the train who appeared to be quite kind:

   F. were not trustworthy at all.
   G. were not, perhaps, as kind as they seemed.
   H. were themselves quite sad.
   J. actually found Lewis to be quite charming.

9. The passage implies that most of the things Lewis Barber Fletcher did in his life were:

   A. extremely unusual and challenging.
   B. personally quite painful for him.
   C. done in a businesslike manner.
   D. material for gossip at his office.

10. When Edward tried to imagine what his father had been like as a child, the most moving image depicted his father as being:

   F. businesslike but sad.
   G. trusting yet nervous.
   H. untrusting and anxious.
   J. suspicious and angry.

Sample Passage II

PROSE FICTION: This passage is adapted from Milan Kundera's novel *The Book of Laughter and Forgetting* (©1980 by Alfred A. Knopf, Inc.). This story takes place in 1968 in what was then known as Czechoslovakia.

Soon after the Russians occupied my country in 1968, I lost the privilege of working. No one was allowed to hire me. At about that time some young friends started paying me regular visits. They were so
5 young that the Russians did not have them on their lists yet and they could remain in editorial offices, schools, and film studios. These fine young friends, whom I will never betray, suggested I use their names as a cover for writing radio and television scripts, plays, articles,
10 columns, film treatments—anything to earn a living. I accepted a few of their offers, but most I turned down. I couldn't have gotten to them all, for one thing, and then too, it was dangerous. Not for me, for them. The secret police wanted to starve us out, cut off all means
15 of support, force us to capitulate and make public confessions. They kept their eyes out for all the pitiful little escape routes we used to avoid encirclement, and they meted out severe punishments to the friends who gave me their names.

20 One of those generous donors was a girl by the name of R. Shy, delicate, and intelligent, she was an editor of an illustrated weekly for young people with a huge circulation. Since at the time the magazine was obliged to print an incredible amount of undigested
25 political claptrap glorifying our brothers the Russians, the editors were constantly looking for something to attract the attention of the crowd. Finally they decided to make an exception and violate the purity of Marxist ideology with an astrology column.

30 When R. asked me to do an astrology column for her magazine under a pseudonym, I was delighted, of course, and I instructed her to explain to the editorial board that the texts would be written by an important nuclear physicist who had requested her not to divulge
35 his name for fear his colleagues would laugh at him. That seemed to give our undertaking a double cover: a nonexistent scientist and his pseudonym.

Which is how, under an assumed name, I came to write a fine, long introductory article on astrology and
40 short, rather silly monthly texts for individual signs, accompanying the latter with my own drawings of Taurus, Aries, Virgo, Pisces. The pay was miserable, the job itself not particularly amusing or remarkable. The only amusing part of it was my existence, the exis-
45 tence of a man erased from history, literary reference books, even the telephone book, a corpse brought back to life in the amazing reincarnation of a preacher sermonizing hundreds of thousands of young socialists on the great truths of astrology.

50 One day R. announced to me that the editor-in-chief was all excited about his astrologer and wanted a personal horoscope from him. That fascinated me. The editor-in-chief owed his job at the magazine entirely to the Russians. He had spent half his life taking
55 Marxism-Leninism courses in Prague and Moscow both!

"He was a little ashamed to tell me," laughed R. "He certainly wouldn't want it to get around he believed in medieval superstitions or anything. He just
60 can't help himself."

"Fine, fine," I said. I was happy. I knew the man well. Besides being R.'s boss, he was a member of the highest Party committee dealing with hiring and firing, and he had ruined the lives of many of my friends.

65 "He wants complete anonymity. All I'm supposed to give you is his date of birth. You have no idea who he is."

"Even better." That was just what I wanted to hear.

"He says he'll give you a hundred crowns."

70 "A hundred crowns?" I laughed. "Who does he take me for, the cheapskate!"

He sent me a thousand crowns. I filled ten pages with a description of his character and future. I spent a whole week on the opus and consulted regularly with
75 R. After all, a horoscope can greatly influence, even dictate, the way people act. It can recommend they do certain things, warn them against doing others, and bring them to their knees by hinting at future disasters.

R. and I had a good laugh over it later. She
80 claimed he had improved. He yelled less. He had begun to have qualms about his hardheadedness—his horoscope warned against it. He made as much as he could out of the speck of kindness left in him, and staring out into nothingness, his eyes would show signs of sadness,
85 the sadness of a man who has come to realize that the stars hold nothing but suffering in store for him.

11. According to the first paragraph, some of the narrator's friends were especially important to him because:
   A. the use of their names enabled the narrator to make a living.
   B. they told him all he needed to know about the editor-in-chief.
   C. they kept him informed of the clandestine movements of the secret police.
   D. they took the time to discuss events of intellectual import with the narrator.

12. It can reasonably be inferred from the passage that the narrator worked very carefully on the editor-in-chief's horoscope because the narrator:

F. wanted to earn his thousand crowns fair and square.
G. hoped to affect the editor-in-chief's actions.
H. had always wanted to do the editor-in-chief a favor.
J. did not want the editor-in-chief to know he was a nuclear scientist.

13. It can reasonably be inferred from the passage that a true Marxist would view astrology as:

A. a scientific method.
B. a tool for predicting events.
C. a foolish superstition.
D. an interesting ideology.

14. When the narrator asserts that "a horoscope can greatly influence, even dictate, the way people act" (lines 75–76), he means that to some people a horoscope:

F. indicates to them how they should act.
G. forces them to change their personalities completely.
H. enables them to be more creative.
J. causes behavioral changes to subside.

15. According to the passage, prior to beginning his astrological column, the narrator knew that the editor-in-chief had:

A. ruined the lives of many of his friends.
B. been teaching classes in Marxism in Prague.
C. held a deep and abiding interest in astrology.
D. been a member of the secret police.

16. According to the passage, the narrator's monthly articles about individual astrological signs are best characterized as:

F. ludicrous but financially richly rewarding.
G. quite remarkable in terms of their literary style.
H. silly and insignificant yet very popular.
J. very popular with his audience and intellectually stimulating.

17. According to the passage, the methods employed by the secret police involved which of the following?

I. Surveillance
II. Isolation
III. Execution

A. I only
B. II only
C. I and II only
D. II and III only

18. According to the passage, including an astrology column in a Marxist magazine would be:

F. an example of political claptrap.
G. in conformity with the purity of Marxist ideology.
H. a purification of Marxist journalistic practice.
J. inconsistent with pure Marxist ideology.

19. As he is depicted in the passage, the editor-in-chief is best described as a man who became:

A. a good bit more cynical about astrological predictions.
B. more cheerful as he looked toward the future.
C. less easygoing than before but more professional overall.
D. much easier to work with but overall less happy.

20. The narrator was able to write a long and thorough horoscope for the editor-in-chief because he, the narrator, had:

F. been well informed about the editor-in-chief's past.
G. spent a month producing that opus.
H. been certain that his horoscope could dictate future actions.
J. earned 1,000—and not 100—crowns for his work.

Sample Passage III

SOCIAL SCIENCE: This passage is adapted from the article "Japan's Tansu: Cabinetry of the 18th and 19th Centuries" by Rosy Clarke (©1985 by W.R.C. Smith Publishing Company).

The Japanese, always pressed for room on their island empire, have long been masters at utilizing space. This is especially evident in the native handmade Japanese cabinetry known as *tansu,* produced from
5 about 1750 to 1900. A prolific range of wooden tansu was created for a variety of needs, and a diverse group of pieces emerged, ranging from small, portable medicine chests to giant trunks on wheels.

Prior to Japan's Edo Period (1603–1867), owner-
10 ship of furniture was limited to the nobility. Primarily, these were black-and-gold lacquered pieces of Chinese inspiration. But with the demise of Japan's feudal society and the rise of a moneyed merchant class by the mid–Edo Period, furniture in Japan took on its own
15 personality, as craftsmen enjoyed the freedom to create original designs that combined function and beauty. Today, examples of these skillfully constructed chests tell us much about the lifestyle and accoutrements of people during the Edo Period and the Meiji Era
20 (1868–1912).

The greatest demand was for clothing and merchants' chests; within these two categories, hundreds of stylistic variations occurred. Most clothing tansu were constructed with four long drawers for kimono storage
25 and a small door compartment that opened to two or three tiny drawers for personal items. The chests were usually built in two pieces that stacked, a design that allowed for easy portability. A favorite wood used to build clothing tansu was paulownia, noted for its light
30 weight and subtle, natural sheen. In the Edo Period, it was customary for Japanese fathers to plant a paulownia tree when a daughter was born. When she married, the tree was cut down and made into a trousseau chest.

35 Merchants' chests, used to store documents, writing brushes, inkstones and money, were usually constructed of thick zelkova or chestnut. Unlike clothing tansu, which were kept inside a sliding door closet in a home, a merchant's chest was in full view of
40 customers. Thus, shop tansu was an important indicator of a shopkeeper's prosperity.

Some styles were surprisingly large, an example being the staircase tansu. Japanese homes and shops were often built with lofts, and for easy access from the
45 ground floor, a freestanding staircase was designed by clever craftsmen who incorporated compartments and drawers throughout for maximum utility. Around six feet high, most staircase chests were made in two sections that stacked, though many one-piece chests were
50 also produced. Because of the great amount of wood needed to build a staircase tansu, steps, risers and case were made of softwood, and hardwood was used for doors and drawer fronts.

Many households, especially rural homes, kept
55 large kitchen tansu to store food and crockery. The wood of these practical kitchen chests was rarely finished, and those in original condition show a lovely natural patina developed from years of exposure to the smoke and heat of the cooking area. Kitchen tansu were
60 designed strictly for utility with sliding door compartments, inner shelves and numerous small drawers. Like staircase tansu, they display a minimum of ironwork and rarely show locking drawers or doors.

After 1900, modern techniques replaced the
65 original handcrafted construction methods. Sand-cast iron handles, for example, are common on furniture made from about 1890 to 1920. Traditional designs—dragons, cherry blossoms and mythical personalities—that were once etched by hand onto lock plates became
70 simplified as machine-pressed patterns appeared. Thick pieces of wood originally used became thinner around 1900, when improved wood planing techniques resulted in mass-produced tansu of diminished quality. And the amazing range of handproduced, naturally pigmented
75 lacquer finishes that hallmarked earlier tansu all but disappeared by about 1920. With rapid industrialization at hand, many of Japan's artisans abandoned their traditional crafts.

Appreciated today for their beauty, simplicity and
80 functionality, tansu are now showing up in homes in America and Europe. But relatively few exceptional examples of the thousands produced now remain. Those pieces available document a special part of Japanese history and culture as well as the remarkable sense of
85 space and design of Japan's unknown craftsmen.

21. The author states that the result of mass production techniques on the tansu was:

   A. diminished quality.
   B. thicker pieces of wood.
   C. renewed popularity.
   D. greater variety.

22. The passage states that although handmade tansu were designed and used for many purposes, most were:

   F. fancy black-and-gold finished pieces.
   G. kitchen cabinets.
   H. clothing and merchants' chests.
   J. staircase chests.

23. According to the passage, the original popularity of tansu resulted primarily from the:

    A. desire to display clothing and other personal items.
    B. need to make good use of space.
    C. need to disguise a merchant's wealth.
    D. desire to be different from the Chinese.

24. According to the passage, modern production methods caused which of the following changes in the tansu?

       I. Sand-cast iron handles
      II. Simplification of traditional designs
     III. Thinner wood

    F. II only
    G. III only
    H. I and II only
    J. I, II, and III

25. As it is used in the passage, the word *patina* (line 58) most nearly means the:

    A. design carved in the wood of the chests.
    B. original finish applied to the chest.
    C. destruction of the wood by smoke and heat.
    D. surface appearance of the wood.

26. The author claims that by studying examples of hand-crafted Japanese tansu that are still available today, scholars can learn about which of the following?

       I. How mass production first began in Japan
      II. How Japanese industrialists developed short-cuts in building furniture
     III. How the Japanese lived during the Edo Period and the Meiji Era

    F. II only
    G. III only
    H. I and II only
    J. I, II, and III

27. According to the account of tansu-making in the passage, improved wood-planing techniques resulted in:

    A. a need to change the types of wood used.
    B. the need to apply thicker wood finishes.
    C. the use of thinner wood.
    D. a renewed interest in black-and-gold lacquered finishes.

28. The passage suggests that the Japanese tansu had changed by the mid–Edo Period in which of the following ways?

    F. It reflected increased creative freedom of the craftsmen.
    G. It became a symbol of status and wealth for the nobility.
    H. It became less important to the merchant class.
    J. It became much larger.

29. According to the passage, the Chinese influence on Japanese furniture-making is reflected in which of the following characteristics of some Japanese furniture?

       I. The use of space
      II. The black and gold lacquer
     III. The use of paulownia wood

    A. II only
    B. III only
    C. I and II only
    D. I, II, and III

30. The passage indicates about tansu that they were:

       I. used for aesthetic purposes only.
      II. indicative of financial status.
     III. hidden from view because they held important documents.

    F. I only
    G. II only
    H. I and II only
    J. II and III only

Sample Passage IV

NATURAL SCIENCE: This passage is adapted from the article "Probing the Cycle of Sleeping and Waking" by Edmund L. Andrews (©1990 by The New York Times).

It looks like a typical power plant control room, complete with back issues of Nuclear Engineering magazine. Operators sit at a console, studying computer screens that display ever-changing plant indicators. The
5 lights are low, the sotto voce chatter is mostly technical and the computer hum is often the loudest sound in the room.

But there is one big difference here: This control center is designed to monitor the technicians, not the
10 other way around. Each worker wears electrodes taped to his or her scalp, the outside corner of each eye and to their chins, to catch them if they fall asleep. If workers get drowsy, nearby recording equipment will log their sluggish brainwaves and their logy eye movements.

15 When they finish their shift, the workers will walk through a door into a cozy compartment featuring a living room, an eating area, a kitchenette and bedrooms. Only two features are unusual: The video cameras over each bed and the absence of any windows
20 or outside sound. Some of these workers spend weeks without seeing daylight.

Welcome to the world of circadian research, the inquiry into the rhythms of sleep and wakefulness. Why do a disproportionate number of crashes, explosions,
25 derailments and other debacles of human error occur in the wee hours of the morning? How can workers on rotating shifts lead lives that are less miserable and more productive? Is there a cure for jet lag?

Circadian researchers argue that the answers lie in
30 the biological pacemakers that regulate the daily cycles of human activity. They believe that a person's daily rhythms are controlled in large part by a small cluster of brain cells called the superchiasmatic nucleus. Located above the nerves linking the eye with the brain,
35 these cells are believed to help synchronize cyclical changes in body temperatures, hormone rhythms and sleep-wake cycles. By understanding these natural clocks, they say, it is possible to devise better strategies for the armies of people who must contend with a
40 24-hour world.

"People who work shifts have special problems," said David Hayward, manager of an electrical generation and transmission control facility. "They have social problems and physical problems. If you have a
45 better understanding of why these things occur, you can do something about it, and you're going to have better workers."

A growing body of research documents the toll such schedules can take. A study by the Battelle
50 Memorial Institute, for example, found that more than 60 percent of accidents in nuclear plants occur during night shifts. The accidents at Three Mile Island and Chernobyl, as well as the Bhopal chemical plant explosion in India, all took place during pre-dawn hours.

55 "We've created a world which now operates around the clock, but people still have a 9-to-5 mentality," said Dr. Martin Moore-Ede, founder of the Institute for Circadian Physiology. "Seventy to eighty percent of people who work night shifts will admit to
60 falling asleep on the job. They'll fall asleep in airline cockpits. They'll fall asleep in nuclear power plant control rooms. They'll fall asleep in oil refineries, in hospitals and on board ships."

Circadian researchers argue that particular strat-
65 egies can make it easier to reset the internal clocks. It turns out, for example, that adjusting to clockwise schedule rotations—from day shift to evening to night—is twice as fast as adjusting counterclockwise. Because the light signals of night and day are basic
70 cues for the system, said Dr. Moore-Ede, travelers can use controlled exposure to light to adjust to new time zones within a few hours.

"Circadian rhythms also suggest that truck drivers might be better off with longer hours at different
75 times," said Dr. Moore-Ede. Statistics indicate that accidents are correlated far more closely with the time of day than with the number of hours driven. But current law fosters the practice of driving at bad times, because truckers must stop for eight hours of rest after
80 every ten hours of road time. "If, instead, truckers always started out at 7 A.M., and drove 14 hours," said Dr. Moore-Ede, "they could work the same schedule every day and would never have to drive during the deadly pre-dawn period." Yet they would cover the
85 same number of total miles.

"Napping strategies" offer even additional possibilities. One emerging buzz phrase is "anchor sleep," designed to help workers who must constantly readjust to new schedules. The idea is to sleep one four-hour
90 segment at the same time every day, and to catch the remaining rest in shorter increments when they are convenient. "Anchor hours," according to the institute, can keep a person on an even keel.

31. The passage suggests that which of the following incidents is(are) likely to be of considerable interest to circadian researchers?

    I. A nuclear power plant accident that occurs at 4 A.M. because of worker fatigue.
    II. The closing of an automobile assembly line because of declining product demand.
    III. A chemical plant explosion happening at 2 A.M. because of mistakes made by technicians on duty.

  A. III only
  B. I and II only
  C. I and III only
  D. I, II, and III

32. According to the passage, researchers believe that a person's daily rhythms are mainly controlled by:

  F. circadian research.
  G. the superchiasmatic nucleus.
  H. sluggish brainwaves.
  J. hormone rhythms.

33. According to the passage, napping strategies were developed to:

  A. assist workers who must often adjust to new schedules.
  B. help those who work night shifts at power plants.
  C. make four hours of sleep per day suffice for most workers.
  D. allow workers to avoid clockwise shift rotations.

34. According to the information provided in the passage, circadian research is most accurately defined as being:

  F. the study of the frequency of night-shift accidents.
  G. the regulation of a person's daily rhythms.
  H. inquiry into the rhythms of sleep and wakefulness.
  J. the study of how rotating shifts make workers more productive.

35. It seems reasonable to infer from the passage that the idea behind "anchor sleep" (line 87) is that:

  A. a person needs at least four hours of uninterrupted sleep daily.
  B. four hours of sleep per day is all a person really needs.
  C. when you sleep for more than four hours, you can avoid napping strategies.
  D. it will suit perfectly those who work fixed schedules.

36. It can be reasonably inferred from the passage that which of the following is(are) approximately synonymous with the term *biological pacemakers* (line 30)?

    I. Natural clocks
    II. Rotating shifts
    III. Cyclical changes
    IV. Anchor sleep

  F. I only
  G. II only
  H. I, II, and IV only
  J. I, II, III, and IV

37. The passage suggests that solutions for reducing the accidents that occur in nuclear power plants may derive from:

  A. studying manufacturing plants during day shifts.
  B. various federal regulations.
  C. revising our notions of anchor sleep.
  D. circadian research studies of plant workers.

38. One of the main observations made in the next-to-last paragraph (lines 73–85) is that:

  F. current law can be seen as encouraging truck drivers to drive at unsafe times.
  G. truck drivers should work different hours every day.
  H. truck drivers find it difficult to cover their required daily mileage.
  J. the accidents truck drivers have occur when they've driven more than 14 hours.

39. It can reasonably be inferred from the passage that, if circadian researchers can reach a deep understanding of the body's natural clocks, then night-shift workers will:

  A. be able to obtain anchor sleep much more easily.
  B. have exactly the same problems as day-shift workers.
  C. have to learn to live without accidents.
  D. be employed much more productively than previously.

40. The fourth paragraph (lines 22–28) poses several questions that, it can reasonably be inferred from the passage, might best be answered by:

  F. making sure that workers do not get drowsy.
  G. referring to circadian researchers' work.
  H. stabilizing each person's daily rhythms.
  J. reducing worker misery and increasing worker productivity.

Sample Passage V

NATURAL SCIENCE: This passage is adapted from Jonathan Evan Maslow's *The Owl Papers* (©1983 by Jonathan Maslow). In this selection, the term *ornithologists* refers to scientists who specialize in the study of birds.

The owl's astounding auditory powers are probably second to none among living things. If you spent a cold, dark, sleeting January afternoon standing in front of the Great Horned Owl cage at the Bronx Zoo, as I
5 did recently, you couldn't fail to notice that listening, for the owl, is hardly a passive activity. Take this grand old Great Horned perched on the barkless diorama stump the zoo has provided it, staring right through me as if I didn't exist. The bird's head rarely remains still
10 for more than a few seconds. It dips, bobs, swivels, cranes forward, stretches up, twists down, retreats into the neck, rather like a radar scanner constantly repositioning. I hear nothing but the falling sleet. The owl is picking up sounds humans can't hear—too faint, or out
15 of our frequency range. In fact, aside from the eyes, beak, and mouth, a sound scanner is exactly what the owl's face is—a large saucer designed to transmit and amplify sound waves to the ears and brain. The rounded facial disks, which give the grand old Great Horned its
20 appealing, semihuman appearance, are actually composed of short, stiff layers of feathers. These feathers, controlled by the facial muscles, are oriented to oncoming sound waves. The facial disks are bordered by a narrow trough, where the sound waves are caught,
25 concentrated, and funneled to the ears, hidden behind the disks (the owl's horns are actually false ears, having nothing to do with hearing). Like human ears, the owl's ear has a pre-aural flap, the operculum. But in an improvement over man, the bird can move the flap
30 forward or backward like a cowl, orienting the ear to the sound source. Again, the actual and relative size of the ears is enormous. In a species like the Barn Owl, the outer ear reaches from the top of the cranium all the way down to the lower jaw. The eardrums within
35 are equally great.

For more than a century, anatomists have noted that owl ears are neither symmetrically placed on the skull nor of the same size. The left ear is generally larger, lower, and opens downward, while the right ear
40 is smaller, higher on the skull, and opens upward. They are also set relatively far apart, since the facial disks are so large. These asymmetries cause sound waves to arrive a fraction of a second later at one ear than the other. The sound will thus be slightly louder in the ear
45 nearer the sound source, and the two ears will receive slightly different tonal messages. Using this information for comparison, the owl triangulates to form a precise impression of the sound's point of origin.

There is still another specialization to owl's
50 hearing, a rare one in nature: owls hear higher-frequency sounds better than the lower-pitched sounds made by their own voices. Almost all other animals hear their own tonal range best. One need not be too clever to guess which animals most consistently pro-
55 duce the high-pitched sounds owl ears are especially

sensitive to: mice, rats, shrews, voles, rabbits, and the whole host of squeakers the owl hunts. It seems likely that the owl developed this ability to hear rodents best solely to do in more squeakers. But what if the cunning
60 mouse makes nary a peep? Observant naturalists have noted that dry spells in the weather are accompanied by a marked increase in the owl's nightly catch, as read in their pellets, while precipitation decreases hunting success. In very rainy weather, many owls apparently
65 won't even attempt to hunt. When modern ornithologists took these observations into the lab, they analyzed sounds made by rodents scurrying through dry leaves. They found that important components of these rustling and crackling sounds are high-pitched in the very same
70 frequency range owls hear most efficiently. Then they analyzed the sound of mice chewing. And chewing, too, it turned out, produces high-frequency sounds. Which helps explain why people have reported seeing owls suddenly plunge into perfectly undisturbed, deep snow-
75 drifts and come back up with mice in their talons.

41. According to the passage, the size and arrangement of its ears on its head enables an owl to:

   A. compare tonalities with other animals.
   B. balance its rather sizable facial disks.
   C. funnel sound into its ears more easily.
   D. fix the exact location of a sound.

42. As it is used in line 62, the word *marked* most nearly means:

   F. noticeable.
   G. slight.
   H. scientific.
   J. written down.

43. According to the passage, anatomists studying the size and position of the ears of owls have realized that an owl's ears are:

   A. precisely symmetrical but not the same size on either side.
   B. asymmetrical on the owl's head but identically sized.
   C. larger on the right than the left and asymmetrically placed on the owl's head.
   D. asymmetrically placed on the owl's head and of differing sizes.

44. According to the passage, all of the following contribute to the owl's extraordinary sound scanning EXCEPT its:

   F. facial muscles.
   G. operculum.
   H. beak.
   J. feathers.

45. According to the passage, the Great Horned Owl's horns are:

   A. immensely beautiful and delicate.
   B. a secondary pair of ears that catch lower-frequency sounds.
   C. hidden behind rather substantial facial disks.
   D. not ears, even though they look like ears.

46. According to the passage, an owl that dives into a snowbank and emerges holding a mouse was able to capture its prey most probably because the:

   F. owl heard the mouse in the snowbank, figured out its location, and attacked.
   G. owl was actually able to see into the snowbank and spot the mouse.
   H. mouse made a noise in a tonal range identical to the owl's tonal range.
   J. owl read the mouse's pellets and realized exactly where it would be.

47. The passage suggests that one quite unusual feature of owl hearing is that the owl:

   A. enjoys the low-pitched sound of its own voice.
   B. can usually guess at a sound's point of origin.
   C. hears its own tonal range best.
   D. does not hear its own tonal range best.

48. The author of the passage feels that the feature which contributes to the Great Horned Owl's somewhat human appearance is its:

   F. operculum.
   G. pre-aural flap.
   H. facial disks.
   J. asymmetrical ears.

49. The author of the passage compares the ears of owls and humans, and states that one way in which an owl's ears are superior is that the owl:

   A. has a pre-aural flap, which triangulates.
   B. uses them for low-frequency hearing.
   C. can direct its operculum at the sound source.
   D. has a larger left ear than right ear.

50. One inference that can be made from the passage is that owls can hear higher frequency sounds better than lower frequency sounds because:

   F. owls triangulate to learn the exact origin of a sound in their habitat.
   G. an owl's prey makes high-pitched noises.
   H. high-frequency sounds are more audible for most animals.
   J. most animals hear their own tonal range best.

Sample Passage VI

HUMANITIES: This passage is adapted from *A Guide to Orchestral Music* by Ethan Mordden (©1980 by Ethan Mordden). In this selection, Beethoven refers to Ludwig van Beethoven, a German composer during the early nineteenth century. Haydn and Mozart were both Austrian composers during the late eighteenth century.

"I don't want to know anything about your whole system of ethics," he once wrote. "*Power* is the morality of men who stand out from the rest, and it is also mine."

5 Power was Beethoven's ethic, power of such presumption that the musical forms of his day were not large enough to contain that ethic. Beethoven made them titanic. Power: this was the morality of his symphonic outlook, power to extend the limits of the sym-
10 phony, to free it for more imposing articulations of human will than his predecessors Haydn and Mozart could conceive of. Inheriting a model from them, one of precision, balance, and tensile beauty, Beethoven evolved it over the course of a quarter-cen-
15 tury into a grander form, no less precise but capable of greater drama, building a music of ideas as well as of melodies. With his Third Symphony, he fulfilled the symphony's potential for tragic poetry. With his Fifth, he devised a unity of heroic transformation through the
20 use of one basic theme that grows more triumphant from movement to movement. With his Ninth, he idealized ecumenical communion, an elitist's populism, using text and singers to celebrate the fraternity of mankind.

25 Classicism was, on one level, a preference for equilibrium. Romanticism was a rage for power. Beethoven spanned the two eras, and by the time of his death he had so fully remotivated the symphony as a musicoemotional form that one may safely call his the
30 single most significant achievement in the development of the Romantic Symphony, with its dramatic and heroic focus. No less famous for his expansion of the piano sonata and the string quartet, Beethoven remains the quintessential composer for many listeners.

35 Biographers have emphasized Beethoven the wretched man—uncouth, bad-tempered, sometimes malign in his business and personal relationships, and [physically ill] (this to explain his loss of hearing, aggravated from a worrisome nuisance in his twenties
40 to total deafness in his fifties). The catalogue of Beethoven's squabbles with publishers, musicians, patrons, family, and friends is inexhaustible, it seems. But all this is of little assistance in placing Beethoven the creator: a man's achievements far outweigh a man.

45 Moreover, we can only admire the man who dramatizes himself in such noble music as this. His work was a statement on man, on life: on power. Thus, his Third Symphony, the "Eroïca," marked a major break with the "moderation" of Classicism. Similarly,
50 Beethoven's sole opera, *Fidelio,* revitalized the genre known as "rescue opera" with a saga of tyranny over-thrown by faith and endurance, capped by a scene of the liberation of political prisoners that has never been equalled for humanistic exhilaration. Power made him
55 reinvent the very usage of music, its form and content.

It was Vincent D'Indy, a composer of a later era, who divided Beethoven's oeuvre into three periods: Imitation, Externalization, and Reflection. This is astutely observed. Beethoven's Imitation is the appren-
60 ticeship of a traveler learning the routes. His Externalization (the period covering Symphonies 3 through 8, the last two piano concertos, and the violin concerto) is that of the pioneer who strikes out on his own. The Reflection is that of the discoverer laureate,
65 retraversing his old trails to seek their profoundest mysteries. This third period, that of the last five piano sonatas, the last five string quartets, the Missa Solemnis (Solemn Mass), and the Ninth Symphony, is one of sublimation, of perfecting the innovations.
70 Rather than break further with tradition, Beethoven draws closer to it, fulfilling his personal language to the utmost while working toward an abstraction of the forms that he had overthrown—the Ninth as the ultimate symphony, the Missa Solemnis as the ultimate
75 Mass, the "Hammerklavier" as the ultimate piano sonata.

Musicians argue over whether Beethoven might be thought of as a Classicist or a Romantic; but what is important is that he supervised, in music, the transition
80 from one to the other. The key, of course, is in the word "power." Beethoven's was a time of great upheaval, a revolutionary time in many ways. A new urgency inflamed life, thought, and art—a need to force wide the structures set up in the past. Romantics were the
85 agents provocateurs as poets and politicians; Romantic art had to develop more complex forms than were known to—or needed by—Classicism. "In the beginning," says Goethe's Faust, "was the Deed." This is what Beethoven means by power.

51. The main idea of the passage is that:

A. the distinction between the Classical period of music and the Romantic period of music is artificial.

B. the music of the Classical period is far superior to the music of the Romantic period.

C. Beethoven was such a masterful musician that he virtually transformed the musical forms of his day.

D. Beethoven was a power-hungry individual who sublimated his music to his quest for political power.

52. According to the passage, composer Vincent D'Indy classified Beethoven's career into three periods. The first period is known as the:

   F. Externalization period.
   G. Romantic period.
   H. Imitation period.
   J. Classical period.

53. The attitude of the author of the passage toward Beethoven is apparently one of:

   A. admiration.
   B. disdain.
   C. ambivalence.
   D. envy.

54. As it is used in line 8 of the passage, the word *titanic* most nearly means:

   F. colossal.
   G. doomed.
   H. understandable.
   J. grotesque.

55. The passage suggests that one of the main themes of Beethoven's *Fidelio* is that:

   A. all prisoners are, in essence, political prisoners.
   B. faith and human endurance can defeat tyranny.
   C. the liberation of prisoners is a politically wise move.
   D. humanistic exhilaration can be a dangerous force.

56. In the third paragraph of the passage, the statement that "Beethoven remains the quintessential composer for many listeners" (lines 33–34) means that many people consider Beethoven to be:

   F. the standard against which all other composers are measured.
   G. a tyrannical composer who forced his views on his listeners.
   H. the model of a supremely successful and modest composer.
   J. a composer who showed extraordinary promise, but who did not live up to that promise.

57. According to the passage, what distinguishes Beethoven's Fifth Symphony?

   A. It used text and singers to celebrate the unity of mankind.
   B. It created unity by taking one basic theme and using it in each movement.
   C. It created an idealized ecumenical communion.
   D. It combined opera and symphonic music to create a totally new musical form.

58. According to the passage, which of the following of Beethoven's works belong(s) to the Externalization period?

     I. The Missa Solemnis
     II. The Fifth Symphony
     III. The Ninth Symphony

   F. I only
   G. II only
   H. I and II only
   J. II and III only

59. According to the passage, Beethoven composed how many operas?

   A. None
   B. One
   C. Between five and ten
   D. More than ten

60. According to the passage, Beethoven's biographers would probably agree with which of the following statements?

     I. Beethoven was more concerned with pleasing his musical patrons than he was with his own artistic integrity.
     II. Beethoven had frequent disagreements with his family and friends.
     III. Beethoven was exemplary in all aspects of his business relationships.

   F. I only
   G. II only
   H. I and II only
   J. I and III only

Answer Key for Reading Test Sample Items

1.	C	21.	A	41.	D
2.	J	22.	H	42.	F
3.	A	23.	B	43.	D
4.	F	24.	J	44.	H
5.	D	25.	D	45.	D
6.	J	26.	G	46.	F
7.	C	27.	C	47.	D
8.	G	28.	F	48.	H
9.	C	29.	A	49.	C
10.	H	30.	G	50.	G
11.	A	31.	C	51.	C
12.	G	32.	G	52.	H
13.	C	33.	A	53.	A
14.	F	34.	H	54.	F
15.	A	35.	A	55.	B
16.	H	36.	F	56.	F
17.	C	37.	D	57.	B
18.	J	38.	F	58.	G
19.	D	39.	D	59.	B
20.	F	40.	G	60.	G

ACT Assessment Science Reasoning Test

The ACT Assessment Science Reasoning Test asks you to answer 40 multiple-choice questions in 35 minutes. The questions measure the interpretation, analysis, evaluation, reasoning, and problem-solving skills associated with science. The test is made up of seven test units, each of which consists of a passage containing scientific information followed by a number of multiple-choice questions.

Content of the ACT Assessment Science Reasoning Test

The categories of the Science Reasoning Test parallel the content of courses commonly taught in grades 7 through 12 and in the entry level at colleges and universities. Each test unit consists of one of the following categories (the topics included in each category are given in parentheses):

- **Biology** (cell biology, botany, zoology, microbiology, ecology, genetics, and evolution)
- **Earth/Space Sciences** (geology, meteorology, oceanography, astronomy, and environmental sciences)
- **Chemistry** (atomic theory, inorganic chemical reactions, chemical bonding, reaction rates, solutions, equilibriums, gas laws, electrochemistry, organic chemistry, biochemistry, and properties and states of matter)
- **Physics** (mechanics, energy, thermodynamics, electromagnetism, fluids, solids, and light waves)

You do not need advanced knowledge in these subjects, but you may need some background knowledge—scientific facts or terms—to answer some of the questions. Most high school students who have completed two years of science coursework will have all the background knowledge they need to successfully understand the passages on the Science Reasoning Test.

You do not need advanced mathematical skills for the Science Reasoning Test, but you may need to make minimal arithmetic computations in order to answer some questions. The use of calculators is **not** permitted on the Science Reasoning Test. The passages of the Science Reasoning Test are concise and clear; you should have no trouble understanding them. The test emphasizes scientific reasoning skills rather than recall of scientific content, skill in mathematics, or reading ability.

Basic arithmetic will be necessary to answer some questions.

Format of the ACT Assessment Science Reasoning Test

The scientific information presented in each passage of the ACT Science Reasoning Test is conveyed in one of three different formats. The **Data Representation** format requires you to understand, evaluate, and interpret information presented in graphic or tabular form. The **Research Summaries** format asks you to comprehend, evaluate, analyze, and interpret the design of an experiment. The **Conflicting Viewpoints** format requires you to evaluate two or three alternative theories, hypotheses, or viewpoints on a specific observable phenomenon. The approximate proportion of the ACT Science Reasoning Test devoted to each of the three formats is given in the chart on page 43 at the beginning of this chapter.

You'll find examples of the kinds of passages that you're likely to find in each of the formats in the pages that follow.

The example Science Reasoning Test passages and questions in this section are representative of those you'll encounter in the ACT Science Reasoning Test. The following chart illustrates the content area, format, and topic covered by each sample passage given in the remainder of this section.

Passage	Content Area	Format	Topic of Passage
I	Earth/Space Sciences	Data Representation	Galaxies
II	Chemistry	Data Representation	Solubility
III	Physics	Research Summaries	Electrical Circuits
IV	Biology	Conflicting Viewpoints	Species Richness

Data Representation format

This type of format presents scientific information in charts, tables, graphs, and diagrams similar to those found in science journals and texts. In the sample passages in this section (Sample Passage I on page 147 and Sample Passage II on page 150) are examples of tables and graphs used in actual Data Representation passages administered to students.

The questions you'll find in the Data Representation format ask you to interpret charts and tables, read graphs, interpret scatter plots, and analyze information presented in diagrams. There are five example Data Representation questions presented with each sample Data Representation passage.

Sample Passage I

Edwin Hubble first studied the relationship between the distances to galaxies and the speed at which they are moving away from us. Table 1 lists the velocities, distances from Earth, and apparent diameters of nine of the millions of galaxies in the universe. (Note: The apparent diameter of a galaxy is the angular width as seen from Earth. Angular width is often measured in arcseconds.) Figure 1 shows a plot of velocity versus distance for those galaxies.

Table 1			
Galaxy	Velocity (km/sec)	Distance from Earth (Mpc)*	Apparent diameter (arcseconds)†
1	800	1.0	560
2	1,100	2.0	155
3	2,200	2.8	124
4	2,800	6.9	107
5	3,200	7.2	88
6	4,700	9.8	60
7	5,200	11.7	41
8	11,000	21.7	35
9	19,300	33.6	16

* 1 megaparsec (Mpc) = 3.26 million light-years
1 light-year = 9.5×10^{12} km
† 1 arcsecond = 1/3,600 of a degree

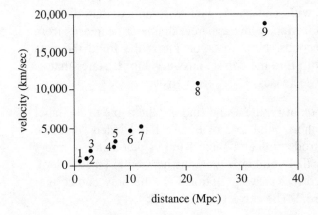

Figure 1

1. If the galaxies are taken in order from 1 through 9, what is the relationship between distance from Earth and apparent diameter?

   A. Distance and diameter both decrease.
   B. Distance and diameter both increase.
   C. As distance increases, diameter decreases.
   D. As distance decreases, diameter stays the same.

2. The horizontal axis of Figure 1 represents which of the following variables?

   F. Velocity
   G. Distance from Earth
   H. Galaxy number
   J. Apparent diameter

3. According to the data provided, the velocity of a galaxy is measured to be 12,000 km/sec. What is the approximate distance to this galaxy?

   A. 5 Mpc
   B. 11 Mpc
   C. 20 Mpc
   D. 23 Mpc

4. Based on the data provided, what is the apparent relationship between the velocity and distance from Earth of these galaxies?

   F. Velocity decreases with distance.
   G. Velocity decreases with the square of the distance.
   H. Velocity increases as distance increases.
   J. Velocity increases as distance decreases.

5. A *quasar* is a starlike object found at great distances from Earth. If a hypothetical quasar 39 Mpc from Earth follows the same relationship as the galaxies in Figure 1, what, if anything, could one hypothesize about its velocity?

   A. It would be traveling slower than the galaxies in Figure 1.
   B. It would be traveling faster than the galaxies in Figure 1.
   C. It would be traveling at the same average speed as the galaxies in Figure 1.
   D. One cannot hypothesize about its velocity without more information.

Sample Passage I

This Data Representation passage is an Earth/Space Sciences unit on galaxies. It contains a paragraph of approximately 100 words and two depictions of data: Table 1 and Figure 1. The data were collected by the astronomer Edwin Hubble, who first studied the relationship between the distance to galaxies and the speed at which they are moving away from Earth.

Examine Table 1 and notice that the four columns represent nine specific galaxies, the velocity in km/sec of the galaxies, the distance of the galaxies from Earth in Mpc, and the apparent diameter of the galaxies in arcseconds. Some units of measurement that may be new to you are marked in the table with a (*) or a (†). (At the bottom of the table you'll find the [*] and the [†] with the explanations of the units in their equivalent units of measurement.) For a given galaxy, you should be able to read across the rows of the table and find specific values for velocity, distance from Earth, and apparent diameter. You should also be able to determine general trends and relationships and make interpolations about the galaxies.

Examine Figure 1 and notice that it is a plot of velocity versus distance for the nine galaxies listed in Table 1. You should be able to see the labels on both the horizontal axis (x-axis) and the vertical axis (y-axis). This graph is no different than a graph you would draw in a math class. Notice that the galaxies are listed as numbered dots on the graph. As you examine Figure 1, you should be able to determine approximately the velocity in km/sec and the distance in Mpc for any given galaxy. You should also be able to determine general trends, figure out relationships between galaxies, and make extrapolations.

Question 1 asks you to determine the relationship between the distance from Earth and the apparent diameter of the galaxies. You must look at Table 1 to determine the answer. Notice that Table 1 shows the distance and the apparent diameter relationships for Galaxies 1–9. If you look at the galaxies in order, starting with Galaxy 1, you will notice that distance increases from 1 Mpc to 33.6 Mpc, while apparent diameter decreases from 560 arcseconds to 16 arcseconds. Now that you know the trend the data follow, look at options **A–D** to find the correct answer. Only **C** states that as distance increases, diameter decreases. The correct answer is **C.**

Question 2 asks you to look at Figure 1 and find out the name of the label for the horizontal axis. The horizontal axis of Figure 1 is labeled "distance (Mpc)." Both Passage I's introduction and Table 1 tell us that *distance* refers to distance from Earth. Now that you know what the horizontal label is, look at options **F–J** to find the correct answer. Option **G** is the only choice that mentions "distance from Earth." The correct answer is **G.**

Question 3 asks you to determine the distance to a galaxy whose velocity is 12,000 km/sec. You must look at Table 1 to determine the answer. First look at the column labeled "Velocity (km/sec)" and find 12,000 km/sec. You will be able to find 11,000 km/sec and 19,300 km/sec, but not 12,000 km/sec. Don't worry! The value 12,000 km/sec is greater than 11,000 km/sec, but less than 19,300 km/sec. Knowing this, you can now go to the column labeled "Distance from Earth (Mpc)" and determine that at 11,000 km/sec the distance from Earth is 21.7 Mpc, and that at 19,300 km/sec the distance from Earth is 33.6 Mpc. So the approximate distance from Earth for this galaxy is between 21.7 Mpc and 33.6 Mpc. Look at the answer choices and find the number between 21.7 Mpc and 33.6 Mpc. The only number between these two values is 23 Mpc, so the correct answer is **D.**

Question 4 asks you to determine the relationship between the velocity and the distance from Earth of Galaxies 1–9. You must look at Table 1 to find the answer. First, determine what happens to the velocity as you proceed, in order, from Galaxy 1 to Galaxy 9 in Table 1. The velocity increases from Galaxy 1 to Galaxy 9. Then determine what happens to the distance from Earth as you proceed, in order, from Galaxy 1 to Galaxy 9 in Table 1. The distance from Earth increases from Galaxy 1 to Galaxy 9. Now you know that velocity increases as distance increases. Look at the answer choices and select the answer that states that "velocity increases as distance increases." The correct answer is **H.**

Question 5 deals with quasars. Notice that the word *quasar* is italicized and defined for you. It is not essential that you be familiar with quasars; what's important here is that the quasar mentioned in the question follows the same relationship as the galaxies in Figure 1. The question tells you that the quasar is 39 Mpc from Earth. Figure 1 shows us that the farther away from Earth a galaxy is, the greater its velocity. Galaxy 9, the farthest galaxy shown, is 33.6 Mpc from Earth and is traveling at 19,300 km/sec. If the quasar is even farther from Earth than Galaxy 9, it must be traveling even faster than 19,300 km/sec. A speed above 19,300 km/sec would mean that the quasar would be traveling faster than any of the galaxies shown in Figure 1. Look at the options and select the answer that states that the galaxy "would be traveling faster than the galaxies in Figure 1." The only option that states this is option **B,** so the correct answer is **B.**

Sample Passage II

Solubility is a measure of the quantity of a substance that will dissolve in a quantity of water (H_2O) or other liquid. The substance that dissolves is called the *solute* and the liquid that is doing the dissolving is called the *solvent*. If a substance does not dissolve in a particular solvent, it is considered *insoluble*.

Solubilities can be displayed on a graph called a solubility curve. The figure shows the solubility of a variety of solutes in water over a range of temperatures.

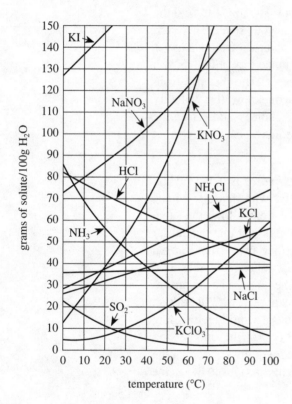

temperature (°C)

Figure adapted from Henry Dorin, *Chemistry: The Study of Matter*, 3rd ed. ©1987 by Prentice Hall, Inc.

6. A solution is *saturated* at a particular temperature if it contains as much solute as it can dissolve. A beaker containing 100 g of H_2O at 36°C would contain a saturated solution if it contained which of the following amounts of $NaNO_3$ dissolved in water?

   F. 74 g
   G. 87 g
   H. 100 g
   J. 124 g

7. According to the figure, which of the following solutes exhibits the largest change in solubility for any 10°C change in temperature?

   A. KI
   B. $NaNO_3$
   C. HCl
   D. KNO_3

8. Which of the following statements about the relationship, if any, between the solubility of the given solutes and temperature is consistent with the data in the figure?

   F. The solubility of a majority of solutes increases when temperature decreases.
   G. The solubility of a majority of solutes increases when temperature increases.
   H. The solubility of a majority of solutes decreases when the temperature is held constant.
   J. There is no relationship between the solubility of a solute and the temperature.

9. Based on the information in the figure, which of the following solutes has the highest solubility at temperatures below 40°C ?

   A. SO_2
   B. HCl
   C. KNO_3
   D. KI

10. If 10 g each of KNO_3, KCl, NaCl, and $KClO_3$ were stirred into 4 separate beakers, each containing 100 g of H_2O at 10°C, which of these solutes would NOT be expected to completely dissolve under these conditions?

   F. KNO_3
   G. KCl
   H. NaCl
   J. $KClO_3$

Sample Passage II

This passage is another example of the Data Representation format. It is a chemistry passage that discusses solubility. Notice that the word *solubility* is italicized and defined for you. Other important words that you need to understand to answer the questions in this passage are also italicized and defined—*solute*, *solvent*, and *insoluble*. You need to make sure you understand the definitions of these terms before proceeding to analyze the graph of the solubility curve. Notice that the graph shows the solubility of a variety of solutes. The solutes are represented as chemical formulas. It is not important that you know exactly what KI is or what $KClO_3$ is in order to answer the questions; however, it is very important that you be able to read the graph. Notice that the horizontal axis (*x*-axis) depicts temperature from $0°C$ to $100°C$. The vertical axis (*y*-axis) shows the number of grams of solute, from 0 g to 150 g, that can dissolve in 100 g of H_2O.

Question 6 defines a saturated solution as a solution that contains as much solute as it can dissolve at a particular temperature. The question then asks you to determine what amount of $NaNO_3$ would be needed to form a saturated solution in a beaker containing 100 g of H_2O at $36°C$. To answer this question you must find $36°C$ on the *x*-axis of the graph and move upward along the graph until you reach the curved line labeled $NaNO_3$. From the point that $36°C$ intersects the curve for $NaNO_3$, move across to the left to read the number of grams off the vertical axis (*y*-axis). The answer is 100 g, so the correct answer is **H.**

Question 7 asks you to analyze the graph and determine which solute shows the largest change in solubility for any $10°C$ change in temperature. To solve this question you must look at the curved lines on the graph and find the steepest one. Remember from mathematics that the slope is defined as the change in *y* over the change in *x*—so the greater the change in the grams of solute that can be dissolved in 100 g of H_2O per $10°C$, the steeper the line. Look at the curves for each of the solutes given as options and determine which one is steepest. The solute with the steepest slope is KNO_3, so the correct answer is **D.**

Question 8 refers to the graph and asks about relationships between solubility and temperature. Look at the graph and notice that it shows that for three solutes, solubility decreases as the temperature increases. For the remaining seven solutes, the graph shows that solubility increases as the temperature increases. The seven solutes whose solubility increases as temperature increases constitute a majority (more than half) of the solutes. You should look for the option that states that "the solubility of a majority of solutes increases when temperature increases." Option **G** is the only one that states this relationship.

Question 9 asks which of the given solutes (SO_2, HCl, KNO_3, and KI) has the highest solubility at temperatures below 40°C. You must examine the graph from a temperature range of 0°C to 40°C and determine which solute is soluble between those temperatures. KI shows a solubility of approximately 127 g per 100 g of H_2O and it shows an increasing trend as the temperature increases to 40°C. None of the other solutes (SO_2, HCl or KNO_3) have a solubility as high as KI in the temperature range of 0°C to 40°C. The correct answer is **D.**

Question 10 asks you to predict which of the four solutes will not dissolve under the same conditions. It is important to recognize that one of the conditions, 100 g of H_2O, is the same condition used to rate solubilities in the figure. Because the passage defines solubility as the quantity of a substance that will dissolve in a quantity of water, you know that the lines in the figure represent the maximum amount of each solute that will dissolve in 100 g of H_2O at a given temperature. Once you know the maximum amount of a solute that will dissolve in 100 g of H_2O at a given temperature, you know that any amount of that solute below that maximum will dissolve in 100 g of H_2O at that given temperature. The question specifies 10 g of each solute at 10°C. Locate this point on the graph. For 10 g of a particular solute not to be completely soluble at 10°C, part of that solute's curve would have to lie below the point you just located. The line for $KClO_3$ is the only line that is below 10 g at 10°C. Look at the answer choices to find $KClO_3$. The correct answer is **J.**

Research Summaries format

This type of format provides descriptions of one or more related experiments or studies similar to those conducted by scientists. The research descriptions include the purpose for the experiment, experimental designs, results, and conclusions. The results may be depicted with graphs or tables. Sample Passage III provides an example of the Research Summaries format that shows the results of three different experiments using electrical circuits.

The questions you'll find in the Research Summaries format ask you to comprehend, evaluate, analyze, and interpret the design of the experiments and to analyze the experimental results. There are five example Research Summaries questions in Sample Passage III.

For example, you may be asked to consider a series of experiments testing Archimedes' principle regarding a body immersed in a liquid.

Sample Passage III

Electrical components in a circuit are characterized by 3 basic quantities: current (I) in amps, resistance (R) in ohms, and voltage (V) in volts. *Current* is the rate at which charge flows. *Resistance* is analogous to friction; that is, it is the resistance to the flow of current through a circuit. *Voltage* is the energy per unit charge lost or gained as charges pass through a circuit component. When a charge encounters resistance, electrical energy is converted to heat.

To discover various relationships between current, resistance, voltage, and heat loss in a circuit, students performed experiments using the simple circuit below.

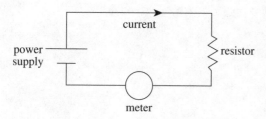

Experiment 1

A resistor with constant resistance of 50 ohms was inserted into the circuit. The voltage of the power supply was varied, and the resulting current flowing through the circuit was measured (see Table 1).

Table 1	
Voltage (volts)	Current (amps)
10	0.2
20	0.4
30	0.6
40	0.8
50	1.0

Experiment 2

The 50-ohm resistor was waterproofed and submerged in a thermally insulated beaker of water. The voltage of the power supply was varied to produce constant currents through the resistor. In each trial, a different current was allowed to flow through the resistor for 15 minutes, then the temperature rise of the water was measured and recorded in Table 2. The initial temperature of the water was 25°C in all trials.

Table 2	
Current (amps)	Temperature increase (°C)
0.0	0.0
0.2	0.9
0.4	3.4
0.6	7.7
0.8	13.8
1.0	21.5

Experiment 3

In this experiment, several different resistors were individually submerged in the water for 15 minutes, as in Experiment 2. This time, the current was held constant at 1.0 amp. The temperature increase of the water was measured and recorded in Table 3. Again, the initial temperature of the water in all trials was 25°C.

Table 3	
Resistance (ohms)	Temperature increase (°C)
10	4.3
20	8.6
30	12.9
40	17.2
50	21.5

11. The trial in Experiment 3 that best supports the results of Experiment 2 was when the resistance was:

   A. 20 ohms.
   B. 30 ohms.
   C. 40 ohms.
   D. 50 ohms.

12. Which of the following graphs of resistance versus temperature increase best shows the results of Experiment 3 ?

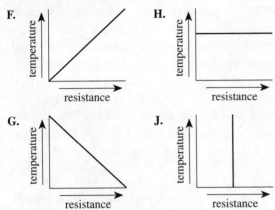

F.

temperature / resistance

H.

temperature / resistance

G.

temperature / resistance

J.

temperature / resistance

13. If a current of 1.2 amps had flowed through the resistor in Experiment 2, which of the following temperature increases would have probably resulted?

   A.   1.2°C
   B.   22.5°C
   C.   31.0°C
   D.   53.4°C

14. The same resistor was used, and the time duration was held constant in all trials in Experiment 2 so that the:

   F.   current would be kept below a dangerous level.
   G.   relationship between resistance and time could be evaluated.
   H.   relationship between current and temperature increase could be evaluated.
   J.   results could be compared with those of Experiment 1.

15. Which of the following hypotheses was tested in Experiment 1 ?

   A.   Current is directly related to resistance.
   B.   Current is directly related to voltage.
   C.   Temperature increase is directly related to current.
   D.   Temperature increase is directly related to resistance.

Sample Passage III

This Research Summaries passage is a physics unit on the topic of electrical circuits. It contains an introductory paragraph about electrical circuits followed by descriptions of three experiments. The terms you need to understand concerning electrical circuits are in italics and defined—*current*, *resistance*, and *voltage*. It is important that you become familiar with these terms so that you can understand the experiments. Notice that each term is designated with a letter and by specific units of measurement. Do not spend a lot of time on this information—it will be presented in each of the experiments. You should, however, examine the diagram of a simple electrical circuit in order to understand the experimental setup for the experiments that follow.

There are three experiments in this passage. Each experiment has a control, a variable or variables, and a specific value that is measured by the students. You should examine these experiments to determine exactly what was measured, what the control was, and what the variable or variables were.

Examine the information provided.

In Experiment 1, resistance was held constant and served as the control. The voltage of the power supply was varied. The students measured the resulting current.

In Experiment 2, resistance was held constant and served as the control. The voltage of the power supply was varied and the current was varied. The students measured the temperature increase in the water.

In Experiment 3, current was held constant and served as the control. The resistance was varied. The students measured the temperature increase.

Question 11 asks you to analyze the trials in Experiment 3 and compare them to the results of Experiment 2. Specifically, it asks you to select the resistance in Experiment 3 that best supports the results of Experiment 2. You need to look at the results of Experiment 2 in Table 2 and find a temperature value that is identical to a result in Experiment 3 in Table 3. This value is 21.5°C. Then find the value for resistance in Table 3 that is associated with a temperature increase of 21.5°C. This value is 50 ohms. Look at the options to find 50 ohms. The correct answer is **D.**

Question 12 asks you to select the graph of resistance versus temperature that best shows the results of Experiment 3. According to Table 3, for every 10-ohm increase in resistance, the temperature increases 4.3°C. This means that temperature is increasing linearly with resistance. Of the four graphs listed, only graph **F** shows this relationship. Graph **G** shows temperature decreasing as resistance increases. Graph **H** shows temperature remaining constant as resistance increases. Graph **J** shows temperature increasing while resistance remains constant. Experiment 3 does not show any of the relationships depicted in graphs **G, H,** and **J.** The correct answer is **F.**

Question 13 asks you to determine the temperature increase that would probably have resulted if a current of 1.2 amps had flowed through the resistor in Experiment 2. To solve this problem, you must use Table 2 to see how the temperature increases change as each 0.2 amp of current is added. The difference between the temperature increases at 0.2 amp and 0.0 amp is 0.9°C – 0.0°C = 0.9°C. The difference between the temperature increases at 0.4 amp and 0.2 amp is 3.4°C – 0.9°C = 2.5°C. The difference between the temperature increases at 0.6 amp and 0.4 amp is 7.7°C – 3.4°C = 4.3°C. The difference between the temperature increases at 0.8 amp and 0.6 amp is 13.8°C – 7.7°C = 6.1°C. The difference between the temperature increases at 1.0 amp and 0.9 amp is 21.5°C – 13.8°C = 7.7°C. Notice that each difference between temperature increases is larger than the one before, by either 1.6°C or 1.8°C. Following this pattern, the differences between the temperature increases at 1.2 amps and 1.0 amp should be greater than the difference between the temperature increases at 1.0 amp and 0.8 amp, which is 7.7°C. How much greater? This, too, should follow the pattern: it should be either 1.6°C or 1.8°C greater. So the temperature increase at 1.2 amps should be 21.5°C + 7.7°C + 1.6°C = 30.8°C, or 21.5°C + 7.7°C + 1.6°C = 31.0°C. Look at the options and find the value closest to one of these. That value is 31.0°C, so the correct answer is **C.**

Question 14 asks you to evaluate the scientific procedure used in Experiment 2. You are asked to understand why the same resistor was used and why the time duration was held constant in Experiment 2. First you need to realize that the resistor and time are constants in this experiment. The students measured the temperature increase in the water as it related to changing current. The only way students could make these measurements would be to have some controls in the experiment: the same resistor and the time duration of 15 minutes. To find the correct answer choice you must find one that says something about "the relationship between current and temperature increase." The only option that states this relationship is option **H.**

Question 15 asks you to select the hypothesis that was tested in Experiment 1. Go back to Experiment 1 and analyze it. In Experiment 1, the voltage was varied and the resulting current was measured at a constant resistance. No other quantities were varied in Experiment 1. Therefore, the results of Experiment 1 allow us to determine whether current is related to voltage. The results show that it is. Only option **B** mentions that current is related to voltage.

Conflicting Viewpoints format

This type of format provides two or three alternative theories, hypotheses, or viewpoints on a specific observable phenomenon. These conflicting viewpoints are based on different premises or incomplete data and are inconsistent with one another. Sample Passage IV, a biology passage on species richness, is an example of the Conflicting Viewpoints format. Notice that this passage presents the theories of three different ecologists.

The questions you'll find in the Conflicting Viewpoints format ask you to understand, analyze, evaluate, and compare two or three theories, hypotheses, or viewpoints. There are five example Conflicting Viewpoints questions presented with Sample Passage IV.

Sample Passage IV

Ecologists are interested in understanding what determines the *species richness* (number of different species) of *plant communities* (all the plants living within a given area). Ecologists agree that the resources necessary for all plants to survive are light, water, carbon dioxide, nitrogen, and phosphorus. However, ecologists disagree on how factors in the environment affect plant species richness. Three ecologists discuss their theories.

Ecologist 1

The species richness of a plant community is determined by the amounts of available resources. Plants compete for resources that are in short supply. As a result of competition, no species attains high enough abundance to eliminate any other. Therefore, a plant community with limited resources will have high species richness. To explain species richness, it is necessary to examine the competitive relationships between plant species.

Ecologist 2

The species richness of a plant community is determined by the amounts of available resources. When a resource is in short supply, those species that are *competitively superior* (use the resource most efficiently) increase in abundance. Eventually, these dominant species become so abundant that some other species are eliminated, resulting in lower species richness. A plant community with limited resources will be composed of a few dominant species, each in high abundance, and some rare species in low abundance. To explain species richness, it is necessary to examine dominant species for the adaptations that allow them to acquire and use resources more efficiently than rare species in an environment limited in resources.

Ecologist 3

The species richness of a plant community is determined by the *herbivores* (plant-eating animals) present. Herbivores encounter dominant species more often than rare species. Consequently, dominant species are eaten more often. A plant community will be composed of many species because the abundances of dominant species are kept low enough to allow the coexistence of species that would otherwise be eliminated. The more herbivores present, the greater the chance of high plant species richness. To explain species richness, it is necessary to examine the factors that affect the number of herbivores.

16. Which of the following statements about the factors which affect species richness would be consistent with the theories of Ecologists 1 and 2 ?

    F. The amounts of available resources determine the species richness of plant communities.
    G. The number of herbivores determines the species richness of plant communities.
    H. The number of herbivores and the amounts of available resources both determine the species richness of plant communities.
    J. Competition has no effect on the species richness of plant communities.

17. According to the theory of Ecologist 2, it can be concluded that when resources are diminished:

    A. no plant species occurs in high abundance.
    B. plant species richness increases.
    C. plant species richness decreases.
    D. competition between plant species decreases.

18. Which of the following is a criticism that Ecologist 2 would make of the theory of Ecologist 1 ?

    F. It ignores adaptations which make some plant species better competitors.
    G. Resources are never in short supply.
    H. Plant species do not compete for limited resources.
    J. The role of herbivores is ignored.

19. In an experiment, all of the herbivores in a plant community were removed. According to the theory of Ecologist 3, one would predict that the species richness of the plant community would:

    A. increase, because the number of dominant species would increase.
    B. increase, because rare species would increase in abundance and eliminate other species.
    C. decrease, because dominant species would increase in abundance and eliminate other species.
    D. decrease, because rare species would increase in abundance and eliminate other species.

20. Which of the following assumptions about herbivores was made by Ecologist 3 ?

    F. As the number of herbivores decreases, plant species richness increases.
    G. Herbivores have no effect on plant species richness.
    H. Herbivores prefer to eat individuals of rare plant species.
    J. All plant species are equally preferred food sources for herbivores.

Sample Passage IV

This Conflicting Viewpoints passage is a biology unit on the topic of species richness of a plant community. The introductory paragraph italicizes and defines the terms *species richness* and *plant communities*. It is important that you understand the meaning of these terms as you work through this passage. Also, you should find the primary reason for the disagreement between the ecologists: they disagree on how factors in the environment affect plant species richness.

You should carefully read each ecologist's theory and determine the viewpoint of each on plant species richness. Also, make sure you understand the similarities and differences in each of the viewpoints.

Ecologist 1 states that the species richness of a plant community is determined by the amount of available resources. This ecologist tries to explain species richness in terms of the competitive relationships between plant species.

Ecologist 2 also indicates that the species richness of a plant community is determined by the amounts of available resources. This ecologist states that in order to explain species richness, it is necessary to examine dominant species for the adaptations that allow them to acquire and use resources more effectively than other plants.

Ecologist 3 states that the species richness of a plant community is determined by the herbivores present. The more herbivores present, the greater the chance of high species richness. Ecologist 3 indicates that in order to explain species richness, it is necessary to examine the factors that affect the number of herbivores.

Question 16 asks you to select the statement about the factors that affect species richness that would be consistent with the theories of Ecologists 1 and 2. You need to examine the viewpoints of Ecologist 1 and Ecologist 2. Ecologist 1 states that species richness is determined by the amounts of available resources. Ecologist 2 also states that species richness is determined by the amounts of available resources. Look at the options and select the one that states that the amounts of available resources determine the species richness. Only option **F** states this.

Question 17 asks you to examine the theory of Ecologist 2 and determine what happens when resources are diminished. Review the viewpoint of Ecologist 2: that when a resource is in short supply, those species that use the resource most effectively increase, and that species richness will eventually be lower. Look at the options and select the one that states that plant species richness will be lower or decrease. Only option **C** makes this statement.

Question 18 asks you to find a criticism that Ecologist 2 would make concerning the theory of Ecologist 1. Ecologist 2 argues that some species are better competitors for limited resources than other species. Ecologist 2 would criticize Ecologist 1 because Ecologist 1 does not take into account differences in the competitive abilities of different species. **G** is incorrect because both ecologists recognize that resources can be limited. **H** is incorrect because both ecologists agree that plant species compete for resources that are in short supply. **J** is incorrect because both Ecologist 1 and Ecologist 2 ignore the role of herbivores. Because Ecologist 2 argues that some species are better competitors for limited resources, we can assume from the discussion of Ecologist 2 that Ecologist 1 ignores adaptations. The only option that deals with adaptations is option **F,** so the correct answer is **F.**

Question 19 asks you to predict an outcome based on the viewpoint of Ecologist 3. You need to predict what would happen to the species richness of a plant community if all the herbivores were removed. Ecologist 3 suggests that the action of herbivores keeps the abundances of dominant species low enough to allow the coexistence of rarer species that would otherwise be excluded from the plant community by the dominant species. If all of the herbivores were removed, one would expect that the dominant species would increase in abundance, thereby excluding other species. Therefore, in the absence of herbivores, one would expect that the species richness of the plant community would decrease. Look for an option that states that the species richness would decrease because dominant species would increase and eliminate other species. Option **C** says this, so the correct answer is **C.**

Question 20 asks you to determine Ecologist 3's assumption about herbivores. Ecologist 3 states that because herbivores encounter dominant species more often than they encounter rare species, dominant species are eaten more often than rarer species. If plants are eaten in relation only to their abundance, then one can infer from this that the plants must be equally preferred as food sources. Look for the option that states that all plants are equally preferred as food sources. The only option that states this is option **J,** so the correct answer is **J.**

	Answer Key for Science Reasoning Test Sample Items	
1. C	8. G	15. B
2. G	9. D	16. F
3. D	10. J	17. C
4. H	11. D	18. F
5. B	12. F	19. C
6. H	13. C	20. J
7. D	14. H	

Strategies for Taking the ACT Science Reasoning Test

General strategies

It's important to read text, graphs, and tables carefully and thoughtfully so that you'll understand clearly what you're being asked. Then you can determine the information needed to solve the problem and the information given in the passage that will help you find the answer. You may find it helpful to underline important information or to make notes in the margins of your test booklet. Unless you're instructed otherwise, it's okay to write in the test booklet, and that may help you find key information more quickly as you answer the questions.

Pace yourself

Remember, you have 35 minutes to read seven passages and their accompanying questions. That's about 5 minutes for each passage and the accompanying questions. You can think of it as 40 questions in 35 minutes, or a little less than a minute per question. If you're like most people, you'll find some of the units more familiar and probably easier than some of the others, so it's a good idea to try to work fast enough to allow yourself time to come back to any questions you have trouble answering the first time.

Learn specific strategies for Data Representation passages

When reading graphs and tables, you should be able to identify axis labels, find information in keys, identify the variable shown, determine relationships between variables (direct, inverse, or other relationships), interpolate between data points, extrapolate a data trend, make hypotheses or predictions from the data presented, translate data from one presentation form into another, and determine if new information is consistent with presented data.

An example of an inverse relationship is that the closer it gets to lunchtime, the slower clocks seem to run.

Learn specific strategies for Research Summaries passages

When working with a Research Summaries passage, you should be able to understand scientific processes. This includes identifying the designs of experiments, identifying assumptions and hypotheses underlying the experiments, identifying controls and variables, determining the effects of altering the experiments, identifying similarities and differences between the studies, identifying the strengths and weaknesses of the experiments, developing other experiments that will test the same hypothesis, making hypotheses or predictions from research results, and creating models from research results.

Learn specific strategies for Conflicting Viewpoints passages

When working with a Conflicting Viewpoints passage, you should be able to interpret the viewpoints, theories, or hypotheses; determine their strengths and weaknesses; determine their similarities and differences; find out how new information affects the viewpoints; and determine how alternate viewpoints explain the same phenomenon.

Think about how you can use the information in graphs and diagrams

Graphs and diagrams illustrate data in ways that can be very useful if you follow a few rules. First, it's important to identify what is being displayed in the graph or diagram (pig iron, nuclear missiles, concentration of cytoplasm, etc.). What units of measurement are used (meters, pounds, kilometers per hour, etc.)? Graphs usually have captions or labels that provide this information; diagrams generally have a key or legend or other short explanation of the information presented. Many graphs consist of two axes (horizontal and vertical), both of which will be labeled. Remember, the first thing to find out about any graph or diagram is exactly what the numbers represent.

Pig iron.

Once you've identified what is being presented in a graph or diagram, you can begin to look for trends in the data. The main reason for using a graph or diagram to present information is to show how one characteristic of the data tends to influence one or more other characteristics.

For a coordinate graph, notice how a change on the horizontal axis (or *x*-axis) relates to the position of the variable on the vertical axis (or *y*-axis). If the curve shown angles upward from lower left to upper right (as in Figure 1a), then as the variable shown on the *x*-axis increases, so does the variable on the *y*-axis (a direct relationship). An example of a direct relationship is that a person's weight increases as his or her height increases. If the curve goes from the upper left to the lower right (as in Figure 1b), then as the variable on the *x*-axis increases, the variable on the *y*-axis decreases (an inverse relationship). An example of an inverse relationship is that the more players there are on a soccer team, the less time each of them gets to play (assuming everyone gets equal playing time). If the graph shows a vertical or horizontal line (as in Figure 1c), the characteristics are probably unrelated.

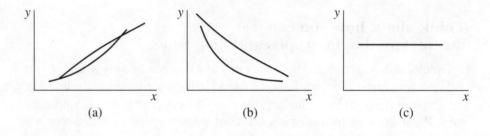

(a)　　　　　(b)　　　　　(c)

Figure 1

Sometimes, a question will ask you to estimate a value for one characteristic based on a given value of another characteristic that is beyond the limits of the curve shown on the graph. In this case, the solution will require you to extrapolate, or extend, the graph. If the curve is a relatively straight line, just use your pencil to extend that line far enough for the value called for to be included. If the graphed line is a curve, use your best judgement to extend the line to follow the apparent pattern. Figure 2 shows how to extend both types of graphs.

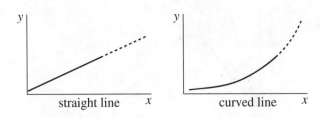

Figure 2

Another type of graph problem asks you to estimate a value that falls between two known values on a curve. This process is called interpolation and, if the curve is shown, it amounts to finding a point on the curve that corresponds to a given value for one characteristic and reading the value for the other characteristic. (For example, "For a given x, find y.") If only scattered points are shown on the graph, draw a "best-fit line," a line that comes close to all of the points. Use this line to estimate the middle value. Figure 3 shows how to construct a best-fit line.

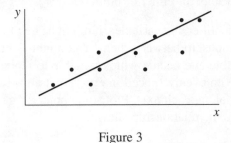

Figure 3

One very useful kind of graph shows more than one curve on the same pair of axes. Such a graph might be used when the results of a number of experiments are compared or when an experiment involves more than two variables. Analysis of this sort of graph requires that you determine the relationship shown by each curve and then determine how the curves are related to one another. Figure 4 shows a graph with multiple curves.

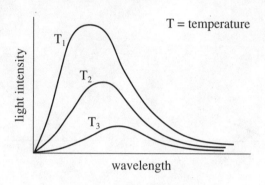

Figure 4

Think about how you can use the information in tables

While graphs and diagrams offer ways of illustrating data, sometimes you will have to work from raw data presented in a table. To understand what a table is showing you, you need to identify the information or data presented. You need to know two things: how the quantity has been measured (in grams, quarts, hectares, etc.) and what purpose the information or data serve in the experiment. Generally, experiments intentionally vary one characteristic (the independent variable) to see how it affects another (the dependent variable). Tables may report results for either or both.

Once you have identified the variables, it might be helpful to sketch a graph to illustrate the relationship between them. You might sketch an *x*-axis and a *y*-axis next to the table and decide which variable to represent on each axis. Mark off the axes with evenly spaced intervals that allow all of the numbers for a category to fit along each axis. Plot some points. Again, draw a best-fit line and characterize the relationship shown.

As with graphs and diagrams, you may be asked to look for trends in the data. For example, do the numbers representing the dependent variable increase or decrease as the numbers representing the independent variable increase or decrease? If no pattern is clear, you may want to refer to a rough graph as discussed above. You may also need to make predictions about values of quantities between the data points shown (interpolation), or beyond the limits of those shown on the table (extrapolation). Another type of problem may require you to compare data from multiple columns of a table. A simple explanation of the numbers may be enough to see a relationship, but you may find it helpful to sketch a graph containing a curve for each category. The curves may be compared as described above in "Think about how you can use the information in graphs and diagrams" (page 163).

Develop a problem-solving method

Because you have only a limited time in which to take the Science Reasoning Test, you may find it helpful to work out a general problem-solving method that you can use for all or most of the questions. The method described here is certainly not the only way to solve the problems, but it is one that works for most science problems. If you can see a way to adapt this method, or if you can work out your own approach, use the method that works best for you.

One approach to solving problems is to break the process into a series of smaller steps. After you have read the passage, take a careful look at the question and restate it in your own words to make sure you have the problem clearly in mind. Next, decide what information you need to solve the problem. Examine the information given in the passage and decide what sort of information you have, including data presented in the passage and scientific concepts and assumptions underlying the experiments, arguments, or conclusions. Sort and assemble the information necessary for a conclusion and logically think through your answer, then compare it to the possible answers. This problem-solving method may be described in four steps:

1. **Restate the problem.**
2. **Decide what information is needed.**
3. **Find needed information in the passage.**
4. **Think through your answer.**

Moving to the Next Step

The information in this chapter should give you a good idea of what to expect on the ACT test. The example passages and questions in this chapter, taken from previous ACT tests and representing each of the four content areas that make up the ACT Assessment, were used to illustrate some of the different types of questions you can expect to see when you take the ACT test. At this point, you may want to consider two different strategies for continuing to study for the ACT test: study in more depth some of the topics that have been covered in this chapter, perhaps with a study group or a teacher, or continue in this book and take the practice tests in Chapter 5 to see how you're progressing in your preparation for the ACT test.

Part 3: Practice Tests and Scoring

5

Practice ACT Tests

In this chapter, you'll find two complete practice ACT tests and explanatory answers for the questions on those tests. In order to make the best use possible of the materials offered here, you may want to take a minute to familiarize yourself with the format of this large chapter before you continue.

Practice Test 1 is first, with the individual tests in the same order as they will be on the actual test: the English Test, the Mathematics Test, the Reading Test, and the Science Reasoning Test. Following each complete practice test, you will find the explanatory answers for the questions on that test. The explanatory answers follow the same pattern as the individual tests (English, Mathematics, Reading, and Science Reasoning). Answer sheets that you can tear out and use to record your answers for the practice tests follow each set of Science Reasoning Test explanatory answers. (The practice tests and the answer sheets are somewhat smaller than they are on the actual test.)

How should you use the practice tests? Use the materials to fit your needs and abilities. Here are some possibilities:

■ **Take all four tests in the first practice test.** If you feel confident about your test-taking skills and just want some quick practice, you might work through Practice Test 1, timing yourself to simulate actual test conditions. After you complete the four tests of Practice Test 1, check your answers against the answer key in Chapter 6 (pages 537–541) or against the explanatory answers that accompany each individual test. You'll probably want to refer to the explanatory answers for any questions you answer incorrectly.

■ **Take selected tests within the first practice test.** If you feel more confident about some content areas than you do about others, you may want to first take the tests in Practice Test 1 that you feel confident about, then refer to Chapter 4 to review the format and content of the tests you feel less confident about before you take those tests. So, for example, if you feel comfortable in every content area except English, you may want to refer to Chapter 4 and review the English Test before you take it in Practice Test 1.

■ **Go back and reread other chapters.** Your results on Practice Test 1 should give you an idea about what to do next, whatever strategy you decide to use. If your scores indicate that you need work in a certain content area, refer to Chapter 4 for more assistance. You may also want to ask your teacher in that content area for help. If you feel you need to better understand the ACT test or any of the four individual tests, the information and strategies in Chapters 3 and 4 may be helpful to you.

■ **Practice Test 2.** After you work through Practice Test 1 and complete any further work you feel you need, take Practice Test 2 to see how your additional studying has helped you. You'll find the answer key for Practice Test 2 on pages 548–552 in Chapter 6, or you can use the explanatory answers that accompany each individual test.

Now you know the contents of this chapter, and you have some ideas about how to use it. Think about your abilities and the time you have available for practice, then decide how you can best use the materials in this chapter. You will probably want to use the information and strategies presented in Chapters 1, 3, and 4 as you work through Practice Tests 1 and 2. Finally, remember that the contents of this book are here for one purpose: to help you do your very best on the ACT test.

Practice Test 1

Your Signature (do not print): _____

Print Your Name Here: _____

Your Social Security Number or ACT ID Number:

☐☐☐ – ☐☐ – ☐☐☐☐

 ACT Assessment

DIRECTIONS

This booklet contains tests in English, Mathematics, Reading, and Science Reasoning. These tests measure skills and abilities highly related to high school course work and success in college. *CALCULATORS MAY BE USED ON THE MATHEMATICS TEST ONLY.*

The questions in each test are numbered, and the suggested answers for each question are lettered. On the answer document, the rows of ovals are numbered to match the questions, and the ovals in each row are lettered to correspond to the suggested answers.

For each question, first decide which answer is best. Next, locate on the answer document the row of ovals numbered the same as the question. Then, locate the oval in that row lettered the same as your answer. Finally, fill in the oval completely. Use a soft lead pencil and make your marks heavy and black. *DO NOT USE A BALLPOINT PEN.*

Mark only one answer to each question. If you change your mind about an answer, erase your first mark thoroughly before marking your new answer. For each question, make certain that you mark in the row of ovals with the same number as the question.

Only responses marked on your answer document will be scored. Your score on each test will be based only on the number of questions you answer correctly during the time allowed for that test. You will NOT be penalized for guessing. *IT IS TO YOUR ADVANTAGE TO ANSWER EVERY QUESTION EVEN IF YOU MUST GUESS.*

You may work on each test ONLY when your test supervisor tells you to do so. If you finish a test before time is called for that test, you should use the time remaining to reconsider questions you are uncertain about in that test. You may NOT look back to a test on which time has already been called, and you may NOT go ahead to another test. To do so will disqualify you from the examination.

Lay your pencil down immediately when time is called at the end of each test. You may NOT for any reason fill in ovals for a test after time is called for that test. To do so will disqualify you from the examination.

Do not fold or tear the pages of your test booklet.

DO NOT OPEN THIS BOOKLET UNTIL TOLD TO DO SO.

P.O. BOX 168
IOWA CITY, IA 52243-0168

1 ■ ■ ■ ■ ■ ■ ■ ■ ■ 1

ENGLISH TEST
45 Minutes—75 Questions

DIRECTIONS: In the five passages that follow, certain words and phrases are underlined and numbered. In the right-hand column, you will find alternatives for each underlined part. You are to choose the one that best expresses the idea, makes the statement appropriate for standard written English, or is worded most consistently with the style and tone of the passage as a whole. If you think the original version is best, choose "NO CHANGE."

You will also find questions about a section of the passage, or about the passage as a whole. These questions do not refer to an underlined portion of the passage, but rather are identified by a number or numbers in a box.

For each question, choose the alternative you consider best and fill in the corresponding oval on your answer document. Read each passage through once before you begin to answer the questions that accompany it. You cannot determine most answers without reading several sentences beyond the question. Be sure that you have read far enough ahead each time you choose an alternative.

PASSAGE I

Diane Boyd, Wildlife Biologist

[1]

They call her Diane of the Wolves. Wildlife
 _____
      1

biologist Diane Boyd studies wolves in their native

habitat in a remote wilderness in the Northwest.

It being her base, Boyd's eighty-year-old cabin is
_____
                    2

thirty-five miles from the nearest paved road. It has

little running water, electricity, or phone, and
_____
  3

Glacier National Park is just across the river that

flows past her cabin door.
       4

    cabin's [2]

Because of her isolation, Boyd has had to

become self-sufficient. She heats the cabin with
                                          _____
                                            5

firewood she chops herself, and hunts wild game
_____
          6

for food. Much of her time is spent trapping wolves

in order to radio-collar (put a tracking device on)

them. Once a wolf is collared, its movements are
                                 _____
                                     7

easy to follow and record. And though she often

comes across dangerous grizzlies, Boyd carries no

weapon as she makes the rounds of her traps.

1. **A.** NO CHANGE
   B. Wolves, wildlife
   C. Wolves. Wildlife,
   D. Wolves, specializing in wildlife

2. **F.** NO CHANGE
   G. Her base is an eighty-year-old cabin
   H. Being an eighty-year-old cabin, it is her base
   J. Boyd's cabin, it being an eighty-year-old base, is

3. **A.** NO CHANGE
   B. less
   C. few
   D. no

4. **F.** NO CHANGE
   G. passed her cabin
   H. passed her cabin's
   J. past her cabins'

5. **A.** NO CHANGE
   B. cabin which is her base
   C. cabin, her home base
   D. cabin, which is eighty years old

6. **F.** NO CHANGE
   G. firewood, she chops herself
   H. firewood she chops, herself
   J. firewood she chops herself

7. **A.** NO CHANGE
   B. whereby its
   C. so that
   D. their

GO ON TO THE NEXT PAGE.

1 ■ ■ ■ ■ ■ ■ ■ ■ ■ 1

While checking her traps, she packs supplies.
                                   8

[3]

[1] The first wolf Boyd collared was Sage, a
big gray wolf so strong he has crossed the
Continental Divide twice in the dead of winter.
[2] One winter afternoon, on a routine flight
to check on her wolves, Boyd spotted Sage in a
hunter's trap. [3] She knew that if the hunter didn't
kill him, freezing or starvation soon would. [4] If
Sage died, Boyd's research on this animal would end
unhappily after only four years, it was after landing,
                                              9

Boyd and a fellow, biologist drove fifty miles in a
                            10
four-wheel-drive pickup. [5] They then traveled
through deep snow on snowmobiles in order to
reach Sage. ⬚11

[4]

[1] They approached the half-frozen wolf,
sedated him, and wrapped him in a sleeping bag.
[2] The sky was dark by the time the two biologists
had began working. [3] They used the warmth of
   12
their bare hands to restore circulation to Sage's
frozen right foot. [4] Just before daylight, they fitted
the recovered wolf with a new radio collar and set
him free. ⬚13

[5]

A few days later, Boyd noticed Sage and five
of his pup's playful wrestling on the side of a
          14

8. Which of the alternatives best provides new, specific details about the equipment Diane Boyd uses for the purpose of trapping and collaring wolves?
   F. NO CHANGE
   G. To manage the wolves, she packs a four-foot pole, tranquilizers, and a hypodermic needle.
   H. Safely collaring a wolf requires equipment, which she brings with her when she checks her traps.
   J. Although she doesn't bring weapons, she arms herself with equipment.

9. A. NO CHANGE
   B. years so then after
   C. years. After
   D. years, after

10. F. NO CHANGE
    G. fellow biologist, drove fifty miles
    H. fellow biologist drove fifty miles
    J. fellow biologist, drove fifty miles,

11. The writer wants to add the following explanation of Sage's name to Paragraph 3:

    Boyd named the wolf for his air of wisdom and experience.

    This sentence would most logically be placed:

    A. before Sentence 1.
    B. after Sentence 1.
    C. after Sentence 2.
    D. after Sentence 5.

12. F. NO CHANGE
    G. have begun
    H. begun
    J. began

13. Which of the following sequences of sentences will make Paragraph 4 most logical?
    A. 1, 2, 4, 3
    B. 1, 4, 3, 2
    C. 2, 1, 3, 4
    D. 2, 3, 1, 4

14. F. NO CHANGE
    G. pup's playfully wrestling
    H. pups' wrestling playfully
    J. pups wrestling playfully

GO ON TO THE NEXT PAGE.

1 ■ ■ ■ ■ ■ ■ ■ ■ ■ **1**

mountain. Sage's rescue had been a <u>success after all!</u>
<u>15</u>

15. The writer wants to link the essay's opening and concluding sentences. Which of the alternatives most successfully achieves this effect?
  A. NO CHANGE
  B. success even so.
  C. success, which was predictable.
  D. success, and Diane of the Wolves had earned her nickname once again.

PASSAGE II

World Trade: Lost in Translation?

As American businesses explore overseas

<u>markets. They</u> learn firsthand how language
<u>16</u>

16. F. NO CHANGE
  G. markets, they
  H. markets; they
  J. markets and

<u>differences</u> can stand in the way of trade. After
<u>17</u>
experiencing a period of slow gasoline sales in a

new foreign market, an American oil company

learned that its name in the foreign nation's language

means "stalled car." A major American car

<u>manufacturer, you see,</u> found out that the name of
<u>18</u>

17. A. NO CHANGE
  B. differences, which
  C. differences that
  D. differences of which

18. F. NO CHANGE
  G. manufacturer, as proof,
  H. manufacturer
  J. manufacturer, consequently,

one of its models being <u>converted into hard cash</u>
<u>19</u>
in South America is a Spanish word meaning "ugly

old woman." Blunders like these illustrate that an

important step in breaking down barriers to

international trade is to break down language

barriers.

19. A. NO CHANGE
  B. sold over the counter
  C. traded for the local currency
  D. offered for sale

The many countries of Western Europe have

always faced this problem. Overcoming it is

one of the tasks of the European Economic

<u>Community or Common Market</u> an organization
<u>20</u>

20. F. NO CHANGE
  G. Community, or Common Market;
  H. Community, or Common Market,
  J. Community or, Common Market,

<u>founded at its start</u> to promote trade among
<u>21</u>
nations in that part of the world. But it's a difficult

21. A. NO CHANGE
  B. which was begun and founded
  C. that it organized
  D. formed

GO ON TO THE NEXT PAGE.

1 ■ ■ ■ ■ ■ ■ ■ ■ ■ **1**

task. When one of the European Economic

Community's (EEC's) twelve official languages

are used at a meeting, translation must be available
_____
22

to the other delegates. 23 Finding translators

for English, French, and German is relatively easy.

But finding them for languages like Danish,

Portuguese, and, especially, Greek has proven

more difficult. In fact, when it was
_____
24

almost two decades ago becoming clear that
_____
25
Greece would join the Common Market,

officials began to look for translators three years

in advance. The results of their search were

disappointing to this day, it is almost impossible
_____
26
for them to find translators who can turn Greek

into, say, Danish.
27

For example

    Then, a standing joke among language
_____
28
officials at EEC headquarters begins

with the interrogation of someone by asking the
_____
29
question "What is a Great Dane?" With a rueful

smile, someone is likely to respond, "Any Dane

who knows how to speak Greek?" All that's needed

22. F. NO CHANGE
   G. is used
   H. are being used
   J. are in use

23. At this point, the writer is considering the addition of the following sentence:

    Brussels, the home of EEC headquarters, is the lively and modern capital of Belgium.

Would this be a logical and relevant addition to the essay?

   A. Yes, because it serves to establish the setting for the essay.
   B. Yes, because it helps to legitimize the EEC by mentioning its main headquarters.
   C. No, because the official languages of Belgium aren't mentioned as "problem" languages.
   D. No, because it sheds no new light on the problem of language barriers in the EEC.

24. F. NO CHANGE
   G. (Do NOT begin new paragraph) Furthermore,
   H. (Begin new paragraph) In fact,
   J. (Begin new paragraph) Furthermore,

25. A. NO CHANGE
   B. (Place after *clear*)
   C. (Place after *join*)
   D. (Place after *began*)

26. F. NO CHANGE
   G. disappointing, and
   H. disappointing and
   J. so disappointing

27. A. NO CHANGE
   B. into say,
   C. into, say
   D. into,

28. F. NO CHANGE
   G. A
   H. For instance, a
   J. Eventually, a

29. A. NO CHANGE
   B. by asking someone to answer the
   C. by commencing with the introductory
   D. with the

GO ON TO THE NEXT PAGE.

1 ■ ■ ■ ■ ■ ■ ■ ■ ■ **1**

to turn that smile into a look of <u>despair, is a</u> reminder that Turkey, whose language is not widely studied in Western Europe, may someday become a member of the Common Market.

30. F. NO CHANGE
G. despair, was
H. despair is
J. despair, would be

PASSAGE III

Central Park

[1]

While New <u>Yorker's</u> sometimes take Central Park for granted, visitors are often astonished to

31. A. NO CHANGE
B. Yorker's,
C. Yorkers
D. Yorkers'

discover <u>the</u> size and variety. Nestled in the very center of the nation's largest city are 843 acres of wooded and landscaped grounds containing lakes and ponds, bogs and meadows, a castle, a zoo, and an enormous range of wildlife. Though it seems to have always been there, Central Park represents only the most recent in a series of <u>altering</u>

32. F. NO CHANGE
G. its
H. it's
J. their

33. A. NO CHANGE
B. changes,
C. changing
D. OMIT the underlined portion.

transformations of <u>this part of the country.</u>

34. At this point, the writer would like to provide specific geographical information about the area where Central Park is located. Which alternative does that best?

F. NO CHANGE
G. these parts.
H. this part of the island of Manhattan.
J. this part that resulted in Central Park.

[2]

[1] About 450 million years ago, <u>what is now park</u> rested on the floor of an ancient sea. [2] After aeons of erosion, accelerated by the

35. A. NO CHANGE
B. that which is now park, but was not then
C. that park, which then was not one,
D. it wasn't a park then, but it

Ice <u>Age and</u> the landscape began to assume its modern appearance. [3] By the time European settlers arrived, the entire island was an oak-and-chestnut woodland, <u>it is</u> populated by black bears, wolves, and beavers. [4] Within the next 200 years, however, the forests were cleared for farming, and the animals were eliminated by hunters and trappers.

36. F. NO CHANGE
G. Age;
H. Age,
J. Age, and

37. A. NO CHANGE
B. it was
C. they found it
D. OMIT the underlined portion.

GO ON TO THE NEXT PAGE.

1 ■ ■ ■ ■ ■ ■ ■ ■ ■ **1**

[5] By the mid-nineteenth century, central

Manhattan, being barren of trees, creating a
___
38

desolate area of swamps, hovels, and pigsties.

[6] Over 200 million years ago, the shifting of the

earth's surface squeezed present-day Manhattan up

into mountains over 12,000 feet high. ☐39☐

[3]

In 1857 Frederick Olmsted and Calvert

Vaux were given the enormous task of transforming
___
40

this area into a park. Their intention was

to finish the park within two years. They undertook
___
41

the project with confidence and enterprise, overturning
___
42

nearly five million cubic yards of rock and earth.

Olmsted and Vaux hired local land developers
___
43

to help plan the park's landscape.
___
43

[4]

Today in Central Park, natural beauty and

human engineering work together. Although the
___
44

genius of Olmsted and Vaux, once a landscape barely
___
45

38. F. NO CHANGE
   G. Manhattan being
   H. Manhattan, which was
   J. Manhattan was

39. For the sake of logic and coherence, Sentence 6 should be placed:

   A. where it is now.
   B. before Sentence 1.
   C. before Sentence 2.
   D. before Sentence 5.

40. F. NO CHANGE
   G. were gave
   H. was given
   J. been given

41. At this point, the writer wants to provide readers with a general description of Vaux and Olmsted's vision of the finished park. Assuming all are true, which alternative does that best?

   A. NO CHANGE
   B. to find new techniques for land development by experimenting with new machinery and new ideas in land design.
   C. to create the park using the most economical means they could.
   D. not to create a formal garden with meticulously trimmed hedges, as in the European tradition, but a natural-looking landscape.

42. F. NO CHANGE
   G. they overturn
   H. they overturned
   J. they having overturned

43. At this point, the writer would like to emphasize the enormousness of the project. Assuming all are true, which alternative does that best?

   A. NO CHANGE
   B. Another 700,000 cubic yards of topsoil had to be brought from New Jersey before the landscapers could plant their 17,000 trees and shrubs.
   C. The result is a park that attracts tourists from all over the world.
   D. Many workers from the New York area contributed to the park's development.

44. F. NO CHANGE
   G. Considering
   H. Through
   J. Despite

45. A. NO CHANGE
   B. a once-bare landscape
   C. a once barely landscape
   D. a once, bare landscape

GO ON TO THE NEXT PAGE.

1 ■ ■ ■ ■ ■ ■ ■ ■ **1**

was transformed into an oasis in the center of
urban life.

Item 46 poses a question about the essay as a whole.

46. Suppose the writer were to eliminate Paragraph 1. This omission would cause the essay as a whole to lose primarily:
    F. relevant details about the current attractions in Central Park.
    G. irrelevant details about the current attractions in Central Park.
    H. historical information regarding the creation of Central Park.
    J. an irrelevant anecdote about the tourists in Central Park.

PASSAGE IV

My Most Memorable Meal

[1]

Recently I came across a series of magazine
articles which various people described their most
            47

memorable eating experiences. Out of all those
                                        48
people who were interviewed many of those people
            48

raved about the perfect seven-course meal they
                              49
had once been served in a grand and expensive
restaurant. Some reminisced about romantic
picnics. Meals made memorable by the
      50

diner's companions; rather than by the
      51

47. A. NO CHANGE
    B. that
    C. in which
    D. OMIT the underlined portion.

48. F. NO CHANGE
    G. Out of all the ones they interviewed, many of those people
    H. Of the ones that were interviewed, out of those, many of them
    J. Many of those interviewed

49. A. NO CHANGE
    B. meals, that
    C. meals, which
    D. meals,

50. F. NO CHANGE
    G. picnics; meals
    H. picnics—meals
    J. picnics meals

51. A. NO CHANGE
    B. diners' companions
    C. diners companions'
    D. diners companions

GO ON TO THE NEXT PAGE.

1 ■ ■ ■ ■ ■ ■ ■ ■ ■ ■ 1

food consumed. 52

[2]

While reading these entertaining memoirs, I was myself moved to rummage through old memories in search of remarkable meals. My first meal at the college dormitory came to mind, (the name of it was Goodhue) but it was hardly
___
53
memorable for its excellence. I considered the string of Thanksgiving dinners I've enjoyed, but, and perhaps by design, no one of them stand
——
54

out as unusual. 55

[3]

Then I remembered the night I tasted the Sri Lankan holiday dish called *lampries*. Served in a rough cottage in the Sri Lankan jungle, with lizards climbing the whitewashed walls and the innkeeper's dog leaping affectionately into my lap, the meal was certainly not remarkable for its formal elegance. It was, however, the more complex, elaborate, and
___
56
delicious concoction I've ever eaten.

[4]

It took the innkeeper and the cook all day to prepare the spicy rice and four fiery curries that compose *lampries*. They began grinding the spices while we guests were having breakfast, and it wasn't

52. Some interviewees in the magazine articles spoke about home cooking; some about gorging themselves on desserts when they were children; and some about picnic food. The writer wishes to add another example at the end of Paragraph 1 in order to show the range of experience covered. Which of the following sentences would best further the writer's purpose of capturing the diversity of the experiences described?

   F. Others recalled childhood feasts on ice cream or cake.
   G. When eating a seven-course meal, most diners must take care not to overindulge in appetizers.
   H. Grand restaurants make any meal memorable.
   J. Picnics—whether romantic or merely expedient—usually are composed of the same predictable dishes: bread, wine, cheese, pickles.

53. **A.** NO CHANGE
   B. (the name of which was Goodhue)
   C. (Goodhue was its name)
   D. OMIT the underlined portion.

54. **F.** NO CHANGE
   G. stands
   H. have stood
   J. were standing

55. The writer wishes to add another relevant example to Paragraph 2 without straying from the purpose of cataloguing a variety of meals, none of which can be more remarkable than the *lampries* meal described later in the essay. Which of the following sentences does that best?

   A. In my family, all Thanksgiving dinners are created equal.
   B. Surely, though, the most remarkable meal I've ever eaten, better and more exotic than all those curries, was the pure, elegant meal I had as part of a formal Japanese tea ceremony.
   C. There was the first meal I ever cooked all by myself, but oozy scrambled eggs and blackened toast are not memoir material.
   D. Dormitory food is, at best, bland and starchy.

56. **F.** NO CHANGE
   G. the most
   H. more
   J. OMIT the underlined portion.

GO ON TO THE NEXT PAGE.

1 ■ ■ ■ ■ ■ ■ ■ ■ ■ **1**

until late <u>afternoon that</u> the innkeeper began
57
cooking the curries. Then the cook layered them

onto huge, green banana leaves, which she bundled

up and tied into packets for the final baking.

[5]

All four rooms of the cottage were filled with the

rich curry aromas of cinnamon, saffron, and mystery.

The innkeeper brought out cold drinks and split a

fresh <u>pineapple. With two strokes of her machete, we</u>
58
took our places, and with great ceremony the cook

brought in the *lampries*—one fat packet for each of

us. Inside was a mixture so unforgettably hot and

exotic it shocked us, but we kept eating.

57. A. NO CHANGE
B. afternoon. That
C. afternoon, that
D. afternoon, thats when

58. F. NO CHANGE
G. pineapple. With two strokes of her machete we
H. pineapple, with two strokes of her machete, we
J. pineapple with two strokes of her machete. We

Items 59 and 60 pose questions about the essay as a whole.

---

59. The writer wishes to include the following sentence in the essay:

> That evening, while standing out back listening to the eerie noises of the awakening night jungle, I peered in through the kitchen window to watch the innkeeper give each of the curries one final meditative stir.

That sentence will fit most smoothly and logically into Paragraph:

A. 2, before the first sentence.
B. 3, after the last sentence.
C. 4, before the last sentence.
D. 5, after the last sentence.

60. The writer wishes to make the details more lush and complete in order to help the reader virtually see, smell, and taste the *lampries*. Where should the writer place the following sentence?

> "Are you hungry? Are you hungry?" chanted the innkeeper, and the dog barked with excitement as we cut the strings and undid the wrappings.

That sentence should be added to Paragraph:

F. 3, before the second sentence.
G. 3, after the third sentence.
H. 4, after the last sentence.
J. 5, before the last sentence.

PASSAGE V

Japanese Comic Books

When Americans think of comic books, they

often think of children's magazines starring Donald

Duck and Superman. In Japan, however, comic

books are among the most popular art forms,

GO ON TO THE NEXT PAGE.

1 ■ ■ ■ ■ ■ ■ ■ ■ **1**

which are being read by almost the entire
_____
                    61
population.

Japanese comic books, called *manga,*

look in appearance very different
_____
        62

then American comics. Whereas most American
____
 63

comics are small magazines. Japanese comics
                 _____
                    64
often resemble big-city telephone books, sometimes

600 pages long. They are often published weekly—

there are also Korean and Chinese comics—and
_____
                    65
contain many serialized stories. The most popular

stories are collected into permanent books.

Usually, American comic books are mostly
_____
   66
about superheroes, a wide variety of stories appear in

Japanese comics. There are adventure stories as in

the U.S., but they are drawn in a very unique
         _____
                    67
style, unlike anything done in the American stories.
_____
                    67

[68] In the U.S., comic books have

61. **A.** NO CHANGE
    B. those being read in their entirety
    C. read
    D. OMIT the underlined portion.

62. **F.** NO CHANGE
    G. look
    H. look and appear
    J. seem to appear to look

63. **A.** NO CHANGE
    B. like
    C. for
    D. from

64. **F.** NO CHANGE
    G. magazines,
    H. for magazines.
    J. magazines and

65. Which of the alternatives provides the contrast most
    appropriate and relevant to the essay?
    A. NO CHANGE
    B. newspapers are usually published daily—
    C. American comics are usually issued on a monthly
        basis—
    D. European comics are becoming more popular in
        America—

66. **F.** NO CHANGE
    G. While
    H. However,
    J. OMIT the underlined portion.

67. Which of the alternative clauses would most effectively
    support the assertion made in the previous sentence
    about the variety of stories in Japanese comics?
    A. NO CHANGE
    B. there are also stories about sports, romance, work,
        history, school, and fashion.
    C. American readers might find some of them diffi-
        cult to understand, even in translation.
    D. the most popular stories in Japanese comics are in
        the category of science fiction.

68. Which of the following would provide the best transi-
    tion here, guiding the reader from the topic of the
    previous paragraph to the new topic of this paragraph?
    F. Many people in Japan read comic books and also
        go to the movies.
    G. As can be seen, there are many topics covered in
        Japanese comic books.
    H. Very few females, young or old, read American
        comic books.
    J. The varied subjects of Japanese *manga* attract a
        wide readership.

GO ON TO THE NEXT PAGE.

1 ■ ■ ■ ■ ■ ■ ■ ■ 1

traditionally been geared to either children or

teenage boys, and circulations rarely exceed

300,000. In Japan, therefore, males and females

of all ages read comics regularly, and there are

comics produced for distinct interests and age

groups. *Manga* can be found in waiting rooms,

barber shops, bus stations—almost anywhere.

We read on the train by businesspeople on the way

to work and by children coming home from school.

Circulations can easily soar into the millions.

In fact, 27 percent of all books and

magazines produced in Japan are comic

books. Comic book creators in Japan are superstars

comparable to America's most famous music and

television stars.

    The comics industry is changing in the U.S.,

becoming much more like that of Japanese comics.

New kinds of stories for adults, as well as, children

are now being written, and some series are being

collected into permanent book format. However,

American comics have a long way to go before

they reach the level of artistic and cultural acceptance

that comics have achieved in Japan.

69. **A.** NO CHANGE
    B. along
    C. from
    D. with

70. **F.** NO CHANGE
    G. as well,
    H. on the other hand,
    J. consequently,

71. **A.** NO CHANGE
    B. They
    C. You
    D. They are

72. **F.** NO CHANGE
    G. magazines, produced in Japan,
    H. magazines, produced in Japan
    J. magazines produced in Japan,

73. **A.** NO CHANGE
    B. that of the Japanese.
    C. Japanese comics.
    D. that of the Japanese comics industry.

74. **F.** NO CHANGE
    G. adults as well as,
    H. adults as well as
    J. adults, as well as

GO ON TO THE NEXT PAGE.

1 ■ ■ ■ ■ ■ ■ ■ ■ **1**

Item 75 poses a question about the essay as a whole.

75. Suppose the writer had been assigned to write a brief essay detailing some specific way in which Japan has been influenced by American culture. Would this essay successfully fulfill the assignment?

A. No, because the essay suggests instead that the Japanese have been innovative leaders in developing the comic book as a popular art form.

B. No, because the essay does not give any specific examples of actual Japanese comic books.

C. Yes, because the U.S. does exert considerable influence on Japanese culture today, although the same is not true for the business world.

D. Yes, because the essay suggests that there are adventure stories in Japanese comic books, just as there are in American comic books.

END OF TEST 1

STOP! DO NOT TURN THE PAGE UNTIL TOLD TO DO SO.

2   **2**

MATHEMATICS TEST
60 Minutes—60 Questions

DIRECTIONS: Solve each problem, choose the correct answer, and then fill in the corresponding oval on your answer document.

Do not linger over problems that take too much time. Solve as many as you can; then return to the others in the time you have left for this test.

You are permitted to use a calculator on this test. You may use your calculator for any problems you choose, but some of the problems may best be done without using a calculator.

Note: Unless otherwise stated, all of the following should be assumed.

1. Illustrative figures are NOT necessarily drawn to scale.
2. Geometric figures lie in a plane.
3. The word *line* indicates a straight line.
4. The word *average* indicates arithmetic mean.

---

1. On a math test, 12 students earned an A. This number is exactly 25% of the total number of students in the class. How many students are in the class?

   A. 15
   B. 16
   C. 21
   D. 30
   E. 48

2. In the figure below, points A, E, and D are on the same line. What is the measure of $\angle CED$?

   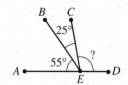

   F. 80°
   G. 90°
   H. 100°
   J. 110°
   K. 140°

3. What is the fifth term of the arithmetic sequence 8, 6, 4, … ?
   A. −2
   B. 0
   C. 4
   D. 8
   E. 16

4. What value of x solves the following proportion?

$$\frac{9}{6} = \frac{x}{8}$$

   F. $5\frac{1}{3}$

   G. $6\frac{3}{4}$

   H. $10\frac{1}{2}$

   J. 11

   K. 12

DO YOUR FIGURING HERE.

GO ON TO THE NEXT PAGE.

2   **2**

5. If point C bisects line segment $\overline{AB}$, then which of the following congruences must hold?

A. $\overline{CA} \cong \overline{AB}$
B. $\overline{CB} \cong \overline{AB}$
C. $\overline{AC} \cong \overline{BA}$
D. $\overline{BC} \cong \overline{BA}$
E. $\overline{AC} \cong \overline{CB}$

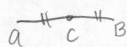

6. Three pieces of wire, each 2.8 meters long, are cut from the end of a wire 90 meters long. How many meters of wire are left?

F. 81.6
G. 82.6
H. 83.2
J. 83.6
K. 87.2

7. If $x = -3$, then $12 - 2(x + 1) = ?$

A. 4
B. 7
C. 16
D. 19
E. 20

8. $-|-10| - (-10) = ?$

F. −100
G. −20
H. 0
J. 20
K. 100

9. Umberto's mother expects an increase of 5% in her current annual salary of $36,000. What would her new annual salary be?

A. $36,005
B. $36,180
C. $37,800
D. $41,000
E. $54,000

10. If $x^3 = 20$ (and x is a real number), then x lies between which two consecutive integers?

F. 2 and 3
G. 3 and 4
H. 4 and 5
J. 5 and 6
K. 6 and 7

GO ON TO THE NEXT PAGE.

2   **2**

DO YOUR FIGURING HERE.

11. If $78 - x = 234$, then $x = ?$

A. -312
B. -156
C. 3
D. 156
E. 312

12. In a laboratory experiment, Amoeba A lives 5 hours longer than Amoeba B, and Amoeba B lives twice as long as Amoeba C. If n is the lifespan of Amoeba C in hours, what is the lifespan of Amoeba A, in terms of n ?

F. $5 + 2n$
G. $7 + n$
H. $7n$
J. $10n$
K. $2(5 + n)$

13. In the standard (x,y) coordinate plane, 3 corners of a rectangle are $(1,-1)$, $(-4,-1)$, and $(1,-4)$. Where is the rectangle's fourth corner?

A. $(1,4)$
B. $(-1,4)$
C. $(-1,1)$
D. $(-1,-4)$
E. $(-4,-4)$

14. Which of the following is a simplified form of $3x - 3y + 2x$?

F. $3(x - y + 2)$
G. $(x - y)(3 + 2x)$
H. $x(5 - 3y)$
J. $x - 3y$
K. $5x - 3y$

15. In the parallelogram below, what is the measure of $\angle DAC$?

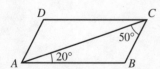

A. $20°$
B. $30°$
C. $40°$
D. $50°$
E. $70°$

GO ON TO THE NEXT PAGE.

2   **2**

16. What is the slope of any line parallel to the line $3x + 5y = 8$?

   DO YOUR FIGURING HERE.

   F. -3

   G. $-\frac{3}{5}$

   H. $\frac{3}{8}$

   J. 3

   K. 8

17. If $x > 0$ and $2x^2 - 5x - 12 = 0$, then $x = $?

   A. $\frac{3}{2}$

   B. 2

   C. 4

   D. 5

   E. 12

18. The lengths of the sides of a triangle are 3, 8, and 9 inches. How many inches long is the shortest side of a similar triangle that has a perimeter of 60 inches?

   F. 9
   G. 11
   H. 20
   J. 24
   K. 27

19. Jeans that normally sell for $35.95 are on sale for 25% off. How much do they cost during the sale, to the nearest dollar?

   A. $ 9
   B. $11
   C. $26
   D. $27
   E. $29

20. Which of the following is a factored form of $4x^3y + 4xy^3$?

   F. $4x^3y^3(y + x)$
   G. $4xy(x^2 + y^2)$
   H. $8xy(x^2 + y^2)$
   J. $4x^3y^3$
   K. $8x^4y^4$

21. If $2x - y = 6$, and $x + 4y = 12$, what is the value of y ?

   A. -6
   B. 0
   C. 1
   D. 2
   E. 3

GO ON TO THE NEXT PAGE.

2   **2**

22. There are 16 ounces in a pound. If 1.5 pounds of hamburger costs $2.88, what is the cost per ounce?

F. $0.12
G. $0.18
H. $0.88
J. $1.92
K. $4.32

DO YOUR FIGURING HERE.

23. The 2 squares in the figure below have the same dimensions. The vertex of one square is at the center of the other square. What is the area of the shaded region, in square inches?

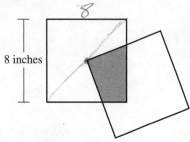

8 inches

A. 4
B. 8
C. 16
D. 32
E. 64

24. A salesperson earns $(6h + 0.05t)$ dollars, where h is the number of hours worked, and t is the total amount of her sales. What does she earn for working 10 hours with $230.80 in sales?

F. $ 71.54
G. $ 74.54
H. $175.40
J. $251.80
K. $295.80

$6 \cdot 10 + 0.$

GO ON TO THE NEXT PAGE.

2   **2**

25. A floor has the dimensions shown below. How many square feet of carpeting are needed to cover the entire floor?

(Note: All angles are right angles.)

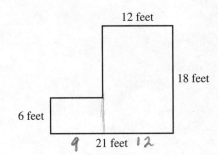

12 feet

18 feet

6 feet

9   21 feet 12

A.   57
B.   72
C.   162
D.   270
E.   324

26. Which of the following is the graph of the solution set of $x - 1 < -2$? $x < -1$

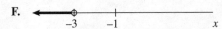

F.

    −3   −1 x

G.

    −3   −1 x

H.

    −3   −1 x

J.

    −3   −1 x

K.

        −1   3 x

27. Which of the following is less than $\frac{3}{4}$?

A. $\frac{5}{6}$ .75

B. $\frac{5}{7} = .71$

C. $\frac{6}{8}$

D. $\frac{8}{10}$

E. $\frac{10}{13}$

GO ON TO THE NEXT PAGE.

DO YOUR FIGURING HERE.

28. What is the area, in square meters, of a right triangle with sides of length 8 meters, 15 meters, and 17 meters?

   F. 40

   G. 60

   H. 68

   J. 120

   K. $127\frac{1}{2}$

29. When the marching band is arranged in rows of 4 people each, the last row is one person short. When it is arranged in rows of 5, the last row is still one person short. When arranged in rows of 6, the last row is *still* one person short. What is the least possible number of people in the marching band?

   A. 11
   B. 14
   C. 59
   D. 89
   E. 119

30. A triangle has sides of length 2.5 feet and 4 feet. Which of the following CANNOT be the length of the third side, in feet?

   F. 1
   G. 2
   H. 3
   J. 4
   K. 5

31. For all $a > 0$, $\frac{1}{a} + \frac{2}{3} = ?$

   A. $\frac{2}{3a}$

   B. $\frac{3}{3a}$

   C. $\frac{3 + 2a}{3a}$

   D. $\frac{3}{3 + a}$

   E. $\frac{3 + 2a}{3 + a}$

GO ON TO THE NEXT PAGE.

2   **2**

32. In the right triangle below, how long is side $\overline{AB}$?

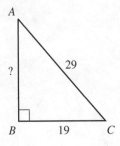

F. $\sqrt{29^2 - 19^2}$

G. $\sqrt{29^2 + 19^2}$

H. $29^2 - 19^2$

J. $29^2 + 19^2$

K. $29 - 19$

33. If the length of a square is increased by 1 inch and the width is increased by 2 inches, a rectangle is formed. If each side of the original square is x inches long, what is the area of the new rectangle, in square inches?

A. $2x + 3$

B. $4x + 6$

C. $x^2 + 2$

D. $x^2 + 3x + 2$

E. $x^2 + 3x + 3$

34. If $\sin \alpha = \frac{12}{13}$, and $\cos \alpha = \frac{5}{13}$, then $\tan \alpha = ?$

F. $\frac{5}{12}$

G. $\frac{7}{13}$

H. $\frac{12}{5}$

J. $\frac{17}{13}$

K. $\frac{60}{13}$

35. Which of the following best describes the graph on the number line below?

A. $|x| = -1$

B. $|x| < 0.5$

C. $-2 < x < 0$

D. $-0.5 < x < -1.5$

E. $-0.5 > x > -1.5$

GO ON TO THE NEXT PAGE.

2 △ △ △ △ △ △ △ △ △ **2**

36. A performance was rated on a 3-point scale by an audience. A rating of 1 was given by 30% of the audience, a rating of 2 by 60%, and a rating of 3 by 10%. To the nearest tenth, what was the average of the ratings?

DO YOUR FIGURING HERE.

F. 1.2
G. 1.5
H. 1.8
J. 2.0
K. 2.2

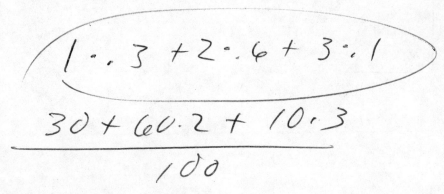

$$\frac{1\cdot .3 + 2\cdot .6 + 3\cdot .1}{30 + 60\cdot 2 + 10\cdot 3}$$
$$100$$

37. In the right triangle below, if $\overline{BC}$ is 4 inches long, how many inches long is $\overline{AB}$?

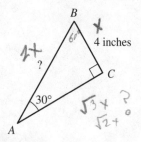

A. 4
B. $4\sqrt{2}$
C. $4\sqrt{3}$
D. 6
E. 8

38. What is the largest possible product for 2 even integers whose sum is 38 ?

F. 72
G. 76
H. 136
J. 280
K. 360

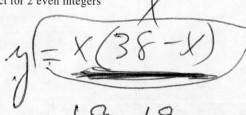

$y = x(38 - x)$

$19 \cdot 19$

GO ON TO THE NEXT PAGE.

2 △ △ △ △ △ △ △ △ △ 2

39. In the figure below, lines *j* and *k* are parallel, lines *m* and *n* are parallel, and the measures of 2 angles are shown. What is the measure of ∠*x* ?

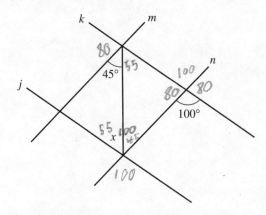

A. 45°
B. 55°
C. 65°
D. 75°
E. 80°

40. In the (*x*,*y*) coordinate plane, what is the *y*-intercept of the line 6*x* − 2*y* = 6 ?

F. −3
G. −2
H. 0
J. 3
K. 6

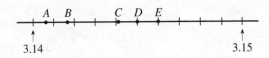

41. Among the points graphed on the number line below, which is closest to π ?

(Note: π ≈ 3.1415926)

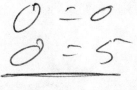

A. *A*
B. *B*
C. *C*
D. *D*
E. *E*

42. For what value of *a* would the following system of equations have an infinite number of solutions?

$$2x - y = 6$$
$$8x - 4y = 3a$$

F. 2
G. 6
H. 8
J. 18
K. 24

$y = mx + b$

$8x - 4(2x - 6) = 3a$

$8x - 8x + 24 = 3a$

$24 = 3a$

GO ON TO THE NEXT PAGE.

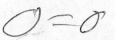

2   **2**

43. The expression $(180 - x)$ is the degree measure of a nonzero acute angle if and only if:

- **A.** $0 < x < 45$
- **B.** $0 < x < 90$
- **C.** $45 < x < 90$
- **D.** $90 < x < 135$
- **E.** $90 < x < 180$

DO YOUR FIGURING HERE.

44. If $x + y = -2$, and $x - y = -3$, then $x^2 - y^2 = ?$

- **F.** 13
- **G.** 6
- **H.** 5
- **J.** −5
- **K.** −6

45. The sides of a triangle are 5, 12, and 13 inches long. What is the angle between the 2 shortest sides?

- **A.** 30°
- **B.** 45°
- **C.** 60°
- **D.** 90°
- **E.** 120°

46. In the standard (x,y) coordinate plane, if the x-coordinate of each point on a line is 4 less than twice its y-coordinate, the slope of the line is:

- **F.** −4
- **G.** −2
- **H.** $\dfrac{1}{2}$
- **J.** 2
- **K.** 4

GO ON TO THE NEXT PAGE.

2 △ △ △ △ △ △ △ △ △ 2

47. From a hot air balloon, the angle between a radio antenna straight below and the base of the library downtown is 57°, as shown below. If the distance between the radio antenna and the library is 1.3 miles, how many miles high is the balloon?

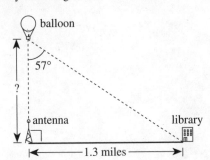

A. 1.3 sin 57°

B. 1.3 tan 57°

C. $\dfrac{1.3}{\sin 57°}$

D. $\dfrac{1.3}{\cos 57°}$

E. $\dfrac{1.3}{\tan 57°}$

48. Two numbers have a greatest common factor of 4 and a least common multiple of 24. Which of the following could be the pair of numbers?

F. 4 and 8
G. 4 and 12
H. 8 and 12
J. 8 and 24
K. 12 and 24

49. Listed below are 5 functions, each denoted $g(x)$ and each involving a real number constant $c \geq 2$. If $f(x) = 2^x$, which of these 5 functions yields the greatest value for $f(g(x))$, for all $x > 1$?

A. $g(x) = cx$

B. $g(x) = \dfrac{c}{x}$

C. $g(x) = \dfrac{x}{c}$

D. $g(x) = x - c$

E. $g(x) = \log_c x$

GO ON TO THE NEXT PAGE.

2

50. Line segments $\overline{AB}$, $\overline{BC}$, and $\overline{CD}$, which represent the 3 dimensions of the rectangular box shown below, have lengths of 4 inches, 3 inches, and 5 inches, respectively. What is the sine of $\angle DAC$?

DO YOUR FIGURING HERE.

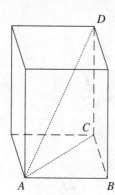

F. 1

G. $\frac{4}{5}$

H. $\frac{\sqrt{2}}{2}$

J. $\frac{3}{5}$

K. $\frac{3\sqrt{2}}{10}$

51. A certain circle has an area of π square inches. How many inches long is its radius?

A. $\frac{1}{2}$

B. 1

C. 2

D. $\frac{\pi}{2}$

E. π

52. The equation of line s below is $y = mx + b$. Which of the following could be an equation for line t ?

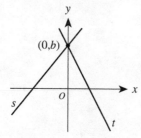

F. $y = 2mx$
G. $y = 2mx + b$
H. $y = 2mx - b$
J. $y = -2mx + b$
K. $y = -2mx - b$

GO ON TO THE NEXT PAGE.

2 △ △ △ △ △ △ △ △ △ **2**

53. The equation $x^2 - 10x + k = 0$ has only one solution
for x. What is the value of k ?

   A.   0
   B.   5
   C.   10
   D.   20
   E.   25

DO YOUR FIGURING HERE.

54. In the standard (x,y) coordinate plane, what is the
slope of the line that passes through the origin and the
point $\left(\frac{1}{2}, \frac{2}{3}\right)$?

   F. $\frac{1}{2}$

   G. $\frac{1}{3}$

   H. $\frac{2}{3}$

   J. $\frac{3}{4}$

   K. $\frac{4}{3}$

55. If A, B, and C are real numbers, and if $ABC = 1$, which
of the following conditions *must* be true?

   A. AB is equal to $\frac{1}{C}$

   B. A, B, and C must all be positive

   C.   Either $A = 1$, $B = 1$, or $C = 1$

   D.   Either $A = 0$, $B = 0$, or $C = 0$

   E.   Either $A < 1$, $B < 1$, or $C < 1$

56. The length of a rectangle is $(x + 5)$ units and its width is
$(x + 7)$ units. Which of the following expresses the
remaining area of the rectangle, in square units, if a
square, x units in length, is removed from the interior of
the rectangle?

   F.   12
   G.   35
   H. $2x + 12$
   J. $12x + 35$
   K. $x^2 + 12x + 35$

GO ON TO THE NEXT PAGE.

2 △ △ △ △ △ △ △ △ △ **2**

DO YOUR FIGURING HERE.

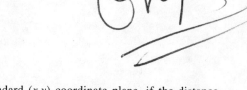

57. What is the smallest positive value for x where $y = \sin 2x$ reaches its maximum?

A. $\frac{\pi}{4}$

B. π

C. $\frac{3\pi}{2}$

D. 2π

E. $\frac{5\pi}{2}$

58. In the standard (x,y) coordinate plane, if the distance between points $(8,a)$ and $(a,1)$ is 5 coordinate units, which of the following could be the value of a ?

F. 5
G. 3
H. −3
J. −4
K. −5

59. Martin has an empty bag and puts in 3 red marbles. He now wants to put in enough green marbles so the probability of drawing a red marble at random from the bag is $\frac{1}{4}$. How many green marbles should he put in?

A. 1
B. 3
C. 5
D. 9
E. 12

60. How many different integer values of n satisfy the inequality $\frac{1}{13} < \frac{2}{n} < \frac{1}{10}$?

F. 1
G. 2
H. 3
J. 4
K. 5

END OF TEST 2

STOP! DO NOT TURN THE PAGE UNTIL TOLD TO DO SO.

DO NOT RETURN TO THE PREVIOUS TEST.

3 ████████████████████████████████ **3**

READING TEST
35 Minutes—40 Questions

DIRECTIONS: There are four passages in this test. Each passage is followed by several questions. After reading a passage, choose the best answer to each question and fill in the corresponding oval on your answer document. You may refer to the passages as often as necessary.

Passage I

PROSE FICTION: This passage is adapted from Paule Marshall's short story "Reena" (©1983 by The Feminist Press).

We met—Reena and myself—at the funeral of her aunt who had been my godmother and whom I had also called aunt, Aunt Vi, and loved, for she and her house had been, respectively, a source of understanding and a
5 place of calm for me as a child. Reena entered the church where the funeral service was being held as though she, not the minister, were coming to officiate, sat down among the immediate family up front, and turned to inspect those behind her. I saw her face then.

10 It was a good copy of the original. The familiar mold was there, that is, and the configuration of bone beneath the skin was the same despite the slight fleshiness I had never seen there before, her features had even retained their distinctive touches: the positive set
15 to her mouth, the assertive lift to her nose, the same insistent, unsettling eyes which when she was angry became as black as her skin—and this was total, unnerving, and very beautiful. Yet something had happened to her face. It was different despite its sameness.
20 Aging even while it remained enviably young. Time had sketched in, very lightly, the evidence of the twenty years.

Her real name had been Doreen, a standard for girls among West Indians (her mother, like my parents,
25 was from Barbados), but she had changed it to Reena on her twelfth birthday—"As a present to myself"—and had enforced the change on her family by refusing to answer to the old name. "Reena. With two e's!" she would say and imprint those e's on your mind with the
30 indelible black of her eyes and a thin threatening finger that was like a quill.

She and I had not been friends through our own choice. Rather, our mothers, who had known each other since childhood, had forced the relationship. And from
35 the beginning, I had been at a disadvantage. For Reena, as early as the age of twelve, had had a quality that was unique, superior, and therefore dangerous. She seemed defined, even then, all of a piece, the raw edges of her adolescence smoothed over; indeed, she seemed to have
40 escaped adolescence altogether and made one dazzling leap from childhood into the very arena of adult life.

At thirteen, for instance, she was reading Zola, Hauptmann, Steinbeck, while I was still in the thrall of the Little Minister and Lorna Doone. When I could
45 only barely conceive of the world beyond Brooklyn, she was talking of the Civil War in Spain, lynchings in the South, Hitler in Poland—and talking with the outrage and passion of a revolutionary. I would try, I remember, to console myself with the thought that she
50 was really an adult masquerading as a child, which meant that I could not possibly be her match.

For her part, Reena put up with me and was, by turns, patronizing and impatient. I merely served as the audience before whom she rehearsed her ideas and the
55 yardstick by which she measured her worldliness and knowledge.

"Do you realize that this stupid country supplied Japan with the scrap iron to make the weapons she's now using against it?" she had shouted at me once.

60 I had not known that.

Just as she overwhelmed me, she overwhelmed her family, with the result that despite a half dozen brothers and sisters who consumed quantities of bread and jam whenever they visited us, she behaved like an only
65 child and got away with it. Her father, a gentle man with skin the color of dried tobacco and with the nose Reena had inherited jutting out like a crag from his nondescript face, had come from Georgia and was always making jokes about having married a for-
70 eigner—Reena's mother being from the West Indies. When not joking, he seemed slightly bewildered by his large family and so in awe of Reena that he avoided her. Reena's mother, a small, dry, formidably black woman, was less a person to me than the abstract prin-
75 ciple of force, power, energy. She was alternately strict and indulgent with Reena and, despite the inconsistency, surprisingly effective.

1. Of the persons mentioned in the passage, which of the following had the greatest positive effect on the narrator as a child?

A. Reena's minister
B. Reena's father
C. Aunt Vi's godmother
D. Aunt Vi

GO ON TO THE NEXT PAGE.

3   3

2. In order to ensure that her family would call her Reena, and not Doreen, Reena would:

    I. point at them threateningly.
    II. start crying loudly.
    III. shout and stamp her feet.
    IV. stare meaningfully.

  F. I and II only
  G. I and IV only
  H. II and IV only
  J. I, II, and IV only

3. It can reasonably be inferred from the passage that Reena's mother, as compared with Reena's father, was a:

  A. more strict and much funnier parent.
  B. more retiring and less authoritative parent.
  C. more forceful and effective parent.
  D. less argumentative and more gentle parent.

4. Reena's talking about which of the following subjects intimidated the narrator?

    I. Hitler in Poland
    II. The Civil War in Spain
    III. The thrall of the Little Minister

  F. I only
  G. II only
  H. III only
  J. I and II only

5. As it is described in the first paragraph, Reena's entrance into the church suggests that Reena is a woman who:

  A. is quite confident.
  B. is used to officiating at funerals.
  C. is deeply unhappy.
  D. has changed remarkably.

6. Reena apparently had the sort of character that her father found it necessary to:

  F. discipline her severely.
  G. keep her at a distance.
  H. praise her constantly.
  J. humor her endlessly.

7. The narrator's point of view is that of:

  A. a child.
  B. an adolescent.
  C. a psychologist.
  D. an adult.

8. The statement that Reena had a half dozen brothers and sisters yet "behaved like an only child and got away with it" (lines 64–65) supports the narrator's feeling that Reena:

  F. was completely and utterly selfish.
  G. had been her best friend for years.
  H. did not like her brothers and sisters.
  J. could overwhelm just about anyone.

9. According to the narrator, adolescence is a stage usually characterized by:

  A. raw edges.
  B. abstract principles.
  C. dazzling leaps.
  D. impatient patronizing.

10. The fifth paragraph (lines 52–56) suggests that Reena's relationship with the narrator was primarily characterized by:

  F. Reena's patience with the narrator.
  G. Reena's exploitation of the narrator.
  H. the narrator's devotion to Reena.
  J. the narrator's increasing worldliness.

GO ON TO THE NEXT PAGE.

3

3

Passage II

SOCIAL SCIENCE: This passage is adapted from Jack Weatherford's *Indian Givers: How the Indians of America Transformed the World* (©1988 by Jack McIver Weatherford).

Egalitarian democracy and liberty as we know them today owe little to Europe. They are not Greco-Roman derivatives somehow revived by the French in the eighteenth century. They entered modern western
5 thought as American Indian notions translated into European language and culture.

In language, custom, religion, and written law, the Spaniards descended directly from ancient Rome, yet they brought nothing resembling a democratic tradition
10 with them to America. The French and Dutch who set-tled parts of North America also settled many other parts of the world that did not become democratic. Democracy did not spring up on French-speaking Haiti any more than in Southern Africa, where the British
15 and Dutch settled about the same time that they settled in North America.

Even the Netherlands and Britain, the two show-cases for European democracy, had difficulty grafting democracy onto monarchical and aristocratic systems
20 soaked in the strong traditions of class privilege. During the reign of George III of Great Britain, while the United States was fighting for its independence, only one person in twenty could vote in England. And in Ireland no Catholic could hold office or vote. In
25 their centuries of struggle to suppress the Irish, the British possibly encumbered their own democratic development.

American anglophiles occasionally point to the signing of the Magna Carta by King John on the battle-
30 field of Runnymede in 1215 as the start of civil liberties and democracy in the English-speaking world. This document, however, merely moved slightly away from monarchy and toward oligarchy by increasing the power of the aristocracy. It continued the traditional
35 European vacillation between government by a single strong ruler and by an oligarchic class. An oligarchy is not an incipient democracy, and a step away from monarchy does not necessarily mean a step toward democracy. In the same tradition, the election of the
40 pope by a college of cardinals did not make the Vatican into a democratic institution, nor did the Holy Roman Empire become a democracy merely because a congress of aristocrats elected the emperor.

When the Dutch built colonies in America, power
45 in their homeland rested securely in the hands of the aristocracy and the burghers, who composed only a quarter of the population. A city such as Amsterdam fell under the rule of a council of thirty-six men, none of whom was elected; instead each council member
50 inherited his office and held it until death.

Henry Steele Commager wrote that during the Enlightenment "Europe was ruled by the wellborn, the rich, the privileged, by those who held their places by divine favor, inheritance, prescription, or purchase."
55 The philosophers and thinkers of the Enlightenment became quite complacent and self-congratulatory because the "enlightened despots" such as Catherine of Russia and Frederick of Prussia read widely and showed literary inclinations. Too many philosophers
60 became court pets and because of that believed that Europe was moving toward enlightened democracy. As Commager explained it, Europe only imagined the Enlightenment, but America enacted it. This Enlightenment grew as much from its roots in Indian
65 culture as from any other source.

When Americans try to trace their democratic her-itage back through the writings of French and English political thinkers of the Enlightenment, they often forget that these people's thoughts were heavily shaped
70 by the democratic traditions and the state of nature of the American Indians. The concept of the "noble savage" derived largely from writings about the American Indians, and even though the picture grew romanticized and distorted, the writers were only
75 romanticizing and distorting something that really did exist. The Indians did live in a fairly democratic condi-tion, they were egalitarian, and they did live in greater harmony with nature.

The modern notions of democracy based on egali-
80 tarian principles and a federated government of over-lapping powers arose from the unique blend of European and Indian political ideas and institutions along the Atlantic coast between 1607 and 1776. Modern democracy as we know it today is as much the
85 legacy of the American Indians, particularly the Iroquois and the Algonquians, as it is of the British set-tlers, of French political theory, or of all the failed efforts of the Greeks and Romans.

The discovery of new forms of political life in
90 America freed the imaginations of Old World thinkers to envision utopias, socialism, communism, anarchism, and dozens of other social forms. Scarcely any political theory or movement of the last three centuries has not shown the impact of this great political awakening that
95 the Indians provoked among the Europeans.

11. According to the passage, two Native American peo-ples who contributed greatly to the development of modern democracy were the:

A. Iroquois and the Cherokee.
B. Iroquois and the Algonquians.
C. Algonquians and the Seminoles.
D. Cherokee and the Cheyenne.

GO ON TO THE NEXT PAGE.

3 ▬▬▬▬▬▬▬▬▬▬▬▬▬▬▬▬▬▬▬▬▬▬ **3**

12. The author of the passage would most likely agree with which of the following statements?

   F. European political thinkers of the sixteenth century created the notion of a completely egalitarian society.
   G. The efforts of the Spaniards to create a democratic society in the New World failed due to the unfavorable climate of the New World.
   H. American Indians generally are not given as much credit as they deserve with regard to their contribution to modern democratic political theory.
   J. The roots of modern democracy can be traced directly back to the Holy Roman Empire.

13. Historian Henry Steele Commager's belief that "Europe only imagined the Enlightenment, but America enacted it" (lines 62–63) refers to the idea, presented in the passage, that:

   A. European political thinkers wrote a great deal about democracy and liberty, but democracy and liberty did not really manifest themselves until European and Native American political ideas met in the New World.
   B. European political thinkers lived utopian lives that prevented them from seeing the monarchical excesses of European society.
   C. the Dutch and Spanish political thinkers had a history of democratic traditions, but they were not able to translate their ideas into a workable democracy in America.
   D. Native Americans, when introduced to the democratic ideals of European political thinkers, readily adopted the Europeans' political philosophies.

14. One of the main ideas of the passage is that:

   F. democracy and liberty are political ideas derived primarily from the Greeks and Romans of the ancient world.
   G. the French and the Dutch who settled in America were the primary sources of democracy in the New World.
   H. modern democracy evolved from the interaction of Native American and European political thought in colonial America.
   J. Native Americans were initially opposed to the democratic traditions that the Europeans brought to the New World.

15. It can be inferred from the sixth paragraph (lines 51–65) that historian Henry Steele Commager would agree with the statement that, during the Enlightenment, Europe was mainly ruled by:

   A. a democratic majority.
   B. a college of cardinals.
   C. the aristocratic class.
   D. the intellectual elite.

16. The passage argues that at the time of European contact with Native Americans in the 1600s, the political systems of Native Americans could best be characterized as being:

   F. essentially nonexistent.
   G. ruled by a few Indian chiefs who were similar to Europe's "enlightened despots."
   H. a monarchical system of government.
   J. fairly democratic and egalitarian.

17. The passage specifies that the law of which of the following countries descended directly from that of ancient Rome?

   A. Britain
   B. France
   C. The Netherlands
   D. Spain

18. According to the fourth paragraph (lines 28–43), the signing of the Magna Carta:

   I. increased the power of the English aristocracy.
   II. decreased the power of the English monarchy.
   III. created the first truly democratic government in England.

   F. I only
   G. I and II only
   H. I and III only
   J. II and III only

19. According to the passage, the attitude of some philosophers of the Enlightenment toward European monarchs and their governments was often:

   A. not critical enough, because the philosophers were on too friendly terms with the monarchs.
   B. not critical enough, because the philosophers needed to justify European expansion in North America.
   C. too critical, because the philosophers personally disliked the monarchs.
   D. too critical, because the philosophers didn't understand Greco-Roman ideas well enough to develop sound theories.

20. According to the passage, at the same time they settled in North America, the British and the Dutch also settled in:

   I. Haiti.
   II. South Africa.
   III. Greece.

   F. I only
   G. II only
   H. I and II only
   J. I and III only

GO ON TO THE NEXT PAGE.

3   3

Passage III

HUMANITIES: This passage is adapted from Annie Dillard's *The Writing Life* (©1989 by Annie Dillard).

When you write, you lay out a line of words. The line of words is a miner's pick, a woodcarver's gouge, a surgeon's probe. You wield it, and it digs a path you follow. Soon you find yourself deep in new territory. Is
5 it a dead end, or have you located the real subject? You will know tomorrow, or this time next year.

You make the path boldly and follow it fearfully. You go where the path leads. At the end of the path, you find a box canyon. You hammer out reports, dis-
10 patch bulletins.

The writing has changed, in your hands, and in a twinkling, from an expression of your notions to an epistemological tool. The new place interests you because it is not clear. You attend. In your humility,
15 you lay down the words carefully, watching all the angles. Now the earlier writing looks soft and careless. Process is nothing; erase your tracks. The path is not the work. I hope your tracks have grown over; I hope birds ate the crumbs; I hope you will toss it all and not
20 look back.

The line of words is a hammer. You hammer against the walls of your house. You tap the walls, lightly, everywhere. After giving many years' attention to these things, you know what to listen for. Some of
25 the walls are bearing walls; they have to stay, or every-thing will fall down. Other walls can go with impunity; you can hear the difference. Unfortunately, it is often the bearing wall that has to go. It cannot be helped. There is only one solution, which appalls you, but there
30 it is. Knock it out. Duck.

Courage utterly opposes the bold hope that this is such fine stuff the work needs it, or the world. Courage, exhausted, stands on bare reality: this writing weakens the work. You must demolish the work and start over.
35 You can save some of the sentences, like bricks. It will be a miracle if you can save some of the paragraphs, no matter how excellent in themselves or hard-won. You can waste a year worrying about it, or you can get it over with now. (Are you a woman, or a mouse?)

40 The part you must jettison is not only the best-written part; it is also, oddly, that part which was to have been the very point. It is the original key passage, the passage on which the rest was to hang, and from which you yourself drew the courage to begin.

45 Putting a book together is interesting and exhila-rating. It is sufficiently difficult and complex that it engages all your intelligence. It is life at its most free. Your freedom as a writer is not freedom of expression in the sense of wild blurting; you may not let it rip. It is
50 life at its most free, if you are fortunate enough to be able to try it, because you select your materials, invent your task, and pace yourself.

The obverse of this freedom, of course, is that your work is so meaningless, so fully for yourself alone, and
55 so worthless to the world, that no one except you cares whether you do it well, or ever. You are free to make several thousand close judgment calls a day. Your freedom is a by-product of your days' triviality.

Here is a fairly sober version of what happens in
60 the small room between the writer and the work itself. It is similar to what happens between a painter and a canvas.

First you shape the vision of what the projected work of art will be. The vision, I stress, is no marvelous
65 thing: it is the work's intellectual structure and aes-thetic surface. It is a chip of mind, a pleasing intellec-tual object. It is a vision of the work, not of the world. It is a glowing thing, a blurred thing of beauty. Its structure is at once luminous and translucent; you can
70 see the world through it.

Many aspects of the work are still uncertain, of course; you know that. You know that if you proceed you will change things and learn things, that the form will grow under your hands and develop new and richer
75 lights. But that change will not alter the vision or its deep structures; it will only enrich it. You know that, and you are right.

But you are wrong if you think that in the actual writing, or in the actual painting, you are filling in the
80 vision. You cannot fill in the vision. You cannot even bring the vision to light. You are wrong if you think you can in any way take the vision and tame it to the page. The page is jealous and tyrannical; the page is made of time and matter; the page always wins. The
85 vision is not so much destroyed, exactly, as it is, by the time you have finished, forgotten.

21. As it is used in line 47, the word *engages* most nearly means:

A. demands.
B. defeats.
C. envisions.
D. ensures.

22. The author compares the interaction between writers and their work to that in all of the following occupa-tions EXCEPT:

F. surgeon.
G. miner.
H. painter.
J. musician.

GO ON TO THE NEXT PAGE.

3 ═══════════════════════════════════ **3**

23. The author suggests that the best-written part of a piece of writing is often, ironically, the part of a piece of writing that the writer:

  A. finds most painful.
  B. must throw away.
  C. feels is most dramatic.
  D. produced in a wild burst.

24. Which of the following best states the main point of the passage?

  F. Writers need to be aggressive and intellectual.
  G. The path is really the same thing as the work.
  H. Writing is a humbling and transforming experience.
  J. In writing, it is crucial that you consider your audience.

25. The main emphasis of the third paragraph (lines 11–20) regarding the nature of the act of writing is on:

  A. why writers need to learn humility.
  B. keeping the line of words from being altered.
  C. how a writer's perception of her work changes.
  D. how writing expresses notions of the self.

26. As it is used in line 9, the phrase *hammer out* most nearly means:

  F. break.
  G. write.
  H. erase.
  J. remove.

27. An analogy made in the passage is that sentences are to writing as:

  A. courage is to bare reality.
  B. bearing walls are to vision.
  C. bricks are to building.
  D. painting is to freedom.

28. The author claims that putting a book together is life at its most free because:

  F. you select your own materials, task, and pace.
  G. you can fully express your inner self.
  H. nothing is more intellectually demanding.
  J. you create something valued by the entire world.

29. The author of the passage describes the vision as:

  I. a chip of mind.
  II. the by-product of your day's triviality.
  III. a glowing thing.

  A. II only
  B. III only
  C. I and II only
  D. I and III only

30. The author asserts that it will be a miracle if, during the course of revision, the writer is able to salvage:

  F. some of the bricks.
  G. any of the words.
  H. some of the paragraphs.
  J. all of the path.

GO ON TO THE NEXT PAGE.

Passage IV

NATURAL SCIENCE: This passage is adapted from Frank Close, Michael Marten, and Christine Sutton's *The Particle Explosion* (©1987 by Frank Close, Michael Marten, and Christine Sutton).

The detector is a kind of ultimate microscope, which records what happens when a [subatomic] particle strikes another particle, either in a fixed target such as a lump of metal or a chamber filled with a gas
5 or liquid, or in an on-coming beam in a collider. The 1950s and 60s were the age of the bubble chamber, so called because electrically charged particles moving through it produce trails of tiny bubbles in the liquid filling the chamber. [But today most] experiments are
10 based on electronic detectors.

Detectors rarely record *all* the particle collisions that occur in a particular experiment. Usually collisions occur thousands of times a second and no equipment can respond quickly enough to record all the associated
15 data. Moreover, many of the collisions may reveal mundane 'events' that are relatively well understood. So the experimenters often define beforehand the types of event that may reveal the particles they are trying to find, and program the detector accordingly. This is
20 what a major part of the electronics in a detector is all about. The electronics form a filter system, which decides within a split second whether a collision has produced the kind of event that the experimenters have defined as interesting and which should therefore be
25 recorded by the computer. Of the thousands of collisions per second, only one may actually be recorded. One of the advantages of this approach is its flexibility: the filter system can always be reprogrammed to select different types of event.

30 Often, computer graphics enable the events to be displayed on computer monitors as images, which help the physicists to discover whether their detector is functioning in the correct way and to interpret complex or novel events.

35 Imaging has always played an important role in particle physics. In earlier days, much of the data was actually recorded in photographic form—in pictures of tracks through cloud chambers and bubble chambers, or even directly in the emulsion of special photographic
40 film. Many of these images have a peculiar aesthetic appeal, resembling abstract art. Even at the subatomic level nature presents images of itself that reflect our own imaginings.

The essential clue to understanding the images of
45 particle physics is that they show the *tracks* of the particles, not the particles themselves. What a pion, for instance, really looks like remains a mystery, but its passage through a substance—solid, liquid, or gas—can be recorded. Particle physicists have become as adept at
50 interpreting the types of track left by different particles as the American Indians were at interpreting the tracks of an enemy.

A number of simple clues immediately narrows down the possibilities. For instance, many detectors are
55 based around a magnet. This is because the tracks of electrically-charged particles are bent in a magnetic field. A curving track is the signature of a charged particle. And if you know the direction of the magnetic field, then the way that the track curves—to left or
60 right, say—tells you whether the particle is positively or negatively charged. The radius of curvature is also important, and depends on the particle's velocity and mass. Electrons, for instance, which are very lightweight particles, can curve so much in a magnetic field
65 that their tracks form tight little spirals.

Most of the subatomic zoo of particles have brief lives, less than a billionth of a second. But this is often long enough for the particle to leave a measurable track. Relatively long-lived particles leave long tracks,
70 which can pass right through a detector. Shorter-lived particles, on the other hand, usually decay visibly, giving birth to two or more new particles. These decays are often easily identified in images: a single track turns into several tracks.

75 Neutral particles present more of a headache to experimenters. Particles without an electric charge leave no tracks in a detector, so their presence can be deduced only from their interactions or their decay products. If you see two tracks starting at a common
80 point, apparently arising from nowhere, you can be almost certain that this is where a neutral particle has decayed into two charged particles.

Our perception of nature has deepened not only because the accelerators have increased in power, but
85 also because the detection techniques have grown more sophisticated. The quality of particle imagery and the range of information it provides have both improved over the years.

31. The main idea of the passage is that:
  A. most particle collisions are "mundane" events.
  B. bubble chambers were constructed to capture high-energy particles.
  C. the technology for detecting particle images is improving.
  D. the detection of particle images has direct application to the study of nuclear energy.

32. The passage states that magnets affect atomic particles by:
  F. influencing the direction particles travel.
  G. turning particles into negatively charged electrons.
  H. increasing the life of particles.
  J. causing positive and negative particles to collide.

GO ON TO THE NEXT PAGE.

3 ▬▬▬▬▬▬▬▬▬▬▬▬▬▬▬▬▬▬▬▬▬ **3**

33. The passage states that which of the following particles leaves a long track?

    A. A positively charged particle
    B. A negatively charged particle
    C. A short-lived particle
    D. A long-lived particle

34. As it is used in line 46, the word *pion* precisely refers to:

    F. an image.
    G. a track.
    H. a particle.
    J. a molecule.

35. According to the passage, which of the following CANNOT be tracked electronically by experimenters?

    A. Electrically charged particles
    B. Pion particles
    C. Negatively charged particles
    D. Neutral particles

36. Which of the following statements would the authors most likely agree with?

    F. Most tracking of electrically charged particles is difficult and inaccurate.
    G. Tracking of electrically charged particles is still primitive because of unclear photographs.
    H. Short-lived particles are easier to track than long-lived particles.
    J. Electrically charged particles can be tracked with the right equipment and careful observation.

37. What, according to the passage, is one effect of charged particles passing through a bubble chamber?

    A. Collisions of the particles as they are stopped by the bubbles
    B. Computer images that can be greatly enhanced
    C. Photographs of the actual particles
    D. Patterns of tiny bubbles in the liquid filling the chamber

38. The passage suggests that the greatest difference between experiments done with a bubble chamber and those done with electronic detectors is that:

    F. bubble chambers are much better at tracking the particles.
    G. electronic detectors can track pions.
    H. electronic detectors are more selective of the particle events.
    J. electronic detectors can photograph the particles themselves.

39. How does the analogy likening the detector to the microscope function in the passage?

    A. It suggests that the detector, like the microscope, reveals to scientists a part of reality not easily seen.
    B. It presents the differences and similarities in the way a detector works compared to a microscope.
    C. It proves that all instruments are ultimately the same in the way that they function in a laboratory.
    D. It introduces the argument in the passage that all detectors, whether microscope, bubble chamber, or collider, present images that resemble abstract art.

40. What is the main idea of the second paragraph (lines 11–29)?

    F. Even the best detectors still miss most of the important collisions in an experiment.
    G. New technology allows scientists to select the collisions they want to record.
    H. Despite the new technology, detectors still record mostly mundane events.
    J. Scientists can now use computers to record virtually all the collisions in an experiment.

END OF TEST 3

STOP! DO NOT TURN THE PAGE UNTIL TOLD TO DO SO.

DO NOT RETURN TO A PREVIOUS TEST.

4 ○ ○ ○ ○ ○ ○ ○ ○ ○ **4**

SCIENCE REASONING TEST

35 Minutes—40 Questions

DIRECTIONS: There are seven passages in this test. Each passage is followed by several questions. After reading a passage, choose the best answer to each question and fill in the corresponding oval on your answer document. You may refer to the passages as often as necessary.

You are NOT permitted to use a calculator on this test.

Passage I

Bacteria reproduce by a process in which a single cell divides into two cells. The average time required for bacteria to divide and their population to double is called the *generation time*. Table 1 presents the generation time for a variety of bacteria at a given temperature.

Bacterial population growth occurs in a series of distinct steps referred to as a *bacterial growth curve*. It consists of 4 phases, which reflect changes in the cells' environment and metabolism over time. See Figure 1.

Table 1			
Bacterium	Growth medium	Temperature (°C)	Generation time (min)
Clostridium botulinum	glucose broth	37	35
Escherichia coli	glucose broth	37	17
Lactobacillus acidophilus	milk	37	66
Mycobacterium tuberculosis	synthetic medium	37	792
Pseudomonas aeruginosa	glucose broth	37	31
Shigella dysenteriae	milk	37	23
Staphylococcus aureus	glucose broth	37	32
Streptococcus lactis	lactose broth	30	48
Streptococcus lactis	glucose milk	37	26
Streptococcus lactis	peptone milk	37	37
Streptococcus pneumoniae	glucose broth	37	30
Xanthomonas campestris	glucose broth	25	74

Table adapted from P. L. Altman and D. S. Dittmer, eds., *Biology Data Book.* ©1972 by Pergamon Press PLC.

GO ON TO THE NEXT PAGE.

4 ◯ ◯ ◯ ◯ ◯ ◯ ◯ ◯ **4**

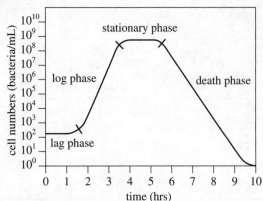

Figure 1

1. On the basis of the data presented in Table 1, if *Streptococcus lactis* was placed in a test tube containing growth medium at 37°C, one would predict its generation time to most likely be:

  A. less than 10 min.
  B. between 10 and 15 min.
  C. between 15 and 25 min.
  D. between 25 and 40 min.

2. The bacterial population increases most rapidly during which of the following phases?

  F. Lag phase
  G. Log phase
  H. Stationary phase
  J. Death phase

3. Based on the data presented in Table 1, which of the following bacteria growing in glucose broth took the longest time to double its population?

  A. *Pseudomonas aeruginosa*
  B. *Staphylococcus aureus*
  C. *Streptococcus pneumoniae*
  D. *Xanthomonas campestris*

4. Samples of growth medium containing milk were inoculated with the microorganisms depicted in Table 1 and put in an environmental chamber at 37°C. Which of the following bacteria would take closest to 1 hour to double its population?

  F. *Lactobacillus acidophilus*
  G. *Mycobacterium tuberculosis*
  H. *Shigella dysenteriae*
  J. *Streptococcus lactis*

5. Which of the following hypotheses about bacterial populations is supported by the data presented in Figure 1 ?

  A. Bacteria populations change at a constant rate throughout all the growth phases.
  B. Bacteria begin to increase immediately after transfer to a new growth medium.
  C. Bacteria begin to decrease immediately after transfer to a new growth medium.
  D. Bacteria require a period of adjustment before they begin to reproduce in a new growth medium.

GO ON TO THE NEXT PAGE.

4 ◯ ◯ ◯ ◯ ◯ ◯ ◯ ◯ ◯ 4

Passage II

Scientists noted an increase in plant growth in a lake. Increased growth of lake weeds and algae is usually the result of an increased input of nutrients, especially phosphates and nitrates. Nitrates are easily carried by water moving through the soil (*groundwater*) or streams. Phosphates can attach to soil or stream sediment particles. To determine the primary source of nutrients entering the lake, scientists conducted the following experiments.

Experiment 1

Scientists deduced that one source of phosphates and nitrates was seepage from wastewater systems buried in the soil near houses adjacent to the lake. Sampling wells were placed in locations where samples of groundwater, flowing from houses toward the lake, could be obtained daily. The results are presented in Table 1.

Table 1		
Date	Phosphate concentration (mg/L)	Nitrate concentration (mg/L)
House 1		
May 2	7.4	17.2
May 3	8.4	17.9
May 4	8.0	18.3
May 5	7.7	17.5
May 6	7.2	21.7
House 2		
May 2	9.1	22.8
May 3	9.7	25.1
May 4	11.8	22.5
May 5	9.1	21.3
May 6	8.8	18.2

Experiment 2

Scientists suspected that another source of nutrients was the runoff from nearby farm lands where fertilizers were applied. Water and suspended-sediment samples were obtained from two streams that flowed into the lake. These streams intercept surface runoff from the farm lands during rainfall and snowmelt. The results are depicted in Table 2.

Table 2			
Date	Suspended sediment concentration (mg/L)	Phosphate concentration (mg/L)	Nitrate concentration (mg/L)
Stream 1			
May 2	14.1	8.6	37.4
May 3	16.4	10.3	36.3
May 4	477.2	45.8	38.9
May 5	1,080.9	90.2	61.1
May 6	568.6	50.3	58.2
Stream 2			
May 2	8.3	7.6	10.7
May 3	15.5	15.2	24.8
May 4	25.1	27.3	27.4
May 5	17.2	16.9	21.6
May 6	8.3	10.4	11.1

6. How do the designs of Experiments 1 and 2 differ in terms of the sampling procedure?

   F. In Experiment 1, sampling was performed daily, whereas in Experiment 2, sampling was performed weekly.
   G. In Experiment 1, groundwater was sampled, whereas in Experiment 2, stream water was sampled.
   H. In Experiment 1, suspended sediment concentration was sampled, whereas in Experiment 2, suspended sediment concentration was not sampled.
   J. In Experiment 1, only nitrate concentration was sampled, whereas in Experiment 2, only phosphate concentration was sampled.

7. In order to obtain more information about the relationship between phosphates, nitrates, and plant growth, which of the following procedures should be performed next?

   A. Studying how the lake weeds grow in water maintained at different temperatures
   B. Growing algae in water samples containing several different phosphate and nitrate concentrations
   C. Adding large amounts of phosphates and nitrates to the soil of House 1
   D. Decreasing the amount of irrigation used by local farmers

GO ON TO THE NEXT PAGE.

4 ◯ ◯ ◯ ◯ ◯ ◯ ◯ ◯ ◯ **4**

8. Scientists suspected that fertilizers applied to farm lands also contaminated groundwater, which in turn increased nutrient input into the lake. In order to best test this hypothesis, which of the following should the scientists do next?

F. Sample water from three different streams
G. Measure the increase in algae and plant growth in the lake
H. Increase the amount of fertilizer applied to nearby farm lands
J. Vary the amount of fertilizer applied to nearby farm lands and sample groundwater flowing toward the lake in these fields

9. What was the scientists' hypothesis concerning lake plant growth in Experiment 1 ?

A. Wastewater from houses increases lake plant growth.
B. Runoff from farm lands decreases lake plant growth.
C. Rain falling in the vicinity of the houses and lake decreases lake plant growth.
D. Lake sediments release nitrates and phosphates into areas where plants are least abundant.

10. Given the results of Experiments 1 and 2, all of the following measures would reduce the input of phosphorus and nitrogen into the lake EXCEPT:

F. increasing the number of houses surrounding the lake.
G. limiting surface runoff and erosion on upstream farm lands.
H. limiting fertilizer application on upstream farm lands.
J. installing pipes to carry wastewater to a central treatment facility.

11. As phosphates move farther from their source, they are more likely to be adsorbed by the soil (removed from the water). Which of the following would most likely be the approximate phosphate concentration for House 1 on May 3 if the sampling well were closer to the wastewater system of the house?

A. 6.0 mg/L
B. 7.0 mg/L
C. 8.0 mg/L
D. 9.0 mg/L

GO ON TO THE NEXT PAGE.

4 ○ ○ ○ ○ ○ ○ ○ ○ **4**

Passage III

Motor vehicle exhaust is a significant source of several air pollutants, including the nitrogen oxides, NO_2 and NO. Scientists performed two experiments to investigate the levels and behavior of these pollutants and naturally occurring gases in the atmosphere near busy roadways.

Experiment 1

Scientists studied how NO_2 levels vary with vehicle use. They measured NO_2 levels hourly for a 24-hour period, 10 meters (m) downwind from six roadways. Each roadway had a combination of a different speed limit and *vehicle usage* (approximate number of vehicles per day). An average NO_2 value for each roadway was calculated in parts per billion (ppb). The results are in Table 1.

Table 1		
Roadway speed limit (km/hr)	Vehicle usage (vehicles/day)	Average NO_2 level (ppb)
60	10,000 20,000 30,000	5 9 13
100	10,000 20,000 30,000	8 13 22

Experiment 2

Next, the levels of NO_2 and NO were measured at 0, 50, and 100 m downwind from the 100 km/hr roadway which averaged 30,000 vehicles per day. The level of NO_2 decreased from 30 ppb at 0 m to 17 ppb at 100 m. The level of NO decreased from 150 ppb at 0 m to 42 ppb at 100 m.

(Note: The levels of NO_2 and NO that would be found far from pollution sources are 15 ppb and 35 ppb, respectively.)

Experiment 3

Ozone (O_3) is a naturally occurring gas in the atmosphere. Levels of ozone, in parts per million (ppm) were taken at various distances downwind from the 100 km/hr roadway which averaged 30,000 vehicles per day. The results are in Table 2.

(Note: The naturally occurring ozone concentration is 0.12 ppm.)

Table 2	
Distance from roadway (m)	Ozone level (ppm)
0	0.0075
50	0.02
100	0.04
150	0.075
200	0.09

12. Which of the following factors was varied in Experiment 3?

   F. Background concentration of NO_2
   G. Background level of ozone
   H. Distance from roadway
   J. Speed limit

13. According to the experimental results, one way to reduce levels of NO_2 in an area would be to:

   A. reduce the levels of naturally occurring ozone near roadways.
   B. lower speed limits on the roadways.
   C. raise speed limits on the roadways.
   D. require installation of ozone filters in motor vehicle exhaust systems.

14. According to the experimental results, if one compared ozone levels near a major highway to those in a remote wilderness location, ozone levels:

   F. near the highway would be higher than at the wilderness location.
   G. near the highway would be lower than at the wilderness location.
   H. near the highway would be the same as those in the wilderness location.
   J. would be detectable only near the highway.

GO ON TO THE NEXT PAGE.

4 ○ ○ ○ ○ ○ ○ ○ ○ ○ **4**

15. Carbon monoxide (CO) is another pollutant associated with motor vehicle exhaust. If carbon monoxide behaves like the nitrogen oxides in the experiments, one would expect that carbon monoxide levels:

A. would decrease over time.
B. would stay the same over time.
C. are higher near roadways than farther away from them.
D. are lower near roadways than farther away from them.

16. According to the results of the experiments, as distance from the roadway increases:

F. NO$_2$ and ozone levels both increase.
G. NO$_2$ levels increase and ozone levels decrease.
H. NO$_2$ levels increase and ozone levels stay the same.
J. NO$_2$ levels decrease and ozone levels increase.

17. A certain roadway has a speed limit of 100 km/hr and an average vehicle usage of 100,000 vehicles per day. One would predict that 10 m downwind from this roadway NO$_2$ levels are:

A. less than 8 ppb.
B. between 8 and 13 ppb.
C. between 13 and 22 ppb.
D. above 22 ppb.

GO ON TO THE NEXT PAGE.

4 ◯ ◯ ◯ ◯ ◯ ◯ ◯ ◯ **4**

Passage IV

The following experiments were done to study factors that affect the precession of a top. *Precession* is the revolution of a top around an imaginary line perpendicular to the surface at the point of contact (see Figure 1).

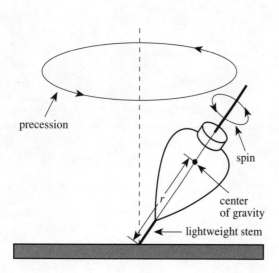

precession

spin

center
of gravity

lightweight stem

r

Figure 1

Experiment 1

An electric motor was attached to a top and used to give the top a known spin rate or number of revolutions per minute (rpm). Once the desired spin rate was achieved, the motor was removed and the number of precessions per minute was counted. The process was repeated using different spin rates. The results are recorded in Table 1.

Table 1	
Spin rate (rpm)	Precession rate (rpm)
350	16
500	11
700	8
1,100	5

Experiment 2

The distance from the surface to the top's center of gravity (r) was varied by changing the length of the lightweight stem on the top from Experiment 1. The electric motor was used to generate the same spin rate in each trial. The measured precession rate is given in Table 2.

Table 2	
r (inches)	Precession rate (rpm)
2	7.5
3	11
4	15
5	19

Experiment 3

A scientist took the top from Experiment 1 to the Moon. It was found that for a given spin rate and stem length, the precession rate was approximately one-sixth that on Earth. For example, a precession rate of 12 rpm on Earth would be approximately 2 rpm on the Moon.

18. Based on the results of Experiment 2, one can conclude that the precession rate of a top increases as the stem:

   F. decreases in length.
   G. increases in length.
   H. remains the same length.
   J. doubles in mass.

19. Which of the following graphs best represents the change in precession rate with increasing spin rate as shown in Experiment 1 ?

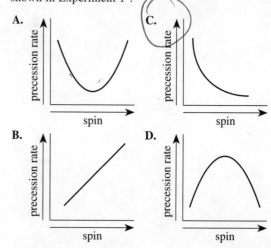

GO ON TO THE NEXT PAGE.

4

20. The scientist conducting Experiment 3 hypothesizes that precession rate is related to gravity. The best way to confirm this hypothesis would be to repeat the experiment on:

F. several different planets with varying gravities.
G. one other planet with the same gravity as Earth.
H. a planet without an atmosphere.
J. Earth using various spin rates.

21. If the spin rate used in Experiment 2 was 500 rpm, what is most likely the value of *r* in Experiment 1 ?

A. 3 inches
B. 4 inches
C. 5 inches
D. 6 inches

22. If the techniques of Experiment 1 had not been perfected first, how would this have affected Experiment 2 ?

F. The mass of the top would have been a factor.
G. The spin rate might not have been the same in each trial.
H. The top's mass may have redistributed itself.
J. The top's shape may have changed.

23. How would one best investigate the effect of a top's mass on the precession rate if the spin rate is constant?

A. Use tops of different colors
B. Use tops that are the same size, have the same shape, and are made from different metals
C. Try different tops and test them on both the Earth and Moon
D. Try tops with equal mass but stems of different lengths

GO ON TO THE NEXT PAGE.

4 ◯ ◯ ◯ ◯ ◯ ◯ ◯ ◯ ◯ **4**

Passage V

Lightning is a visible electrical emission that often occurs in a cloud that has positive charges at the top and negative charges at the base (bottom). Two theories attempt to explain the mechanisms by which thunderstorm clouds become electrically charged and produce lightning.

Gravitational Theory

As shown in Stage I of Figure 1, in a *mature thunderstorm cloud* (a cloud beginning to precipitate), most precipitation particles, which may include raindrops, snow, or ice crystals, are initially *neutral* (no charge). As the larger particles (water droplets or ice crystals) in the upper regions of such a cloud fall due to gravity, they pass and rub against the smaller particles (see Stage II). The friction between them generates static electricity and places a negative charge on the larger particles as they settle to the cloud base. The smaller particles, which become positively charged through this process, rise to the top of the cloud (see Stage III). This separation of the positive and negative charges within the cloud is necessary for lightning formation.

Convective Theory

In this theory, the wind circulation within thunderstorm clouds is believed to cause the charge separation. Near the ground, some air molecules are positively charged. As *updrafts* (vertically rising currents of air) from the surface initiate the development of thunderstorm clouds, they also carry these positive charges aloft into the cloud (see Stage I of Figure 2). Initially, the entire cloud has a positive charge (Stage II). Negatively charged particles in the atmosphere are attracted toward the positively charged cloud and form a layer of negative charge around the edges of the cloud (Stage III). Strong downdrafts form as precipitation begins to fall and the thunderstorm reaches its mature state (Stage IV). These downdrafts strip the layer of negative charge from the cloud edge and carry it downward toward the base. The net effect of the convective circulation is to carry positively charged particles from the atmosphere to the cloud top and deposit negatively charged particles from the cloud's edge at the base of the cloud. This process continues through the remainder of the cloud's life cycle.

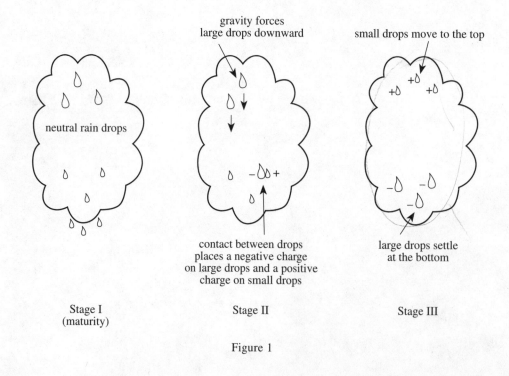

gravity forces
large drops downward

small drops move to the top

neutral rain drops

contact between drops
places a negative charge
on large drops and a positive
charge on small drops

large drops settle
at the bottom

Stage I
(maturity)

Stage II

Stage III

Figure 1

GO ON TO THE NEXT PAGE.

4 ○ ○ ○ ○ ○ ○ ○ ○ **4**

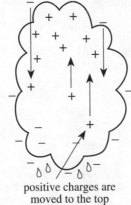

neutral cloud

updrafts carry
positively charged air
molecules toward cloud
Stage I

cloud becomes
positively charged

+ +
+ +
+
+ +
+ + +
+ + +

Stage II

negatively charged
particles are attracted
to positive cloud

$\boxed{-}$

downdrafts of precipitation
move negative charges
toward the bottom

Stage III

Stage IV
(maturity)

positive charges are
moved to the top
of the cloud by updrafts

Figure 2

24. Which of the following represents an example of a cloud in which supporters of both theories would agree lightning would NOT occur?

F. A cloud with large precipitation particles colliding with other smaller precipitation particles
G. A cloud with updrafts and downdrafts moving charged particles from the atmosphere
H. A cloud that only contains neutral particles
J. A cloud with positive charges at the top of the cloud and negative charges at the base of the cloud

25. About which of the following points do the two theories differ?

A. Height of thunderstorm clouds
B. Initial location of charges in the cloud
C. Whether precipitation forms
D. Amount of rainfall produced

26. According to the Gravitational Theory, the concentration of negative charge at the cloud base is greatest:

F. when the raindrops inside the cloud are large.
G. when the raindrops inside the cloud are small.
H. when no rain is falling inside the cloud.
J. after a lightning strike.

27. A research aircraft flies through the center of a mature thunderstorm cloud at a constant altitude and finds that most of the particles in that region are negatively charged. Both theories would agree that:

A. no circulation is present to carry positively charged particles upward from the ground.
B. most of the positively charged particles are suspended above this region.
C. strong updrafts are occurring only at levels above this region.
D. the entire cloud is negatively charged.

28. Florida experiences more thunderstorms than any other state. The Convective Theory would suggest that these storms most likely result from which of the following?

F. A high negative charge in the air just above the ground
G. A greater attractive force between positive and negative charges in this region
H. A high frequency of updrafts over Florida
J. A low frequency of updrafts over Florida

29. If a cloud consisted entirely of ice crystals, which of the following statements about this cloud would support the Gravitational Theory?

A. Only the ice crystals with positive charge would fall and create a separation of charge.
B. Positively charged ice crystals would attract negatively charged ice crystals from the atmosphere.
C. The larger ice crystals would fall more rapidly than the smaller ice crystals and become negatively charged.
D. Downdrafts cause the ice crystals to fall and therefore gain negative charge.

30. Lightning usually occurs when electrical current flows from regions of negative charge to regions with positive charge. Based on the Convective Theory, which lightning path is NOT possible?

F. Within a cloud from base to top
G. From the base of one cloud to the top of another
H. Cloud top to the ground
J. Cloud base to a positively charged region of the atmosphere

GO ON TO THE NEXT PAGE.

4 ○ ○ ○ ○ ○ ○ ○ ○ **4**

Passage VI

An atom has a *nucleus*, which consists of *protons* (positively charged particles) and *neutrons* (uncharged particles), surrounded by one or more *electrons* (negatively charged particles) which move in *orbits* (see Figure 1).

Table 1					
Element	Z	n	r($\times 10^{-8}$ cm)	I (eV)	E (eV)
H	1	4	8.5	0.85	12.7
H	1	3	4.8	1.5	12.1
H	1	2	2.1	3.4	10.2
He$^+$	2	4	4.2	3.4	51.0
He$^+$	2	3	2.4	6.0	48.4
He$^+$	2	2	1.1	13.6	40.9
Li^{+2}	3	4	2.8	7.7	115.0
Li^{+2}	3	3	1.6	13.6	109.0
Li^{+2}	3	2	0.7	30.5	91.9
Be^{+3}	4	4	2.1	13.6	204.0
Be^{+3}	4	3	1.2	24.2	194.0
Be^{+3}	4	2	0.5	54.2	163.0

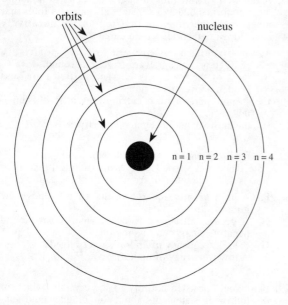

Figure 1

Note: Drawing is NOT to scale.

Table 1 contains data for several neutral and charged atoms containing only one electron. Table 1 includes the number of protons (Z); the identification of the initial orbit (n); the radius of the orbit (r); the energy (I, in electron volts, or eV) to remove an electron from the atom; and the energy (E) of a photon emitted when an electron falls from its initial orbit to the orbit where n = 1.

31. For a given value of Z, the data indicate that as n increases, I:

A. increases.
B. increases, then decreases.
C. decreases.
D. decreases, then increases.

32. According to Table 1, for element H, n = 5, the most likely value for I would be:

F. 0.54 eV.
G. 0.90 eV.
H. 2.7 eV.
J. 3.4 eV.

33. According to the information provided in the passage, an atom has a net positive charge when it has more:

A. neutrons than protons.
B. protons than neutrons.
C. protons than electrons.
D. electrons than neutrons.

GO ON TO THE NEXT PAGE.

4   **4**

34. The hypothesis that for a given value of n, r decreases as net positive charge increases, is supported by the data for:

    F. H and He^+ only.
    G. H and Li^{+2} only.
    H. H, He^+, and Li^{+2} only.
    J. H, He^+, Li^{+2}, and Be^{+3}.

35. The most energetic photons will be emitted when an electron falls from orbit:

    A. n = 2 to n = 1 in He^+.
    B. n = 2 to n = 1 in Be^{+3}.
    C. n = 4 to n = 1 in H.
    D. n = 4 to n = 1 in Be^{+3}.

GO ON TO THE NEXT PAGE.

4 ◯ ◯ ◯ ◯ ◯ ◯ ◯ ◯ ◯ 4

Passage VII

Consider the following reaction:

$$H_2 (g) + I_2 (g) \rightleftharpoons 2HI (g)$$

At *chemical equilibrium*, the formation of hydrogen iodide gas (HI) occurs at the same rate as the formation of hydrogen (H_2) and iodine (I_2) gases.

At equilibrium, the equilibrium constant, (K_{eq}), is the ratio of the square of the HI concentration ([HI]) to the product of the concentrations of H_2 and I_2. The table below shows the data collected while varying either the temperature or the initial reactant concentrations.

Trial	Temperature (°C)	K_{eq}	Initial [H_2] (mol/L*)	Initial [I_2] (mol/L)	Initial [HI] (mol/L)	Final [H_2] (mol/L)	Final [I_2] (mol/L)	Final [HI] (mol/L)
1	360	66.0	0.50	0.50	0	0.099	0.099	0.802
2	380	61.9	0.50	0.50	0	0.100	0.100	0.800
3	400	57.7	0.50	0.50	0	0.106	0.106	0.788
4	420	53.7	0.50	0.50	0	0.109	0.109	0.782
5	440	50.5	0.50	0.50	0	0.110	0.110	0.780
6	460	46.8	0.50	0.50	0	0.113	0.113	0.774
7	400	57.7	1.00	1.00	0	0.208	0.208	1.584
8	420	53.7	1.00	1.00	0	0.214	0.214	1.572
9	400	57.7	1.00	0.50	0	0.529	0.029	0.942
10	400	57.7	0.50	1.00	0	0.029	0.529	0.942
11	400	57.7	0.75	0.25	0	0.508	0.008	0.484
12	400	57.7	0.25	0.75	0	0.008	0.508	0.484
13	400	57.7	0.15	0.85	0	0.002	0.702	0.296

Table 1

* mol/L = moles/liter

Table adapted from Ralph H. Petrucci, *General Chemistry-Principles and Modern Applications.* ©1985 by Macmillan Publishing Company.

36. Which of the following pairs of trials in the table shows that reversing the initial concentrations of H_2 and I_2 at the same temperature gives the same final concentration of HI ?

F. Trials 1 and 2
G. Trials 7 and 8
H. Trials 8 and 11
J. Trials 9 and 10

37. Based on the information in the table, as the initial concentrations of H_2 and I_2 are both doubled, the final concentration of HI:

A. decreases by one-half.
B. decreases by one-fourth.
C. increases by one-fourth.
D. increases by two times.

GO ON TO THE NEXT PAGE.

4 ○ ○ ○ ○ ○ ○ ○ ○ ○ **4**

38. According to the table, increasing the reaction temperature, while keeping the total initial concentration of reactants constant, would result in which, if any, of the following concentration changes?

  F. A decrease in the initial concentration of H_2 and I_2
  G. A decrease in the final concentration of HI
  H. An increase in the initial concentration of H_2 and I_2
  J. No changes in the final concentration of the product

39. Based on the data in the table, which of the following statements best represents the relationship that exists between the K_{eq} of a reaction and the temperature of that reaction?

  A. The K_{eq} value decreases as the temperature is increased.
  B. The K_{eq} value decreases then levels off as the temperature is increased.
  C. The K_{eq} value stays the same as the temperature is increased.
  D. The K_{eq} value increases as the temperature is increased.

40. Based on the information in the table, if the scientist had repeated the experiment at 400°C and started with 2.0 mol/L each of H_2 and I_2, the final concentration of HI would be closest to:

  F. 0.35 mol/L.
  G. 0.70 mol/L.
  H. 1.50 mol/L.
  J. 3.00 mol/L.

END OF TEST 4

STOP! DO NOT RETURN TO ANY OTHER TEST.

Passage I

Question 1. The best answer is A.

A is the best answer because it provides punctuation (a period) that creates two complete sentences.

B is incorrect because the comma and no conjunction between two independent clauses creates a comma splice.

C is incorrect. It creates two complete sentences, but the comma in the second sentence interrupts Diane Boyd's title of "wildlife biologist."

D is incorrect because it creates a nonsensical sentence, the second half of which reads, in part, "specializing in wildlife biologist Diane Boyd." This option does not clearly state that Diane Boyd's specialty is studying wolves.

Question 2. The best answer is G.

F is incorrect because it suggests the illogical idea that Boyd's cabin is located 35 miles from the nearest road because of the fact that it is her base. There is no support in the passage for this idea.

G is the best answer because it clearly and logically states that Boyd's cabin is old and far from a road.

H is incorrect because it is grammatically awkward and unclear. *It* has no clear antecedent—does it refer to the "eighty-year-old cabin," or "a remote wilderness in the Northwest"?

J is incorrect because it is too wordy—"it being" is unnecessary—and because it doesn't clearly state that Boyd's cabin is her base.

Question 3. The best answer is D.

A is incorrect because while "little running water" and "little electricity" might make sense under some circumstances, "little phone" is an illogical idea (it is not used in this context as a physical description of a small telephone; it refers to "little phone service," which makes no sense—you either have phone service or you don't).

B is incorrect because it starts to make three comparisons but doesn't complete them: less running water than what? less electricity than what? less phone than what? In addition, "less phone" is a nonsensical idea.

C is incorrect because it makes three nonsensical pairings: what is few running water? few electricity? few phone?

D is the best answer because this option makes three pairings that make sense: the cabin has no running water, no electricity, and no phone.

Question 4. The best answer is F.

F is the best answer because it uses the correct form of *past* in an adverbial phrase modifying *flows.*

G is incorrect. *Passed,* the past tense of the verb *to pass,* is a homophone of *past,* but the two words don't have the same meaning. *Passed* doesn't make sense in this context.

H is incorrect because it contains the word *passed,* which is the past tense of the verb *to pass. Passed* is a homophone of *past,* but the two words don't have the same meaning. *Passed* doesn't make sense in this context.

J is incorrect because it uses the word *cabins',* the plural possessive form of *cabin,* but only one cabin is being discussed.

Question 5. The best answer is A.

A is the best answer because it does not contain an unneeded description of the cabin.

B is not the best answer because it elaborates unnecessarily on which cabin is being discussed—the essay has already mentioned that the cabin is Boyd's base.

C is incorrect because it elaborates unnecessarily on which cabin is being discussed. Furthermore, the descriptive clause "her home base" needs to be followed by a comma to be correctly punctuated.

D is incorrect because it elaborates unnecessarily on which cabin is being discussed. Furthermore, the descriptive clause "which is eighty years old" needs to be followed by a comma to be correctly punctuated.

Question 6. The best answer is J.

F is incorrect because it implies that Boyd chops her own body rather than her firewood.

G is incorrect because it implies that Boyd chops her own body rather than her firewood.

H is incorrect because it contains an unneeded comma between *chops* and *herself.* What does "herself and hunts wild game" mean?

J is the best answer because it makes it clear that Boyd chops the wood and hunts wild game.

Question 7. The best answer is A.

A is the best answer because it is the appropriate singular possessive pronoun to stand in for "the wolf's."

B is incorrect because it turns the main clause of the sentence ("its movements are easy to follow") into a dependent clause, making the entire construction a sentence fragment.

C is incorrect because it has no subject, so it is nonsensical.

D is incorrect because *their* (a plural possessive pronoun), does not agree in number with "a wolf," which is singular.

Question 8. The best answer is G.

F is not the best answer because the essay has already mentioned that Boyd checks her traps, and *supplies* is not very specific.

G is the best answer because it names specific equipment that Boyd carries "to manage the wolves," thereby providing new, specific details, which is what the question asks for.

H is incorrect because it mentions equipment without providing any details, and includes the subordinate clause "when she checks her traps," which provides almost the same information as "as she makes the rounds of her traps" in the previous sentence.

J is incorrect because it repeats the information that Boyd carries no weapon while checking her traps (it was mentioned in the preceding sentence), and it mentions equipment but doesn't provide any specific details.

Question 9. The best answer is C.

A is incorrect because it causes a comma splice. Furthermore, it is unclear what *it* refers to.

B is incorrect because it causes a run-on sentence.

C is the best answer because it provides punctuation (a period) that creates two complete sentences.

D is incorrect because it joins two complete sentences with a comma and no coordinating conjunction, creating a comma splice.

Question 10. The best answer is H.

F is incorrect because it contains an unnecessary comma separating the adjective *fellow* from the noun it modifies, *biologist.* It implies that Boyd and "a fellow" drove the 50 miles, with the word *biologist* left as an unclear reference.

G is incorrect because it contains an unnecessary comma separating the subject ("Boyd and a fellow biologist") from the verb (*drove*).

H is the best answer because it does not contain any unnecessary commas, and the sentence's meaning is therefore clear.

J is incorrect because it contains an unnecessary comma separating the subject ("Boyd and a fellow biologist") from the verb (*drove*). The comma after *miles* is also unnecessary, although it doesn't make the option incorrect.

Question 11. The best answer is B.

A is incorrect because it is illogical: if the proposed sentence is put in front of Sentence 1, then Paragraph 3 explains Sage's name before we know who "the wolf" is.

B is the best answer because the proposed new sentence gives details about Boyd's reasons for naming the first wolf she collared. It makes sense to provide details about why Boyd gave the wolf the name "Sage" as soon as possible after the wolf is first mentioned in the essay.

C is incorrect because it is a weaker choice than **B.** Sentence 2 offers new information that would interrupt the logical flow of the paragraph if the new sentence were inserted after Sentence 2. It would be better to explain why Boyd named the wolf "Sage" immediately after the wolf is mentioned in Sentence 1.

D is incorrect because it is a weaker choice than **B.** Sentences 2 through 5 offer new information that would interrupt the logical flow of the paragraph if the new sentence were inserted after Sentence 5. It makes sense to provide details about why Boyd gave the wolf the name "Sage" immediately after the wolf is mentioned in the essay.

Question 12. The best answer is J.

F is incorrect because *began* is not the correct form of the past participle of *begin* for use here with *had. Begun* should be used instead.

G is incorrect. It would work if the paragraph were written in the present tense; however, it is written in the past tense.

H is incorrect because *begun* is a form of the verb *begin* that requires *have* or *had* to accompany it. The word *begun* is not used by itself in standard English.

J is the best answer because it is in the past tense, as is the rest of the paragraph.

Question 13. The best answer is C.

A is incorrect. Sentence 2 should logically be the first sentence, as it refers to the beginning of the biologists' work. Furthermore, Sentence 4 cannot logically be placed anywhere but last in the paragraph because the action described in the paragraph begins with the sky turning dark and ends "just before daylight."

B is incorrect. Sentence 2 should logically be the first sentence because it refers to the beginning of the biologists' work. Furthermore, Sentence 4 cannot logically be placed anywhere but last in the paragraph because the action described in the paragraph begins with the sky turning dark and ends "just before daylight."

C is the best answer. Sentence 2 should logically be the first sentence because it refers to the beginning of the biologists' work. Sentence 3 refers to physical contact between the biologists and the wolf and should therefore be placed after Sentence 1, which refers to how the biologists approached the wolf. Sentence 4 cannot logically be placed anywhere but last in the paragraph because the action described in the paragraph begins with the sky turning dark and ends "just before daylight."

D is incorrect. Sentence 3 refers to physical contact between the biologists and the wolf, and should therefore be placed after Sentence 1, which refers to how the biologists approached the wolf.

Question 14. The best answer is J.

F is incorrect. *Pup's* has two possible meanings: it is either the possessive of *pup*, or it is a contraction meaning "pup is." If *pup's* is possessive, it does not make sense in the context of this sentence. If *pup's* is a contraction, it causes the sentence to be grammatically incorrect.

G is incorrect. *Pup's* has two possible meanings: it is either the possessive of *pup* or it is a contraction meaning "pup is." If *pup's* is possessive, it does not make sense in the context of this sentence. If *pup's* is a contraction, it causes the sentence to be grammatically incorrect.

H is incorrect because no possessive usage is needed here. This option causes the sentence to mean that Boyd noticed Sage and five "wrestling playfully" belonging to Sage's pups, which makes no sense.

J is the best answer because it is the only option that makes sense. This option causes the sentence to mean that Boyd noticed Sage and five of Sage's pups, who were wrestling in a playful manner.

Question 15. The best answer is D.

A is incorrect because nothing in it refers to the essay's opening sentence.

B is incorrect because nothing in it refers to the essay's opening sentence.

C is incorrect because nothing in it refers to the essay's opening sentence.

D is the best answer because it refers to "Diane of the Wolves," which is Diane Boyd's nickname, mentioned in the essay's opening sentence.

Passage II

Question 16. The best answer is G.

F is incorrect. The punctuation (a period) creates the sentence fragment "As American businesses explore overseas markets."

G is the best answer. It forms a complete sentence composed of a dependent clause and an independent clause separated by a comma.

H is incorrect. The punctuation (a semicolon) is preceded by a dependent clause and followed by an independent clause. A semicolon should not be used between a dependent clause and an independent clause.

J is incorrect. It is a sentence fragment.

Question 17. The best answer is A.

A is the best answer because it forms a complete sentence with unambiguous meaning.

B is incorrect because it turns the rest of the sentence into a dependent clause, which results in a nonsensical fragment.

C is incorrect because it turns the entire sentence into a dependent clause: American businesses learn how language differences (the ones that can stand in the way of trade) do what? This option turns the sentence into a fragment.

D is incorrect because it contains the awkward usage "differences of which can stand," which is redundant: the "of which" (what kind of differences) refers to language differences, but that has already been stated in the sentence.

Question 18. The best answer is H.

F is incorrect because it contains the overly casual and unneeded "you see."

G is incorrect because it adds the phrase "as proof," which doesn't fit with the meaning of the sentence since this sentence is not offered as proof of the preceding sentence. This sentence is a second example of how language differences can cause difficulties for businesses.

H is the best answer because it does not try to relate this sentence to the previous one as evidence of it or the effect of it: this sentence is given as a second example of the point made in the paragraph's opening two sentences.

J is incorrect. By adding *consequently,* this option attempts to convince the reader that the car manufacturer's discovery of its mistake was somehow a cause of the discovery made by the oil company, but that is not the case.

Question 19. The best answer is D.

A is incorrect. It misuses the idiom of turning something "into hard cash" by making it appear literal (the rather formal "being converted" has this effect). Even if the idiom were used correctly, it is too casual in tone for this passage.

B is incorrect. It uses an idiom that (in this case) sounds ridiculous, because automobiles cannot be sold over a counter. That silliness and the informality of the expression "to sell over the counter" are too casual in tone for this passage.

C is not the best answer because it is overly wordy and complicated and tells readers something they don't need to know.

D is the best answer because it is straightforward and clear in its meaning; it does not introduce an inappropriate tone to the passage.

Question 20. The best answer is H.

F is incorrect because it does not contain any punctuation to clarify the sentence's meaning. Does "Common Market" mean the same thing as "European Economic Community," or is overcoming a language barrier problem the task of *either* the Common Market *or* the European Economic Community? Clarifying punctuation is needed.

G is incorrect because by placing a semicolon after "or Common Market," it renders the rest of the sentence meaningless. The phrase beginning with "an organization" cannot stand on its own, as it must because it follows a semicolon.

H is the best answer. By using commas to set off "or Common Market," it makes it clear that "Common Market" is another name for the "European Economic Community."

J is incorrect because by leaving the *or* out of the part set off by commas, it makes the sentence nonsensical: the task of overcoming the language barrier problem is, with this punctuation, one of the tasks of the European Economic Community *or* an organization formed to promote trade (looking ahead to the next question), but the phrase beginning with "an organization" is a description of the European Economic Community.

Question 21. The best answer is D.

A is incorrect because it is redundant: an organization is always founded at its start; it is impossible to found one later in its existence.

B is incorrect because it is redundant (*begun* and *founded* mean the same thing here).

C is incorrect because it is not clear from the context who or what *it* refers to.

D is the best answer because it avoids redundancy and unclear references and is therefore the best answer of all the options.

Question 22. The best answer is G.

F is incorrect because it uses *are,* a plural verb form, but the subject, *one,* is singular.

G is the best answer because it uses *is,* which is a singular verb form, with the singular subject *one.*

H is incorrect because it uses *are,* a plural verb form, but the subject, *one,* is singular.

J is incorrect because it uses *are,* a plural verb form, but the subject, *one,* is singular.

Question 23. The best answer is D.

A is incorrect because the proposed sentence tells us nothing new or relevant about the problem of languages in the European Economic Community, but instead digresses from the paragraph's subject. This option is untrue; the sentence does not establish a setting for the essay (the essay is not set in Brussels).

B is incorrect because the proposed sentence does not tell us anything new or relevant about the problem of languages in the European Economic Community. Mentioning that the EEC headquarters is in "the lively and modern capital of Belgium" does little to legitimize the EEC.

C is incorrect because although it correctly states that the proposed sentence would not be a logical and relevant addition to the essay, the stated reason is meaningless, given that neither the essay nor the proposed sentence states what the official languages of Belgium are.

D is the best answer because it correctly states that the proposed sentence shouldn't be added to the essay because it adds no information about the problem of language barriers in the European Economic Community, which is the paragraph's topic.

Question 24. The best answer is F.

F is the best answer because "in fact" introduces a detail that elaborates on the previous sentence. No new paragraph is needed here because this sentence and the following sentence continue the discussion of Greek and Danish translation, the topic of the previous sentence.

G is incorrect. *Furthermore* doesn't make sense as a transitional word here because the sentence doesn't extend the discussion in a new direction, but rather provides more depth to the current topic.

H is incorrect because no new paragraph is needed here: the sentence continues with the discussion of Greek and Danish translation.

J is incorrect because no new paragraph is needed here: the sentence continues the discussion of Greek and Danish translation. *Furthermore* doesn't make sense as an introductory word here because the sentence doesn't extend the discussion in a new direction—it provides more depth to the current topic.

Question 25. The best answer is B.

A is incorrect because it leaves readers with the awkward sense that something (*it*) happened almost two decades ago, but it doesn't say what *it* was.

B is the best answer because the moment being referred to in the phrase "almost two decades ago" is the moment when it first became clear that Greece would be joining the Common Market.

C is incorrect because the moment being referred to in the phrase "almost two decades ago" is the moment when it first became obvious that Greece would be joining the Common Market, not the moment that Greece would actually join the Common Market—the officials were alerted to the need to look for translators when it became obvious that Greece would be joining the Common Market. The tense shift is also awkward and nonstandard in this option: "would join almost two decades ago" looks forward and backward at the same time.

D is incorrect because the moment being referred to in the phrase "almost two decades ago" is the moment when it first became obvious that Greece would be joining the Common Market, not the moment that Greece would actually join the Common Market. The sentence explains that the officials began to look for translators three years before Greece actually joined the Common Market.

Question 26. The best answer is G.

F is incorrect because it makes it unclear when the disappointment occurred and whether or not the disappointment might still be occurring. This option also creates a comma splice.

G is the best answer because it contains the needed comma before the coordinating conjunction *and* that separates the two independent clauses.

H is incorrect because it is missing the comma needed before the coordinating conjunction *and* that separates two independent clauses.

J is incorrect because adding the word *so* makes it sound as though the day itself suffered the disappointment.

Question 27. The best answer is A.

A is the best answer because it sets off *say,* used here to mean "for example," with commas on either side.

B is incorrect because it is nonsensical. What does "Greek into say" mean? The comma following *say* makes that phrase a unit, but it does not make sense as a unit.

C is incorrect because it is missing the comma needed after *say,* which is used to mean "for example" here.

D is incorrect because it contains an unneeded comma separating a preposition, *into,* from its object, *Danish.*

Question 28. The best answer is G.

F is incorrect because it contains the transitional word *then,* which doesn't work in this context. The preceding sentence is in the present tense, as is the current sentence.

G is the best answer because there is no need for any of the transitional words or phrases that the other options suggest.

H is incorrect because the transitional phrase "for instance" indicates that the current sentence will give an example of something mentioned in the preceding sentence, but that doesn't happen.

J is incorrect because the transitional word *eventually* doesn't fit with the present-tense style of the essay.

Question 29. The best answer is D.

A is incorrect because it is extremely wordy, and it contains redundancies (*interrogation, asking,* and *question* refer to the same thing).

B is incorrect because it is unnecessarily wordy.

C is incorrect because it is extremely wordy, and it contains redundancies (*begins, commencing,* and *introductory* refer to the same thing).

D is the best answer. Unlike the other options, it contains no redundancies and is not unnecessarily wordy.

Question 30. The best answer is H.

F is incorrect because it contains an unnecessary comma separating the subject, "all that's needed," from the verb *is.*

G is incorrect because it contains an unnecessary comma separating the subject, "all that's needed," from the verb *was.*

H is the best answer because it contains no unnecessary comma separating the subject, "all that's needed," from the verb *is.*

J is incorrect because it contains an unnecessary comma separating the subject, "all that's needed," from the verb phrase *would be.*

Passage III

Question 31. The best answer is C.

A is incorrect because the sentence clearly refers to people who live in New York, and no use of the singular form of the possessive is required.

B is incorrect because the sentence clearly refers to people who live in New York, and no use of the singular form of the possessive is required. Furthermore, this option contains an unneeded comma separating the subject "New Yorkers" from the verb *take*.

C is the best answer because the sentence clearly refers to people who live in New York, correctly designated by "New Yorkers."

D is incorrect because the sentence clearly refers to people who live in New York, and no use of the plural form of the possessive is required.

Question 32. The best answer is G.

F is incorrect because it contains an unclear reference: the size and variety of what? the New Yorkers? the park? something in the park?

G is the best answer because it correctly and clearly uses the singular possessive pronoun *its* to refer to the size and variety of Central Park.

H is incorrect because it contains the contraction for "it is," which makes the sentence nonsensical ("to discover it [Central Park] is size and variety").

J is incorrect because it makes it sound as if visitors are astonished at the size and variety of New Yorkers, a declaration that may be true but is clearly not the intention of this sentence. If this were the intention, the mention of Central Park would seem out of place in the first part of the sentence; it is obvious from the context that mention of Central Park is the main purpose of the sentence.

Question 33. The best answer is D.

A is incorrect because it is redundant (*altering* and *transformations* refer to the same thing).

B is incorrect because it is redundant (*changes* and *transformations* refer to the same thing).

C is incorrect because it is redundant (*changing* and *transformations* refer to the same thing).

D is the best answer because it omits the redundancies offered in the other options.

Question 34. The best answer is H.

F is incorrect because it provides vague, rather than specific, geographical information about the park's location.

G is incorrect because it provides vague, rather than specific, geographical information about the park's location.

H is the best answer because it provides specific geographical information about Central Park's location—the fact that Central Park is part of the island of Manhattan.

J is incorrect because it states an obvious fact: Central Park is the most recent development of "this part," which is Central Park.

Question 35. The best answer is A.

A is the best answer because it makes it clear that the land being discussed is park now (but not 450 million years ago), and that the land rested on the floor of an ancient sea 450 million years ago.

B is incorrect because it is wordy and awkward: what does "but was not then rested on the floor" mean?

C is incorrect because it is wordy, convoluted, and ambiguous. The sentence says "that park . . . rested," which implies that it was a park 450 million years ago, yet the awkward "which then was not one" contradicts that implication.

D is incorrect because it is extremely awkward: it interrupts itself. Also, *but* seems to contradict something (did it formerly rest on something other than the floor of an ancient sea?).

Question 36. The best answer is H.

F is incorrect because it uses a coordinating conjunction (*and*) to pretend that landscape is another thing that accelerated the erosion, which is nonsensical. The *and* could also be trying to turn the sentence into a series of items, but this is unsuccessful because the items are not parallel (the first two are adverbial phrases, and the last is an independent phrase with a subject and a verb).

G is incorrect. By proposing a semicolon, it implies that the first part of the sentence is complete and can stand alone, but the first part is composed of two adverbial phrases, so no subject and verb are present.

H is the best answer because it correctly allows the adjectival phrase "accelerated by the Ice Age" to modify "aeons of erosion." Both phrases are followed by commas preceding the subject of the sentence, "the landscape."

J is incorrect because it uses a coordinating conjunction (*and*) to attach an independent clause ("the landscape began to assume its modern appearance") with an adverbial phrase ("after aeons of erosion") followed by an adjectival phrase ("accelerated by the Ice Age") instead of with another independent phrase. The *and* could also be trying to turn the sentence into a series of items, but this is unsuccessful because the items are not parallel (the first two are adverbial phrases, the last is an independent phrase with a subject and verb).

Question 37. The best answer is D.

A is incorrect because it makes the second half of the sentence into an independent clause. Because the two independent halves are joined by a comma without a coordinating conjunction (for example, *and*), a comma splice occurs. Furthermore, there is a time shift: the island was an oak-and-chestnut woodland, but is it currently populated by black bears, wolves, and beavers? The context makes it clear that this interpretation is not intended.

B is incorrect because it makes the second half of the sentence an independent clause. Because the two independent halves are joined by a comma without a coordinating conjunction (for example, *and*), a comma splice occurs.

C is incorrect because it makes the second half of the sentence an independent clause. Because the two independent halves are joined by a comma without a coordinating conjunction (for example, *and*), a comma splice occurs.

D is the best answer because it correctly allows the phrase beginning with *populated* to simply modify *woodland.*

Question 38. The best answer is J.

F is incorrect because it consists of only a series of clauses modifying each other; there is no verb in the sentence.

G is incorrect because it consists of only a series of clauses modifying each other; there is no verb in the sentence.

H is incorrect because it consists of only a series of clauses modifying each other; there is no verb in the sentence.

J is the best answer because it supplies the verb *was,* which is needed to form a complete sentence.

Question 39. The best answer is C.

A is incorrect because it illogically has the "over 200 million years ago" sentence following the discussion of the land's modern appearance.

B is incorrect because it illogically has the "over 200 million years ago" sentence preceding the discussion of the land's appearance 450 years ago.

C is the best answer because it correctly places the descriptions in chronological order, with the "450 million years ago" sentence first, the "over 200 million years ago" sentence next, and the "modern appearance" sentence last.

D is incorrect because it illogically has the "over 200 million years ago" sentence following the discussion of the land's modern appearance.

Question 40. The best answer is F.

F is the best answer because it contains the correct form of the verb phrase "to be given."

G is incorrect because it contains an incorrect form of the verb phrase "to be given." The simple past tense *gave* is a verb that must take a direct object (as in "Olmsted and Vaux gave the task to someone").

H is incorrect because it uses *was*, which is singular, but the subject is "Frederick Olmsted and Calvert Vaux," which is plural.

J is incorrect because in order to be correct, it requires a form of *have* (for example, "have been given," "had been given"). And even if the *have* or *had* were present, this option would represent an unneeded shift in tense from the rest of the paragraph.

Question 41. The best answer is D.

A is incorrect because it discusses the project deadline, not Vaux and Olmsted's vision of the finished park.

B is incorrect because it discusses machinery, not Vaux and Olmsted's vision of the finished park.

C is incorrect because it discusses saving money, not Vaux and Olmsted's vision of the finished park.

D is the best answer because it discusses Vaux and Olmsted's vision of the finished park as having a natural-looking landscape.

Question 42. The best answer is F.

F is the best answer because it correctly avoids introducing a subject (and thus a comma splice) into the second half of the sentence, instead allowing it to simply modify the first half.

G is incorrect because it contains a tense shift (from past to present) and introduces a comma splice—two independent clauses fastened together by a comma with no coordinating conjunction (such as *and*).

H is incorrect because it introduces a comma splice—two independent clauses fastened together by a comma with no coordinating conjunction (such as *and*).

J is incorrect because it contains a tense shift that doesn't make sense in context: this version of the sentence implies that the turning over of the rock and earth caused Olmsted and Calvert to undertake the project with confidence and enterprise.

Question 43. The best answer is B.

A is not the best answer because it is general and bland, with no statistics to stress the enormousness of the project.

B is the best answer because it contains statistics that emphasize with specific numbers the enormousness of the project.

C is not the best answer because the number of tourists today does not stress the enormousness of the project.

D is not the best answer because the fact that "many workers" helped develop the park does not stress the enormousness of the project as strongly as **B**.

Question 44. The best answer is H.

F is incorrect because it is nonsensical: "Although the genius. . ." has no verb accompanying it (such as, "although the genius of Olmsted and Vaux astounds us, . . ."). The phrase means nothing as it stands.

G is incorrect because it sounds as though the rest of the sentence will be about the genius of the designers rather than the success of their plans. The sentence seems to lead us to a conclusion (for example, "considering their genius, of course the park was a success," or, "considering their genius, it's a wonder the park succeeded"). The second half of the sentence is not in response to "considering their genius," but merely a statement about the park's transformation.

H is the best answer because it achieves the correct tone and sense that credits the park's transformation to the genius of its designers.

J is incorrect because it makes it sound as if the park succeeded in spite of the work of Olmsted and Vaux rather than as a result of their work.

Question 45. The best answer is B.

A is incorrect because it implies that the landscape almost couldn't make its transformation ("barely was transformed") or that it wasn't completely transformed, when it was in fact a work-intensive, time-consuming, thorough transformation that took place, as is clear from the passage.

B is the best answer because it joins two adjectives to make a single descriptive term to describe the landscape as having been bare at one time.

C is incorrect because it uses an adverb (*barely*) where an adjective should be used.

D is incorrect because an unneeded comma separates the adjectives. Taken separately, a "bare landscape" makes sense, but what is a "once landscape?"

Question 46. The best answer is F.

F is the best answer because the first paragraph discusses the current attractions of the park, rather than historical information.

G is incorrect because the first paragraph contains many details that are relevant to understanding the entire passage.

H is incorrect because the first paragraph discusses the current attractions of the park, rather than historical information.

J is incorrect because the first paragraph contains many details that are relevant to understanding the entire passage. The first paragraph does not contain an anecdote, which is a short narrative, or story, of an incident.

Passage IV

Question 47. The best answer is C.

A is incorrect because it is missing a reference to point directly to the magazine articles; it sounds vaguely as if people are describing magazine articles rather than food.

B is incorrect because it is missing a reference to point directly to the magazine articles; it sounds vaguely as if people are describing magazine articles rather than food.

C is the best answer because it contains the needed reference to point directly to the magazine articles where people described their eating experiences. The preposition *in* is the pointer, and *which* is the pronoun standing in for the magazine articles.

D is incorrect because it is missing a reference to point directly to the magazine articles; it sounds vaguely as if people are describing magazine articles rather than food.

Question 48. The best answer is J.

F is incorrect because it is extremely wordy. The repetition of "those people" is awkward and unnecessary.

G is incorrect because it is wordy and awkward. It contains the nonspecific pronoun *ones*. Furthermore, who, exactly, does *they* refer to?

H is incorrect because it is wordy and extremely awkward. It contains the nonspecific pronoun *ones,* and instead of saying "the ones who were interviewed," it says "the ones that were interviewed." It is also redundant, with "of the ones" and "out of those" serving the same function.

J is the best answer because it avoids wordiness and redundancy and is clear and to the point.

Question 49. The best answer is A.

A is the best answer because the singular *meal* matches the singular "once been served" and the singular *restaurant* later in the sentence.

B is incorrect because there is an unneeded comma in the middle of the noun phrase "meals that they had once been served," and because *meal,* not *meals,* is correct (see the explanation for **A** above).

C is incorrect because there is an unneeded comma in the middle of the noun phrase "meals which they had once been served," and because *meal,* not *meals,* is correct (see the explanation for **A** above).

D is incorrect because there is an unneeded comma in the middle of the noun phrase "meals they had once been served," which creates a comma splice. In addition, *meal,* not *meals,* is correct (see the explanation for **A** above).

Question 50. The best answer is H.

F is incorrect because it ignores the connection between picnics and the description of the picnics. It causes a sentence fragment, beginning with *Meals,* to be formed.

G is incorrect because it ignores the connection between picnics and the description of the picnics by separating the two parts of the sentence with a semicolon. The portion following the semicolon would need to be an independent clause in order for this punctuation to work, but the clause has no verb.

H is the best answer because it acknowledges the connection between picnics and the description of the picnics by separating them with only a dash.

J is incorrect because it creates the nonsensical compound noun "picnics meals."

Question 51. The best answer is B.

A is incorrect because it uses the singular possessive form of *diner,* but the sentence begins with *some,* which is plural: several of the people interviewed reminisced about their companions. Furthermore, there is an unneeded semicolon following *companions,* which would have to be followed by an independent clause in order to be correct. (The phrase following the semicolon is lacking a subject and verb.)

B is the best answer because it shows that the companions belong to the diners by using the plural possessive form of *diner.*

C is incorrect because it indicates that the companions own something called *rather,* which is nonsensical, and it fails to show that the companions belong to the diners.

D is incorrect because it fails to show that the companions belong to the diners.

Question 52. **The best answer is F.**

F is the best answer because it brings in a new area of discussion, thus broadening the range of experiences mentioned in the paragraph.

G is incorrect because it discusses a fancy meal served in a grand restaurant, which has already been discussed in the paragraph. This option does nothing to capture the diversity of experiences mentioned in the question.

H is incorrect because it discusses grand restaurants, which have already been discussed in the paragraph. This option does nothing to capture the diversity of experiences mentioned in the question.

J is incorrect because it discusses picnics, which have already been discussed in the paragraph. This option does nothing to capture the diversity of experiences mentioned in the question.

Question 53. **The best answer is D.**

A is incorrect because it contains information that is completely unnecessary. In addition, it is unclear whether Goodhue was the name of the meal or the college dormitory.

B is incorrect because it contains information that is completely unnecessary. In addition, it is unclear whether Goodhue was the name of the meal or the college dormitory.

C is incorrect because it contains information that is completely unnecessary. In addition, it is unclear whether Goodhue was the name of the meal or the college dormitory.

D is the best answer because it avoids mentioning unnecessary information.

Question 54. The best answer is G.

F is incorrect because it contains the plural form of the verb, but the subject, "no one," is singular.

G is the best answer because it contains the singular form of the verb, which agrees with "no one," the singular subject.

H is incorrect because *have* is a plural verb form, but the subject, "no one," is singular.

J is incorrect because *were* is a plural verb form, but the subject, "no one," is singular.

Question 55. The best answer is C.

A is incorrect because it refers to material already covered and thus adds nothing to the range of food already mentioned.

B is incorrect because it refers to a new meal, but it is described as the most remarkable meal the writer has ever eaten, which contradicts the description of the lampries meal as the most remarkable. Furthermore, the reference to "those curries" is mysterious here because the curries have not yet been mentioned.

C is the best answer because it contains an example of another meal that, like the ones already listed in the paragraph, was unremarkable. Its new details, however, make it worthy of mention in the paragraph.

D is incorrect because it refers to material already covered and thus adds nothing to the range of food already mentioned.

Question 56. The best answer is G.

F is incorrect because using *more* makes it a comparison, but there is no object to compare to (more complex, elaborate, and delicious than what?).

G is the best answer because it contains the superlative *most,* which is needed. A superlative is needed because of the "I've ever" later in the sentence (the best I've ever eaten, the worst I've ever eaten, the most burned, the least fresh, etc.). This option also contains the needed article *the* to accompany *concoction.*

H is incorrect because it makes a comparison without another object to compare to (more complex, elaborate, and delicious than what?).

J is incorrect because it is missing an article (*the, a,* or *an*) to accompany *concoction.* Also, a superlative is needed because of the "I've ever" later in the sentence (the best I've ever eaten, the worst I've ever eaten, the most burned, the least fresh, etc.).

Question 57. The best answer is A.

A is the best answer because it contains no unneeded punctuation separating the verb *was* (which is contracted with *not*) from its object, "that the innkeeper began cooking." The adverbial phrase "[not] until late afternoon" (the *not* is contained in the contraction *wasn't*) modifies the verb and requires no commas before or after it.

B is incorrect because it leaves the first sentence unfinished: what wasn't until late afternoon? Also, the phrase beginning with *that* is a sentence fragment.

C is incorrect because it separates the verb *was* (which is contracted with *not*) from its object ("that the innkeeper began cooking") with an unneeded comma.

D is incorrect because it separates the verb *was* (which is contracted with *not*) from its object ("that the innkeeper began cooking") with an unneeded comma. The adverbial phrase "[not] until late afternoon" (the *not* is contained in the contraction *wasn't*) modifies the verb and requires no commas before or after it. Furthermore, this option contains a nonword (*thats*).

Question 58. The best answer is J.

F is incorrect because it makes it seem as if the diners grabbed the machete and made two swift strokes, perhaps at their seats. It is clear from the previous sentence, however, that the innkeeper split the pineapple, which would have required the use of her machete.

G is incorrect because it makes it seem as if the diners grabbed the machete and made two swift strokes (in the air?) before taking their seats. It is clear from the previous sentence, however, that the innkeeper split the pineapple, which would have required the use of her machete.

H is incorrect because its commas make the sentence's meaning ambiguous: who was splitting what with the machete? Does the phrase "with two strokes of her machete" belong with the material preceding it or the material following it?

J is the best answer because it makes it clear that the machete was used by the innkeeper to split the pineapple.

Question 59. The best answer is C.

A is incorrect because it would tell us about the cook before we even know that the lampries exist. The references to "that evening" could refer back to the time when the writer was reading a series of magazine articles, but the reference to the innkeeper and her actions would be completely mysterious.

B is incorrect because it would tell us about the cook and her spoon before we even know what the cook is doing. The "final meditative stir" would be a mysterious reference at this point in the essay.

C is the best answer because it describes food preparation in a logical order: after the cook gives the curries a final stir, she ladles them onto banana leaves, bundles them, and ties them for their final baking.

D is incorrect because it would tell us about stirring the uneaten curries after we have read about eating them, which is clearly out of order.

Question 60. The best answer is J.

F is incorrect. Paragraph 3 deals with the setting in which the narrator ate the lampries meal. The given sentence, which describes the narrator and the other guests preparing to eat the lampries, best fits in Paragraph 5, which describes the meal itself.

G is incorrect. See the explanation for **F**.

H is incorrect. Paragraph 4 deals with the cooking of the lampries meal. The last sentence describes the cook tying lampries into packets "for the final baking." A description of the guests untying the packets is most appropriate in Paragraph 5, which describes the guests eating the lampries.

J is the best answer. Paragraph 5 describes the guests eating the lampries, so it is the best place for the given sentence, which describes the guests preparing to eat.

Passage V

Question 61. The best answer is C.

A is incorrect because it is wordy and awkward: does *which* refer to comic books or art forms?

B is incorrect because it is wordy and awkward: does *those* refer to comic books or art forms? Also, "in their entirety" is an unneeded detail at this point.

C is the best answer because it forms an adjectival phrase that clearly refers to comic books.

D is incorrect because it states that the comic books are being produced by almost everyone rather than being read by almost everyone.

Question 62. The best answer is G.

F is incorrect because it is redundant (*look* and *in appearance* refer to the same thing).

G is the best answer because it is free of redundancies and is thus the best answer choice.

H is incorrect because it is redundant (*look* and *appear* refer to the same thing).

J is incorrect because it is redundant (*to appear* and *look* refer to the same thing).

Question 63. The best answer is D.

A is incorrect because it contains *then,* which is a time reference, but there is no time being pointed to (it is not relevant at this point to ask "different when").

B is incorrect because it contradicts itself, with *different* paired with its opposite, *like.*

C is incorrect because it implies nonsensically that Japanese comics look one way in Japan and another way in America. Clearly this is not what's intended, as can be learned from the context.

D is the best answer because it uses the correct idiom "different from." It thus makes clear what is different: Japanese comic books and American comic books.

Question 64. The best answer is G.

F is incorrect because it sets up a comparison beginning with *whereas,* but the comparison is never completed. What is left is a sentence fragment followed by a complete sentence.

G is the best answer because it sets up a comparison beginning with *whereas* and completes the thought by showing how American comics and Japanese comics differ.

H is incorrect because it sets up a comparison beginning with *whereas,* but the comparison is never completed. What is left is a sentence fragment followed by a complete sentence.

J is incorrect because it sets up a comparison beginning with *whereas,* but the comparison is never completed. What is created is a long sentence fragment.

Question 65. The best answer is C.

A is incorrect because it does not continue the comparison that contrasts Japanese and American comics; it inserts material that is not relevant at this point in the essay.

B is incorrect because it does not continue the comparison that contrasts Japanese and American comics; it inserts material that is not relevant at this point in the essay.

C is the best answer because it continues the comparison that contrasts Japanese and American comics by showing their difference in publication frequency.

D is incorrect because it does not continue the comparison that contrasts Japanese and American comics; it inserts material that is not relevant at this point in the essay.

Question 66. The best answer is G.

F is incorrect because it causes the first phrase to become independent, making the entire sentence two independent (and seemingly unrelated) clauses fastened together by a comma, which creates a comma splice. Furthermore, this option fails to continue the comparison between the two types of comics.

G is the best answer because it continues the comparison of the two types of comics by setting up the first part of the comparison ("while this is true, that is true in this other instance . . .").

H is incorrect because it implies that the first phrase is in response to and contrasted with the previous sentence, but this is not the case. A new subject is introduced in this sentence: the subject matter in the two types of comics.

J is incorrect because it causes the first phrase to become independent, making the entire sentence two independent (and seemingly unrelated) phrases fastened together by a comma, which creates a comma splice. Furthermore, this option fails to continue the comparison between the two types of comics.

Question 67. The best answer is B.

A is incorrect because it fails to give examples of other kinds of stories, as required by the question; the previous sentence asserts that "a wide variety of stories appear in Japanese comics."

B is the best answer because it lists types of stories that are examples of the wide variety of stories found in Japanese comics, as requested by the question.

C is incorrect because it fails to give examples of other kinds of stories, as required by the question; the previous sentence asserts that "a wide variety of stories appear in Japanese comics."

D is incorrect because it fails to give examples of other kinds of stories, as required by the question; the previous sentence asserts that "a wide variety of stories appear in Japanese comics."

Question 68. The best answer is J.

F is incorrect because it introduces a new, unrelated topic—going to the movies—that does not refer to the previous paragraph or guide the reader to the new topic of this paragraph, the comic's readers.

G is incorrect because it restates the topic of the previous paragraph without adding any new or interesting information, and it does not guide the reader to the new topic of this paragraph, the comic's readers.

H is incorrect because it introduces a new topic—the gender of American comic book readers—which does not refer to the previous paragraph at all, so it does not provide a transition from paragraph to paragraph, as requested by the question.

J is the best answer because it combines the topic of the variety of stories with that of the stories' readership, thus best providing a transition from one paragraph to the next.

Question 69. The best answer is A.

A is the best answer because it provides the correct preposition for use with *geared* in this context, where the phrase is used to mean "made appealing to." "Geared to" is an English idiom.

B is incorrect because it presents the incorrect preposition for use with *geared* in this context, where the phrase is used to mean "made appealing to." The phrase "geared along" is not an English idiom.

C is incorrect because it presents the incorrect preposition for use with *geared* in this context, where the phrase is used to mean "made appealing to." The phrase "geared from" is not an English idiom.

D is incorrect because it presents the incorrect preposition for use with *geared* in this context, where the phrase is used to mean "made appealing to." The phrase "geared with" is not an English idiom.

Question 70. The best answer is H.

F is incorrect because it fails to complete the comparison being made between the age of readers of American comics and that of readers of Japanese comics. Instead, this option implies that this sentence is the result of what is stated in the previous sentence, but the context makes it clear that this is not the case.

G is incorrect because it fails to complete the comparison being made between the age of readers of American comics and that of readers of Japanese comics. Instead, this option implies that this sentence is another example of what is stated in the previous sentence, but the context makes clear that this is not the case.

H is the best answer because it makes it clear that a comparison is being made between the age of readers of American comics and that of readers of Japanese comics, and that this sentence offers information that contrasts with that in the previous sentence.

J is incorrect because it fails to complete the comparison being made between the age of readers of American comics and that of readers of Japanese comics. Instead, this option implies that this sentence is the result of what is stated in the previous sentence, but the context makes clear that this is not the case.

Question 71. The best answer is D.

A is incorrect. This option makes sense until you reach the phrases "by businesspeople" and "by children." It's not clear who *we* would be, riding on Japanese trains, when the third-person point of view has been used in the rest of the essay.

B is incorrect. This option makes sense until you reach the phrases "by businesspeople" and "by children." It's not immediately clear who *they* would be, suddenly riding on Japanese trains: looking back to the previous sentence, it appears that *they* refers to either *manga* or the various reading locations, neither of which make sense in this context.

C is incorrect. It makes sense until you reach the phrases "by businesspeople" and "by children," at which point it's clear that it is the businesspeople and children who are doing the reading, which eliminates this option. It's not clear why *you* would be used here, when the third-person point of view has been used in the rest of the essay.

D is the best answer because it is the only choice that makes it clear that the businesspeople and children do the reading. It is clear that in this option, *they* refers to the comic books.

Question 72. The best answer is F.

F is the best answer because it makes it clear that comic books make up 27 percent of the material that is produced in Japan. There are no unneeded commas in this option, thus allowing the sentence's meaning to be easily understood.

G is incorrect because it implies that all books and magazines (in the world, presumably) are produced in Japan, but 27 percent of them are comics.

H is incorrect because it contains an unneeded comma that separates the adjectival phrase "produced in Japan" from "books and magazines," the nouns the phrase is meant to modify. This comma also serves to separate the sentence's subject from its verb.

J is incorrect because it contains an unneeded comma that separates the sentence's subject from its verb.

Question 73. The best answer is B.

A is incorrect because it implies that comics, rather than people, own the comics industry in Japan.

B is the best answer because it makes it clear that people, rather than comics, own the comics industry in Japan.

C is incorrect because it fails to compare the comics industry of the U.S. with the comics industry of Japan: it instead compares the comics industry of the U.S. with the Japanese comics themselves.

D is incorrect because it is wordy and awkward. It implies that the comics industry owns the comics industry, which is a strange way to state the case.

Question 74. The best answer is H.

F is incorrect because it implies that children are being written, which is nonsensical. When *as* is used in the comparison "as well as" (which is equivalent to "in addition to"), no comma is needed before or after the second *as* (for example, "we invited the boys as well as the girls").

G is incorrect because it contains an unneeded comma following *as* (see the explanation for **F**).

H is the best answer because it avoids adding unneeded commas and does not imply the nonsensical notion that children are being written, as **F** and **J** do.

J is incorrect because it contains an unneeded comma separating *adults* from what is in addition to them, *children*. **J** also implies that children are being written, which is nonsensical.

Question 75. The best answer is A.

A is the best answer because it correctly states that the essay would not successfully fulfill the assignment described in the question; the Japanese comics industry has influenced the American comics industry, not the other way around.

B is incorrect because although it is correct in stating that the essay would not successfully fulfill the assignment described in the question, it can be rejected because the reason given is silly: if the essay had included specific examples of Japanese comic books (by listing their titles, presumably), it still would not fulfill the assignment of detailing a "way in which Japan has been influenced by American culture."

C is incorrect because it contains a statement that is general, vague, probably untrue, and not supported by anything in the essay.

D is incorrect because it has an extremely narrow focus, singling out as it does a single point mentioned only briefly in the essay. The sentence does not even attempt to prove that it is the appearance of adventure stories in American comics that causes adventure stories to appear in Japanese comics, which is just as well, because the essay makes it clear in the final paragraph that it is American comics that are being influenced by Japanese comics, not the reverse.

Question 1. The correct answer is E.

Basically, you're trying to answer the question "25% of what is 12 ?" Translated into symbols with x representing what you're trying to find, the equation is 25% of x = 12 or $0.25x = 12$. So, $x = \dfrac{12}{0.25} = 48$.

A is incorrect because if 15 is the number of students in the class, 25% of 15 would be the number of students who earned A's. But 25% of 15 is $0.25(15) = 3.75$, and the number of students who earned A's is 12. Possibly you used the numbers from the problem, multiplied $0.25(12)$, and got 3. Then, realizing that 3 was too small, you added 12 to get 15.

B is incorrect because if 16 is the number of students in the class, 25% of 16 would be the number of students who earned A's. But 25% of 16 is $0.25(16) = 4$, and the number of students who earned A's is 12. Possibly you solved the problem thinking that 75% of the students in the class earned A's because 75% of 16 is $0.75(16)$, or 12.

C is incorrect because if 21 is the number of students in the class, 25% of 21 would be the number of students who earned A's. But 25% of 21 is $0.25(21) = 5.25$, and the number of students who earned A's is 12. Possibly you thought that if 25% of the students earned A's then 75% of the students in the class earned other grades; 75% of 12 is $0.75(12)$ or 9. You might have thought 12 earned A's and 9 earned other grades, so there were 12 + 9, or 21, students in the class.

D is incorrect because if 30 is the number of students in the class, 25% of 30 would be the number of students who earned A's. But 25% of 30 is $0.25(30) = 7.5$, and the number of students who earned A's is 12. Possibly you tried to find 25% of 12, but made a decimal point error and multiplied $2.5(12)$ instead of $0.25(12)$.

E is correct, as explained above.

Question 2. The correct answer is H.

Because A, E, and D are on a straight line, the sum of the measures of $\angle AEB$, $\angle BEC$, and $\angle CED$ is $180°$, so $55° + 25° + m\angle CED = 180°$ and $m\angle CED = 180° - (55° + 25°) = 100°$.

F is incorrect because the sum of the measures of $\angle AEB$ and $\angle BEC$ and $80°$ must be $180°$ since A, E, and D are on a straight line. But the sum of the measures of $\angle AEB$ and $\angle BEC$ and $80°$ is $55° + 25° + 80° = 160°$. The angle measure you found is the measure of the supplement of angle $\angle CED$, not the measure of $\angle CED$.

G is incorrect because the sum of the measures of $\angle AEB$ and $\angle BEC$ and $90°$ must be $180°$ since A, E, and D are on a straight line. But the sum of the measures of $\angle AEB$ and $\angle BEC$ and $90°$ is $55° + 25° + 90° = 170°$. Possibly you thought that $\angle CED$ looked like a right angle from the figure.

H is correct, as explained above.

J is incorrect because the sum of the measures of $\angle AEB$ and $\angle BEC$ and $110°$ must be $180°$ since A, E, and D are on a straight line. But the sum of the measures of $\angle AEB$ and $\angle BEC$ and $110°$ is $55° + 25° + 110° = 190°$. Perhaps you made an addition error and didn't carry when you added $55° + 25°$.

K is incorrect because the sum of the measures of $\angle AEB$ and $\angle BEC$ and $140°$ must be $180°$ since A, E, and D are on a straight line. But the sum of the measures of $\angle AEB$ and $\angle BEC$ and $140°$ is $55° + 25° + 140° = 220°$.

Question 3. The correct answer is B.

The given sequence is arithmetic, so obtain each term by adding a constant to the previous term. The constant in this sequence is -2 because $8 + -2 = 6$, $6 + -2 = 4$. So the first term is 8, the second term is 6, the third term is 4, and, continuing, the fourth term is $4 + -2 = 2$, and the fifth term is $2 + -2 = 0$.

A is incorrect because -2 is the sixth term of the sequence, not the fifth term. As discussed above, the constant in this sequence is -2. So the sixth term of the sequence is the fifth term, 0, plus the constant, -2, or $0 + -2 = -2$.

B is correct, as explained above.

C is incorrect because 4 is the third term of the sequence, not the fifth term. The first three terms are given—the first term is 8, the second term is 6, and the third term is 4.

D is incorrect because 8 is the first term of the sequence, not the fifth term. The first term is given and is 8.

E is incorrect because 16 is not a term of the sequence at all. The first term is 8, and it is the largest term of the sequence, so 16 isn't a term of the sequence.

MATHEMATICS ■ PRACTICE TEST 1 ■ EXPLANATORY ANSWERS

Question 4. The correct answer is K.

To find the value of x, multiply both sides of the equation by 48 (or use the shortcut of cross multiplying) and get $9 \cdot 8 = 6x$, so $72 = 6x$, $\frac{72}{6} = x$, and $12 = x$.

F is incorrect because $\frac{5\frac{1}{3}}{8}$ does not equal $\frac{9}{6}$, or 1.5. $\frac{5\frac{1}{3}}{8}$ is less than 1 because its numerator, $5\frac{1}{3}$, is less than its denominator, 8. Since $5\frac{1}{3}$ is the solution for $9x = 48$, perhaps you set the product of the numerators of the two ratios equal to the product of the denominators.

G is incorrect because $\frac{6\frac{3}{4}}{8}$ does not equal $\frac{9}{6}$, or 1.5. $\frac{6\frac{3}{4}}{8}$ is less than 1 because its numerator, $6\frac{3}{4}$, is less than its denominator, 8. Since $6\frac{3}{4}$ is the solution for $54 = 8x$, perhaps you took $\frac{9}{6}$ as $6 \cdot 9$ and $\frac{x}{8}$ as $8x$.

H is incorrect because $\frac{10\frac{1}{2}}{8}$ does not equal $\frac{9}{6}$, or 1.5. $\frac{10\frac{1}{2}}{8}$ is 1.3125 (divide 10.5 by 8 on your calculator). Perhaps you were trying to get a number that is $1\frac{1}{2}$ times 8 (since 9 is $1\frac{1}{2}$ times 6 on the other side of the equation) and made a computation error that gave you $10\frac{1}{2}$.

J is incorrect because $\frac{11}{8}$ does not equal $\frac{9}{6}$, or 1.5. $\frac{11}{8}$ is 1.375 (divide 11 by 8 on your calculator). Perhaps in getting 11, you thought that since 9 is 3 more than 6 on the left side, x should be 3 more than 8.

K is correct, as explained above.

Question 5. The correct answer is E.

If C bisects $\overline{AB}$, then C is the midpoint of $\overline{AB}$. This means that the length of $\overline{AC}$ is half the length of $\overline{AB}$ and the length of $\overline{CB}$ is half the length of $\overline{AB}$, so $\overline{AC}$ and $\overline{CB}$ are the same length. Segments that have the same length are congruent, so $\overline{AC} \cong \overline{CB}$.

A is incorrect because if C bisects $\overline{AB}$, then C is the midpoint of $\overline{AB}$. This means that the length of $\overline{AC}$ (which is the same as $\overline{CA}$) is half the length of $\overline{AB}$. Therefore $\overline{CA}$ and $\overline{AB}$ are not congruent because they are not the same length.

B is incorrect because if C bisects $\overline{AB}$, then C is the midpoint of $\overline{AB}$. This means that the length of $\overline{CB}$ is half the length of $\overline{AB}$. Therefore $\overline{CB}$ and $\overline{AB}$ are not congruent because they are not the same length.

C is incorrect because if C bisects $\overline{AB}$, then C is the midpoint of $\overline{AB}$. This means that the length of $\overline{AC}$ is half the length of $\overline{AB}$ (which is the same as $\overline{BA}$). Therefore $\overline{AC}$ and $\overline{BA}$ are not congruent because they are not the same length.

D is incorrect because if C bisects $\overline{AB}$, then C is the midpoint of $\overline{AB}$. This means that the length of $\overline{CB}$ (which is the same as $\overline{BC}$) is half the length of $\overline{AB}$ (which is the same as $\overline{BA}$). Therefore $\overline{BC}$ and $\overline{BA}$ are not congruent because they are not the same length.

E is correct, as explained above.

Question 6. The correct answer is F.

Three pieces of wire, each 2.8 meters long, have a total length 3(2.8) or 8.4 meters. If the length of the whole wire is 90 meters long and the 3 pieces have a total length of 8.4 meters, the remaining wire has a length of 90 – 8.4, or 81.6 meters.

F is correct, as explained above.

G is incorrect because if 82.6 meters were left, then the lengths of the 3 pieces that were cut off would total 90 – 82.6, or 7.4 meters. But 3 pieces each 2.8 meters long have a total length of 8.4 meters. Your error might have been in computation.

H is incorrect because if 83.2 meters were left, then the lengths of the 3 pieces that were cut off would total 90 – 83.2, or 6.8 meters. But 3 pieces each 2.8 meters long have a total length of 8.4 meters. Your error might have been in computation.

J is incorrect because if 83.6 meters were left, then the lengths of the 3 pieces that were cut off would total 90 – 83.6, or 6.4 meters. But 3 pieces each 2.8 meters long have a total length of 8.4 meters. Your error might have been in computation.

K is incorrect because if 87.2 meters were left, then the lengths of the 3 pieces that were cut off would total 90 – 87.2, or 2.8 meters. This would mean that only 1 piece 2.8 meters long was cut from the wire instead of 3 pieces.

Question 7. The correct answer is C.

Substituting -3 for x gives $12 - 2(-3 + 1) = 12 - 2(-2) = 12 + 4 = 16$.

A is incorrect because $12 - 2(x + 1)$ has a value of 4 when $x = 3$ since $12 - 2(3 + 1) = 12 - 2(4) = 12 - 8 = 4$. You might have substituted 3 instead of -3 for x.

B is incorrect because $12 - 2(x + 1)$ has a value of 7 when $x = \frac{3}{2}$ since $12 - 2\left(\frac{3}{2} + 1\right) = 12 - 2\left(\frac{5}{2}\right) = 12 - 5 = 7$. You might have treated $12 - 2(x + 1)$ as $12 - 2x + 1$ and substituted 3 instead of -3 for x in order to get 7.

C is correct, as explained above.

D is incorrect because $12 - 2(x + 1)$ has a value of 19 when $x = -\frac{9}{2}$ since $12 - 2\left(-\frac{9}{2} + 1\right) = 12 - 2\left(-\frac{7}{2}\right) = 12 - (-7) = 19$. You might have treated $12 - 2(x + 1)$ as $12 - 2x + 1$ in order to get 19.

E is incorrect because $12 - 2(x + 1)$ has a value of 20 when $x = -5$ since $12 - 2(-5 + 1) = 12 - 2(-4) = 12 - (-8) = 20$. You might have treated $12 - 2(x + 1)$ as $12 + 2(x + 1)$ and substituted 3 instead of -3 for x in order to get 20.

Question 8. The correct answer is H.

The absolute value of -10 is 10, so $|-10| = 10$. Then $-|-10| = -10$ and $-|-10| - (-10) = -10 - (-10) = 0$ since -10 is being subtracted from itself. Or, using what you know about subtracting a negative, $-10 - (-10) = -10 + 10 = 0$.

F is incorrect because $|-10| = 10$, so $-|-10| = -10$ and $-|-10| - (-10) = -10 - (-10) = -10 + 10 = 0$, not -100. To get -100, you might have multiplied in the last step instead of adding.

G is incorrect because $|-10| = 10$, so $-|-10| = -10$ and $-|-10| - (-10) = -10 - (-10) = -10 + 10 = 0$, not -20. To get -20, you might have dropped a minus sign and computed $-10 - (10)$ instead of $-10 - (-10)$.

H is correct, as explained above.

J is incorrect because $|-10| = 10$, so $-|-10| = -10$ and $-|-10| - (-10) = -10 - (-10) = -10 + 10 = 0$, not 20. To get 20, you might have dropped a minus sign and computed $10 + 10$ instead of $-10 + 10$.

K is incorrect because $|-10| = 10$, so $-|-10| = -10$ and $-|-10| - (-10) = -10 - (-10) = -10 + 10 = 0$, not 100. To get 100, you might have multiplied -10 and -10 instead of subtracting them.

Question 9. The correct answer is C.

Umberto's mother expects a 5% increase in her salary of $36,000. The decimal form of 5% is 0.05, so the increase Umberto's mother expects is 0.05(36,000), or $1,800. Her new salary will be her current salary plus the expected increase, so her new salary will be $36,000 + $1,800, or $37,800.

A is incorrect because a new salary of $36,005 means that her salary increase is only $5, but 5% of $36,000, or 0.05(36,000), is $1,800. You might have mistaken 5% for $5.

B is incorrect because a new salary of $36,180 means that her salary increase is only $180, but 5% of $36,000, or 0.05(36,000), is $1,800. You might have made a decimal point error in converting 5% to its decimal form.

C is correct, as explained above.

D is incorrect because a new salary of $41,000 means that her salary increase is $5,000, but 5% of $36,000, or 0.05(36,000), is $1,800. You might have thought that percent involved thousands so that 5% meant 5,000.

E is incorrect because a new salary of $54,000 means that her salary increase is $18,000, but 5% of $36,000, or 0.05(36,000), is $1,800. You might have made a decimal point error in converting 5% to its decimal form.

Question 10. The correct answer is F.

The solution of the equation $x^3 = 20$ is $x = \sqrt[3]{20}$ since $(\sqrt[3]{20})^3 = 20$. On a calculator that does cube roots, $\sqrt[3]{20} \approx 2.714$ so $x \approx 2.714$, which is between 2 and 3. Without a calculator, $\sqrt[3]{8} = 2$ since $2^3 = 8$, and $\sqrt[3]{27} = 3$ since $3^3 = 27$. So, cube roots of numbers between 8 and 27 are between 2 and 3, and since 20 is between 8 and 27, $\sqrt[3]{20}$ is between 2 and 3.

F is correct, as explained above.

G is incorrect because, if x lies between 3 and 4, then x^3 lies between $3^3 = 27$ and $4^3 = 64$. But 20 does not lie between 27 and 64.

H is incorrect because, if x lies between 4 and 5, then x^3 lies between $4^3 = 64$ and $5^3 = 125$. But 20 does not lie between 64 and 125.

J is incorrect because, if x lies between 5 and 6, then x^3 lies between $5^3 = 125$ and $6^3 = 216$. But 20 does not lie between 126 and 216.

K is incorrect because, if x lies between 6 and 7, then x^3 lies between $6^3 = 216$ and $7^3 = 343$. But 20 does not lie between 216 and 343.

Question 11. The correct answer is B.

If $78 - x = 234$, then subtracting 78 from both sides gives $-x = 156$. Multiplying both sides by -1 gives $(-1)(-x) = (-1)(156)$ or $x = -156$.

A is incorrect because $78 - (-312) = 78 + 312 = 390$, not 234. Instead of subtracting 78 from both sides of $78 - x = 234$, you might have added 78 to both sides.

B is correct, as explained above.

C is incorrect because $78 - 3 = 75$, not 234. You may have treated $78 - x = 234$ as $78x = 234$ and then divided both sides by 78 to get 3.

D is incorrect because $78 - 156 = -78$, not 234. You may have treated $78 - x = 234$ as $78 + x = 234$ and then subtracted 78 from both sides to get 156.

E is incorrect because $78 - 312 = -234$, not 234. You may have treated $78 - x = 234$ as $x - 78 = 234$ and then added 78 to both sides.

Question 12. The correct answer is F.

If the lifespan of Amoeba C is n hours, Amoeba B lives $2n$ hours because it lives twice as long as Amoeba C. Amoeba A lives 5 hours longer than Amoeba B, so Amoeba A lives $2n + 5$ hours.

F is correct, as explained above.

G is incorrect because if Amoeba A lives $7 + n$ hours and this is 5 hours longer than Amoeba B, then Amoeba B lives $2 + n$ hours. But this is 2 hours more than Amoeba C, not twice as long as Amoeba C's lifespan of n hours. You might have interpreted "twice as long" as "2 hours longer."

H is incorrect because if Amoeba A lives $7n$ hours and this is 5 hours longer than Amoeba B, then Amoeba B lives $7n - 5$ hours. But this is not twice as long as Amoeba C's lifespan of n hours. You might have gotten $5 + 2n$ and treated it as $(5 + 2)n$ in order to get $7n$ as your answer.

J is incorrect because if Amoeba A lives $10n$ hours and this is 5 hours longer than Amoeba B, then Amoeba B lives $10n - 5$ hours. But this is not twice as long as Amoeba C's lifespan of n hours. You might have interpreted "5 hours longer" as "5 times as long" in order to get $10n$ as your answer.

K is incorrect because if Amoeba A lives $2(5 + n) = 10 + 2n$ hours and this is 5 hours longer than Amoeba B, then Amoeba B lives $5 + 2n$ hours. But this is not twice as long as Amoeba C's lifespan of n hours. You might have thought that Amoeba C lives n hours, Amoeba B lives 5 hours longer than Amoeba C, and Amoeba A lives twice as long as Amoeba B in order to get $2(5 + n)$ as your answer.

Question 13. The correct answer is E.

The graph below shows the location of $(1,-1)$, $(-4,-1)$, and $(1,-4)$. These 3 points determine adjacent sides of the rectangle—one horizontal and one vertical. The fourth corner of the rectangle must be where the horizontal line through $(1,-4)$ intersects the vertical line through $(-4,-1)$.

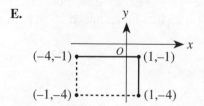

A is incorrect because, as shown by the graph below, (1,–1), (1,–4), and (1,4) are collinear. Three corners of a rectangle cannot all be on the same line.

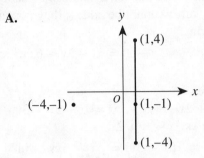

B is incorrect because, as shown by the graph below, the quadrilateral with corners at (1,–1), (–4,–1), (1,–4), and (–1,4) is not a rectangle.

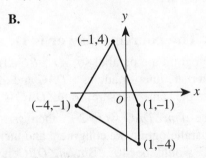

C is incorrect because, as shown by the graph below, the quadrilateral with corners at (1,–1), (–4,–1), (1,–4), and (–1,1) is not a rectangle.

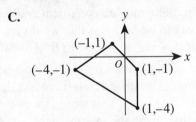

D is incorrect because, as shown by the graph below, the quadrilateral with corners at (1,–1), (–4,–1), (1,–4), and (–1,–4) is not a rectangle.

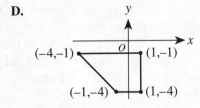

E is correct, as explained above.

Question 14. The correct answer is K.

In $3x - 3y + 2x$, $3x$ and $2x$ are like terms and can be added to get $5x$. The term with y and the terms with x cannot be added; they contain different variables and so are not like terms.

F is incorrect because $3(x - y + 2) = 3x - 3y + 6$, which is not the same as $3x - 3y + 2x$.

G is incorrect because
$(x - y)(3 + 2x) = x(3 + 2x) - y(3 + 2x) = 3x + 2x^2 - 3y - xy$,
which is not the same as $3x - 3y + 2x$.

H is incorrect because $x(5 - 3y) = 5x - 3xy$, which is not the same as $3x - 3y + 2x$.

J is incorrect because $x - 3y$ is the same as $3x - 3y - 2x$, not $3x - 3y + 2x$.

K is correct, as explained above.

Question 15. The correct answer is D.

The sides of a parallelogram are parallel so $\overline{AD} \parallel \overline{BC}$. The diagonal $\overline{AC}$ is a transversal and the alternate interior angles $\angle DAC$ and $\angle ACB$ are congruent. Congruent angles have the same measure, so $m\angle DAC$ is 50°.

A is incorrect because if $m\angle DAC$ were 20°, then $m\angle DAB$ would be 40°. Opposite angles of a parallelogram are congruent and therefore have the same measure, so $m\angle DBC$ would be 40°. But $m\angle DBC$ is at least 50° since $m\angle DBC = m\angle DCA + m\angle BCA$ and $m\angle BCA$ is 50°.

B is incorrect because if $m\angle DAC$ were 30°, then $m\angle DAB$ would be 50°. Opposite angles of a parallelogram are congruent and therefore have the same measure, so $m\angle DBC$ would be 50°. But this would mean that $m\angle DCA$ is 0° since $m\angle DBC = m\angle DCA + m\angle BCA$ and $m\angle BCA$ is 50°.

C is incorrect because if $m\angle DAC$ were 40°, then $m\angle DAB$ would be 60°. Opposite angles of a parallelogram are congruent and therefore have the same measure, so $m\angle DBC$ would be 60°. This would mean that $m\angle DCA$ is 10°, but $m\angle DCA$ is 20° since the alternate interior angles $\angle DCA$ and $\angle CAB$ are congruent and congruent angles have the same measure.

D is correct, as explained above.

E is incorrect because if $m\angle DAC$ were 70°, then $m\angle DAB$ would be 90°. Opposite angles of a parallelogram are congruent and therefore have the same measure, so $m\angle DBC$ would be 90°. This would mean that $m\angle DCA$ is 40°, but $m\angle DCA$ is 20° since the alternate interior angles $\angle DCA$ and $\angle CAB$ are congruent and congruent angles have the same measure.

Question 16. The correct answer is G.

The slope of a line can be found by writing the equation in slope-intercept form, $y = mx + b$, where m is the slope of the line. So, if $3x + 5y = 8$, then $5y = 8 - 3x$ and $y = \frac{8}{5} + -\frac{3}{5}x$. The slope of the line with equation $3x + 5y = 8$ is then $-\frac{3}{5}$. Parallel lines have equal slopes, so the slope of any line parallel to the line with equation $3x + 5y = 8$ is also $-\frac{3}{5}$.

F is incorrect because parallel lines have equal slopes and -3 isn't equal to $-\frac{3}{5}$, the slope of the line with equation $3x + 5y = 8$. Perhaps in trying to get the slope-intercept form, you got as far as $5y = 8 - 3x$, but didn't do the last step.

G is correct, as explained above.

H is incorrect because parallel lines have equal slopes and $\frac{3}{8}$ isn't equal to $-\frac{3}{5}$, the slope of the line with equation $3x + 5y = 8$. Perhaps you learned that when an equation has the form $Ax + By = C$, the slope is $-\frac{A}{B}$ and the y-intercept is $\frac{C}{B}$, and you remembered the formulas incorrectly.

J is incorrect because parallel lines have equal slopes and 3 isn't equal to $-\frac{3}{5}$, the slope of the line with equation $3x + 5y = 8$. Perhaps you learned that when an equation has the form $Ax + By = C$, the slope is $-\frac{A}{B}$ and the y-intercept is $\frac{C}{B}$, and you remembered the formulas incorrectly and thought the slope was A.

K is incorrect because parallel lines have equal slopes and 8 isn't equal to $-\frac{3}{5}$, the slope of the line with equation $3x + 5y = 8$. Perhaps you learned that when an equation has the form $Ax + By = C$, the slope is $-\frac{A}{B}$ and the y-intercept is $\frac{C}{B}$, and you remembered the formulas incorrectly and thought the slope was C.

Question 17. The correct answer is C.

If you solve the equation $2x^2 - 5x - 12 = 0$ by factoring, you get $(2x + 3)(x - 4) = 0$. Then, $2x + 3 = 0$ so $x = -\frac{3}{2}$ or $x - 4 = 0$ so $x = 4$. Since $x > 0$ is given as a condition, $x = 4$ is the correct answer.

If you solve the equation using the quadratic formula, then

$$x = \frac{-(-5) \pm \sqrt{(-5)^2 - 4(2)(-12)}}{2(2)} = \frac{5 \pm \sqrt{25 - (-96)}}{4} = \frac{5 \pm \sqrt{121}}{4} = \frac{5 \pm 11}{4} \text{ so}$$

$x = -\frac{3}{2}$ or $x = 4$. Then, since $x > 0$ is given as a condition, $x = 4$ is the correct answer.

A is incorrect because $2\left(\frac{3}{2}\right)^2 - 5\left(\frac{3}{2}\right) - 12 = -15$, not 0. You might have factored incorrectly and got $2x - 3$ as a factor or you might have made a sign error in solving $2x + 3 = 0$.

B is incorrect because $2(2)^2 - 5(2) - 12 = -14$, not 0. You might have factored incorrectly and got $x - 2$ as a factor or, in using the quadratic formula, you might have used a instead of $2a$ as the denominator.

C is correct, as explained above.

D is incorrect because $2(5)^2 - 5(5) - 12 = 13$, not 0. You might have remembered only part of the quadratic formula and set x equal to $-b$.

E is incorrect because $2(12)^2 - 5(12) - 12 = 216$, not 0. You might have thought that the solution of a quadratic equation is the opposite of the constant term.

Question 18. The correct answer is F.

If x represents the length of the shortest side of the similar triangle, x corresponds to the side of length 3 of the given triangle. Thus one ratio in the proportion is $\frac{x}{3}$. The perimeter of the given triangle is $3 + 8 + 9 = 20$, and the perimeter of the similar triangle is 60. The other ratio of the proportion is $\frac{60}{20}$, and the proportion is $\frac{x}{3} = \frac{60}{20}$. This simplifies to $\frac{x}{3} = 3$. Multiplying both sides by 3 gives $x = 9$.

F is correct, as explained above.

G is incorrect because the perimeter of the given triangle is $3 + 8 + 9 = 20$ and the perimeter of the similar triangle is 60, making the sides of the similar triangle 3 times as long as those of the given triangle. No side of the similar triangle can be 11 inches long because 11 isn't 3 times any of the side lengths of the given triangle ($11 \neq 3 \cdot 3$, $11 \neq 3 \cdot 8$, and $11 \neq 3 \cdot 9$).

H is incorrect because the perimeter of the given triangle is $3 + 8 + 9 = 20$ and the perimeter of the similar triangle is 60, making the sides of the similar triangle 3 times as long as those of the given triangle. No side of the similar triangle can be 20 inches long because 20 isn't 3 times any of the side lengths of the given triangle ($20 \neq 3 \cdot 3$, $20 \neq 3 \cdot 8$, and $20 \neq 3 \cdot 9$). You might have started by finding that the perimeter of the given triangle is 20 and chose that as your answer.

J is incorrect because the perimeter of the given triangle is $3 + 8 + 9 = 20$ and the perimeter of the similar triangle is 60, making the sides of the similar triangle 3 times as long as those of the given triangle. By answering 24, you might have been thinking of the length of the second-longest side of the similar triangle ($24 = 3 \cdot 8$), not the length of the shortest side.

K is incorrect because the perimeter of the given triangle is $3 + 8 + 9 = 20$ and the perimeter of the similar triangle is 60, making the sides of the similar triangle 3 times as long as those of the given triangle. By answering 27, you might have been thinking of the length of the longest side of the similar triangle ($27 = 3 \cdot 9$), not the length of the shortest side.

Question 19. The correct answer is D.

To calculate the amount that was taken off the normal price during the sale, you need to find 25% of $35.95. This amounts to finding $\frac{1}{4}$ of $35.95, or (0.25)(35.95), which is $8.99. Thus $8.99 was taken off the normal price and $35.95 − $8.99 = $26.96. Rounding to the nearest dollar gives the sale price, $27.

A is incorrect because 25% of $35.95 is $8.99, which is $9 to the nearest dollar, and this is the amount off, not the sale price.

B is incorrect because if the jeans cost $11 during the sale, then the amount taken off the normal price would be $24.95. This is more than half of $39.95 and would mean that the normal price was reduced by more than 50%, not just 25%.

C is incorrect because if the jeans cost $26 during the sale, then the amount taken off the normal price would be $9.95. This is more than 25% because 25% of $35.95 is $8.99. You might have gotten $26.96 as the sale price and rounded it down to $26 instead of rounding it up to the nearest dollar.

D is correct, as explained above.

E is incorrect because if the jeans cost $29 during the sale, then the amount taken off the normal price would be $6.95. This is less than 25% because 25% of $35.95 is $8.99.

Question 20. The correct answer is G.

The greatest common factor of the terms is $4xy$ because each term has at least one factor of 4, at least one factor of x, and at least one factor of y. Factoring the $4xy$ out of $4x^3y$ leaves x^2, and factoring $4xy$ out of $4xy^3$ leaves y^2. Therefore $4x^3y + 4xy^3 = 4xy(x^2 + y^2)$.

F is incorrect because $4x^3y^3(y + x) = 4x^3y^4 + 4x^4y^3$, not $4x^3y + 4xy^3$. You might have found the least common multiple of the terms instead of the greatest common factor.

G is correct, as explained above.

H is incorrect because $8xy(x^2 + y^2) = 8x^3y + 8xy^3$, not $4x^3y + 4xy^3$.

J is incorrect because $4x^3y$ and $4xy^3$ are not like terms and cannot be added together to obtain one term.

K is incorrect because $4x^3y$ and $4xy^3$ are not like terms and cannot be added together to obtain one term. You might have added the coefficients and multiplied x^3y and xy^3.

Question 21. The correct answer is D.

Solving the second equation for x gives $x = 12 - 4y$. Then substituting x into the first equation gives $2(12 - 4y) - y = 6$. Then, $24 - 8y - y = 6$, $24 - 9y = 6$, $-9y = -18$, $y = 2$.

A is incorrect because if $y = -6$, then from $2x - y = 6$, $2x - (-6) = 6$ so $2x = 0$ and $x = 0$. But, from $x + 4y = 12$, $x + 4(-6) = 12$ so $x = 36$. There is no point with y-coordinate -6 that satisfies both equations, so y cannot be -6.

B is incorrect because if $y = 0$, then from $2x - y = 6$, $2x - 0 = 6$ so $2x = 6$ and $x = 3$. But, from $x + 4y = 12$, $x + 4(0) = 12$ so $x = 12$. There is no point with y-coordinate 0 that satisfies both equations, so y cannot be 0.

C is incorrect because if $y = 1$, then from $2x - y = 6$, $2x - 1 = 6$ so $2x = 7$ and $x = \frac{7}{2}$. But, from $x + 4y = 12$, $x + 4(1) = 12$ so $x = 8$. There is no point with y-coordinate 1 that satisfies both equations, so y cannot be 1.

D is correct, as explained above.

E is incorrect because if $y = 3$, then from $2x - y = 6$, $2x - 3 = 6$ so $2x = 9$ and $x = \frac{9}{2}$. But, from $x + 4y = 12$, $x + 4(3) = 12$ so $x = 0$. There is no point with y-coordinate 3 that satisfies both equations, so y cannot be 3.

Question 22. The correct answer is F.

The amount of hamburger given, 1.5 pounds, is 1.5(16), or 24, ounces. Dividing $2.88 by 24 ounces gives $0.12 per ounce.

F is correct, as explained above.

G is incorrect because 1.5 pounds, or 24 ounces, of hamburger at $0.18 per ounce would cost $4.32, not $2.88. You might have found the cost per ounce assuming that 1 pound, not 1.5 pounds, of hamburger costs $2.88.

H is incorrect because 1.5 pounds, or 24 ounces, of hamburger at $0.88 per ounce would cost $21.12, not $2.88.

J is incorrect because 1.5 pounds, or 24 ounces, of hamburger at $1.92 per ounce would cost $46.08, not $2.88. You might have found the cost per pound by dividing 2.88 by 1.5.

K is incorrect because if 1.5 pounds, or 24 ounces, of hamburger cost only $2.88, a single ounce could not cost $4.32.

Question 23. The correct answer is C.

By looking at the figure below, where the vertices of one square have been labeled and auxiliary lines have been drawn, you can see that square *ABCD* is divided into 4 congruent pieces and the shaded region (the overlap of *ABCD* and the other square) is one of these pieces. Therefore, the area of the shaded region is $\frac{1}{4}$ of the area of *ABCD*. Since *ABCD* is 8 inches on a side, its area is 8(8) = 64 square inches and the area of the shaded region is $\frac{1}{4}(64)$ = 16 square inches.

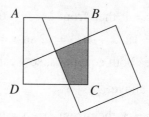

A is incorrect because if the area of the shaded region were only 4 square inches, then the shaded region would be only $\frac{4}{64}$, or $\frac{1}{16}$, of the square. Clearly, there would have to be much less overlap between the two squares to make this so. You might have thought that you should take half of the length of a side of the square.

B is incorrect because if the area of the shaded region were only 8 square inches, then the shaded region would be only $\frac{8}{64}$, or $\frac{1}{8}$, of the square. Clearly, there would have to be much less overlap between the two squares to make this so. You might have thought that the area of the shaded region would be the same numerically as the side length.

C is correct, as explained above.

D is incorrect because if the area of the shaded region were 32 square inches, then the shaded region would be $\frac{32}{64}$, or $\frac{1}{2}$, of the square. Clearly, there would have to be much more overlap between the two squares to make this so. Perhaps you found the perimeter of one square and thought this would be the same numerically as the area of the shaded region.

E is incorrect because 64 square inches is the area of the whole square, not the area of the shaded region.

Question 24. The correct answer is F.

The expression $6h + 0.05t$ basically says that the salesperson makes \$6 per hour and makes a commission of 5% on her total sales. Substituting 10 for h and 230.80 for t gives $6(10) + 0.05(230.80) = 60 + 11.54 = 71.54$.

F is correct, as explained above.

G is incorrect because \$74.54 is the value of $(6h + t)(0.05)$ when $h = 10$ and $t = 230.80$ since $(60 + 230.80)(0.05) = (290.80)(0.05) = 74.54$. You might have given her commission on her hourly wages in addition to her total sales.

H is incorrect because \$175.40 is the value of $6h + 0.5t$ when $h = 10$ and $t = 230.80$ since $6(10) + 0.5(230.80) = 60 + 115.40 = 175.40$. You might have given her 50% commission instead of 5%.

J is incorrect because if the salesperson worked only 10 hours, her hourly wages would have been \$60, leaving \$251.80 – \$60 = \$191.80 as her commission. With her sales only \$230.80, this means that her commission was over 80%.

K is incorrect because \$295.80 is the value of $(6 + 0.5)h + t$ since $(6 + 0.5)(10) + 230.80 = 65 + 230.80 = 295.80$. You might have attempted to add 5% to the hourly wage, added 0.5 instead, and then added that to the salesperson's total sales.

Question 25. The correct answer is D.

As shown in the figure below, the floor can be divided into two rectangles—one 12 feet by 18 feet and the other 6 feet by 9 feet. The area of the floor is the sum of the areas of the pieces, which are 12(18) = 216 and 6(9) = 54. The area of the floor is 216 + 54 = 270 square feet.

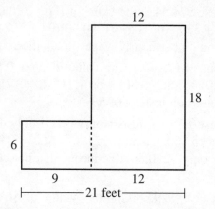

A is incorrect because 57 = 12 + 18 + 21 + 6, the sum of all the dimensions given on the original figure, and this is part of the perimeter of the floor, not the area.

B is incorrect because 72 square feet is the area of a rectangle that is 6 feet by 12 feet. Although two of the dimensions marked on the figure are 6 feet and 12 feet, the floor is not a 6-foot-by-12-foot rectangle.

C is incorrect because 162 square feet is the area of a rectangle that is 9 feet by 18 feet. Although 9 feet and 18 feet are dimensions of parts of the floor, the floor is not a 9-foot-by-18-foot rectangle.

D is correct, as explained above.

E is incorrect because 324 square feet is the area of a square that is 18 feet on a side. Although one of the dimensions marked on the figure is 18 feet, the floor is not an 18-foot-by-18-foot square.

Question 26. The correct answer is G.

To solve the inequality $x - 1 < -2$, add 1 to both sides of the inequality to get $x < -1$. This set includes all numbers to the left of -1 on the number line, with an open dot at -1 to show that -1 is not included in the set.

F is incorrect because it shows the graph of $x < -3$. You might have subtracted 1 from both sides of the inequality instead of adding 1.

G is correct, as explained above.

H is incorrect because it shows the graph of $-3 < x < -1$. You might have thought you were solving an inequality with absolute values because they frequently have solutions that are all numbers between two other numbers.

J is incorrect because it shows the graph of $x > -1$. You might have thought that the inequality to be solved was $x - 1 > -2$.

K is incorrect because it gives the graph of $-1 < x < 3$. You might have thought that the inequality to be solved was $|x - 1| < 2$.

Question 27. The correct answer is B.

The decimal for $\frac{3}{4}$, found by dividing 3 by 4, is 0.75. The decimal for $\frac{5}{7}$, found by dividing 5 by 7, is $0.\overline{714285}$ and $0.\overline{714285} < 0.75$.

A is incorrect because the decimal for $\frac{3}{4}$, found by dividing 3 by 4, is 0.75. The decimal for $\frac{5}{6}$, found by dividing 5 by 6, is $0.8\overline{3}$ and $0.8\overline{3} \not< 0.75$.

B is correct, as explained above.

C is incorrect because $\frac{6}{8} = \frac{3}{4}$, so $\frac{6}{8} \not< \frac{3}{4}$.

D is incorrect because the decimal for $\frac{3}{4}$, found by dividing 3 by 4, is 0.75. The decimal for $\frac{8}{10}$, found by dividing 8 by 10, is 0.8 and $0.8 \not< 0.75$.

E is incorrect because the decimal for $\frac{3}{4}$, found by dividing 3 by 4, is 0.75. The decimal for $\frac{10}{13}$, found by dividing 10 by 13, is $0.\overline{769230}$, and $0.\overline{769230} \not< 0.75$.

Question 28. The correct answer is G.

The area of a triangle is given by the formula $A = \frac{1}{2}bh$. For a right triangle, b is the length of one leg and h is the length of the other leg. Because the legs are the shortest two sides of a right triangle, the legs of the given triangle are 8 meters and 15 meters. The area is therefore $\frac{1}{2}(8)(15) = 60$ square meters.

F is incorrect because $40 = 8 + 15 + 17$; adding the lengths of the sides gives the perimeter, not the area.

G is correct, as explained above.

H is incorrect because $68 = \frac{1}{2}(8)(17)$, but 8 and 17 are not the two legs of the right triangle; 17 is the length of the hypotenuse, which is the longest side.

J is incorrect because $120 = 8(15)$, which is the area of a rectangle that is 8 meters by 15 meters. You might have forgotten the factor of $\frac{1}{2}$ in the formula for the area of a triangle, $A = \frac{1}{2}bh$.

K is incorrect because $127\frac{1}{2} = \frac{1}{2}(15)(17)$, but 15 and 17 are not the two legs of the right triangle; 17 is the length of the hypotenuse, which is the longest side.

Question 29. The correct answer is C.

Say that the band has n members. If it had 1 more member (so it had $n + 1$ members), then the members could be arranged in rows of 4, 5, or 6, and no row would be short. This means that $n + 1$ is divisible by 4, 5, and 6. The least number that is divisible by 4, 5, and 6 is 60 ($60 \div 4 = 15$, $60 \div 5 = 12$, and $60 \div 6 = 10$) so $n + 1 = 60$ and $n = 59$.

A is incorrect because 11 people arranged in rows of 5 leaves the last row with only 1 person; the last row would have to have 4 people in order to be 1 short.

B is incorrect because 14 people arranged in rows of 4 leaves the last row with only 2 people; the last row would have to have 3 people in order to be 1 short.

C is correct, as explained above.

D is incorrect because 89 people arranged in rows of 4 leaves the last row with only 1 person; the last row would have to have 3 people in order to be 1 short.

E is incorrect because, even though arranging 119 people in rows of 4, 5, or 6 always leaves the last row 1 person short, this is also true for 59 people, and so 119 is not the smallest possible number of people that could be in the band.

Question 30. The correct answer is F.

The sum of the lengths of any two sides of a triangle must be greater than the length of the third side. Since $1 + 2.5 \not> 4$, 1 cannot be the length of the third side.

F is correct, as explained above.

G is incorrect because the sum of the lengths of any two sides of a triangle must be greater than the length of the third side. The third side can have length 2 because $2 + 2.5 > 4$, $2 + 4 > 2.5$, and $2.5 + 4 > 2$.

H is incorrect because the sum of the lengths of any two sides of a triangle must be greater than the length of the third side. The third side can have length 3 because $3 + 2.5 > 4$, $3 + 4 > 2.5$, and $2.5 + 4 > 3$.

J is incorrect because the sum of the lengths of any two sides of a triangle must be greater than the length of the third side. The third side can have length 4 because $4 + 2.5 > 4$, and $4 + 4 > 2.5$.

K is incorrect because the sum of the lengths of any two sides of a triangle must be greater than the length of the third side. The third side can have length 5 because $5 + 2.5 > 4$, $5 + 4 > 2.5$, and $2.5 + 4 > 5$.

Question 31. The correct answer is C.

When adding fractions, you need to find the common denominator, which in this problem is $3a$. Then $\frac{1}{a} + \frac{2}{3} = \frac{1 \cdot 3}{a \cdot 3} + \frac{2 \cdot a}{3 \cdot a} = \frac{3 + 2a}{3a}$.

A is incorrect because $\frac{2}{3a}$ is $\frac{1}{a} \cdot \frac{2}{3}$, not $\frac{1}{a} + \frac{2}{3}$. You might have thought that you needed to multiply the fractions.

B is incorrect because $\frac{3}{3a} = \frac{1}{a}$, not $\frac{1}{a} + \frac{2}{3}$. You might have determined that the common denominator for the fractions should be $3a$, converted $\frac{1}{a}$ to a fraction with that common denominator, and then thought you were finished with the problem.

C is correct, as explained above.

D is incorrect because $\frac{3}{3 + a} = \frac{1 + 2}{a + 3}$, but adding numerators and adding denominators is not the correct way to add fractions.

E is incorrect because, although the numerator is correct, the denominator should be $3a$, not $3 + a$. You might have written the wrong operation symbol in the denominator.

Question 32. **The correct answer is F.**

By the Pythagorean theorem, the sum of the squares of the lengths of the legs of a right triangle equals the square of the length of the hypotenuse. If x stands for the length of $\overline{AB}$, applying the Pythagorean theorem to $\triangle ABC$ gives $19^2 + x^2 = 29^2$. Then $x^2 = 29^2 - 19^2$ and $x = \sqrt{29^2 - 19^2}$.

F is correct, as explained above.

G is incorrect because applying the Pythagorean theorem to $\triangle ABC$ gives $19^2 + x^2 = 29^2$. Then $x^2 = 29^2 - 19^2$ and $x = \sqrt{29^2 - 19^2}$, not $\sqrt{29^2 + 19^2}$. You might have thought that the Pythagorean theorem says that the difference of the squares of the lengths of the legs of a right triangle equals the square of the length of the hypotenuse.

H is incorrect because $29^2 - 19^2$ is the square of the length of the missing side. You probably forgot to take the square root as your final step.

J is incorrect because applying the Pythagorean theorem to $\triangle ABC$ gives $19^2 + x^2 = 29^2$. Then $x^2 = 29^2 - 19^2$, not $29^2 + 19^2$. Also, the length of $\overline{AB}$ is $\sqrt{29^2 - 19^2}$. You might have thought that the Pythagorean theorem says that the difference of the squares of the lengths of the legs of a right triangle equals the square of the length of the hypotenuse and you probably forgot to take the square root as your final step.

K is incorrect because $29 - 19 = 10$ and 10 cannot be the length of $\overline{AB}$. The sum of the lengths of any two sides of a triangle must be greater than the third side, and $10 + 19 \not> 29$. You might have found the length of $\overline{AB}$ to be $\sqrt{29^2 - 19^2}$ and then took the square root of $29^2 - 19^2$ term by term.

Question 33. The correct answer is D.

If the square is x inches on a side and the length is increased by 1 inch, the length of the new figure is $x + 1$. If the width is increased by 2 inches, the width of the new figure is $x + 2$. The area of the new figure is the product of the length and the width of the new figure, and so the area is $(x + 1)(x + 2) = x^2 + 3x + 2$.

A is incorrect because $2x + 3$ is $(x + 1) + (x + 2)$, and the area of a rectangle is the product of the dimensions, not the sum.

B is incorrect because $4x + 6$ is $2[(x + 1) + (x + 2)]$, which is the perimeter of the new figure, not the area.

C is incorrect because the area is $(x + 1)(x + 2) = x^2 + 3x + 2$, not $x^2 + 2$. You probably forgot the middle term when multiplying $(x + 1)$ and $(x + 2)$.

D is correct, as explained above.

E is incorrect because the area is $(x + 1)(x + 2) = x^2 + 3x + 2$, not $x^2 + 3x + 3$. You may have added the last terms, 1 and 2, instead of multiplying them.

Question 34. The correct answer is H.

Because $\tan \alpha = \dfrac{\sin \alpha}{\cos \alpha}$, $\tan \alpha = \dfrac{\frac{12}{13}}{\frac{5}{13}} = \dfrac{12}{13} \cdot \dfrac{13}{5} = \dfrac{12}{5}$.

F is incorrect because $\dfrac{5}{12} = \dfrac{\frac{5}{13}}{\frac{12}{13}} = \dfrac{\cos \alpha}{\sin \alpha} = \cot \alpha \neq \tan \alpha$.

G is incorrect because $\dfrac{7}{13} = \dfrac{12}{13} - \dfrac{5}{13} = \sin \alpha - \cos \alpha$ and $\tan \alpha = \dfrac{\sin \alpha}{\cos \alpha}$, not $\sin \alpha - \cos \alpha$.

H is correct, as explained above.

J is incorrect because $\dfrac{17}{13} = \dfrac{12}{13} + \dfrac{5}{13} = \sin \alpha + \cos \alpha$ and $\tan \alpha = \dfrac{\sin \alpha}{\cos \alpha}$, not $\sin \alpha + \cos \alpha$.

K is incorrect because $\dfrac{60}{13} = 13\left(\dfrac{12}{13} \cdot \dfrac{5}{13}\right) = 13(\sin \alpha)(\cos \alpha) \neq \tan \alpha$. You might have forgotten to invert the divisor before you multiplied the fractions and neglected to multiply the denominators.

Question 35. The correct answer is E.

The graph indicates all numbers between, but not including, –1.5 and –0.5. This set of numbers is represented algebraically by the inequality $-1.5 < x < -0.5$ or $-0.5 > x > -1.5$.

A is incorrect because the solution to $|x| = -1$ is the empty set since the absolute value of a number can never be negative.

B is incorrect because the numbers that satisfy $|x| < 0.5$ are between, but do not include, –0.5 and 0.5. The numbers shown on the graph are between –1.5 and –0.5.

C is incorrect because the graph indicates all numbers between –1.5 and –0.5, not all numbers between –2 and 0.

D is incorrect because the set of numbers that are greater than –0.5 and less than –1.5 at the same time is the empty set.

E is correct, as explained above.

Question 36. The correct answer is H.

In order to find the average rating, assume that there were n people who rated the performance. Since 30% of the audience gave a rating of 1, there were $\frac{30n}{100}$ ratings of 1. Since 60% gave a rating of 2, there were $\frac{60n}{100}$ ratings of 2. Since 10% gave a rating of 3, there were $\frac{10n}{100}$ ratings of 3. The average of the ratings is

$$\frac{1\left(\frac{30n}{100}\right) + 2\left(\frac{60n}{100}\right) + 3\left(\frac{10n}{100}\right)}{n} = \frac{\frac{1(30n) + 2(60n) + 3(10n)}{100}}{n} = \frac{30n + 120n + 30n}{100n}$$

$$= \frac{180n}{100n} = 1.8.$$

F is incorrect because $1.2 = 2(0.60)$. You may have thought that, since 2 is in the middle of the ratings, 60% of 2 would be the average rating.

G is incorrect because $1.5 = 2(0.60) + 3(0.10)$. You may have thought that the ratings of 1 didn't count.

H is correct, as explained above.

J is incorrect because 2 is the average of 1, 2, and 3 since $2 = \frac{1 + 2 + 3}{3}$. You may have assumed that equal percentages of people gave each of the ratings.

K is incorrect because 2.2 would be the average rating if 30% of the audience had given a rating of 1, 20% gave a rating of 2, and 50% gave a rating of 3, but these are not the percentages given in the problem.

Question 37. The correct answer is E.

In 30°-60°-90° triangles, like $\triangle ABC$, the length of the hypotenuse (the side opposite the right angle) is twice the length of the side opposite the 30° angle. Here, $\overline{BC}$, the side opposite the 30° angle, is 4 inches long, so $\overline{AB}$, the hypotenuse, is 2(4) = 8 inches long.

A is incorrect because if $\overline{AB}$ were 4 inches long, then $\triangle ABC$ would be isosceles with congruent base angles $\angle A$ and $\angle C$. Clearly a 30° angle and a 90° angle cannot be congruent. You might have been thinking about a 45°-45°-90° triangle.

B is incorrect because if $\overline{AB}$ were $4\sqrt{2}$ inches long, then by the Pythagorean theorem, $\overline{AC}$ would be $\sqrt{(4\sqrt{2})^2 - 4^2} = \sqrt{32 - 16} = 4$. Then $\triangle ABC$ would be isosceles with congruent base angles $\angle A$ and $\angle B$. But if $\angle A$ and $\angle B$ are both 30°, then the angle sum of $\triangle ABC$ would be 30° + 30° + 90° = 150°, and the angle sum must be 180°. You might have been thinking about a 45°-45°-90° triangle.

C is incorrect because in 30°-60°-90° triangles, like $\triangle ABC$, the length of the side opposite the 60° angle is $\sqrt{3}$ times the length of the side opposite the 30° and so $\overline{AC}$ is $4\sqrt{3}$. The hypotenuse, $\overline{AB}$, cannot be the same length as one of the legs of a right triangle. You might have interchanged the $1:2:\sqrt{3}$ ratios you learned for 30°-60°-90° triangles.

D is incorrect because in 30°-60°-90° triangles the sides have to be in the ratio $1:2:\sqrt{3}$ and 6 is not $4 \cdot 1$, $4 \cdot 2$, or $4 \cdot \sqrt{3}$.

E is correct, as explained above.

Question 38. The correct answer is K.

If m and n are the two even numbers, $m + n = 38$ and you want to find the maximum value for mn. If $m + n = 38$ then $n = 38 - m$, and then $mn = m(38 - m) = 38m - m^2$. If you consider $f(x) = 38x - x^2$, the graph will be a parabola that turns downward. The maximum value will occur at the vertex of the parabola or where $x = -\dfrac{38}{2(-1)} = 19$. But 19 can't be m since m is even, so pick the even number closest to 19. If you pick 18, then $m = 18$ and $n = 38 - 18 = 20$. On the other hand, if you pick 20, then $m = 20$ and $n = 38 - 20 = 18$. In either case, $mn = 360$.

F is incorrect because, while $72 = 2 \cdot 36$ and $2 + 36 = 38$, there are other numbers that have a sum of 38 and give a larger product. Therefore, 72 is not the largest.

G is incorrect because the only two even numbers whose product is 76 are 2 and 38 and their sum is not 38. Possibly you took the numbers from the problem and multiplied them.

H is incorrect because, while $136 = 4 \cdot 34$ and $4 + 34 = 38$, there are other numbers that have a sum of 38 and give a larger product. Therefore, 136 is not the largest.

J is incorrect because, while $280 = 10 \cdot 28$ and $10 + 28 = 38$, there are other numbers that have a sum of 38 and give a larger product. Therefore, 280 is not the largest.

K is correct, as explained above.

Question 39. The correct answer is B.

On the figure below, certain points have been labeled for reference. Line k is a transversal that cuts parallel lines n and m, so $\angle ABD$ and $\angle BCE$ are corresponding angles and are therefore congruent and have the same measure. Then, $100° = m\angle BCE = 45° + m\angle DCB$ so $m\angle DCB = 55°$. The line through C and D is a transversal that cuts parallel lines j and k so $\angle DCB$ and $\angle CDE$ are alternate interior angles and are therefore congruent and have the same measure. Since $m\angle DCB = 55°$, $m\angle CDE = 55°$ and so $m\angle x = 55°$.

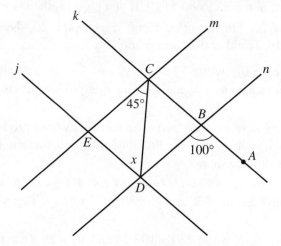

A is incorrect because if $m\angle x = 45°$, then $m\angle CED = 90°$ since the angle sum of $\triangle CED$ must be $180°$. But the sum of the measures of $\angle BCE$ and $\angle CED$ must be $180°$ since lines j and k are parallel, so $m\angle CED = 180° - (55° + 45°) = 80°$. But $\angle CED$ cannot have measures of both $80°$ and $90°$.

B is correct, as explained above.

C is incorrect because if $m\angle x = 65°$, then $m\angle CED = 70°$ since the angle sum of $\triangle CED$ must be $180°$. But the sum of the measures of $\angle BCE$ and $\angle CED$ must be $180°$ since lines j and k are parallel, so $m\angle CED = 180° - (55° + 45°) = 80°$. But $\angle CED$ cannot have measures of both $70°$ and $80°$.

D is incorrect because if $m\angle x = 75°$, then $m\angle CED = 60°$ since the angle sum of $\triangle CED$ must be $180°$. But the sum of the measures of $\angle BCE$ and $\angle CED$ must be $180°$ since lines j and k are parallel, so $m\angle CED = 180° - (55° + 45°) = 80°$. But $\angle CED$ cannot have measures of both $60°$ and $80°$.

E is incorrect because if $m\angle x = 80°$, then $m\angle CED = 55°$ since the angle sum of $\triangle CED$ must be $180°$. But the sum of the measures of $\angle BCE$ and $\angle CED$ must be $180°$ since lines j and k are parallel, so $m\angle CED = 180° - (55° + 45°) = 80°$. But $\angle CED$ cannot have measures of both $55°$ and $80°$. You might have given the measure of $\angle CED$ instead of the measure of $\angle x$.

Question 40. The correct answer is F.

The y-intercept can be obtained easily from $y = mx + b$ (the slope-intercept form for the equation of a line), where the y-intercept is given by b. To solve the equation $6x - 2y = 6$ for y, subtract $6x$ from both sides to get $-2y = -6x + 6$, then divide both sides by -2 to get $y = 3x - 3$. The y-intercept is -3.

F is correct, as explained above.

G is incorrect because if the y-intercept were -2, then $(0,-2)$ would satisfy the equation $6x - 2y = 6$. But $6(0) - 2(-2) = 4$, not 6. You might have thought that the coefficient of the y-term gives the y-intercept.

H is incorrect because if the y-intercept were 0, then $(0,0)$ would satisfy the equation $6x - 2y = 6$. But $6(0) - 2(0) = 0$, not 6. You might have tried to subtract $6x$ from both sides and thought that $6 - 6x$ gave 0.

J is incorrect because if the y-intercept were 3, then $(0,3)$ would satisfy the equation $6x - 2y = 6$. But $6(0) - 2(3) = -6$, not 6. You might have made a sign error.

K is incorrect because if the y-intercept were 6, then $(0,6)$ would satisfy the equation $6x - 2y = 6$. But $6(0) - 2(6) = -12$, not 6. You might have thought that the coefficient of the x-term gives the y-intercept.

Question 41. The correct answer is B.

On the number line graph, the interval between 3.14 and 3.15 is divided into 10 equal parts so the tick marks are at 3.140, 3.141, 3.142, 3.143, 3.144, 3.145, 3.146, 3.147, 3.148, 3.149, and 3.150. Point A is between 3.140 and 3.141, slightly closer to 3.141 than to 3.140 so its coordinate is about 3.1406. Point B is between 3.141 and 3.142, slightly closer to 3.142, so its coordinate is about 3.1416. Point C is only slightly greater than 3.144, so its coordinate is about 3.1441. Points D and E are right on tick marks, so their coordinates are 3.145 and 3.146, respectively. Since $\pi \approx 3.1415926$, 3.1416 is closer to π than is 3.1406, 3.1441, 3.145, or 3.146.

A is incorrect because π is between 3.141 and 3.142 and point A is between 3.140 and 3.141. Point B is closer to π because it is between 3.141 and 3.142.

B is correct, as explained above.

C is incorrect because π is between 3.141 and 3.142 and point C is between 3.144 and 3.145. Point B is closer to π because it is between 3.141 and 3.142.

D is incorrect because π is between 3.141 and 3.142 and point D is right at 3.145. Point B is closer to π because it is between 3.141 and 3.142.

E is incorrect because π is between 3.141 and 3.142 and point E is right at 3.146. Point B is closer to π because it is between 3.141 and 3.142.

Question 42. The correct answer is H.

In order for a system of two linear equations to have an infinite number of solutions, the equations must represent the same line. In slope-intercept form, the first equation is $y = 2x - 6$ and the second equation is $y = 2x - \frac{3a}{4}$. The slopes are the same and the y-intercepts must be the same, so $6 = \frac{3a}{4}$.

Cross multiplying gives $24 = 3a$, so $a = 8$.

F is incorrect because if a is 2, then the second equation becomes $8x - 4y = 6$, which is $y = 2x - \frac{3}{2}$. The first equation in slope-intercept form is $y = 2x - 6$. The two lines have the same slopes but different intercepts. They are not the same line, but instead are parallel and never intersect. Therefore, the system of equations has no solution. You might have thought that the constant terms had to be equal.

G is incorrect because if a is 6, then the second equation becomes $8x - 4y = 18$, which is $y = 2x - \frac{9}{2}$. The first equation in slope-intercept form is $y = 2x - 6$. The two lines have the same slopes but different intercepts. They are not the same line, but instead are parallel and never intersect. Therefore, the system of equations has no solution. You may have thought that the constant terms needed to be equal so the left side of the second equation should be 6, but didn't set $3a$ equal to 6.

H is correct, as explained above.

J is incorrect because if a is 18, then the second equation becomes $8x - 4y = 54$, which is $y = 2x - \frac{27}{2}$. The first equation in slope-intercept form is $y = 2x - 6$. The two lines have the same slopes but different intercepts. They are not the same line, but instead are parallel and never intersect. Therefore, the system of equations has no solution. You might have multiplied the 6 by the 3 of $3a$.

K is incorrect because if a is 24, then the second equation becomes $8x - 4y = 72$, which is $y = 2x - 18$. The first equation in slope-intercept form is $y = 2x - 6$. The two lines have the same slopes but different intercepts. They are not the same line, but instead are parallel and never intersect. Therefore, the system of equations has no solution. You might have known that the constant for the second equation needed to be 24 but neglected to set $3a$ equal to 24.

Question 43. The correct answer is E.

Nonzero acute angles have measures between 0° and 90°. Therefore, if $(180 - x)$ is the degree measure of an acute angle, then $0 < 180 - x < 90$. To solve for x, subtract 180° from all members of the inequality and get $-180 < -x < -90$. Then, multiply all members of the inequality by -1 (and remember to reverse the direction of the inequality symbols) and get $90 < x < 180$. On the other hand, if $90 < x < 180$, then $-180 < -x < -90$, and $0 < 180 - x < 90$, so $180 - x$ is the measure of an acute angle. Thus, both parts of the "if and only if" statement are true for option **E**.

A is incorrect because if $0 < x < 45$, then $-45 < -x < 0$, and $135 < 180 - x < 180$, so $180 - x$ is not between 0 and 90 and is not the measure of an acute angle.

B is incorrect because if $0 < x < 90$, then $-90 < -x < 0$, and $90 < 180 - x < 180$, so $180 - x$ is not between 0 and 90 and is not the measure of an acute angle.

C is incorrect because if $45 < x < 90$, then $-90 < -x < -45$, and $90 < 180 - x < 135$, so $180 - x$ is not between 0 and 90 and is not the measure of an acute angle.

D is incorrect because, for example, if $180 - x = 30$, then $180 - x$ is the measure of an acute angle, but if $180 - x = 30$, then $x = 150$, and 150 is not between 90 and 135. So the statement "If $180 - x$ is the measure of an acute angle, then $90 < x < 135$" isn't necessarily true.

E is correct, as explained above.

Question 44. The correct answer is G.

If $x - y = -2$ and $x + y = -3$, then $(x - y)(x + y) = (-2)(-3)$. But $(x - y)(x + y) = x^2 - y^2$ and $(-2)(-3) = 6$, so $x^2 - y^2 = 6$.

F is incorrect because $13 = (-2)^2 + (-3)^2$ and so $x^2 - y^2$ should equal $(x + y)^2 + (x - y)^2$ by substitution. But $(x + y)^2 + (x - y)^2 = x^2 + 2xy + y^2 + x^2 - 2xy + y^2 = 2x^2 + 2y^2$, and $2x^2 + 2y^2 \neq x^2 - y^2$. You might have thought that $x^2 - y^2$ was the sum of the squares of -2 and -3.

G is correct, as explained above.

H is incorrect because if $x^2 - y^2 = 5$, then possible values for x and y are 3 and 2, respectively, since $3^2 - 2^2 = 5$. Then $x + y$ should equal -2, and $x - y$ should equal -3, but $3 + 2 \neq -2$ and $3 - 2 \neq -3$. You might have thought that $x^2 - y^2$ was the sum of the absolute values of -2 and -3.

J is incorrect because if $x^2 - y^2 = -5$, then possible values for x and y are 2 and 3, respectively, since $2^2 - 2^2 = -5$. Then $x + y$ should equal -2, and $x - y$ should equal -3, but $2 + 3 \neq -2$ and $2 - 3 \neq -3$. You might have thought that $x^2 - y^2$ was the sum of -2 and -3.

K is incorrect because if $x^2 - y^2 = -6$, then possible values for x and y are 0 and $\sqrt{6}$, respectively, since $0^2 - (\sqrt{6})^2 = -6$. Then $x + y$ should equal -2, and $x - y$ should equal -3, but $0 + \sqrt{6} \neq -2$ and $0 - \sqrt{6} \neq -3$. You might have made a sign error in multiplying -2 and -3.

Question 45. The correct answer is D.

If you recognize 5, 12, and 13 as a Pythagorean triple, then you know that $5^2 + 12^2 = 13^2$, so the triangle with sides of 5, 12, and 13 inches is a right triangle. The two shortest sides are the legs, so the angle between the two shortest sides is a right angle and has measure 90°. If you don't recognize 5, 12, and 13 as a Pythagorean triple, you can use the law of the cosines: $c^2 = a^2 + b^2 - 2ab \cos \angle C$, where $\angle C$ is the angle formed by the sides with lengths a and b. Then $13^2 = 5^2 + 12^2 - 2(5)(12) \cos \angle C$. This gives $0 = -2(5)(12) \cos \angle C$, so $\cos \angle C = 0$ and $\angle C$ is 90°.

A is incorrect because if the angle between the shortest sides is 30°, then the longest side is opposite the 30° angle. At least one of the other angles of the triangle has to be greater than 30° in order for the angle sum of the triangle to be 180° (if they were all 30° or less, the angle sum would be at most 90°). So one of the shorter sides will be opposite an angle greater than 30°. This contradicts the theorem that says the longer the side of a triangle the greater the angle opposite that side.

B is incorrect because if the angle between the shortest sides is 45°, then the longest side is opposite the 45° angle. At least one of the other angles of the triangle has to be greater than 45° in order for the angle sum of the triangle to be 180° (if they were all 45° or less, the angle sum would be at most 135°). So one of the shorter sides will be opposite an angle greater than 45°. This contradicts the theorem that says the longer the side of a triangle the greater the angle opposite that side.

C is incorrect because if the angle between the shortest sides is 60°, then the longest side is opposite the 60° angle. One of the other angles of the triangle has to be greater than 60° and the third must be less than 60° in order for the angle sum of the triangle to be 180° (if they were all 60° the triangle would be equilateral and there wouldn't be a shortest or a longest side). So one of the shorter sides will be opposite the angle greater than 60°. This contradicts the theorem that says the longer the side of a triangle the greater the angle opposite that side.

D is correct, as explained above.

E is incorrect because if the angle between the shortest sides is 120°, then the longest side is opposite the 120° angle, and the law of the cosines gives the square of this side as $5^2 + 12^2 - 2(5)(12)\cos 120° = 25 + 144 - 120(-0.5) = 229$. So the longest side is $\sqrt{229}$. This contradicts the fact that the longest side of the triangle is 13 inches long.

| MATHEMATICS ■ PRACTICE TEST 1 ■ EXPLANATORY ANSWERS |

Question 46. The correct answer is H.

"The x-coordinate is 4 less than twice the y-coordinate" in symbols is

$x = 2y - 4$. So $2y = x + 4$ and $y = \frac{1}{2}x + 2$. This is the slope-intercept form of

the equation, so the slope of the line is $\frac{1}{2}$, the coefficient of the x-term in the

slope-intercept form.

F is incorrect because if the slope were -4, then the coefficient of x would be -4 when the coefficient of y was 1. This would mean that the coefficient of y would be $-\frac{1}{4}$ when the coefficient of x was 1. But "the x-coordinate is 4 less than twice the y-coordinate" says that when the coefficient of x is 1, the coefficient of y is 2.

G is incorrect because if the slope were -2, then the coefficient of x would be -2 when the coefficient of y was 1. This would mean that the coefficient of y would be $-\frac{1}{2}$ when the coefficient of x was 1. But "the x-coordinate is 4 less than twice the y-coordinate" says that when the coefficient of x is 1, the coefficient of y is 2.

H is correct, as explained above.

J is incorrect because if the slope were 2, then the coefficient of x would be 2 when the coefficient of y was 1. This would mean that the coefficient of y would be $\frac{1}{2}$ when the coefficient of x was 1. But "the x-coordinate is 4 less than twice the y-coordinate" says that when the coefficient of x is 1, the coefficient of y is 2.

K is incorrect because if the slope were 4, then the coefficient of x would be 4 when the coefficient of y was 1. This would mean that the coefficient of y would be $\frac{1}{4}$ when the coefficient of x was 1. But "the x-coordinate is 4 less than twice the y-coordinate" says that when the coefficient of x is 1, the coefficient of y is 2.

Question 47. The correct answer is E.

Since the length of one leg of the right triangle is given and you're trying to find the length of the other leg, the tangent ratio, which involves the legs, is the best trigonometric ratio to use. If h stands for the length of the leg you're trying to find, $\tan 57° = \dfrac{1.3}{h}$ since 1.3 is the length of the side opposite the 57° angle and h is the length of the side adjacent to the 57° angle. Solving for h gives $h \tan 57° = 1.3$ and $h = \dfrac{1.3}{\tan 57°}$

A is incorrect because 1.3 sin 57° would be the answer if you were looking for the length of the side opposite the 57° angle and the length of the hypotenuse of the triangle were 1.3. In this problem, 1.3 is the length of the side opposite the 57° angle and you're looking for the length of the side adjacent the 57° angle.

B is incorrect because 1.3 tan 57° would be the answer if you were looking for the length of the side opposite the 57° angle and 1.3 were the length of the side adjacent to the 57° angle. In this problem, 1.3 is the length of the side opposite the 57° angle and you're looking for the length of the side adjacent the 57° angle.

C is incorrect because $\dfrac{1.3}{\sin 57°}$ would be the answer if you were looking for the length of the hypotenuse of the triangle. In this problem you're looking for the length of the side adjacent the 57° angle.

D is incorrect because $\dfrac{1.3}{\cos 57°}$ would be the answer if you were looking for the length of the hypotenuse of the triangle and 1.3 were the length of the side adjacent the 57° angle. In this problem, 1.3 is the length of the side opposite the 57° angle, but you're looking for the length of the side adjacent the 57° angle.

E is correct, as explained above.

Question 48. The correct answer is H.

If 4 is the greatest common factor of the two numbers, then both numbers have a factor of 4. Since 24 is the least common multiple of the two numbers, and $24 = 4 \cdot 2 \cdot 3$, one of the numbers must have another factor of 2 and one must have a factor of 3. So one number has 3 factors of 2 and could be 8 while the other has a factor of 4 and a factor of 3 and could be 12.

F is incorrect because 8, not 24, is the least common multiple of 4 and 8.

G is incorrect because 12, not 24, is the least common multiple of 4 and 12.

H is correct, as explained above.

J is incorrect because 8, not 4, is the greatest common factor of 8 and 24.

K is incorrect because 12, not 4, is the greatest common factor of 12 and 24.

Question 49. The correct answer is A.

In all cases, $f(g(x))$ will be $2^{g(x)}$. Exponential functions with base 2 are increasing and so $f(g(x))$ will have the greatest value when the exponent $g(x)$ is the largest. A way to examine the relative size of the five functions $g(x)$ is to look at their graphs. Since $c \geq 2$, the graphs below show $g(x)$ when $c = 2$. Clearly, $g(x) = 2x$ yields the greatest values for $f(g(x))$ for all $x > 1$. The conclusion would be the same for every value of $c \geq 2$.

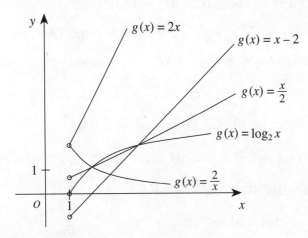

A is correct, as explained above.

B is incorrect because, for example, if $c = 2$ and $x = 4$, $f(g(x))$ when $g(x) = cx$ is $2^8 = 256$ and the value of $f(g(x))$ when $g(x) = \frac{c}{x}$ is $2^{\frac{1}{2}} \approx 1.414$, then clearly $f(g(x))$ does not have the greatest values for $g(x) = \frac{c}{x}$.

C is incorrect because, for example, if $c = 2$ and $x = 4$, $f(g(x))$ when $g(x) = cx$ is $2^8 = 256$ and the value of $f(g(x))$ when $g(x) = \frac{x}{c}$ is $2^2 = 4$, then clearly $f(g(x))$ does not have the greatest values for $g(x) = \frac{x}{c}$.

D is incorrect because, for example, if $c = 2$ and $x = 4$, $f(g(x))$ when $g(x) = cx$ is $2^8 = 256$ and the value of $f(g(x))$ when $g(x) = x - c$ is $2^2 = 4$, then clearly $f(g(x))$ does not have the greatest values for $g(x) = x - c$.

E is incorrect because, for example, if $c = 2$ and $x = 4$, $f(g(x))$ when $g(x) = cx$ is $2^8 = 256$ and the value of $f(g(x))$ when $g(x) = \log_c x$ is $2^2 = 4$, then clearly $f(g(x))$ does not have the greatest values for $g(x) = \log_c x$.

Question 50. The correct answer is H.

The bottom of the box is a rectangle with sides $\overline{AB}$ and $\overline{BC}$ and dimensions 4 inches and 3 inches, respectively. $\overline{AC}$ is the diagonal of this rectangle and has length $\sqrt{4^2 + 3^2}$ = 5 inches. Then $\triangle ACD$ is a right triangle with right angle $\angle ACD$. The legs of $\triangle ACD$, $\overline{AC}$ and $\overline{CD}$, are each 5 inches long, so the hypotenuse, $\overline{AD}$, is $\sqrt{5^2 + 5^2}$ = $2\sqrt{5}$ inches long. Then sin $\angle DAC$ is the length of the leg opposite side $\angle DAC$ over the length of the hypotenuse, so sin $\angle DAC = \dfrac{5}{5\sqrt{2}} = \dfrac{1}{\sqrt{2}} = \dfrac{\sqrt{2}}{2}$.

F is incorrect because 1 is tan $\angle DAC$, not sin $\angle DAC$.

G is incorrect because $\dfrac{4}{5}$ is sin $\angle ACB$, and $\angle ACB \not\equiv \angle DAC$ because $\triangle ACD$ is an isosceles right triangle and $\triangle ACB$ isn't.

H is correct, as explained above.

J is incorrect because $\dfrac{3}{5}$ is sin $\angle CAB$, and $\angle CAB \not\equiv \angle DAC$ because $\triangle ACD$ is an isosceles right triangle and $\triangle ACB$ isn't.

K is incorrect because $\dfrac{3\sqrt{2}}{10} < \dfrac{\sqrt{2}}{2}$ so $\dfrac{3\sqrt{2}}{10}$ is the sine of an angle that has measure less than 45°. But $\triangle ACD$ is isosceles, so $\angle DAC$ is a 45° angle. Therefore $\dfrac{3\sqrt{2}}{10}$ cannot be the sine of $\angle DAC$.

Question 51. The correct answer is B.

You can find the area of a circle by using the formula $A = \pi r^2$. If $A = \pi$, then $\pi = \pi r^2$ so $r^2 = 1$ and $r = 1$.

A is incorrect because a circle with radius $\frac{1}{2}$ has area $\pi\left(\frac{1}{2}\right)^2$ or $\frac{1}{4}\pi$. The area of the circle in this problem is π. You might have used the formula for the circumference, $C = 2\pi r$, instead of the formula for the area, $A = \pi r^2$.

B is correct, as explained above.

C is incorrect because a circle with radius 2 has area $\pi(2)^2$ or 4π. The area of the circle in this problem is π. You might have thought that you needed to give the diameter, which is twice the radius.

D is incorrect because a circle with radius $\frac{\pi}{2}$ has area $\pi\left(\frac{\pi}{2}\right)^2$ or $\frac{\pi^3}{4}$. The area of the circle in this problem is π.

E is incorrect because a circle with radius π has area $\pi(\pi)^2$ or π^3. The area of the circle in this problem is π.

Question 52. The correct answer is J.

From the graph, it is clear that line t has the same y-intercept as line s because both lines go through the point $(0,b)$ on the y-axis. Options **F, H,** and **K** can be eliminated since these do not have b as their y-intercept. The slope of line s is positive since line s slants to the right and so $m > 0$. The slope of line t is negative since line t slants to the left. The slope of the line in option **G** is positive since the slope is $2m$, where $m > 0$, so **G** can be eliminated. The only option left is **J,** and the slope of the line given in **J** is negative since it is $-2m$, where $m > 0$.

F is incorrect because the y-intercept is 0, not b.

G is incorrect because the slope of line t must be negative, and the slope in this answer choice is $2m$, which is positive, since $m > 0$.

H is incorrect because the y-intercept is $-b$, not b, and the slope of line t must be negative; the slope in this answer choice is $2m$, which is positive, since $m > 0$.

J is correct, as explained above.

K is incorrect because the y-intercept is $-b$, not b.

Question 53. The correct answer is E.

If the equation $x^2 - 10x + k = 0$ has only one solution, then $x^2 - 10x + k$ is a perfect square. Since $x^2 - 10x$ are the first two terms of $(x - 5)^2$, k must be the last term of $(x - 5)^2$, so $k = 25$.

A is incorrect because if $k = 0$, then the equation is $x^2 - 10x = 0$ and then $x(x - 10) = 0$. But this equation has two solutions: $x = 0$ and $x = 10$.

B is incorrect because if $k = 5$, then the equation is $x^2 - 10x + 5 = 0$. The expression $x^2 - 10x + 5$ is not factorable so you can use the quadratic formula to get two solutions: $x = \dfrac{10 \pm \sqrt{(-10)^2 - 4(1)(5)}}{2(1)} = \dfrac{10 \pm \sqrt{80}}{2}$.

C is incorrect because if $k = 10$, then the equation is $x^2 - 10x + 10 = 0$. The expression $x^2 - 10x + 10$ is not factorable so you can use the quadratic formula to get two solutions: $x = \dfrac{10 \pm \sqrt{(-10)^2 - 4(1)(10)}}{2(1)} = \dfrac{10 \pm \sqrt{60}}{2}$.

D is incorrect because if $k = 20$, then the equation is $x^2 - 10x + 20 = 0$. The expression $x^2 - 10x + 20$ is not factorable so you can use the quadratic formula to get two solutions: $x = \dfrac{10 \pm \sqrt{(-10)^2 - 4(1)(20)}}{2(1)} = \dfrac{10 \pm \sqrt{20}}{2}$.

E is correct, as explained above.

Question 54. The correct answer is K.

The slope of a line through two points (x_1, y_1) and (x_2, y_2) is given by $\frac{y_1 - y_2}{x_1 - x_2}$.

Applying this formula to $\left(\frac{1}{2}, \frac{2}{3}\right)$ and $(0,0)$ gives $\dfrac{\frac{2}{3} - 0}{\frac{1}{2} - 0} = \frac{2}{3} \cdot \frac{2}{1} = \frac{4}{3}$.

F is incorrect because if $\frac{1}{2}$ were the slope, the equation of the line would be

$y = \frac{1}{2}x$ since the line goes through the origin. But $\left(\frac{1}{2}, \frac{2}{3}\right)$ isn't on this line.

G is incorrect because if $\frac{1}{3}$ were the slope, the equation of the line would be

$y = \frac{1}{3}x$ since the line goes through the origin. But $\left(\frac{1}{2}, \frac{2}{3}\right)$ isn't on this line.

H is incorrect because if $\frac{2}{3}$ were the slope, the equation of the line would be

$y = \frac{2}{3}x$ since the line goes through the origin. But $\left(\frac{1}{2}, \frac{2}{3}\right)$ isn't on this line.

J is incorrect because if $\frac{3}{4}$ were the slope, the equation of the line would be

$y = \frac{3}{4}x$ since the line goes through the origin. But $\left(\frac{1}{2}, \frac{2}{3}\right)$ isn't on this line.

Possibly you used $\frac{x_1 - x_2}{y_1 - y_2}$ in finding the slope.

K is correct, as explained above.

Question 55. The correct answer is A.

If $ABC = 1$, then $C \neq 0$ (if $C = 0$, then $ABC = 0$) and so both sides of the equation can be divided by C. This gives $AB = \dfrac{1}{C}$.

A is correct, as explained above.

B is incorrect because if $A = -1$, $B = -1$, and $C = 1$, then $ABC = (-1)(-1)(1) = 1$, but A, B, and C are not all positive.

C is incorrect because if $A = \dfrac{1}{2}$, $B = 3$, and $C = \dfrac{2}{3}$, then $ABC = \dfrac{1}{2} \cdot 3 \cdot \dfrac{2}{3} = 1$, but none of A, B, or C is 1.

D is incorrect because if $A = 0$, $B = 0$, or $C = 0$, then $ABC = 0$, so if $ABC = 1$, then none of A, B, or C can be 0.

E is incorrect because if $A = 1$, $B = 1$, and $C = 1$, then $ABC = (1)(1)(1) = 1$, but none of A, B, or C is less than 1.

Question 56. The correct answer is J.

The area of the original rectangle is $(x + 5)(x + 7) = x^2 + 12x + 35$. If a square of side length x is removed, the area removed is x^2, and the remaining area of the rectangle is $x^2 + 12x + 35 - x^2 = 12x + 35$.

F is incorrect because if only 12 square units remain, then $x^2 + 12x + 23$ square units were removed since $12 + (x^2 + 12x + 23) = x^2 + 12x + 35$. But the area that was removed was x^2. You might have multiplied $(x + 5)(x + 7)$ incorrectly and got $x^2 + 12$.

G is incorrect because if 35 square units remain, then $x^2 + 12x$ square units were removed since $35 + (x^2 + 12x) = x^2 + 12x + 35$. But the area that was removed was x^2. You might have multiplied $(x + 5)(x + 7)$ incorrectly and got $x^2 + 35$.

H is incorrect because if $2x + 12$ square units remain, then $x^2 + 10x + 23$ square units were removed since $(2x + 12) + (x^2 + 10x + 23) = x^2 + 12x + 35$. But the area that was removed was x^2. You might have multiplied $(x + 5)(x + 7)$ incorrectly and got $x^2 + 2x + 12$.

J is correct, as explained above.

K is incorrect because if $x^2 + 12x + 35$ square units are left, then 0 square units were removed since $x^2 + 12x + 35$ was the area of the rectangle before the square was removed. You might have found the area of the original rectangle and thought you were finished with the problem.

Question 57. The correct answer is A.

The smallest value for x where the sine function reaches its maximum value, 1, is $\frac{\pi}{2}$. If $2x = \frac{\pi}{2}$, then $x = \frac{\pi}{4}$.

A is correct, as explained above.

B is incorrect because if $x = \pi$, $\sin 2x = \sin(2\pi) = 0$. But the maximum value of the sine function is 1.

C is incorrect because if $x = \frac{3\pi}{2}$, $\sin 2x = \sin(3\pi) = -1$. But the maximum value of the sine function is 1.

D is incorrect because if $x = 2\pi$, $\sin 2x = \sin(4\pi) = 0$. But the maximum value of the sine function is 1.

E is incorrect because if $x = \frac{5\pi}{2}$, $\sin 2x = \sin(5\pi) = -1$. But the maximum value of the sine function is 1.

Question 58. The correct answer is F.

Using the distance formula, the distance between $(8,a)$ and $(a,1)$ is $\sqrt{(8-a)^2+(a-1)^2}$. This distance is 5, so $\sqrt{(8-a)^2+(a-1)^2}=5$ and $(8-a)^2+(a-1)^2=25$. Then, $64-16a+a^2+a^2-2a+1=25$, $2a^2-18a+65=25$, $2a^2-18a+40=0$, and finally $a^2-9a+20=0$. Factoring gives $(a-4)(a-5)=0$ and so $a=4$ or $a=5$, and 5 is option **F**.

F is correct, as explained above.

G is incorrect because if $a=3$, then the distance between $(8,3)$ and $(3,1)$ using the distance formula is $\sqrt{(8-3)^2+(3-1)^2}=\sqrt{25+4}=\sqrt{29}$, and $\sqrt{29}\neq5$.

H is incorrect because if $a=-3$, then the distance between $(8,-3)$ and $(-3,1)$ using the distance formula is $\sqrt{(8-(-3))^2+(-3-1)^2}=\sqrt{121+16}=\sqrt{137}$, and $\sqrt{137}\neq5$.

J is incorrect because if $a=-4$, then the distance between $(8,-4)$ and $(-4,1)$ using the distance formula is $\sqrt{(8-(-4))^2+(-4-1)^2}=\sqrt{144+25}=\sqrt{169}=13$, and $13\neq5$.

K is incorrect because if $a=-5$, then the distance between $(8,-5)$ and $(-5,1)$ using the distance formula is $\sqrt{(8-(-5))^2+(-5-1)^2}=\sqrt{169+36}=\sqrt{205}$, and $\sqrt{205}\neq5$.

Question 59. The correct answer is D.

If there are n marbles in the bag (3 red and the rest green) then the probability of drawing a red marble is $\frac{3}{n}$. But the probability of drawing a red marble is $\frac{1}{4}$, so $\frac{3}{n} = \frac{1}{4}$ and $n = 12$. If there are already 3 marbles in the bag, 9 green marbles need to be added so that the bag has a total of 12 marbles.

A is incorrect because if 1 green marble is added to the bag, the bag will have 4 marbles—3 red and 1 green. The probability of drawing a red marble is $\frac{3}{4}$, not $\frac{1}{4}$. Perhaps you were thinking that the probability of a green marble needed to be $\frac{1}{4}$.

B is incorrect because if 3 green marbles are added to the bag, the bag will have 6 marbles—3 red and 3 green. The probability of drawing a red marble is $\frac{3}{6}$, or $\frac{1}{2}$, not $\frac{1}{4}$.

C is incorrect because if 5 green marbles are added to the bag, the bag will have 8 marbles—3 red and 5 green. The probability of drawing a red marble is $\frac{3}{8}$, not $\frac{1}{4}$.

D is correct, as explained above.

E is incorrect because if 12 green marbles are added to the bag, the bag will have 15 marbles—3 red and 12 green. The probability of drawing a red marble is $\frac{3}{15}$, or $\frac{1}{5}$, not $\frac{1}{4}$.

Question 60. The correct answer is K.

Intuitively, since $\frac{1}{13} = \frac{2}{26}$ and $\frac{1}{10} = \frac{2}{20}$, all of $\frac{2}{25}, \frac{2}{24}, \frac{2}{23}, \frac{2}{22}$, and $\frac{2}{21}$ will be between $\frac{2}{26}$ and $\frac{2}{20}$. So, $\frac{2}{n}$ is between $\frac{1}{13}$ and $\frac{1}{10}$ for 5 integer values of n.

Mathematically, since $\frac{2}{n}$ lies between the 2 positive fractions $\frac{1}{13}$ and $\frac{1}{10}$, n must be positive, so multiplying by n will not change the direction of the inequality symbols. The given inequality $\frac{1}{13} < \frac{2}{n} < \frac{1}{10}$ is short for $\frac{1}{13} < \frac{2}{n}$ and $\frac{2}{n} < \frac{1}{10}$. If you multiply both sides of $\frac{1}{13} < \frac{2}{n}$ by $13n$ (which is positive since n is positive), you get $n < 26$. If you multiply both sides of $\frac{2}{n} < \frac{1}{10}$ by $10n$ (which is positive since n is positive), you get $20 < n$. Combining these results you get $20 < n < 26$. Five integers (21, 22, 23, 24, and 25) satisfy this inequality.

F is incorrect because 21, 22, 23, 24, and 25 all satisfy this inequality ($\frac{1}{13} \approx 0.077$, $\frac{2}{25} = 0.08$, $\frac{2}{24} = 0.083$, $\frac{2}{23} \approx 0.087$, $\frac{2}{22} \approx 0.09$, $\frac{2}{21} \approx 0.095$, $\frac{1}{10} = 0.1$).

G is incorrect because 21, 22, 23, 24, and 25 all satisfy this inequality ($\frac{1}{13} \approx 0.077$, $\frac{2}{25} = 0.08$, $\frac{2}{24} = 0.083$, $\frac{2}{23} \approx 0.087$, $\frac{2}{22} \approx 0.09$, $\frac{2}{21} \approx 0.095$, $\frac{1}{10} = 0.1$).

H is incorrect because 21, 22, 23, 24, and 25 all satisfy this inequality ($\frac{1}{13} \approx 0.077$, $\frac{2}{25} = 0.08$, $\frac{2}{24} = 0.083$, $\frac{2}{23} \approx 0.087$, $\frac{2}{22} \approx 0.09$, $\frac{2}{21} \approx 0.095$, $\frac{1}{10} = 0.1$).

J is incorrect because 21, 22, 23, 24, and 25 all satisfy this inequality ($\frac{1}{13} \approx 0.077$, $\frac{2}{25} = 0.08$, $\frac{2}{24} = 0.083$, $\frac{2}{23} \approx 0.087$, $\frac{2}{22} \approx 0.09$, $\frac{2}{21} \approx 0.095$, $\frac{1}{10} = 0.1$).

K is correct, as explained above.

Passage I

Question 1. The best answer is D.

A is incorrect because a minister (it is not clear whether the minister is Reena's minister) is mentioned only briefly, in line 7, and no influence on the narrator is implied or stated. When the narrator mentions being "in the thrall of the Little Minister" (lines 43–44), it is clear from the context that she is referring to a character from a children's book.

B is incorrect because the passage doesn't mention Reena's father influencing the narrator at all. The relationship between Reena's father and Reena is discussed in the last paragraph of the passage, however.

C is incorrect because there is no character in the passage referred to as Aunt Vi's godmother. Aunt Vi was the narrator's godmother (line 2).

D is the best answer. The narrator loved Aunt Vi (line 3) and considered her "a source of understanding and a place of calm for me as a child" (lines 3–5).

Question 2. The best answer is G.

F is incorrect because although Reena is described as pointing at her family threateningly (option I), there is no mention of her crying loudly (option II). Reena is described as saying, not shouting or crying, what she wanted (line 29).

G is the best answer because Reena did point threateningly (option I) and stare meaningfully (option IV) at her family, as described in lines 29–31.

H is incorrect because although option IV is correct, option II, crying loudly, is inaccurate (see the explanation for **F**).

J is incorrect because although options I and IV are correct (see the explanation for **G**), option II, crying loudly, is inaccurate (see the explanation for **F**).

Question 3. The best answer is C.

A is incorrect because although Reena's mother is described as sometimes being strict (line 75) and Reena's father is not, there is no mention of Reena's mother being a funnier parent than Reena's father. Reena's father is described as making jokes (lines 68–70), while Reena's mother is described as "dry" (line 73).

B is incorrect because Reena's father was more retiring and less authoritative than Reena's mother. Reena's father was "so in awe of Reena that he avoided her" (lines 72–73). Reena's mother, in contrast, was formidable, forceful, powerful, and often strict (lines 73–75).

C is the best answer because lines 74–77 describe Reena's mother as "the abstract principle of force, power, energy" and as "surprisingly effective." Reena's father, on the other hand, is described as "so in awe of Reena that he avoided her" (lines 72–73).

D is incorrect because it more accurately describes Reena's father than her mother, who was forceful, powerful, and energetic (line 75), rather than gentle.

Question 4. The best answer is J.

F is incorrect because although it includes Hitler in Poland (option I), the discussion of which the narrator mentions in line 47 as intimidating to her, it fails to include the Civil War in Spain (option II), listed in line 46. Lines 44–51 describe the narrator's feeling of intimidation.

G is incorrect because although option II is correct (see the explanation for **F**), option I, which is also correct (see the explanation for **F**) is not included.

H is incorrect because the passage does not mention Reena talking about the "thrall of the Little Minister" (option III). The passage does say that the narrator was "in the thrall of the Little Minister" (lines 43–44).

J is the best answer because it includes Hitler in Poland (option I) and the Civil War in Spain (option II), both of which are subjects Reena discusses with the narrator (lines 46–47), and it does not include option III, which is incorrect (see the explanation for **H**).

Question 5. The best answer is A.

A is the best answer because in the first paragraph Reena is described as entering the church as if "she, not the minister, were coming to officiate" (line 7). Acting as if she is in charge, even though the event is a funeral and she is not, in fact, in charge, indicates that Reena is very confident.

B is incorrect because there is no evidence that Reena has ever officiated at a funeral or that she will officiate at this funeral. The passage does say that Reena entered the church "as though she, not the minister, were coming to officiate" (lines 6–7), but this is not the same as saying that Reena is used to officiating at funerals.

C is incorrect because there is no indication in the passage that Reena is deeply unhappy. She entered the church confidently and began inspecting the other people in the church (lines 5–9).

D is incorrect because the first paragraph says nothing about Reena having changed.

Question 6. The best answer is G.

F is incorrect because there is no evidence in the passage that Reena's father disciplined her at all. Rather, he avoided her (lines 72–73).

G is the best answer because Reena's father was "so in awe of Reena that he avoided her" (lines 72–73).

H is incorrect because there is no evidence in the passage that Reena's father praised her.

J is incorrect because there is no evidence in the passage that Reena's father humored Reena at all. Reena's father "was always making jokes" (lines 68–69), but joking is not the same as humoring.

Question 7. The best answer is D.

A is incorrect because the passage takes place when Reena and the narrator are adults attending a funeral (see the explanation for **B**). The narrator looks back at their childhood relationship.

B is incorrect because the narrator looks back at Reena and the narrator's relationship; the narrator mentions what it was like when Reena was twelve and thirteen. The narrator mentions "the evidence of the twenty years" that have passed (lines 21–22). Given that so much time has passed, the narrator must be an adult.

C is incorrect. Although the narrator's reflection on Reena and herself is in some ways psychological, there is no mention in the passage of the narrator's occupation, and it cannot be deduced or even inferred that the narrator is a psychologist.

D is the best answer because the narrator and Reena attended Aunt Vi's funeral as adults, and the narrator is looking back at both that event and at their earlier relationship from an adult's point of view. The narrator describes Reena's aging (lines 20–22), and the passage of time is mentioned in the phrase "the evidence of the twenty years" (lines 21–22).

Question 8. The best answer is J.

F is incorrect because although Reena is described as overwhelming her family, there is no evidence that she was selfish: she was concerned about social issues involving people other than herself or people she knew (she talked "with the outrage and passion of a revolutionary," about social issues in Spain, the South, and Poland, according to lines 45–47), which shows a compassionate side to her personality.

G is incorrect because the passage makes it clear that the narrator had not seen Reena for a long time and that they met again at the funeral for Aunt Vi. They had been out of contact, which does not indicate a close friendship. Also, the friendship had been pushed on them initially by their mothers (lines 32–34), and the narrator had "been at a disadvantage" in the relationship (line 35). Reena is described as putting up with the narrator and acting patronizing and impatient with her (lines 52–53), which further suggests that the two children were not best friends.

H is incorrect because the passage does not mention or suggest that Reena had a negative attitude toward her brothers and sisters, although it does say that Reena "overwhelmed her family" (lines 61–62).

J is the best answer because lines 61–62 describe Reena as overwhelming her family and the narrator. Reena's father was "so in awe of Reena that he avoided her" (lines 72–73).

Question 9. The best answer is A.

A is the best answer because in lines 38–39, the narrator describes Reena as having "the raw edges of her adolescence smoothed over." The narrator describes Reena as being unusual in this (lines 36–37 say that she "had a quality that was unique"), implying that others experience adolescence as a time of raw edges.

B is incorrect because there is no mention in the passage of the narrator believing that most adolescents believe in or understand abstract principles. The passage does suggest that Reena understood abstract principles such as justice and peace (lines 44–48 and 57–59), but Reena is described as an exceptional adolescent, one who seemed to the narrator to have skipped adolescence and entered directly into adulthood (lines 38–41).

C is incorrect because Reena is described as having "seemed to have escaped adolescence altogether and made one dazzling leap from childhood into the very arena of adult life" (lines 39–41), but the point of the passage is to describe her uniqueness. Her behavior is not described as typical or usual for adolescents.

D is incorrect because the passage does not suggest that adolescence is a stage usually characterized by impatient patronizing. Reena exhibited impatient patronizing behavior toward the narrator (lines 52–53), but as mentioned in the explanation for **C**, Reena is not depicted as the typical adolescent.

Question 10. The best answer is G.

F is incorrect because Reena is described as exhibiting impatience with the narrator (lines 52–53).

G is the best answer because Reena used the narrator as "the audience before whom she rehearsed her ideas and the yardstick by which she measured her worldliness and knowledge" (lines 53–56). Reena was "by turns, patronizing and impatient" (lines 52–53) rather than treating the narrator as an equal in their relationship.

H is incorrect because there is no evidence of the narrator feeling any affection or devotion to Reena in the passage. The narrator had not chosen to be friends with Reena (lines 32–33) and was aware of the role each of them played in their relationship: "from the beginning, I had been at a disadvantage" (lines 34–35). The narrator recalls merely serving as an audience for Reena's patronizing lectures (lines 53–54); she does not comment on any positive feelings toward Reena.

J is incorrect because the narrator states in line 51, "I could not possibly be her match," which was a recognition that there was no use trying to become as worldly as Reena. The passage does not suggest that the narrator became any more worldly during the two children's time spent together.

Passage II

Question 11. The best answer is B.

A is incorrect. The Cherokee are not mentioned in the passage.

B is the best answer because lines 84–88 state that modern democracy is a "legacy of the American Indians, particularly the Iroquois and the Algonquians, [as much] as it is of the British settlers, of French political theory, or of all the failed efforts of the Greeks and Romans."

C is incorrect. The Seminoles are not mentioned in the passage.

D is incorrect. Neither the Cherokee nor the Cheyenne are mentioned in the passage.

Question 12. The best answer is H.

F is incorrect because in the first paragraph the passage states that egalitarian democracy "entered modern western thought as American Indian notions translated into European language and culture." The seventh paragraph (lines 66–78) says that French and English political thinkers' thoughts were heavily influenced by American Indians, and the eighth paragraph (lines 79–88) states that "modern notions of democracy based on egalitarian principles . . . arose from the unique blend of European and Indian political ideas and institutions."

G is incorrect because in lines 9–10 the author states that the Spaniards "brought nothing resembling a democratic tradition with them to America." In addition, the passage does not say that the climate was unfavorable in the New World.

H is the best answer because the main point of the passage is that egalitarian democracy and liberty "entered modern western thought as American Indian notions translated into European language and culture" (lines 4–6). And in lines 66–71, the passage says that "When Americans try to trace their democratic heritage back through the writings of French and English political thinkers of the Enlightenment, they often forget that these people's thoughts were heavily shaped by the democratic traditions and the state of nature of the American Indians."

J is incorrect because the passage does not say that the roots of democracy can be traced to the Holy Roman Empire. Rather, the Holy Roman Empire's practice of having a congress of aristocrats elect an emperor is given as an example of a practice that did not make the empire a democracy (lines 41–43).

Question 13. The best answer is A.

A is the best answer. The passage mentions the "writings of French and English political thinkers" (lines 67–68) and says that "modern notions of democracy . . . arose from the unique blend of European and Indian political ideas and institutions along the Atlantic coast between 1607 and 1776" (lines 79–83).

B is incorrect because there is no evidence that European political thinkers lived utopian lives. Many of them lived at court, where they could see firsthand the excesses of monarchical life.

C is incorrect. The passage says that "the Spaniards . . . brought nothing resembling a democratic tradition with them to America" (lines 7–10). The second paragraph (lines 7–16) gives examples of Dutch settlements that were not democratic, and the fifth paragraph (lines 44–50) says that at the time that the Dutch built colonies in America, their political tradition was one of aristocratic, minority rule, not democracy.

D is incorrect because the passage states that American Indians were living in democratic conditions before the Europeans arrived in America. No mention is made of the Europeans teaching the Indians democratic ideals; rather, in lines 4–6 the passage says that Indians influenced European democratic thought.

Question 14. The best answer is H.

F is incorrect because in lines 2–3 the passage states that democracy is not a Greco-Roman derivative, and in lines 87–88 it mentions "the failed efforts of the Greeks and Romans."

G is incorrect because in lines 10–12 the passage states that the French and Dutch settled many parts of the world that did not become democratic, suggesting that they were not sources of democracy in America.

H is the best answer because the passage describes the interaction of American Indian thought and practice with European language and culture that resulted in democratic practices and institutions along the Atlantic coast of America during the 1600s and 1700s. The eighth paragraph (lines 79–88) especially emphasizes this.

J is incorrect because there is no mention of the American Indians being opposed to democratic traditions; rather, they were already practicing democracy when the Europeans arrived in America. American Indians influenced French and English political thinkers (lines 66–71).

Question 15. The best answer is C.

A is incorrect because Henry Steele Commager makes no mention of a democratic majority ruling Europe; he labels the rulers as "the wellborn, the rich, the privileged" (lines 52–53), which describes the aristocratic class, not a democratic majority.

B is incorrect because the college of cardinals served only to elect the pope (lines 39–40), who is in charge of the Vatican. The passage does not suggest that the pope or a college of cardinals ruled Europe.

C is the best answer because in lines 52–54 the author quotes Henry Steele Commager as describing the European rulers during the Enlightenment as "the wellborn, the rich, the privileged . . . those who held their places by divine favor, inheritance, prescription, or purchase." This describes the aristocratic class.

D is incorrect because while philosophers may have held a somewhat privileged position at court, there is no evidence in the passage that they ruled Europe. Many "became court pets" (line 60); they weren't leaders or rulers themselves.

Question 16. The best answer is J.

F is incorrect because in lines 76–77 the passage describes the Native Americans as living in a "fairly democratic condition" and as being "egalitarian."

G is incorrect because the passage does not describe any Native American chiefs who were similar to Europe's "enlightened despots." The passage says that egalitarian democracy and liberty "entered modern western thought as American Indian notions translated into European language and culture" (lines 4–6), which suggests that American Indian chiefs were not despots.

H is incorrect because the passage does not mention any Native American societies with a monarchical system of government.

J is the best answer because in lines 76–77 the author writes that the Indians lived in "a fairly democratic condition" and calls them "egalitarian."

Question 17. The best answer is D.

A is incorrect because there is no evidence in the passage that British law descended directly from that of ancient Rome.

B is incorrect because there is no evidence in the passage that French law descended directly from that of ancient Rome.

C is incorrect because there is no evidence in the passage that Dutch law descended directly from that of ancient Rome.

D is the best answer because in lines 7–8 the passage states that "In language, custom, religion, and written law, the Spaniards descended directly from ancient Rome."

Question 18. The best answer is G.

F is not the best answer because although option I is correct (see the explanation for **G**), option II, which is also correct (see the explanation for **G**), is not included here.

G is the best answer because both option I and option II are correct. According to lines 31–34, the signing of the Magna Carta increased the power of the English aristocracy (option I) and slightly decreased the power of the English monarchy (option II). Option III is not correct (see the explanation for **H**).

H is incorrect because although option I is correct (see the explanation for **G**), it includes option III, which is not correct. The signing of the Magna Carta did not create a democracy; it merely weakened the monarchy's rule slightly while increasing the power of the aristocracy. The passage states that "a step away from monarchy does not necessarily mean a step toward democracy" (lines 37–39).

J is incorrect because although option II is correct (see the explanation for **G**), option III, which is not correct (see the explanation for **H**), is also included.

Question 19. The best answer is A.

A is the best answer because the passage says that some philosophers "became court pets" (line 60) who became complacent and self-congratulatory because they were pleased that the "enlightened despots" (line 57) read widely and had literary inclinations. The philosophers' complacency led them to believe that Europe was moving toward an enlightened democracy when it was not (lines 59–61).

B is incorrect because there is no mention in the passage of philosophers trying to justify European expansion in North America.

C is incorrect because the passage doesn't mention that any philosophers disliked the monarchs. Rather, "Too many philosophers became court pets and because of that believed that Europe was moving toward enlightened democracy" (lines 59–61).

D is incorrect because there is no evidence in the passage to suggest that philosophers could not understand Greco-Roman ideas or develop sound theories.

Question 20. The best answer is G.

F is incorrect because the passage does not say that the British and the Dutch settled in Haiti (option I). The passage suggests that the French settled Haiti (lines 10–14).

G is the best answer because lines 14–16 mention the British and Dutch settling in South Africa (option II) at "about the same time that they settled in North America."

H is incorrect because although option II is correct (see the explanation for **G**), option I, Haiti, is incorrect (see the explanation for **F**).

J is incorrect because both option I, Haiti (see the explanation for **F**), and option III, Greece, are incorrect—the passage doesn't suggest that the British or the Dutch settled in either country.

Passage III

Question 21. The best answer is A.

A is the best answer; the context of "engages" makes it clear that the task of putting together a book requires, or demands, all of the writer's intelligence because it is such a difficult and complex task.

B is incorrect because there is no evidence that the author believes assembling a book defeats the writer's intelligence, although she does say that "the page always wins" (line 84). The author says that while putting a book together, the writer will "learn things" (line 73), which suggests that putting a book together enhances, rather than defeats, the writer's intelligence.

C is incorrect because a task cannot envision (that is, see in its imagination) intelligence; only a person can do that.

D is incorrect because a task cannot ensure (that is, make certain or guarantee) all of the writer's intelligence. Only the writer, if anybody, can do that.

Question 22. The best answer is J.

F is incorrect because in lines 1–3 the author compares the writer's "line of words" to "a surgeon's probe."

G is incorrect because in lines 1–2 the author compares the writer's "line of words" to "a miner's pick."

H is incorrect because in lines 59–62 the author says that "what happens . . . between the writer and the work itself. . . . is similar to what happens between a painter and a canvas."

J is the best answer because the author does not compare the interaction between writers and their work to that of the work of a musician anywhere in the passage.

Question 23. The best answer is B.

A is incorrect because the author states that the writer draws courage, not pain, from the best-written part (lines 42–44).

B is the best answer because in lines 40–41 the author states that the writer must jettison, or throw away, the best-written part.

C is incorrect because there is no mention in the passage that the best-written part of a piece is the most dramatic part.

D is incorrect because one of the points of the passage is that writing is a process that takes time. Lines 48–49 state that one's freedom as a writer "is not freedom of expression in the sense of wild blurting."

Question 24. The best answer is H.

F is incorrect because the author mentions a writer's humility (line 14); she does not discuss any need to be aggressive. There is nothing in the passage to indicate that the author believes writers must be intellectual, either. The passage is addressed to a universal "you," that is, anyone who wishes to write seriously. The writer's work is described as having an "intellectual structure" (line 65), which is the shape of the writer's vision.

G is incorrect because as it is described in the second paragraph (lines 7–10), the path is the process of following one's thoughts until one arrives at what one wants to say, at which point one will "hammer out reports." The path is the direction one's thoughts take, not the actual writing produced. "The path is not the work," according to lines 17–18.

H is the best answer because the passage clearly presents writing as a humbling and transforming experience. The sentence in lines 14–16 says that a writer writes from a standpoint of humility, or humbleness. Lines 21–39 further imply that humility is needed when a writer tears down, rewrites, and revises. The constant need to revise and rewrite one's words requires the courage to demolish what one has already written. Through this process the writer learns, as described throughout the passage, which clearly implies a mental transformation.

J is incorrect because this passage is about the relationship between the writer and her or his work, not the writer and the audience. In lines 54–56 the author states that the work is "fully for yourself alone" and that "no one except you cares whether you do it well, or ever."

Question 25. The best answer is C.

A is incorrect because the third paragraph doesn't say anything about why writers need to learn humility. In fact, the third paragraph doesn't say that writers need to learn humility at all. Rather, the third paragraph suggests that humility results naturally from the fact that the writing changes "from an expression of your notions to an epistemological tool" (lines 12–13).

B is incorrect because the author encourages the writer to "toss it all and not look back" (lines 19–20), which would involve altering the line of words.

C is the best answer because the third paragraph (lines 11–20) focuses on how a writer will suddenly perceive the work differently. The author says that the writing has changed "in your hands, and in a twinkling" (lines 11–12), and that earlier writing has changed, too—it looks "soft and careless" (line 16).

D is incorrect because the third paragraph does not focus on how writing expresses notions of the self. In lines 12–13 the author says that the writing has changed "from an expression of your notions to an epistemological tool."

Question 26. The best answer is G.

F is incorrect. At this point in the essay, the writer is discussing the act of writing and going "where the path leads" (line 8). In this context, "breaking" a report doesn't make much sense.

G is the best answer. The phrase *hammer out* describes what the writer does in "a box canyon" (line 9). At the point that the phrase *hammer out* is used, the passage is describing the process of writing. Because of this, it can be assumed that the phrase *hammer out* and the word *dispatch* refer to the way in which the writer writes "reports" and "bulletins," so the best definition of *hammer out* is *write*.

H is incorrect. The context of the phrase *hammer out* is a description of the writing process (see the explanations for **F** and **G**). The author makes no reference to erasing writing at the point in the passage where the phrase *hammer out* is used.

J is incorrect. Up to the point where the phrase *hammer out* is used, the passage doesn't mention removing any writing. The best meaning for *hammer out* is *write* (see the explanation for **G**).

Question 27. The best answer is C.

A is incorrect. The statement in lines 32–33 indicates that "Courage, exhausted, stands on bare reality," but no such statement is made about sentences "standing on" writing.

B is incorrect. In the fourth paragraph, lines 21–30, the passage compares bearing walls to the ideas that one has held the longest or is most sure of, which one must use as the support for the work one is producing. Vision, on the other hand, is called "a chip of mind" (line 66) that helps a writer see the world.

C is the best answer because the author says, "You can save some of the sentences, like bricks" (line 35).

D is incorrect because in lines 59–62 the author compares painting to "the work itself," that is, to the writing, not to freedom.

Question 28. The best answer is F.

F is the best answer because in lines 49–52 the author says that putting a book together "is life at its most free, . . . because you select your materials, invent your task, and pace yourself."

G is incorrect because the author says that the writer's freedom "is not freedom of expression in the sense of wild blurting; you may not let it rip" (lines 48–49).

H is incorrect because although the author says that putting a book together engages all of one's intelligence (lines 45–47), she does not claim that it is the most intellectually demanding task there is.

J is incorrect because in line 55 the author reminds the writer that the work is "worthless to the world."

Question 29. The best answer is D.

A is incorrect because option II is incorrect. It is freedom, not the vision, that is described as the by-product of the writer's days' triviality (line 58).

B is not the best answer because while it includes option III, which is correct (see the explanation for **D**), it does not include option I, which is also correct (see the explanation for **D**).

C is incorrect because although it includes option I, which is correct (see the explanation for **D**), it includes option II, which is incorrect (see the explanation for **A**).

D is the best answer because the vision is described as "a chip of mind" (option I) in line 66 and as "a glowing thing" (option III) in line 68.

Question 30. The best answer is H.

F is incorrect. In line 35, the passage mentions that some of the "bricks"—the sentences—will be saved, but it says nothing about this being miraculous.

G is incorrect. Some of the words will be salvaged if some of the sentences, containing the words, will be saved (see the explanation for **A**), but the passage doesn't say that this is a miracle.

H is the best answer. The passage says that "It will be a miracle if you can save some of the paragraphs" (lines 35–36).

J is incorrect because "the path is not the work" (lines 17–18), and it is the work that is revised by the writer.

Passage IV

Question 31. The best answer is C.

A is incorrect because although the passage mentions that many particle collisions are mundane events (lines 15–16), that part of the passage is very small. It precedes a much longer discussion of how a variety of types of events are recorded.

B is incorrect because although bubble chambers are mentioned in lines 5–9 as a technology of the 1950s and 1960s, they are not a subject of the entire passage. Electronic detectors are discussed at much greater length.

C is the best answer. Lines 5–10 establish that the technology for detecting particle images has changed, and most of the passage explores what the current technology is like. Lines 85–88 reinforce the idea that the technology has improved over time.

D is incorrect because nuclear energy is not mentioned in the passage.

Question 32. The best answer is F.

F is the best answer, as stated in lines 55–57: the magnetic field causes charged particles to leave curving tracks.

G is incorrect. Negatively charged particles are discussed in lines 58–62, and charged particles are said to result from the disintegration of neutral particles (lines 79–82), but the passage does not state anywhere that magnets cause particles to turn into negatively charged electrons. And while you might be aware that electrons are negatively charged, the passage does not state or imply that electrons are negatively charged.

H is incorrect. There is no support for this statement in the passage. The seventh paragraph (lines 66–74) talks about long-lived and shorter-lived particles, and the sixth paragraph (lines 53–65) discusses the effect of magnets on the tracks of charged molecules, but the passage never says anything about magnets increasing (or decreasing) the life of particles.

J is incorrect. There is no support for this statement in the passage. The passage talks about detectors that detect particle collisions, but it does not say whether positive and negative particles ever collide. Magnets are discussed in the sixth paragraph (lines 53–65), which focuses on the effect of magnets on the particle tracks of "electrically-charged particles." The sixth paragraph doesn't say anything about magnets affecting the life of particles.

Question 33. The best answer is D.

A is incorrect. The sixth paragraph (lines 53–65) discusses the direction of a positively charged particle's track. However, the passage says nothing about the length of a positively charged particle's track.

B is incorrect. The sixth paragraph (lines 53–65) discusses the direction, but not the length, of the track of a negatively charged particle.

C is incorrect because in lines 70–71 the passage states that shorter-lived particles decay visibly. The "on the other hand" in line 71 is in contrast to the previous statement about long-lived particles leaving long tracks.

D is the best answer, as stated in line 69: "Relatively long-lived particles leave long tracks, . . ."

Question 34. The best answer is H.

F is incorrect. Particle tracks are often "displayed on computer monitors as images" (line 31); pions are particles whose tracks can be recorded, but pions have never been seen, as stated in the fifth paragraph (lines 44–52).

G is incorrect. As stated in the fifth paragraph (lines 44–52), the tracks that particles leave are visible through the use of a detector. A pion is a type of particle whose tracks can be seen; however, the appearance of a pion "remains a mystery" (line 47).

H is the best answer. As the fifth paragraph (lines 44–52) makes clear, a pion is a type of particle, the tracks of which can be recorded by an electronic detector.

J is incorrect. The passage makes no mention of molecules. The sentence in which the word *pion* appears (lines 46–49) is preceded and followed by sentences about particle physics, and it is clear from the context that a pion is a type of particle.

Question 35. The best answer is D.

A is incorrect because lines 55–57 discuss the tracks of electrically charged particles.

B is incorrect because the fifth paragraph (lines 44–52) makes clear that pions themselves cannot be seen, although their tracks can be recorded by electronic detectors.

C is incorrect because lines 55–65 discuss the tracks of negatively charged particles.

D is the best answer. Neutral particles—particles without an electric charge—"leave no tracks in a detector" (line 77). Particles can be tracked by experimenters only if they leave tracks.

Question 36. The best answer is J.

F is incorrect because the passage is about the sophistication of today's particle detectors. The passage does not describe tracking as difficult or inaccurate.

G is incorrect. Photographs were used in the past to record the tracks of particles (lines 36–40). Today, electronic detectors are used (lines 9–10).

H is incorrect. The seventh paragraph (lines 66–74) talks about the tracks that both short- and long-lived particles leave, but it doesn't say that either kind is easier or harder to track.

J is the best answer. The passage is about the technology used to track particles and how it has improved. The second paragraph (lines 11–29) discusses how scientists can program their equipment so that they can capture the most useful information. In lines 49–52 the authors state that particle physicists have become extremely adept at interpreting particle tracks.

Question 37. The best answer is D.

A is incorrect because there is no mention in the passage of bubbles stopping particles as they move through the chamber. The bubbles indicate the path of a particle moving through a bubble chamber (lines 7–9).

B is incorrect. As stated in the first paragraph, bubble chambers were used in the 1950s and 1960s in conjunction with photographic equipment; computer images are used in today's electronic detectors (lines 30–31).

C is incorrect. It is possible to photograph the tracks that electrically charged particles make in chambers (lines 36–38), but "the images . . . show the *tracks* of the particles, not the particles themselves" (lines 44–46).

D is the best answer. Lines 7–9 describe electrically charged particles producing trails of bubbles in the liquid filling the chamber.

Question 38. The best answer is H.

F is incorrect. The passage doesn't say that bubble chambers are better at tracking particles than electronic devices.

G is incorrect. In the fifth paragraph (lines 44–52), the passage mentions that pions, a type of particle, can be tracked; nowhere is it suggested that pions could not be tracked in bubble chambers.

H is the best answer. Lines 21–29 describe how scientists filter out the images they are not interested in, recording only a fraction of the events that occur.

J is incorrect because, as stated in lines 44–46, it is the tracks of particles that are visible, not the particles themselves. Also, electronic detectors do not photograph the particles' tracks; rather, they produce computerized images of the tracks.

Question 39. The best answer is A.

A is the best answer because when the passage compares the detector to "a kind of ultimate microscope" (line 1), the word "ultimate" tells readers that the detector is very powerful, like the best microscope that could be imagined. Indeed, a detector is so powerful that it can record the tracks of subatomic particles, most of which exist for "less than a billionth of a second" (line 67). These particles could never be seen by the naked eye.

B is incorrect because microscopes are not mentioned again after line 1 of the passage. There is no ongoing comparison of microscopes and detectors in the passage.

C is incorrect because the passage presents no evidence for this statement. Detectors are compared to microscopes in line 1, but no further comparisons are made. It can most reasonably and easily be inferred that each instrument in a laboratory has its own use, so the statement can be rejected as nonsensical.

D is incorrect because there is no mention in the passage of using microscopes for particle detection, and because it is bubble chamber images rather than electronic detector images that are said to resemble abstract art (lines 36–41).

Question 40. The best answer is G.

F is incorrect. Although "no equipment can respond quickly enough to record all the associated data" from the thousands of collisions each second (lines 13–15), most collisions are not missed, but rather screened out by the scientists who program the detectors, as stated in lines 17–19.

G is the best answer because the second paragraph (lines 11–29) describes how scientists program electronic detectors to record only a fraction of the events that occur; it is the collisions that interest the scientists.

H is incorrect. According to the second paragraph (lines 11–29), scientists program the electronic detectors to screen out mundane collisions. The detectors are programmed to record only the collisions that are defined as interesting.

J is incorrect. Lines 13–15 state that "no equipment can respond quickly enough to record all the associated data" from the thousands of collisions that occur each second.

Passage I

Question 1. The correct answer is D.

In Table 1, *Streptococcus lactis* is grown at 37°C in two different growth mediums. In glucose milk, generation time is 26 min; in peptone milk it is 37 min. Therefore, the predicted generation time should include these two values.

A is incorrect because the range of values is below both values from Table 1.

B is incorrect because the range is too low to include either value from Table 1.

C is incorrect because the range is too low to include either value from Table 1.

D is correct because both 26 and 37 min, the generation times from Table 1, are included within the range of the answer.

Question 2. The correct answer is G.

The question refers to Figure 1, which shows the phases of bacterial population growth.

F is incorrect because population growth does not occur during the lag phase (the curve is flat).

G is correct because population growth increases most rapidly during the log phase, as shown by the rising curve.

H is incorrect because population growth does not occur (the curve is flat) during the stationary phase.

J is incorrect because the population decreases (the curve goes down) during the death phase.

Question 3. The correct answer is D.

Based on information in the passage, the generation time is the time needed for bacteria to double their population. According to the last column of Table 1, the generation times for the four bacteria listed are, respectively, 31, 32, 30, and 74 min. The largest of these values (that is, the longest generation time) is 74, which corresponds to **D**.

A is incorrect because it is shorter than **B** and **D**.

B is incorrect because it is shorter than **D**.

C is incorrect because it is shorter than **A**, **B**, and **D**.

D is correct because it is the longest value.

Question 4. The correct answer is F.

Based on the values for generation time (time to double the population) in Table 1, the four bacterial populations doubled at the following rates (in min): 66, 792, 23, and 26. Of these values, the only option close to 1 hour (60 min) is **F,** 66 min.

F is correct because it is approximately 1 hour.

G is incorrect because it is much greater than 1 hour (more than 13 hours).

H is incorrect because it is less than 1/2 hour.

J is incorrect because it is less than 1/2 hour.

Question 5. The correct answer is D.

The question refers to Figure 1, which shows the phases of bacterial population growth.

A is incorrect because the graph in Figure 1 shows differing, not constant, rates of change throughout the growth phases.

B is incorrect because there is a lag phase at the beginning where growth does not occur, indicating that the bacteria do not begin to increase immediately after transfer to a new medium.

C is incorrect because bacteria do not begin to decrease until the death phase (the last phase of the cycle).

D is correct because the lag phase of no growth during the first 2 hours, before the population begins to increase, supports the hypothesis that a period of adjustment (no growth) is needed before reproduction begins.

Passage II

Question 6. The correct answer is G.

F is incorrect because sampling was performed daily in both experiments, not daily in Experiment 1 and weekly in Experiment 2.

G is correct because the descriptions of the experiments state that groundwater was sampled in Experiment 1 and that water and suspended sediment from streams were sampled in Experiment 2.

H is incorrect because it is backward. Suspended sediment was not sampled in Experiment 1, but was sampled in Experiment 2.

J is incorrect because both phosphate and nitrate concentrations were sampled in both experiments.

Question 7. The correct answer is B.

The question requires you to determine the next experimental step that should be taken to better understand how phosphates and nitrates relate to plant growth. Of the four options, **B** describes an experiment involving all three of these factors.

A is incorrect because it measures the effect of temperature, not nitrates and phosphates, on plant growth.

B is correct because it involves growing plants (algae) under controlled concentrations of nitrates and phosphates. This would allow the researcher to determine how much plant growth occurs at specific concentrations of nitrates and phosphates.

C is incorrect. It does not include any observations or measurements of plants, or any controlled applications of nitrates or phosphates. Also, it would not provide more information because it does not measure a variable or test a new hypothesis.

D is incorrect because it does not involve use of plants, phosphates, or nitrates. Thus, there is no way to test the relationship among these three factors.

Question 8. The correct answer is J.

The question asks you to determine how best to test the effects of fertilizer on the amount of phosphates and nitrates found in groundwater near farms.

F is incorrect because it does not involve addition of fertilizer or measurement of groundwater.

G is incorrect because, although it measures an effect of increased nutrient input (increased plant growth), it does not measure groundwater as a source of nutrient input, and it does not directly measure nutrient amounts.

H is incorrect because, although it involves adding nutrients (fertilizer) to the farmlands, the nutrients are not measured or controlled, and levels of nutrients in the groundwater are not tested.

J is correct because an experimental variable (amount of fertilizer added to farmland) is varied in a controlled way, and the results of changes in this variable (nutrient levels in groundwater) are then measured. Because the groundwater flows toward the lake, increases in nutrient content of groundwater would be expected to cause increases in nutrient input to the lake. The experiment tests this hypothesis.

Question 9. The correct answer is A.

The scientists observed an increase in plant growth in a lake, and looked for sources of nutrients that could be causing the growth. According to the description of Experiment 1, they hypothesized that wastewater could be entering the lake from the wastewater systems of houses near the lake.

A is correct because it agrees with the description of Experiment 1 given in the passage.

B is incorrect because Experiment 1 deals with groundwater samples from houses, not runoff from farmland. Also, plant growth was increasing, not decreasing, and the hypothesis must reflect this.

C is incorrect because wastewater from houses, not rainfall, is considered in the hypothesis, and because plant growth is increasing, not decreasing.

D is incorrect because the experiment deals with groundwater, not lake sediments.

Question 10. The correct answer is F.

The question requires you to pick the one option that, according to the results of Experiments 1 and 2, would not reduce input of nitrogen and phosphorus into the lake.

F is correct because increasing the number of houses around the lake would increase the nitrogen and phosphorus entering the groundwater, and therefore entering the lake.

G is incorrect because these actions would decrease the amounts of both nitrogen and phosphorus entering the lake by reducing the amount of runoff from farmland that enters the lake.

H is incorrect because this action would decrease the amount of nitrogen and phosphorus entering the lake by reducing the amount of these chemicals introduced into the nearby farmland, which eventually enters the lake.

J is incorrect because this action would decrease the amount of nitrogen and phosphorus entering the groundwater, and therefore the lake, by reducing the amount of runoff into the lake.

Question 11. The correct answer is D.

The question states that the farther phosphates move from their source, the more phosphorus will be adsorbed by soil (and therefore removed from the water). Conversely, we can assume that closer to the source, fewer phosphates will be adsorbed, and phosphorus concentrations will be higher. According to Table 1, the phosphorus concentration at House 1 on May 3 was 8.4 mg/L. If the sampling had been done closer to the house, less phosphorus would have been adsorbed by the soil and the water concentration would have been higher than 8.4 mg/L. **D** is the only answer higher than 8.4 mg/L.

A is incorrect because it is less that 8.4 mg/L.

B is incorrect because it is less that 8.4 mg/L.

C is incorrect because it is less that 8.4 mg/L.

D is correct because it is greater than 8.4 mg/L.

Passage III

Question 12. The correct answer is H.

The factor that is varied in an experiment is the factor that the researcher purposely changed in order to measure the effect of this change. In this experiment, distance from the roadway was varied so that the researcher could measure the change in ozone level at each distance.

F is incorrect because background concentration of NO_2 is a natural, constant factor, not one that can be varied.

G is incorrect because background concentration of ozone is a natural, constant factor, not one that can be varied.

H is correct because researchers varied the distance from the roadway from 0 to 200 m.

J is incorrect because the speed limit on the roadway was fixed at 100 km/hr.

Question 13. The correct answer is B.

According to the results of Experiment 1, NO_2 levels on the 60 km/hr highway were lower than those on the 100 km/hr highway. Thus, we would expect that lowering the speed limit would reduce NO_2 levels in an area.

A is incorrect because reducing the naturally occurring ozone would have no effect on NO_2 levels.

B is correct because according to Experiment 1, NO_2 levels have been shown to be lower in areas with lower speed limits.

C is incorrect because according to Experiment 1, raising speed limits would increase, not reduce, NO_2 levels.

D is incorrect because ozone filters would not affect levels of NO_2.

Question 14. The correct answer is G.

Ozone levels are compared in Experiment 3, which shows that ozone levels increase as the distance from the roadway increases. The passage gives the naturally occurring ozone concentration as 0.12 ppm, which is higher than the ozone level 200 m from the roadway.

F is incorrect because the highway level of ozone would be lower, not higher, than the wilderness (naturally occurring) level.

G is correct, based on values in Table 2 compared to the naturally occurring ozone level of 0.12 ppm.

H is incorrect because the values near the highway would be lower than, not the same as, those in the wilderness location.

J is incorrect; because wilderness values are higher than values near the highway, they would be easily detectable.

Question 15. The correct answer is C.

This question requires you to determine what the values of nitrogen oxides are doing under certain conditions and to assume that carbon monoxide (CO) will do the same thing. You need to look through the experiments for data relating to changes in nitrogen oxides over time (options **A** and **B**) and changes in nitrogen oxides at varying distances from the roadway (options **C** and **D**).

A is incorrect because none of the three experiments show changes in nitrogen oxides over time.

B is incorrect because none of the three experiments show changes in nitrogen oxides over time.

C is correct. According to Experiment 2, the levels of both NO and NO_2 are highest at the roadway (0 m) and decrease farther away. Therefore, if CO acted in the same way as nitrogen oxides, it would also show this pattern.

D is incorrect because it is the opposite of the results shown in Experiment 2, and, according to the question, you are expected to assume that CO acts in the same way as nitrogen oxides.

Question 16. The correct answer is J.

To answer the question, you must look at Experiment 2 for NO_2 levels and Experiment 3 for ozone levels. According to Experiment 2, NO_2 decreases from 30 ppb at 0 m to 17 ppb at 100 m. According to Experiment 3 (Table 2), ozone increased from 0.0075 ppm at 0 m to 0.04 ppm at 100 m. (These two experiments can be compared because both sets of measurements were made under the same conditions—a 100 km/hr roadway with an average of 30,000 vehicles/day.)

F is incorrect because NO_2 levels should decrease.

G is incorrect because both values are opposite from what they should be, based on Experiments 1 and 2. NO_2 levels should decrease, and ozone levels should increase.

H is incorrect because NO_2 levels should decrease, and ozone levels should increase rather than stay the same.

J is correct, based on the values in Experiments 2 and 3 (see the explanation above).

Question 17. The correct answer is D.

To answer this question, you must use the results from Experiment 1. This experiment uses the same conditions described in the question (a speed limit of 100 km/hr; measurements of NO_2 levels taken 10 m downwind). The NO_2 values for highways with 10, 20, and 30 thousand vehicles per day were 8, 13, and 22 ppb of NO_2, respectively. Therefore, the value of 100,000 vehicles per day must be much higher than 22 ppb.

A is incorrect because it is less than 22 ppb.

B is incorrect because it is less than 22 ppb.

C is incorrect because it is less than 22 ppb.

D is correct because it is greater than 22 ppb, which agrees with the results of Experiment 1, as described in the explanation above.

Passage IV

Question 18. The correct answer is G.

The stem length is defined by the length of r in Table 2. As the stem length (r) increases, the precession rate increases.

F is incorrect because it is the opposite of what is shown in Table 2 (that is, precession decreases as the stem length decreases).

G is correct, based on Table 2. Precession increases as the stem length increases.

H is incorrect because Table 2 shows that as the stem increases, the precession rate increases. Thus, if the stem remains the same length, the precession rate should not change.

J is incorrect because the length of r, not mass, is the factor varied in this experiment.

Question 19. The correct answer is C.

The values in Table 1 show that as spin rate increases, precession rate decreases. Of the four graphs, **C** is the only one that shows the relationship.

A is incorrect because it shows precession rate decreasing then increasing with increasing spin.

B is incorrect because it shows precession rate increasing rather than decreasing with increasing spin.

C is correct; it shows a rapid decrease in precession rate, then a continued decrease at a slower rate as spin rate increases. If the numbers in Table 1 were plotted, the curve would resemble this.

D is incorrect because it shows an increase in precession rate followed by a decrease with increasing spin. This pattern does not occur in Table 1.

Question 20. The correct answer is F.

The best way to determine whether gravity affects precession rate is to measure precession rate at several different gravities. **F** is the only option in which gravity is varied.

F is correct. If precession rate varies in a predictable way in relation to the gravity of the different planets, this would confirm the hypothesis that precession rate is related to gravity.

G is incorrect because if the two planets tested have the same gravity, gravity is not being varied and the effect of varying gravity is therefore not being tested.

H is incorrect because the hypothesis relates to gravity, not to the presence or absence of an atmosphere.

J is incorrect because the hypothesis relates to gravity, not to spin rates.

Question 21. The correct answer is A.

This question requires you to take information from Table 1 (precession rate at a spin rate of 500 rpm, which is 11), and relate it to Experiment 2. The precession rate of 11 rpm occurred at a value of *r* of 3 inches (Table 1); therefore the value of *r* in Experiment 1 must have been 3 inches.

A is correct, based on comparisons of Tables 1 and 2 (see the explanation above).

B is incorrect. According to the two tables, a value of *r* of 4 inches would result in a precession rate of 15 rpm, which occurs at a spin rate of between 350 and 500 rpm, not at 500 rpm.

C is incorrect. A value of *r* of 5 inches would result in a precession rate of 19 rpm, which would occur at a spin rate of less than 350 rpm.

D is incorrect. A value of *r* of 6 inches is higher than shown on Table 2, but based on the trend in the table, the precession rate would be higher than 19 rpm, and the resulting spin rate would therefore have to be much lower than 350 rpm.

Question 22. The correct answer is G.

Experiment 1 involved using an electric motor to give the top a known spin rate. The motor had to be adjusted to a different power to produce each spin rate. If these adjustments were not perfected, the spin rate could not have been measured accurately and therefore might not have been kept constant in Experiment 2. This would have introduced error into the results.

F is incorrect because mass was not a factor in Experiment 1.

G is correct because if the spin rate could not be measured accurately, it could have varied from trial to trial.

H is incorrect because nothing in either experiment affected distribution of the top's mass.

J is incorrect because nothing in either experiment affected the top's shape.

Question 23. The correct answer is B.

Because different metals have different masses, you could test the effect of mass by varying the metal from which the top is made. Keeping the tops the same size and shape would insure that the only variable is mass.

A is incorrect because color is unrelated to mass.

B is correct, as explained above.

C is incorrect because *different* is too vague (different in what way?), and also because testing tops on both Earth and the Moon would not affect the tops' mass, only their weight due to gravity.

D is incorrect because this tests different centers of gravity (due to different stem lengths), but does not test mass because mass remains constant as stem length is changed.

Passage V

Question 24. **The correct answer is H.**

You are asked to choose the description of the only type of cloud in which lightning would not occur, according to supporters of both theories. The answer depends on the basic definition of lightning, which is accepted by supporters of both hypotheses. Since lightning is defined as an electrical phenomenon that only occurs in clouds having positively and negatively charged particles (see the first paragraph of the passage), any cloud having only neutral particles could not produce lightning.

F is incorrect. Supporters of the Gravitational Theory would say that lightning could occur under these conditions, since they assume that charged particles are created by the collision of large and small precipitation particles.

G is incorrect. Supporters of the Convective Theory would say that lightning could occur under these conditions because they assume that updrafts from the surface move positively charged particles into the clouds.

H is correct; supporters of both theories would agree that no lightning can form if only neutral particles are present. They agree that positive and negative particles are necessary; they disagree on how the charged particles are formed, not on whether they are present.

J is incorrect; this is the exact situation in which lightning does occur, according to both theories.

Question 25. The correct answer is B.

The theories deal with where and how charges are initiated in the cloud. In the Gravitational Theory, the neutral particles become charged as large and small particles rub against each other within the cloud. In the Convective Theory, updrafts carry positive charges from ground level into the cloud, and negative charges are attracted to the edges of the cloud from the surrounding atmosphere.

A is incorrect because neither theory deals with the height of clouds.

B is correct, as explained above.

C is incorrect because both theories deal with whether lightning, not precipitation, forms.

D is incorrect. Again, neither theory deals with precipitation (either occurrence or amount); instead, they deal with whether lightning forms.

Question 26. The correct answer is F.

According to the Gravitational Theory, large drops fall to the bottom of the cloud, becoming negatively charged as they fall.

F is correct because according to the Gravitational Theory, large particles are associated with negative charges, and according to the theory, they would accumulate at the base of the cloud.

G is incorrect because according to the Gravitational Theory, small particles tend to be positively, not negatively, charged, and according to the theory, small particles tend to gather at the top of a thunderstorm cloud.

H is incorrect because according to the Gravitational Theory, rain (droplets) must be falling inside the cloud for negatively charged particles to collect at the bottom.

J is incorrect because the passage does not say anything about the concentration of charged particles after a lightning strike.

Question 27. The correct answer is B.

According to both the Convective Theory and the Gravitational Theory, negative charges are found near the bottom of mature thunderstorm clouds. As both Figure 1 and Figure 2 show, positive charges are found above the region of the cloud in which negative charges are found.

A is incorrect because this would be accepted by the Convective Theory only. Surface updrafts are not a factor in the Gravitational Theory.

B is correct, as described above.

C is incorrect because this relates only to the Convective Theory, not to the Gravitational Theory.

D is incorrect because neither would agree with this. Both theories would assume that both positive and negative charges exist within the cloud.

Question 28. The correct answer is H.

The Convective Theory states that updrafts drive positively charged surface particles upward into clouds, initiating charging of the cloud and formation of lightning.

F is incorrect because according to the Convective Theory, air just above the ground has a positive, not a negative, charge.

G is incorrect because attractive forces between charges are defined by laws of chemistry, not by the region in which the charges are found. The passage does not mention increased or decreased attractive force between charged particles as a factor in lightning formation.

H is correct because updrafts are believed to carry positive charges into clouds, causing lightning. More updrafts would lead to more lightning, and therefore more thunderstorms.

J is incorrect because a low frequency of updrafts, according to the supporters of the Convective Theory, would lead to fewer thunderstorms.

Question 29. The correct answer is C.

The description of the Gravitational Theory states that neutral particles fall due to gravity. Larger (heavier) particles would fall faster and reach the bottom of the cloud first, and these are the particles that become negatively charged.

A is incorrect because according to the theory, particles are neutral when they begin to fall; separation of charge occurs because of the interaction of particles as they fall.

B is incorrect because this statement describes a major assumption of the Convective, not the Gravitational, Theory.

C is correct because gravity results in larger ice crystals falling more rapidly than smaller crystals, and the Gravitational Theory states that the larger particles become negatively charged as they fall.

D is incorrect because according to the Gravitational Theory, gravity rather than downdrafts cause ice crystals to fall, and they gain negative charge as they fall.

Question 30. The correct answer is H.

According to the question, the path of lightning must be from negatively charged regions to positively charged regions. The Convective Theory states that updrafts move positive charges from the ground to the tops of clouds, and downdrafts move negative charges toward the bottoms of clouds. This question asks for the lightning path that is not possible; that is, in which situation is the described path not from negative to positive?

F is incorrect because lightning is possible in this situation since the base of the cloud is negatively charged and the top is positively charged.

G is incorrect because the base of the cloud is negative and the top of the other cloud is positive, so lightning could follow this path.

H is correct because in this situation the lightning would originate from a positive region; the passage states that lightning always flows from negative to positive.

J is incorrect because the cloud base is negative, so the lightning path could occur from the cloud base to a positively charged region of the atmosphere.

Passage VI

Question 31. The correct answer is C.

For any given value of Z, say 1, as n increases, in this case from 2 to 4, I decreases, in this case from 3.4 to 0.85. This pattern is the same as Z = 2, 3, and 4.

A is incorrect because this is the opposite of the trend in Table 1.

B is incorrect because the data show only a decrease, not an increase at first.

C is correct because Table 1 shows a continuous decrease for I for each given value of Z.

D is incorrect because the data show only a decrease, not a decrease followed by an increase.

Question 32. The correct answer is F.

According to Table 1, as values for n increase, values for I decrease. So for n = 5, we would expect the value for I to be less than the value of n = 4, which is 0.85 eV. The only answer less than 0.85 is **F,** or 0.54 eV.

F is correct, based on the reasoning given in the explanation above.

G is incorrect because the value 0.90 eV is more than 0.85 eV.

H is incorrect because the value 2.7 eV is more than 0.85 eV.

J is incorrect because the value 3.4 eV is more than 0.85 eV.

Question 33. The correct answer is C.

The description of Table 1 states that atoms in the table contain only 1 electron. Column 2 shows the number of protons (Z) in each atom. The H atoms, which have only 1 proton (equal to the number of electrons) have no charge, while those with more than 1 proton (He, Li, and Be) all have positive charges.

A is incorrect because excess protons, not neutrons, are associated with a positive charge.

B is incorrect because it is the number of protons compared to electrons, not neutrons, that determines the charge.

C is correct because Table 1 shows that positive charges occur in atoms having more than 1 proton (that is, more protons than electrons).

D is incorrect; because electrons have a negative charge, more electrons than neutrons would give the atom a negative charge. Excess protons must be present for an atom to have a net positive charge.

Question 34. The correct answer is J.

To determine this answer, you must choose a given value of n (say 4) and look at the values of r for each of the four types of atom. The four types of atom show increasing net positive charges (H = 0, He = 1, Li = 2, Be = 3). The values of r (column 4) for the four respective types of atoms when n = 4 are: 8.5, 4.2, 2.8, 2.1. This shows a decrease as net positive charge increases. The same trend holds when n = 3 and n = 2.

F is incorrect; the data for all four elements, not just two, support the hypothesis.

G is incorrect; the data for all four elements, not just two, support the hypothesis.

H is incorrect; the data for all four elements, not just three, support the hypothesis.

J is correct; r decreases as net positive charge increases for all four elements at any given value of n in Table 1.

Question 35. The correct answer is D.

Energy of photons produced when electrons fall to the orbit where n = 1 is given in the last column of Table 1. The larger the value of E, the more energetic the photon. Therefore, in this answer, you are looking for the situation that produces the largest value of E.

A is incorrect. The value of E for He^+ when n = 2 is 40.9 eV. This is lower than the value for Be^{+3} when n = 2 and when n = 4.

B is incorrect. The value of E for Be^{+3} when n = 2 is 163.0 eV. This is lower than the value for Be^{+3} when n = 4.

C is incorrect. The value of E for H when n = 4 is 12.7 eV. This is lower than the value for He^+ when n = 2 and for Be^{+3} when n = 2 and when n = 4.

D is correct. The value of E for Be^{+3} when n = 4 is 204.0 eV. This is the highest of the four options.

Passage VII

Question 36. The correct answer is J.

Initial concentrations are given in columns 4 and 5 of the table. To determine the answer, you must look at the values in these two columns for each pair of trials to determine in which pair of trials the initial concentrations are reversed.

F is incorrect because the initial concentrations of H_2 and I_2 are the same in the two trials. Also, in Trials 1 and 2 the temperature and the final concentration are not the same.

G is incorrect because the initial concentrations of H_2 and I_2 are the same in the two trials. Also, in Trials 7 and 8 the temperature and the final concentration are not the same.

H is incorrect because the initial concentrations of H_2 and I_2 in these two trials are different, but they are not reversed. Also, in Trials 8 and 11 the temperature and the final concentration are not the same.

J is correct because in Trial 9, the initial concentration of H_2 is 1.00 and the initial concentration of I_2 is 0.50, while in Trial 10 these values are reversed. Also, in Trials 9 and 10 the temperature and the final concentration are the same.

Question 37. The correct answer is D.

To determine this answer, you must look at columns 4 and 5 to find trials where initial concentrations of H_2 and I_2 are doubled, then compare the final concentrations of HI (last column) for each pair. There are two such pairs of values: Trials 3 and 7 (at 400°C) and Trials 4 and 8 (at 420°C). Both pairs of trials show that the final concentration of HI doubles (increases by two times) when the initial concentrations are doubled.

A is incorrect because as the initial concentrations double, the final concentration of HI increases.

B is incorrect because as the initial concentrations double, the final concentration of HI increases.

C is incorrect because the final concentration of HI increases by more than one-fourth.

D is correct because according to the table, as the initial concentration of H_2 and I_2 are doubled, the final concentration of HI increases by two times (doubles) from 0.788 to 1.584 mol/L (Trials 3 and 7) and from 0.782 to 1.572 mol/L (Trials 4 and 8).

Question 38. The correct answer is G.

To determine this answer, you must look at Trials 1–6, in which temperatures are changed while initial concentrations of reactants (H_2 and I_2) are kept constant.

F is incorrect. H_2 and I_2 are the reactants, and the question states that the initial concentrations of the reactants are kept constant.

G is correct. HI is the product. The table shows that, as the temperature increases from 360°C to 460°C, the final concentration of HI decreases slightly from 0.802 to 0.774 mol/L.

H is incorrect. H_2 and I_2 are the reactants, and the question states that the initial concentrations of the reactants are kept constant.

J is incorrect. The product, HI, does show a small change (a decrease).

Question 39. The correct answer is A.

To determine the answer, you must compare the K_{eq} values (column 3) at different temperatures (column 2) in Trials 1–6, where temperature is varied.

A is correct because the table shows that as temperature increases from 360°C to 460°C, the K_{eq} decreases from 66.0 to 46.8.

B is incorrect because K_{eq} does not level off, but continues to decrease throughout the range of temperatures shown on the table.

C is incorrect because K_{eq} does not stay the same, but decreases markedly as the temperature increases.

D is incorrect because it is the opposite of the trend shown in the table.

Question 40. The correct answer is J.

The table shows that doubling the initial concentrations doubles the amount of final product (compare Trials 3 and 7). If the initial concentrations are doubled from 1.00 to 2.00 mol/L, the final concentration of HI would be expected to double from slightly more than 1.5 mol/L to slightly more than 3.0 mol/L.

F is incorrect; this is less than the amount produced from initial concentrations of 1.00 mol/L. It is unrealistic to expect that if you double the concentrations of reactants you would get less final product.

G is incorrect; this is less than the amount produced from initial concentrations of 1.00 mol/L. It is unrealistic to expect that if you double the concentrations of reactants you would get less final product.

H is incorrect; this is about the same as the amount produced from initial concentrations of 1.00 mol/L.

J is correct; this shows a doubling of the final product when the reactants are doubled.

Practice Test 2

Your Signature (do not print): _____

Print Your Name Here: _____

Your Social Security Number
or ACT ID Number:

☐☐☐ – ☐☐ – ☐☐☐☐

ACT Assessment

DIRECTIONS

This booklet contains tests in English, Mathematics, Reading, and Science Reasoning. These tests measure skills and abilities highly related to high school course work and success in college. *CALCULATORS MAY BE USED ON THE MATHEMATICS TEST ONLY.*

The questions in each test are numbered, and the suggested answers for each question are lettered. On the answer document, the rows of ovals are numbered to match the questions, and the ovals in each row are lettered to correspond to the suggested answers.

For each question, first decide which answer is best. Next, locate on the answer document the row of ovals numbered the same as the question. Then, locate the oval in that row lettered the same as your answer. Finally, fill in the oval completely. Use a soft lead pencil and make your marks heavy and black. *DO NOT USE A BALLPOINT PEN.*

Mark only one answer to each question. If you change your mind about an answer, erase your first mark thoroughly before marking your new answer. For each question, make certain that you mark in the row of ovals with the same number as the question.

Only responses marked on your answer document will be scored. Your score on each test will be based only on the number of questions you answer correctly during the time allowed for that test. You will NOT be penalized for guessing. *IT IS TO YOUR ADVANTAGE TO ANSWER EVERY QUESTION EVEN IF YOU MUST GUESS.*

You may work on each test ONLY when your test supervisor tells you to do so. If you finish a test before time is called for that test, you should use the time remaining to reconsider questions you are uncertain about in that test. You may NOT look back to a test on which time has already been called, and you may NOT go ahead to another test. To do so will disqualify you from the examination.

Lay your pencil down immediately when time is called at the end of each test. You may NOT for any reason fill in ovals for a test after time is called for that test. To do so will disqualify you from the examination.

Do not fold or tear the pages of your test booklet.

DO NOT OPEN THIS BOOKLET UNTIL TOLD TO DO SO.

P.O. BOX 168
IOWA CITY, IA 52243-0168

1 ▪ ▪ ▪ ▪ ▪ ▪ ▪ ▪ ▪ 1

ENGLISH TEST
45 Minutes—75 Questions

DIRECTIONS: In the five passages that follow, certain words and phrases are underlined and numbered. In the right-hand column, you will find alternatives for each underlined part. You are to choose the one that best expresses the idea, makes the statement appropriate for standard written English, or is worded most consistently with the style and tone of the passage as a whole. If you think the original version is best, choose "NO CHANGE."

You will also find questions about a section of the passage, or about the passage as a whole. These questions do not refer to an underlined portion of the passage, but rather are identified by a number or numbers in a box.

For each question, choose the alternative you consider best and fill in the corresponding oval on your answer document. Read each passage through once before you begin to answer the questions that accompany it. You cannot determine most answers without reading several sentences beyond the question. Be sure that you have read far enough ahead each time you choose an alternative.

PASSAGE I

A Natural Wonder

You sit in the bright silver moonlight on a beach where its 10,000 miles from home. You are on the east
$\underline{\quad\quad}$
1
coast of Malaysia. You hear the soft, steady sound of the surf and feel the gentle touch of the warm breeze against your skin. Barefoot, you wiggle your toes into the damp sand. You cross your arms and lean forward against your upraised knees. You are waiting.

Then they come out of the sea, and are three
$\underline{\quad\quad\quad}$
2
massive turtles. They are giant leatherback turtles, seven feet long and weighing 1,000 to 1,500 pounds. They can live to be more than a hundred years old. [3] Each year they return here to lay their eggs, in the place where they themselves were hatched.

You watch as each of them slowly dig a hole and fill
$\underline{\quad\quad\quad\quad\quad\quad}$
4

1. **A.** NO CHANGE
   B. and its
   C. it's
   D. OMIT the underlined portion.

2. **F.** NO CHANGE
   G. they are
   H. you see
   J. OMIT the underlined portion.

3. Given that all are true, which of the following sentences, if added here, would most vividly describe the turtles' appearance and their movement from the water to the beach?
   A. They are the largest living turtle in the world and are covered with a tough outer shell that looks like leather.
   B. Eventually there appear three enormous turtles on the beach in front of you.
   C. They look like huge living rocks creeping almost imperceptibly onto the sand in front of you.
   D. There in front of you are three of the largest turtles you've ever seen.

4. **F.** NO CHANGE
   G. they each slowly dig a hole and fill
   H. they each slowly digs a hole and fills
   J. they slowly dig a hole and fills

GO ON TO THE NEXT PAGE.

1 ■ ■ ■ ■ ■ ■ ■ ■ ■ 1

it, one egg at a time, in which there are over a hundred

eggs. The eggs are bright white and about two inches in

diameter. You were watching as each turtle then slowly,

laboriously, buries the eggs, turning in circle after circle,

pushing sand back into the holes with surprisingly

efficient flippers.

[1] You notice that the turtles' eyes are covered

with a shiny liquid. [2] You know that this liquid has

a scientific explanation: they keep they're eyes

moist and clear of particles. [3] It looks as if they've

been crying. [4] Nevertheless, you may prefer to

think of them as emotional teary-eyed, over

creating new life. ☐ 11

The process takes hours, but you remain

quiet and still. It is all being watched by you. You

are looking at the sight of these odd, slow, determined

beings and their prehistoric ritual. And one realizes that

there is nothing quite as astounding as witnessing one of

life's more subtle and elusive natural wonders.

5. A. NO CHANGE
B. there are
C. with
D. OMIT the underlined portion.

6. F. NO CHANGE
G. watch
H. had watched
J. watched

7. A. NO CHANGE
B. until the eggs are buried with surprisingly efficient flippers, pushing sand back into the holes, turning in circle after circle.
C. turning in circle after circle with surprisingly efficient flippers until the eggs are buried pushing sand back into the holes.
D. turns in circle after circle, back into the holes pushing sand until they are buried with surprisingly efficient flippers.

8. F. NO CHANGE
G. turtle's eyes
H. turtles eyes
J. turtles' eye's

9. A. NO CHANGE
B. it keeps its
C. it keeps their
D. they keep its

10. F. NO CHANGE
G. them as emotional, teary-eyed over
H. them, as emotional, teary-eyed over
J. them as, emotional teary-eyed over,

11. Which of the following sequences of sentences makes this paragraph most logical?
A. NO CHANGE
B. 1, 3, 2, 4
C. 2, 1, 4, 3
D. 3, 2, 1, 4

12. F. NO CHANGE
G. All of it is watched by you.
H. You watch it all.
J. Watching all of it is you.

13. Which of the choices best emphasizes the writer's intense involvement in witnessing this process?
A. NO CHANGE
B. watching
C. immersed in
D. curious in

14. Which of the choices is most consistent with the style established in the essay?
F. NO CHANGE
G. it is then apparent
H. one can see
J. you realize

GO ON TO THE NEXT PAGE.

1 ■ ■ ■ ■ ■ ■ ■ ■ ■ **1**

Question 15 asks about the essay as a whole.

15. Suppose the writer had been assigned to write an essay explaining the reproductive methods of different species of turtles. Would this essay successfully fulfill the assignment?

A. Yes, because the essay focuses on the turtles and their egg-laying process.

B. Yes, because the essay describes the reproductive methods of giant leatherback turtles.

C. No, because the essay restricts its focus to the writer's experience of witnessing the egg-laying process of giant leatherback turtles.

D. No, because the essay omits mention of any turtle behavior connected with their means of reproduction.

PASSAGE II

Prepared for Anything

My mother is a justice of the peace; that means she has the power to perform weddings. She has to be

prepared for anything, because weddings these days can range from formal evening gown affairs to barefoot frolics during which the bride's dog might play the part of the ring bearer. She loves them all.
                              17

Mom keeps a crazy conglomeration of wedding gear; rubber boots; a swanky, black formal; blue jeans;
                              18
dignified dresses, in three pastel colors; sneakers; beach
                              18
sandals, and a ski hat. Every item—except that ski hat— has come in handy at least once.

The rubber-boot wedding until now was one
                              19
of the most exciting and, despite the boots, romantic ceremonies so far. It took place on a wide pond. When Mom arrived, the guests had already been ferried

16. F. NO CHANGE
   G. put on the ball and chain.
   H. join couples up in matrimonial wedlock.
   J. do the nuptial thing.

17. Which of the choices best introduces a central theme of the essay and provides an appropriate transition between the first and second paragraphs?

   A. NO CHANGE
   B. Or, a younger brother could be ring bearer.
   C. The bride usually has a maid or matron of honor.
   D. But it is usually the father who gives the bride away.

18. F. NO CHANGE
   G. gear; rubber boots, a swanky, black formal, blue jeans, dignified dresses in three pastel colors, sneakers,
   H. gear: rubber boots; a swanky black formal; blue jeans; dignified dresses, in three pastel colors; sneakers;
   J. gear: rubber boots, a swanky black formal, blue jeans, dignified dresses in three pastel colors, sneakers,

19. A. NO CHANGE
   B. (Place after *was*)
   C. (Place after *ceremonies*)
   D. OMIT the underlined portion.

GO ON TO THE NEXT PAGE.

1 ■ ■ ■ ■ ■ ■ ■ ■ **1**

out to a leaky, flat-bottomed boat made
                                  ___
                                   20

festive with flowers and pink balloons. 21

They may be more expensive, but helium balloons do
_____
                        22
look festive. My mother and the bridesmaids, all suitably
_____
    22
booted, paddled out in a canoe. Finally, dramatically, the

bride and her parents arrived under sail. 23

24 Except for the beach setting, the bride had

informed her, everything was to be traditional. The bride

wore a long, queenly gown and veil, but she had not

considered on the wind, which would have lifted her veil

clean off if my mother hadn't had the good sense to hold

it on. In the wedding photograph Mom appears to be

blessing the bride of whom a slightly harried expression
                     _____
                                    25
is disclosed by the wind.

Thus Mom's favorite weddings was a wonderful
____
 26
blending of cultures and traditions: the bride and groom

were Hungarian immigrants dressed in American denim;

the ceremony of two-minute duration which was in
_____
                        27
English was followed by hours of Hungarian celebrations.

20. **F.** NO CHANGE
    G. boat for it has been made
    H. boat, which it was made
    J. boat. Making it

21. Given that all are true, which of the following sentences, if added here, would best enhance the narration of events in this paragraph?
    A. Festivity is a good thing at weddings.
    B. The groom and best man rowed up in a dinghy.
    C. The bride and parents came later.
    D. The bride didn't come in a flat-bottomed boat.

22. **F.** NO CHANGE
    G. Flowers are also expensive, but they do look festive.
    H. Helium balloons come in many colors.
    J. OMIT the underlined portion.

23. Which of the following sentences, if added here, would best conclude the paragraph and support the main idea of the paragraph as expressed in its first sentence?
    A. By the time the wedding was over, everyone was damp.
    B. The crows cawed across the pond, the water sloshed, and the mosquitoes bit remorselessly.
    C. My mother said not even all those wet galoshes undermined the romance of the starlit evening.
    D. A flute duet performed by friends of the bride was nearly drowned out by the hiss of the wind in their dresses.

24. Which of the following sentences best continues to develop and support the theme of the essay while providing a smooth transition between the preceding paragraph and this one?
    F. One of my mother's favorite weddings was held in the desert and another at the seashore.
    G. My mother's second maritime wedding demanded the swanky formal and the sandals.
    H. My mother sported a swanky formal and sandals.
    J. My mother likes strange weddings.

25. **A.** NO CHANGE
    B. which a slightly harried expression
    C. a slightly harried expression of whom
    D. whose slightly harried expression

26. **F.** NO CHANGE
    G. Therefore,
    H. Nevertheless,
    J. Another of

27. **A.** NO CHANGE
    B. two-minute ceremony
    C. two-minute ceremony that took only a minute and was
    D. ceremony that took two minutes and that was

GO ON TO THE NEXT PAGE.

1 ■ ■ ■ ■ ■ ■ ■ ■ ■ 1

Yet the wedding Mom dreams of performing; she
hopes will take place at the foot of a ski run. She

imagines my brother and his bride skiing down the

mountain to join she and their guests. Mom,

however, will be wearing a ski hat.

28. F. NO CHANGE
    G. performing she
    H. performing, and she
    J. performing

29. A. NO CHANGE
    B. her and their guests.
    C. their guests and she.
    D. there guests and herself.

30. F. NO CHANGE
    G. nevertheless,
    H. of course,
    J. whoever,

PASSAGE III

Marian Anderson in Concert

It has been said that Marian Anderson's concerts
were much like communal celebrations than singing
events. Her voice had extraordinary range and power,

but equally moving was her presence on stage.
Sincerely, gracious, always in full command of her art,
she seemed completely absorbed in every song she sang.

There is perhaps no superior example of her
ability to reach out to an audience than the concert she

gave on Easter Sunday in 1939. It was, therefore,
originally scheduled to be given at Constitution Hall

in Washington, D.C. But several weeks before the

engagement, the organization that owned the hall

canceled the contract because members objected to
an African American singing there.

The decision created controversy that spread

throughout the country. When word of what happened

reached the president's wife, Eleanor Roosevelt, her first

response was to resign from the organization. The second

thing she did was to arrange for Anderson to sing before

31. A. NO CHANGE
    B. more as
    C. more like
    D. OMIT the underlined portion.

32. F. NO CHANGE
    G. Sincere, gracious,
    H. Sincere graciously,
    J. Sincere, gracious

33. A. NO CHANGE
    B. better of an
    C. better
    D. good

34. F. NO CHANGE
    G. was, however,
    H. was, in fact,
    J. was

35. A. NO CHANGE
    B. canceled, the contract;
    C. canceled the contract;
    D. canceled, the contract,

36. F. NO CHANGE
    G. did: was
    H. did was,
    J. did, was

GO ON TO THE NEXT PAGE.

1 ■ ■ ■ ■ ■ ■ ■ ■ ■ **1**

the nation, her listening audience, from the steps of the
_____
37

Lincoln Memorial.

Anderson wrote that she was in her autobiography
                                _____
                                        38
so nervous she barely remembered that day. Before

her a sea of faces stretched all the way to the

Washington Monument, and behind her

towered the statue of Abraham Lincoln.
_____
                  39
She was introduced to Supreme Court

justices members, of the House, and Senate, executive
_____
              40
department heads, and other dignitaries. Then she

walked over to the bank of microphones.

Anderson began by singing the national anthem,
_____
                        41
after which she sang several opera pieces and spirituals.
_____
                        41
Her splendid voice was broadcast into homes all across the

country. With her mastery of various musical styles and

the richness and control of her renditions, she made that

Easter Sunday one of the nicest days of the year.
              _____
                            42

Whether performing Verdi at the Metropolitan

Opera or singing folk spirituals on one of many concert
                                   _____
                                         43
tours, Anderson embraced her audiences with the same

37. Which choice most effectively explains how Anderson
was able to sing "before the nation"?
  - **A.** NO CHANGE
  - **B.** in front of the radio,
  - **C.** via radio,
  - **D.** across the dial,

38. F. NO CHANGE
  - **G.** (Place after *wrote*)
  - **H.** (Place after *nervous*)
  - **J.** (Place after *day* and end sentence with a period)

39. A. NO CHANGE
  - **B.** Abraham Lincoln towered as a statue.
  - **C.** was towering the statue of Abraham Lincoln.
  - **D.** the statue of Abraham Lincoln was towered.

40. F. NO CHANGE
  - **G.** justices members of the House
  - **H.** justices, members of the House,
  - **J.** justices, members of the House

41. A. NO CHANGE
  - **B.** After she sang several opera pieces and spirituals,
Anderson began by singing the national anthem.
  - **C.** Anderson began by singing the national anthem,
after she sang several opera pieces and spirituals.
  - **D.** By singing the national anthem, Anderson began
and then sang several opera pieces and spirituals.

42. Which choice would most effectively summarize the
event's impact as it has been described here?
  - **F.** NO CHANGE
  - **G.** a very important religious holiday.
  - **H.** a nationwide celebration of song.
  - **J.** the dream of a musical connoisseur.

43. A. NO CHANGE
  - **B.** many of one's
  - **C.** one out of her
  - **D.** any one of those

GO ON TO THE NEXT PAGE.

1 ■ ■ ■ ■ ■ ■ ■ ■ **1**

largeness of spirit. When she retired in 1965, [44] she

had won over not only their acclaim but their enduring
affection.

44. The writer is considering adding the following phrase at this point in the essay:

> decades after making one of her several concert tours on the European continent,

Would this phrase be a relevant and appropriate addition to the essay, and why?

 F. Yes, because it informs the reader that she continued to perform long after that European tour.
 G. Yes, because it helps the reader to form a historical reference for her European concert tours.
 H. Yes, because it draws the link between the extreme pressures of those tours and her eventual retirement.
 J. No, because it is vague and implies a significance to those tours unsupported by the rest of the essay.

45. A. NO CHANGE
 B. earned the winnings of
 C. been the winner in
 D. won

PASSAGE IV

> The following paragraphs may or may not be in the most logical order. Each paragraph is numbered in brackets, and item 60 will ask you to choose the most logical placement for Paragraph 4.

Clouds and Their Silver Linings

[1]

History is not merely remembering the good that came before. What's nostalgia. Small doses of nostalgia

may be harmless but enough, anything beyond that can

get awfully dangerous awfully fast. [48]

46. F. NO CHANGE
 G. Its
 H. That's
 J. Thats

47. A. NO CHANGE
 B. enough harmless, but
 C. harmless enough, however,
 D. harmless enough, but

48. Which of the following, if added here, would most effectively serve to summarize one of the main ideas of the essay?

 F. People who accept mere nostalgia as history often deny or ignore long-term problems that need attention.
 G. Those who don't believe in history are nostalgic—they realize that life is made up of both good and bad.
 H. The number of people who have accepted mere nostalgia as history has begun to decrease in recent years.
 J. In this essay, we will attempt to examine the intricate relationship between nostalgia and history.

GO ON TO THE NEXT PAGE.

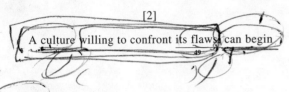

1 ▪ ▪ ▪ ▪ ▪ ▪ ▪ ▪ 1

[2]

A culture willing to confront its flaws can begin
49

to find remedies for it. The American Revolution
50

involving the original thirteen colonies was the outgrowth
51

of a focused attack on an unjust system. The same goes for

the abolition, women's rights, and civil rights movements.
52

In contrast, every constructive social movement in United
53

States history has resulted less from preening over

successes than from examining failures.

[3]

More recently, American culture during the 1980s,
54

typified by the popular song "Don't Worry, Be Happy,"
55

fostered a host of domestic problems. Many health experts

will tell you that if our leaders had initially taken the

AIDS epidemic seriously, the disease would not be the

problem that it is today. And many economists will tell

you that the savings-and-loan scandal, which will cost

United States taxpayers more than the entire Vietnam

War, could only have occurred during a time of

irresponsible confidence, when too many people

wanted to ignore any negative information.

49. A. NO CHANGE
    B. it's flaws
    C. it's flaws,
    D. its flaws

50. F. NO CHANGE
    G. for them.
    H. of them.
    J. for themselves.

51. A. NO CHANGE
    B. that occurred in what was to become the United States
    C. that took place in what was then the thirteen colonies
    D. OMIT the underlined portion.

52. F. NO CHANGE
    G. abolition, womens' rights
    H. abolition women's rights,
    J. abolition, womens rights

53. A. NO CHANGE
    B. In fact,
    C. Besides,
    D. For example,

54. F. NO CHANGE
    G. culture, derived from the same Latin root as the word *cultivate* is,
    H. culture, by which we do not mean "aesthetic taste or refinement,"
    J. social patterns, traits, and products that are the sum of American culture

55. The writer intends here to provide an example of 1980s American culture superficially celebrating the positive. Given that all of the statements are true, which choice would best accomplish the writer's goal?

    A. NO CHANGE
    B. when the baby boomers became the "thirty-something" crowd,
    C. which was certainly not an easy time for everybody,
    D. despite a worldwide trend toward greater democratic freedom,

GO ON TO THE NEXT PAGE.

1 ■ ■ ■ ■ ■ ■ ■ ■ ■ 1

[4]

Sadly, the converse is equally true: a culture that blinds itself to flaws and dwells on the positive can create serious trouble for itself. Many historians believe that the self-indulgence and nationalism of the 1920s, for example, led directly to the Great Depression, which entertained breadlines and dust bowls.
56

[5]

As the philosopher George Santayana said "Those
57
who cannot remember the past are condemned to repeat it." In their effort to dwell on only the upbeat aspects of history, the people peddling like in nostalgia are distorting
58
the past, and remembering it. The more distorted our past
59
becomes, the more doomed we are to repeat it. Or, to put it another way, the more we look at the silver lining and ignore the clouds, the more likely we are to be caught in the rain with no umbrella.

56. **F.** NO CHANGE
    G. Depression, when they suffered breadlines and dust bowls.
    H. Depression, a time of breadlines and dust bowls.
    J. breadlines and dust bowls of the Depression.

57. **A.** NO CHANGE
    B. philosopher, George Santayana said
    C. philosopher, George Santayana, said
    D. philosopher George Santayana said,

58. **F.** NO CHANGE
    G. peddling nostalgia
    H. peddling nostalgia like a bicycle
    J. nostalgia peddling

59. **A.** NO CHANGE
    B. nor
    C. as their
    D. not

> Question 60 asks about the essay as a whole.

60. For the sake of the unity and coherence of this essay, Paragraph 4 should be placed:

    F. where it is now.
    G. after Paragraph 1.
    H. after Paragraph 2.
    J. after Paragraph 5.

PASSAGE V

A Schedule for Success

[1]

Japanese students observe a rigorous annually
61
schedule. Beginning in the second week of

April and extending through the following March. The
62

61. **A.** NO CHANGE
    B. an annual rigorously
    C. an annual rigorous
    D. a rigorous annual

62. **F.** NO CHANGE
    G. April, which extends the school year
    H. April, their school year extends
    J. April and extends

GO ON TO THE NEXT PAGE.

1 ▪ ▪ ▪ ▪ ▪ ▪ ▪ ▪ ▪ 1

students have no long breaks or full summer vacations. [63]

[2]

[1] Japanese students finish their first term at the end of July and go on vacation until the beginning of September. [2] Then students return for their third term. [3] The second term ends on December 25 for the upcoming New Year's holiday. [64]

[3]

The Japanese school system consists of six years of elementary, three years of middle, and three years of high school. Although high school is not compulsory,
_____
65

attendees have become virtually universal. Acceptance
_____
66

into the best Japanese high schools however, are highly
                                _____
                                67
competitive.

[4]

Japanese students have mixed attitudes toward
_____
68
school. Attending school six days a week,
_____
68

taking as many as nine courses during a term.
_____
69

Typical, a ninth-grader takes Japanese, social studies,
_____
70
mathematics, science, music, fine arts, physical education,

63. The writer wishes to open Paragraph 1 with a sentence that will define the topic and begin to sharpen the focus on the particular subject of this essay. Given that all are true, which of the following would most effectively accomplish this?

   A. Japan is a populous island nation located along what is commonly known as the Pacific Rim.
   B. The economic "miracle" that has taken place on the island nation of Japan has its roots in a strong educational system.
   C. The economic growth that began in Japan in the 1960s has resulted in the third-highest gross national product in the world.
   D. Every presidential candidate that comes before the public points out the importance to the nation of a healthy educational system.

64. Which of the following provides the most logical ordering of the sentences in Paragraph 2?

   F. NO CHANGE
   G. 1, 3, 2
   H. 2, 1, 3
   J. 3, 1, 2

65. A. NO CHANGE
   B. school, although,
   C. school, although
   D. school and although

66. F. NO CHANGE
   G. the number of attendants has
   H. attendants have
   J. attendance has

67. A. NO CHANGE
   B. schools, however, is
   C. schools, however, are
   D. schools however, is

68. Which choice most effectively and appropriately introduces the subject of Paragraph 4?

   F. NO CHANGE
   G. Students in Japan have been given the option to learn beyond the classroom.
   H. Japanese students generally have a heavy course load.
   J. After all, Japanese students are just like you and me.

69. A. NO CHANGE
   B. as many as nine courses may be taken
   C. they take as many as nine courses
   D. nine courses are taken by as many as possible

70. F. NO CHANGE
   G. Typically, a
   H. A typically
   J. A typical,

GO ON TO THE NEXT PAGE.

1 ■ ■ ■ ■ ■ ■ ■ ■ **1**

English, and homemaking or workshop are taken. The
                                    ‾‾‾‾‾‾‾‾‾‾
                                         71
greatest emphasis, however, is on the basic skills of

writing, reading, and mathematical abilities and aptitudes.
                     ‾‾‾‾‾‾‾‾‾‾‾‾‾‾‾‾‾‾‾‾‾‾‾‾‾‾‾‾‾‾
                                    72

[5]

Because each major Japanese corporation recruits
                                          ‾‾‾‾‾‾‾
                                            73
new employees by arrangement from particular

universities year after year, getting into the right
           ‾‾‾‾‾‾‾‾‾‾‾‾‾‾‾‾
university is important for students. Therefore, most

parents encourage their children to attend *jukus,* or private

preparatory schools, on weeknights and Sundays. The

extra work helps the students to score well on entrance

exams, which determine what universities they may

attend. Once accepted into college, students are almost

guaranteed graduation and a good job afterward.

[6]

With this emphasis on education, Japan has

attained one of the highest literacy rates in the

world; about 99 percent. Meanwhile, Japan's educational
‾‾‾‾‾‾‾‾‾‾‾
     74

system and its business community have joined forces to
          ‾‾‾
          75
ensure that a steady supply of well-prepared youth

continue to enter the work force.

71. A. NO CHANGE
 B. workshop is also taken.
 C. workshop can be taken.
 D. workshop.

72. F. NO CHANGE
 G. the subject where math skills are practiced.
 H. basic mathematical computations.
 J. mathematics.

73. A. NO CHANGE
 B. recruits, on an annual basis,
 C. annually recruits
 D. each year recruits

74. F. NO CHANGE
 G. world about,
 H. world: about
 J. world about

75. A. NO CHANGE
 B. it's
 C. their
 D. its'

END OF TEST 1

STOP! DO NOT TURN THE PAGE UNTIL TOLD TO DO SO.

2   2

MATHEMATICS TEST
60 Minutes—60 Questions

DIRECTIONS: Solve each problem, choose the correct answer, and then fill in the corresponding oval on your answer document.

Do not linger over problems that take too much time. Solve as many as you can; then return to the others in the time you have left for this test.

You are permitted to use a calculator on this test. You may use your calculator for any problems you choose, but some of the problems may best be done without using a calculator.

Note: Unless otherwise stated, all of the following should be assumed.

1. Illustrative figures are NOT necessarily drawn to scale.
2. Geometric figures lie in a plane.
3. The word *line* indicates a straight line.
4. The word *average* indicates arithmetic mean.

---

1. A *stone* is a unit of weight equivalent to 14 pounds. If a person weighs 177 pounds, how many stone, to the nearest tenth, does this person weigh?

   A. 247.8
   B. 126.4
   C. 79.1
   D. 12.6
   E. 7.9

2. To keep up with rising expenses, a motel manager needs to raise the $30.00 room rate by 18%. What will be the new rate?

   F. $30.18
   G. $31.80
   H. $33.00
   J. $35.40
   K. $48.00

3. Contributions to a charity are made by each of 5 companies as indicated in the table below.

Company	A	B	C	D	E
Contribution in dollars	0	300	300	180	270

   What is the average of the contributions made by the 5 companies?

   A. $187.50
   B. $210.00
   C. $250.00
   D. $262.50
   E. $350.00

DO YOUR FIGURING HERE.

GO ON TO THE NEXT PAGE.

2 △ △ △ △ △ △ △ △ △ **2**

DO YOUR FIGURING HERE.

4. Car A travels 60 miles per hour for $1\frac{1}{2}$ hours; Car B *80* travels 40 miles per hour for 2 hours. What is the *difference* between the number of miles traveled by Car A and the number of miles traveled by Car B ?

   F. 0
   G. 10
   H. 80
   J. 90
   K. 170

5. Which of the following is a value of t for which $(t - 3)(t + 2) = 0$?

   A. 2
   B. 3
   C. 5
   D. 6
   E. 7

6. In the parallelogram $ABCD$ shown below, $\overline{AD}$ is 6 inches long. If the parallelogram's perimeter is 34 inches, how many inches long is $\overline{AB}$?

   F. 28
   G. 22
   H. 17
   J. 11
   K. $5\frac{2}{3}$

7. If the measure of each interior angle in a regular polygon is 90°, how many sides does the polygon have?

   A. 3
   B. 4
   C. 6
   D. 8
   E. 12

8. For all nonzero r, t, and z values, $\frac{16r^3tz^5}{-4rt^3z^2} = ?$

   F. $-\frac{4z^3}{r^2t^2}$
   G. $-\frac{4r^2z^3}{t^2}$
   H. $-\frac{4rz}{t}$
   J. $-4r^4t^4z^7$
   K. $-4r^2t^2z^3$

GO ON TO THE NEXT PAGE.

2   **2**

9. In the figure below, X and Y lie on the sides of $\triangle ABC$, and $\overline{XY}$ is parallel to $\overline{AB}$. What is the measure of $\angle C$?

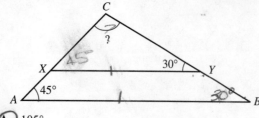

- **A.** 105°
- **B.** 115°
- **C.** 125°
- **D.** 135°
- **E.** 150°

10. $|-3| \cdot |2| = ?$

- **F.** −6
- **G.** −5
- **H.** −1
- **J.** 5
- **K.** 6

11. A TV station conducted a telephone poll seeking viewers' reactions to a new show. Of the 750 people who answered, 500 liked the new show, 100 disliked it, and the rest were undecided. What percent of those who answered were undecided about the new show?

- **A.** 20%
- **B.** 25%
- **C.** $66\frac{2}{3}\%$
- **D.** 80%
- **E.** 150%

12. Two whole numbers have a greatest common factor of 6 and a least common multiple of 36. Which of the following pairs of whole numbers will satisfy the given conditions?

- **F.** 4 and 9
- **G.** 9 and 12
- **H.** 12 and 15
- **J.** 12 and 18
- **K.** 18 and 24

13. If $x = -2$ and $y = 3$, then $x^3y + xy^3 = ?$

- **A.** −30
- **B.** −36
- **C.** −48
- **D.** −78
- **E.** −108

DO YOUR FIGURING HERE.

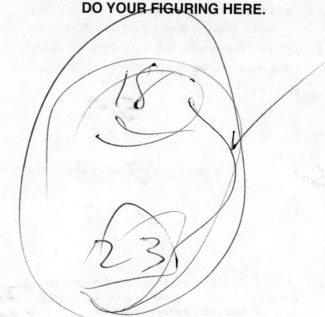

GO ON TO THE NEXT PAGE.

2 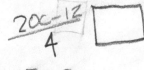 **2**

14. How many units long is 1 side of a square with perimeter $20c - 12$ units?

   F. $20c - 12$
   G. $20c - 3$
   H. $8c$
   J. $5c - 12$
   K. $5c - 3$

DO YOUR FIGURING HERE.

$$\frac{20c - 12}{4}$$

$5c - 3$

15. If $(x + k)^2 = x^2 + 22x + k^2$ for all real numbers x, then $k = ?$

   A. 11
   B. 22
   C. 44
   D. 88
   E. 176

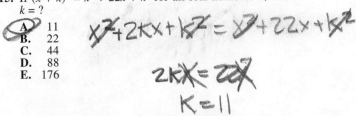

$x^2 + 2kx + k^2 = x^2 + 22x + k^2$

$2kx = 22x$

$k = 11$

16. Before his interview, Ben bought 1 suit and 2 shirts, all on sale. The suit, regularly \$260, was 20% off, and the shirts, regularly \$30 each, were 30% off. What was the total price of the 3 items Ben bought?

(Note: Assume there is no sales tax.)

   F. \$220
   G. \$229
   H. \$240
   J. \$250
   K. \$270

$$\begin{array}{r} 208 \\ + 42 \\ \hline 250 \end{array}$$

17. Which of the following expressions gives the slope of the line connecting the points $(6,8)$ and $(-4,-10)$ in the standard (x,y) coordinate plane?

   A. $\dfrac{8 + (-10)}{-6 - (-4)}$

   B. $\dfrac{8 + (-10)}{-4 + 6}$

   C. $\dfrac{8 - (-10)}{6 - (-4)}$

   D. $\dfrac{8 - (-10)}{-4 - 6}$

   E. $\dfrac{8 - (-10)}{-6 + 4}$

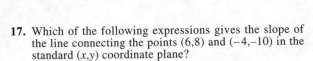

$$\frac{8 - (-10)}{6 - (-4)}$$

18. In the standard (x,y) coordinate plane, how many times does the graph of $y = (x + 1)(x - 2)(x + 3)(x + 4)$ intersect the x-axis?

   F. 10
   G. 6
   H. 4
   J. 3
   K. 1

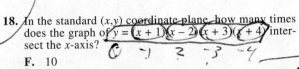

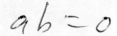

$ab = 0$

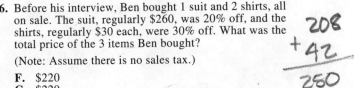

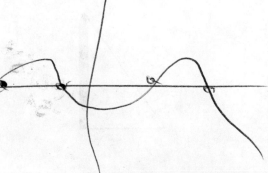

GO ON TO THE NEXT PAGE.

2   **2**

19. Which of the following is a simplified version equivalent to $\dfrac{3 + 6x}{9x}$?

    A. $\dfrac{2x + 1}{3x}$

    B. $\dfrac{1 + 6x}{3x}$

    C. 1

    D. 2

    E. $\dfrac{7}{3}$

DO YOUR FIGURING HERE.

20. Four students about to purchase concert tickets for $18.50 for each ticket discover that they may purchase a block of 5 tickets for $80.00. How much would each of the 4 save if they can get a fifth person to join them and the 5 people equally divide the price of the 5-ticket block?

    F. $ 1.50
    G. $ 2.50
    H. $ 3.13
    J. $10.00
    K. $12.50

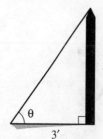

21. What is the sum of the polynomials $3a^2b + 2a^2b^2$ and $-ab^2 + a^2b^2$?

    A. $3a^2b - ab^2 + 3a^2b^2$
    B. $3a^2b - ab^2 + 2a^2b^2$
    C. $2a^2b + 3a^2b^2$
    D. $2a^2b^3 + 2a^4b^4$
    E. $-3a^3b^3 + 2a^4b^4$

22. An object 4 feet tall casts a 3-foot shadow when the angle of elevation of the sun is θ (see figure below). What is tan(θ) ?

    F. $\dfrac{3}{4}$

    G. 1

    H. $\dfrac{4}{3}$

    J. 7

    K. 12

GO ON TO THE NEXT PAGE.

2   **2**

23. Mary was x years old 10 years ago. How old will she be 6 years from now?

- **A.** $x + 6$
- **B.** $(x - 10) + 6$
- **C.** $(x + 10) - 6$
- **D.** $(x - 10) - 6$
- **E.** $(x + 10) + 6$

DO YOUR FIGURING HERE.

24. Which of the following is a factor of $x^2 - 5x - 6$?

- **F.** $(x - 1)$
- **G.** $(x + 2)$
- **H.** $(x - 2)$
- **J.** $(x - 3)$
- **K.** $(x - 6)$

25. What is the length, in centimeters (cm), of the hypotenuse of a right triangle with legs measuring 5 cm and 12 cm ?

- **A.** 7
- **B.** 13
- **C.** 17
- **D.** $\sqrt{17}$
- **E.** $\sqrt{119}$

26. Which of the following expressions is a simplified form of $(-2a^5)^2$?

- **F.** $-4a^{10}$
- **G.** $-4a^7$
- **H.** $-2a^{10}$
- **J.** $4a^7$
- **K.** $4a^{10}$

$4a^{10}$

$-(-2)^2$

$-(2)^2 = -4$

27. The *specific gravity* of a substance is the ratio of the weight of the substance to the weight of an equal volume of water. If 1 cubic foot of water weighs 62.5 pounds, what is the specific gravity of a liquid that weighs 125 pounds per cubic foot?

- **A.** 1
- **B.** 1.25
- **C.** 2
- **D.** 6.25
- **E.** 125

28. If $2x + 1 = -3$, what is the value of $x^2 - 3x$?

- **F.** -10
- **G.** -2
- **H.** 2
- **J.** 5
- **K.** 10

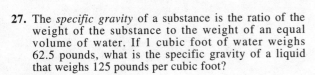

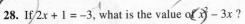

$(-2)^2$

$x = -2$

GO ON TO THE NEXT PAGE.

2   **2**

29. Which of the following is the graph of the solution set for $3(2 + x) < 3$?

DO YOUR FIGURING HERE.

A.

B.

C.

D.

E.

30. Which of the following equations has y varying directly as the square of w and inversely as the cube of t ?

F. $\dfrac{y^2}{t^3} = w$

G. $\dfrac{w^2}{t^3} = y$

H. $\dfrac{t^2}{w^3} = y$

J. $\dfrac{\sqrt{w}}{\sqrt[3]{t}} = y$

K. $\dfrac{w^2}{y^3} = t$

31. Points $A(-3,-4)$ and $B(7,-2)$ determine line segment $\overline{AB}$ in the standard (x,y) coordinate plane. If the midpoint of $\overline{AB}$ is $(a,-3)$, what is the value of a ?

A. 2
B. −4
C. 4
D. −5
E. 5

32. If the graphs of $y = 2x$ and $y = mx + 1$ are parallel in the standard (x,y) coordinate plane, then $m = $?

F. −1

G. 0

H. $\dfrac{1}{2}$

J. 1

K. 2

GO ON TO THE NEXT PAGE.

2 △ △ △ △ △ △ △ △ △ **2**

33. When 4 times x is increased by 7, the result is less than 19. Which of the following is a graph of the real numbers x that satisfy this relationship?

DO YOUR FIGURING HERE.

A.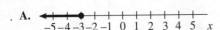

B. ⬤ (circled)

C.

D.

E.

$4x + 7 < 19$

$4x < 12$

$x < 3$

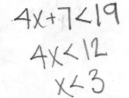

34. It costs 90 cents to purchase x apples and 68 cents to purchase y oranges. Which of the following is an expression for the cost, in cents, of 5 apples and 7 oranges?

F. $\dfrac{90}{5+x} + \dfrac{68}{7+y}$

G. $7\left(\dfrac{90}{x}\right) + 5\left(\dfrac{68}{y}\right)$

H. $5\left(\dfrac{x}{90}\right) + 7\left(\dfrac{y}{68}\right)$

J. $5\left(\dfrac{90}{x}\right) + 7\left(\dfrac{68}{y}\right)$

K. $5\left(\dfrac{68}{x}\right) + 7\left(\dfrac{90}{x}\right)$

35. When graphed in the standard (x,y) coordinate plane, 3 points from among $(-12,3)$, $(-8,2)$, $(-3,2)$, $(1,2)$, and $(5,1)$ lie on the same side of the line $y + x = 0$. Which 3 points are they?

A. $(-12,3)$, $(-8,2)$, $(-3,2)$
B. $(-12,3)$, $(-8,2)$, $(1,2)$
C. $(-12,3)$, $(-3,2)$, $(5,1)$
D. $(-12,3)$, $(1,2)$, $(5,1)$
E. $(-3,2)$, $(1,2)$, $(5,1)$

GO ON TO THE NEXT PAGE.

2   **2**

DO YOUR FIGURING HERE.

36. What is the cosine of angle A in right triangle $\triangle ABC$ below?

F. $\dfrac{2}{\sqrt{5}}$

G. $\dfrac{2}{3}$

H. $\dfrac{\sqrt{5}}{3}$

J. $\dfrac{\sqrt{5}}{2}$

K. $\dfrac{3}{\sqrt{5}}$

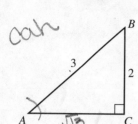

[handwritten: cah; $3^2 + 2^2 =$; $9 + 4 = 13$; $\dfrac{\sqrt{13}}{3}$; ?]

37. The graph of the solution set for the system of linear equations below is a single line in the standard (x,y) coordinate plane.

$$18x - 30y = 54$$
$$6x + \ ky = 18$$

What must be the value of k?

A. -10

B. -6

C. $-\dfrac{1}{3}$

D. $\dfrac{3}{5}$

E. 3

[handwritten: $18x - 30y = 54$; $-3(6x + ky = 18)$; $-18x - 3ky = -54$]

38. Doctors use the term *maximum heart rate* (*MHR*) when referring to the quantity found by starting with 220 beats per minute and subtracting 1 beat per minute for each year of a person's age. Doctors recommend exercising 3 or 4 times each week for at least 20 minutes with your heart rate increased from its *resting heart rate* (*RHR*) to its *training heart rate* (*THR*), where

$$THR = RHR + .65(MHR - RHR)$$

Which of the following is closest to the *THR* of a 43-year-old person whose *RHR* is 54 beats per minute?

F. 197

G. 169

H. 162

J. 134

K. 80

[handwritten: train, rest, max, rest; THR = 54 + .65(177 - 54)]

GO ON TO THE NEXT PAGE.

2   **2**

39. Martina's teacher told her to be sure NOT to calculate $(a + b)^2$ as $a^2 + b^2$. But Martina thinks that sometimes that calculation works. After working for a while, she shows that $(a + b)^2$ equals $a^2 + b^2$ if and only if:

A. $a = 0$
B. $b = 0$
C. $a = 0$ and $b = 0$
D. $a = 0$ or $b = 0$
E. a and b have the same sign

DO YOUR FIGURING HERE.

40. In the figure below, $\overline{CD}$ is an altitude of equilateral triangle $\triangle ABC$. If $\overline{CD}$ is $6\sqrt{3}$ units long, how many units long is $\overline{AC}$?

F. $3\sqrt{3}$
G. 6
H. 12
J. $12\sqrt{3}$
K. 36

41. What is the perimeter, in feet (ft), of the figure below?

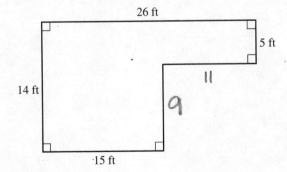

A. 60
B. 75
C. 80
D. 130
E. 364

GO ON TO THE NEXT PAGE.

2 △ △ △ △ △ △ △ △ △ **2**

42. Right triangle $\triangle ABC$ is inscribed in a circle with center M, shown below, and C can be any point on the circle other than A or B. Which of the following is the most direct explanation of why $\triangle MCA$ is isosceles?

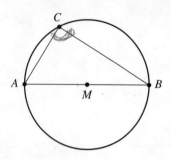

F. 2 sides are radii of the circle
G. Side-angle-side congruence
H. Angle-side-angle congruence
J. Angle-angle-angle similarity
K. The Pythagorean theorem

43. A square 2 feet on a side is cut out of a circle with radius 10 feet as shown in the figure below. Which of the following expressions gives the area of the shaded region, in square feet?

$OA = \pi r^2$

$\pi(10-2)^2$

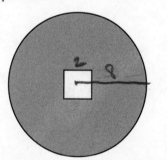

A. $\pi(10 - 2^2)$
B. $\pi(10 - 2)^2$
C. $\pi(10 - 1)^2$
D. $\pi 10^2 - 1^2$
E. $\pi 10^2 - 2^2$

GO ON TO THE NEXT PAGE.

2   **2**

44. The inside dimensions of a rectangular picture frame are $15\frac{1}{2}$ inches by 24 inches and the outside dimensions are 20 inches by $28\frac{1}{2}$ inches, as shown below.

DO YOUR FIGURING HERE.

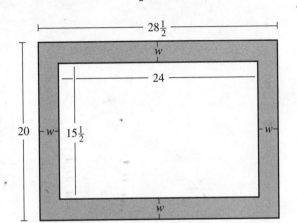

What is the width (w), in inches, of the picture frame?

F. $1\frac{1}{8}$

G. 2

H. $2\frac{1}{4}$

J. $2\frac{1}{2}$

K. $4\frac{1}{2}$

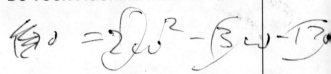

45. The area of a rectangular floor is 170 square feet. The length of the floor is 3 feet less than twice the width. How many feet wide is the floor?

A. 8.5
B. 10
C. 14
D. 15
E. 17

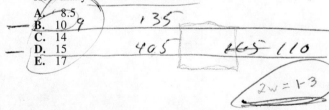

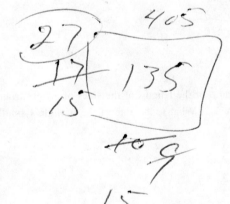

46. For the area of a square to double, the new side lengths must be the old side lengths multiplied by:

F. $\sqrt{2}$

G. 2

H. 4

J. $\sqrt{8}$

K. 8

GO ON TO THE NEXT PAGE.

2   **2**

DO YOUR FIGURING HERE.

47. If $\log_x 81 = 4$, then $x = ?$

   A. 3

   B. 9

   C. $\frac{81}{4}$

   D. $\frac{81}{\log 4}$

   E. 81^4

48. If $A = \begin{bmatrix} 2 & -4 \\ 6 & 0 \end{bmatrix}$ and $B = \begin{bmatrix} -2 & 4 \\ -6 & 0 \end{bmatrix}$, then $A - B = ?$

   F. $\begin{bmatrix} 0 & 0 \\ 0 & 0 \end{bmatrix}$

   G. $\begin{bmatrix} 1 & 0 \\ 0 & 1 \end{bmatrix}$

   H. $\begin{bmatrix} 0 & -8 \\ 0 & 0 \end{bmatrix}$

   J. $\begin{bmatrix} -4 & 0 \\ -12 & 0 \end{bmatrix}$

   K. $\begin{bmatrix} 4 & -8 \\ 12 & 0 \end{bmatrix}$

49. If a and b are real numbers, and $a > b$ and $b < 0$, then which of the following inequalities must be true?

   A. $a > 0$

   B. $a < 0$

   C. $a^2 > b^2$

   D. $a^2 < b^2$

   E. $b^2 > 0$

50. The ratio of the lengths of the sides of a right triangle is $1 : \sqrt{3} : 2$. What is the sine of the triangle's smallest angle?

   F. $\frac{1}{4}$

   G. $\frac{1}{2}$

   H. $\frac{\sqrt{3}}{2}$

   J. $\frac{\sqrt{3}}{3}$

   K. 1

GO ON TO THE NEXT PAGE.

2 △ △ △ △ △ △ △ △ △ **2**

51. What is the amplitude of the graph of the equation $y + 2 = 3 \sin(4\theta)$?

    (Note: The amplitude is $\frac{1}{2}$ the difference between the maximum and the minimum values of y.)

    A. 2
    B. 3
    C. 4
    D. 5
    E. 6

DO YOUR FIGURING HERE.

52. Each of the following determines a unique plane in 3-dimensional Euclidean space EXCEPT:

    F. 1 line and 1 point NOT on the line.
    G. 2 distinct parallel lines.
    H. 2 intersecting perpendicular lines.
    J. 2 lines intersecting in more than 1 point.
    K. 3 distinct points NOT on the same line.

53. The measure of the vertex angle of an isosceles triangle is $(x - 20)°$. The base angles each measure $(2x + 30)°$. What is the measure in degrees of one of the base angles?

    A. 8°

    B. 28°

    C. $42\frac{1}{2}°$

    D. $47\frac{1}{2}°$

    E. 86°

54. In decorating baskets for a retirement party, Rudy needs the following amounts of ribbon for each basket:

number of ribbons	length (inches)
5	8
3	16
2	10

    If the ribbon costs $0.98 per yard, which of the following would be the approximate cost of ribbon for 10 baskets?

    (Note: 1 yard = 36 inches)

    F. $ 3
    G. $ 9
    H. $30
    J. $35
    K. $90

GO ON TO THE NEXT PAGE.

55. The formula for the surface area (S) of a rectangular solid (shown below) is $S = 2lw + 2lh + 2wh$, where l represents the length, w the width, and h the height of the solid. Doubling each of the dimensions (l, w, and h) will increase the surface area to how many times its original size?

DO YOUR FIGURING HERE.

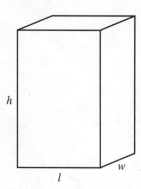

- **A.** 2
- **B.** 4
- **C.** 6
- **D.** 8
- **E.** 24

56. The average of a set of five integers is 16. When a sixth number is included in the set, the average of the set increases to 18. What is the sixth number?

- **F.** 18
- **G.** 20
- **H.** 21
- **J.** 24
- **K.** 28

57. Which of the following is an equation of the largest circle that can be inscribed in the ellipse with equation $\dfrac{(x-1)^2}{9} + \dfrac{(y+3)^2}{16} = 1$?

- **A.** $(x-1)^2 + (y+3)^2 = 144$
- **B.** $(x-1)^2 + (y+3)^2 = 16$
- **C.** $(x-1)^2 + (y+3)^2 = 9$
- **D.** $x^2 + y^2 = 16$
- **E.** $x^2 + y^2 = 9$

GO ON TO THE NEXT PAGE.

2   **2**

58. One of the graphs below is that of $y = Ax^3$, where A is a constant. Which one?

DO YOUR FIGURING HERE.

F.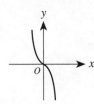

J.

G.

K.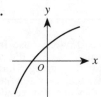

H.

59. How many points do the graphs of all 3 of the following equations have in common?

$$-x = y - 3$$
$$-x = -y - 3$$
$$3x = -3y + 2$$

A. 0
B. 1
C. 2
D. 3
E. Infinitely many

60. In 3 fair coin tosses, what is the probability of obtaining exactly 2 tails?

(Note: In a fair coin toss the 2 outcomes, heads and tails, are equally likely.)

F. $\frac{1}{3}$

G. $\frac{3}{8}$

H. $\frac{1}{2}$

J. $\frac{2}{3}$

K. $\frac{7}{8}$

END OF TEST 2

STOP! DO NOT TURN THE PAGE UNTIL TOLD TO DO SO.

DO NOT RETURN TO THE PREVIOUS TEST.

3 _____ **3**

READING TEST

35 Minutes—40 Questions

DIRECTIONS: There are four passages in this test. Each passage is followed by several questions. After reading a passage, choose the best answer to each question and fill in the corresponding oval on your answer document. You may refer to the passages as often as necessary.

Passage I

PROSE FICTION: This passage is adapted from Virginia Woolf's *To The Lighthouse* (©1955 by Leonard Woolf).

It could not last, she knew, but at the moment her eyes were so clear that they seemed to go round the table unveiling each of these people, and their thoughts and their feelings, without effort like a light stealing
5 under water so that its ripples and the reeds in it and the minnows balancing themselves, and the sudden silent trout are all lit up hanging, trembling. So she saw them; she heard them; but whatever they said had also this quality, as if what they said was like the movement
10 of a trout when, at the same time, one can see the ripple and the gravel, something to the right, something to the left; and the whole is held together; for whereas in active life she would be netting and separating one thing from another; she would be saying she liked the
15 Waverley novels or had not read them; she would be urging herself forward; now she said nothing. For the moment, she hung suspended.

"Ah, but how long do you think it'll last?" said somebody. It was as if she had antennae trembling out
20 from her, which, intercepting certain sentences, forced them upon her attention. This was one of them. She scented danger for her husband. A question like that would lead, almost certainly, to something being said which reminded him of his own failure. How long
25 would he be read—he would think at once. William Bankes (who was entirely free from all such vanity) laughed, and said he attached no importance to changes in fashion. Who could tell what was going to last—in literature or indeed in anything else?

30 "Let us enjoy what we do enjoy," he said. His integrity seemed to Mrs. Ramsay quite admirable. He never seemed for a moment to think, But how does this affect me? But then if you had the other temperament, which must have praise, which must have encourage-
35 ment, naturally you began (and she knew that Mr. Ramsay was beginning) to be uneasy; to want somebody to say, Oh, but your work will last, Mr. Ramsay, or something like that. He showed his uneasiness quite clearly now by saying, with some irritation, that, any-
40 how, Scott (or was it Shakespeare?) would last him his lifetime. He said it irritably. Everybody, she thought, felt a little uncomfortable, without knowing why. Then

Minta Doyle, whose instinct was fine, said bluffly, absurdly, that she did not believe that any one really
45 enjoyed reading Shakespeare. Mr. Ramsay said grimly that very few people liked it as much as they said they did. But, he added, there is considerable merit in some of the plays nevertheless, and Mrs. Ramsay saw that it would be all right for the moment anyhow;
50 he would laugh at Minta, and she, Mrs. Ramsay saw, realising his extreme anxiety about himself, would, in her own way, see that he was taken care of, and praise him, somehow or other. But she wished it was not necessary. Anyhow, she was free now to listen to what
55 Paul Rayley was trying to say about books one had read as a boy. They lasted, he said. He had read some of Tolstoi at school. There was one he always remembered, but he had forgotten the name. Russian names were impossible, said Mrs. Ramsay. "Vronsky," said
60 Paul. He remembered that because he always thought it such a good name for a villain. "Vronsky," said Mrs. Ramsay; "Oh, *Anna Karenina*," but that did not take them very far; books were not in their line. No, Charles Tansley would put them both right in a second about
65 books, but it was all so mixed up with, Am I saying the right thing? Am I making a good impression? that, after all, one knew more about him than about Tolstoi, whereas, what Paul said was about the thing, simply, not himself, nothing else. Like all stupid people, he had
70 a kind of modesty too, a consideration for what you were feeling, which, once in a way at least, she found attractive. Now he was thinking, not about himself or about Tolstoi, but whether she was cold, whether she would like a pear.

75 No, she said, she did not want a pear. Indeed she had been keeping guard over the dish of fruit (without realising it) jealously, hoping that nobody would touch it. Her eyes had been going in and out among the curves and shadows of the fruit, among the rich purples
80 of the lowland grapes, then over the horny ridge of the shell, putting a yellow against a purple, a curved shape against a round shape, without knowing why she did it, or why, every time she did it, she felt more and more serene; until, oh, what a pity that they should do it—a
85 hand reached out, took a pear, and spoilt the whole thing.

GO ON TO THE NEXT PAGE.

3 ▆▆▆▆▆▆▆▆▆▆▆▆▆▆▆▆▆▆▆▆▆ 3

1. Which author is described as less enjoyable to read than people are willing to admit?

   A. Scott
   B. Ramsay
   C. Shakespeare
   D. Tolstoi

2. What danger does Mrs. Ramsay sense at one point in the conversation?

   F. That she will be forced to pay attention to what is being said
   G. That her husband will miss an important change in literature
   H. That she will be seen as vain
   J. That something will be said to make her husband feel a failure

3. It is most reasonable to infer that Mrs. Ramsay hopes no one will touch the dish of fruit primarily because:

   A. it is beautiful and calming.
   B. she knows her children want it.
   C. she is afraid her husband will get angry.
   D. she wants the pear for herself.

4. Given the way he is presented in the passage, William Bankes can best be described as:

   F. amiable and self-confident.
   G. vain and insecure.
   H. kind but vain.
   J. self-confident and selfish.

5. The first paragraph suggests that the "she" who is looking around the dinner table feels unusually:

   A. awkward and unsure of what's happening.
   B. aware of what others are thinking and feeling.
   C. on display like a fish in an aquarium.
   D. like a character in the Waverley novels.

6. Which of the following conclusions about the relationship between Mr. and Mrs. Ramsay is best supported by the details in the passage?

   F. She admires his integrity and he respects her modesty.
   G. They are bored and uncomfortable with each other and only stay together for their children.
   H. She is jealous and selfish and he is unhappy.
   J. He is insecure and requires a lot of attention, which she usually gives.

7. What does the narrator suggest is a central characteristic of Charles Tansley?

   A. Stupidity
   B. Modesty
   C. Self-absorption
   D. Forgetfulness

8. Which person does Mrs. Ramsay admire for having integrity?

   F. Mr. Ramsay
   G. Mr. Rayley
   H. Minta Doyle
   J. Mr. Bankes

9. Mrs. Ramsay would most likely agree with which of the following characterizations of Paul Rayley?

   A. He is stupid but considerate.
   B. He is a vain intellectual.
   C. He is modest and smart.
   D. He is vain and worried about making a good impression.

10. One can reasonably infer from the passage that on the occasion of this dinner Mrs. Ramsay is feeling:

    F. detached and analytical.
    G. frightened and uneasy.
    H. giddy and happy.
    J. irritated and insecure.

GO ON TO THE NEXT PAGE.

3 ▬▬▬▬▬▬▬▬▬▬▬▬▬▬▬▬ **3**

Passage II

SOCIAL SCIENCE: This passage is adapted from *Loose Canons*, a collection of essays by Henry Louis Gates, Jr. (©1992 by Henry Louis Gates, Jr.).

What is multiculturalism, and why are they saying such terrible things about it? We've been told it threatens to fragment American culture into a warren of ethnic enclaves, each separate and inviolate. We've been
5 told that it menaces the Western tradition of literature and the arts. We've been told it aims to politicize the school curriculum, replacing honest historical scholarship with a "feel good" syllabus designed solely to bolster the self-esteem of minorities. The alarm has been
10 sounded, and many scholars and educators—liberals as well as conservatives—have responded to it. After all, if multiculturalism is just a pretty name for ethnic chauvinism, who needs it?

There is, of course, a liberal rejoinder to these
15 concerns, which says that this isn't what multiculturalism is—or at least not what it ought to be. The liberal pluralist insists that the debate has been miscast from the beginning and that it is worth setting the main issues straight.

20 There's no denying that the multicultural initiative arose, in part, because of the fragmentation of American society by ethnicity, class, and gender. To make it the culprit for this fragmentation is to mistake effect for cause. Mayor Dinkins's metaphor about New
25 York as a "gorgeous mosaic" is catchy but unhelpful, if it means that each culture is fixed in place and separated by grout. Perhaps we should try to think of American culture as a conversation among different voices—even if it's a conversation that some of us
30 weren't able to join until recently. Perhaps we should think about education, as the conservative philosopher Michael Oakeshott proposed, as "an invitation into the art of this conversation in which we learn to recognize the voices," each conditioned, as he says, by a different
35 perception of the world. Common sense says that you don't bracket 90 percent of the world's cultural heritage if you really want to learn about the world.

To insist that we "master our own culture" before learning others only defers the vexed question: What
40 gets to count as "our" culture? What makes knowledge worth knowing? Unfortunately, as history has taught us, an Anglo-American regional culture has too often masked itself as universal, passing itself off as our "common culture," and depicting different cultural traditions
45 ditions as "tribal" or "parochial." So it's only when we're free to explore the complexities of our hyphenated American culture that we can discover what a genuinely common American culture might actually look like. Common sense reminds us that we're *all*
50 ethnics, and the challenge of transcending ethnic chauvinism is one we all face.

Granted, multiculturalism is no magic panacea for our social ills. We're worried when Johnny can't read.

We're worried when Johnny can't add. But shouldn't
55 we be worried, too, when Johnny tramples gravestones in a Jewish cemetery or scrawls racial epithets on a dormitory wall? It's a fact about this country that we've entrusted our schools with the fashioning and refashioning of a democratic polity; that's why the
60 schooling of America has always been a matter of political judgment. But in America, a nation that has theorized itself as plural from its inception, our schools have a very special task.

The society we have made simply won't survive
65 without the values of tolerance. And cultural tolerance comes to nothing without cultural understanding. In short, the challenge facing America in the next century will be the shaping, at long last, of a truly common public culture, one responsive to the long-silenced cultures
70 tures of color. If we relinquish the ideal of America as a plural nation, we've abandoned the very experiment that America represents.

11. The main point of the last paragraph is that the values upon which America is based demand that its citizens need to be:

A. more scholarly.
B. more tolerant.
C. less idealistic.
D. more experimental.

12. The author of the passage finds Mayor Dinkins's metaphor (line 25) unhelpful because that metaphor suggests that each culture in America:

F. should probably be blended together.
G. exists separately from one another.
H. seems to embody cultural pluralism.
J. attacks the concept of ethnic chauvinism.

GO ON TO THE NEXT PAGE.

3   **3**

13. The author of the passage appears to feel that the answer to the question "What gets to count as 'our' culture?" should be provided by:

A. most Anglo-Americans.
B. a few liberal pluralists.
C. a range of cultural perspectives.
D. concerned scholars and educators.

14. As it is used in line 62, the word *inception* most nearly means:

F. politics.
G. beginnings.
H. idealism.
J. multiculturalism.

15. One of the main points made in the third paragraph (lines 20–37) is that education demands that people:

A. learn to master their own culture.
B. learn to see the world from new perspectives.
C. find a way to define American regional culture.
D. bracket 90 percent of the world's cultures.

16. The author implies that it is not unusual for the dominant culture in our country to look at different cultural traditions as:

F. parochial.
G. typical.
H. universal.
J. multicultural.

17. According to the passage, only by hearing the many different voices in American culture can we know what:

A. panacea will make American culture fully multicultural.
B. is so appealing about Dinkins's "gorgeous mosaic" metaphor.
C. distinguishes tribal from parochial in American culture.
D. a genuinely common American culture might look like.

18. The author states that because we have entrusted the task of "fashioning and refashioning a democratic polity" to our schools, education has become:

F. democratic.
G. irrelevant.
H. multicultural.
J. political.

19. The author states that America was founded upon the notion of being:

I. a truly plural nation.
II. a "gorgeous mosaic."
III. responsive to the cultures of color.

A. I only
B. II only
C. I and II only
D. II and III only

20. The author's comment about cultures that are "long-silenced" refers to groups that:

F. have little interest in contributing to American cultural growth.
G. deliberately avoided discussing the subject of multiculturalism.
H. the dominant group has tried to exclude from shaping American culture.
J. rarely felt it necessary to comment on the course of American culture.

GO ON TO THE NEXT PAGE.

3 ████████████████████████████████ **3**

Passage III

HUMANITIES: This passage is adapted from Lindsay Heinsen's "The Southern Artist: Kreg Kallenberger" (©1991 by Southern Accents, Inc.).

As the Ozarks reach west from Missouri and Arkansas, they give their final gasps north of Tulsa and then collapse onto the Great Plains. The gasps are the Osage Hills. It's a hard, undomesticated landscape of
5 low, bald elevations, red clay, and scrub oak. The Osage Hills have cast no spell over Tulsa's real-estate developers who, in boom times, have pushed the city relentlessly southward onto the plains. "This is forgotten country," says a man who grew up in its shadow.
10 "Most Tulsa residents don't know it's here." Yet the Osage Hills have found at least one contemporary poet in sculptor Kreg Kallenberger. A soft-spoken man of forty, Kallenberger moved to Tulsa at the age of one and has seldom left since. From the foothills, it's a
15 short drive down Apache Street to his home and studio on Reservoir Hill. There, he reworks the burnt hills and blasted sky in the cool medium of glass.

Kallenberger's Osage sculptures would look at home on the shelves of a Rocky Mountain minerals
20 shop, surrounded by geodes. Most are long wedges of cast optical crystal, glacial melon slices weighing as much as fifty pounds. On the tops and sides, they are all precision—sliced, notched, and polished. Yet this refinement has a raw edge. The rugged bottoms are
25 peaks and valleys, stained with the colors and vistas of the nearby hills. As Kallenberger readies them for a February show at Boca Raton's Habatat Galleries, Osage works are strewn about the studio. They seem to have been sliced from the foothills with sky intact, as if
30 God were gathering landscape samples for the next world.

These are works of time-consuming craftsmanship: when Kallenberger says, "I rarely leave the house," one believes him. His intensity and background
35 in engineering may be prerequisites for sculptors working with glass. The days are spent lugging crystal ingots, tinkering with the furnace, sketching, fabricating molds, monitoring the slow processes of heating, cooling, grinding, and polishing. His chosen wedge
40 shape is particularly vulnerable to the cooling process, which lasts up to three weeks; if the power fails or the equipment settings are inaccurate, the result is fracture. "This is not a predictable industry," he says. "You base this success on the last failure." He completed just
45 twelve Osage pieces last year.

The sculptor's reputation has taken off in the past six or seven years. He now has regular one-man shows at the two Habatat Galleries, located at Farmington Hills near Detroit and in Boca Raton. Through Habatat,
50 he has attended the influential New Art Forms show at Chicago's Navy Pier each autumn. And in 1984, on the strength of his Interlock and Cuneiform series, he received a National Endowment for the Arts Fellowship Grant. He is represented in Tulsa by M. A.

55 Doran Gallery, and his works are in the Detroit Institute of Arts, Atlanta's High Museum of Art, and the Museum of Fine Arts, Boston.

In April of [1990], Kallenberger was featured in the Detroit Habatat's Eighteenth Annual International
60 Invitational exhibition. Ferdinand Hampson, who cofounded the gallery with Tom and Linda Boone, says, "These are theoretically the greatest artists in glass today, and Kreg dominated the show in sales and critical opinion."

65 Kallenberger's current themes emerged with the Titanic series in the mid-eighties. The wedges of his earlier Cuneiform series reappeared, elongated and deeper. Key details—a scoop or notch, a pair of black circles—appeared on the thin top edge, in contrast with
70 the deep and massive whole. Along came the rough edges, controlled fractures, eventually stained by hand.

The optical effects of the Osage sculptures are dazzling. As one walks around each piece, its transparent volume suddenly fills up with the refracted land-
75 scape of the bottom edge—a sculpture filled with an image. "The glass just does that," he says. The power of basic shapes is his focus, as are contrasts of texture and color.

Oddly, the charisma of glass exerts a special fasci-
80 nation for men. "It seems to be made through mysterious processes," Kallenberger says. Among his audience are "CEOs [Chief Executive Officers of corporations] who've never bought sculpture or any art before." Presented with identical shapes in bronze and glass,
85 this hypothetical male CEO will prefer the latter. Why? "Because he *thinks* he knows how the bronze shape is made. It's made sort of like his car is made. It's metal—you can hammer on it, weld it. He looks at the same form in glass and has no idea how it was made.
90 Men look at a piece and say, 'How did you *do* that?'"

21. The passage indicates Kallenberger's sculptures are most vulnerable to damage during which part of their production?

    A. Mold fabrication
    B. Heating process
    C. Cooling period
    D. Grinding procedure

22. Kallenberger says that by his observation male CEOs frequently like what kind of art pieces best?

    F. Brass sculpture
    G. Geodes
    H. Paintings
    J. Glass sculpture

GO ON TO THE NEXT PAGE.

3   **3**

23. The phrase "reworks the burnt hills and blasted sky in the cool medium of glass" (lines 16–17) implies that:

    A. Kallenberger is doing some landscaping around his house with his sculptures to make his home cooler and nicer.

    B. there is an interesting contrast between the stark, hot, rough landscape that Kallenberger captures in his sculpture and the cool, smooth texture of glass.

    C. Kallenberger is using glass windows and skylights in his house and studio to cool them off.

    D. there are more fires in the hills around Kallenberger's studios than in the mountains where he gets his glass.

24. It is reasonable to infer that Kallenberger calls his Osage sculptures Osage because:

    F. the process comes from an artist named Osage.

    G. the crystal comes from the Osage Hills.

    H. Osage is the place he was born.

    J. the Osage Hills inspire his work.

25. When was Kallenberger's Titanic series of works produced?

    A. After the Cuneiform series

    B. Before the Cuneiform series

    C. In April of 1990

    D. After the Detroit Habatat Eighteenth Annual International Invitational

26. Which of the following is NOT characteristic of the Osage sculptures?

    F. They are modern geometric designs.

    G. They would be at home in a minerals shop.

    H. They look like reworkings of the burnt hills.

    J. They are often colored to resemble the Osage Hills.

27. As it is used in line 2, the word *gasps* most nearly means:

    A. deep sighs.

    B. small mountains.

    C. wide valleys.

    D. profound fatigue.

28. The passage suggests that Kallenberger's early training for another profession has proven to be:

    F. a hindrance to his work as an artist.

    G. not significant in his work as an artist.

    H. useful in the technical part of his work as an artist.

    J. helpful in developing his artistic sensibility.

29. The passage suggests that much of the visual power of Kallenberger's sculptures comes from the:

    A. perfect smoothness of all the sides of the sculptures.

    B. pure white transparency of the sculptures.

    C. way the rough bottom edge is refracted in the sculptures.

    D. contrast between the glass and bronze parts of the sculpture.

30. The passage suggests that Kallenberger's sculptures come from:

      I. pieces of natural mineral in the Ozarks.

     II. geodes in a Rocky Mountain minerals shop.

    III. cast glass that is heated, cooled, and polished.

    F. I only

    G. III only

    H. I and II only

    J. I, II, and III

GO ON TO THE NEXT PAGE.

3 ████████████████████ 3

Passage IV

NATURAL SCIENCE: This passage is adapted from the article "Butterflies and Bad Taste: Rethinking a Classic Tale of Mimicry" by Tim Walker (©1991 by Science Service, Inc.).

Picture a bird searching for a midafternoon snack—perhaps a butterfly.

Suddenly, the bird spies a bright orange butterfly. But instead of attacking, the bird ignores it. Why?
5 Because the bird remembers what happened the last time it ate a bright orange butterfly: It vomited.

So the butterfly survives and continues on its way, courtesy of the bright orange warning that nature painted on its wings.

10 But was this a false warning? Did the butterfly's color trick the bird into passing up what would have actually made a tasty hors d'oeuvre? If the orange butterfly was a viceroy, *Limenitis archippus,* most biologists would have answered yes. For more than a
15 century, the conventional wisdom has held that this winged insect cloaks a very appetizing body behind the colors of a toxic monarch butterfly, *Danaus plexippus.*

New research indicates, however, that the viceroy has successfully deceived scientists, not birds.
20 Entomologists have long labored under the assumption that the viceroy's orange warning colors were just a bluff. Now, two zoologists have demonstrated that to discerning birds, the viceroy can taste just as foul as the noxious monarch.

25 Nineteenth-century English naturalist Henry Walter Bates first put forth the idea that a species of tasty butterfly could protect itself by evolving to mimic a toxic species. One species' exploitation of another's protection system has been called Batesian mimicry
30 ever since.

And for most of this century, biology textbooks have touted the viceroy-monarch relationship as the classic example of Batesian mimicry—a truism that must now be reconsidered.

35 David B. Ritland and Lincoln P. Brower have conducted an avian taste test. The test aimed to determine which butterfly species, if any, were noxious to the birds. Because these snacks lacked wings, the birds had to base their selections on the taste of the butterflies'
40 bodies alone.

The birds found the viceroy just as unappetizing as the monarch.

Why had no one challenged the viceroy's avian palatability before?

45 One reason, says entomologist Austin P. Platt, is that the viceroy evolved from a group of tasty admiral butterflies. "So it was just widely held that the viceroy itself was also palatable," he explains.

During the last several years, however, a few
50 experiments began to cast doubt on the viceroy's supposed tastiness. But those experiments used whole butterflies, Ritland says, which meant that the taste-testing birds could have rejected the viceroys because of their orange wings and not because of any noxious
55 taste.

Moreover, many biologists believed butterflies couldn't manufacture their own toxic chemicals to defend themselves from predators; instead, the insects had to absorb the toxins of poisonous plants during
60 their caterpillar stage. And viceroy larvae don't feed on toxic plants.

The adult monarch's chemical defense, however, does depend on toxins in the milkweed plants on which its caterpillars feed, Brower notes. Because monarch
65 caterpillars incorporate the heart toxins, called cardiac glycosides, that milkweeds rely on for their own defense against herbivores, eating a monarch can "really set a bird's heart jumping," he observes.

But the toxicity of an individual monarch depends
70 on the variety of milkweed it ate as a caterpillar, Brower says. A bird that eats a monarch butterfly that dined as a caterpillar on a mildly toxic variety of milkweed will not be poisoned. But a monarch caterpillar feeding on a strongly toxic milkweed variety will
75 become a truly toxic butterfly, potentially deadly to any bird that eats one and doesn't vomit it back up.

Viceroy caterpillars, in contrast, feed on nontoxic willows, and this suggests that viceroy butterflies somehow manufacture their own chemical defense. The
80 observation supports a new view that not all butterflies depend on plant poisons for their defenses.

For example, Ritland and Brower's results suggest that the viceroy may actually be a "Mullerian" mimic of the monarch. This kind of mutually advantageous
85 mimicry is named for the 19th-century German-born Brazilian zoologist, Fritz Muller, who first described how two or more equally distasteful butterfly species gain greater protection from predators by evolving the same general appearance.

90 Brower explains the advantage: If each of two chemically protected species has a different wing-color pattern, then a bird will have to eat many individuals of each species before it learns to avoid both. But if both species evolve the same color pattern, then only half as
95 many of each species need succumb.

GO ON TO THE NEXT PAGE.

3 ▬▬▬▬▬▬▬▬▬▬▬▬▬▬▬▬▬▬▬▬ 3

31. The reason that Ritland and Brower's work is forcing reconsideration of a long-standing theory of the relationship between viceroy and monarch butterflies is that their experiment demonstrated that the birds:

A. were not made ill by either viceroy or monarch bodies.
B. would only eat butterflies whose wings were still attached.
C. found viceroy bodies to be no tastier than those of monarchs.
D. preferred the monarch bodies, contrary to the theory.

32. According to the passage, viceroy caterpillars feed on:

  I. milkweed.
  II. nontoxic willows.
  III. mildly toxic willows.

F. I only
G. II only
H. I and II only
J. I and III only

33. According to David Ritland, recent experiments testing the palatability of viceroy butterflies (lines 49–55) were flawed primarily because the experimenters:

A. didn't remove the butterflies' wings.
B. doubted the tastiness of viceroys from the outset.
C. didn't include monarch butterflies in the experiments for comparison.
D. followed the widely held belief that viceroys taste like admiral butterflies.

34. The passage suggests that the toxicity of the monarch butterfly is primarily a result of the:

F. amount of milkweed that the monarch butterfly eats.
G. ability of the monarch butterfly to manufacture its own poison.
H. variety of milkweed that the monarch caterpillar ate.
J. color of the monarch butterfly's wings.

35. Which of the following best describes the question that remains unanswered from Ritland and Brower's research, as it is presented in the passage?

A. Why had no scientists discovered the toxicity of viceroy butterflies before?
B. How do viceroy butterflies manufacture the toxic chemicals in their system?
C. Why are some adult monarchs more poisonous than others?
D. How are birds affected by the poison contained in monarch butterflies?

36. It can be inferred from the passage that after a bird eats a monarch butterfly, all of the following could reasonably happen EXCEPT that the bird:

F. dies within a short period of time.
G. experiences a drastically increased heart rate.
H. immediately vomits the butterfly and dies.
J. vomits the butterfly and then survives.

37. According to the passage, the main difference between Batesian and Mullerian mimicry is that:

A. Mullerian mimicry offers greater protection for two inedible species through their resemblance, while Batesian mimicry protects an edible species because it looks like a poisonous one.
B. Batesian mimicry offers mutual protection for two unappetizing species, while Mullerian mimicry serves to protect an edible species simply because it resembles a poisonous species.
C. Batesian mimicry involves a predator species exploiting a prey species, while Mullerian mimicry involves cooperation between two species.
D. Batesian mimicry requires that the bad-tasting species be actually tasted by the predator, while Mullerian mimicry does not.

38. If scientists conclude that Mullerian mimicry does provide an adequate explanation for the coloring of viceroy butterflies, which of the following would the mimicry be serving to protect?

  I. Admiral butterflies
  II. Monarch butterflies
  III. Viceroy butterflies

F. II only
G. III only
H. I and II only
J. II and III only

GO ON TO THE NEXT PAGE.

3 **3**

39. According to the passage, biologists were convinced until recently that viceroy butterflies could NOT be toxic because the biologists believed that:

  A. butterflies could only become toxic if their larvae ate toxic plants.
  B. butterflies had to manufacture their own poisons.
  C. viceroy butterflies defended themselves by means of mimicry.
  D. viceroy caterpillars fed on only milkweed plants.

40. According to evidence presented in the passage, the fact that Batesian mimicry was the readily accepted explanation for the similarity of the viceroy's appearance to that of the monarch is likely due to the mistaken belief that:

  F. the two species of butterflies were considered to be closely related.
  G. butterfly coloring was a function of the food that the caterpillars eat.
  H. Mullerian mimicry always involved one tasty and one distasteful species.
  J. viceroys must taste good because they were evolved from another palatable species.

END OF TEST 3

STOP! DO NOT TURN THE PAGE UNTIL TOLD TO DO SO.

DO NOT RETURN TO A PREVIOUS TEST.

4 ○ ○ ○ ○ ○ ○ ○ ○ 4

SCIENCE REASONING TEST

35 Minutes—40 Questions

DIRECTIONS: There are seven passages in this test. Each passage is followed by several questions. After reading a passage, choose the best answer to each question and fill in the corresponding oval on your answer document. You may refer to the passages as often as necessary.

You are NOT permitted to use a calculator on this test.

Passage I

Two artificial marshes were built to help reduce the amounts of iron and manganese in, and the acidity of, water seeping into a stream from a coal mine site (see Figure 1). Table 1 shows precipitation, in centimeters (cm); flow rate, in liters per minute (L/min); pH (acidity); and iron and manganese content, in milligrams per liter (mg/L), of inlet and outlet water over 5 days.

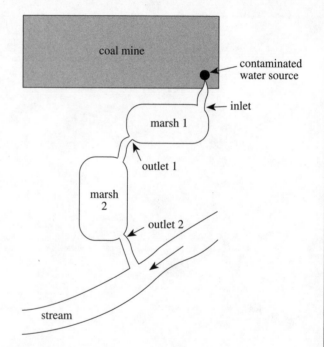

Figure 1

		Flow rate (L/min)			pH			Iron (mg/L)			Manganese (mg/L)		
Day	Precipitation (cm)	Inlet	Outlet 1	Outlet 2	Inlet	Outlet 1	Outlet 2	Inlet	Outlet 1	Outlet 2	Inlet	Outlet 1	Outlet 2
1	0	110	105	100	5.5	5.8	6.5	100	50	5.2	6.4	6.4	6.3
2	0	100	95	90	5.4	6.0	6.4	110	56	5.0	6.5	6.5	6.4
3	4.5	110	295	420	5.5	6.6	7.4	100	65	22.7	6.4	4.3	2.2
4	trace	130	190	250	5.4	6.4	6.8	90	47	10.2	6.3	5.5	4.7
5	0	150	145	140	5.5	6.1	6.5	80	42	7.1	6.0	6.0	5.9

Table 1

GO ON TO THE NEXT PAGE.

4 ◯ ◯ ◯ ◯ ◯ ◯ ◯ ◯ **4**

Water having a higher level of iron or manganese or a lower pH than the values given in Table 2 is said to be contaminated.

Table 2		
Allowed contaminant levels		
pH	Iron (mg/L)	Manganese (mg/L)
6.0	3.5	2.0

1. Which of the following figures best represents the iron concentrations at Outlet 2 for the 5-day period?

A.
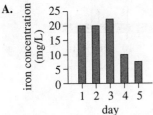

B.
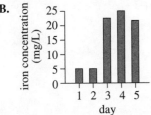

C.

D.
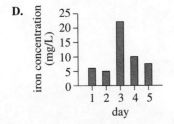

2. Which of the following statements best explains why the manganese level was at its lowest on Day 3 at Outlet 2 ?

   F. Manganese is used as a nutrient by the plants in the marshes.
   G. Manganese levels are lowered through dilution with rainwater.
   H. Manganese cannot be dissolved in water.
   J. Manganese is no longer seeping from the coal mine site.

3. Which of the following statements about Outlet 1 and Outlet 2 flow rates is supported by the data in Table 1 ?

   A. Outlet 1 and 2 flow rates both increased during heavy rain.
   B. Outlet 1 and 2 flow rates both decreased during heavy rain.
   C. Outlet 1 and 2 flow rates did not change during heavy rain.
   D. Outlet 1 and 2 flow rates returned to their Day 2 levels the day after the heavy rain.

4. According to the information provided in Tables 1 and 2, on any given day, the water leaving the marshes at Outlet 2 is contaminated with respect to:

   F. iron only.
   G. manganese only.
   H. iron and manganese only.
   J. manganese and pH only.

5. According to the data, which of the following actions would be most useful in reducing the iron levels in water released to the stream to a level below the allowed contaminant level given in Table 2 ?

   A. Building a third marsh
   B. Removing the second marsh
   C. Removing the marshes entirely
   D. Rerouting the stream

GO ON TO THE NEXT PAGE.

4 ◯ ◯ ◯ ◯ ◯ ◯ ◯ ◯ **4**

Passage II

An acid-base titration involves slowly adding a measured amount of acid to a solution containing a base and an indicator. The indicator, a dye, signals the *endpoint* (exact point where the acid has consumed all of the base) by changing colors as the solution goes from basic to acidic. The pH scale is a relative measure of the strength of acids and bases (see Figure 1). Table 1 shows the amount of acid required to reach the endpoint of different basic solutions containing various natural indicators.

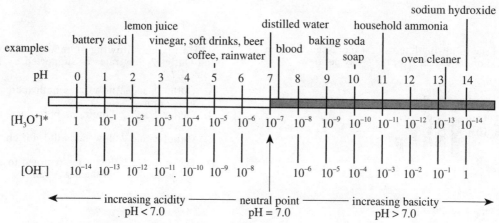

Figure 1

Table 1							
Natural indicator	Initial color	Initial pH	Volume of acid added (mL)			Final color	Final pH
			Trial 1	Trial 2	Trial 3		
Apple	red	8.5	17.1	17.2	17.0	yellow	5.5
Beets	red	10.0	12.2	11.9	12.4	purple	6.0
Blueberry	purple	8.0	18.6	18.5	18.1	green	6.0
Grape juice	red	9.5	10.4	10.3	10.9	green	6.5
Onion	colorless	8.5	11.2	11.8	11.4	yellow	5.5
Red cabbage	red	8.0	26.2	26.8	25.9	pink	4.0
Spinach	green	9.0	21.3	20.8	21.1	yellow	6.0
Tea	orange	11.0	19.4	20.2	19.8	yellow	5.0

Figure adapted from J. Dudley Herron et al., *Heath Chemistry.*
©1987 by D.C. Heath and Company.

GO ON TO THE NEXT PAGE.

6. Based on the information in Table 1, which of the following indicators experienced the greatest change in pH during the titration?

   F. Spinach
   G. Tea
   H. Beets
   J. Apple

7. According to Figure 1, which of the following solutions is the most acidic?

   A. Oven cleaner
   B. Baking soda
   C. Lemon juice
   D. Rainwater

8. Which of the following statements about the pH of the basic solutions before and after the titration is consistent with the data in Table 1 ?

   F. The pH of a solution is lower after the titration because of the addition of a base.
   G. The pH of a solution is lower after the titration because of the addition of an acid.
   H. The pH of a solution is higher before the titration because of the addition of an acid.
   J. The pH of a solution is higher before the titration because of the addition of the indicator.

9. If the solutions were reversed and the base was added to an acid solution in the presence of an indicator, based on the information in Table 1, one would predict which of the following results?

   A. The pH changes in the opposite direction, but the same color change occurs.
   B. The pH changes in the opposite direction and the colors would be reversed.
   C. The pH changes in the same direction, but the colors would be reversed.
   D. The pH changes in the same direction and the same color change occurs.

10. Strongly acidic or basic solutions have pH values near either end of the pH scale. According to the data in Table 1, which of the following indicators changes at the most acidic pH ?

   F. Grape juice
   G. Onion
   H. Red cabbage
   J. Tea

GO ON TO THE NEXT PAGE.

4 ○ ○ ○ ○ ○ ○ ○ ○ **4**

Passage III

Many individuals past the age of 45 develop *osteoporosis,* which makes the bones less dense and is characterized by a net loss of calcium in the bones. Although osteoporosis occurs in men, it is more common in women. Several hypotheses have been proposed to explain the onset of osteoporosis.

Dietary Hypothesis

Calcium from food is absorbed into the bloodstream by the small intestine. Vitamin D is necessary for this process. Most Americans ingest too little calcium and vitamin D in their diet. In a study of individuals 18–25 years old, it was shown that the majority had significantly low levels of calcium in their blood. When these individuals received daily supplements of 1,500 mg of calcium and 400 units of vitamin D, their blood calcium levels increased to normal levels. If insufficient levels of calcium and vitamin D are supplied by the diet, dietary supplements should be taken to avoid osteoporosis.

Estrogen Hypothesis

Estrogens, hormones produced primarily in the ovaries in women and, to a much lesser degree, in the adrenal glands in both sexes, and *androgens,* produced in the testes in men, are required for the deposition of calcium into bone. Androgen levels in men remain relatively constant throughout life; estrogen levels in women slowly decline after the onset of *menopause* (the time when a woman's ability to reproduce ends), which usually occurs between the ages of 45 and 55. As a result, the bones of postmenopausal women lose calcium.

Scientists compared the bone density of 4 groups of postmenopausal women. Each group took a dietary supplement. The results are shown in the table.

Group	Supplements	Change in bone density
A	estrogen	+2.3%
B	500 mg calcium	−1.0%
C	estrogen + 500 mg calcium	+2.3%
D	sugar	−1.0%

Exercise Hypothesis

Lack of exercise results in calcium loss from bones, whereas regular weight-bearing exercise can increase bone density. One study showed that 8 weeks of weight training added calcium and hardened bones in both postmenopausal women and men over the age of 45. Since body weight is supported by water, 8 weeks of swimming had no effect on bone density. Both groups followed the same high-calcium diet. Vitamin D intake was not measured.

11. To accept the evidence presented in the Dietary Hypothesis, one must assume that low blood levels of calcium are indicative of:

A. low bone levels of calcium.
B. low bone levels of estrogen.
C. high intestinal levels of vitamin D.
D. high blood levels of vitamin D.

12. One advantage of the Estrogen Hypothesis is that, of the three hypotheses, it *best* explains why osteoporosis is more common in which of the following groups?

F. Men over the age of 45 rather than in women over the age of 45
G. Men over the age of 45 rather than in men under the age of 45
H. Women over the age of 45 rather than in men over the age of 45
J. Women under the age of 45 rather than in women over the age of 45

13. According to the Estrogen Hypothesis, premenopausal women who have had their ovaries surgically removed should exhibit:

A. increased calcium levels in their bones.
B. increased estrogen levels in their blood.
C. gradual loss of calcium from their bones.
D. gradual reduction in vitamin D levels in their blood.

GO ON TO THE NEXT PAGE.

4 ◯ ◯ ◯ ◯ ◯ ◯ ◯ ◯ **4**

14. Which of the following is a criticism that supporters of the Dietary Hypothesis would make of the experimental results cited in the Exercise Hypothesis?

  F. Too much calcium was added to the diets of the test subjects in both groups.
  G. Blood vitamin D levels in the two groups were not monitored.
  H. Estrogen supplements should have been given to each group of individuals.
  J. Osteoporosis is more common in premenopausal women than in postmenopausal women.

15. Assume that increased blood calcium levels result in increased bone density. How would supporters of the Estrogen Hypothesis explain the experimental results presented in the Dietary Hypothesis?

  A. The test subjects probably had below-normal blood calcium levels.
  B. The test subjects did not perform any weight-bearing exercise.
  C. The test subjects probably had normal estrogen and androgen levels.
  D. The test subjects were given too low a dosage of vitamin D.

16. How would supporters of the Dietary Hypothesis explain the results for Group B in the experiment cited in the Estrogen Hypothesis?

  F. Vitamin D supplements should not have been taken by this group.
  G. Insufficient calcium was added to the diet to increase bone density.
  H. Estrogen supplements should have been taken to increase bone density.
  J. Too much estrogen was added to the diet of this group to affect bone density.

17. The experiments cited in the Estrogen Hypothesis and in the Exercise Hypothesis are similar in that each:

  A. test subject was given an estrogen supplement.
  B. test subject was given a calcium supplement.
  C. test subject was given a vitamin D supplement.
  D. woman tested was postmenopausal.

GO ON TO THE NEXT PAGE.

4 ○ ○ ○ ○ ○ ○ ○ ○ **4**

Passage IV

Three studies were conducted to examine the relationship between ants and the acacia trees they inhabit.

Study 1

Table 1 shows the results of a comparison between a species of acacia tree that is inhabited by ants (ant trees) and a species that is not inhabited by ants (non-ant trees).

Table 1		
	Ant trees	Non-ant trees
Leaves	bitter-tasting chemicals absent protein-bodies present	bitter-tasting chemicals present protein-bodies absent
Thorns	specialized hollow thorns on stems	no specialized thorns
Ants	specific ant species living in thorns	no ants living on trees
Extrafloral nectaries*	present	absent
Trunk	surrounded by bare ground	surrounded by many other plants

*Nectar-producing (sugar-producing) structures located outside the flowers

Study 2

Table 2 shows the results of a comparison between acacia ants and a closely related ant species that does not inhabit acacia trees.

Table 2		
	Acacia ants	Non-acacia ants
Aggressiveness	very aggressive	very aggressive
Active periods	active day and night	active during daylight only
Diet	protein-bodies nectar	do not eat living plants
Nest site	only in the thorns of ant trees	in the ground

Study 3

Acacia trees were divided into three groups. Acacia ants were removed from the trees in Group A, but were left on the trees in Group B. Group C consisted of a species of non-ant acacia tree. All the trees were initially healthy and of similar size. The number of trees still alive in each group 300 days after the start of the study is shown in Table 3.

Table 3					
	Group A		Group B		Group C	
Day	alive	dead	alive	dead	alive	dead
1	38	0	39	0	40	0
300	10	28	28	11	30	10

Trees in Group A were killed by plant-eating insects and large mammals that ate the leaves on lower branches. There was no evidence that trees in Groups B and C were killed by grazing animals.

18. How is the design of Study 1 different from the design of Study 2 ?

   F. In Study 1, acacia ants were removed from acacia trees, but not in Study 2.
   G. In Study 1, plant characteristics were examined, while in Study 2, ant characteristics were examined.
   H. In Study 1, acacia ants were examined, while in Study 2, non-acacia ants were examined.
   J. In Study 1, ant characteristics were examined, while in Study 2, plant characteristics were examined.

19. On the basis of the experimental results, one can generalize that which of the following characteristics protects non-ant acacias from being eaten by insects or grazing animals?

   A. Bitter-tasting chemicals
   B. Protein bodies
   C. Extrafloral nectaries
   D. Specialized hollow thorns

GO ON TO THE NEXT PAGE.

4

20. From the results of Study 2 the researchers would hypothesize that the ground surrounding the ant acacia trees was bare of vegetation because the:

F. acacia ants killed the plants growing near the ant acacia trees.
G. acacia ants killed the plants growing near the non-ant acacia trees.
H. non-acacia ants killed the plants growing near the non-ant acacia trees.
J. non-acacia ants killed the ant acacia trees.

21. Can any conclusions about the relationship between plants and insects be drawn from the observations made on acacias and ants?

A. Yes; the behavior of different insect species toward plants seems to be the same.
B. Yes; some plants apparently provide shelter for the insects that protect them.
C. No; plants apparently have the same species of insects living on them.
D. No; insects are rarely associated with plants.

22. Researchers removed all the insects from a tree that is different from the acacia. A comparison showed that few leaves were eaten both before and after removal of the insects. Which of the following conclusions about the insects and the tree best explains these results?

F. The leaves were protected from grazing by some factor other than the insects.
G. Numerous vines grew over the tree and covered the leaves and stems.
H. The tree was unable to defend its leaves from attacks by grazing animals.
J. Aggressive insects attacked any potential grazers on the leaves of this tree.

23. Which of the following conclusions about the function of protein bodies and extrafloral nectaries would be consistent with the results of the studies?

A. Protein bodies are used to deter grazing animals, while extrafloral nectaries are used as a food source by acacia ants.
B. Extrafloral nectaries are used to deter grazing animals, while protein bodies are used as a food source by acacia ants.
C. Both protein bodies and extrafloral nectaries are used to deter grazing animals.
D. Both protein bodies and extrafloral nectaries are used as food sources by acacia ants.

GO ON TO THE NEXT PAGE.

Passage V

A *solution* is a mixture of at least two substances. The *solvent* does the dissolving and the *solute* is dissolved by the solvent.

Some solutions containing solutes, called *electrolytes*, can conduct electricity because they can carry an electric charge when in solution; whereas *nonelectrolytes* cannot carry an electric charge. An *ammeter* is a device used to measure the current carried by a solution (see Figure 1).

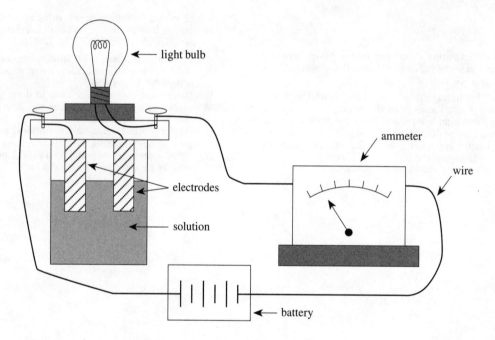

Figure 1

The following experiments were performed to test the hypothesis that either increasing the amount of solute or the temperature of the solution will increase the solution's conductivity.

Experiment 1

The solutions consisted of 5.0 grams (g) of each solute dissolved in 100 milliliters (mL) of water at 20°C. The water was also tested without any solute. The results are shown in Table 1.

Table 1	
Solute	Ammeter reading (milliamps)
Water (H_2O)	0.0
Hydrogen chloride (HCl)	5.9
Sugar ($C_{12}H_{22}O_{11}$)	0.0
Potassium chloride (KCl)	2.9
Sodium fluoride (NaF)	5.0
Magnesium acetate ($Mg(C_2H_3O_2)_2$)	2.1

GO ON TO THE NEXT PAGE.

4 ◯ ◯ ◯ ◯ ◯ ◯ ◯ ◯ **4**

Experiment 2

Experiment 1 was repeated, except the amount of solute of each solution was increased to 10.0 g in 100 mL of water at 20°C. The results are shown in Table 2.

Table 2	
Solute	Ammeter reading (milliamps)
Water (H_2O)	0.0
Hydrogen chloride (HCl)	11.4
Sugar ($C_{12}H_{22}O_{11}$)	0.0
Potassium chloride (KCl)	5.5
Sodium fluoride (NaF)	8.5
Magnesium acetate ($Mg(C_2H_3O_2)_2$)	3.4

Experiment 3

Experiment 2 was repeated at 50°C. The results are shown in Table 3.

Table 3	
Solute	Ammeter reading (milliamps)
Water (H_2O)	0.0
Hydrogen chloride (HCl)	1.7
Sugar ($C_{12}H_{22}O_{11}$)	0.0
Potassium chloride (KCl)	7.4
Sodium fluoride (NaF)	12.0
Magnesium acetate ($Mg(C_2H_3O_2)_2$)	4.7

24. The experimental results for each of the following solutes supports the scientist's hypothesis that increasing the amount of solute increases the conductivity of a solution EXCEPT the results for:

   F. HCl.
   G. $C_{12}H_{22}O_{11}$.
   H. KCl.
   J. $Mg(C_2H_3O_2)_2$.

25. According to the results of all 3 experiments, which of the following solutions of $Mg(C_2H_3O_2)_2$ would be expected to conduct the most electricity?

   A.   2 g in   200 mL of   5°C H_2O
   B. 10 g in   100 mL of   5°C H_2O
   C. 10 g in   100 mL of 15°C H_2O
   D. 20 g in 1,000 mL of   2°C H_2O

26. If a scientist dissolved both 10 g of $C_{12}H_{22}O_{11}$ and 10 g of KCl in 100 mL of H_2O at 50°C, the ammeter would read approximately:

   F.   0.0 milliamps.
   G.   1.7 milliamps.
   H.   7.4 milliamps.
   J.   8.9 milliamps.

27. If Experiment 3 was repeated and the temperature of the H_2O was increased to 80°C, the conductivity of the solutions with electrolytes would most likely:

   A. decrease with the exception of HCl.
   B. remain constant.
   C. increase only.
   D. increase with the exception of HCl.

28. Which of the following best explains why H_2O was tested in all three experiments?

   F. To determine if H_2O is the solute or the solvent
   G. To determine the amount of conductivity contributed by the solvent
   H. To determine if H_2O will dissolve all of the salts equally
   J. To prove that H_2O is a good conductor of electricity

29. On the basis of the experimental results, which of the following effects would be most appropriate to test next to gain additional information about conductivity?

   A. The effect of temperature on conductivity
   B. The effect of solute color on conductivity
   C. The effect of water on conductivity
   D. The effect of different solvents on conductivity

GO ON TO THE NEXT PAGE.

4 ○ ○ ○ ○ ○ ○ ○ ○ 4

Passage VI

Various chains were released from rest with their lower end touching a scale that measured the force, in newtons (N), of the chain on the scale pan (see Figure 1). A *newton* is the force required to accelerate a 1-kilogram mass at a rate of 1.0 m/sec^2. The mass of the chain, its total length (L), the momentary length of chain on the pan (x), as well as the momentary weight of the portion of the chain on the pan, were also measured. The results are shown in Table 1.

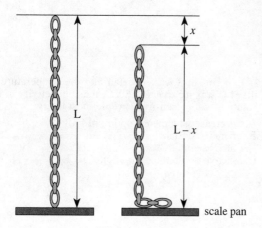

Figure 1

Table 1					
Trial	Mass of chain (g)	Total length of chain (m)	Momentary length on scale pan (m)	Momentary weight on scale pan (N)	Force on scale pan (N)
1	250	0.5	0.1	0.49	1.47
2	250	0.5	0.2	0.98	2.94
3	250	0.5	0.3	1.47	4.41
4	250	0.5	0.4	1.96	5.88
5	500	0.5	0.1	0.98	2.94
6	500	0.5	0.2	1.96	5.88
7	500	0.5	0.3	2.94	8.82
8	500	0.5	0.4	3.92	11.76
9	750	0.5	0.3	4.41	13.23
10	750	1.0	0.5	3.67	11.01
11	1,000	0.5	0.3	5.88	17.64
12	1,000	1.0	0.5	4.90	14.70
13	1,000	1.5	1.0	6.53	19.60
14	1,000	2.0	1.5	7.35	22.05

Figure 1 and Table 1 adapted from John R. Gordon and Raymond A. Serway, *Physics for Scientists and Engineers with Modern Physics,* 3rd edition. ©1990 by Saunders College Publishing.

GO ON TO THE NEXT PAGE.

4

30. In Trials 5–8, as the momentary length of chain on the pan increases, the momentary weight of the chain on the pan:

F. increases.
G. decreases.
H. remains constant.
J. increases and then decreases.

31. Which of the following trials best supports the hypothesis that doubling the mass of a chain while keeping the length of chain on the pan constant doubles the force on the pan?

A. Trials 1 and 4
B. Trials 2 and 9
C. Trials 2 and 14
D. Trials 3 and 7

32. Based on the data in Table 1, if a chain with a mass of 1,250 g and a total length of 2.0 m were used, in which of the following ranges would the force on the pan be if $x = 1.5$ m ?

F. 5.88 N to 14.72 N
G. 14.73 N to 19.58 N
H. 19.59 N to 22.04 N
J. Greater than 22.05 N

33. Which of the following trials uses the chain with the largest mass per unit length?

A. Trials 5–8
B. Trial 9
C. Trial 11
D. Trial 14

34. If, in Trials 1–4, the entire length of chain (0.5 m) would have been allowed to drop on the scale pan, the momentary weight on the pan for this new trial would have been approximately:

F. 1.0 N.
G. 1.5 N.
H. 2.0 N.
J. 2.5 N.

GO ON TO THE NEXT PAGE.

4 ◯ ◯ ◯ ◯ ◯ ◯ ◯ ◯ ◯ **4**

Passage VII

Early on May 18, 1980, Mount St. Helens violently erupted, expelling a huge cloud of volcanic ash. Most of the ash fell to Earth on May 18, as the cloud moved rapidly away from the volcano. The following studies examined the ashfall.

Study 1

Researchers measured the depth of uncompacted ash, in millimeters (mm), at hundreds of stations in Washington, Idaho, and Montana. Only ash that had fallen on manufactured objects such as roofs and cars was measured. The results are shown in Figure 1.

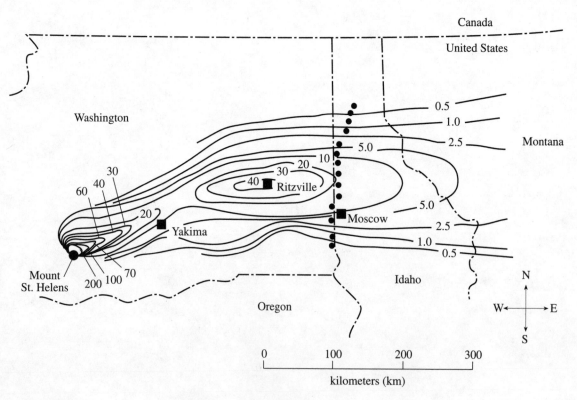

Figure 1

GO ON TO THE NEXT PAGE.

4 ○ ○ ○ ○ ○ ○ ○ ○ ○ **4**

Study 2

The thickness of the ash layer on manufactured objects was measured at 14 stations along a north-south line passing near Moscow, Idaho (see Figure 1).

Researchers found that ash deposits east of Yakima, Washington, were composed of two different layers. The thin lower layer (1–2 mm) was made of dark gray ash composed of sand-sized particles of fragmented volcanic rock, and, above that, a thicker layer of lighter-colored ash was composed of smaller (silt-sized) particles (see Figure 2).

It was believed that the dark ash formed during the initial eruption, when rock from the mountain was pulverized, whereas the lighter-colored ash formed later in the eruption as molten rock (magma) inside the volcano was violently expelled.

Study 3

Samples of volcanic ash were collected along a line of stations stretching from the volcano to western Montana. Figure 3 shows the calculated average particle size of the samples at each station.

(Note: The average grain size in Figure 3 includes particles of both dark and light ash.)

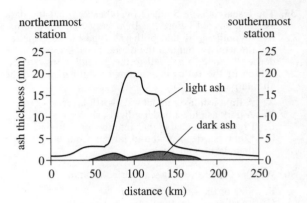

Figure 2

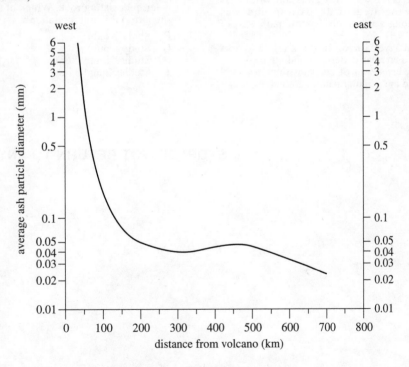

Figure 3

Figures adapted from A. M. Sarna-Wojcicki et al., "Areal Distribution, Thickness, Mass, Volume, and Grain Size of Air-fall Ash from the Six Major Eruptions of 1980." ©1982 by the U. S. Geological Survey.

GO ON TO THE NEXT PAGE.

35. The researchers in Study 2 hypothesized that the dark ash was ejected before the light gray ash. An alternative hypothesis is that both ash types were expelled simultaneously, but that the darker particles were more dense ("heavier") and fell to the ground more rapidly. Which of the following findings would *disprove* the alternative hypothesis?

A. A light ash layer under a dark ash layer
B. A dark ash layer under a light ash layer
C. Light ash ejected higher into the air than dark ash
D. Light ash deposits found farther from the volcano than dark ash deposits

36. Which of the following was varied in Study 3 ?

F. Size of the sample taken
G. Location of sites from which ash samples were taken
H. Method of determining the average ash particle diameter
J. Mass of ash particles per cubic millimeter of ash

37. Do the results of Study 1 support the hypothesis that volcanic ash rises into the atmosphere and settles out evenly in a fairly circular region around the erupting volcano?

A. No; the ash layer varied in thickness and was deposited mainly east of the peak.
B. No; the ash layer was of a constant thickness throughout the area of deposition and was deposited along a relatively narrow path east of the peak.
C. Yes; the ash layer varied in thickness and was deposited in a circular pattern around the peak.
D. Yes; the ash layer was of constant thickness and was deposited in a circular pattern around the peak.

38. Based on Study 3, what can one conclude about how average ash particle diameter changed with distance from Mount St. Helens?

   I. It decreased between 50 and 200 km.
   II. It increased between 325 and 450 km.
   III. It decreased between 500 and 700 km.

F. I only
G. II only
H. III only
J. I, II, and III

39. If Study 2 were repeated along a north-south line passing through Ritzville, Washington (shown in Figure 1), compared to the results from the line passing through Moscow, those from Ritzville would show:

A. a maximum thickness of ash greater than 25 mm.
B. no dark ash at any of the measurement sites.
C. no light ash at any of the measurement sites.
D. a thinner ash layer in the center part of the line than at the ends of it.

40. Investigators believed that most of the deposited ash resulted from fragmentation of new rock formed during the eruption rather than fragmentation of much older, preexisting rock. Which of the following studies support(s) this interpretation?

F. Study 2 only
G. Study 3 only
H. Studies 1 and 2 only
J. Studies 2 and 3 only

END OF TEST 4

STOP! DO NOT RETURN TO ANY OTHER TEST.

Passage I

Question 1. The best answer is D.

A is incorrect. As it is used here, *where* is a subordinating conjunction, so it should introduce a subordinate clause. However, it only introduces the phrase "its 10,000 miles from home." Also, *its* is a possessive pronoun, indicating in this context that either the moonlight or the beach possesses "10,000 miles from home," which doesn't make sense.

B is incorrect. *Its* is a possessive pronoun, so when **B** is inserted in the sentence, the sentence says that you are not only sitting on a beach, you are also sitting on the 10,000 miles from home that belong to *it* (the beach). This doesn't make sense.

C is incorrect. Inserting *it's* (it is) into the sentence creates a second main clause within the sentence—"it's 10,000 miles from home." Because there is no punctuation between the two main clauses of the sentence, **C** creates an unacceptable fused sentence.

D is the best answer. Using this option, the phrase "10,000 miles from home" modifies *beach,* making it clear that the beach is 10,000 miles from your home.

Question 2. The best answer is J.

F is not the best answer because it suggests that *they*—the turtles—are only turtles once they come out of the sea.

G is incorrect because it creates an independent clause, "they are three massive turtles," that is separated from the other independent clause in the sentence by only a comma. This creates a comma splice.

H is incorrect because it forms an independent clause, "you see three massive turtles," that is separated from the other independent clause in the sentence ("Then they come out of the sea") by only a comma. This creates a comma splice.

J is the best answer. It separates the noun phrase "three massive turtles" from the rest of the sentence, making it clear that the *they* in the beginning of the sentence refers to the turtles.

Question 3. The best answer is C.

A is incorrect because even though it describes the turtles' appearance somewhat vividly—"a tough outer shell that looks like leather"—it doesn't describe the turtles' movement from the water to the beach.

B is incorrect because its description of the turtles (*enormous*) is not very vivid, and it says that the turtles simply appear on the beach, which doesn't describe their movement very vividly.

C is the best answer because its description of the turtles and their movements—"huge living rocks creeping almost imperceptibly"—is the most vivid of any of the options.

D is incorrect because its description of the turtles—"three of the largest turtles you've ever seen"—is less vivid than the other options, and it doesn't describe the turtles' movement at all.

Question 4. The best answer is G.

F is incorrect because the singular subject *each* requires the verb forms *digs* and *fills*.

G is the best answer because the third-person plural subject *they* requires the verb forms *dig* and *fill*.

H is incorrect because the third-person plural subject *they* requires the verb forms *dig* and *fill*.

J is incorrect because "they slowly dig a hole" makes it sound as if the turtles dig one hole together (which the rest of the paragraph suggests is not true) and because the third-person plural subject *they* requires the verb form *fill,* not *fills.*

Question 5. The best answer is C.

A is incorrect because the subordinate clause "in which there are over a hundred eggs" seems to modify "one egg at a time" rather than *it* (the hole). Even if "in which there are over a hundred eggs" were clearly modifying *it,* this option would be incorrect because it would make it appear that there were already over a hundred eggs in the hole, when in fact the turtles lay their eggs one at a time in freshly dug holes.

B is incorrect because it creates an independent clause, "there are over a hundred eggs," that is separated from the rest of the sentence (an independent clause and a subordinate clause) by only a comma, creating a comma splice.

C is the best answer because it supplies the preposition *with,* which makes the sentence's meaning clear: each turtle fills its hole with over a hundred eggs by laying one egg at a time.

D is incorrect because the phrase it creates—"over a hundred eggs"—does not clearly modify any part of the sentence. Although it is possible to infer that the more than a hundred eggs referred to are turtle eggs that were just laid, it is impossible to be sure.

Question 6. The best answer is G.

F is incorrect because it uses a different tense—the past progressive—than the rest of the essay. This tense shift is unnecessary and confusing.

G is the best answer because it uses the present tense, the same tense that is used throughout the essay.

H is incorrect because it changes the tense from the present tense used throughout the essay to the present perfect tense, making it sound as if you saw the turtles bury their eggs at some time in the past.

J is incorrect because it changes the tense from the present tense used throughout the essay to the past tense, making it sound as if the turtles buried their eggs earlier, when in fact the sentence is describing them laying their eggs.

Question 7. The best answer is A.

A is the best answer because it accurately and unambiguously describes each turtle using its flippers to push the sand and bury the eggs. This option makes far more sense than any of the others.

B is incorrect because it is in the passive voice, but the rest of the sentence (and the essay) is in the active voice. This is an unnecessary, confusing shift in voice.

C is incorrect because this option makes it appear that the eggs push sand into the holes while they (the eggs) are being buried. This makes little sense because it implies that the eggs are capable of moving on their own and burying themselves.

D is incorrect because it is confusing: does *they* refer to the eggs, the holes, or the turtles themselves?

Question 8. The best answer is F.

F is the best answer because it uses the plural possessive noun *turtles'* and the plural noun *eyes* to refer to the eyes of all of the turtles. The rest of the paragraph refers to all three of the turtles at once, so this sentence should too.

G is incorrect. It is possessive but singular, so it refers to the eyes of only one turtle. The rest of the paragraph refers to all three turtles, so this sentence should too.

H is incorrect because it doesn't contain the possessive form of the plural *turtles,* which is needed to make clear that the eyes belonging to the turtles are being discussed.

J is incorrect because *turtles'* and *eye's* are both possessive: they make the reader expect to find out what the one eye that belongs to all three turtles (a nonsensical idea) possesses. However, there is nothing in the sentence that refers to what the eye possesses.

Question 9. The best answer is C.

A is incorrect because it is unclear whether *they* refers to the turtles or the liquid. The liquid should be referred to in this part of the sentence, but *they*, a plural pronoun, isn't the right pronoun to use to refer to "the liquid," which is singular.

B is incorrect because although it correctly uses *it* to refer to the liquid, it then uses the singular possessive pronoun *its* to modify *eyes*. By saying "its eyes," the sentence refers to the eyes of only one of the turtles, although the rest of the paragraph refers to all three turtles.

C is the best answer because it correctly uses *it* to refer to the liquid and *their* to refer to the turtles' eyes, making it clear that the liquid protects the eyes of the turtles.

D is incorrect because it is not clear who or what *they* refers to. Furthermore, *its* is singular, but there are three turtles described throughout the paragraph.

Question 10. The best answer is G.

F is incorrect because it is improperly punctuated. There should be a comma between the coordinate adjectives *emotional* and *teary-eyed,* and there should not be a comma interrupting the adjectival phrase "teary-eyed over creating new life," which should be treated as a single unit.

G is the best answer because it correctly separates the coordinate adjectives *emotional* and *teary-eyed* with a comma, while avoiding unnecessary punctuation elsewhere. This option makes it clear that the writer thinks that you may want to consider the turtles as emotional animals who are teary-eyed over their egg-laying.

H is incorrect because *as* is used as a preposition in this sentence. There should be no comma between *them* and *as* because the prepositional phrase should not be set off from the rest of the sentence.

J is incorrect because it contains two incorrect commas and is missing one comma. There should not be a comma between the preposition *over* and its object ("creating new life"), nor should there be a comma between the preposition *as* and its object ("emotional teary-eyed"). There should be a comma between *emotional* and *teary-eyed.*

Question 11. The best answer is B.

A is incorrect because although it is correct to place Sentence 1 as the first sentence, Sentence 3 should follow Sentence 1 since Sentence 3 elaborates on the shiny liquid that Sentence 1 mentions. Sentence 4's *nevertheless* refers to Sentence 2's explanation, so those two sentences should not be interrupted by Sentence 3.

B is the best answer because it correctly places Sentence 1 first, which mentions the "shiny liquid" that is also referred to by the other three sentences. Sentence 2's "this liquid" reference would be unclear if that sentence appeared first. Sentence 3 follows Sentence 1 logically and clearly: Sentence 1 describes something that the reader notices, and Sentence 3 describes what it looks like. Sentences 2 and 4 should also be kept together, as the explanation for **A** describes.

C is incorrect because the first sentence must be Sentence 1, as the explanation for **A** describes. Sentence 2's "this liquid" reference would be unclear if that sentence appeared first. Sentence 4 makes little sense following Sentence 1, as it does here. Sentence 4 should follow Sentence 2, as the explanation for **A** describes.

D is incorrect because the first sentence must be Sentence 1. Sentence 3's "they've been crying" would be an unclear reference if that sentence appeared first: would it be referring to the turtles, the eggs, or the flippers of the previous paragraph?

Question 12. The best answer is H.

F is incorrect because it uses the passive voice. The rest of the essay is in the active voice; there is no compelling reason to use the passive voice here.

G is incorrect because it uses the passive voice. The rest of the essay is in the active voice; there is no compelling reason to use the passive voice here.

H is the best answer because it correctly places the emphasis of the sentence on the activity of watching, rather than on the person doing the watching (as **J** does), and it uses the active verb *watch* rather than the passive verb phrase "being watched" that the other options use.

J is incorrect because it places the subject, *you*, at the end of the sentence, thereby emphasizing it. However, it is the watching that is important in this sentence, not *you*. The inverted subject-verb order is awkward here.

Question 13. The best answer is C.

A is incorrect because intense involvement goes beyond merely looking at something.

B is incorrect because intense involvement goes beyond merely watching something.

C is the best answer because "immersed in" implies complete engagement in watching.

D is incorrect because intense involvement, as mentioned in the question, goes beyond mere curiosity about something. Also, the preposition *in* makes this answer nonsensical in view of the question: it implies that the viewer is a curious sight when seen from the point of view of the turtles, but the turtles' point of view is not given in the essay.

Question 14. The best answer is J.

F is incorrect because it shifts from the second-person, present-tense style used throughout the essay.

G is incorrect because it shifts from the second-person, present-tense style used throughout the essay.

H is incorrect because it shifts from the second-person, present-tense style used throughout the essay.

J is the best answer because it maintains the second-person, present-tense style used throughout the essay.

Question 15. The best answer is C.

A is incorrect because the turtles in the essay are from one species, leatherbacks, not several different species, and only one part of their reproductive methods, egg-laying, is discussed.

B is incorrect because the essay discusses only one part of the reproductive process (egg-laying) of one species of turtle, leatherbacks.

C is the best answer because the essay doesn't fulfill the assignment. The essay's focus is restricted to one species of turtle and the writer's personal experience in witnessing a single part of the reproductive process, egg-laying.

D is incorrect because a part of the turtle reproductive process is discussed in the essay.

Passage II

Question 16. The best answer is F.

F is the best answer because it maintains the essay's tone and is accurate and straightforward.

G is incorrect because it is colloquial and inappropriate in tone when compared with the rest of the essay.

H is incorrect because it is redundant, and it contains the word *up,* which is not needed.

J is incorrect because it is colloquial and inappropriate in tone when compared with the rest of the essay.

Question 17. The best answer is A.

A is the best answer because it introduces the idea that the narrator's mother enjoys her job very much, which is a theme that is central to the essay. It provides a transition to the next paragraph, which begins to explain how the narrator's mother responds to the varied types of weddings described in the first paragraph.

B is incorrect because it includes a detail that neither introduces a theme nor provides a transition.

C is incorrect because it changes the subject of the essay abruptly.

D is incorrect because it changes the subject of the essay abruptly.

Question 18. The best answer is J.

F is incorrect because the words "wedding gear" introduce a list; they are not part of the list, as the semicolon after *gear* suggests.

G is incorrect because the items following "wedding gear" are examples of wedding gear, so *gear* must be followed by a colon in order to introduce the list.

H is incorrect because the items of the list should be separated by commas. (The comma after *sandals* indicates that the rest of the items in the list should be separated by commas too.)

J is the best answer because the colon following *gear* introduces the items in the list of examples of wedding gear. The items of the list should be separated by the same type of punctuation, in this case commas (see the explanation for **H**).

Question 19. The best answer is D.

A is incorrect because it implies that the writer will go on to describe an amazing wedding that has been taking place until now, but that does not occur.

B is incorrect because it implies that the writer will go on to describe an amazing wedding taking place now, but that does not occur.

C is incorrect because it is awkward and makes no sense: when is "until now so far"?

D is the best answer because nothing in the paragraph justifies the appearance of "until now" in the sentence.

Question 20. The best answer is F.

F is the best answer because it correctly modifies *boat* with the adjectival phrase "made festive with flowers and pink balloons."

G is incorrect because it is awkward; the subordinate clause (beginning with *which*) contains a time shift.

H is incorrect because it is awkward; the subordinate clause it creates (beginning with *which*) contains a time shift and an unclear reference, and is in the passive voice.

J is incorrect because it creates a sentence fragment ("Making it festive with flowers and pink balloons"). There is no subject or complete verb in the fragment.

Question 21. The best answer is B.

A is incorrect because it does not enhance the narration of events; it states a bland opinion.

B is the best answer; it enhances the narration of events by describing how the groom and best man arrive at the wedding that is being described.

C is incorrect because it repeats what the final sentence of the paragraph states, in a less interesting way.

D is incorrect because it is neither interesting nor descriptive, and it doesn't enhance the narration of events. It partly repeats the paragraph's last sentence.

Question 22. The best answer is J.

F is incorrect. It mentions that helium balloons are "more expensive," but it isn't clear whether the balloons that are mentioned in the preceding paragraph were helium balloons or not. Option **F** also contains unnecessary detail: expense isn't mentioned anywhere else in the essay, and there is no reason to include such detail here. This paragraph focuses on the exciting wedding; discussion of mundane details is out of place.

G is incorrect because it is confusing. It says that "flowers are also expensive," but the essay doesn't discuss the expense of any activities or items.

H is incorrect because it contains unnecessary detail: the fact that the balloons come in many colors does not add anything to the narration at this point. The subject of this paragraph is the rubber-boot wedding; a discussion of the varieties of helium balloons is out of place.

J is the best answer because the balloons and flowers don't warrant further comment; they are minor details whose expense or color are not worth noting here.

Question 23. The best answer is C.

A is incorrect because it fails to mention the rubber boots or the romantic nature of the ceremony, which are the main ideas of the first sentence of the paragraph.

B is incorrect because it not only fails to mention the rubber boots that are a prominent part of the first sentence of the paragraph, but it also makes the event seem more noisy and uncomfortable than romantic.

C is the best answer because it supports the main idea of the first sentence of the paragraph: the romantic nature of the ceremony. The rubber boots that are mentioned in the first sentence are described again in this option: "all those wet galoshes."

D is incorrect because it not only fails to mention the boots that are a prominent part of the first sentence of the paragraph, it also makes the event seem unromantic.

Question 24. The best answer is G.

F is incorrect because it fails to support the clothing theme that is used to tie all of the paragraphs together. There is no other mention of the desert wedding, so its inclusion in the paragraph's opening sentence is unnecessary.

G is the best answer because it ties this new paragraph to the rest of the essay by mentioning two more items from the list of clothing in the second paragraph. The third paragraph mentions the rubber boots; this option mentions the formal and sandals. The wedding described in the fourth paragraph took place on a beach, not a pond, so it must be made clear that it is a different wedding from the one described in the third paragraph, which this option does.

H is incorrect because it fails to make clear that it refers to a different wedding from the one described in the third paragraph.

J is incorrect because it fails to support the clothing theme that is used to tie all of the paragraphs together. It also restates an obvious point of the essay (see question 17) that doesn't need restating.

Question 25. The best answer is D.

A is incorrect because it is awkward; "of whom" seems, by the construction of the sentence, to refer to *expression,* which makes no sense.

B is incorrect because it makes no sense: to whom or what does *which* refer?

C is incorrect because it contains awkward, nonstandard usage.

D is the best answer because it makes it clear that it is the bride's expression that is slightly harried.

Question 26. The best answer is J.

F is incorrect because it implies a cause-effect relationship being explained, when no such relationship is present. There is no contrast being set up; the fifth paragraph continues the essay's focus on weddings that the narrator's mother has presided over.

G is incorrect because it implies a cause-effect relationship being explained, when no such relationship is present. There is no previous point that explains why the next sentence is true; the fifth paragraph continues the essay's focus on weddings that the narrator's mother has presided over.

H is incorrect because it implies a cause-effect relationship being explained, when no such relationship is present. There is no contrast being set up; the fifth paragraph continues the essay's focus on weddings that the narrator's mother has presided over.

J is the best answer because it begins the paragraph by introducing a wedding that the paragraph goes on to describe.

Question 27. The best answer is B.

A is not the best answer because it has the same meaning as **B**, "two-minute ceremony," but **A** is wordier.

B is the best answer because it is clear and concise.

C is incorrect because it is silly (how can a two-minute ceremony take only a minute?) and creates a sentence fragment.

D is incorrect because it creates a confusing sentence fragment.

Question 28. The best answer is G.

F is incorrect because it contains punctuation (a semicolon) that should separate two independent clauses; however, the clause before the semicolon is a fragment (it has no verb), and the clause following the semicolon is nonsensical (what does she hope will take place?).

G is the best answer because the subordinate noun clause "the wedding Mom dreams of performing" indicates (without any interrupting punctuation) what Mom hopes will take place at the foot of a ski run.

H is incorrect because it contains punctuation (a comma) and a conjunction (*and*) which together should separate two independent clauses; however, the clause before the comma is a subordinate clause (a noun clause) and the clause following the semicolon is nonsensical (what does she hope will take place?).

J is incorrect because it indicates that the wedding is doing the hoping, which is nonsensical.

Question 29. The best answer is B.

A is incorrect because the prepositional phrase "to join" requires the objective form *her*, not the subjective form *she*.

B is the best answer because it contains the objective form *her* required by the prepositional phrase "to join," and because it contains the correct possessive form *their*.

C is incorrect because the prepositional phrase "to join" requires the objective form *her*, not the subjective form *she*.

D is incorrect because it contains the reflexive *there* instead of the correct possessive *their*. The use of the pronoun *herself* in this sentence is also awkward.

Question 30. The best answer is H.

F is incorrect because it implies that there is a contrast being made with a previous statement—for example, the groom and bride not wearing ski hats, but Mom wearing one anyway—but no such statement is provided.

G is incorrect because it implies that there is a contrast being made with a previous statement—the groom and bride not wearing ski hats, for example, but Mom wearing one anyway—but no such statement is provided.

H is the best answer because the entire essay supports the idea that Mom would wear a ski hat to this particular type of wedding, so the use of "of course" reinforces the writer's attitude about Mom's on-the-job behavior. This choice fits with the style and content of the rest of the essay.

J is incorrect because it is nonsensical. To whom does *whoever* refer? How does it relate to Mom?

Passage III

Question 31. The best answer is C.

A is incorrect because the *than* later in the sentence makes this choice nonsensical: "much like . . . than" has no meaning.

B is incorrect because the *than* later in the sentence makes this choice nonsensical: "more as . . . than" has no meaning.

C is the best answer because the phrase "more like . . . than" sets up a comparison between Marian Anderson's concerts, communal celebrations, and singing events.

D is incorrect because the *than* later in the sentence makes this choice nonsensical: "concerts were celebrations . . . than" has no meaning.

Question 32. The best answer is G.

F is incorrect because it uses the adverb *sincerely* in a list of adjectives describing *she* (Marian Anderson).

G is the best answer because it uses the adjectives *sincere* and *gracious* to modify *she* (Marian Anderson), and it separates the adjectives and the following adjectival phrase from each other correctly.

H is incorrect because it uses the adverb *graciously* in a list of adjectives modifying *she* (Marian Anderson).

J is incorrect because it omits the comma needed to separate the adjective *gracious* from the following adjectival phrase.

Question 33. The best answer is C.

A is incorrect because the *than* later in the sentence makes this choice nonsensical: what does "no superior example . . . than" mean?

B is incorrect because it is a colloquial phrase that incorrectly includes "of an." This essay is not written with a colloquial tone.

C is the best answer because the phrase "no better example . . . than" sets up the description of the best example of Anderson's ability to reach out to an audience.

D is incorrect because the *than* later in the sentence makes this choice nonsensical: what does "no good example . . . than" mean?

Question 34. The best answer is J.

F is incorrect because there is no previously stated reason for *therefore* to point to.

G is incorrect because *however* suggests that the Easter Sunday concert was scheduled to be given at Constitution Hall despite something. However, there is nothing to suggest that this is so.

H is incorrect because there is nothing needing to be emphasized that would require an "in fact."

J is the best answer because it sets up a straightforward statement of fact about the original concert location.

Question 35. The best answer is A.

A is the best answer because it does not contain any unnecessary punctuation.

B is incorrect because it introduces an unnecessary comma between the verb *canceled* and its object, "the contract." It also introduces an unnecessary semicolon between the *because* clause and what the clause explains (canceling the contract).

C is incorrect because it separates the *because* clause from what it explains (canceling the contract) with an unnecessary semicolon.

D is incorrect because it introduces an unnecessary comma between the verb *canceled* and its object, "the contract." It also introduces an unnecessary comma between the *because* clause and what the clause explains (canceling the contract).

Question 36. The best answer is F.

F is the best answer because it does not contain any unnecessary punctuation.

G is incorrect because it introduces unnecessary punctuation (a colon) between the subject ("the second thing she did") and verb (*was*).

H is incorrect because it introduces unnecessary punctuation (a comma) between *was* and "to arrange."

J is incorrect because it introduces unnecessary punctuation (a comma) between the subject ("the second thing she did") and verb (*was*).

Question 37. The best answer is C.

A is incorrect because it fails to mention the radio. The use of the radio explains how Anderson was able to sing "before the nation."

B is incorrect because it describes Anderson standing in front of a radio, which is not a way she would have transmitted her voice to the nation.

C is the best answer because "via radio"—by radio—is a method a person could use to "sing before the nation."

D is incorrect because it is unclear. With no other mention of radio, it's not necessarily clear that the radio is involved, a fact that is crucial at this point.

Question 38. The best answer is G.

F is incorrect because it suggests that Anderson was nervous in her autobiography rather than on the day of her concert at the Lincoln Memorial. This does not make sense.

G is the best answer because it makes it clear that Anderson was nervous on the day of her performance at the Lincoln Memorial, which is suggested by the next sentence.

H is incorrect because it has Anderson nervous in her autobiography rather than on the day of her concert at the Lincoln Memorial. It does not make sense that she would be nervous in her autobiography but not in real life.

J is incorrect because it has Anderson barely remembering something in her autobiography and nervous on the day of writing rather than nervous on her performance day. Although it is possible that Anderson could have been so nervous that she had trouble remembering a day, **G** makes the most sense.

Question 39. The best answer is A.

A is the best answer because it is the clearest of the options. It correctly uses *towered,* which parallels *stretched* earlier in the sentence. This option makes clear that Lincoln is represented by a statue.

B is incorrect because its meaning is not completely clear. Does it mean that Abraham Lincoln towered like a statue behind Anderson? (This meaning could not be true; Lincoln was not alive in 1939, when the concert took place.) Or does it mean that a statue of Abraham Lincoln towered behind Anderson? This makes sense, but the option is not worded as clearly as it could be, if the second meaning is intended.

C is incorrect because it uses *towering,* which isn't parallel to *stretched* earlier in the sentence.

D is incorrect because it unnecessarily switches from active voice to passive voice. Also, *towered* doesn't have a meaning that allows it to be used as it is in this option.

Question 40. The best answer is J.

F is incorrect. The list of persons must be separated by commas, and the first people on the list are Supreme Court justices, so there must be a comma following *justices.* The next people on the list are members of the House and Senate, so the commas following *members* and *House* are both incorrect.

G is incorrect because the list of persons must be separated by commas, and the first people on the list are Supreme Court justices, so there must be a comma following *justices.*

H is incorrect because the second group of people on the list are members of the House and Senate, so the comma following *House* is incorrect.

J is the best answer because it uses commas correctly to separate the list of persons to whom Anderson was introduced.

Question 41. The best answer is A.

A is the best answer because it indicates the correct order of Anderson's performance: she began by singing the national anthem and then she sang opera pieces and spirituals.

B is incorrect because it uses *began by* and *after*, which are silly and nonsensical. This option seems to imply that Anderson sang opera pieces and spirituals before the program really began, but there is nothing in the essay to suggest that this makes sense.

C is incorrect because it says that Anderson began singing "after she sang several opera pieces and spirituals." This is confusing: how could she begin singing after she already sang?

D is incorrect because it is odd and unclear: it seems to imply that singing the national anthem helped Anderson sing the opera pieces and spirituals.

Question 42. The best answer is H.

F is incorrect because it is a bland, subjective statement that says nothing about the event's impact.

G is incorrect because it is not supported in the essay. Although the concert was on Easter Sunday, not all of the selections that Anderson sung were religious, and the event itself was not connected to a religious celebration. Also, Easter is already "a very important religious holiday," and any one singer would not make it more or less religiously important.

H is the best answer because it summarizes the event's nationwide impact as a celebration, a description supported by the rest of the essay.

J is incorrect because it isn't supported in the essay. The concert was enjoyed by people of all types across the country. Furthermore, what makes a "musical connoisseur" is subjective—it would have to be defined in the essay, but it is not.

Question 43. The best answer is A.

A is the best answer because it correctly characterizes Anderson as singing on many concert tours.

B is incorrect because it says that Anderson sang on "many of one's concert tours," but who is *one*?

C is not the best answer because "one out of her" is awkward. Option **A** more clearly expresses that Anderson performed many concert tours, even though only one concert is described in detail in this passage.

D is incorrect because it implies that several tours have been described in the essay ("any one of those"), but that isn't the case.

Question 44. The best answer is J.

F is incorrect because it implies that "that European tour" has been emphasized in the essay, but in fact it has not previously been mentioned.

G is incorrect because it is untrue; no references to her European tours can be found in the essay.

H is incorrect because it is untrue. No links between tour pressures and Anderson's retirement have been established in the essay.

J is the best answer because European tours haven't been previously discussed, so it doesn't make sense to mention one of the European tours so briefly here, in conjunction with her retirement.

Question 45. The best answer is D.

A is incorrect because it deviates from the standard English usage of the phrase "to win acclaim." One doesn't "win over" acclaim.

B is incorrect because it deviates from the standard English usage of the phrase "to win acclaim." One doesn't "earn the winnings of" acclaim.

C is incorrect because it deviates from the standard English usage of the phrase "to win acclaim." One doesn't find oneself "the winner in" acclaim.

D is the best answer because it contains the standard English usage of the phrase "to win acclaim."

Passage IV

Question 46. The best answer is H.

F is incorrect because it implies that the sentence "what's nostalgia" is a question, but there is no question mark to indicate that this is so. The context of the sentence makes that question unlikely.

G is incorrect. Although it is possessive, it says that *nostalgia* belongs to *it.* However, the essay doesn't make clear what *it* is. In any case, "Its nostalgia" is a sentence fragment.

H is the best answer because it is the correct form of the contraction of "that is," and it makes an independent clause that defines what "merely remembering the good that came before" is.

J is incorrect because *thats* has no meaning in this context.

Question 47. The best answer is D.

A is incorrect because a comma after *enough* forms a comma splice. Also, what does it mean for something to be "harmless but enough"?

B is incorrect because it contains nonstandard usage: what does "enough harmless" mean in this context?

C is incorrect because it requires a semicolon before the transitional expression *however* in order to avoid ambiguity.

D is the best answer because it contains the needed comma before the conjunction *but,* which joins the sentence's two independent clauses.

Question 48. The best answer is F.

F is the best answer because it makes an assertion that is explored in the remainder of the essay, making this summation one of the essay's main ideas.

G is incorrect because it contradicts one of the main ideas of the essay. The first paragraph asserts that nostalgia involves remembering only "the good that came before," not realizing "that life is made up of both good and bad."

H is incorrect because it makes an assertion that is not supported by anything in the essay.

J is incorrect because it makes an assertion that is not supported by anything in the essay.

Question 49. The best answer is D.

A is incorrect because it contains an unnecessary comma separating the sentence's subject ("A culture willing to confront its flaws") from its predicate ("can begin to find remedies for them").

B is incorrect because it contains the contraction *it's* (it is) rather than the possessive form *its,* which is needed here.

C is incorrect because it contains the contraction *it's* (it is) rather than the possessive form *its,* which is needed here. Furthermore, there is an unnecessary comma separating the subject of the sentence from its predicate (see the explanation for **A**).

D is the best answer because it contains *its,* the possessive form needed here (to refer to the culture's flaws), and does not contain any unnecessary punctuation.

Question 50. The best answer is G.

F is incorrect because in this option *it,* a singular pronoun, refers to a plural antecedent, *flaws.* To be correct, the pronoun that refers to *flaws* must be plural—*them.*

G is the best answer because the plural pronoun *them* refers properly to its plural antecedent *flaws.* This option also contains *for,* which is the standard preposition after *remedy.*

H is incorrect because it contains nonstandard usage. One doesn't find a remedy *of* something, but rather *for* something.

J is incorrect. The plural reflexive pronoun *themselves* is used here as a pronoun referring to the antecedent *flaws,* which is not standard usage.

Question 51. The best answer is D.

A is incorrect because there is no reason to explain where the American Revolution occurred or who was involved in it.

B is incorrect because there is no reason to explain where the American Revolution occurred.

C is incorrect because there is no reason to explain where the American Revolution occurred; it is common knowledge that the Revolution took place in the thirteen colonies, and mentioning that does not advance the essay.

D is the best answer because it eliminates **A,** which is unneeded, and avoids adding any of the information in the other options, which are also unneeded.

Question 52. The best answer is F.

F is the best answer because it contains the correct plural possessive form *women's* and the commas that correctly separate the series of three examples in the sentence.

G is incorrect because it contains the incorrect possessive form. *Women* is a plural noun; its possessive form is *women's,* not *womens'*.

H is incorrect because it is missing a comma following *abolition,* the first item in a series of three examples in the sentence.

J is incorrect because it is missing an apostrophe before the *s* in *womens* that would indicate the possessive form for the rights of women.

Question 53. The best answer is B.

A is incorrect because it implies that something in the current sentence is being contrasted with something in the previous statements, but the current sentence actually supports the previous statements.

B is the best answer because it correctly emphasizes that the current sentence makes a point that is suggested by the preceding statements.

C is incorrect because it implies that the current sentence contains another example of a culture confronting its flaws, when in fact the sentence makes a conclusion about constructive social movements.

D is incorrect because it implies that the current sentence contains an example of something stated in the previous statements, which is not the case.

Question 54. The best answer is F.

F is the best answer because it does not attempt to define the word *culture,* as the other options do. The definition is not needed at this point in the essay.

G is incorrect because there is no reason to define the word *culture* here, much less discuss that it shares a root with a word not even used in the essay. This option indicates that American culture is derived from a Latin root, which is nonsensical—only a word could be derived from a Latin root.

H is incorrect because there is no reason to define the word *culture* here, much less indicate what the definition is not.

J is incorrect because there is no reason to define the word *culture* at this point in the essay. The reader should understand that *culture* means "social patterns, traits, and products"—there is no need to say it directly.

Question 55. The best answer is A.

A is the best answer because it says that American culture during the 1980s was typified, or represented, by a pop song that invites listeners to stop worrying and simply be happy, which is a superficial celebration of the positive and therefore fulfills the writer's goal.

B is incorrect because it does not mention celebrating anything, superficially or otherwise, so this option would not accomplish the writer's goal.

C is incorrect because it does not provide an example of anyone celebrating anything, superficially or otherwise, so this option would not accomplish the writer's goal.

D is incorrect because it does not provide an example of anyone celebrating anything, superficially or otherwise, so this option would not accomplish the writer's goal.

Question 56. The best answer is H.

F is incorrect because the Great Depression did not *entertain* anything (as in provide entertainment for, show hospitality to, or take into consideration).

G is incorrect because it contains a nonspecific *they*. Who suffered? The historians?

H is the best answer because it contains a short, accurate description of the Great Depression.

J is incorrect because if this option is used, the proper noun "Great breadlines" is formed. What are "Great breadlines"?

Question 57. The best answer is D.

A is incorrect because it is missing the needed comma after *said,* before the quoted material.

B is incorrect because there should be no commas before or after "George Santayana," since he is the philosopher being referred to. In addition, this option is missing the needed comma after *said,* and before the quoted material.

C is incorrect because there should be no commas before or after "George Santayana," because he is the philosopher being referred to. In addition, this option is missing the needed comma after *said.*

D is the best answer because it does not contain any unnecessary punctuation, and it does contain the needed comma after *said.*

Question 58. The best answer is G.

F is incorrect because in this context *peddling* needs an object (what, exactly, are the people peddling?), and it lacks one here. Additionally, the idea of people peddling (something) "in nostalgia" makes no sense.

G is the best answer because it is the standard usage of *peddling;* in this context it means something like *promoting.*

H is incorrect because in this sentence *peddling* is used in the sense of *promoting;* "promoting nostalgia like a bicycle" makes no sense.

J is incorrect because in order to convey that "the people" are peddling nostalgia, the normal word order would be "peddling nostalgia," not "nostalgia peddling."

Question 59. The best answer is D.

A is incorrect because it eliminates the intended distinction between distorting the past (for instance, when being nostalgic) and remembering it accurately.

B is incorrect because it makes no sense. The sentence contrasts nostalgia—"distorting the past"—with "remembering it [nostalgia]." *Nor* does not make the contrast.

C is incorrect because it contains *their* instead of *they're*, which would be needed here. Even if *they're* were used here, though, there would have to be no comma before *as* in order for this option to work.

D is the best answer because it clearly makes the intended distinction between distorting the past (when being nostalgic) and remembering it accurately. *Not* (an adverb) is paired with the *are* that occurs earlier in the sentence.

Question 60. The best answer is H.

F is not the best answer because Paragraph 4 says that "a culture that blinds itself to flaws and dwells on the positive can create serious trouble for itself," and that this statement is the *converse* of something. For the sake of unity and coherence, then, Paragraph 4 should be placed immediately after the paragraph that "a culture . . . itself" is the converse of. Paragraph 3 does not contain that statement.

G is not the best answer because Paragraph 4 says that "a culture that blinds itself to flaws and dwells on the positive can create serious trouble for itself," and that this statement is the *converse* of something. For the sake of unity and coherence, then, Paragraph 4 should be placed immediately after the paragraph that contains a statement that is the converse of "a culture . . . itself." Paragraph 1 does not contain that statement.

H is the best answer because Paragraph 2 contains the *converse* mentioned in the first sentence of Paragraph 4 ("a culture that blinds itself to flaws and dwells on the positive can create serious trouble for itself"). By placing Paragraph 4 immediately after Paragraph 2, the essay becomes unified and coherent.

J is not the best answer because Paragraph 4 says that "a culture that blinds itself to flaws and dwells on the positive can create serious trouble for itself," and that this statement is the *converse* of something. For the sake of unity and coherence, then, Paragraph 4 should be placed immediately after the paragraph that contains a statement that is the converse of "a culture . . . itself." Paragraph 5 does not contain that description.

Passage V

Question 61. The best answer is D.

A is incorrect because it uses the adverb *annually* to modify the noun *schedule*. The adjective *annual* should be used instead.

B is incorrect because it uses the adverb *rigorously* instead of the needed adjective *rigorous* to modify the noun *schedule*. Even if *rigorous* were used, however, this would not be the best option.

C is incorrect because it does not make clear whether the schedule is rigorous only once a year or throughout the year.

D is the best answer because it uses the adjectives *annual* and *rigorous* to modify the noun *schedule*. This option makes clear that the students' schedule is a rigorous, year-round one.

Question 62. The best answer is H.

F is incorrect because it is a sentence fragment: there is no subject and no verb, just an adverbial clause.

G is incorrect because it does not form a complete sentence, but rather is a sentence fragment: there is no subject.

H is the best answer because it forms a complete sentence composed of an adjective clause (the first part of the sentence, before the comma) and an independent clause.

J is incorrect because it forms a sentence fragment; it also contains the nonparallel verbs *beginning* and *extends*.

Question 63. The best answer is B.

A is incorrect because it does not refer to the Japanese educational system, which should be mentioned in order to define the topic.

B is the best answer because it introduces the essay's topic by mentioning the educational system in Japan and its effect on the economic system of the country.

C is incorrect because there is no mention of the educational system in Japan, which is needed in order to define the essay's topic.

D is incorrect because it does not make it clear that it is the Japanese educational system being discussed. This option does not "sharpen the focus."

Question 64. The best answer is G.

F is incorrect because the students' terms are mentioned out of order (the first term is in the first sentence, the third term is in the second sentence, and the second term is in the third sentence).

G is the best answer because the students' terms are mentioned in the order they occur during the school year (the first term is in the first sentence, the second term is in the second sentence, and the third term is in the third sentence).

H is incorrect because the students' terms are mentioned out of order (the third term is in the first sentence, the first term is in the second sentence, and the second term is in the third sentence).

J is incorrect because the students' terms are mentioned out of order (the second term is in the first sentence, the first term is in the second sentence, and the third term is in the third sentence).

Question 65. The best answer is A.

A is the best answer because it correctly breaks the information into two complete sentences. There is no ambiguity of meaning when the information is divided this way.

B is incorrect because it forms a run-on sentence with a comma splice. It is impossible to know, on first reading, whether the phrase beginning with *although* applies to what precedes it or what follows it. The comma following *although* further confuses the reading.

C is incorrect because it forms a run-on sentence with a comma splice. It is impossible to know, on first reading, whether the dependent clause beginning with *although* applies to what precedes it or what follows it.

D is incorrect. In order for this option to work, it would require a comma before the conjunction *and.*

Question 66. The best answer is J.

F is incorrect because it indicates that the *attendees* (students) have become universal. What are "universal attendees"?

G is incorrect because it indicates that the "number of attendants" is universal. What are attendants, in the context of this paragraph?

H is incorrect because it indicates that the *attendants* have become universal.

J is the best answer because it indicates that school attendance has become universal, which makes sense in the context of the sentence.

Question 67. The best answer is B.

A is incorrect because the sentence's subject, *acceptance,* is singular, so the verb must be the singular *is.* Furthermore, *however* must be preceded and followed by commas.

B is the best answer because it pairs the singular subject, *acceptance,* with the singular verb *is,* and contains commas before and after *however,* as needed.

C is incorrect because the sentence's subject, *acceptance,* is singular, so the verb must be the singular *is.*

D is incorrect because *however* must be preceded and followed by commas.

Question 68. The best answer is H.

F is incorrect because Paragraph 4 does not deal with the subject of Japanese students' mixed attitudes toward school.

G is incorrect because it introduces the subject of learning beyond the classroom, but there is no discussion in Paragraph 4 of learning outside the classroom.

H is the best answer because it is supported by the information contained in the rest of the paragraph.

J is incorrect. It may or may not be true, but there is no support for it in the essay.

Question 69. The best answer is C.

A is incorrect because it is a sentence fragment.

B is incorrect because it is written in passive voice and it does not specify who does the attending or the course-taking.

C is the best answer because it has a subject, *they,* that refers to Japanese students, and it is a complete sentence that uses the active rather than passive voice.

D is incorrect because it is written in passive voice, and it implies that the courses attend school rather than the students.

Question 70. The best answer is G.

F is incorrect because it contains the adjective *typical,* but the adverb *typically* is needed, to modify *takes.*

G is the best answer because it correctly uses the adverb *typically* to modify the verb *takes.*

H is incorrect because it tries unsuccessfully to use the adverb *typically* as an adjective.

J is incorrect because it contains an unnecessary comma that separates the adjective *typical* from the noun it modifies, *ninth-grader.*

Question 71. The best answer is D.

A is incorrect because *takes* (earlier in the sentence) does not need to be supplemented by "are taking."

B is incorrect because *takes* (earlier in the sentence) does not need to be supplemented by "is also taken."

C is incorrect because *takes* (earlier in the sentence) does not need to be supplemented by "can be taken."

D is the best answer because it lets the verb *takes* stand alone in the sentence.

Question 72. The best answer is J.

F is incorrect because it is redundant. This option is part of a list of basic skills that are emphasized, but one *has* (or "does not have") basic skills in mathematics, not in math abilities and aptitudes.

G is incorrect because it is an unneeded and inadequate definition of mathematics. It would be better if it were replaced by the name of the subject, *mathematics*.

H is incorrect because it is redundant—"basic skills" is echoed in "basic computations."

J is the best answer because it gives the name of the subject, *mathematics*.

Question 73. The best answer is A.

A is the best answer because it says that each major corporation recruits, but does not mention how often—that information is given later in the sentence.

B is incorrect because it is redundant; since the sentence contains the phrase "year after year," it does not need to add "on an annual basis."

C is incorrect because it is redundant; since the sentence contains the phrase "year after year," it does not need to add "annually."

D is incorrect because it is redundant; since the sentence contains the phrase "year after year," it does not need to add "each year."

Question 74. The best answer is H.

F is incorrect because it makes the second half of the sentence ("about 99 percent") into a fragment. There must be a subject and predicate following the semicolon.

G is incorrect because it obscures the meaning of the sentence by putting a comma in the middle of the adverbial phrase "about 99 percent."

H is the best answer because by placing a colon after "one of the highest literacy rates in the world," it shows that "about 99 percent" is the literacy rate that is being referred to.

J is incorrect because it is ambiguous: should one read "the world about" as a unit? What would that mean, in this sentence?

Question 75. The best answer is A.

A is the best answer because it contains *its,* the correct possessive singular pronoun to represent *Japan* and show that the "business community" referred to is Japan's business community.

B is incorrect because it contains *it's* (it is), which makes no sense in this context.

C is incorrect because *their* is a plural pronoun, but it refers to Japan's business community, which is singular.

D is incorrect because *its'* is not a word.

Question 1. The correct answer is D.

Since 1 stone is equivalent to 14 pounds, $\frac{1}{14}$ stone is equivalent to 1 pound and $177\left(\frac{1}{14}\right)$ stone is equivalent to 177 pounds. So, a person who weighs 177 pounds weighs $\frac{177}{14}$, or 12.6, stone.

A is incorrect because, since 1 stone equals 14 pounds, a person who weighs 247.8 stone weighs 14(247.8) or 3,469.2 pounds, not 177 pounds. You might have multiplied 14(177), instead of dividing 177 by 14, and when the result was 2,478, which seemed unreasonable, put in a decimal to make the answer 247.8, which seemed more reasonable.

B is incorrect because, since 1 stone equals 14 pounds, a person who weighs 126.4 stone weighs 14(126.4) or 1,769.6 pounds, not 177 pounds. Since $177 \div 14 = 12.64$, you might have made a decimal point error.

C is incorrect because, since 1 stone equals 14 pounds, a person who weighs 79.1 stone weighs 14(79.1) or 1,107.4 pounds, not 177 pounds. You might have divided 14 by 177, and when the result was 0.0791, which seemed unreasonable, moved the decimal point to make the answer 79.1, which seemed more reasonable.

D is correct, as explained above.

E is incorrect because, since 1 stone equals 14 pounds, a person who weighs 7.9 stone weighs 14(7.9) or 110.6 pounds, not 177 pounds. You might have divided 14 by 177, and when the result was 0.0791, which seemed unreasonable, moved the decimal point to make the answer 7.9, which seemed more reasonable.

Question 2. The correct answer is J.

The increase in the room rate is 18%, which, as a decimal, is 0.18, and 18% of $30.00 is 0.18(30.00), or $5.40. The new rate is the old rate plus the amount of the increase, so the new rate is $30.00 + $5.40, or $35.40.

F is incorrect because an increase of $0.18 is less than 1% of $30.00 (1% of $30.00 is $0.30). You might have interpreted 18% to mean $0.18.

G is incorrect because an increase of $1.80 is less than 10% of $30.00 (10% of $30.00 is $3.00). You might have made a decimal point error in converting 18% to a decimal.

H is incorrect because an increase of $3.00 is 10% of $30.00, not 18%.

J is correct, as explained above.

K is incorrect because an increase of $18.00 is more than 50% of $30.00 (50% of $30.00 is $15.00). You might have interpreted 18% to mean $18.00.

Question 3. The correct answer is B.

The average of 5 numbers is the sum of the 5 numbers divided by 5. So the average of the 5 companies' contributions is

$$\frac{0 + 300 + 300 + 180 + 270}{5} = \frac{1,050}{5} = 210.$$

A is incorrect because $187.50 = \frac{750}{4} = \frac{300 + 180 + 270}{4}$. You might have thought that the contribution of 0 didn't count at all and that the second occurrence of 300 (that is, Company C's contribution) shouldn't be counted in the total of the contributions, but Company C should be included in the number of companies contributing.

B is correct, as explained above.

C is incorrect because $250.00 = \frac{750}{3} = \frac{300 + 180 + 270}{3}$. You might have thought that the contribution of 0 and the second occurrence of 300 didn't count at all.

D is incorrect because $262.50 = \frac{1,050}{4} = \frac{300 + 300 + 180 + 270}{4}$. You might have thought that the contribution of 0 didn't count at all.

E is incorrect because $350.00 = \frac{1,050}{3} = \frac{300 + 300 + 180 + 270}{3}$. You might have thought that the contribution of 0 didn't count at all and that you should divide by 3 since there were only 3 distinct amounts contributed by the other 4 companies.

Question 4. The correct answer is G.

According to the relationship $D = rt$, where D is the distance traveled, r is the rate, and t is the time, traveling 60 miles per hour for $1\frac{1}{2}$ hours means that Car A traveled $60\left(1\frac{1}{2}\right)$ or 90 miles. Car B, by traveling 40 miles per hour for 2 hours, traveled 40(2) or 80 miles. The difference between the number of miles Car A traveled and the number of miles Car B traveled is $90 - 80 = 10$ miles.

F is incorrect because if the cars traveled the same number of miles, making the difference in the miles they traveled 0, then Car A would have had to go slower to cover fewer than 90 miles or Car B would have had to go faster to cover more than 90 miles.

G is correct, as explained above.

H is incorrect because 80 is the number of miles traveled by Car B only.

J is incorrect because 90 is the number of miles traveled by Car A only.

K is incorrect because 170 is the sum, not the difference, of the numbers of miles traveled by Cars A and B.

Question 5. The correct answer is B.

If $(t - 3)(t + 2) = 0$, then $t - 3 = 0$, so $t = 3$, or $t + 2 = 0$, so $t = -2$. Option **B** is 3.

A is incorrect because if $t = 2$, then $(t - 3)(t + 2) = (2 - 3)(2 + 2) = (-1)(4) = -4$, not 0. You might have made a sign error in solving $t + 2 = 0$.

B is correct, as explained above.

C is incorrect because if $t = 5$, then $(t - 3)(t + 2) = (5 - 3)(5 + 2) = 2(7) = 14$, not 0.

D is incorrect because if $t = 6$, then $(t - 3)(t + 2) = (6 - 3)(6 + 2) = 3(8) = 24$, not 0.

E is incorrect because if $t = 7$, then $(t - 3)(t + 2) = (7 - 3)(7 + 2) = 4(9) = 36$, not 0.

Question 6. The correct answer is J.

The perimeter of a parallelogram is twice the sum of the measures of two adjacent sides. This is the same as the sum of the measures of all four sides since opposite sides of a parallelogram are congruent and therefore have the same measure. So, if the perimeter of parallelogram $ABCD$ is 34 inches and one side is 6 inches long, $34 = 2(6 + x)$, where x is the length of $\overline{AB}$, the side adjacent to $\overline{AD}$. Then $17 = 6 + x$ and $x = 11$.

F is incorrect because if $\overline{AB}$ were 28 inches long, the perimeter of $ABCD$ would be $6 + 28 + 6 + 28 = 68$, not 34. You might have thought that the perimeter of a parallelogram was the sum of two adjacent sides.

G is incorrect because if $\overline{AB}$ were 22 inches long, the perimeter of $ABCD$ would be $6 + 22 + 6 + 22 = 56$, not 34. You might have taken 12 from 34 to account for sides $\overline{AD}$ and $\overline{BC}$ without realizing that 22 represents the sum of the measures of $\overline{AB}$ and $\overline{DC}$, not just the measure of $\overline{AB}$.

H is incorrect because if $\overline{AB}$ were 17 inches long, the perimeter of $ABCD$ would be $6 + 17 + 6 + 17 = 46$, not 34. You might have thought that the measure of $\overline{AB}$ was half of the perimeter.

J is correct, as explained above.

K is incorrect because if $\overline{AB}$ were $5\frac{2}{3}$ inches long, the perimeter of $ABCD$ would be $6 + 5\frac{2}{3} + 6 + 5\frac{2}{3} = 23\frac{1}{3}$, not 34. You might have confused perimeter with area because $5\frac{2}{3}(6) = 34$.

Question 7. The correct answer is B.

The formula $S = 180(n - 2)$ relates S, the sum of the measures of the angles of a regular polygon, to n, the number of sides the polygon has. A regular polygon of n sides has n congruent angles, so $S = n\alpha$, where α is the measure of one of the angles. Then $n\alpha = 180(n - 2)$. In this problem, $\alpha = 90°$, so $n(90) = 180(n - 2)$, $90n = 180n - 360$, $-90n = -360$, $n = 4$.

A is incorrect because if the regular polygon had three sides, it would be an equilateral triangle. The measure of each angle of an equilateral triangle is 60°, not 90°.

B is correct, as explained above.

C is incorrect because if each of the angles of a regular hexagon (6 sides) were 90°, then the angle sum of the hexagon would be 6(90°) = 540°. But drawing three diagonals of a regular hexagon divides it into four triangles, each of which has angle sum 180°, so the angle sum of a regular pentagon is 4(180) = 720°. Therefore, the angles of a regular hexagon cannot be 90° angles.

D is incorrect because if each of the angles of a regular octagon (8 sides) were 90°, then the angle sum of the octagon would be 8(90°) = 720°. But drawing five diagonals of a regular octagon divides it into six triangles, each of which has angle sum 180°, so the angle sum of a regular octagon is 6(180) = 1,080°. Therefore, the angles of a regular octagon cannot be 90° angles.

E is incorrect because if each of the angles of a regular dodecagon (12 sides) were 90°, then the angle sum of the dodecagon would be 12(90°) = 1,080°. But drawing nine diagonals of a regular dodecagon divides it into ten triangles, each of which has angle sum 180°, so the angle sum of a regular dodecagon is 10(180) = 1,800°. Therefore, the angles of a regular dodecagon cannot be 90° angles.

Question 8. The correct answer is G.

First, $\dfrac{16r^3tz^5}{-4rt^3z^2} = \dfrac{16}{-4} \cdot \dfrac{r^3}{r} \cdot \dfrac{t}{t^3} \cdot \dfrac{z^5}{z^2}$. Then, $\dfrac{16}{-4} = -4$, and using the property of

exponents that says $\dfrac{a^m}{a^n} = a^{m-n}$, $\dfrac{r^3}{r} = r^{3-1} = r^2$, $\dfrac{t}{t^3} = t^{1-3} = t^{-2} = \dfrac{1}{t^2}$, and

$\dfrac{z^5}{z^2} = z^{5-2} = z^3$. So, $\dfrac{16r^3tz^5}{-4rt^3z^2} = -4 \cdot r^2 \cdot \dfrac{1}{t^2} \cdot z^3 = -\dfrac{4r^2z^3}{t^2}$.

F is incorrect because $\dfrac{r^3}{r} = r^{3-1} = r^2$, not $\dfrac{1}{r^2}$. You might have subtracted the

exponents in the wrong order.

G is correct, as explained above.

H is incorrect because $\dfrac{r^3}{r} = r^{3-1} = r^2$, not r; $\dfrac{t}{t^3} = t^{1-3} = t^{-2} = \dfrac{1}{t^2}$, not $\dfrac{1}{t}$; and

$\dfrac{z^5}{z^2} = z^{5-2} = z^3$, not z.

J is incorrect because $\dfrac{r^3}{r} = r^{3-1} = r^2$, not r^4; $\dfrac{t}{t^3} = t^{1-3} = t^{-2} = \dfrac{1}{t^2}$, not t^4; and

$\dfrac{z^5}{z^2} = z^{5-2} = z^3$, not z^7. You might have added exponents instead of subtracting.

K is incorrect because $\dfrac{t}{t^3} = t^{1-3} = t^{-2} = \dfrac{1}{t^2}$, not t^2. You might have dropped

the minus sign on the exponent.

Question 9. The correct answer is A.

Because $\overline{AB}$ and $\overline{XY}$ are parallel, $\angle CXY$ and $\angle CAB$ are corresponding angles, and corresponding angles are congruent. The measure of $\angle CXY$ is $45°$ since congruent angles have the same measure. The sum of the measures of the angles of a triangle is $180°$, so $\angle C$'s measure is $180° - (45° + 30°) = 180° - 75° = 105°$.

A is correct, as explained above.

B is incorrect because if $\angle C$ were a $115°$ angle, then the measure of $\angle CXY$ would be $180° - (30° + 115°)$, or $35°$. But the measure of $\angle CXY$ is $45°$ because $\angle CXY$ and $\angle CAB$ are corresponding angles and as such are congruent and have the same measure, which is $45°$.

C is incorrect because if $\angle C$ were a $125°$ angle, then the measure of $\angle CXY$ would be $180° - (30° + 125°)$, or $25°$. But the measure of $\angle CXY$ is $45°$ because $\angle CXY$ and $\angle CAB$ are corresponding angles and as such are congruent and have the same measure, which is $45°$.

D is incorrect because if $\angle C$ were a $135°$ angle, then the measure of $\angle CXY$ would be $180° - (30° + 135°)$, or $15°$. But the measure of $\angle CXY$ is $45°$ because $\angle CXY$ and $\angle CAB$ are corresponding angles and as such are congruent and have the same measure, which is $45°$. You might have neglected to include the measure of $\angle CYX$ when you computed the angle sum for $\triangle CXY$.

E is incorrect because if $\angle C$ were a $150°$ angle, then the measure of $\angle CXY$ would be $180° - (30° + 150°)$, or $0°$. But this is impossible. You might have neglected to include the measure of $\angle CXY$ when you computed the angle sum for $\triangle CXY$.

Question 10. The correct answer is K.

The absolute value of –3 is 3 (that is, $|-3| = 3$), and the absolute value of 2 is 2 (that is, $|2| = 2$) so $|-3| \cdot |2| = 3 \cdot 2 = 6$.

F is incorrect because if the product were negative, one of the factors would have to be negative, and the absolute value of a number is never negative. You might have disregarded the absolute value.

G is incorrect because if the product were negative, one of the factors would have to be negative, and the absolute value of a number is never negative. Also, a product involving 3 or –3 and 2 or –2 would have to be 6 or –6, not 5 or –5. You might have thought that the absolute value made a number have the opposite sign, and you might have added instead of multiplying.

H is incorrect because if the product were negative, one of the factors would have to be negative, and the absolute value of a number is never negative. Also, a product involving 3 or –3 and 2 or –2 would have to be 6 or –6, not 1 or –1. You might have disregarded the absolute value, and you might have added instead of multiplying.

J is incorrect because a product involving 3 or –3 and 2 or –2 would have to be 6 or –6, not 5 or –5. You might have added the absolute values instead of multiplying them.

K is correct, as explained above.

Question 11. The correct answer is A.

If, out of the 750 people who answered the telephone poll, 500 liked the new show and 100 disliked it, then the number of people who were undecided is $750 - (500 + 100) = 150$. The percent who were undecided is $\frac{150}{750} \times 100$, or 20%.

A is correct, as explained above.

B is incorrect because the number of people who were undecided is $750 - (500 + 100) = 150$ and 25% of 750 is $0.25(750) = 187.5$, not 150.

C is incorrect because the number of people who were undecided is $750 - (500 + 100) = 150$ and $66\frac{2}{3}\%$ of 750 is $0.\overline{6}(750) = 500$, not 150. You might have given the percent of people who liked the new show instead of the percent of people who were undecided.

D is incorrect because the number of people who were undecided is $750 - (500 + 100) = 150$ and 80% of 750 is $0.8(750) = 600$, not 150. You might have given the percent of people who were not undecided instead of the percent of people who were undecided.

E is incorrect because the number of people who were undecided is $750 - (500 + 100) = 150$ and 150% of 750 is $1.5(750) = 1,125$, not 150.

Question 12. The correct answer is J.

If 6 is the greatest common factor of the two numbers, then both numbers have a factor of 6. Since 36 is the least common multiple of the two numbers, and $36 = 6 \cdot 2 \cdot 3$, one of the numbers must have another factor of 2 and one must have a factor of 3. So one number has a factor of 6 and a factor of 2 and could be 12 while the other has a factor of 6 and a factor of 3 and could be 18.

F is incorrect because 6 is not a factor of 4 or 9, so 6 cannot be the greatest common factor of 4 and 9.

G is incorrect because 6 is not a factor of 9, so 6 cannot be the greatest common factor of 9 and 12.

H is incorrect because 6 is not a factor of 15, so 6 cannot be the greatest common factor of 12 and 15.

J is correct, as explained above.

K is incorrect because 36 is not a multiple of 24, so 36 cannot be the least common multiple of 18 and 24.

Question 13. The correct answer is D.

If $x = -2$ and $y = 3$, then
$x^3y + xy^3 = (-2)^3(3) + (-2)(3)^3 = (-8)(3) + (-2)(27) = -24 + (-54) = -78$.

A is incorrect because
$(-2)^3(3) + (-2)(3)^3 = (-8)(3) + (-2)(27) = -24 + (-54) = -78$, not -30.
You might have thought that $(-2)^3(3)$ was 24, instead of -24, because
$24 + (-54)$ gives the answer of -30.

B is incorrect because
$(-2)^3(3) + (-2)(3)^3 = (-8)(3) + (-2)(27) = -24 + (-54) = -78$, not -36.
You might have used the exponents as coefficients, because
$3(-2)(3) + 3(-2)(3) = -36$.

C is incorrect because
$(-2)^3(3) + (-2)(3)^3 = (-8)(3) + (-2)(27) = -24 + (-54) = -78$, not -48.
You might have found the value of $x^3y + x^3y$, because
$(-2)^3(3) + (-2)^3(3) = -48$.

D is correct, as explained above.

E is incorrect because
$(-2)^3(3) + (-2)(3)^3 = (-8)(3) + (-2)(27) = -24 + (-54) = -78$, not -108.
You might have found the value of $xy^3 + xy^3$, because
$(-2)(3)^3 + (-2)(3)^3 = -108$.

Question 14. The correct answer is K.

The perimeter of a square is given by $P = 4s$, where s is the length of the side

of the square. So, $s = \dfrac{P}{4}$. If the perimeter of the given square is $20c - 12$, then

the side of the square is $\dfrac{20c - 12}{4} = \dfrac{4(5c - 3)}{4} = 5c - 3$.

F is incorrect because if the side of the square were $20c - 12$, then the perimeter would be $4(20c - 12)$ or $80c - 48$, not $20c - 12$.

G is incorrect because if the side of the square were $20c - 3$, then the perimeter would be $4(20c - 3)$ or $80c - 12$, not $20c - 12$. You might have neglected to divide every term by 4.

H is incorrect because if the side of the square were $8c$, then the perimeter would be $4(8c)$ or $32c$, not $20c - 12$. You might have tried to subtract 12 from $20c$.

J is incorrect because if the side of the square were $5c - 12$, then the perimeter would be $4(5c - 12)$ or $20c - 48$, not $20c - 12$. You might have neglected to divide every term by 4.

K is correct, as explained above.

Question 15. The correct answer is A.

If $(x + k)^2 = x^2 + 22x + k^2$, then, because
$(x + k)^2 = x^2 + 2kx + k^2$, $x^2 + 22x + k^2 = x^2 + 2kx + k^2$.
Equating the coefficients of the middle terms gives $2k = 22$ or $k = 11$.

A is correct, as explained above.

B is incorrect because when $k = 22$, $(x + k)^2 = (x + 22)^2 = x^2 + 44x + k^2$, not $x^2 + 22x + k^2$.

C is incorrect because when $k = 44$, $(x + k)^2 = (x + 44)^2 = x^2 + 88x + k^2$, not $x^2 + 22x + k^2$. You might have gotten as far as $2k = 22$ and then multiplied by 2 instead of dividing.

D is incorrect because when $k = 88$, $(x + k)^2 = (x + 88)^2 = x^2 + 176x + k^2$, not $x^2 + 22x + k^2$.

E is incorrect because when $k = 176$, $(x + k)^2 = (x + 176)^2 = x^2 + 352x + k^2$, not $x^2 + 22x + k^2$.

Question 16. The correct answer is J.

The price of the suit after the discount is $260 – 0.20($260), or $208. The price of each shirt after the discount is $30 – 0.30($30), or $21. The total price of the suit and two shirts Ben bought is $208 + 2($21), or $250.

F is incorrect because it includes the discount on all three items, but it includes the price of only one shirt in the total price. The discount on the suit is 0.20($260) = $52 and the discount on the shirts is 0.30($60) = $18, so the total discount is $70. The regular price of the suit and one shirt is $290, and $290 – $70 = $220.

G is incorrect because it is the price for the suit and only one shirt. The price of the suit after the discount is $208, the price of a shirt after the discount is $21, and $208 + $21 = $229.

H is incorrect because it is the total price of the suit and two shirts after everything was discounted 25%, the average of 20% and 30% (that is, ($260 + $30 + $30) – 0.25($260 + $30 + $30) = $240).

J is correct, as explained above.

K is incorrect because it is the total price of the suit and two shirts after a $20 discount. ($260 + $30 + $30) – $20 = $270.

Question 17. The correct answer is C.

The slope of a line through two points (x_1, y_1) and (x_2, y_2) is given by $\frac{y_1 - y_2}{x_1 - x_2}$.
Applying this formula to $(6,8)$ and $(-4,-10)$ gives $\frac{8 - (-10)}{6 - (-4)}$.

A is incorrect because the numerator has $y_1 + y_2$ instead of $y_1 - y_2$ and the first point is taken as $(-6,8)$ instead of $(6,8)$.

B is incorrect because the numerator has $y_1 + y_2$ instead of $y_1 - y_2$ and the denominator has $x_2 + x_1$ instead of $x_1 - x_2$.

C is correct, as explained above.

D is incorrect because the denominator has $x_2 - x_1$ instead of $x_1 - x_2$.

E is incorrect because the first point is taken as $(-6,8)$ instead of $(6,8)$.

Question 18. The correct answer is H.

The graph of $y = (x + 1)(x - 2)(x + 3)(x + 4)$ crosses the x-axis at points where $y = 0$. When $y = 0$, $(x + 1)(x - 2)(x + 3)(x + 4) = 0$. Solving for x gives $x + 1 = 0$ or $x = -1$, $x - 2 = 0$ or $x = 2$, $x + 3 = 0$ or $x = -3$, and $x + 4 = 0$ or $x = -4$. Therefore, there are 4 points on the graph with y-coordinate 0: $(-1,0)$, $(2,0)$, $(-3,0)$, and $(-4,0)$.

F is incorrect because the equation $(x + 1)(x - 2)(x + 3)(x + 4) = 0$ has 4 solutions ($x = -1$, $x = 2$, $x = -3$, and $x = -4$), so there are 4 points on the graph where the graph intersects the x-axis. You might have thought you needed to add 1, 2, 3, and 4.

G is incorrect because the equation $(x + 1)(x - 2)(x + 3)(x + 4) = 0$ has 4 solutions ($x = -1$, $x = 2$, $x = -3$, and $x = -4$), so there are 4 points on the graph where the graph intersects the x-axis. You might have thought that you needed to add 1, -2, 3, and 4.

H is correct, as explained above.

J is incorrect because the equation $(x + 1)(x - 2)(x + 3)(x + 4) = 0$ has 4 solutions ($x = -1$, $x = 2$, $x = -3$, and $x = -4$), so there are 4 points on the graph where the graph intersects the x-axis.

K is incorrect because the equation $(x + 1)(x - 2)(x + 3)(x + 4) = 0$ has 4 solutions ($x = -1$, $x = 2$, $x = -3$, and $x = -4$), so there are 4 points on the graph where the graph intersects the x-axis. You might have been thinking of the number of times the graph crosses the y-axis.

Question 19. The correct answer is A.

To simplify $\dfrac{3+6x}{9x}$, you can begin by factoring the numerator and the denominator so $\dfrac{3+6x}{9x} = \dfrac{3(1+2x)}{3(3x)}$, then $\dfrac{3(1+2x)}{3(3x)} = \dfrac{3}{3} \cdot \dfrac{1+2x}{3x} = \dfrac{1+2x}{3x}$ since $\dfrac{3}{3}$ is 1 and $1 \cdot a = a$ no matter what a is. Then $\dfrac{1+2x}{3x} = \dfrac{2x+1}{3x}$ since the commutative property says that order of the addition doesn't matter.

A is correct, as explained above.

B is incorrect because $\dfrac{1+6x}{3x}$ is not equivalent to $\dfrac{3+6x}{9x}$; if $x = 1$, $\dfrac{1+6x}{3x} = \dfrac{7}{3}$ and $\dfrac{3+6x}{9x} = 1$. You might not have factored a 3 out of each term of the numerator.

C is incorrect because $\dfrac{3+6x}{9x}$ equals 1 only when $x = 1$. When $x = 2$, for example, $\dfrac{3+6x}{9x} = \dfrac{5}{6}$. You might have thought that it was all right to combine 3 and $6x$ to get $9x$, but 3 and $6x$ aren't like terms and cannot be combined.

D is incorrect because $\dfrac{3+6x}{9x}$ equals 2 only when $x = \dfrac{1}{4}$. When $x = 2$, for example, $\dfrac{3+6x}{9x} = \dfrac{5}{6}$. You might have multiplied 6 and $3x$ to get $18x$ and then reduced $\dfrac{18x}{9x}$ to 2.

E is incorrect because $\dfrac{3+6x}{9x}$ equals $\dfrac{7}{3}$ only when $x = \dfrac{1}{5}$. When $x = 2$, for example, $\dfrac{3+6x}{9x} = \dfrac{5}{6}$.

Question 20. The correct answer is G.

If the block of 5 tickets costs $80.00, each ticket in the block costs $16.00 since $80.00 ÷ 5 = $16.00. Individual tickets cost $18.50 so each person could save $18.50 – $16.00, or $2.50, by buying a block ticket.

F is incorrect because $1.50 reflects the assumption that the block of tickets has only 4 tickets. Then each ticket would be $20.00 because 4($20.00) is $80.00 and the difference is $20.00 – $18.50, or $1.50.

G is correct, as explained above.

H is incorrect because $3.13 is the amount each of 4 people would save if 5 tickets were purchased at the individual ticket price compared to the block price: $3.13 = $\frac{5(18.50) - 80.00}{4}$.

J is incorrect because the savings would be $10.00 per person only if the block of 5 tickets cost $42.50. Then each ticket in the block would cost $8.50 and the savings would be $10.00 over the individual price of $18.50.

K is incorrect because $12.50 is the difference in price for 5 tickets purchased for $18.50 each and 5 tickets purchased in a block for $80.00. You might have neglected to divide by 5 as your last step.

Question 21. The correct answer is A.

In the sum of $3a^2b + 2a^2b^2$ and $-ab^2 + a^2b^2$, only $2a^2b^2$ and a^2b^2 are like terms (terms with identical variables raised to the same powers) and can be added to get $3a^2b^2$. The other two terms, $3a^2b$ and $-ab^2$, are not like terms (one has a^2 and the other has only a, for example) and cannot be combined, so the sum of $3a^2b + 2a^2b^2$ and $-ab^2 + a^2b^2$ is $3a^2b - ab^2 + 3a^2b^2$.

A is correct, as explained above.

B is incorrect because it doesn't include a^2b^2 in the sum.

C is incorrect because it treats $-ab^2$ as $-a^2b$ and combines it with $3a^2b$.

D is incorrect partly because it treats $2a^2b^2 + a^2b^2$ as $(2a^2b^2)(a^2b^2)$.

E is incorrect because it treats $2a^2b^2 + a^2b^2$ as $(2a^2b^2)(a^2b^2)$ and $3a^2b + -ab^2$ as $(3a^2b)(-ab^2)$.

Question 22. The correct answer is H.

The tangent of an angle of a right triangle is defined as the measure of the side opposite the angle over the measure of the side adjacent to the angle. In this problem, the side opposite the angle θ has measure 4 feet and the side adjacent to θ has measure 3 feet. Therefore, $\tan(\theta) = \frac{4}{3}$.

F is incorrect because it gives the measure of the side adjacent to θ over the measure of the side opposite θ.

G is incorrect because it treats θ as a 45° angle (because tan 45° = 1).

H is correct, as explained above.

J is incorrect because it gives the sum of the measure of the side opposite θ and the measure of the side adjacent to θ instead of the ratio of the measure of the side opposite θ to the measure of the side adjacent to θ.

K is incorrect because it gives the product of the measure of the side opposite θ and the measure of the side adjacent to θ instead of the ratio of the measure of the side opposite θ to the measure of the side adjacent to θ.

Question 23. The correct answer is E.

If Mary was x years old 10 years ago, she is $x + 10$ years old now, and 6 years from now she will be $(x + 10) + 6$.

A is incorrect because, for example, if $x = 5$, Mary was 5 years old 10 years ago, so she's 15 years old now, and in 6 years, she will be 21. But the value of $x + 6$ when $x = 5$ is 11. You might have let x be Mary's age now instead of her age 10 years ago.

B is incorrect because, for example, if $x = 5$, Mary was 5 years old 10 years ago, so she's 15 years old now, and in 6 years, she will be 21. But the value of $(x - 10) + 6$ when $x = 5$ is 1.

C is incorrect because, for example, if $x = 5$, Mary was 5 years old 10 years ago, so she's 15 years old now, and in 6 years, she will be 21. But the value of $(x + 10) - 6$ when $x = 5$ is 9.

D is incorrect because, for example, if $x = 5$, Mary was 5 years old 10 years ago, so she's 15 years old now, and in 6 years, she will be 21. But the value of $(x - 10) - 6$ when $x = 5$ is –11.

E is correct, as explained above.

Question 24. The correct answer is K.

The expression $x^2 - 5x - 6$ in factored form is $(x - 6)(x + 1)$, and $(x - 6)$ is option **K.**

F is incorrect because $x^2 - 5x - 6$ in factored form is $(x - 6)(x + 1)$ and $(x - 1)$ is not one of the factors. You might have made a sign error.

G is incorrect because $x^2 - 5x - 6$ in factored form is $(x - 6)(x + 1)$ and $(x + 2)$ is not one of the factors.

H is incorrect because $x^2 - 5x - 6$ in factored form is $(x - 6)(x + 1)$ and $(x - 2)$ is not one of the factors.

J is incorrect because $x^2 - 5x - 6$ in factored form is $(x - 6)(x + 1)$ and $(x - 3)$ is not one of the factors.

K is correct, as explained above.

Question 25. The correct answer is B.

If you recognize 5 and 12 as two members of a Pythagorean triple, you immediately know that the other member is 13, so the measure of the hypotenuse of the right triangle is 13 centimeters. If you don't recognize 5 and 12 as two members of a Pythagorean triple, you can use the Pythagorean theorem, which says that the square of the length of the hypotenuse of a right triangle is equal to the sum of the squares of the lengths of the legs. So, the length of the hypotenuse is $\sqrt{5^2 + 12^2} = \sqrt{169} = 13$ centimeters.

A is incorrect because 7 is the difference in the measures of the two legs of the right triangle.

B is correct, as explained above.

C is incorrect because 17 is the sum of the measures of the two legs of the right triangle.

D is incorrect because $\sqrt{17} \approx 4.12$ and $4.12 < 5$, so the hypotenuse would be shorter than the shorter leg of the triangle. But the hypotenuse is the longest side of a right triangle. You may have neglected to square the lengths of the legs when using the Pythagorean theorem.

E is incorrect because $\sqrt{119} \approx 10.91$ and $10.91 < 12$, so the hypotenuse would be shorter than one of the legs of the triangle. But the hypotenuse is the longest side of a right triangle. You may have subtracted instead of adding when using the Pythagorean theorem.

Question 26. The correct answer is K.

Using the rule of exponents that says $(ab)^n = (a^n)(b^n)$, $(-2a^5)^2 = (-2)^2 \cdot (a^5)^2$. Then, using the rule that says $(a^m)^n = a^{mn}$, $(a^5)^2 = a^{10}$. Since $(-2)^2 = 4$, $(-2a^5)^2 = 4a^{10}$.

F is incorrect because squared quantities are always positive and $-4a^{10}$ is negative. You might have treated $(-4)^2$ as $-(4^2)$.

G is incorrect because squared quantities are always positive and $-4a^7$ is positive only when $a < 0$. Also, the exponent should be 10, not 7. You might have treated $(-4)^2$ as $-(4^2)$ and added the exponents instead of multiplying them.

H is incorrect because squared quantities are always positive and $-2a^{10}$ is negative. You might have treated $(-2a^5)^2$ as $-2(a^5)^2$.

J is incorrect because squared quantities are always positive and $4a^7$ is positive only when $a > 0$. Also, the exponent should be 10, not 7. You might have added the exponents instead of multiplying them.

K is correct, as explained above.

Question 27. The correct answer is C.

The specific gravity of the liquid is the ratio of the weight of the liquid to the weight of an equal volume of water. A cubic foot of the liquid weighs 125 pounds and a cubic foot of water weighs 62.5 pounds, so the specific gravity of the liquid is $\frac{125}{62.5} = 2$.

A is incorrect because if the specific gravity of the liquid were 1, then water would weigh 125 pounds per cubic foot since $\frac{125}{125} = 1$. But water weighs 62.5 pounds per cubic foot.

B is incorrect because if the specific gravity of the liquid were 1.25, then water would weigh 100 pounds per cubic foot since $\frac{125}{100} = 1.25$. But water weighs 62.5 pounds per cubic foot.

C is correct, as explained above.

D is incorrect because if the specific gravity of the liquid were 6.25, then water would weigh 20 pounds per cubic foot since $\frac{125}{20} = 6.25$. But water weighs 62.5 pounds per cubic foot.

E is incorrect because if the specific gravity of the liquid were 125, then water would weigh 1 pound per cubic foot since $\frac{125}{1} = 125$. But water weighs 62.5 pounds per cubic foot.

Question 28. The correct answer is K.

If $2x + 1 = -3$, then $2x = -4$ and $x = -2$. When $x = -2$,
$x^2 - 3x = (-2)^2 - 3(-2) = 4 + 6 = 10$.

F is incorrect because if $x^2 - 3x = -10$, then x should be -2, but $x^2 - 3x = -10$ has no real solutions (the discriminant is $(-3)2 - 4(1)(10) = 9 - 40$, which is negative). You might have made sign errors.

G is incorrect because if $x^2 - 3x = -2$, then x should be -2, but $x^2 - 3x = -2$ means $x^2 - 3x + 2 = 0$, so $(x - 1)(x - 2) = 0$, so $x = 1$ or $x = 2$. Neither solution is -2. You might have solved $2x + 1 = -3$ and thought you were finished with the problem.

H is incorrect because if $x^2 - 3x = 2$, then x should be -2, but $x^2 - 3x = 2$ means $x^2 - 3x - 2 = 0$ and the solutions for this equation are $\frac{3 \pm \sqrt{17}}{2}$. Neither solution is -2. You might have made a sign error when calculating $(-2)^2$.

J is incorrect because if $x^2 - 3x = 5$, then x should be -2, but $x^2 - 3x = 5$ means $x^2 - 3x - 5 = 0$ and the solutions for this equation are $\frac{3 \pm \sqrt{29}}{2}$. Neither solution is -2.

K is correct, as explained above.

Question 29. The correct answer is C.

If $3(2 + x) < 3$, then $6 + 3x < 3$, $3x < -3$, and $x < -1$. This is the set of numbers to the left of -1, not including -1, which is shown in option **C**.

A is incorrect because, for example, $x = -2$ satisfies the inequality since $3(2 + -2) = 0$ and $0 < 3$, but $x = -2$ is not included in the graph for option **A**. You might not have multiplied each term of $(2 + x)$ by 3 and solved the inequality $6 + x < 3$.

B is incorrect because, for example, $x = -4$ satisfies the inequality since $3(2 + -4) = -6$ and $-6 < 3$, but $x = -4$ is not included in the graph for option **B**. You might not have multiplied each term of $(2 + x)$ by 3 and solved the inequality $6 + x < 3$ and then thought that subtracting 6 from both sides would reverse the inequality symbol.

C is correct, as explained above.

D is incorrect because, for example, $x = -2$ satisfies the inequality since $3(2 + -2) = 0$ and $0 < 3$, but $x = -2$ is not included in the graph for option **D**. You might have divided both sides of $3(2 + x) < 3$ by 3 to get $2 + x < 1$ and then thought subtracting 1 from both sides would reverse the inequality symbol.

E is incorrect because, for example, $x = 0$ is a point on the graph given in option **E**, but $x = 0$ does not satisfy the inequality since $3(2 + 0) = 6$ and $6 \not< 3$. You might not have multiplied each term of $(2 + x)$ by 3 and solved the inequality $6 + x < 3$ by adding 6 instead of subtracting 6.

Question 30. The correct answer is G.

By definition, if one quantity, represented by q_1, varies directly as a second quantity, represented by q_2, and inversely as a third quantity, represented by q_3, then the relationship between the three quantities is $q_1 = k\dfrac{q_2}{q_3}$, where k is a constant of variation. In this problem, a quantity, represented by y, varies directly as the square of a second quantity, represented by w (so the square of w is represented by w^2), and inversely as the cube of a third quantity, represented by t (so the cube of t is represented by t^3), so the relationship between y, w, and t is $y = k\dfrac{w^2}{t^3}$. Since k can be any nonzero number, we can let k be 1 and so the equation is $y = \dfrac{w^2}{t^3}$.

F is incorrect because the equation has w varying directly as the square of y and inversely as the cube of t. You might have switched y and w.

G is correct, as explained above.

H is incorrect because the equation has y varying directly as the square of t and inversely as the cube of w. You might have switched w and t.

J is incorrect because the equation has y varying directly as the square root of w and inversely as the cube root of t. You might have confused "square" with "square root" and "cube" with "cube root."

K is incorrect because the equation has t varying directly as the square of w and inversely as the cube of y. You might have switched y and t.

Question 31. The correct answer is A.

Because you're looking for the value of a and a is the first coordinate of the midpoint, you don't need to spend time finding anything but the first coordinate. By the midpoint formula, the first coordinate of the midpoint of a segment determined by the points (x_1, y_1) and (x_2, y_2) is given by $\frac{x_1 + x_2}{2}$. Therefore, $a = \frac{-3 + 7}{2} = 2$.

A is correct, as explained above.

B is incorrect because if $a = -4$, then the midpoint of $\overline{AB}$ would be $(-4, -3)$, which isn't even on $\overline{AB}$, as shown on the graph below. You might have made a sign error in adding and neglected to divide by 2.

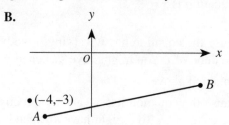

C is incorrect because if $a = 4$, then the midpoint of $\overline{AB}$ would be $(4, -3)$, which isn't even on $\overline{AB}$, as shown on the graph below. You might have neglected to divide by 2.

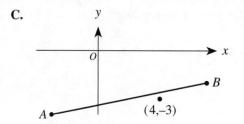

D is incorrect because if $a = -5$, then the midpoint of $\overline{AB}$ would be $(-5,-3)$, which isn't even on $\overline{AB}$, as shown on the graph below. You might have made a sign error in adding.

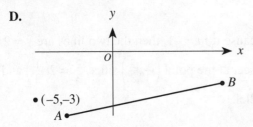

E is incorrect because if $a = 5$, then the midpoint of $\overline{AB}$ would be $(5,-3)$, which isn't even on $\overline{AB}$, as shown on the graph below. You might have made a sign error in adding.

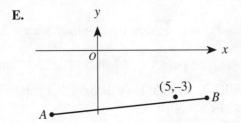

Question 32. The correct answer is K.

Since the equations for the two lines are in slope-intercept form ($y = mx + b$, where the slope is m), the slopes are 2 and m. Parallel lines have equal slopes, so $m = 2$.

F is incorrect because if $m = -1$, then the two lines are $y = 2x$ and $y = -x + 1$. These lines intersect at the point $\left(\frac{1}{3}, \frac{2}{3}\right)$ since $\frac{2}{3} = 2\left(\frac{1}{3}\right)$ and $\frac{2}{3} = -\frac{1}{3} + 1$, so they are not parallel.

G is incorrect because if $m = 0$, then the two lines are $y = 2x$ and $y = 1$. These lines intersect at the point $\left(\frac{1}{2}, 1\right)$ since $1 = 2\left(\frac{1}{2}\right)$ and $1 = 1$, so they are not parallel.

H is incorrect because if $m = \frac{1}{2}$, then the two lines are $y = 2x$ and $y = \frac{1}{2}x + 1$. These lines intersect at the point $\left(\frac{2}{3}, \frac{4}{3}\right)$ since $\frac{4}{3} = 2\left(\frac{2}{3}\right)$ and $\frac{4}{3} = \frac{1}{2}\left(\frac{2}{3}\right) + 1$, so they are not parallel. You might have thought that parallel lines have slopes that are reciprocals of each other.

J is incorrect because if $m = 1$, then the two lines are $y = 2x$ and $y = x + 1$. These lines intersect at the point $(1,2)$ since $2 = 2(1)$ and $2 = 1 + 1$, so they are not parallel.

K is correct, as explained above.

Question 33. The correct answer is D.

Translating from words to symbols gives the inequality $4x + 7 < 19$, so $4x < 12$, and $x < 3$. The set of numbers satisfying $x < 3$ is the set of all numbers that are to the left of 3 on the number line. The number 3 is not included, and an open dot at 3 signifies this.

A is incorrect because, for example, when 4 times 0 is increased by 7, the result, 7, is less than 19, but the graph in this option does not include the number 0. You might have made a sign error and solved the inequality as if it had ≤ instead of <.

B is incorrect because, for example, when 4 times 3 is increased by 7, the result, 19, is not less than 19, but the solid dot at 3 shows that the graph in this option includes the number 3. You might have reversed the meanings of open dots and solid dots.

C is incorrect because, for example, when 4 times 3 is increased by 7, the result, 19, is not less than 19, but the solid dot at 3 shows that the graph in this option includes the number 3. You might have reversed the meanings of open dots and solid dots. Also, for another example, when 4 times 5 is increased by 7, the result, 27, is not less than 19, but the graph in option **C** includes the number 5. You might have solved the inequality as if it had > instead of <.

D is correct, as explained above.

E is incorrect because, for example, when 4 times 5 is increased by 7, the result, 27, is not less than 19, but the graph in this option includes the number 5. You might have solved the inequality as if it had > instead of <.

Question 34. The correct answer is J.

If x apples cost 90 cents, then 1 apple costs $\frac{90}{x}$ cents and 5 apples cost $5\left(\frac{90}{x}\right)$. Similarly, if y oranges cost 68 cents, then 1 orange costs $\frac{68}{y}$ cents and 7 oranges cost $7\left(\frac{68}{y}\right)$. Adding these costs gives $5\left(\frac{90}{x}\right) + 7\left(\frac{68}{y}\right)$, which is the cost of 5 apples and 7 oranges.

F is incorrect. To show this, let's say, for simplicity, that $x = 3$ so 3 apples cost 90 cents, 1 apple costs 30 cents, and 5 apples cost 5(30) or 150 cents. Let's say that $y = 2$ so 2 oranges cost 68 cents, one orange costs 34 cents, and 7 oranges cost 7(34) or 238 cents. The total for all the fruit is $150 + 238$ or 388 cents. But, when $x = 3$ and $y = 2$ are substituted into the expression in option **F,** the result is $\frac{90}{5+3} + \frac{68}{7+2} \approx 11 + 8$ or 19 cents, which is not even close to 388 cents. You might have thought that $5\left(\frac{90}{x}\right)$ is the same as $\frac{90}{5+x}$ and that $7\left(\frac{68}{y}\right)$ is the same as $\frac{68}{7+y}$.

G is incorrect because the expression in option **G** gives the cost, in cents, of 7 apples and 5 oranges. You might have switched the number of apples and oranges.

H is incorrect because if x apples cost 90 cents, then $\frac{x}{90}$ represents the apples that you can buy for 1 cent and $5\left(\frac{x}{90}\right)$ represents the apples that you can buy for 5 cents. Similarly, if y oranges cost 68 cents, then $\frac{y}{68}$ represents the oranges you can buy for 1 cent and $7\left(\frac{y}{68}\right)$ represents the oranges you can buy for 7 cents. The sum of $5\left(\frac{x}{90}\right)$ and $7\left(\frac{y}{68}\right)$ represents the apples and oranges you can buy for 12 cents. That's not what the problem asked for. You might have divided in the wrong order.

J is correct, as explained above.

K is incorrect because it treats 68 cents as the cost of x apples instead of the cost of y oranges and does not use y at all. You may have switched the number of apples and oranges, writing x in both terms instead of writing x in one and y in the other.

Question 35. The correct answer is A.

If you plot the line $y + x = 0$ and the five points, as shown below, it is easy to see that the three that lie on the same side of the line are $(-12,3)$, $(-8,2)$, and $(-3,2)$.

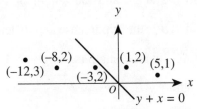

Algebraically, for all points (x,y) in the coordinate plane, either $y = -x$ or $y < -x$ or $y > -x$. The points for which $y = -x$ are on the line $y = -x$ (that is, the line $y + x = 0$) that bisects the second and fourth quadrants; the points for which $y < -x$ are "below" the line; and the points for which $y > -x$ are "above" the line. If you test each of the 5 points that are given, you find that

   $(-12,3)$ is below the line because $3 < -(-12)$ since $3 < 12$;
   $(-8, 2)$ is below the line because $2 < -(-8)$ since $2 < 8$;
   $(-3, 2)$ is below the line because $2 < -(-3)$ since $2 < 3$;
   $(1,2)$ is above the line because $2 > -1$;
   $(5,1)$ is above the line because $1 > -5$.

So the three points that are on the same side of the line are $(-12,3)$, $(-8,2)$, and $(-3,2)$.

A is correct, as explained above.

B is incorrect because, as shown by the graph above, $(1,2)$ is not on the same side of the line as $(-12,3)$ and $(-8,2)$.

C is incorrect because, as shown by the graph above, $(5,1)$ is not on the same side of the line as $(-12,3)$ and $(-3,2)$.

D is incorrect because, as shown by the graph above, $(-12,3)$ is not on the same side of the line as $(1,2)$ and $(5,1)$.

E is incorrect because, as shown by the graph above, $(-3,2)$ is not on the same side of the line as $(1,2)$ and $(5,1)$.

Question 36. The correct answer is H.

To find the cosine of an angle of a right triangle, you need to know the length of the side adjacent to the angle and the length of the hypotenuse of the triangle. In this problem, $\overline{AB}$ is the hypotenuse and its length is given as 3. The side adjacent to $\angle A$ is $\overline{AC}$, but its length is not given. Using the Pythagorean theorem to find the length of $\overline{AC}$ gives $\sqrt{3^2 - 2^2} = \sqrt{5}$. Then, the cosine of $\angle A$ is the ratio of the length of $\overline{AC}$ to the length of $\overline{AB}$, or $\frac{\sqrt{5}}{3}$.

F is incorrect because it gives the tangent of $\angle A$ instead of the cosine.

G is incorrect because it gives the sine of $\angle A$ instead of the cosine.

H is correct, as explained above.

J is incorrect because it gives the cotangent of $\angle A$ (the reciprocal of the tangent of $\angle A$) instead of the cosine.

K is incorrect because it gives the secant of $\angle A$ (the reciprocal of the cosine of $\angle A$) instead of the cosine.

Question 37. The correct answer is A.

In order for the graph of a system of two linear equations to be a single line, their slope-intercept forms must be identical. The first equation is

$18x - 30y = 54$, so $-30y = -18x + 54$, $y = -\dfrac{18}{-30}x + \dfrac{54}{-30}$, and finally

$y = \dfrac{3}{5}x - \dfrac{9}{5}$. The second equation is $6x + ky = 18$, so $ky = -6x + 18$,

$y = -\dfrac{6}{k}x + \dfrac{18}{k}$. Then, $\dfrac{3}{5} = -\dfrac{6}{k}$, $3k = -30$, $k = -10$.

A is correct, as explained above.

B is incorrect because if $k = -6$, then the second equation would be $6x - 6y = 18$. The point $(0,-3)$ satisfies this equation since $6(0) - 6(-3) = 18$, so $(0,-3)$ is on the graph of the second equation. But $(0,-3)$ does not satisfy the first equation because $18(0) - 30(-3) = 90$, not 54, so $(0,-3)$ is not on the graph of the first equation. Therefore, the graphs of the equations cannot be the same line.

C is incorrect because if $k = -\dfrac{1}{3}$, then the second equation would be

$6x - \dfrac{1}{3}y = 18$. The point $(0,-54)$ satisfies this equation since

$6(0) - \dfrac{1}{3}(-54) = 18$, so $(0,-54)$ is on the graph of the second equation. But

$(0,-54)$ does not satisfy the first equation because $18(0) - 30(-54) = 1{,}620$, not 54, so $(0,-54)$ is not on the graph of the first equation. Therefore, the graphs of the equations cannot be the same line.

D is incorrect because if $k = \dfrac{3}{5}$, then the second equation would be

$6x + \dfrac{3}{5}y = 18$. The point $(0,30)$ satisfies this equation since

$6(0) + \dfrac{3}{5}(30) = 18$, so $(0,30)$ is on the graph of the second equation. But $(0,30)$

does not satisfy the first equation because $18(0) - 30(30) = -900$, not 54, so $(0,30)$ is not on the graph of the first equation. Therefore, the graphs of the equations cannot be the same line. You might have found the slope of the line given by the first equation and thought you were finished with the problem.

E is incorrect because if $k = 3$, then the second equation would be $6x + 3y = 18$. The point $(0,6)$ satisfies this equation since $6(0) + 3(6) = 18$, so $(0,6)$ is on the graph of the second equation. But $(0,6)$ does not satisfy the first equation because $18(0) - 30(6) = -180$, not 54, so $(0,6)$ is not on the graph of the first equation. Therefore, the graphs of the equations cannot be the same line.

Question 38. The correct answer is J.

The maximum heart rate (*MHR*) for a 43-year-old person is 220 − 43, or 177. This person's *RHR* is 54. Using the formula *THR* = *RHR* + .65(*MHR* − *RHR*) for this person gives

THR = 54 + .65(177 − 54) = 54 + .65(123) = 54 + 79.95 = 133.95. The answer choice closest to 133.95 is 134.

F is incorrect because 197 ≈ 54 + .65(220) and the calculation using the formula correctly would be 54 + .65[(220 − 43) − 54]. You might have thought the *MHR* was 220 instead of 220 minus the person's age, and you might have neglected to subtract the *RHR* before multiplying by .65.

G is incorrect because 169 ≈ 54 + .65(220 − 43) and the calculation using the formula correctly would be 54 + .65[(220 − 43) − 54]. You might have neglected to subtract the *RHR* before multiplying by .65.

H is incorrect because 162 ≈ 54 + .65(220 − 54) and the calculation using the formula correctly would be 54 + .65[(220 − 43) − 54]. You might have neglected to subtract the person's age from 220 to get the *MHR* before subtracting the *RHR* and multiplying by .65.

J is correct, as explained above.

K is incorrect because 80 ≈ .65[(220 − 43) − 54] and the calculation using the formula correctly would be 54 + .65[(220 − 43) − 54]. You might have neglected to add the *RHR*.

Question 39. The correct answer is D.

If $(a + b)^2 = a^2 + b^2$, then $a^2 + 2ab + b^2 = a^2 + b^2$ and $2ab = 0$. If $2ab = 0$, then $a = 0$ or $b = 0$. Going the other way (since the statement says "if and only if"), there are two parts to the proof:

(1) Assume $a = 0$. Then $(a + b)^2 = (0 + b)^2$ by substitution since $a = 0$
$$= b^2 \text{ since } 0 + b = b$$
$$= 0 + b^2 \text{ since } 0 + b^2 = b^2$$
$$= a^2 + b^2 \text{ since } a^2 = 0 \text{ because } a = 0$$

(2) Assume $b = 0$. Then $(a + b)^2 = (a + 0)^2$ by substitution since $b = 0$
$$= a^2 \text{ since } a + 0 = a$$
$$= a^2 + 0 \text{ since } a^2 + 0 = a^2$$
$$= a^2 + b^2 \text{ since } b^2 = 0 \text{ because } b = 0$$

So, if either $a = 0$ or $b = 0$, then $(a + b)^2 = a^2 + b^2$.

A is incorrect because if, for example, $a = 3$ and $b = 0$, then $(a + b)^2 = (3 + 0)^2 = 3^2 = 9$ and $a^2 + b^2 = 3^2 + 0^2 = 3^2 = 9$ so $(a + b)^2 = a^2 + b^2$ and $a \neq 0$.

B is incorrect because if, for example, $a = 0$ and $b = 3$, then $(a + b)^2 = (0 + 3)^2 = 3^2 = 9$ and $a^2 + b^2 = 0^2 + 3^2 = 3^2 = 9$ so $(a + b)^2 = a^2 + b^2$ and $b \neq 0$.

C is incorrect because if, for example, $a = 0$ and $b = 3$, it is not true that both a and b are 0, and yet $(a + b)^2 = a^2 + b^2$ since $(a + b)^2 = (0 + 3)^2 = 3^2 = 9$ and $a^2 + b^2 = 0^2 + 3^2 = 3^2 = 9$.

D is correct, as explained above.

E is incorrect because if, for example, $a = 1$ and $b = 1$, then a and b have the same sign (both are positive), but $(a + b)^2 = (1 + 1)^2 = 2^2 = 4$ and $a^2 + b^2 = 1^2 + 1^2 = 1 + 1 = 2$ so $(a + b)^2 \neq a^2 + b^2$.

Question 40. The correct answer is H.

An equilateral triangle's 3 angles each measure 60°, so $\triangle ADC$ is a 30°-60°-90° triangle with $\overline{CD}$ $6\sqrt{3}$ units long. For a 30°-60°-90° triangle, if x represents the length of the side opposite the 30° angle, then the lengths of the hypotenuse and the side opposite the 60° angle are $2x$ and $x\sqrt{3}$, respectively. Since $\overline{CD}$, with measure $6\sqrt{3}$, is the side opposite the 60° angle, $x = 6$ and $2x = 2(6) = 12$. The length of the hypotenuse, $\overline{AC}$, is 12 units.

F is incorrect because if $\overline{AC}$ were $3\sqrt{3}$ units long, the hypotenuse of $\triangle ADC$ would be shorter than one of its legs.

G is incorrect because if $\overline{AC}$ were 6 units long, the hypotenuse of $\triangle ADC$ would be shorter than one of its legs. You might have found the length of $\overline{AD}$ instead of the length of $\overline{AC}$.

H is correct, as explained above.

J is incorrect because if $\overline{AC}$ were $12\sqrt{3}$ units long, then by the Pythagorean theorem, $\overline{AD}$ would be $\sqrt{(12\sqrt{3})^2 - (6\sqrt{3})^2} = \sqrt{432 - 108} = 18$, but $18 > 6\sqrt{3}$ and this would mean that the side opposite the 30° angle ($\overline{AD}$) is longer than the side opposite the 60° angle ($\overline{CD}$), which is impossible. You might have thought that $\overline{AD}$ is the side that is $6\sqrt{3}$ units long.

K is incorrect because if $\overline{AC}$ were 36 units long, then by the Pythagorean theorem, $\overline{AD}$ would be $\sqrt{(36)^2 - (6\sqrt{3})^2} = \sqrt{1,296 - 108} \approx 34$, but $34 > 6\sqrt{3}$, which would mean that the side opposite the 30° angle ($\overline{AD}$) is longer than the side opposite the 60° angle ($\overline{CD}$), which is impossible. You might have found the perimeter of $\triangle ADC$ instead of the length of $\overline{AC}$.

Question 41. The correct answer is C.

On the figure below, vertex labels have been added for reference. The perimeter of the figure is the sum of AB, BC, CD, DE, EF, and FA, where AB denotes the length of $\overline{AB}$, BC denotes the length of $\overline{BC}$, and so on. All of these lengths are known except for CD and DE. The sum of CD and EF is the same as AB, so $CD + 15 = 26$ and $CD = 11$. Also, the sum of BC and DE is the same as FA, so $5 + DE = 14$ and $DE = 9$. Finally, the perimeter of the figure is $26 + 5 + 11 + 9 + 15 + 14 = 80$ feet.

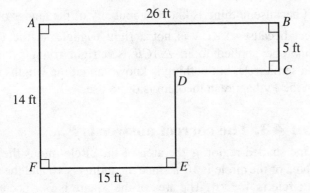

A is incorrect because $60 = 26 + 5 + 15 + 14$ and does not include CD or DE. You might have thought that $\overline{CD}$ and $\overline{DE}$ didn't need to be included in the perimeter because their lengths aren't marked on the figure.

B is incorrect because $75 = 26 + 11 + 9 + 15 + 14$ and does not include the length of $\overline{BC}$. You might have overlooked $\overline{BC}$.

C is correct, as explained above.

D is incorrect because $130 = 26(5)$ and is the area of a rectangle that is 26 feet by 5 feet. You might have confused area and perimeter.

E is incorrect because $364 = 14(26)$ and is the area of a rectangle that is 14 feet by 26 feet. You might have confused area and perimeter.

Question 42. The correct answer is F.

If A and C are points on the circle and M is the center, then both $\overline{MA}$ and $\overline{MC}$ are radii of the circle. All radii of a circle are the same length, so $\overline{MA} \cong \overline{MC}$, and $\triangle MCA$ is isosceles by definition.

F is correct, as explained above.

G is incorrect because nothing is known about any of the angles of $\triangle MCA$.

H is incorrect because nothing is known about any of the angles of $\triangle MCA$.

J is incorrect because nothing is known about any of the angles of $\triangle MCA$.

K is incorrect because $\triangle MCA$ is not a right triangle so the Pythagorean theorem cannot be applied to it. $\triangle ACB$ is a right triangle because it is inscribed in a semicircle, but nothing is known about the lengths of the sides of $\triangle ACB$, so the Pythagorean theorem is of no use.

Question 43. The correct answer is E.

The area of the shaded region is the area of the circle minus the area of the square. The area of the circle is $10^2\pi$ since the radius is 10 and the formula for the area of a circle is $A = \pi r^2$. The area of the square is 2^2 since each side of the square is 2 feet long. The area of the shaded region is then $10^2\pi - 2^2$ (or $\pi 10^2 - 2^2$).

A is incorrect because $\pi(10 - 2^2) = 10\pi - 2^2\pi$; 10π is the circumference of a semicircle with radius 10, not the area of a circle with radius 10. The area of a square of side length 2 feet does not have a factor of π.

B is incorrect because $\pi(10 - 2)^2 = \pi(8^2)$; this is the area of a circle with radius 8 feet, not the area of the shaded region.

C is incorrect because $\pi(10 - 1)^2 = \pi(9^2)$; this is the area of a circle with radius 9 feet, not the area of the shaded region.

D is incorrect because $\pi(10^2) - 2^2$ is the area of a shaded region that results from cutting a square with 1 foot sides from a circle of radius 10 feet.

E is correct, as explained above.

Question 44. The correct answer is H.

From the figure, you can see that $20 = 15\frac{1}{2} + 2w$, so $2w = 20 - 15\frac{1}{2} = 4\frac{1}{2}$. Then $w = 4\frac{1}{2} \div 2 = 2\frac{1}{4}$.

F is incorrect because if $w = 1\frac{1}{8}$ then one outside dimension of the frame would be $1\frac{1}{8} + 15\frac{1}{2} + 1\frac{1}{8} = 17\frac{3}{4}$, but neither of the outside dimensions of the frame is $17\frac{3}{4}$.

G is incorrect because if $w = 2$ then one outside dimension of the frame would be $2 + 15\frac{1}{2} + 2 = 19\frac{1}{2}$, but neither of the outside dimensions of the frame is $19\frac{1}{2}$.

H is correct, as explained above.

J is incorrect because if $w = 2\frac{1}{2}$ then one outside dimension of the frame would be $2\frac{1}{2} + 15\frac{1}{2} + 2\frac{1}{2} = 20\frac{1}{2}$, but neither of the outside dimensions of the frame is $20\frac{1}{2}$. You might have made a computation error in dividing $4\frac{1}{2}$ by 2.

K is incorrect because if $w = 4\frac{1}{2}$ then one outside dimension of the frame would be $4\frac{1}{2} + 15\frac{1}{2} + 4\frac{1}{2} = 24\frac{1}{2}$, but neither of the outside dimensions of the frame is $24\frac{1}{2}$.

Question 45. The correct answer is B.

The length of the floor is 3 feet less than twice the width. If w represents the width of the floor, then the length of the floor is $2w - 3$. The area of a rectangle is its length times its width, so $w(2w - 3)$ is the area of the floor. But the area of the floor is 170 square feet, so $w(2w - 3) = 170$. Then, $2w^2 - 3w - 170 = 0$, $(2w + 17)(w - 10) = 0$, so $2w = -17$, $w = -\dfrac{17}{2}$ or $w - 10 = 0$, $w = 10$. Since the width of the floor cannot be negative, the width is 10 feet.

A is incorrect because if the width of the floor is 8.5 feet, then the length is $2(8.5) - 3 = 14$. But then the area is $14(8.5) = 119$, not 170 square feet. You might have made a sign error.

B is correct, as explained above.

C is incorrect because if the width of the floor is 14 feet, then the length is $2(14) - 3 = 25$. But then the area is $14(25) = 350$, not 170 square feet.

D is incorrect because if the width of the floor is 15 feet, then the length is $2(15) - 3 = 27$. But then the area is $15(27) = 405$, not 170 square feet.

E is incorrect because if the width of the floor is 17 feet, then the length is $2(17) - 3 = 31$. But then the area is $17(31) = 527$, not 170 square feet.

Question 46. The correct answer is F.

If the area of the original square is x^2, then doubling the area gives $2x^2$, but $2x^2 = (\sqrt{2}x)^2$ and so the side of the new square is $\sqrt{2}x$, or the old side length multiplied by $\sqrt{2}$.

F is correct, as explained above.

G is incorrect because if the side length of the original square is x, then its area is x^2, and if the new square has side length $2x$, its area is $(2x)^2 = 4x^2$. The area of the new square is 4 times the area of the old square, not double.

H is incorrect because if the side length of the original square is x, then its area is x^2, and if the new square has side length $4x$, its area is $(4x)^2 = 16x^2$. The area of the new square is 16 times the area of the old square, not double.

J is incorrect because if the side length of the original square is x, then its area is x^2, and if the new square has side length $\sqrt{8}x$, its area is $(\sqrt{8}x)^2 = 8x^2$. The area of the new square is 8 times the area of the old square, not double.

K is incorrect because if the side length of the original square is x, then its area is x^2, and if the new square has side length $8x$, its area is $(8x)^2 = 64x^2$. The area of the new square is 64 times the area of the old square, not double.

Question 47. The correct answer is A.

By definition, $\log_b c = d$ if and only if $b^d = c$. Therefore, $\log_x 81 = 4$ means $x^4 = 81$. Because $81 = 3^4$, $x = 3$.

A is correct, as explained above.

B is incorrect because if $x = 9$, $9^2 = 81$ so $\log_x 81 = \log_9 81 = 2$, not 4.

C is incorrect because if $x = \dfrac{81}{4}$, $\left(\dfrac{81}{4}\right)^1 = \dfrac{81}{4}$ and $\left(\dfrac{81}{4}\right)^2 \approx 410$, and $\dfrac{81}{4} < 81 < 410$, so when $x = \dfrac{81}{4}$, $\log_x 81$ is between 1 and 2 and is not 4.

D is incorrect because if $x = \dfrac{81}{\log 4}$, $\left(\dfrac{81}{\log 4}\right)^0 = 1$ and $\left(\dfrac{81}{\log 4}\right)^1 \approx 135$, and $1 < 81 < 135$, so when $x = \dfrac{81}{\log 4}$, $\log_x 81$ is between 0 and 1 and is not 4.

E is incorrect because if $x = 81^4$, $(81^4)^{\frac{1}{4}} = 81$, so when $x = 81^4$, $\log_x 81 = \dfrac{1}{4}$, not 4.

Question 48. The correct answer is K.

To find the difference of two matrices, $A - B$, you subtract entries in B from corresponding entries in A. Therefore, the entries in the first row of $A - B$ are $2 - (-2) = 4$ and $-4 - 4 = -8$. The entries in the second row are $6 - (-6) = 12$ and $0 - 0 = 0$.

F is incorrect because if $A - B$ were the zero matrix (the matrix with all entries 0), A and B would have to be equal. Matrices are equal when their corresponding entries are equal. A and B are not equal because corresponding entries of A and B have opposite signs. You might have added the matrices instead of subtracting them.

G is incorrect because each entry of $A - B$ should be an entry of A with the corresponding entry of B subtracted from it. Therefore, the first entry of $A - B$ should be $2 - (-2) = 4$, not 1. Since the entries of A are opposite in sign from the entries of B, you may have thought that A and B were inverses of each other, but in that case, their product, not their difference, would be $\begin{bmatrix} 1 & 0 \\ 0 & 1 \end{bmatrix}$.

H is incorrect because each entry of $A - B$ should be an entry of A with the corresponding entry of B subtracted from it. Therefore, the first entry of $A - B$ should be $2 - (-2) = 4$, not 0. You might have added the entries in the first column of B to the corresponding entries of A instead of subtracting.

J is incorrect because each entry of $A - B$ should be an entry of A with the corresponding entry of B subtracted from it. Therefore, the second entry in the first row of $A - B$ should be $-4 - 4 = -8$, not 0. You might have added the second entry in the first column of B to the corresponding entry of A instead of subtracting.

K is correct, as explained above.

Question 49. The correct answer is E.

If $a > b$ and $b < 0$, a could be positive (for example, $4 > -5$) or negative (for example, $-4 > -5$). Likewise, a^2 could be greater than b^2 (for example, $6 > -5$ and $36 = 6^2 > (-5)^2 = 25$) or a^2 could be less than b^2 (for example, $4 > -5$ and $16 = 4^2 < (-5)^2 = 25$). But since the square of a negative number is always positive, $b^2 > 0$ must be true.

A is incorrect because if, for example, $a = -4$ and $b = -5$, then $a > b$ and $b < 0$, but $a \not> 0$.

B is incorrect because if, for example, $a = 4$ and $b = -5$, then $a > b$ and $b < 0$, but $a \not< 0$.

C is incorrect because if, for example, $a = -4$ and $b = -5$, then $a > b$ and $b < 0$, but $a^2 \not> b^2$ because $a^2 = (-4)^2 = 16$, $b^2 = 5^2 = 25$ and $16 \not> 25$.

D is incorrect because if, for example, $a = 6$ and $b = -5$, then $a > b$ and $b < 0$, but $a^2 \not< b^2$ because $a^2 = 6^2 = 36$, $b^2 = 5^2 = 25$ and $36 \not< 25$.

E is correct, as explained above.

Question 50. The correct answer is G.

Since the sides of the given right triangle are in the ratio $1:\sqrt{3}:2$, the sides have length x, $x\sqrt{3}$, and $2x$, for some positive value of x. Since the smallest angle of a triangle is opposite the smallest side, the length of the side opposite the smallest angle is x. The hypotenuse of the triangle is $2x$ since the hypotenuse of a right triangle is the longest side. By definition, the sine of an angle is the length of the side opposite the angle over the length of the hypotenuse, so the sine of the smallest angle of the given triangle is $\frac{x}{2x} = \frac{1}{2}$.

F is incorrect because if the sine of the smallest angle were $\frac{1}{4}$, then the length of the side opposite that angle would be x for some positive value of x, and the length of the hypotenuse would be $4x$. By the Pythagorean theorem, the length of the third side would be $\sqrt{(4x)^2 - x^2} = \sqrt{16x^2 - x^2} = \sqrt{15x^2} = x\sqrt{15}$. The ratio of the lengths of the sides would then be $1:\sqrt{15}:4$, not $1:\sqrt{3}:2$.

G is correct, as explained above.

H is incorrect because if the sine of the smallest angle were $\frac{\sqrt{3}}{2}$, then the length of the side opposite that angle would be $x\sqrt{3}$ for some positive value of x, and the length of the hypotenuse would be $2x$ (and the sine of the angle would be $\frac{x\sqrt{3}}{2x} = \frac{\sqrt{3}}{2}$). By the Pythagorean theorem, the length of the third side would be $\sqrt{(2x)^2 - (x\sqrt{3})^2} = \sqrt{4x^2 - 3x^2} = \sqrt{x^2} = x$. But $x\sqrt{3}$ is the length of the smallest side (since it is opposite the smallest angle) and yet $x\sqrt{3}$ is greater than x. You might have given the cosine of the smallest angle.

J is incorrect because if the sine of the smallest angle were $\frac{\sqrt{3}}{3}$, then the length of the side opposite that angle would be $x\sqrt{3}$ for some positive value of x, and the length of the hypotenuse would be $3x$ (and the sine of the angle would be $\frac{x\sqrt{3}}{3x} = \frac{\sqrt{3}}{3}$). By the Pythagorean theorem, the length of the third side would be $\sqrt{(3x)^2 - (x\sqrt{3})^2} = \sqrt{9x^2 - 3x^2} = \sqrt{6x^2} = \sqrt{6}x$. The ratio of the lengths of the sides would then be $\sqrt{3}:\sqrt{6}:3$, not $1:\sqrt{3}:2$. You might have given the tangent of the smallest angle, not the sine.

K is incorrect because $\sin 90° = 1$ and the smallest angle of a right triangle cannot be a 90° angle. You may have given the length of the smallest side, instead of the sine of the smallest angle.

Question 51. The correct answer is B.

The equation $y + 2 = 3 \sin(4\theta)$ can be written as $y = 3 \sin(4\theta) - 2$. Since $-1 \leq \sin(4\theta) \leq 1$ (values of sine always range from -1 to 1, inclusive), $-3 \leq 3 \sin(4\theta) \leq 3$, and $-5 \leq 3 \sin(4\theta) - 2 \leq 1$, the difference between the maximum and minimum values of $y = 3 \sin(4\theta) - 2$ is $1 - (-5) = 6$. The amplitude is then $\frac{1}{2}(6) = 3$.

A is incorrect because if the amplitude of the graph of $y + 2 = 3 \sin(4\theta)$ were 2, then the difference between the maximum and minimum values of y would be 4. But $-1 \leq \sin(4\theta) \leq 1$, so $-5 \leq 3 \sin(4\theta) - 2 \leq 1$ and $1 - (-5) = 6$, not 4. You might have made a sign error and got 4 instead of 6 as the difference of 1 and -5.

B is correct, as explained above.

C is incorrect because if the amplitude of the graph of $y + 2 = 3 \sin(4\theta)$ were 4, then the difference between the maximum and minimum values of y would be 8. But $-1 \leq \sin(4\theta) \leq 1$, so $-5 \leq 3 \sin(4\theta) - 2 \leq 1$ and $1 - (-5) = 6$, not 8.

D is incorrect because if the amplitude of the graph of $y + 2 = 3 \sin(4\theta)$ were 5, then the difference between the maximum and minimum values of y would be 10. But $-1 \leq \sin(4\theta) \leq 1$, so $-5 \leq 3 \sin(4\theta) - 2 \leq 1$ and $1 - (-5) = 6$, not 10.

E is incorrect because if the amplitude of the graph of $y + 2 = 3 \sin(4\theta)$ were 6, then the difference between the maximum and minimum values of y would be 12. But $-1 \leq \sin(4\theta) \leq 1$, so $-5 \leq 3 \sin(4\theta) - 2 \leq 1$ and $1 - (-5) = 6$, not 12. You might have neglected to divide by 2 as your last step.

Question 52. The correct answer is J.

In 3-dimensional Euclidean space, 2 lines that intersect in more than 2 points cannot be distinct (different) lines because 2 distinct lines can intersect in at most 1 point. Therefore, 2 lines that intersect in more than 1 point are really only 1 line. Since a plane is determined by 3 noncollinear points and 1 line does not contain 3 noncollinear points, 1 line (or 2 lines that intersect in more than 1 point) cannot determine a unique plane.

F is incorrect because a point not on a given line and 2 points from the line are 3 points that are noncollinear and any 3 noncollinear points determine a unique plane. Therefore, 1 line and 1 point not on the line determine a unique plane.

G is incorrect because 1 point on one of the parallel lines and 2 points from the other parallel line are 3 points that are noncollinear and any 3 noncollinear points determine a unique plane. Therefore, 2 distinct parallel lines determine a unique plane.

H is incorrect because 1 point from one of the perpendiculars (as long as it is not the point where the 2 lines intersect) and 2 points from the other are 3 points that are noncollinear and any 3 noncollinear points determine a unique plane. Therefore, 2 intersecting perpendicular lines determine a unique plane.

J is correct, as explained above.

K is incorrect because 3 distinct points not on the same line are 3 points that are noncollinear and any 3 noncollinear points determine a unique plane. Therefore, 3 distinct points not on the same line determine a unique plane.

Question 53. The correct answer is E.

The measure of the vertex angle is $(x - 20)°$ and the measure of each base angle is $(2x + 30)°$, so the sum of the measures of the triangle's angles is $(x - 20)° + 2(2x + 30)°$. The sum of the measures of the angles of a triangle is $180°$, so $(x - 20)° + 2(2x + 30)° = 180°$, $5x + 40 = 180$, $5x = 140$, $x = 28$. Therefore, the base angles are each $(2(28) + 30)° = 86°$.

A is incorrect because if the measure of one base angle were $8°$, then $(2x + 30)° = 8°$, so $2x + 30 = 8$, $2x = -22$, $x = -11$. Then the measure of the vertex angle would be $(x - 20)° = (-11 - 20) = -33°$, which is impossible. You might have given the measure of the vertex angle.

B is incorrect because if the measure of one base angle were $28°$, then $(2x + 30)° = 28°$, so $2x + 30 = 28$, $2x = -2$, $x = -1$. Then the measure of the vertex angle would be $(x - 20)° = (-1 - 20) = -21°$, which is impossible. You might have found the value for x and thought you were finished with the problem.

C is incorrect because if the measure of one base angle were $42\frac{1}{2}°$, then $(2x + 30)° = 42\frac{1}{2}°$, so $2x + 30 = 42\frac{1}{2}$, $2x = 12\frac{1}{2}$, $x = 6\frac{1}{4}$. Then the measure of the vertex angle would be $(x - 20)° = (6\frac{1}{4} - 20) = -13\frac{1}{4}°$, which is impossible.

D is incorrect because if the measure of one base angle were $47\frac{1}{2}°$, then $(2x + 30)° = 47\frac{1}{2}°$, so $2x + 30 = 47\frac{1}{2}$, $2x = 17\frac{1}{2}$, $x = 8\frac{3}{4}$. Then the measure of the vertex angle would be $(x - 20)° = (8\frac{3}{4} - 20) = -11\frac{1}{4}°$, which is impossible.

E is correct, as explained above.

Question 54. The correct answer is H.

Each basket requires $5(8) + 3(16) + 2(10) = 108$ inches of ribbon, which is 3 yards of ribbon since there are 36 inches per yard. Ten baskets require $10(3) = 30$ yards. If the ribbon costs $0.98 per yard, that's about $1.00 per yard, so the 30 yards of ribbon for 10 baskets will cost about $30.

F is incorrect because if the ribbon costs $0.98 per yard, you could buy about 3 yards for $3 and that's enough ribbon for only one basket since each basket takes $5(8) + 3(16) + 2(10) = 108$ inches, or 3 yards of ribbon.

G is incorrect because if the ribbon costs $0.98 per yard, you could buy about 9 yards for $9 and that's enough ribbon for only 3 baskets since each basket takes $5(8) + 3(16) + 2(10) = 108$ inches, or 3 yards of ribbon. You might have divided 108 by 12 instead of 36 and got 9 yards, which, at $0.98 per yard, would cost approximately $9.

H is correct, as explained above.

J is incorrect because if the ribbon costs $0.98 per yard, you could buy about 35 yards for $35 and that's enough ribbon for more than 11 baskets since each basket takes $5(8) + 3(16) + 2(10) = 108$ inches, or 3 yards. Rudy needs ribbon for only 10 baskets.

K is incorrect because if the ribbon costs $0.98 per yard, you could buy about 90 yards for $90 and that's enough ribbon for 30 baskets since each basket takes $5(8) + 3(16) + 2(10) = 108$ inches, or 3 yards. Rudy needs ribbon for only 10 baskets. You might have divided 108 by 12 instead of 36 and got 9 yards, instead of 3 yards, of ribbon for each basket.

Question 55. The correct answer is B.

If the dimensions are l, w, and h, doubling each dimension gives $2l$, $2w$, and $2h$. The surface area of the new figure is
$$2(2l)(2w) + 2(2l)(2h) + 2(2w)(2h) = 8lw + 8lh + 8wh = 4(2lw + 2lh + 2wh),$$
which is 4 times the original surface area.

A is incorrect because if the new surface area were twice the old, then
$$2(2lw + 2lh + 2wh) = 2(2lw) + 2(2lh) + 2(2wh)$$
$$= 2(\sqrt{2}l)(\sqrt{2}w) + 2(\sqrt{2}l)(\sqrt{2}h) + 2(\sqrt{2}w)(\sqrt{2}h),$$
and each dimension has been multiplied by $\sqrt{2}$, not 2.

B is correct, as explained above.

C is incorrect because if the new surface area were 6 times the old, then
$$6(2lw + 2lh + 2wh) = 2(6lw) + 2(6lh) + 2(6wh)$$
$$= 2(\sqrt{6}l)(\sqrt{6}w) + 2(\sqrt{6}l)(\sqrt{6}h) + 2(\sqrt{6}w)(\sqrt{6}h),$$
and each dimension has been multiplied by $\sqrt{6}$, not 2.

D is incorrect because if the new surface area were 8 times the old, then
$$8(2lw + 2lh + 2wh) = 2(8lw) + 2(8lh) + 2(8wh)$$
$$= 2(\sqrt{8}l)(\sqrt{8}w) + 2(\sqrt{8}l)(\sqrt{8}h) + 2(\sqrt{8}w)(\sqrt{8}h),$$
and each dimension has been multiplied by $\sqrt{8}$, not 2. You might have been thinking of the volume of the new figure, which will be 8 times greater than the volume of the original figure.

E is incorrect because if the new surface area were 24 times the old, then
$$24(2lw + 2lh + 2wh) = 2(24lw) + 2(24lh) + 2(24wh)$$
$$= 2(\sqrt{24}l)(\sqrt{24}w) + 2(\sqrt{24}l)(\sqrt{24}h) + 2(\sqrt{24}w)(\sqrt{24}h),$$
and each dimension has been multiplied by $\sqrt{24}$, not 2.

Question 56. The correct answer is K.

If the average of 5 integers is 16, then the sum of the 5 integers is 5(16) = 80. If the average of 6 integers is 18, then the sum of the 6 integers is 6(18) = 108. The sum of the 6 integers is 28 more than the sum of the 5 integers (108 – 80, or 28), so the sixth integer is 28.

F is incorrect because if the sixth number were 18, then the sum of the 6 integers would be the sum of the first 5 integers, 5(16), plus 18, or 5(16) + 18 = 80 + 18 = 98. Then the average of the 6 integers would be $\frac{98}{6}$ or $16\frac{1}{3}$, not 18.

G is incorrect because if the sixth number were 20, then the sum of the 6 integers would be the sum of the first 5 integers, 5(16), plus 20, or 5(16) + 20 = 80 + 20 = 100. Then the average of the 6 integers would be $\frac{100}{6}$ or $16\frac{2}{3}$, not 18.

H is incorrect because if the sixth number were 21, then the sum of the 6 integers would be the sum of the first 5 integers, 5(16), plus 21, or 5(16) + 21 = 80 + 21 = 101. Then the average of the 6 integers would be $\frac{101}{6}$ or $16\frac{5}{6}$, not 18.

J is incorrect because if the sixth number were 24, then the sum of the 6 integers would be the sum of the first 5 integers, 5(16), plus 24, or 5(16) + 24 = 80 + 24 = 104. Then the average of the 6 integers would be $\frac{104}{6}$ or $17\frac{1}{3}$, not 18.

K is correct, as explained above.

Question 57. The correct answer is C.

The length of the major axis of the ellipse is 8 (that is, $2\sqrt{16}$), the length of the minor axis is 6 (that is, $2\sqrt{9}$), and the center of the ellipse is (1,–3). Since a circle inscribed in the ellipse must be contained completely within the ellipse and touch the ellipse in as many points as possible, the center of the circle must be (1,–3), the same as the center of the ellipse, and the diameter of the circle must be the same length as the minor axis, which is 6. Therefore the radius of the largest circle that can be inscribed in an ellipse is 3. The equation is $(x - 1)^2 + (y + 3)^2 = 3^2$ or $(x - 1)^2 + (y + 3)^2 = 9$.

A is incorrect because the radius of this circle is $\sqrt{144} = 12$ and the diameter is 24, so this circle has a diameter that is larger than the major axis of the ellipse, and the ellipse will be completely contained inside the circle.

B is incorrect because the radius of this circle is $\sqrt{16} = 4$ and the diameter is 8, so this circle has a diameter that is the same length as the major axis of the ellipse and the ellipse will be inside the circle, touching it at (1,1) and (1,–7).

C is correct, as explained above.

D is incorrect because this circle and the ellipse intersect at two points. The point (1,1) is on the ellipse (because $\frac{(1 - 1)^2}{9} + \frac{(1 + 3)^2}{16} = 0 + \frac{16}{16} = 1$) and inside the circle (because $1^2 + 1^2 < 16$), but (1,–7) is on the ellipse (because $\frac{(1 - 1)^2}{9} + \frac{(-7 + 3)^2}{16} = 0 + \frac{16}{16} = 1$) and outside the circle (because $1^2 + (-7)^2 > 16$). So in tracing the ellipse from (1,1) to (1,–7) and back to (1,1) you go from inside the circle to outside the circle and back to inside the circle, thus crossing the circle twice.

E is incorrect because this circle and the ellipse intersect at two points. The point (1,1) is on the ellipse (because $\frac{(1 - 1)^2}{9} + \frac{(1 + 3)^2}{16} = 0 + \frac{16}{16} = 1$) and inside the circle (because $1^2 + 1^2 < 9$), but (1,–7) is on the ellipse (because $\frac{(1 - 1)^2}{9} + \frac{(-7 + 3)^2}{16} = 0 + \frac{16}{16} = 1$) and outside the circle (because $1^2 + (-7)^2 > 9$). So in tracing the ellipse from (1,1) to (1,–7) and back to (1,1) you go from inside the circle to outside the circle and back to inside the circle, thus crossing the circle twice.

Question 58. The correct answer is F.

Assume that $A \neq 0$ because if A were 0, the equation would be $y = 0$, and none of the graphs given is the graph of the x-axis. The graph of $y = Ax^3$ passes through $(0,0)$ (since $A \cdot 0^3 = A \cdot 0 = 0$) and no other point on the x-axis because $y = 0$ only if $x = 0$. The graphs given in options **G** and **K** do not pass through $(0,0)$ and the graph given in option **H** crosses the x-axis at least 3 times. Therefore, options **G, H,** and **K** can be eliminated. From the graph in option **F,** A is negative because there are points on the graph such that $x < 0$ and $y > 0$. But $x^3 < 0$ when $x < 0$, so A must be negative to make Ax^3 positive. If we assume for convenience that A is -1, then some points on $y = Ax^3$ would be $(-3,27)$, $(-2,8)$, $(-1,1)$, $(0,0)$, $(1,-1)$, $(2,-8)$, $(3,-27)$. It seems reasonable that these points are on the graph in option **F.** For the graph in option **J,** A is positive because there are points on the graph such that $x > 0$ and $y > 0$. If we assume, for convenience that $A = 1$, then the graph of $y = x^3$ would contain $(-3,-27)$, $(-2,-8)$, $(-1,-1)$, $(0,0)$, $(1,1)$, $(2,8)$, and $(3,27)$. The y-coordinates of these points seem to be increasing faster than the y-coordinates of the points on the graph of option **J** so this graph doesn't appear to be the graph of $y = Ax^3$. Option **F** must be the graph of $y = Ax^3$.

F is correct, as explained above.

G is incorrect because the graph of $y = Ax^3$ must pass through $(0,0)$ (because if $x = 0$, then $y = 0$), and this graph does not pass through $(0,0)$.

H is incorrect because the graph of $y = Ax^3$ passes through $(0,0)$ (because $A \cdot 0^3 = A \cdot 0 = 0$) and no other point on the x-axis (because $y = 0$ only if $x = 0$). This graph crosses the x-axis at least 3 times.

J is incorrect because for this graph, if we assume, for convenience, that $A = 1$, then the graph of $y = x^3$ would contain $(-3,-27)$, $(-2,-8)$, $(-1,-1)$, $(0,0)$, $(1,1)$, $(2,8)$, and $(3,27)$. The y-coordinates of these points are increasing faster than the y-coordinates of the points on this graph.

K is incorrect because the graph of $y = Ax^3$ must pass through $(0,0)$ (because if $x = 0$, then $y = 0$), and this graph does not pass through $(0,0)$.

Question 59. The correct answer is A.

The equations in slope-intercept form are $y = -x + 3$, $y = x - 3$, and $y = -x + \frac{2}{3}$.

Since $y = -x + 3$ and $y = -x + \frac{2}{3}$ have the same slope, -1, and different intercepts, 3 and $\frac{2}{3}$, respectively, they are distinct parallel lines and never intersect. Since these two lines have 0 points in common, all 3 lines have 0 points in common.

A is correct, as explained above.

B is incorrect because even though it is possible for 3 lines to contain 1 point in common, these 3 lines don't because the first and third lines are parallel and have 0 points in common. In slope-intercept form, they are $y = -x + 3$ and $y = -x + \frac{2}{3}$. They have the same slope, -1, and different intercepts, 3 and $\frac{2}{3}$, respectively, and so they are distinct, parallel lines and never intersect.

C is incorrect because the 3 lines are distinct (they all have different y-intercepts) and it is impossible for 3 distinct lines to intersect in 2 points. Any 2 distinct lines can intersect in at most 1 point and if 2 distinct lines can't have 2 points in common, 3 distinct lines can't either.

D is incorrect because the 3 lines are distinct (they all have different y-intercepts) and it is impossible for 3 distinct lines to intersect in 3 points. Any 2 distinct lines can intersect in at most 1 point and if 2 distinct lines can't have 3 points in common, 3 distinct lines can't either.

E is incorrect because the 3 lines are distinct (they all have different y-intercepts) and it is impossible for 3 distinct lines to intersect in infinitely many points. Any 2 distinct lines can intersect in at most 1 point and if 2 distinct lines can't have infinitely many points in common, 3 distinct lines can't either.

Question 60. The correct answer is G.

In 3 fair coin tosses, there are 8 equally likely outcomes: HHH, HHT, HTH, HTT, THH, THT, TTH, and TTT. Three of these outcomes (HTT, THT, and TTH) contain exactly 2 tails, so the probability of obtaining exactly 2 tails is $\frac{3}{8}$.

F is incorrect because in 3 fair coin tosses, there are 8 equally likely outcomes (HHH, HHT, HTH, HTT, THH, THT, TTH, and TTT) and 3 of these outcomes (HTT, THT, and TTH) contain exactly 2 tails, so the probability of obtaining exactly 2 tails is $\frac{3}{8}$.

G is correct, as explained above.

H is incorrect because in 3 fair coin tosses, there are 8 equally likely outcomes (HHH, HHT, HTH, HTT, THH, THT, TTH, and TTT) and 3 of these outcomes (HTT, THT, and TTH) contain exactly 2 tails, so the probability of obtaining exactly 2 tails is $\frac{3}{8}$. You might have been thinking of the probability of getting a tail on 1 fair coin toss because that probability is $\frac{1}{2}$.

J is incorrect because in 3 fair coin tosses, there are 8 equally likely outcomes (HHH, HHT, HTH, HTT, THH, THT, TTH, and TTT) and 3 of these outcomes (HTT, THT, and TTH) contain exactly 2 tails, so the probability of obtaining exactly 2 tails is $\frac{3}{8}$.

K is incorrect because in 3 fair coin tosses, there are 8 equally likely outcomes (HHH, HHT, HTH, HTT, THH, THT, TTH, and TTT) and 3 of these outcomes (HTT, THT, and TTH) contain exactly 2 tails, so the probability of obtaining exactly 2 tails is $\frac{3}{8}$. You might have been thinking of the probability of getting at least 1 tail because that probability is $\frac{7}{8}$.

Passage I

Question 1. The best answer is C.

A is incorrect because Scott is only mentioned in lines 40–41, when Mr. Ramsay says that "Scott (or was it Shakespeare?) would last him his lifetime."

B is incorrect because although Mr. Ramsay is insecure about his work (lines 35–38), the passage does not suggest that anyone finds his work less enjoyable to read than they wish to admit.

C is the best answer because lines 43–47 say that "Minta Doyle . . . said bluffly, absurdly, that she did not believe that any one really enjoyed reading Shakespeare. Mr. Ramsay said grimly that very few people liked it as much as they said they did."

D is incorrect because Tolstoi is mentioned only as an author Paul Rayley read at school (lines 56–57).

Question 2. The best answer is J.

F is incorrect because there is no evidence in the passage that Mrs. Ramsay is ever in danger of being forced to pay attention. Mrs. Ramsay's attention is extremely focused, anyway—so much so that she thinks she can tell what others are feeling and thinking (lines 1–17).

G is incorrect because there is no discussion in the passage of an important change in literature that Mrs. Ramsay's husband must attend to.

H is incorrect because there is no discussion in the passage of what the others think of Mrs. Ramsay or of Mrs. Ramsay being in danger of being seen as vain.

J is the best answer because lines 21–24 say that "She [Mrs. Ramsay] scented danger for her husband. A question like that would lead, almost certainly, to something being said which reminded him [Mr. Ramsay] of his own failure."

Question 3. The best answer is A.

A is the best answer because lines 79–82 describe the beauty of the curves and shadows, the rich colors, and the textures and shapes of the fruit, and lines 83–84 say that every time Mrs. Ramsay looked at the fruit, "she felt more and more serene."

B is incorrect because the passage does not mention whether Mrs. Ramsay has children.

C is incorrect because the passage does not suggest that Mr. Ramsay would get angry if anyone touched the fruit.

D is incorrect because although Paul Rayley asks Mrs. Ramsay "whether she would like a pear" (lines 73–74), in line 75 the passage states that Mrs. Ramsay "did not want a pear."

Question 4. The best answer is F.

F is the best answer because William Bankes is described in lines 25–33 as free of vanity, amused by clothing fashions, and determined to "enjoy what we do enjoy." He does not need to worry about how everything affects him. The "other temperament"—that is, the kind of temperament different from William Bankes—lacks confidence and "must have encouragement" (lines 33–35), but Mr. Bankes doesn't need such constant praise and reassurance.

G is incorrect because Mr. Bankes is described as "free from all such vanity" (line 26). Furthermore, Mr. Bankes is contrasted with the "other tempera- ment," which lacks confidence and "must have encouragement" (lines 33–35).

H is incorrect because Mr. Bankes is described as "free from all such vanity" (line 26).

J is incorrect because although Mr. Bankes is self-confident (see the explana- tion for F), there is no evidence in the passage that he is selfish.

Question 5. The best answer is B.

A is incorrect because "she" (Mrs. Ramsay) is not unsure at all. Rather, she has a heightened awareness of her surroundings, and feels as if she can tell what others are thinking and feeling (lines 1–17).

B is the best answer because in the first paragraph the passage says that "her eyes were so clear that they seemed to go round the table unveiling each of these people, and their thoughts and their feelings, without effort like a light stealing under water" (lines 1–5).

C is incorrect because in the first paragraph, "she" (Mrs. Ramsay) is described as being engrossed in watching and analyzing others. She does not feel as if she is on display herself; rather, Mrs. Ramsay's eyes feel "so clear that they seemed to go round the table unveiling each of these people, and their thoughts and their feelings, without effort like a light stealing under water so that its ripples and the reeds in it and the minnows balancing themselves, and the sudden silent trout are all lit up hanging, trembling" (lines 2–7).

D is incorrect because the Waverley novels are only mentioned once in lines 14–15, and their characters are not mentioned at all.

Question 6. The best answer is J.

F is incorrect because it is not supported by details in the passage. Mrs. Ramsay admires Mr. Bankes' integrity (lines 30–31), but the passage does not suggest that she admires Mr. Ramsay's integrity, or that Mr. Ramsay admires her modesty.

G is incorrect because the passage does not suggest that Mr. and Mrs. Ramsay are bored with each other or that they have children.

H is incorrect. Mrs. Ramsay is described as "keeping guard over the dish of fruit . . . jealously" (lines 76–77), but that does not mean that she is a jealous person—she wanted the arrangement to stay intact so that she could continue to enjoy looking at it. Mrs. Ramsay worries about Mr. Ramsay's reactions to the conversation, which could be described as an unselfish attitude. Mr. Ramsay says something "irritably" (line 41), but that doesn't necessarily mean that he is unhappy.

J is the best answer. Mrs. Ramsay pays a lot of attention to her husband: she is alert to danger to his ego (lines 21–24), and she admires William Bankes' confidence and recognizes that confidence is a trait her husband doesn't possess (lines 33–41). Mrs. Ramsay notes when "it would be all right for the moment anyhow" (line 49) and at that point Mrs. Ramsay considers herself "free now" (line 54), which implies that Mrs. Ramsay feels an obligation to be attentive to Mr. Ramsay's needs.

Question 7. The best answer is C.

A is incorrect because when the passage says that "Charles Tansley would put them both right in a second about books" (lines 63–65) it suggests that he is intelligent, at least where books are concerned.

B is incorrect because in lines 65–67 the passage says that Charles Tansley's main concern is whether he's said the right thing or made a good impression, neither of which are indications of modesty.

C is the best answer because lines 65–67 say that Charles Tansley's main concern is whether he says the right thing and makes a good impression, both of which indicate an absorption with himself rather than with others.

D is incorrect because the passage does not suggest that Charles Tansley is forgetful.

Question 8. The best answer is J.

F is incorrect because the statement "His integrity seemed to Mrs. Ramsay quite admirable" (lines 30–31) follows a description of William Bankes, not Mr. Ramsay.

G is incorrect because the statement "His integrity seemed to Mrs. Ramsay quite admirable" (lines 30–31) follows a description of William Bankes, not Mr. Rayley.

H is incorrect because the statement "His integrity seemed to Mrs. Ramsay quite admirable" (lines 30–31) follows a description of William Bankes, not Minta Doyle.

J is the best answer because the statement "His integrity seemed to Mrs. Ramsay quite admirable" (lines 30–31) follows a description of William Bankes.

Question 9. The best answer is A.

A is the best answer because the passage says the following about Paul Rayley: "Like all stupid people, he had . . . a consideration for what you were feeling, which, once in a way at least, she [Mrs. Ramsay] found attractive" (lines 69–72).

B is incorrect because the passage doesn't suggest that Mrs. Ramsay thinks of Paul Rayley as vain. Rather, "he had a kind of modesty . . . she found attractive" (lines 69–72). Rayley is not seen as intellectual by Mrs. Ramsay, either: she compares him to "all stupid people" (line 69).

C is incorrect because although Paul Rayley is described as having "a kind of modesty" (line 70), he is described as being "Like all stupid people" (line 69), not as being smart.

D is incorrect. Paul Rayley is described as having "a kind of modesty" (line 70) and as being unconcerned with making a good impression: he is described as talking "about the thing, simply, not himself, nothing else" (lines 68–69).

Question 10. The best answer is F.

F is the best answer because throughout the passage, Mrs. Ramsay is described as analyzing her husband and the people speaking. She says nothing and merely listens to others' conversation, remaining detached from the social occasion.

G is incorrect because the passage does not describe Mrs. Ramsay as being frightened at any time. Mr. Ramsay, not Mrs. Ramsay, is described as feeling uneasy (lines 38–39 say that "He showed his uneasiness quite clearly now. . . .").

H is incorrect because the passage describes Mrs. Ramsay as observing and not speaking, not as giddy. The passage doesn't mention whether she is happy or unhappy.

J is incorrect because Mrs. Ramsay is not described as being irritable or insecure. Mr. Ramsay is described as insecure, however: in lines 34–35 he is described as needing praise and encouragement, which are signs of insecurity.

Passage II

Question 11. The best answer is B.

A is incorrect because the last paragraph does not mention scholarly endeavors.

B is the best answer because the last paragraph says that "The society we have simply won't survive without the values of tolerance" (lines 64–65). The paragraph further states that America must be "responsive to the long-silenced cultures of color" (lines 69–70), which is another plea for tolerance.

C is incorrect because the last paragraph does not mention a need for less idealism. In fact, it calls for more idealism—it says, in its last sentence, that "If we relinquish the ideal of America as a plural nation, we've abandoned the very experiment that America represents." The *if* in this sentence makes it clear that the author believes that America has not relinquished "the ideal of America as a plural nation." In the last paragraph, the author calls for America to live up to "the ideal of America as a plural nation."

D is incorrect because the last paragraph does not mention a need for America to be more experimental. The author does refer to "the experiment that America represents" in the last sentence of the last paragraph, however.

Question 12. The best answer is G.

F is incorrect because the author does not think that Mayor Dinkins's metaphor suggests that each culture in America "should probably be blended together," but rather that it suggests that the cultures exist separately from one another (see the explanation for **G**).

G is the best answer. The author says that "Mayor Dinkins's metaphor about New York as a 'gorgeous mosaic' is catchy but unhelpful, if it means that each culture is fixed in place and separated by grout" (lines 24–27). A mosaic is a design made by setting pieces of material of varied colors in a design; the pieces of material are sometimes held in place using grout, a kind of mortar. So, the author finds Mayor Dinkins's metaphor unhelpful because it suggests that each piece of the mosaic—each culture—exists separately, separated from the others as if by grout.

H is incorrect because the author does not think that Mayor Dinkins's metaphor suggests that each culture in America "seems to embody cultural pluralism," but rather that it suggests that each culture exists separately (see the explanation for **G** above).

J is incorrect because Mayor Dinkins's metaphor does not suggest that each culture in America "attacks the concept of ethnic chauvinism," but rather that each culture in America exists separately from one another (see the explanation for **G**).

Question 13. The best answer is C.

A is incorrect because in lines 41–43 the author says that "Unfortunately, as history has taught us, an Anglo-American regional culture has too often masked itself as universal, . . ."

B is incorrect because the author does not say anything about "a few liberal pluralists" defining "our" culture. The author does mention "liberal pluralists" in the sentence that begins "The liberal pluralist . . ." (lines 16–19).

C is the best answer because in lines 27–29 the author says, "Perhaps we should try to think of American culture as a conversation among different voices." And in lines 46–48 the author suggests we should explore the complexities of our different cultural perspectives to discover "a genuinely common American culture."

D is incorrect because the author does not propose anywhere in the passage that scholars and educators should decide what counts as part of "our" culture. In the fifth paragraph (lines 52–63), the author does discuss a function of schools in our society: "fashioning and refashioning of a democratic polity."

Question 14. The best answer is G.

F is incorrect because *inception* cannot be used to mean "politics."

G is the best answer because *inception* can be used to mean "beginnings."

H is incorrect because *inception* cannot be used to mean "idealism."

J is incorrect because *inception* cannot be used to mean "multiculturalism."

Question 15. The best answer is B.

A is incorrect because the author discusses understanding culture as an invitation into the art of conversation (lines 29–34), not as something to be mastered.

B is the best answer because the author discusses understanding culture as an invitation into the art of conversation (lines 29–34). The author invites us to learn to "recognize the voices," which is best paraphrased as "see the world from new perspectives."

C is incorrect because the author discusses understanding culture as an invitation into the art of conversation (lines 29–34), not as a need to define a regional culture. The author says that "Perhaps we should try to think of American culture as a conversation among different voices" (lines 27–29), and he discusses American culture (line 28), not regional culture, in this paragraph.

D is incorrect because in lines 35–37 the author states that "you don't bracket 90 percent of the world's cultural heritage if you really want to learn about the world."

Question 16. The best answer is F.

F is the best answer because according to the author, "an Anglo-American regional culture has too often masked itself as universal" and depicted other cultures as "parochial" (lines 42–45).

G is incorrect because in lines 42–45 the author states that "an Anglo-American regional culture has too often masked itself as universal, passing itself off as our 'common culture.'" Cultural traditions different from the dominant Anglo-American regional culture would not, therefore, be labeled "typical" by that culture because that culture would consider itself "universal," or typical.

H is incorrect because in lines 42–45 the author states that an Anglo-American regional culture has often called itself universal, "passing itself off as our 'common culture.'" The dominant culture, therefore, looks at itself as universal.

J is incorrect because in lines 42–45 the author states that an Anglo-American regional culture has often called itself universal, "passing itself off as our 'common culture.'" The different cultural traditions would not, therefore, be labeled "multicultural" by the dominant culture.

Question 17. The best answer is D.

A is incorrect because there is no support for this statement anywhere in the passage.

B is incorrect because there is no support for this statement anywhere in the passage.

C is incorrect because there is no support for this statement anywhere in the passage.

D is the best answer because lines 45–49 state, "it's only when we're free to explore the complexities of our hyphenated American culture that we can discover what a genuinely common American culture might actually look like."

Question 18. The best answer is J.

F is incorrect because there is no support for this statement anywhere in the passage.

G is incorrect because there is no support for this statement anywhere in the passage.

H is incorrect because there is no support for this statement anywhere in the passage.

J is the best answer because lines 59–61 state, "that's why the schooling of America has always been a matter of political judgment."

Question 19. The best answer is A.

A is the best answer because the author states that America was founded upon the notion of being "a truly plural nation" (option I): in lines 61–62, the author describes America as "a nation that has theorized itself as plural from its inception." The passage's final sentence also supports option I—it refers to "the ideal of America as a plural nation."

B is incorrect because the "gorgeous mosaic" (option II) is a description of New York that the author says is possibly "unhelpful" as a metaphor for America (line 25). The author does not say that America was founded upon the notion of being a "gorgeous mosaic."

C is incorrect because although option I is correct (see the explanation for **A**), option II is incorrect (see the explanation for **B**).

D is incorrect because option II is incorrect (see the explanation for **B**), as is option III: the author does not say that America was founded upon the notion of being "responsive to the cultures of color," although lines 68–70 suggest that "a truly common public culture" would be "responsive to the long-silenced cultures of color."

Question 20. The best answer is H.

F is incorrect. The passage does not suggest that the cultures described as being "long-silenced" (line 69) have little interest in contributing to American cultural growth. Having little interest in contributing to cultural growth is different from being silenced by outside forces, as the passage implies has happened to "the long-silenced cultures of color" (lines 69–70).

G is incorrect. The passage does not suggest that the cultures described as "long-silenced" (line 69) have deliberately avoided discussing the subject of multiculturalism. Deliberately avoiding the subject of multiculturalism is different from being silenced by outside forces, as the passage implies has happened to "the long-silenced cultures of color" (lines 69–70).

H is the best answer because the passage implies that the "long-silenced cultures of color" (lines 69–70) have not been included in "a truly common public culture" (lines 68–69). (The last paragraph makes clear that the author would like to see "a truly common public culture" that is "responsive to the long-silenced cultures of color.") The "long-silenced" groups had to have been silenced by some force; the passage suggests that the dominant culture ("Anglo-American regional culture," discussed in lines 41–45) has tried to exclude groups.

J is incorrect. The passage does not suggest that the groups described as "long-silenced" rarely felt it necessary to comment on the course of American culture. Not feeling it necessary to comment on the course of culture is different from being deliberately silenced by outside forces, as the passage implies has happened to "the long-silenced cultures of color" (lines 69–70).

Passage III

Question 21. The best answer is C.

A is incorrect because there is no support for this choice in the passage.

B is incorrect because there is no support for this choice in the passage.

C is the best answer because lines 40–42 explain that the sculptures are "particularly vulnerable to the cooling process," when fractures result from power failures or inaccurate settings.

D is incorrect because there is no support for this choice in the passage.

Question 22. The best answer is J.

F is incorrect. The last paragraph explains why CEOs like bronze sculpture less than glass sculpture.

G is incorrect. The passage does not give any information about whether CEOs like geodes. The passage does say that Kallenberger's Osage sculptures "would look at home on the shelves of a Rocky Mountain minerals shop, surrounded by geodes" (lines 18–20).

H is incorrect. The passage does not mention whether CEOs like paintings.

J is the best answer. The last paragraph explains that CEOs prefer glass sculpture over bronze sculpture because the CEOs have "no idea" how the glass sculpture is made.

Question 23. The best answer is B.

A is incorrect because the passage does not mention whether Kallenberger is doing any landscaping around his house.

B is the best answer because as it is used here, *reworks* most nearly means "revises," which implies a contrast between the original entities—the "burnt hills and blasted sky" (lines 16–17)—and their appearance in the finished sculptures, which are made in "the cool medium of glass."

C is incorrect because the passage does not mention how Kallenberger maintains the internal climate in his house and studio.

D is incorrect because the terms "burnt hills" and "blasted sky" (lines 16–17) are used metaphorically to describe a landscape created by a hot, dry climate—they do not refer to the occurrence of fires in the hills. Furthermore, the passage does not mention where Kallenberger gets his glass.

Question 24. The best answer is J.

F is incorrect because the passage does not mention any artist named Osage. Kallenberger lives in the Osage Hills, according to the first paragraph.

G is incorrect because the passage does not specify where Kallenberger gets the crystal he uses.

H is incorrect because the passage does not mention a place named Osage. Kallenberger lives in the Osage Hills near Tulsa, where he moved at the age of one (lines 10–14).

J is the best answer because the second paragraph (lines 18–31) details similarities between Kallenberger's Osage sculptures and the surrounding Osage Hills: the "rugged bottoms" of the sculptures are "peaks and valleys, stained with the colors and vistas of the nearby hills," and the sculptures "seem to have been sliced from the foothills with sky intact."

Question 25. The best answer is A.

A is the best answer because line 67 identifies the Cuneiform series as "earlier" than the Titanic series.

B is incorrect because line 67 identifies the Cuneiform series as "earlier" than the Titanic series.

C is incorrect because lines 65–66 suggest that Kallenberger sculpted the Titanic series in the mid-eighties (mid-1980s).

D is incorrect because lines 65–66 suggest that Kallenberger sculpted the Titanic series in the mid-eighties (mid-1980s), and the Detroit Invitational exhibition was in 1990 (lines 58–60).

Question 26. The best answer is F.

F is the best answer because the crystal sculptures are described as "melon slices" (line 21) and as containing "peaks and valleys" (line 25). They are not described as having geometric designs.

G is incorrect because in lines 18–20 the passage describes the sculptures as pieces that "would look at home on the shelves of a Rocky Mountain minerals shop," so this option accurately describes the Osage sculptures.

H is incorrect because in lines 16–17 the passage describes the sculptures as looking like reworkings of the burnt Osage Hills, so this option accurately describes the Osage sculptures.

J is incorrect because in lines 25–26 the passage describes the sculptures as "stained with the colors and vistas of the nearby hills" (that is, the Osage Hills), so this option accurately describes the Osage sculptures.

Question 27. The best answer is B.

A is incorrect because in line 2 the word *gasps* is not used in its literal sense—as a type of breath—but as a metaphor (see the explanation for **B**).

B is the best answer because lines 3–4 make clear that the word *gasps* in line 2 refers to the Osage Hills, the end of the Ozarks. (The Osage Hills come just before the Ozarks "collapse onto the Great Plains.")

C is incorrect because lines 3–4 state explicitly that "the gasps are the Osage Hills."

D is incorrect because this option is not supported anywhere in the passage. Furthermore, lines 3–4 state explicitly that "the gasps are the Osage Hills."

Question 28. The best answer is H.

F is incorrect because lines 34–36 say that Kallenberger's background in engineering may be a prerequisite for glass sculpting, so his training clearly has not been a hindrance.

G is incorrect because lines 34–36 say that Kallenberger's background in engineering may be a prerequisite for glass sculpting, so his training clearly has not been insignificant.

H is the best answer because lines 34–36 say that Kallenberger's background in engineering may be a prerequisite for working in glass, so his training clearly has been useful in his work as an artist, sculpting glass.

J is incorrect because although lines 34–36 say that Kallenberger's background in engineering may be a prerequisite for working in glass, the passage does not suggest that his engineering background has been helpful in developing Kallenberger's artistic sensibility.

Question 29. The best answer is C.

A is incorrect. The bottoms of Kallenberger's sculptures are rugged, with peaks and valleys, not smooth (lines 24–25).

B is incorrect because the sculptures are "stained with the colors . . . of the nearby hills" (lines 25–26); the passage never suggests that the sculptures have a quality of "pure white transparency."

C is the best answer because the "refracted landscape of the bottom edge" is the source of the "dazzling" optical effect of the Osage sculptures, as described in lines 72–76.

D is incorrect because the passage does not describe the sculptures as containing any brass. In the final paragraph, brass sculptures are contrasted with Kallenberger's glass sculptures.

Question 30. The best answer is G.

F is incorrect because the passage does not suggest that Kallenberger's sculptures come from "pieces of natural mineral in the Ozarks" (option I); the passage never says where Kallenberger gets his crystal.

G is the best answer because lines 38–39 describe Kallenberger heating, cooling, and polishing his sculptures (option III).

H is incorrect because option I is incorrect (see the explanation for **F**), and the passage never suggests that Kallenberger's sculptures come from geodes in a Rocky Mountain minerals shop (option II). Lines 18–20 only state that Kallenberger's sculptures "would look at home . . . surrounded by geodes."

J is incorrect because although option III is correct (see the explanation for **G**), options I and II are incorrect (see the explanations for **F** and **H**).

Passage IV

Question 31. The best answer is C.

A is incorrect because there is no evidence that the birds ate either kind of butterfly during the experiment. The birds found both types of butterfly unappetizing (lines 41–42); presumably they did not eat the butterflies in order to avoid becoming ill.

B is incorrect because line 38 says that neither species of butterfly in Ritland and Brower's study had wings still attached.

C is the best answer because lines 41–42 indicate that in Ritland and Brower's experiment the birds found both species unappetizing.

D is incorrect because lines 41–42 indicate that in Ritland and Brower's experiment the birds ate neither the viceroys nor the monarchs.

Question 32. The best answer is G.

F is incorrect because viceroy caterpillars do not feed on milkweed (option I); they feed on nontoxic willows (lines 77–78).

G is the best answer because lines 77–78 state explicitly that viceroy caterpillars feed on nontoxic willows (option II).

H is incorrect because although option II is correct (lines 77–78 state that viceroy caterpillars feed on nontoxic willows), option I is incorrect: viceroy caterpillars do not feed on milkweed (see the explanation for **F**).

J is incorrect because option I is incorrect (see the explanation for **F**), and so is option III: "mildly toxic willows" are not mentioned in the passage.

Question 33. The best answer is A.

A is the best answer because the use of whole butterflies instead of those with wings removed meant that the birds could have rejected the butterflies because of their color rather than their taste (lines 49–55).

B is incorrect because lines 47–48 explain that it was widely believed that the viceroy was palatable.

C is incorrect because lines 49–55 imply that the experiments previous to Ritland and Brower's experiment used both species of butterfly with wings attached.

D is incorrect because the passage does not suggest that the mistaken belief, though widely held, figured as a flaw in the experiments that preceded Ritland and Brower's.

Question 34. The best answer is H.

F is incorrect because it is the variety of milkweed that is crucial, not the amount ingested, as explained in lines 69–76.

G is incorrect because the monarch's chemical defense derives from the plants it eats as a caterpillar (lines 62–64).

H is the best answer because, as lines 69–76 explain, it is the toxicity of the variety of milkweed ingested that affects the toxicity of the individual monarch butterfly.

J is incorrect because the color of the monarch's wings is an indication (to birds) that the monarchs are toxic; the wing color does not cause monarchs to be toxic. The monarch's chemical defense derives from the plants it eats as a caterpillar (lines 62–64).

Question 35. The best answer is B.

A is incorrect because the passage explains that scientists were content to assume that viceroys were not toxic because they came from a family of palatable butterflies (lines 45–48).

B is the best answer because lines 77–81 imply that this question continues to perplex scientists, who now suspect that viceroys somehow manufacture their own toxins.

C is incorrect because the passage explains that some adult monarchs are more poisonous because they ate more toxic varieties of milkweed as caterpillars (lines 69–76).

D is incorrect because the second paragraph (lines 3–6) explains that birds learn which varieties of butterfly to avoid eating by recalling past ill effects of eating toxic butterflies.

Question 36. The best answer is H.

F is incorrect because lines 75–76 explain that a toxic monarch is "potentially deadly" to the bird that eats it.

G is incorrect because lines 62–68 explain that the heart toxins ingested by monarchs can "really set a bird's heart jumping."

H is the best answer because lines 75–76 explain that if the bird vomits the butterfly, it will not be poisoned.

J is incorrect because the second paragraph (lines 3–6) explains that birds that eat toxic butterflies become ill and vomit the butterflies; they do not die.

Question 37. The best answer is A.

A is the best answer because it accurately portrays the two types of mimicry. Lines 84–89 support the description of Mullerian mimicry, and lines 25–30 support the description of Batesian mimicry.

B is incorrect because it reverses the definitions of Batesian mimicry (described in lines 25–30) and Mullerian mimicry (described in lines 84–89).

C is incorrect because it fails to use the correct definitions of the two theories and instead invents two definitions.

D is incorrect because it introduces the idea of actual tasting as a requirement for the theories: the actual tasting preceded the formation of the theories and serves to supplement information for future theories. The mimicry that exists can work without any actual tasting going on because the mimicry causes certain behaviors in the birds—that is, avoidance of the butterflies rather than sampling of them.

Question 38. The best answer is J.

F is incorrect because according to the Mullerian theory, if two butterfly species evolve the same color pattern, only half as many butterflies of each species need to die before a bird learns not to eat them, so both monarchs (option II) and viceroys (option III) benefit from this scheme.

G is incorrect because according to the Mullerian theory, if two butterfly species evolve the same color pattern, only half as many butterflies of each species need to die before a bird learns not to eat them, so both monarchs (option II) and viceroys (option III) benefit from this scheme.

H is incorrect because the passage identifies admiral butterflies as tasty (lines 46–47).

J is the best answer because according to the Mullerian theory, if two butterfly species evolve the same color pattern, only half as many butterflies of each species need to die before a bird learns not to eat them, so both monarchs (option II) and viceroys (option III) benefit from this scheme.

Question 39. The best answer is A.

A is the best answer, as stated in lines 56–60.

B is incorrect because paragraph 13 (lines 56–61) makes clear that until recently, many biologists thought that butterflies couldn't manufacture toxic chemicals but rather had to absorb toxins from poisonous plants in order to become toxic.

C is incorrect because mimicry does not necessarily prevent a species from being toxic, as demonstrated by the case of viceroy butterflies, which resemble toxic monarch butterflies and may themselves be toxic.

D is incorrect because viceroy caterpillars feed on nontoxic willows, according to lines 77–78.

Question 40. The best answer is J.

F is incorrect because viceroys belong to the admiral butterfly family, according to lines 46–47. There is no claim made that viceroys and monarchs are closely related.

G is incorrect because the passage does not imply that diet affects wing coloring.

H is incorrect because mimicry involving one tasty and one distasteful species is the essence of Batesian mimicry, not Mullerian mimicry.

J is the best answer because it paraphrases the information in paragraph 11 (lines 45–48).

Passage I

Question 1. The correct answer is D.

The answer to this question is the figure that correctly plots the values given in column 11 of Table 1 (iron in mg/L, for Outlet 2).

A is incorrect because the values for Days 1 and 2 are much too high. They are closer to 20 mg/L than to 5.0 mg/L and 5.2 mg/L, the values given in Table 1.

B is incorrect because the values for Days 4 and 5 are much too high. They are both above 20 mg/L, and the values in Table 1 are approximately 10 mg/L and 7 mg/L.

C is incorrect because the values for Days 1 and 4 are far too high (both are 25 mg/L instead of 5 mg/L and 10 mg/L), and the value for Day 3 is too low (about 5 mg/L instead of 22.7 mg/L).

D is correct because all figure values correspond to those in Table 1.

Question 2. The correct answer is G.

Day 3 differs from other days in amount of rainfall. Manganese levels remain the same at all three measured areas when precipitation is 0. However, on the two days that rain occurred (Days 3 and 4), manganese levels decreased from the inlet to Outlet 1 and then to Outlet 2. The day with the most rain (Day 3) shows the greatest decrease, suggesting that dilution with rainwater was the cause.

F is incorrect because if plant use were causing the decrease, it would occur on all days, not just on Days 3 and 4, as explained above.

G is correct, as explained above.

H is incorrect because if manganese could not be dissolved in water, the values of all measurements would be 0.

J is incorrect because if manganese were no longer seeping from the coal mine site, manganese levels would not be so high after Day 3.

Question 3. The correct answer is A.

To answer this question, you must compare values of flow rates of Outlets 1 and 2 (given in columns 4 and 5 of Table 1). Heavy precipitation occurred on Day 3, so Day 3 should be compared against the other days in those columns.

A is correct. Values for Day 3 at both outlets are much higher than those for Days 1, 2, and 5 (days with no precipitation).

B is incorrect. The values for Day 3 are higher than those for days with no precipitation, indicating an increased, not decreased, flow rate.

C is incorrect. Flow rates did change; they are different for Day 3 than for the other days.

D is incorrect. The flow rates on Day 4, the day after the heavy precipitation, are not equal to the flow rates on Day 2 (190 vs. 95; 250 vs. 90).

Question 4. The correct answer is H.

To show contamination, values for Outlet 2 from Table 1 must be as follows (based on values in Table 2): pH < 6.0 (more acidic), iron > 3.5 mg/L, manganese > 2.0 mg/L. Values for pH at Outlet 2 are higher than 6.0 every day except Day 1, so the water is not contaminated with respect to pH. However, values for iron and manganese are both higher than allowed levels every day.

F is incorrect because both iron and manganese are higher than allowed levels.

G is incorrect because both iron and manganese are higher than allowed levels.

H is correct because both iron and manganese levels show contamination, but pH does not.

J is incorrect because manganese shows contamination, but pH does not.

Question 5. The correct answer is A.

The allowed level of contamination for iron is 3.5 mg/L. According to the iron values in Table 1, the first marsh reduces iron levels from 100 mg/L to 50 mg/L, and the second marsh reduces iron levels from 50 mg/L to 5.2 mg/L (values are for Day 1; values for the other days are similar). Because the two marshes reduce the iron so drastically, it is likely that adding a third marsh would reduce iron levels even further, to below the contaminated range.

A is correct, as explained above.

B is incorrect because if the second marsh were removed entirely, iron levels would not drop from 50 to 5.2 and they certainly would not drop below contaminated levels.

C is incorrect because if the marshes were removed entirely, iron levels would not drop but would remain the same as in the inlet.

D is incorrect because rerouting the stream would have no effect. The presence or absence of marshes, not the position of the stream, determines the iron levels.

Passage II

Question 6. The correct answer is G.

To determine the correct answer, you must find the four natural indicators in column 1 of Table 1 and compare the values for each in column 3 (initial pH) and column 8 (final pH).

F is incorrect because the difference between a pH of 9.0 and a pH of 6.0 is 3.0, which is a smaller difference than **G** and **H**.

G is correct because the difference between a pH of 11.0 and a pH of 5.0 is 6.0, which is the greatest difference of the four choices.

H is incorrect because the difference between a pH of 10.0 and a pH of 6.0 is 4.0, which is a smaller difference than option **G**.

J is incorrect because the difference between a pH of 8.5 and a pH of 5.5 is 3.0, which is a smaller difference than options **G** and **H**.

Question 7. The correct answer is C.

This answer is obtained by comparing the locations of the four options on Figure 1. The option closest to the left end (the direction of increasing acidity) is the correct answer.

A is incorrect because this is the closest to the right end (pH > 13), and is therefore the most basic.

B is incorrect because this is still on the basic end of the scale (pH = 9) and is less acidic than **C** and **D**.

C is correct because of the four options, it is the furthest left on the scale (pH = 2), and therefore is the most acidic.

D is incorrect because although it is on the acidic end of the scale (pH = 5), it is less acidic than **C**.

Question 8. The correct answer is G.

In the passage you are given the information that, during titration, an acid is added to a base. Comparing results from Table 1, initial pH (column 3) compared to final pH (column 8) shows that pH decreases in all cases.

F is incorrect because the final pH is lower in all cases, but acids, not bases, were added.

G is correct because the final pH is lower in all cases, and acids were added.

H is incorrect because the pH is higher before the titration, but not because of the addition of an acid, which would lower the pH.

J is incorrect because the initial pH of the solution is higher, but this is due to the presence of the base, not the indicator.

Question 9. The correct answer is B.

If a base were added to an acid, the pH would go from lower to higher (the solution would become more basic), which is the opposite of what happens in Table 1. The color change is based on the change in pH, so this also would be reversed.

A is incorrect because the pH does change in the opposite direction, but the color change does not stay the same. If pH reverses, color change also does.

B is correct because the pH and the color change would both be reversed since the color change is based on the pH.

C is incorrect because the pH would not change in the same direction; it would go from low to high (acidic to basic) rather than the opposite.

D is incorrect because neither pH nor color change would stay the same, but both would be reversed.

Question 10. The correct answer is H.

The color change in the indicator is how we determine when the final pH has been reached. So the answer is obtained by determining which of the four options is associated with the lowest, or most acidic, pH (see column 8).

F is incorrect because the final pH is 6.5, which is the highest of the four options and therefore the least acidic.

G is incorrect because the final pH is 5.5, which is higher (less acidic) than **H** and **J.**

H is correct because the final pH is 4.0, which is the lowest of the four options.

J is incorrect because the final pH is 5.0, which is higher (less acidic) than **H.**

Passage III

Question 11. The correct answer is A.

A is correct. Osteoporosis is characterized by a net loss of calcium from bones. Because the Dietary Hypothesis considers only blood levels of calcium, it is necessary to assume that low blood levels of calcium indicate low bone levels of calcium.

B is incorrect. The Dietary Hypothesis does not include estrogen in calcium absorption, only vitamin D.

C is incorrect. High intestinal levels of vitamin D would suggest high, not low, blood levels of calcium because vitamin D is necessary for calcium absorption.

D is incorrect. High blood levels of vitamin D would suggest high, not low, blood levels of calcium because vitamin D is necessary for calcium absorption.

Question 12. The correct answer is H.

The introduction states that osteoporosis is more common in women than in men. In the Estrogen Hypothesis, it is explained that estrogen levels slowly decline in women after menopause, which usually occurs between 45 and 55 years of age.

F is incorrect because osteoporosis is more common in women than in men.

G is incorrect because the Estrogen Hypothesis states that androgen levels in men remain relatively constant throughout life.

H is correct. Osteoporosis is more common in women than in men, and estrogen declines in postmenopausal women (those over 45), thus the lack of estrogen would be expected to result in more osteoporosis in this group.

J is incorrect. Osteoporosis is more common in women over 45 (postmenopausal women) than in those under 45 because estrogen levels decrease after menopause.

Question 13. The correct answer is C.

According to the Estrogen Hypothesis, as estrogen levels decrease after menopause, calcium deposition in bones (and therefore bone levels of calcium) slowly declines. Since the ovaries produce estrogen, surgical removal of the ovaries would artificially induce menopause. The women would stop producing estrogen and their bones would be less able to absorb calcium.

A is incorrect because calcium levels in the bones would decrease, not increase, since estrogen is needed for bone deposition of calcium and no estrogen is being produced.

B is incorrect because removal of the ovaries would result in no estrogen production, and therefore blood estrogen levels would decrease, not increase.

C is correct because loss of estrogen would mean loss of ability to absorb calcium, and bones would therefore gradually lose calcium.

D is incorrect because the Estrogen Hypothesis does not consider vitamin D. Also, vitamin D is ingested, not produced by the ovaries, so vitamin D levels would not be affected by removal of the ovaries.

Question 14. The correct answer is G.

Supporters of the Dietary Hypothesis considered the amounts of both calcium and vitamin D in the diet and found in a study that levels of both were significantly low without daily supplementation.

F is incorrect. In the study supporting the Dietary Hypothesis, individuals were given supplements of 1,500 mg of calcium—three times the amount given in the study supporting the Exercise Hypothesis. The criticism would be that too little, not too much, calcium was given.

G is correct. Since, according to the Dietary Hypothesis, vitamin D is necessary for the absorption of calcium into the blood, it would be essential to measure vitamin D levels to determine if they had an effect on bone density levels. Since vitamin D was not monitored, there is no way to tell if the effects on bone density were due to exercise alone, or if vitamin D might also have been a factor.

H is incorrect. Estrogen effects were not considered in the Dietary Hypothesis.

J is incorrect. This statement is incorrect (it is the opposite of what is true), and therefore it cannot be a valid criticism.

Question 15. The correct answer is C.

The test subjects in the study for the Dietary Hypothesis were 18–25 years old, so their blood levels of both estrogen and androgen were most likely normal. Therefore, the low blood levels were due to dietary factors only, and supplementation increased the blood levels to normal. According to supporters of the Estrogen Hypothesis, if the individuals had been older (for example, women over 45), their estrogen levels would have been low, calcium absorption into bones would have been decreased, and osteoporosis would have resulted in spite of dietary supplementation.

A is incorrect because even though this is true and was known at the outset of the experiment for the Dietary Hypothesis, it would not explain why estrogen was not important in this study.

B is incorrect because supporters of the Estrogen Hypothesis do not consider weight-bearing exercise to be an important factor in the formation of osteoporosis.

C is correct because supporters of the Estrogen Hypothesis would explain that, since estrogen levels are normal in 18–25 year-olds, the only factor causing low blood calcium levels would be dietary.

D is incorrect because supporters of the Estrogen Hypothesis do not consider the effect of vitamin D on calcium absorption.

Question 16. The correct answer is G.

Supporters of the Dietary Hypothesis added daily supplements of 1,500 mg of calcium to the diet to get blood levels of calcium up to normal. In the study supporting the Estrogen Hypothesis, only 500 mg of calcium were added, and no effect of calcium supplements was noted. Supporters of the Dietary Hypothesis would argue that a larger calcium supplementation might have resulted in an increase in bone density.

F is incorrect because vitamin D supplements were not taken by this group, so this option is meaningless.

G is correct because the amount of calcium added was only one-third as much as that added in the Dietary Hypothesis study, so supporters of the Dietary Hypothesis would assume that, if more calcium had been added, increased bone density would have occurred.

H is incorrect because supporters of the Dietary Hypothesis would not expect estrogen to be important in determining bone density.

J is incorrect because no estrogen was added to Group B.

Question 17. The correct answer is D.

A is incorrect because only some subjects in the Estrogen Hypothesis study received estrogen supplements, and none in the Exercise Hypothesis study received them.

B is incorrect because only some subjects in the Estrogen Hypothesis study received calcium supplements, and none of those in the Exercise Hypothesis study received them (they followed a high-calcium diet instead).

C is incorrect because no subjects in either group received vitamin D supplements.

D is correct because descriptions of both studies indicate that only postmenopausal women were tested in these two experiments. In the Exercise Hypothesis study, both men and women were tested, but all the women were postmenopausal.

Passage IV

Question 18. The correct answer is G.

The designs of the two studies are described in the sentences preceding the tables.

F is incorrect because acacia ants were not removed from trees in either study.

G is correct because the plants examined in Study 1 were acacia trees (either with or without ants) and the ants in Study 2 were ants that either inhabited acacia trees or did not.

H is incorrect because the focus of Study 1 was trees, not ants, while in Study 2 both acacia ants and non-acacia ants were studied.

J is incorrect because this response reverses the subjects of the studies. Plant, not ant, characteristics were examined in Study 1, and ant, not plant, characteristics were examined in Study 2.

Question 19. The correct answer is A.

According to Table 1, non-ant acacia trees have bitter-tasting chemicals. They do not have protein bodies, extrafloral nectaries, or specialized hollow thorns.

A is correct because non-ant acacia trees have bitter-tasting chemicals, while ant acacia trees do not. Thus, only non-ant acacias could be protected by the chemicals.

B is incorrect because protein bodies are absent from non-ant acacias.

C is incorrect because extrafloral nectaries are absent from non-ant acacias.

D is incorrect because specialized hollow thorns are absent from non-ant acacias.

Question 20. The correct answer is F.

Because the ground surrounding the ant acacia trees was bare, something must have killed the plants under these trees.

F is correct. Because acacia ants inhabit acacia trees, they would be close enough to kill vegetation surrounding these trees.

G is incorrect. Acacia ants do not inhabit or visit non-ant acacia trees; plus, the ground is bare under ant acacia trees (not non-ant trees).

H is incorrect. The question deals with ant acacia trees, not non-ant acacia trees, and with non-acacia ants, not acacia ants.

J is incorrect. Non-acacia ants do not live in or near ant acacia trees; also, the question refers to killing vegetation surrounding the trees, not to killing the trees themselves.

Question 21. The correct answer is B.

A is incorrect because each species' (acacia ants and non-acacia ants) behavior toward plants was different.

B is correct because some plants (for example, acacia trees) provide shelter for the insects that protect them (acacia ants). This is shown in Experiment 3: when acacia ants were removed from ant trees, 28 of the 38 trees were killed by insects and large mammals. When ants live in the trees, many fewer die.

C is incorrect because the ant acacia trees and the non-ant acacia trees have different species of ants living on them.

D is incorrect because only two species each of plants and insects were studied; there is not enough information in these studies to indicate how often insects are associated with plants.

Question 22. The correct answer is F.

F is correct. Since few leaves were eaten either before or after insects were removed, the leaves were protected, but insects apparently were not responsible for the protection.

G is incorrect because nothing in the question or the passage refers to vines.

H is incorrect because few leaves were eaten from the tree, so there is no evidence for attacks by grazing animals or anything else.

J is incorrect because there is no evidence given that either potential grazers or aggressive insects existed on the tree.

Question 23. The correct answer is D.

Study 1 shows that ant trees have both protein bodies and extrafloral nectaries, while non-ant trees do not. Study 2 shows that acacia ants eat both protein bodies and nectar.

A is incorrect because nothing in the studies refers to grazing animals.

B is incorrect because nothing in the studies refers to grazing animals.

C is incorrect because nothing in the studies refers to grazing animals.

D is correct because this information is given in column 2 of Table 2.

Passage V

Question 24. The correct answer is G.

This answer is obtained by comparing the value for each option in Table 1 vs. its value in Table 2, because the only difference between the two experiments was in the amount of solute used. Table 2 has the conductivity values for the higher solute concentration, so, according to the hypothesis, conductivity values should be higher than those in Table 1.

F is incorrect. The conductivity values for HCl are 5.9 (low solute) and 11.4 (high solute). This increase supports the hypothesis.

G is correct. The conductivity value for $C_{12}H_{22}O_{11}$ in both tables is 0.0, so this substance shows no increase in conductivity and is the exception that does not support the hypothesis.

H is incorrect. The conductivity values for KCl are 2.9 (low solute) and 5.5 (high solute), so this increase supports the hypothesis.

J is incorrect. The conductivity values for $Mg(C_2H_3O_2)_2$ are 2.1 (low solute) and 3.4 (high solute), so this increase supports the hypothesis.

Question 25. The correct answer is C.

Experiments 1 and 2 show that the conductivity of $Mg(C_2H_3O_2)_2$ increases as solute concentration increases. Experiments 2 and 3 show that the conductivity increases as temperature increases. Therefore, the solution at the highest concentration and temperature should have the highest conductivity.

A is incorrect. The concentration is 2 g/200 mL (or 1 g/100 mL), which is lower than the concentration in B and C. The temperature of 5°C is lower than the temperature in C.

B is incorrect. The concentration of 10 g/100 mL is as high as the concentration in C, but the temperature is lower.

C is correct. The concentration of 10 g/100 mL is equal to B and higher than A and D, and the temperature of 15°C is higher than B; therefore, this option has the highest concentration and temperature and would be expected to conduct the most electricity.

D is incorrect. The concentration of 20 g/1000 mL (which equals 2 g/100 mL) is lower than B and C, and the temperature of 2°C is the lowest of the four options; therefore, this solution would conduct the least, not the most, electricity.

Question 26. The correct answer is H.

$C_{12}H_{22}O_{11}$ does not conduct electricity (the ammeter reading equals 0.0 under all conditions); therefore, it will not be a factor in determining the answer. The reading for 10 g of KCl in 100 mL of H_2O at 50°C can be found in Table 3. The conductivity of KCl alone will determine the reading.

F is incorrect. This is the reading for $C_{12}H_{22}O_{11}$, not KCl.

G is incorrect. This is the reading for HCl, not KCl.

H is correct. This is the reading for KCl in Table 3, which fits the conditions given in the question.

J is incorrect. This is a larger reading than would be expected.

Question 27. The correct answer is D.

Based on the results in Tables 2 and 3, when the temperature was increased from 20°C to 50°C, ammeter readings for HCl decreased, while readings for KCl, NaF, and $Mg(C_2H_3O_2)_2$ all increased. It would be reasonable to expect the same trend to continue if the temperature was increased from 50°C to 80°C.

A is incorrect. HCl readings decrease, while the others increase; thus, this option is the opposite of what would be expected.

B is incorrect. None of the readings remained constant during the first temperature change; therefore, they would not be expected to do so in a second change.

C is incorrect; readings would not increase only. HCl decreases in the first temperature change and would be expected to do the same in the second change.

D is correct; this is the pattern that occurred in the first temperature change, as explained above.

Question 28. The correct answer is G.

Water was the solvent in these tests; measuring water by itself (without solutes) in the three experiments served as a control to show how much (if any) of the conductivity was due to the solvent.

F is incorrect. Water was chosen, or known, to be the solvent; it was not necessary to determine whether it was the solvent.

G is correct. The "water-only" tests eliminated the experimental variable (the solute) and thus served as controls to determine the effect of the solvent on conductivity.

H is incorrect. Measuring the conductivity of H_2O alone will not test its ability to dissolve solutes.

J is incorrect. Since the conductivity measured for water was 0.0, the tests showed that it is not a conductor of electricity—the opposite of what this option states.

Question 29. The correct answer is D.

A is incorrect; the effect of temperature on conductivity has already been tested in Experiments 2 and 3.

B is incorrect; solute color is related to the individual chemistry of each solute and therefore would not vary unless the solute varied.

C is incorrect; the effect of water on conductivity has been determined in these experiments by measuring the conductivity of the water alone.

D is correct; testing solvents other than water would give additional information about conductivity.

Passage VI

Question 30. The correct answer is F.

This answer can be obtained by comparing the values for Trials 5–8 in columns 4 and 5.

F is correct because as the momentary length increases from 0.1 to 0.4 m, the momentary weight also increases (from 0.98 to 3.92).

G is incorrect because it is the opposite of the trend shown in columns 4 and 5.

H is incorrect because observation of Table 1 shows that the weight values do not remain constant, but increase.

J is incorrect. The weight values continue to increase; they do not increase and then decrease.

Question 31. The correct answer is D.

From Table 1, you must find the pair of options that shows the same length of chain (column 3), but doubles the mass of the chain (column 2). Then you must check the force on the pan (column 6) to be sure it is doubled when the mass is doubled.

A is incorrect. In both Trials 1 and 4, the chain has a mass of 250 g, so mass is not doubled in this option.

B is incorrect. The chain in Trial 2 has a mass of 250 g, while the chain in Trial 9 has a mass of 750 g. Therefore, mass is tripled, not doubled, in this option.

C is incorrect. The chain in Trial 2 has a mass of 250 g, while the chain in Trial 14 has a mass of 1,000 g. Therefore, mass is quadrupled, not doubled, in this option.

D is correct. The chain in Trial 3 has a mass of 250 g, while the chain in Trial 7 has a mass of 500 g. Thus, the mass is doubled, while the length remains constant at 0.5 m. Force on the pan in Trial 3 is 4.41 N, and in Trial 7 is 8.82 N; thus, doubling the mass exactly doubles the force.

Question 32. The correct answer is J.

In Table 1, the force on the scale pan increases as the mass on the pan increases (compare groups of trials in columns 2 and 6). The last four trials (Trials 11–14) show the effect of increasing total length of the chain from 0.5 m to 2.0 m. Length is shown in column 3, momentary length on the scale pan is shown in column 4, and force on the scale pan is shown in column 6.

F is incorrect; a force in this range would occur at a mass of 250–1,000 g and with a total chain length of 0.5–1.0 m.

G is incorrect; a force in this range would occur at a mass of 1,000 g and with a total chain length of 1.0–1.5 m.

H is incorrect; a force in this range would occur at a mass of 1,000 g and with a total chain length of 1.5–2.0 m.

J is correct. Since the force at a chain length of 2.0 m, a momentary length of 1.5 m, and a mass of 1,000 g is 22.05 N, and since we know that force increases as mass increases, it follows that at a higher mass (1,250 g), with all other factors remaining equal, the force would be greater than 22.05 N.

Question 33. The correct answer is C.

Mass per unit length in this situation would best be measured in g/m. Mass (in g) is found in column 2, and total length (in m) is found in column 3. Since not all of the lengths equal 1 m, the ratios must first be converted so that all denominators equal 1 m, and then compared to determine the largest value.

A is incorrect. For Trials 5–8, the mass per unit length is 500 g/0.5 m (or 1,000 g/m), which is smaller than **B** and **C**.

B is incorrect. For Trial 9, the mass per unit length is 750 g/0.5 m (or 1,500 g/m), which is smaller than **C**.

C is correct. For Trial 11, the mass per unit length is 1,000 g/0.5 m (or 2,000 g/m), which is the largest of the four options.

D is incorrect. For Trial 14, the mass per unit length is 1,000 g/2.0 m (or 500 g/m), which is the smallest of the four options.

Question 34. The correct answer is J.

The length allowed to drop on the scale pan is the momentary length, x (column 4). We can see, by comparing column 4 to column 5 (the momentary weight) for Trials 1–4, that the momentary weight increases by approximately 0.5 N for each increase of 0.1 m in length. Because the momentary weight at 0.4 m is approximately 2.0 N, it would be expected that the momentary weight at 0.5 m (the entire length of chain) would be approximately 2.5 N.

F is incorrect. This is the approximate value when $x = 0.2$ m.

G is incorrect. This is the approximate value when $x = 0.3$ m.

H is incorrect. This is the approximate value when $x = 0.4$ m.

J is correct. This value (although not on the chart) would be about 0.5 m greater than the value for $x = 0.4$ m, or 2.5 N.

Passage VII

Question 35. The correct answer is A.

A is correct. If the dark particles are heavier and fall faster, they will always be found under the light particles. If the light particles are found underneath, this disproves the hypothesis.

B is incorrect. This is what would be expected if the hypothesis is true. Since the dark layer is heavier, it would always fall faster and be under the light layer.

C is incorrect. This would also tend to prove the hypothesis. Since light ash is smaller and therefore weighs less, it would be ejected higher into the air than dark ash would.

D is incorrect. This would help to prove the hypothesis because lighter-weight ash would tend to travel farther than darker (heavier) ash.

Question 36. The correct answer is G.

F is incorrect. No information is given about the size of the samples taken.

G is correct. The ash samples were collected at different locations from the volcano to western Montana. The distances from the volcano are plotted on the horizontal axis in Figure 3.

H is incorrect. Average ash particle diameter was calculated for each site (using the same formula for each site) and was a result, not a variable.

J is incorrect. This factor was not a component of the study.

Question 37. The correct answer is A.

A is correct. Based on Figure 1, the ash mainly settled to the east of the volcano rather than encircling it. The numbered lines showing ash thickness in mm indicate that the thickness was much greater very near the volcano and decreased at more distant sites.

B is incorrect. According to Figure 1, the ash was deposited east of the volcano, but the ash thickness was not uniform. It was thicker nearer to the volcano.

C is incorrect because the ash was deposited to the east of the volcano, not in a circle around it.

D is incorrect, both because the ash was not deposited in a circle around the volcano and because the ash layer was not a constant thickness.

Question 38. The correct answer is J.

By observing the direction of the curve in Figure 3, we can determine whether options I, II, and III are true. Average ash particle size decreased rapidly between 50 and 200 km, so option I is true. There is a slight increase between 325 and 450 km (option II is true), and a slight decrease between 500 and 700 km (option III is true).

F is incorrect because all three options are true, not just option I.

G is incorrect because all three options are true, not just option II.

H is incorrect because all three options are true, not just option III.

J is correct because all three options are true, based on the curve in Figure 3.

Question 39. The correct answer is A.

Ritzville is west of Moscow, and the maximum ash thickness is greater there because it is closer to the origin of the volcanic eruption. According to Figure 1, the maximum ash thickness of this new north-south line would be between 30 and 40 mm (that is, greater than 25 mm).

A is correct, as explained above.

B is incorrect because dark ash was found at the sites near Moscow, and we would expect to find even more near Ritzville, which is closer to the volcano.

C is incorrect because light ash was found at the sites near Moscow, and we would expect to find even more near Ritzville, which is closer to the volcano.

D is incorrect because according to the data at the Moscow sites, the ash is thicker near the central portions, and thins out toward the edges.

Question 40. The correct answer is F.

In Study 2, light ash and dark ash are measured separately. The most abundant type is light ash, which was believed to be formed from fragmentation of molten rock during the eruption. The fact that the light ash is the most abundant supports the interpretation described in the question. Studies 1 and 3 do not distinguish between the two types of ash, therefore they do not provide evidence to support this interpretation.

F is correct, as explained above.

G is incorrect because in Study 3 the ash samples contained particles of both light and dark ash, and therefore no distinction between types of ash can be made.

H is incorrect because although Study 2 supports the interpretation, Study 1 does not. In Study 1, only the depth of ash at various distances from the eruption is measured. No measurements of different types of ash were done.

J is incorrect because although Study 2 supports the interpretation, Study 3 does not. The ash samples in Study 3 contained both light and dark ash particles, so no distinction between types of ash can be made.

You may wish to remove this sample answer sheet from the booklet to use in a practice test session.

ACT Assessment Sample Answer Sheet

SIDE 1

NAME, ADDRESS, AND TELEPHONE (Please print.)

Last Name

First Name

MI (Middle Initial)

House Number and Street

City

State

ZIP Code

Area Code / Number

IDENTIFYING INFORMATION

Instructions for Registered Examinees: Your answer sheet will be matched to your registration record using the information you enter in blocks B, C, and D. Enter the information EXACTLY as it appears on your admission ticket, even if any part of the information is missing or incorrect. Fill in the corresponding ovals. Leave block E blank.

Instructions for Standby Examinees: Enter your identifying information in blocks B, C, and D. Fill in the corresponding ovals. (If you do not have a Social Security Number, leave block C blank.) You must also fill in the Standby Testing oval in block E.

SOCIAL SECURITY NUMBER (OR ACT ID NUMBER)

DATE OF BIRTH

Month Day Year

○ Jan.
○ Feb.
○ Mar.
○ Apr.
○ May
○ June
○ July
○ Aug.
○ Sep.
○ Oct.
○ Nov.
○ Dec.

MATCH NAME (FIRST 5 LETTERS OF LAST NAME)

STANDBY TESTING

Fill in this oval ONLY if you turned in a standby registration folder at the test center. This will help ACT to match your answer sheet to your registration record.

○ Yes, I am testing as a standby examinee.

P.O. BOX 168, IOWA CITY, IOWA 52243-0168

Instructions for Registered Examinees: If the information on your admission ticket is complete and correct, do NOT mark in blocks F, G, H, or I. If any corrections are necessary, complete ONLY the block(s) below for which the information on your admission ticket is INCOMPLETE or INCORRECT. Leave the other blocks blank.

Instructions for Standby Examinees: Do NOT mark in blocks F, G, H, or I.

NAME CORRECTION

Last Name

First Name

MI

HIGH SCHOOL CODE CORRECTION

DATE OF BIRTH CORRECTION

Month Day Year

○ Jan.
○ Feb.
○ Mar.
○ Apr.
○ May
○ June
○ July
○ Aug.
○ Sep.
○ Oct.
○ Nov.
○ Dec.

SOCIAL SECURITY NUMBER CORRECTION

BOOKLET NUMBER

FORM

BE SURE TO FILL IN THE CORRECT FORM OVAL.

① ① ① ① ① ①
② ② ② ② ② ②
③ ③ ③ ③ ③ ③
④ ④ ④ ④ ④ ④
⑤ ⑤ ⑤ ⑤ ⑤ ⑤
⑥ ⑥ ⑥ ⑥ ⑥ ⑥
⑦ ⑦ ⑦ ⑦ ⑦ ⑦
⑧ ⑧ ⑧ ⑧ ⑧ ⑧
⑨ ⑨ ⑨ ⑨ ⑨ ⑨
⓪ ⓪ ⓪ ⓪ ⓪ ⓪

TEST 1

	10 Ⓕ Ⓖ Ⓗ Ⓙ	20 Ⓕ Ⓖ Ⓗ Ⓙ	30 Ⓕ Ⓖ Ⓗ Ⓙ	40 Ⓕ Ⓖ Ⓗ Ⓙ	50 Ⓕ Ⓖ Ⓗ Ⓙ	60 Ⓕ Ⓖ Ⓗ Ⓙ	70 Ⓕ Ⓖ Ⓗ Ⓙ
1 Ⓐ Ⓑ Ⓒ Ⓓ	11 Ⓐ Ⓑ Ⓒ Ⓓ	21 Ⓐ Ⓑ Ⓒ Ⓓ	31 Ⓐ Ⓑ Ⓒ Ⓓ	41 Ⓐ Ⓑ Ⓒ Ⓓ	51 Ⓐ Ⓑ Ⓒ Ⓓ	61 Ⓐ Ⓑ Ⓒ Ⓓ	71 Ⓐ Ⓑ Ⓒ Ⓓ
2 Ⓕ Ⓖ Ⓗ Ⓙ	12 Ⓕ Ⓖ Ⓗ Ⓙ	22 Ⓕ Ⓖ Ⓗ Ⓙ	32 Ⓕ Ⓖ Ⓗ Ⓙ	42 Ⓕ Ⓖ Ⓗ Ⓙ	52 Ⓕ Ⓖ Ⓗ Ⓙ	62 Ⓕ Ⓖ Ⓗ Ⓙ	72 Ⓕ Ⓖ Ⓗ Ⓙ
3 Ⓐ Ⓑ Ⓒ Ⓓ	13 Ⓐ Ⓑ Ⓒ Ⓓ	23 Ⓐ Ⓑ Ⓒ Ⓓ	33 Ⓐ Ⓑ Ⓒ Ⓓ	43 Ⓐ Ⓑ Ⓒ Ⓓ	53 Ⓐ Ⓑ Ⓒ Ⓓ	63 Ⓐ Ⓑ Ⓒ Ⓓ	73 Ⓐ Ⓑ Ⓒ Ⓓ
4 Ⓕ Ⓖ Ⓗ Ⓙ	14 Ⓕ Ⓖ Ⓗ Ⓙ	24 Ⓕ Ⓖ Ⓗ Ⓙ	34 Ⓕ Ⓖ Ⓗ Ⓙ	44 Ⓕ Ⓖ Ⓗ Ⓙ	54 Ⓕ Ⓖ Ⓗ Ⓙ	64 Ⓕ Ⓖ Ⓗ Ⓙ	74 Ⓕ Ⓖ Ⓗ Ⓙ
5 Ⓐ Ⓑ Ⓒ Ⓓ	15 Ⓐ Ⓑ Ⓒ Ⓓ	25 Ⓐ Ⓑ Ⓒ Ⓓ	35 Ⓐ Ⓑ Ⓒ Ⓓ	45 Ⓐ Ⓑ Ⓒ Ⓓ	55 Ⓐ Ⓑ Ⓒ Ⓓ	65 Ⓐ Ⓑ Ⓒ Ⓓ	75 Ⓐ Ⓑ Ⓒ Ⓓ
6 Ⓕ Ⓖ Ⓗ Ⓙ	16 Ⓕ Ⓖ Ⓗ Ⓙ	26 Ⓕ Ⓖ Ⓗ Ⓙ	36 Ⓕ Ⓖ Ⓗ Ⓙ	46 Ⓕ Ⓖ Ⓗ Ⓙ	56 Ⓕ Ⓖ Ⓗ Ⓙ	66 Ⓕ Ⓖ Ⓗ Ⓙ	
7 Ⓐ Ⓑ Ⓒ Ⓓ	17 Ⓐ Ⓑ Ⓒ Ⓓ	27 Ⓐ Ⓑ Ⓒ Ⓓ	37 Ⓐ Ⓑ Ⓒ Ⓓ	47 Ⓐ Ⓑ Ⓒ Ⓓ	57 Ⓐ Ⓑ Ⓒ Ⓓ	67 Ⓐ Ⓑ Ⓒ Ⓓ	
8 Ⓕ Ⓖ Ⓗ Ⓙ	18 Ⓕ Ⓖ Ⓗ Ⓙ	28 Ⓕ Ⓖ Ⓗ Ⓙ	38 Ⓕ Ⓖ Ⓗ Ⓙ	48 Ⓕ Ⓖ Ⓗ Ⓙ	58 Ⓕ Ⓖ Ⓗ Ⓙ	68 Ⓕ Ⓖ Ⓗ Ⓙ	
9 Ⓐ Ⓑ Ⓒ Ⓓ	19 Ⓐ Ⓑ Ⓒ Ⓓ	29 Ⓐ Ⓑ Ⓒ Ⓓ	39 Ⓐ Ⓑ Ⓒ Ⓓ	49 Ⓐ Ⓑ Ⓒ Ⓓ	59 Ⓐ Ⓑ Ⓒ Ⓓ	69 Ⓐ Ⓑ Ⓒ Ⓓ	

TEST 2

	8 Ⓕ Ⓖ Ⓗ Ⓙ Ⓚ	16 Ⓕ Ⓖ Ⓗ Ⓙ Ⓚ	24 Ⓕ Ⓖ Ⓗ Ⓙ Ⓚ	32 Ⓕ Ⓖ Ⓗ Ⓙ Ⓚ	40 Ⓕ Ⓖ Ⓗ Ⓙ Ⓚ	48 Ⓕ Ⓖ Ⓗ Ⓙ Ⓚ	56 Ⓕ Ⓖ Ⓗ Ⓙ Ⓚ
1 Ⓐ Ⓑ Ⓒ Ⓓ Ⓔ	9 Ⓐ Ⓑ Ⓒ Ⓓ Ⓔ	17 Ⓐ Ⓑ Ⓒ Ⓓ Ⓔ	25 Ⓐ Ⓑ Ⓒ Ⓓ Ⓔ	33 Ⓐ Ⓑ Ⓒ Ⓓ Ⓔ	41 Ⓐ Ⓑ Ⓒ Ⓓ Ⓔ	49 Ⓐ Ⓑ Ⓒ Ⓓ Ⓔ	57 Ⓐ Ⓑ Ⓒ Ⓓ Ⓔ
2 Ⓕ Ⓖ Ⓗ Ⓙ Ⓚ	10 Ⓕ Ⓖ Ⓗ Ⓙ Ⓚ	18 Ⓕ Ⓖ Ⓗ Ⓙ Ⓚ	26 Ⓕ Ⓖ Ⓗ Ⓙ Ⓚ	34 Ⓕ Ⓖ Ⓗ Ⓙ Ⓚ	42 Ⓕ Ⓖ Ⓗ Ⓙ Ⓚ	50 Ⓕ Ⓖ Ⓗ Ⓙ Ⓚ	58 Ⓕ Ⓖ Ⓗ Ⓙ Ⓚ
3 Ⓐ Ⓑ Ⓒ Ⓓ Ⓔ	11 Ⓐ Ⓑ Ⓒ Ⓓ Ⓔ	19 Ⓐ Ⓑ Ⓒ Ⓓ Ⓔ	27 Ⓐ Ⓑ Ⓒ Ⓓ Ⓔ	35 Ⓐ Ⓑ Ⓒ Ⓓ Ⓔ	43 Ⓐ Ⓑ Ⓒ Ⓓ Ⓔ	51 Ⓐ Ⓑ Ⓒ Ⓓ Ⓔ	59 Ⓐ Ⓑ Ⓒ Ⓓ Ⓔ
4 Ⓕ Ⓖ Ⓗ Ⓙ Ⓚ	12 Ⓕ Ⓖ Ⓗ Ⓙ Ⓚ	20 Ⓕ Ⓖ Ⓗ Ⓙ Ⓚ	28 Ⓕ Ⓖ Ⓗ Ⓙ Ⓚ	36 Ⓕ Ⓖ Ⓗ Ⓙ Ⓚ	44 Ⓕ Ⓖ Ⓗ Ⓙ Ⓚ	52 Ⓕ Ⓖ Ⓗ Ⓙ Ⓚ	60 Ⓕ Ⓖ Ⓗ Ⓙ Ⓚ
5 Ⓐ Ⓑ Ⓒ Ⓓ Ⓔ	13 Ⓐ Ⓑ Ⓒ Ⓓ Ⓔ	21 Ⓐ Ⓑ Ⓒ Ⓓ Ⓔ	29 Ⓐ Ⓑ Ⓒ Ⓓ Ⓔ	37 Ⓐ Ⓑ Ⓒ Ⓓ Ⓔ	45 Ⓐ Ⓑ Ⓒ Ⓓ Ⓔ	53 Ⓐ Ⓑ Ⓒ Ⓓ Ⓔ	
6 Ⓕ Ⓖ Ⓗ Ⓙ Ⓚ	14 Ⓕ Ⓖ Ⓗ Ⓙ Ⓚ	22 Ⓕ Ⓖ Ⓗ Ⓙ Ⓚ	30 Ⓕ Ⓖ Ⓗ Ⓙ Ⓚ	38 Ⓕ Ⓖ Ⓗ Ⓙ Ⓚ	46 Ⓕ Ⓖ Ⓗ Ⓙ Ⓚ	54 Ⓕ Ⓖ Ⓗ Ⓙ Ⓚ	
7 Ⓐ Ⓑ Ⓒ Ⓓ Ⓔ	15 Ⓐ Ⓑ Ⓒ Ⓓ Ⓔ	23 Ⓐ Ⓑ Ⓒ Ⓓ Ⓔ	31 Ⓐ Ⓑ Ⓒ Ⓓ Ⓔ	39 Ⓐ Ⓑ Ⓒ Ⓓ Ⓔ	47 Ⓐ Ⓑ Ⓒ Ⓓ Ⓔ	55 Ⓐ Ⓑ Ⓒ Ⓓ Ⓔ	

TEST 3

	6 Ⓕ Ⓖ Ⓗ Ⓙ	12 Ⓕ Ⓖ Ⓗ Ⓙ	18 Ⓕ Ⓖ Ⓗ Ⓙ	24 Ⓕ Ⓖ Ⓗ Ⓙ	30 Ⓕ Ⓖ Ⓗ Ⓙ	36 Ⓕ Ⓖ Ⓗ Ⓙ
1 Ⓐ Ⓑ Ⓒ Ⓓ	7 Ⓐ Ⓑ Ⓒ Ⓓ	13 Ⓐ Ⓑ Ⓒ Ⓓ	19 Ⓐ Ⓑ Ⓒ Ⓓ	25 Ⓐ Ⓑ Ⓒ Ⓓ	31 Ⓐ Ⓑ Ⓒ Ⓓ	37 Ⓐ Ⓑ Ⓒ Ⓓ
2 Ⓕ Ⓖ Ⓗ Ⓙ	8 Ⓕ Ⓖ Ⓗ Ⓙ	14 Ⓕ Ⓖ Ⓗ Ⓙ	20 Ⓕ Ⓖ Ⓗ Ⓙ	26 Ⓕ Ⓖ Ⓗ Ⓙ	32 Ⓕ Ⓖ Ⓗ Ⓙ	38 Ⓕ Ⓖ Ⓗ Ⓙ
3 Ⓐ Ⓑ Ⓒ Ⓓ	9 Ⓐ Ⓑ Ⓒ Ⓓ	15 Ⓐ Ⓑ Ⓒ Ⓓ	21 Ⓐ Ⓑ Ⓒ Ⓓ	27 Ⓐ Ⓑ Ⓒ Ⓓ	33 Ⓐ Ⓑ Ⓒ Ⓓ	39 Ⓐ Ⓑ Ⓒ Ⓓ
4 Ⓕ Ⓖ Ⓗ Ⓙ	10 Ⓕ Ⓖ Ⓗ Ⓙ	16 Ⓕ Ⓖ Ⓗ Ⓙ	22 Ⓕ Ⓖ Ⓗ Ⓙ	28 Ⓕ Ⓖ Ⓗ Ⓙ	34 Ⓕ Ⓖ Ⓗ Ⓙ	40 Ⓕ Ⓖ Ⓗ Ⓙ
5 Ⓐ Ⓑ Ⓒ Ⓓ	11 Ⓐ Ⓑ Ⓒ Ⓓ	17 Ⓐ Ⓑ Ⓒ Ⓓ	23 Ⓐ Ⓑ Ⓒ Ⓓ	29 Ⓐ Ⓑ Ⓒ Ⓓ	35 Ⓐ Ⓑ Ⓒ Ⓓ	

TEST 4

	6 Ⓕ Ⓖ Ⓗ Ⓙ	12 Ⓕ Ⓖ Ⓗ Ⓙ	18 Ⓕ Ⓖ Ⓗ Ⓙ	24 Ⓕ Ⓖ Ⓗ Ⓙ	30 Ⓕ Ⓖ Ⓗ Ⓙ	36 Ⓕ Ⓖ Ⓗ Ⓙ
1 Ⓐ Ⓑ Ⓒ Ⓓ	7 Ⓐ Ⓑ Ⓒ Ⓓ	13 Ⓐ Ⓑ Ⓒ Ⓓ	19 Ⓐ Ⓑ Ⓒ Ⓓ	25 Ⓐ Ⓑ Ⓒ Ⓓ	31 Ⓐ Ⓑ Ⓒ Ⓓ	37 Ⓐ Ⓑ Ⓒ Ⓓ
2 Ⓕ Ⓖ Ⓗ Ⓙ	8 Ⓕ Ⓖ Ⓗ Ⓙ	14 Ⓕ Ⓖ Ⓗ Ⓙ	20 Ⓕ Ⓖ Ⓗ Ⓙ	26 Ⓕ Ⓖ Ⓗ Ⓙ	32 Ⓕ Ⓖ Ⓗ Ⓙ	38 Ⓕ Ⓖ Ⓗ Ⓙ
3 Ⓐ Ⓑ Ⓒ Ⓓ	9 Ⓐ Ⓑ Ⓒ Ⓓ	15 Ⓐ Ⓑ Ⓒ Ⓓ	21 Ⓐ Ⓑ Ⓒ Ⓓ	27 Ⓐ Ⓑ Ⓒ Ⓓ	33 Ⓐ Ⓑ Ⓒ Ⓓ	39 Ⓐ Ⓑ Ⓒ Ⓓ
4 Ⓕ Ⓖ Ⓗ Ⓙ	10 Ⓕ Ⓖ Ⓗ Ⓙ	16 Ⓕ Ⓖ Ⓗ Ⓙ	22 Ⓕ Ⓖ Ⓗ Ⓙ	28 Ⓕ Ⓖ Ⓗ Ⓙ	34 Ⓕ Ⓖ Ⓗ Ⓙ	40 Ⓕ Ⓖ Ⓗ Ⓙ
5 Ⓐ Ⓑ Ⓒ Ⓓ	11 Ⓐ Ⓑ Ⓒ Ⓓ	17 Ⓐ Ⓑ Ⓒ Ⓓ	23 Ⓐ Ⓑ Ⓒ Ⓓ	29 Ⓐ Ⓑ Ⓒ Ⓓ	35 Ⓐ Ⓑ Ⓒ Ⓓ	

DO NOT SIGN THIS UNTIL YOU HAVE COMPLETED THIS ENTIRE SECTION.

I hereby certify that I have truthfully identified myself on this form. I understand that the consequences of falsifying my identity include cancellation of my scores.

Your Signature

Today's Date

You may wish to remove this sample answer sheet from the booklet to use in a practice test session.

ACT Assessment *Sample Answer Sheet*

SIDE 1

NAME, ADDRESS, AND TELEPHONE (Please print.)

Last Name   First Name   MI (Middle Initial)

House Number and Street

City   State   ZIP Code

Area Code   Number

IDENTIFYING INFORMATION

Instructions for Registered Examinees: Your answer sheet will be matched to your registration record using the information you enter in blocks B, C, and D. Enter the information EXACTLY as it appears on your admission ticket, even if any part of the information is missing or incorrect. Fill in the corresponding ovals. Leave block E blank.

Instructions for Standby Examinees: Enter your identifying information in blocks B, C, and D. Fill in the corresponding ovals. (If you do not have a Social Security Number, leave block C blank.) You must also fill in the Standby Testing oval in block E.

NAME CORRECTION

Instructions for Registered Examinees: If the information on your admission ticket is complete and correct, do NOT mark in blocks F, G, H, or I. If any corrections are necessary, complete ONLY the block(s) below for which the information on your admission ticket is INCOMPLETE or INCORRECT. Leave the other blocks blank.

Instructions for Standby Examinees: Do NOT mark in blocks F, G, H, or I.

MATCH NAME (FIRST 5 LETTERS OF LAST NAME)

SOCIAL SECURITY NUMBER (OR ACT ID NUMBER)

DATE OF BIRTH
Month   Day   Year
○ Jan.
○ Feb.
○ Mar.
○ Apr.
○ May
○ June
○ July
○ Aug.
○ Sep.
○ Oct.
○ Nov.
○ Dec.

STANDBY TESTING

Fill in this oval ONLY if you turned in a standby registration folder at the test center. This will help ACT to match your answer sheet to your registration record.

○ Yes, I am testing as a standby examinee.

P.O. BOX 168, IOWA CITY, IOWA 52243-0168

Last Name   First Name   MI

HIGH SCHOOL CODE CORRECTION

DATE OF BIRTH CORRECTION
Month   Day   Year
○ Jan.
○ Feb.
○ Mar.
○ Apr.
○ May
○ June
○ July
○ Aug.
○ Sep.
○ Oct.
○ Nov.
○ Dec.

SOCIAL SECURITY NUMBER CORRECTION

527

SIDE 2   BOOKLET NUMBER   FORM   BE SURE TO FILL IN THE CORRECT FORM OVAL.

TEST 1

	10 ⒡⒢⒣⒥	20 ⒡⒢⒣⒥	30 ⒡⒢⒣⒥	40 ⒡⒢⒣⒥	50 ⒡⒢⒣⒥	60 ⒡⒢⒣⒥	70 ⒡⒢⒣⒥
1 ⒜⒝©⒟	11 ⒜⒝©⒟	21 ⒜⒝©⒟	31 ⒜⒝©⒟	41 ⒜⒝©⒟	51 ⒜⒝©⒟	61 ⒜⒝©⒟	71 ⒜⒝©⒟
2 ⒡⒢⒣⒥	12 ⒡⒢⒣⒥	22 ⒡⒢⒣⒥	32 ⒡⒢⒣⒥	42 ⒡⒢⒣⒥	52 ⒡⒢⒣⒥	62 ⒡⒢⒣⒥	72 ⒡⒢⒣⒥
3 ⒜⒝©⒟	13 ⒜⒝©⒟	23 ⒜⒝©⒟	33 ⒜⒝©⒟	43 ⒜⒝©⒟	53 ⒜⒝©⒟	63 ⒜⒝©⒟	73 ⒜⒝©⒟
4 ⒡⒢⒣⒥	14 ⒡⒢⒣⒥	24 ⒡⒢⒣⒥	34 ⒡⒢⒣⒥	44 ⒡⒢⒣⒥	54 ⒡⒢⒣⒥	64 ⒡⒢⒣⒥	74 ⒡⒢⒣⒥
5 ⒜⒝©⒟	15 ⒜⒝©⒟	25 ⒜⒝©⒟	35 ⒜⒝©⒟	45 ⒜⒝©⒟	55 ⒜⒝©⒟	65 ⒜⒝©⒟	75 ⒜⒝©⒟
6 ⒡⒢⒣⒥	16 ⒡⒢⒣⒥	26 ⒡⒢⒣⒥	36 ⒡⒢⒣⒥	46 ⒡⒢⒣⒥	56 ⒡⒢⒣⒥	66 ⒡⒢⒣⒥	
7 ⒜⒝©⒟	17 ⒜⒝©⒟	27 ⒜⒝©⒟	37 ⒜⒝©⒟	47 ⒜⒝©⒟	57 ⒜⒝©⒟	67 ⒜⒝©⒟	
8 ⒡⒢⒣⒥	18 ⒡⒢⒣⒥	28 ⒡⒢⒣⒥	38 ⒡⒢⒣⒥	48 ⒡⒢⒣⒥	58 ⒡⒢⒣⒥	68 ⒡⒢⒣⒥	
9 ⒜⒝©⒟	19 ⒜⒝©⒟	29 ⒜⒝©⒟	39 ⒜⒝©⒟	49 ⒜⒝©⒟	59 ⒜⒝©⒟	69 ⒜⒝©⒟	

TEST 2

	8 ⒡⒢⒣⒥Ⓚ	16 ⒡⒢⒣⒥Ⓚ	24 ⒡⒢⒣⒥Ⓚ	32 ⒡⒢⒣⒥Ⓚ	40 ⒡⒢⒣⒥Ⓚ	48 ⒡⒢⒣⒥Ⓚ	56 ⒡⒢⒣⒥Ⓚ
1 ⒜⒝©⒟Ⓔ	9 ⒜⒝©⒟Ⓔ	17 ⒜⒝©⒟Ⓔ	25 ⒜⒝©⒟Ⓔ	33 ⒜⒝©⒟Ⓔ	41 ⒜⒝©⒟Ⓔ	49 ⒜⒝©⒟Ⓔ	57 ⒜⒝©⒟Ⓔ
2 ⒡⒢⒣⒥Ⓚ	10 ⒡⒢⒣⒥Ⓚ	18 ⒡⒢⒣⒥Ⓚ	26 ⒡⒢⒣⒥Ⓚ	34 ⒡⒢⒣⒥Ⓚ	42 ⒡⒢⒣⒥Ⓚ	50 ⒡⒢⒣⒥Ⓚ	58 ⒡⒢⒣⒥Ⓚ
3 ⒜⒝©⒟Ⓔ	11 ⒜⒝©⒟Ⓔ	19 ⒜⒝©⒟Ⓔ	27 ⒜⒝©⒟Ⓔ	35 ⒜⒝©⒟Ⓔ	43 ⒜⒝©⒟Ⓔ	51 ⒜⒝©⒟Ⓔ	59 ⒜⒝©⒟Ⓔ
4 ⒡⒢⒣⒥Ⓚ	12 ⒡⒢⒣⒥Ⓚ	20 ⒡⒢⒣⒥Ⓚ	28 ⒡⒢⒣⒥Ⓚ	36 ⒡⒢⒣⒥Ⓚ	44 ⒡⒢⒣⒥Ⓚ	52 ⒡⒢⒣⒥Ⓚ	60 ⒡⒢⒣⒥Ⓚ
5 ⒜⒝©⒟Ⓔ	13 ⒜⒝©⒟Ⓔ	21 ⒜⒝©⒟Ⓔ	29 ⒜⒝©⒟Ⓔ	37 ⒜⒝©⒟Ⓔ	45 ⒜⒝©⒟Ⓔ	53 ⒜⒝©⒟Ⓔ	
6 ⒡⒢⒣⒥Ⓚ	14 ⒡⒢⒣⒥Ⓚ	22 ⒡⒢⒣⒥Ⓚ	30 ⒡⒢⒣⒥Ⓚ	38 ⒡⒢⒣⒥Ⓚ	46 ⒡⒢⒣⒥Ⓚ	54 ⒡⒢⒣⒥Ⓚ	
7 ⒜⒝©⒟Ⓔ	15 ⒜⒝©⒟Ⓔ	23 ⒜⒝©⒟Ⓔ	31 ⒜⒝©⒟Ⓔ	39 ⒜⒝©⒟Ⓔ	47 ⒜⒝©⒟Ⓔ	55 ⒜⒝©⒟Ⓔ	

TEST 3

	6 ⒡⒢⒣⒥	12 ⒡⒢⒣⒥	18 ⒡⒢⒣⒥	24 ⒡⒢⒣⒥	30 ⒡⒢⒣⒥	36 ⒡⒢⒣⒥
1 ⒜⒝©⒟	7 ⒜⒝©⒟	13 ⒜⒝©⒟	19 ⒜⒝©⒟	25 ⒜⒝©⒟	31 ⒜⒝©⒟	37 ⒜⒝©⒟
2 ⒡⒢⒣⒥	8 ⒡⒢⒣⒥	14 ⒡⒢⒣⒥	20 ⒡⒢⒣⒥	26 ⒡⒢⒣⒥	32 ⒡⒢⒣⒥	38 ⒡⒢⒣⒥
3 ⒜⒝©⒟	9 ⒜⒝©⒟	15 ⒜⒝©⒟	21 ⒜⒝©⒟	27 ⒜⒝©⒟	33 ⒜⒝©⒟	39 ⒜⒝©⒟
4 ⒡⒢⒣⒥	10 ⒡⒢⒣⒥	16 ⒡⒢⒣⒥	22 ⒡⒢⒣⒥	28 ⒡⒢⒣⒥	34 ⒡⒢⒣⒥	40 ⒡⒢⒣⒥
5 ⒜⒝©⒟	11 ⒜⒝©⒟	17 ⒜⒝©⒟	23 ⒜⒝©⒟	29 ⒜⒝©⒟	35 ⒜⒝©⒟	

TEST 4

	6 ⒡⒢⒣⒥	12 ⒡⒢⒣⒥	18 ⒡⒢⒣⒥	24 ⒡⒢⒣⒥	30 ⒡⒢⒣⒥	36 ⒡⒢⒣⒥
1 ⒜⒝©⒟	7 ⒜⒝©⒟	13 ⒜⒝©⒟	19 ⒜⒝©⒟	25 ⒜⒝©⒟	31 ⒜⒝©⒟	37 ⒜⒝©⒟
2 ⒡⒢⒣⒥	8 ⒡⒢⒣⒥	14 ⒡⒢⒣⒥	20 ⒡⒢⒣⒥	26 ⒡⒢⒣⒥	32 ⒡⒢⒣⒥	38 ⒡⒢⒣⒥
3 ⒜⒝©⒟	9 ⒜⒝©⒟	15 ⒜⒝©⒟	21 ⒜⒝©⒟	27 ⒜⒝©⒟	33 ⒜⒝©⒟	39 ⒜⒝©⒟
4 ⒡⒢⒣⒥	10 ⒡⒢⒣⒥	16 ⒡⒢⒣⒥	22 ⒡⒢⒣⒥	28 ⒡⒢⒣⒥	34 ⒡⒢⒣⒥	40 ⒡⒢⒣⒥
5 ⒜⒝©⒟	11 ⒜⒝©⒟	17 ⒜⒝©⒟	23 ⒜⒝©⒟	29 ⒜⒝©⒟	35 ⒜⒝©⒟	

DO NOT SIGN THIS UNTIL YOU HAVE COMPLETED THIS ENTIRE SECTION.

I hereby certify that I have truthfully identified myself on this form. I understand that the consequences of falsifying my identity include cancellation of my scores.

Your Signature

Today's Date

You may wish to remove this sample answer sheet from the booklet to use in a practice test session.

ACT Assessment Sample Answer Sheet

SIDE 1

NAME, ADDRESS, AND TELEPHONE (Please print.)

Last Name

First Name

MI (Middle Initial)

House Number and Street

City

State

ZIP Code

Area Code

Number

IDENTIFYING INFORMATION

Instructions for Registered Examinees: Your answer sheet will be matched to your registration record using the information you enter in blocks B, C, and D. Enter the information EXACTLY as it appears on your admission ticket, even if any part of the information is missing or incorrect. Fill in the corresponding ovals. Leave block E blank.

Instructions for Standby Examinees: Enter your identifying information in blocks B, C, and D. Fill in the corresponding ovals. (If you do not have a Social Security Number, leave block C blank.) You must also fill in the Standby Testing oval in block E.

MATCH NAME
(FIRST 5 LETTERS OF LAST NAME)

SOCIAL SECURITY NUMBER
(OR ACT ID NUMBER)

DATE OF BIRTH

Month   Day   Year

Jan.
Feb.
Mar.
Apr.
May
June
July
Aug.
Sep.
Oct.
Nov.
Dec.

STANDBY TESTING

Fill in this oval ONLY if you turned in a standby registration folder at the test center. This will help ACT to match your answer sheet to your registration record.

○ Yes, I am testing as a standby examinee.

ACT

P.O. BOX 168, IOWA CITY, IOWA 52243-0168

Instructions for Registered Examinees: If the information on your admission ticket is complete and correct, do NOT mark in blocks F, G, H, or I. If any corrections are necessary, complete ONLY the block(s) below for which the information on your admission ticket is INCOMPLETE or INCORRECT. Leave the other blocks blank.

Instructions for Standby Examinees: Do NOT mark in blocks F, G, H, or I.

NAME CORRECTION

Last Name

First Name

MI

HIGH SCHOOL CODE CORRECTION

DATE OF BIRTH CORRECTION

Month   Day   Year

Jan.
Feb.
Mar.
Apr.
May
June
July
Aug.
Sep.
Oct.
Nov.
Dec.

SOCIAL SECURITY NUMBER CORRECTION

Printed in U.S.A.

529

BOOKLET NUMBER

FORM

BE SURE TO FILL IN THE CORRECT FORM OVAL.

TEST 1

	10 Ⓕ Ⓖ Ⓗ Ⓙ	20 Ⓕ Ⓖ Ⓗ Ⓙ	30 Ⓕ Ⓖ Ⓗ Ⓙ	40 Ⓕ Ⓖ Ⓗ Ⓙ	50 Ⓕ Ⓖ Ⓗ Ⓙ	60 Ⓕ Ⓖ Ⓗ Ⓙ	70 Ⓕ Ⓖ Ⓗ Ⓙ
1 Ⓐ Ⓑ Ⓒ Ⓓ	11 Ⓐ Ⓑ Ⓒ Ⓓ	21 Ⓐ Ⓑ Ⓒ Ⓓ	31 Ⓐ Ⓑ Ⓒ Ⓓ	41 Ⓐ Ⓑ Ⓒ Ⓓ	51 Ⓐ Ⓑ Ⓒ Ⓓ	61 Ⓐ Ⓑ Ⓒ Ⓓ	71 Ⓐ Ⓑ Ⓒ Ⓓ
2 Ⓕ Ⓖ Ⓗ Ⓙ	12 Ⓕ Ⓖ Ⓗ Ⓙ	22 Ⓕ Ⓖ Ⓗ Ⓙ	32 Ⓕ Ⓖ Ⓗ Ⓙ	42 Ⓕ Ⓖ Ⓗ Ⓙ	52 Ⓕ Ⓖ Ⓗ Ⓙ	62 Ⓕ Ⓖ Ⓗ Ⓙ	72 Ⓕ Ⓖ Ⓗ Ⓙ
3 Ⓐ Ⓑ Ⓒ Ⓓ	13 Ⓐ Ⓑ Ⓒ Ⓓ	23 Ⓐ Ⓑ Ⓒ Ⓓ	33 Ⓐ Ⓑ Ⓒ Ⓓ	43 Ⓐ Ⓑ Ⓒ Ⓓ	53 Ⓐ Ⓑ Ⓒ Ⓓ	63 Ⓐ Ⓑ Ⓒ Ⓓ	73 Ⓐ Ⓑ Ⓒ Ⓓ
4 Ⓕ Ⓖ Ⓗ Ⓙ	14 Ⓕ Ⓖ Ⓗ Ⓙ	24 Ⓕ Ⓖ Ⓗ Ⓙ	34 Ⓕ Ⓖ Ⓗ Ⓙ	44 Ⓕ Ⓖ Ⓗ Ⓙ	54 Ⓕ Ⓖ Ⓗ Ⓙ	64 Ⓕ Ⓖ Ⓗ Ⓙ	74 Ⓕ Ⓖ Ⓗ Ⓙ
5 Ⓐ Ⓑ Ⓒ Ⓓ	15 Ⓐ Ⓑ Ⓒ Ⓓ	25 Ⓐ Ⓑ Ⓒ Ⓓ	35 Ⓐ Ⓑ Ⓒ Ⓓ	45 Ⓐ Ⓑ Ⓒ Ⓓ	55 Ⓐ Ⓑ Ⓒ Ⓓ	65 Ⓐ Ⓑ Ⓒ Ⓓ	75 Ⓐ Ⓑ Ⓒ Ⓓ
6 Ⓕ Ⓖ Ⓗ Ⓙ	16 Ⓕ Ⓖ Ⓗ Ⓙ	26 Ⓕ Ⓖ Ⓗ Ⓙ	36 Ⓕ Ⓖ Ⓗ Ⓙ	46 Ⓕ Ⓖ Ⓗ Ⓙ	56 Ⓕ Ⓖ Ⓗ Ⓙ	66 Ⓕ Ⓖ Ⓗ Ⓙ	
7 Ⓐ Ⓑ Ⓒ Ⓓ	17 Ⓐ Ⓑ Ⓒ Ⓓ	27 Ⓐ Ⓑ Ⓒ Ⓓ	37 Ⓐ Ⓑ Ⓒ Ⓓ	47 Ⓐ Ⓑ Ⓒ Ⓓ	57 Ⓐ Ⓑ Ⓒ Ⓓ	67 Ⓐ Ⓑ Ⓒ Ⓓ	
8 Ⓕ Ⓖ Ⓗ Ⓙ	18 Ⓕ Ⓖ Ⓗ Ⓙ	28 Ⓕ Ⓖ Ⓗ Ⓙ	38 Ⓕ Ⓖ Ⓗ Ⓙ	48 Ⓕ Ⓖ Ⓗ Ⓙ	58 Ⓕ Ⓖ Ⓗ Ⓙ	68 Ⓕ Ⓖ Ⓗ Ⓙ	
9 Ⓐ Ⓑ Ⓒ Ⓓ	19 Ⓐ Ⓑ Ⓒ Ⓓ	29 Ⓐ Ⓑ Ⓒ Ⓓ	39 Ⓐ Ⓑ Ⓒ Ⓓ	49 Ⓐ Ⓑ Ⓒ Ⓓ	59 Ⓐ Ⓑ Ⓒ Ⓓ	69 Ⓐ Ⓑ Ⓒ Ⓓ	

TEST 2

	8 Ⓕ Ⓖ Ⓗ Ⓙ Ⓚ	16 Ⓕ Ⓖ Ⓗ Ⓙ Ⓚ	24 Ⓕ Ⓖ Ⓗ Ⓙ Ⓚ	32 Ⓕ Ⓖ Ⓗ Ⓙ Ⓚ	40 Ⓕ Ⓖ Ⓗ Ⓙ Ⓚ	48 Ⓕ Ⓖ Ⓗ Ⓙ Ⓚ	56 Ⓕ Ⓖ Ⓗ Ⓙ Ⓚ
1 Ⓐ Ⓑ Ⓒ Ⓓ Ⓔ	9 Ⓐ Ⓑ Ⓒ Ⓓ Ⓔ	17 Ⓐ Ⓑ Ⓒ Ⓓ Ⓔ	25 Ⓐ Ⓑ Ⓒ Ⓓ Ⓔ	33 Ⓐ Ⓑ Ⓒ Ⓓ Ⓔ	41 Ⓐ Ⓑ Ⓒ Ⓓ Ⓔ	49 Ⓐ Ⓑ Ⓒ Ⓓ Ⓔ	57 Ⓐ Ⓑ Ⓒ Ⓓ Ⓔ
2 Ⓕ Ⓖ Ⓗ Ⓙ Ⓚ	10 Ⓕ Ⓖ Ⓗ Ⓙ Ⓚ	18 Ⓕ Ⓖ Ⓗ Ⓙ Ⓚ	26 Ⓕ Ⓖ Ⓗ Ⓙ Ⓚ	34 Ⓕ Ⓖ Ⓗ Ⓙ Ⓚ	42 Ⓕ Ⓖ Ⓗ Ⓙ Ⓚ	50 Ⓕ Ⓖ Ⓗ Ⓙ Ⓚ	58 Ⓕ Ⓖ Ⓗ Ⓙ Ⓚ
3 Ⓐ Ⓑ Ⓒ Ⓓ Ⓔ	11 Ⓐ Ⓑ Ⓒ Ⓓ Ⓔ	19 Ⓐ Ⓑ Ⓒ Ⓓ Ⓔ	27 Ⓐ Ⓑ Ⓒ Ⓓ Ⓔ	35 Ⓐ Ⓑ Ⓒ Ⓓ Ⓔ	43 Ⓐ Ⓑ Ⓒ Ⓓ Ⓔ	51 Ⓐ Ⓑ Ⓒ Ⓓ Ⓔ	59 Ⓐ Ⓑ Ⓒ Ⓓ Ⓔ
4 Ⓕ Ⓖ Ⓗ Ⓙ Ⓚ	12 Ⓕ Ⓖ Ⓗ Ⓙ Ⓚ	20 Ⓕ Ⓖ Ⓗ Ⓙ Ⓚ	28 Ⓕ Ⓖ Ⓗ Ⓙ Ⓚ	36 Ⓕ Ⓖ Ⓗ Ⓙ Ⓚ	44 Ⓕ Ⓖ Ⓗ Ⓙ Ⓚ	52 Ⓕ Ⓖ Ⓗ Ⓙ Ⓚ	60 Ⓕ Ⓖ Ⓗ Ⓙ Ⓚ
5 Ⓐ Ⓑ Ⓒ Ⓓ Ⓔ	13 Ⓐ Ⓑ Ⓒ Ⓓ Ⓔ	21 Ⓐ Ⓑ Ⓒ Ⓓ Ⓔ	29 Ⓐ Ⓑ Ⓒ Ⓓ Ⓔ	37 Ⓐ Ⓑ Ⓒ Ⓓ Ⓔ	45 Ⓐ Ⓑ Ⓒ Ⓓ Ⓔ	53 Ⓐ Ⓑ Ⓒ Ⓓ Ⓔ	
6 Ⓕ Ⓖ Ⓗ Ⓙ Ⓚ	14 Ⓕ Ⓖ Ⓗ Ⓙ Ⓚ	22 Ⓕ Ⓖ Ⓗ Ⓙ Ⓚ	30 Ⓕ Ⓖ Ⓗ Ⓙ Ⓚ	38 Ⓕ Ⓖ Ⓗ Ⓙ Ⓚ	46 Ⓕ Ⓖ Ⓗ Ⓙ Ⓚ	54 Ⓕ Ⓖ Ⓗ Ⓙ Ⓚ	
7 Ⓐ Ⓑ Ⓒ Ⓓ Ⓔ	15 Ⓐ Ⓑ Ⓒ Ⓓ Ⓔ	23 Ⓐ Ⓑ Ⓒ Ⓓ Ⓔ	31 Ⓐ Ⓑ Ⓒ Ⓓ Ⓔ	39 Ⓐ Ⓑ Ⓒ Ⓓ Ⓔ	47 Ⓐ Ⓑ Ⓒ Ⓓ Ⓔ	55 Ⓐ Ⓑ Ⓒ Ⓓ Ⓔ	

TEST 3

	6 Ⓕ Ⓖ Ⓗ Ⓙ	12 Ⓕ Ⓖ Ⓗ Ⓙ	18 Ⓕ Ⓖ Ⓗ Ⓙ	24 Ⓕ Ⓖ Ⓗ Ⓙ	30 Ⓕ Ⓖ Ⓗ Ⓙ	36 Ⓕ Ⓖ Ⓗ Ⓙ
1 Ⓐ Ⓑ Ⓒ Ⓓ	7 Ⓐ Ⓑ Ⓒ Ⓓ	13 Ⓐ Ⓑ Ⓒ Ⓓ	19 Ⓐ Ⓑ Ⓒ Ⓓ	25 Ⓐ Ⓑ Ⓒ Ⓓ	31 Ⓐ Ⓑ Ⓒ Ⓓ	37 Ⓐ Ⓑ Ⓒ Ⓓ
2 Ⓕ Ⓖ Ⓗ Ⓙ	8 Ⓕ Ⓖ Ⓗ Ⓙ	14 Ⓕ Ⓖ Ⓗ Ⓙ	20 Ⓕ Ⓖ Ⓗ Ⓙ	26 Ⓕ Ⓖ Ⓗ Ⓙ	32 Ⓕ Ⓖ Ⓗ Ⓙ	38 Ⓕ Ⓖ Ⓗ Ⓙ
3 Ⓐ Ⓑ Ⓒ Ⓓ	9 Ⓐ Ⓑ Ⓒ Ⓓ	15 Ⓐ Ⓑ Ⓒ Ⓓ	21 Ⓐ Ⓑ Ⓒ Ⓓ	27 Ⓐ Ⓑ Ⓒ Ⓓ	33 Ⓐ Ⓑ Ⓒ Ⓓ	39 Ⓐ Ⓑ Ⓒ Ⓓ
4 Ⓕ Ⓖ Ⓗ Ⓙ	10 Ⓕ Ⓖ Ⓗ Ⓙ	16 Ⓕ Ⓖ Ⓗ Ⓙ	22 Ⓕ Ⓖ Ⓗ Ⓙ	28 Ⓕ Ⓖ Ⓗ Ⓙ	34 Ⓕ Ⓖ Ⓗ Ⓙ	40 Ⓕ Ⓖ Ⓗ Ⓙ
5 Ⓐ Ⓑ Ⓒ Ⓓ	11 Ⓐ Ⓑ Ⓒ Ⓓ	17 Ⓐ Ⓑ Ⓒ Ⓓ	23 Ⓐ Ⓑ Ⓒ Ⓓ	29 Ⓐ Ⓑ Ⓒ Ⓓ	35 Ⓐ Ⓑ Ⓒ Ⓓ	

TEST 4

	6 Ⓕ Ⓖ Ⓗ Ⓙ	12 Ⓕ Ⓖ Ⓗ Ⓙ	18 Ⓕ Ⓖ Ⓗ Ⓙ	24 Ⓕ Ⓖ Ⓗ Ⓙ	30 Ⓕ Ⓖ Ⓗ Ⓙ	36 Ⓕ Ⓖ Ⓗ Ⓙ
1 Ⓐ Ⓑ Ⓒ Ⓓ	7 Ⓐ Ⓑ Ⓒ Ⓓ	13 Ⓐ Ⓑ Ⓒ Ⓓ	19 Ⓐ Ⓑ Ⓒ Ⓓ	25 Ⓐ Ⓑ Ⓒ Ⓓ	31 Ⓐ Ⓑ Ⓒ Ⓓ	37 Ⓐ Ⓑ Ⓒ Ⓓ
2 Ⓕ Ⓖ Ⓗ Ⓙ	8 Ⓕ Ⓖ Ⓗ Ⓙ	14 Ⓕ Ⓖ Ⓗ Ⓙ	20 Ⓕ Ⓖ Ⓗ Ⓙ	26 Ⓕ Ⓖ Ⓗ Ⓙ	32 Ⓕ Ⓖ Ⓗ Ⓙ	38 Ⓕ Ⓖ Ⓗ Ⓙ
3 Ⓐ Ⓑ Ⓒ Ⓓ	9 Ⓐ Ⓑ Ⓒ Ⓓ	15 Ⓐ Ⓑ Ⓒ Ⓓ	21 Ⓐ Ⓑ Ⓒ Ⓓ	27 Ⓐ Ⓑ Ⓒ Ⓓ	33 Ⓐ Ⓑ Ⓒ Ⓓ	39 Ⓐ Ⓑ Ⓒ Ⓓ
4 Ⓕ Ⓖ Ⓗ Ⓙ	10 Ⓕ Ⓖ Ⓗ Ⓙ	16 Ⓕ Ⓖ Ⓗ Ⓙ	22 Ⓕ Ⓖ Ⓗ Ⓙ	28 Ⓕ Ⓖ Ⓗ Ⓙ	34 Ⓕ Ⓖ Ⓗ Ⓙ	40 Ⓕ Ⓖ Ⓗ Ⓙ
5 Ⓐ Ⓑ Ⓒ Ⓓ	11 Ⓐ Ⓑ Ⓒ Ⓓ	17 Ⓐ Ⓑ Ⓒ Ⓓ	23 Ⓐ Ⓑ Ⓒ Ⓓ	29 Ⓐ Ⓑ Ⓒ Ⓓ	35 Ⓐ Ⓑ Ⓒ Ⓓ	

DO NOT SIGN THIS UNTIL YOU HAVE COMPLETED THIS ENTIRE SECTION.

I hereby certify that I have truthfully identified myself on this form. I understand that the consequences of falsifying my identity include cancellation of my scores.

_____
Your Signature

_____
Today's Date

6

Interpreting Your ACT Test Scores

Scoring the Practice Tests

On each of the four ACT tests (English, Mathematics, Reading, and Science Reasoning), the number of questions you answer correctly is called a "raw" score. It's easy to figure out raw scores for the practice tests in this book: Simply count up all your correct answers for each test using the scoring keys on pages 537–541 (Practice Test 1) and 548–552 (Practice Test 2). Then, you can convert your raw scores into scaled scores using the conversion charts on pages 543–544 for Practice Test 1, and pages 553–554 for Practice Test 2. Scaled scores are the scores that ACT reports to students, high schools, colleges, and scholarship agencies. One of the reasons ACT uses scaled scores is to adjust for small differences occurring among different versions of the ACT Assessment. After you've converted your raw scores for the practice tests to scaled scores, you'll want to convert your scaled scores to percentile ranks (see page 547). Percentile ranks, which are explained in the following pages, are useful for interpreting your scores relative to the scores of others who have taken the ACT test.

When scoring each practice test and reviewing your scores, it's important to remember that test scores are only one estimate of your academic skills and knowledge. If, for example, your score on the Mathematics Test isn't as high as you expected, this doesn't necessarily mean you're "no good at math." Instead, it might mean that you need a little more practice in arithmetic calculations, that you could benefit from reviewing some mathematical concepts, that you should work a little faster when you're taking a timed test, or that you simply weren't doing your best work on the practice test. You know your academic strengths and weaknesses—keep them in mind as you evaluate your scores on the practice tests.

Understanding Your ACT Test Results

How ACT scores your test

How does ACT determine the scores it reports for students taking the ACT test? The first step is to do exactly what you are about to do for your practice tests: count the number of questions you answered correctly to determine your raw score. There's no deduction for incorrect answers.

Next, these raw scores are converted to scaled scores—scores that have the same meaning for all versions of the ACT test. The scaled scores range from 1 (low) to 36 (high) for each of the four individual tests and for the Composite score, which is the average of the four test scores.

ACT also computes subscores for areas within the English, Reading, and Mathematics Tests. The subscores range from 1 (low) to 18 (high). Because the four individual test scores are computed independently of the subscores for the tests, the sum of the subscores for a particular test won't necessarily equal the score for that test. For example, the two subscores for the Reading Test won't necessarily add up to the overall score for the Reading Test.

Test scores are just estimates

No test, including the ACT Assessment, can precisely measure educational development. As a result, we estimate the amount of imprecision, or error, in test scores. One estimate for this error is called the "standard error of measurement." On the ACT test, the standard error of measurement (SEM) is about 2 points for each of the test scores and subscores and about 1 point for the Composite score.

Because of the imprecision of test scores, it's best to think of each of your ACT test scores as a range of scores rather than as a precise number. The SEM can be used to estimate ranges for your scores. To do this, just add the SEM to, and subtract it from, each of your scores. For example, if your score on the English Test is 22, your level of English skills and knowledge probably lies somewhere in the interval of 20 to 24 (22 plus or minus 2).

To encourage you to keep the imprecision of test scores in mind, ACT shows error bands corresponding to each of the scores reported on the *ACT Assessment Student Report,* which you'll receive with your ACT test scores. The bands roughly indicate the amount of measurement error involved. Below is an example of the way test scores and error bands (represented by dashed lines for the individual test scores and subscores and by asterisks for the Composite score) are shown on the student report:

KNOWLEDGE AND SKILL AREAS	SCORES (1-36) (1-18)	RANK: PERCENT OF COLLEGE-BOUND STUDENTS AT OR BELOW YOUR SCORES
		1 10 25 50 75 90 99
ENGLISH	24	--- 76----
Usage/Mechanics	13	------- 81 ---------
Rhetorical Skills	12	-------- 75 ---------
MATHEMATICS	17	--- 34 ---
Pre-Algebra/Elem. Alg.	09	------- 41 --------
Alg./Coord. Geometry	10	------ 61 --------
Plane Geometry/Trig.	08	-------- 25 --------
READING	25	--- 75 ----
Soc. Studies/Sciences	10	------ 54 --------
Arts/Literature	14	------ 79 --------
SCIENCE REASONING	18	--- 31 ----
COMPOSITE (Average)	21	**58**

TRACY ARTHUR C
7852 W 46TH ST
WHEAT RIDGE CO 80033

Scores can be compared to the scores earned by different groups of college-bound high school graduates who recently took the ACT as jrs or srs: 58% of jrs/srs tested nationwide and 53% of jrs/srs tested in Colorado scored at or below your Composite score.

H.S. grades you reported: English=A, Math=C, Social Studies=A, Natural Sciences=B.

Using percentile ranks to interpret your scores

In the example above, the imaginary Arthur C. Tracy is given two different kinds of scores, scaled scores and percentile ranks, to describe his performance in the different test areas. Percentile ranks are one way to interpret ACT test scores. A score's percentile rank shows the percentage of college-bound students who scored at or below that score. In the example, Arthur's ACT Composite score is 21. If you look directly to the right of that score, you'll see a 58 with two asterisks (**) on either side of it. This number—the percentile rank for Arthur's Composite score—means that 58% of college-bound students had ACT Composite scores that were the same as or lower than Arthur's Composite score. The error band around 58 is represented by the asterisks. This band indicates the approximate range of measurement error and is used to emphasize that the test scores and percentile ranks are only estimates of Arthur's level of academic skills and knowledge.

Comparing your scores to each other

Another way to interpret your ACT test scores is by comparing them to each other using percentile ranks. You may find it interesting, for example, to compare your percentile ranks for the Science Reasoning and Mathematics Tests to your percentile ranks for the Reading and English Tests. Perhaps you've felt more comfortable and successful in some subject areas than in others. Making comparisons among your ACT test percentile ranks can be especially helpful as you make decisions about the courses you will take in high school and college. A high percentile rank in a particular area may indicate a good chance of success in related college majors and careers. A low percentile rank may indicate that you need to develop your skills more in that area.

It's important to know that scaled scores from the different individual tests can't be directly compared to each other. If you earn scores of 23 on the ACT English and Mathematics Tests, for example, this doesn't necessarily mean that your levels of skill and knowledge in English are the same as they are in mathematics. The percentile ranks corresponding to the scores—not the scores themselves—are probably best for making comparisons among subject areas.

Comparing your scores to your high school grades

Notice that in the *ACT Assessment Student Report* example, the average high school grades Arthur C. Tracy reported when he registered for the ACT test are listed below his scores. After you take the ACT Assessment and receive your student report, you'll want to compare your scores to your high school grades using the percentile ranks. Are your highest grades and highest ACT test scores in the same content areas? If so, you might want to consider college majors that would draw on your areas of greatest strength. On the other hand, if your grades and scores differ, talk with your counselor about possible reasons for the differences.

Comparing your scores to those of enrolled college freshmen

Another way to understand your ACT test scores is by comparing them to the scores of students enrolled at colleges or universities you're interested in attending. This information can be very useful as you make decisions about applying for college. Keep in mind that admissions offices use a number of measures—including high school grades, recommendations, and extra-curricular activities—to determine how students are likely to perform at their schools. Still, knowing that your ACT test scores are similar to those of students already enrolled at a college or university you're considering may make you more confident in applying for admission there. A chart in the *ACT Assessment Student Report* will help you compare your ACT scores to those of freshmen at the schools you indicate when you register for the ACT test. The following chart, for example, indicates that Arthur C. Tracy's ACT Composite score is estimated to rank in the upper quarter of the Composite scores of enrolled freshmen at Beta Community College.

COLLEGE CODE AND NAME	ADMISSIONS POLICY	ESTIMATED RANK OF YOUR ACT COMPOSITE SCORE (ENROLLED FRESHMEN)
9521 UNIVERSITY OF OMEGA	Trad	Middle Half
7111 ALPHA UNIVERSITY	Sel	Middle Half
7222 BETA COMMUNITY COLL	Open	Upper Quarter

Get All the Information You Can

Your *ACT Assessment Student Report* will provide additional information to help you understand your ACT test results and use them in making important decisions about college and exploring possible future careers. With your student report, you'll also receive the booklet *Using Your ACT Assessment Results*, which not only lists activities designed to help you identify and explore career options, but also includes other practical information.

As you approach decisions about college and careers, be sure to take advantage of all the assistance you can find. Talk to your parents, counselors, and teachers; visit your local library; and write directly to colleges you're interested in. The more you can find out about all the educational options available to you and the level of your academic skills and knowledge (using such information as your ACT test results), the better prepared you'll be to make informed college and career choices.

Scoring Keys and Conversion Tables

Practice Test 1

Scoring your practice test involves eight steps.

STEP 1. Write a "1" in the blank for each English Test question that you answered correctly. An example is provided in the box below:

	Key	Subscore Area*		Your answer was
		UM	RH	
1.	A	————		Incorrect
2.	J		1	Correct
3.	B		1	Correct
4.	G	————		Incorrect

English ■ Scoring Key ■ Practice Test 1

	Key	Subscore Area*				Key	Subscore Area*				Key	Subscore Area*	
		UM	RH				UM	RH				UM	RH
1.	A	1			26.	G	1			51.	B		
2.	G		1		27.	A	———			52.	F		1
3.	D	1			28.	G		1		53.	D		1
4.	F	———			29.	D	———			54.	G	1	
5.	A		1		30.	H	1			55.	C		1
6.	J	———			31.	C	———			56.	G	1	
7.	A	1			32.	G	1			57.	A	1	
8.	G		1		33.	D	———			58.	J	———	
9.	C	1			34.	H		1		59.	C		1
10.	H	1			35.	A	———			60.	J		1
11.	B	1			36.	H	———			61.	C	———	
12.	J	1			37.	D	1			62.	G	1	
13.	C		1		38.	J	1			63.	D	———	
14.	J	1			39.	C	———			64.	G	———	
15.	D	1			40.	F	———			65.	C	1	
16.	G	1			41.	D		1		66.	G	———	
17.	A	1			42.	F		1		67.	B	———	
18.	H		1		43.	B		1		68.	J	———	
19.	D	1			44.	H	1			69.	A	1	
20.	H	1			45.	B	1			70.	H	———	
21.	D		1		46.	F	———			71.	D	1	
22.	G	———			47.	C		1		72.	F	———	
23.	D		1		48.	J		1		73.	B	1	
24.	F	1			49.	A	1			74.	H	———	
25.	B	1			50.	H	1			75.	A	1	

* UM = Usage/Mechanics
RH = Rhetorical Skills

STEP 2. Add up the numbers in each subscore area and enter them in the appropriate blanks in the shaded box below:

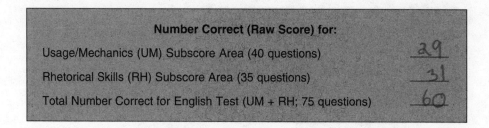

Number Correct (Raw Score) for:	
Usage/Mechanics (UM) Subscore Area (40 questions)	29
Rhetorical Skills (RH) Subscore Area (35 questions)	31
Total Number Correct for English Test (UM + RH; 75 questions)	60

STEP 3. Compute your total number correct for the English Test by adding the numbers you entered in Step 2. Write this total in the appropriate blank in the shaded box above. This is your raw score.

STEP 4. Repeat Steps 1 through 3 for the ACT Mathematics, Reading, and Science Reasoning Tests using the scoring keys on the following pages. Note that the Science Reasoning Test doesn't have subscores, so determine your raw score for that test simply by adding up the number of "1s" you entered.

Mathematics ■ Scoring Key ■ Practice Test 1

	Key	Subscore Area*		
		EA	AG	GT
1.	E	/		
2.	H			/
3.	B		/	
4.	K	/		
5.	E			/
6.	F	/		
7.	C	/		
8.	H	/		
9.	C	/		
10.	F		/	
11.	B	/		
12.	F	/		
13.	E		/	
14.	K	/		
15.	D			/
16.	G		/	
17.	C			/
18.	F			/
19.	D	/		
20.	G	/		
21.	D		/	
22.	F	/		
23.	C	/		
24.	F			/
25.	D			/
26.	G		/	
27.	B			/
28.	G			/
29.	C	/		
30.	F			

	Key	Subscore Area*		
		EA	AG	GT
31.	C		/	/
32.	F			/
33.	D	/		
34.	H			
35.	E		/	
36.	H	/		/
37.	E			/
38.	K			/
39.	B			/
40.	F		/	
41.	B		/	
42.	H		/	
43.	E			
44.	G		/	
45.	D			/
46.	H	/		
47.	E			
48.	H	/		
49.	A			
50.	H			
51.	B			/
52.	J			
53.	E	/		
54.	K	/		
55.	A	/		
56.	J	/		
57.	A			/
58.	F		/	
59.	D	/		
60.	K			

* EA = Pre-Algebra/Elementary Algebra
 AG = Intermediate Algebra/Coordinate Geometry
 GT = Plane Geometry/Trigonometry

Number Correct (Raw Score) for:	
Pre-Alg./Elem. Alg. (EA) Subscore Area (24 questions)	23
Inter. Alg./Coord. Geom. (AG) Subscore Area (18 questions)	15
Plane Geom./Trig. (GT) Subscore Area (18 questions)	13
Total Number Correct for Math Test (EA + AG + GT; 60 questions)	51

Reading ■ Scoring Key ■ Practice Test 1

	Key	SS	AL			Key	SS	AL			Key	SS	AL
1.	D				15.	C				29.	D		
2.	G				16.	J				30.	H		
3.	C				17.	D				31.	C		
4.	J				18.	G				32.	F		
5.	A				19.	A				33.	D		
6.	G				20.	G				34.	H		
7.	D				21.	A				35.	D		
8.	J				22.	J				36.	J		
9.	A				23.	B				37.	D		
10.	G				24.	H				38.	H		
11.	B				25.	C				39.	A		
12.	H				26.	G				40.	G		
13.	A				27.	C							
14.	H				28.	F							

* SS = Social Studies/Sciences
 AL = Arts/Literature

Number Correct (Raw Score) for:

Social Studies/Sciences (SS) Subscore Area (20 questions)   20

Arts/Literature (AL) Subscore Area (20 questions)   16

Total Number Correct for Reading Test (SS + AL; 40 questions)   36

Science Reasoning ■ Scoring Key ■ Practice Test 1

	Key			Key			Key
1.	D		15.	C		29.	C
2.	G		16.	J		30.	H
3.	D		17.	D		31.	C
4.	F		18.	G		32.	F
5.	D		19.	C		33.	C
6.	G		20.	F		34.	J
7.	B		21.	A		35.	D
8.	J		22.	G		36.	J
9.	A		23.	B		37.	D
10.	F		24.	H		38.	G
11.	D		25.	B		39.	A
12.	H		26.	F		40.	J
13.	B		27.	B			
14.	G		28.	H			

Number Correct (Raw Score) for:

Total Number Correct for Science Reasoning Test (40 questions)   _37_

STEP 5. On each of the four tests, the total number of correct responses yields a raw score. Use the conversion table on the following page to convert your raw scores to scaled scores. For each of the four tests, locate and circle your raw score or the range of raw scores that includes it in the conversion table. Then, read across to either outside column of the table and circle the scaled score that corresponds to that raw score. As you determine your scaled scores, enter them in the blanks provided on page 545. The highest possible scaled score for each test is 36. The lowest possible scaled score for any of the four tests is 1.

STEP 6. Compute your Composite score by averaging the four scaled scores. To do this, add your four scaled scores and divide the sum by 4. If the resulting number ends in a fraction, round it off to the nearest whole number. (Round down any fraction less than one-half; round up any fraction that is one-half or more.) Enter this number in the appropriate blank on page 545. This is your Composite score. The highest possible Composite score is 36. The lowest possible Composite score is 1.

Scaled Score Conversion Table
Practice Test 1

Scaled Score	Raw Score				Scaled Score
	English	Mathematics	Reading	Science Reasoning	
36	75	60	40	40	36
35	–	–	39	–	35
34	74	59	38	–	34
33	73	58	37	39	33
32	72	57	–	–	32
31	71	55–56	36	38	31
30	69–70	53–54	35	37	30
29	67–68	51–52	34	36	29
28	65–66	49–50	33	35	28
27	63–64	46–48	32	34	27
26	60–62	44–45	30–31	32–33	26
25	58–59	42–43	29	31	25
24	55–57	40–41	28	29–30	24
23	52–54	38–39	26–27	27–28	23
22	50–51	36–37	25	25–26	22
21	47–49	34–35	23–24	24	21
20	44–46	32–33	22	22–23	20
19	41–43	29–31	20–21	20–21	19
18	39–40	26–28	19	18–19	18
17	36–38	23–25	18	16–17	17
16	33–35	19–22	17	14–15	16
15	30–32	16–18	16	12–13	15
14	28–29	13–15	14–15	11	14
13	25–27	11–12	13	10	13
12	22–24	9–10	11–12	8–9	12
11	19–21	7–8	9–10	7	11
10	16–18	5–6	8	6	10
9	14–15	–	7	5	9
8	12–13	4	6	4	8
7	9–11	3	5	3	7
6	8	–	–	–	6
5	6–7	2	4	2	5
4	4–5	–	3	–	4
3	3	1	2	1	3
2	2	–	1	–	2
1	0–1	0	0	0	1

STEP 7. Now convert your seven raw subscores to scaled subscores using the table below. For each of the seven subscore areas, locate and circle either the raw score or the range of raw scores that includes it in the table. Then read across to either outside column of the table and circle the scaled subscore that corresponds to that raw subscore. As you determine your scaled subscores, enter them in the blanks on page 545. The highest possible scaled subscore is 18. The lowest possible scaled subscore is 1.

Scaled Subscore Conversion Table
Practice Test 1

Scaled Subscore	Raw Scores							Scaled Subscore
	English		**Mathematics**			**Reading**		
	Usage/ Mechanics	Rhetorical Skills	Pre-Alg./ Elem. Alg.	Inter. Alg./ Coord. Geom.	Plane Geom./ Trigonometry	Soc. Studies/ Sciences	Arts/ Literature	
18	39–40	35	23–24	18	18	20	20	18
17	38	34	22	–	–	19	18–19	17
16	36–37	33	–	17	17	18	17	16
15	34–35	31–32	21	16	15–16	17	16	15
14	32–33	30	19–20	14–15	14	16	–	14
13	30–31	27–29	18	12–13	12–13	15	15	13
12	28–29	25–26	17	11	11	13–14	14	12
11	26–27	22–24	16	9–10	10	12	13	11
10	24–25	20–21	14–15	8	8–9	10–11	11–12	10
9	22–23	17–19	12–13	6–7	6–7	8–9	10	9
8	19–21	14–16	10–11	5	5	7	9	8
7	16–18	11–13	8–9	4	4	6	8	7
6	14–15	9–10	6–7	–	3	5	7	6
5	11–13	7–8	5	3	–	4	6	5
4	8–10	5–6	3–4	2	2	3	5	4
3	6–7	4	2	1	–	2	4	3
2	4–5	2–3	1	–	1	1	2–3	2
1	0–3	0–1	0	0	0	0	0–1	1

Your Scaled Scores
Practice Test 1

ACT Test	Your Scaled Score
English	26
Mathematics	29
Reading	31
Science Reasoning	30
Sum of scores	116
Composite score (sum ÷ 4)	29

ACT Test	Your Scaled Subscore
English	
Usage/Mechanics (UM)	12
Rhetorical Skills (RH)	15
Mathematics	
Pre-Algebra/Elem. Algebra (EA)	18
Inter. Algebra/Coord. Geometry (AG)	14
Plane Geometry/Trigonometry (GT)	13
Reading	
Social Studies/Sciences (SS)	18
Arts/Literature (AL)	15

STEP 8. Use the table on the following page to determine your estimated percentile ranks (percent at or below) for each of your scaled scores. In the far left column of the table, circle your scaled score for the English Test (from page 545). Then read across to the percentile rank column for that test; circle or put a check mark beside the corresponding percentile rank. Use the same procedure for the other three tests and for the subscore areas (from page 545). You may find it easier to use the right-hand column of scaled scores for your Science Reasoning Test and Composite scores. As you mark your percentile ranks, enter them in the blanks provided below. You may also find it helpful to compare your performance with the national mean (average) score for each of the four tests, the subscore areas, and the Composite as shown at the bottom of the table.

ACT Test	Your Percentile Rank
English	86
Usage/Mechanics (UM)	73
Rhetorical Skills (RH)	96
Mathematics	96
Pre-Algebra/Elem. Algebra (EA)	99
Inter. Algebra/Coord. Geometry (AG)	93
Plane Geometry/Trigonometry (GT)	85
Reading	93
Social Studies/Sciences (SS)	99
Arts/Literature (AL)	84
Science Reasoning	97

National Distributions of Percentile Ranks (Percent At or Below) for ACT Test Scores

Score	ENGLISH	Usage/Mechanics	Rhetorical Skills	MATHEMATICS	Pre-Algebra/Elem. Alg.	Alg./Coord. Geometry	Plane Geometry/Trig.	READING	Soc. Studies/Sciences	Arts/Literature	SCIENCE REASONING	COMPOSITE	Score
36	99			99				99			99	99	36
35	99			99				99			99	99	35
34	99			99				98			99	99	34
33	99			99				96			99	99	33
32	99			99				95			99	99	32
31	98			98				93			98	99	31
30	97			97				92			97	97	30
29	96			96				90			95	96	29
28	93			94				87			93	93	28
27	90			91				84			91	91	27
26	86			88				80			88	87	26
25	81			84				75			83	83	25
24	76			80				72			77	78	24
23	71			75				66			71	72	23
22	65			69				61			65	65	22
21	59			64				54			56	58	21
20	53			58				47			48	50	20
19	46			50				40			40	42	19
18	39	99	99	42	99	99	99	35	99	99	31	34	18
17	33	99	99	34	98	99	98	28	98	96	24	26	17
16	27	97	98	24	96	98	89	23	95	89	16	19	16
15	21	93	96	16	92	96	96	18	91	84	10	13	15
14	15	88	91	09	87	93	93	14	85	79	06	08	14
13	10	81	84	04	81	88	85	10	78	71	03	04	13
12	07	73	75	02	74	83	78	06	72	62	01	01	12
11	04	65	64	01	65	70	65	03	63	52	01	01	11
10	02	56	53	01	53	61	53	02	54	43	01	01	10
09	01	46	38	01	41	43	39	01	38	35	01	01	09
08	01	36	27	01	30	28	25	01	28	27	01	01	08
07	01	25	17	01	19	17	12	01	20	20	01	01	07
06	01	16	08	01	10	10	08	01	11	13	01	01	06
05	01	08	04	01	05	07	04	01	06	08	01	01	05
04	01	03	01	01	02	04	03	01	03	04	01	01	04
03	01	01	01	01	01	02	01	01	01	02	01	01	03
02	01	01	01	01	01	01	01	01	01	01	01	01	02
01	01	01	01	01	01	01	01	01	01	01	01	01	01
Mean	20.3	10.1	10.4	20.2	10.4	10.0	10.4	21.3	10.6	11.1	21.1	20.9	
S.D.	5.4	3.4	2.9	4.8	3.3	3.0	2.9	6.1	3.4	3.9	4.6	4.7	

Note: These distributions are based on the test scores of 924,663 students who took the ACT test and indicated that they expected to graduate from high school in 1996. Newer versions of the ACT test that were developed after the practice tests in this document will likely have somewhat different conversions of scaled scores to percentile ranks. A copy of current conversions for scaled scores and percentile ranks for the ACT test (the ACT test "norms") can be obtained by contacting ACT.

Scoring Keys and Conversion Tables

Practice Test 2

Scoring your practice test involves eight steps.

STEP 1. Write a "1" in the blank for each English Test question that you answered correctly. An example is provided in the box below:

	Key	Subscore Area*		Your answer was
		UM	RH	
1.	A	————		Incorrect
2.	J		1	Correct
3.	B		1	Correct
4.	G			Incorrect

English ▪ Scoring Key ▪ Practice Test 2

	Key	Subscore Area*				Key	Subscore Area*				Key	Subscore Area*	
		UM	RH				UM	RH				UM	RH
1.	D	1			26.	J		1		51.	D		1
2.	J	1			27.	B		1		52.	F	1	
3.	C		1		28.	G	1			53.	B		1
4.	G	1			29.	B				54.	F		1
5.	C	1			30.	H				55.	A		1
6.	G	1			31.	C	1			56.	H		
7.	A		1		32.	G	1			57.	D	1	
8.	F	1			33.	C				58.	G		1
9.	C	1			34.	J				59.	D	1	
10.	G				35.	A				60.	H		1
11.	B		1		36.	F	1			61.	D	1	
12.	H		1		37.	C	1			62.	H	1	
13.	C		1		38.	G	1			63.	B		1
14.	J		1		39.	A	1			64.	G		1
15.	C		1		40.	J	1			65.	A	1	
16.	F				41.	A		1		66.	J		1
17.	A		1		42.	H	1			67.	B	1	
18.	J	1			43.	A	1			68.	H		1
19.	D		1		44.	J				69.	C		
20.	F	1			45.	D				70.	G	1	
21.	B		1		46.	H	1			71.	D		
22.	J		1		47.	D	1			72.	J		1
23.	C		1		48.	F				73.	A		
24.	G		1		49.	D				74.	H	1	
25.	D	1			50.	G				75.	A	1	

* UM = Usage/Mechanics
  RH = Rhetorical Skills

STEP 2. Add up the numbers in each subscore area and enter them in the appropriate blanks in the shaded box below:

Number Correct (Raw Score) for:	
Usage/Mechanics (UM) Subscore Area (40 questions)	_31_
Rhetorical Skills (RH) Subscore Area (35 questions)	_31_
Total Number Correct for English Test (UM + RH; 75 questions)	_62_

STEP 3. Compute your total number correct for the English Test by adding the numbers you entered in Step 2. Write this total in the appropriate blank in the shaded box above. This is your raw score.

STEP 4. Repeat Steps 1 through 3 for the ACT Mathematics, Reading, and Science Reasoning Tests using the scoring keys on the following pages. Note that the Science Reasoning Test doesn't have subscores, so determine your raw score for that test simply by adding up the number of "1s" you entered.

Mathematics ■ Scoring Key ■ Practice Test 2

	Key	EA	AG	GT
1.	D			
2.	J			
3.	B			
4.	G			
5.	B			
6.	J			
7.	B			
8.	G			
9.	A			
10.	K			
11.	A			
12.	J			
13.	D			
14.	K			
15.	A			
16.	J			
17.	C			
18.	H			
19.	A			
20.	G			
21.	A			
22.	H			
23.	E			
24.	K			
25.	B			
26.	K			
27.	C			
28.	K			
29.	C			
30.	G			

	Key	EA	AG	GT
31.	A			
32.	K			
33.	D			
34.	J			
35.	A			
36.	H			
37.	A			
38.	J			
39.	D			
40.	H			
41.	C			
42.	F			
43.	E			
44.	H			
45.	B			
46.	F			
47.	A			
48.	K			
49.	E			
50.	G			
51.	B			
52.	J			
53.	E			
54.	H			
55.	B			
56.	K			
57.	C			
58.	F			
59.	A			
60.	G			

* EA = Pre-Algebra/Elementary Algebra
  AG = Intermediate Algebra/Coordinate Geometry
  GT = Plane Geometry/Trigonometry

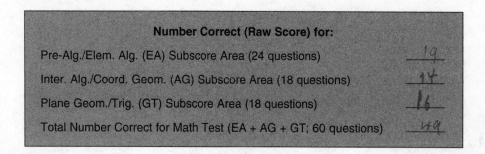

Number Correct (Raw Score) for:	
Pre-Alg./Elem. Alg. (EA) Subscore Area (24 questions)	19
Inter. Alg./Coord. Geom. (AG) Subscore Area (18 questions)	14
Plane Geom./Trig. (GT) Subscore Area (18 questions)	16
Total Number Correct for Math Test (EA + AG + GT; 60 questions)	49

Reading ■ Scoring Key ■ Practice Test 2

	Key	Subscore Area* SS	AL			Key	Subscore Area* SS	AL			Key	Subscore Area* SS	AL
1.	C		✓		15.	B	✓			29.	C		✓
2.	J		✓		16.	F	✓			30.	G		
3.	A		✓		17.	D	✓			31.	C	✓	
4.	F		✓		18.	J	✓			32.	G	✓	
5.	B		✓		19.	A	✓			33.	A	✓	
6.	J		✓		20.	H	✓			34.	H	✓	
7.	C		✓		21.	C		✓		35.	B	✓	
8.	J		✓		22.	J		✓		36.	H	✓	
9.	A		✓		23.	B		✓		37.	A	✓	
10.	F		✓		24.	J		✓		38.	J		
11.	B	✓			25.	A		✓		39.	A		
12.	G	✓			26.	F		✓		40.	J	✓	
13.	C	✓			27.	B		✓					
14.	G	✓			28.	H		✓					

* SS = Social Studies/Sciences
AL = Arts/Literature

Number Correct (Raw Score) for:	
Social Studies/Sciences (SS) Subscore Area (20 questions)	19
Arts/Literature (AL) Subscore Area (20 questions)	19
Total Number Correct for Reading Test (SS + AL; 40 questions)	38

Science Reasoning ■ Scoring Key ■ Practice Test 2

	Key			Key			Key	
1.	D	_____	15.	C	_____	29.	D	_____
2.	G	_____	16.	G	_____	30.	F	_____
3.	A	_____	17.	D	_____	31.	D	_____
4.	H	_____	18.	G	_____	32.	J	_____
5.	A	_____	19.	A	_____	33.	C	_____
6.	G	_____	20.	F	_____	34.	J	_____
7.	C	_____	21.	B	_____	35.	A	_____
8.	G	_____	22.	F	_____	36.	G	_____
9.	B	_____	23.	D	_____	37.	A	_____
10.	H	_____	24.	G	_____	38.	J	_____
11.	A	_____	25.	C	_____	39.	A	_____
12.	H	_____	26.	H	_____	40.	F	_____
13.	C	_____	27.	D	_____			
14.	G	_____	28.	G	_____			

Number Correct (Raw Score) for:

Total Number Correct for Science Reasoning Test (40 questions)   _____

STEP 5. On each of the four tests, the total number of correct responses yields a raw score. Use the conversion table on the following page to convert your raw scores to scaled scores. For each of the four tests, locate and circle your raw score or the range of raw scores that includes it in the conversion table. Then, read across to either outside column of the table and circle the scaled score that corresponds to that raw score. As you determine your scaled scores, enter them in the blanks provided on page 555. The highest possible scaled score for each test is 36. The lowest possible scaled score for any of the four tests is 1.

STEP 6. Compute your Composite score by averaging the four scaled scores. To do this, add your four scaled scores and divide the sum by 4. If the resulting number ends in a fraction, round it off to the nearest whole number. (Round down any fraction less than one-half; round up any fraction that is one-half or more.) Enter this number in the appropriate blank on page 555. This is your Composite score. The highest possible Composite score is 36. The lowest possible Composite score is 1.